Lecture Notes in Computer Science

Commenced Publication in 1973
Founding and Former Series Editors:
Gerhard Goos, Juris Hartmanis, and Jan van Leeuwen

Dorina C. Petriu   Nicolas Rouquette
Øystein Haugen (Eds.)

Model Driven Engineering Languages and Systems

13th International Conference, MODELS 2010
Oslo, Norway, October 3-8, 2010
Proceedings, Part I

 Springer

Volume Editors

Dorina C. Petriu
Carleton University, Department of Systems and Computer Engineering
1125 Colonel By Drive, Ottawa, Ontario, K1S 5BG, Canada
E-mail: petriu@sce.carleton.ca

Nicolas Rouquette
Jet Propulsion Laboratory
Flight Software Systems Engineering and Architecture Group
4800 Oak Grove Drive, Pasadena, CA 91109, USA
E-mail: nicolas.f.rouquette@jpl.nasa.gov

Øystein Haugen
SINTEF IKT
Forskningsveien 1, 0373 Oslo, Norway
E-mail: oystein.haugen@sintef.no

Library of Congress Control Number: 2010935022

CR Subject Classification (1998): D.2, D.3, K.6.3, D.2.9, F.3.3, D.1, D.2.2

LNCS Sublibrary: SL 2 – Programming and Software Engineering

ISSN   0302-9743
ISBN-10   3-642-16144-8 Springer Berlin Heidelberg New York
ISBN-13   978-3-642-16144-5 Springer Berlin Heidelberg New York

springer.com

© Springer-Verlag Berlin Heidelberg 2010

Typesetting: Camera-ready by author, data conversion by Scientific Publishing Services, Chennai, India
Printed on acid-free paper   06/3180

Preface

The MODELS series of conferences is the premier venue for the exchange of innovative technical ideas and experiences focusing on a very important new technical discipline: model-driven software and systems engineering. The expansion of this discipline is a direct consequence of the increasing significance and success of model-based methods in practice. Numerous efforts resulted in the invention of concepts, languages and tools for the definition, analysis, transformation, and verification of domain-specific modeling languages and general-purpose modeling language standards, as well as their use for software and systems engineering.

MODELS 2010, the 13th edition of the conference series, took place in Oslo, Norway, October 3-8, 2010, along with numerous satellite workshops, symposia and tutorials. The conference was fortunate to have three prominent keynote speakers: Ole Lehrmann Madsen (Aarhus University, Denmark), Edward A. Lee (UC Berkeley, USA) and Pamela Zave (AT&T Laboratories, USA).

To provide a broader forum for reporting on scientific progress as well as on experience stemming from practical applications of model-based methods, the 2010 conference accepted submissions in two distinct tracks: Foundations and Applications. The primary objective of the first track is to present new research results dedicated to advancing the state-of-the-art of the discipline, whereas the second aims to provide a realistic and verifiable picture of the current state-of-the-practice of model-based engineering, so that the broader community could be better informed of the capabilities and successes of this relatively young discipline. This volume contains the final version of the papers accepted for presentation at the conference from both tracks.

We received a total of 252 submissions (207 in the Foundations and 45 in the Applications track) from 34 countries; 21% of the papers were co-authored by researchers from different countries, indicating a healthy trend toward international collaboration. The program committees selected a total of 54 papers for presentation at the conference (43 Foundations and 11 Applications) giving a total acceptance rate of 21.3%.

We would like to thank everyone who submitted papers, as well as those who submitted proposals for workshops and tutorials. We would also like to express our gratitude to the large number of volunteers who contributed to the success of the conference. Special thanks are due to Richard van de Stadt for his prompt and unfailing support of CyberChairPRO, the conference management system used for MODELS 2010. Last but not least, we would like to thank our sponsors, ACM, IEEE, SINTEF, and the Department of Informatics at the University of Oslo.

October 2010

Dorina C. Petriu
Nicolas Rouquette
Øystein Haugen

Organization

General Chair

Øystein Haugen   SINTEF and University of Oslo, Norway

Program Chairs

Dorina C. Petriu   Carleton University, Canada
(Foundations Track)
Nicolas Rouquette   NASA, Jet Propulsion Laboratory, USA
(Applications Track)

Local Chair

Birger Møller-Pedersen   University of Oslo, Norway

Publicity and Sponsor Chair

Arne J. Berre   SINTEF and University of Oslo, Norway

International Publicity Chair

Franck Fleurey   SINTEF, Norway

Treasurer

Parastoo Mohagheghi   SINTEF, Norway

Workshop Co-chairs

Juergen Dingel   Queens University, Canada
Arnor Solberg   SINTEF, Norway

Tutorial Co-chairs

Stein Krogdahl   University of Oslo, Norway
Stein-Erik Ellevseth   ABB, Norway

Educators' Symposium Co-chairs

Peter Clarke   Florida International University, USA
Martina Seidl   Vienna University of Technology, Austria

Doctoral Symposium Chair

Bernhard Schätz   Technical University Munich, Germany
Brian Elvesæter   SINTEF and University of Oslo, Norway
(Support)

Panel Chair

Thomas Kühne   Victoria University of Wellington, New Zealand

Exhibition and Demo Chair

Arne Maus   University of Oslo, Norway

Web Chair

Dag Langmyhr   University of Oslo, Norway

Local Room Facilities

Roy Grønmo   SINTEF and University of Oslo, Norway

Student Volunteer Coordinator

Jon Oldevik   SINTEF and University of Oslo, Norway

Program Committee: Foundations Track

Daniel Amyot   University of Ottawa, Canada
Krishnakumar
   Balasubramanian   The MathWorks Inc., USA
Don Batory   University of Texas, USA
Benoit Baudry   INRIA, France
Behzad Bordbar   University of Birmingham, UK
Ruth Breu   University of Innsbruck, Austria
Lionel Briand   Simula Research Lab and University of Oslo,
                              Norway
Jean-Michel Bruel   Université de Toulouse, France
Jordi Cabot   INRIA- Ecole des Mines de Nantes, France

Michel Chaudron   Leiden University, The Netherlands
Tony Clark   Middlesex University, UK
Vittorio Cortellessa   University of L'Aquila, Italy
Krzysztof Czarnecki   University of Waterloo, Canada
Juan de Lara   Universidad Autónoma de Madrid, Spain
Jens Dietrich   Massey University, New Zealand
Juergen Dingel   Queen's University, Canada
Stephane Ducasse   INRIA Lille, France
Keith Duddy   Queensland University of Technology, Australia
Gregor Engels   University of Paderborn, Germany
Franck Fleurey   SINTEF, Norway
Robert B. France   Colorado State University, USA
David Frankel   SAP, USA
Lidia Fuentes   University of Malaga, Spain
Dragan Gasevic   Athabasca University, Canada
Geri Georg   Colorado State University, USA
Sébastien Gérard   CEA LIST, France
Sudipto Ghosh   Colorado State University, USA
Holger Giese   Hasso Plattner Institute at the University of
                             Potsdam, Germany
Tudor Gîrba   University of Bern, Switzerland
Martin Gogolla   University of Bremen, Germany
Susanne Graf   VERIMAG, France
Vincenzo Grassi   University of Rome "Tor Vergata", Italy
Jeff Gray   University of Alabama, USA
John Grundy   Swinburne University of Technology, Australia
Esther Guerra   Universidad Carlos III de Madrid, Spain
Jun Han   Swinburne University of Technology, Australia
Øystein Haugen   SINTEF, Norway
Zhenjiang Hu   National Institute of Informatics, Japan
Heinrich Hussmann   Universität München, Germany
Paola Inverardi   University of L'Aquila, Italy
Jan Jürjens   TU Dortmund and Fraunhofer ISST, Germany
Audris Kalnins   University of Latvia, Latvia
Gerti Kappel   Vienna University of Technology, Austria
Gabor Karsai   Vanderbilt University, USA
Jörg Kienzle   McGill University, Montreal, Canada
Ingolf Krüger   UC San Diego, USA
Thomas Kühne   Victoria University of Wellington, New Zealand
Jochen Küster   IBM Research - Zürich, Switzerland
Yvan Labiche   Carleton University, Canada
Ralf Laemmel   University of Koblenz-Landau, Germany
Michaël Lawley   CSIRO Australian e-Health Research Centre,
                             Australia
Timothy C. Lethbridge   University of Ottawa, Canada

Program Committee: Applications Track

Tony Clark	Middlesex University, UK
Diarmuid Corcoran	Ericsson AB, Sweden
Rik Eshuis	Eindhoven University of Technology, The Netherlands
Huascar Espinoza	European Software Institute, Spain
Andy Evans	Xactium, UK
Geri Georg	Colorado State University, USA
Øystein Haugen	SINTEF, Norway
Steven Kelly	MetaCase, Finland
Jana Koehler	IBM Zurich Research Laboratory, Switzerland
Vinay Kulkarni	Tata Consultancy Services, India
Nikolai Mansourov	KDM Analytics, Canada
Stephen Mellor	Project Technology, Inc., UK
Dragan Milicev	University of Belgrade, Serbia
Hiroshi Miyazaki	Fujitsu, Japan
Juan Carlos Molina Udaeta	CARE Technologies, S.A., Spain
Pierre-Alain Muller	Université de Haute-Alsace, France
Syed Salman Qadri	The Mathworks, Inc., USA
Ina Schieferdecker	TU Berlin/Fraunhofer FOKUS, Germany
Bran Selic	Malina Software Corporation, Canada
Richard Soley	Object Management Group, USA
Ingo Stürmer	Model Engineering Solutions GmbH, Germany
Jun Sun	National University of Singapore, Singapore
François Terrier	CEA-LIST, France
Laurence Tratt	Bournemouth University, UK
Markus Voelter	itemis AG, Germany
Michael von der Beeck	BMW Group, Germany
Thomas Weigert	Missouri University of Science and Technology, USA
Frank Weil	Hengsoft, USA
Jon Whittle	Lancaster University, UK
Ed Willink	Thales Research and Technology Ltd., UK

Steering Committee

Heinrich Hussmann (Chair)
Geri Georg (Vice Chair)
Thomas Baar
Jean Bezivin
Lionel Briand
Jean-Michel Bruel
Krzysztof Czarnecki
Gregor Engels
Øystein Haugen
Rob Pettit
Stuart Kent

Ana Moreira
Pierre-Alain Muller
Óscar Nierstrasz
Dorina Petriu
Gianna Reggio
Matthew Dwyer
Doug Schmidt
Andy Schürr
Perdita Stevens
Jon Whittle

Sponsors

ACM (http://www.acm.org)
IEEE (http://www.ieee.org)
SINTEF (http://www.sintef.no/Home/)
IFI, University of Oslo (http://www.ifi.uio.no/english/)

Additional Reviewers

Saeed Ahmadi-Behnam	Marcos Didonet Del Fabro
Mauricio Alferez	Zinovy Diskin
Shaukat Ali	Frederic Doucet
Hamoud Aljamaan	Mauro Luigi Drago
Andrew Allen	Iulia Dragomir
Carmen Alonso	Zoya Durdik
Michal Antkiewicz	Maged Elaasar
Thorsten Arendt	Romina Eramo
Nesa Asoudeh	Eban Escott
Arun Bahulkar	Sami Evangelista
Kacper Bak	Julie S. Fant
András Balogh	Hanna Farah
Cecilia Bastarrica	Claudiu Farcas
Basil Becker	Stephan Fassbender
Kristian Beckers	Ali Fatolahi
Axel Belinfante	Frederic Fondement
James M. Bieman	Gregor Gabrysiak
Enrico Biermann	Nadia Gámez
Dénes Bisztray	Xiaocheng Ge
Marko Bošković	Christian Gerth
Noury Bouraqadi	Sepideh Ghanavati
Jens Brüning	Martin Giese
Petra Brosch	Thomas Goldschmidt
Frank Brüseke	Cristina Gómez
Erik Burger	László Gönczy
Sergio Campos	Hans Groenniger
Maura Cerioli	Baris Güldali
Dan Chiorean	Tim Gülke
Hyun Cho	Arne Haber
Antonio Cicchetti	Lars Hamann
Selim Ciraci	Brahim Hamid
Rober Clarisó	Ali Hanzala
Peter J. Clarke	Michael Hauck
Benoit Combemale	Regina Hebig
Duc-Hanh Dang	Ramin Hedayati
Sylvain Dehors	Werner Heijstek
Marcus Denker	Michael Henderson

Frank Hernandez
Markus Herrmannsdoerfer
Stephan Hildebrandt
Martin Hirsch
Florian Hoelzl
Sören Höglund
Ákos Horváth
To-Ju Huang
Jeronimo Irazabal
Martin Johansen
Stefan Jurack
Lucia Kapova
Soon-Kyeong Kim
Felix Klar
Dimitrios Kolovos
Dagmar Koss
Mirco Kuhlmann
Thomas Kurpick
Ivan Kurtev
Angelika Kusel
Martin Küster
Scott Uk-Jin Lee
Leen Lambers
Philip Langer
Marius Lauder
Hervé Leblanc
Arne Lindow
Qichao Liu
Alexander De Luca
Markus Luckey
Tomaz Lukman
Carlos Luna
Frederic Massicotte
Max Maurer
Dieter Mayrhofer
Massimiliano Menarini
Marjan Mernik
Raffaela Mirandola
Kim-Sun Mo
Naouel Moha
Maarten de Mol
Ingo Mueller
Gunter Mussbacher
Benjamin Nagel
Stefan Neumann

Ariadi Nugroho
Martin Ochoa
Jon Oldevik
Sebastian Oster
Lars Patzina
Sven Patzina
Ekaterina Pek
Patrizio Pelliccione
Gabriela Perez
Christian Pfaller
Gergely Pintér
Monica Pinto
Alain Plantec
Ernesto Posse
Alireza Pourshahid
Alek Radjenovic
István Ráth
Daniel Ratiu
Irum Rauf
Indrakshi Ray
Holger Rendel
Lukas Renggli
Taylor Riche
Eduardo Rivera
Louis Rose
Sebastian Rose
Judith E. Y. Rossebø
Suman Roychoudhury
Fran J. Ruiz-Bertol
Davide Di Ruscio
Mehrdad Sabetzadeh
Karsten Saller
Pablo Sánchez
Joao Santos
Martin Schindler
Holger Schmidt
Andreas Seibel
Martina Seidl
Filippo Seracini Seyyed Shah
Syed Mohammad Ali Shaw
Carla Silva
Karsten Sohr
Stéphane S. Somé
Michael Spijkerman
Jim Steel

Yu Sun
Andreas Svendsen
Nora Szasz
Jörn Guy Süß
Tian Huat Tan
Massimo Tisi
Catia Trubiani
Sara Tucci-Piergiovanni
Steve Versteeg
Thomas Vogel
Steven Völkel
Sebastian Voss
Ingo Weisemoeller
Konrad Wieland

Manuel Wimmer
Jevon Wright
Yali Wu
Andreas Wübbeke
Yingfei Xiong
Lijun Yu
Tao Yue
Eduardo Zambon
Vadim Zaytsev
Xiaorui Zhang
Manchun Zheng
Celal Ziftci
Karolina Zurowska

Table of Contents – Part I

Session 2a: Verifying Consistency and Conformance

Session 2b: Taming Modeling Complexity

Session 2c: Modeling User-System Interaction

Session 3a: Model-Driven Quality Assurance

Session 3b: Managing Variability

Session 3c: Multi-Modeling Approaches

Table of Contents – Part II

Session 5a: (Meta)Models at Runtime

Session 5b: Requirements Engineering

Session 5c: Slicing and Model Transformations

Keynote 3

Session 6a: Incorporating Quality Concerns in MDD

Session 6b: Model-Driven Engineering in Practice

Session 6c: Modeling Architecture

A Unified Approach to Modeling and Programming

Ole Lehrmann Madsen[1] and Birger Møller-Pedersen[2]

[1] Department of Computer Science, Aarhus University and the Alexandra Institute
Åbogade 34, DK-8200 Århus N, Denmark
ole.l.madsen@cs.au.dk
[2] Department of Informatics, University of Oslo
Gaustadalléen 23, N-0371 Oslo, Norway
birger@ifi.uio.no

Abstract. SIMULA was a language for modeling and programming and provided a unified approach to modeling and programming in contrast to methodologies based on structured analysis and design. The current development seems to be going in the direction of separation of modeling and programming. The goal of this paper is to go back to the future and get inspiration from SIMULA and propose a unified approach. In addition to reintroducing the contributions of SIMULA and the Scandinavian approach to object-oriented programming, we do this by discussing a number of issues in modeling and programming and argue[1] why we consider a unified approach to be an advantage.

1 Introduction

Before the era of object-orientation, software development suffered from the use of different approaches, languages, and representations for analysis, design and implementation as e.g. when using the methodologies of structured analysis and design (SA/SD) [25]. One of the strengths of object-orientation is that it provides a unified approach to modeling as well as to programming, including both a conceptual framework and a set of language mechanisms in support of this.

Current mainstream object-oriented software development, however, seems to be going in the direction of separation of modeling and programming. The numerous technologies and books on object-oriented programming are primarily concerned with the technical aspects of programming and pay very little attention to modeling aspects. New programming languages are apparently defined with no concern for modeling. For modeling languages like UML [9] we see three different developments: informal models in languages that have to be tailored (UML profiled) to specific execution platforms or domains in order to be able to generate more than just skeleton code, executable models in e.g. executable

---

[1] This paper is a position paper accompanying a keynote speech and is therefore not a traditional scientific paper.

D.C. Petriu, N. Rouquette, Ø. Haugen (Eds.): MODELS 2010, Part I, LNCS 6394, pp. 1–15, 2010.
© Springer-Verlag Berlin Heidelberg 2010

UML (fUML) [8], and Domain Specific Languages (DSLs) that are executable by virtue of lending themselves to a specific domain (and often to a framework implemented in some programming language).

Although informal models may play an important role in the development process and DSLs have their mission for domains with specific requirements on syntax and semantics, our main concern is modeling and programming in general purpose languages, as e.g. represented by UML and programming languages like C++ [23], Java [7], and C# [10].

If models are executable one may ask what the principal difference is between a programming language and a modeling language. If the intention is that the users of an executable modeling language are not supposed to handle any generated code in a programming language, then users will require tools for this modeling language that are comparable with the best tools for the best programming languages. They will also require the powerful mechanisms that recently have been added to programming languages (e.g. generics, classes and functions combined, and functions as parameters). Users will also expect to have programming language mechanisms that are used in everyday programming. Otherwise the situation will be (as is the experience with incomplete code generation from models) that code will stay the main artifact, and when things become critical, the model is often dropped and only the code is further developed.

Another issue is efficiency. A lot of effort has been put into making compilers for programming languages that exploit the execution platforms to a maximum. In order to compete, the same would have to be done for an executable modeling language. The alternative would be to rely on code generation to a programming language with efficient code generators, but that implies the risk of ending up with two artifacts.

While programming languages have developed a number of mechanisms not yet found in modeling languages (see above), modeling languages similarly have developed a set of mechanisms that have not found their way into mainstream programming languages (like associations and state machines). In this way programming languages may be seen as a driving force for the development of modeling languages and vice versa.

It has often been emphasized that one of the strengths of object-oriented *programming* is the ability to represent (model) phenomena and concepts from the application domain. Others have questioned the modeling aspect [1,2] by noting that just a small percentage of the code relates to the real world. It is, however, not just modeling of real-world phenomena and concepts that is important – in any application domain, modeling is important, be it the domains of drivers, communication protocols, etc. [19].

All of this makes the case for a unified programming and modeling language, or a programming language with modeling capabilities. Distinguishing between programming and modeling languages blurs the fact the all programming should be modeling in the appropriate domain. Programming should not just be a technical issue about instructing a computer. *To program is to understand*: if models are described in a separate language then programming easily downgrades to just *"getting away with it"*[2] and one looses the advantage of a tight coupling between programming and modeling.

The dual support for modeling and programming may be traced back to SIMULA [4] where one of the main goals was to provide a language for modeling as well as for programming. The focus on modeling and programming has been one of the main characteristics of the Scandinavian School of object-orientation. The authors were involved in making BETA [18], another representative.

The overall purpose of this paper is to go back to the future and get inspiration from some of the ideas, goals and strengths of SIMULA with respect to modeling and programming and outline a unified approach to modeling and programming.

The approach will have to be based upon an analysis of current mainstream programming and modeling languages, identifying candidate elements that should be supported by such a unified approach and how they should be supported by language mechanisms. Similarly, the approach will have to identify and understand programming language mechanisms that do not apply for modeling – and the other way around. Low-level implementation mechanisms may not apply to modeling just as non-executable mechanisms cannot directly become part of a programming language.

2   The Scandinavian Approach to Object-Orientation

2.1   The Contributions from SIMULA

It is well-known that SIMULA (developed by Ole-Johan Dahl and Kristen Nygaard in the sixties) is the first object-oriented programming language, but it is less well-known that the language was designed with support for both programming and modeling, and that it formed the basis for a pure modeling language, DELTA, already in 1973. Nygaard originally worked with operations research and his main motivation for designing a programming language was that he then could describe computer simulations. Dahl on the other hand was a computer scientist with an exceptional talent for programming.[3] Together they formed a unique team that eventually led to the first SIMULA language, SIMULA I, which was a simulation language. Dahl and Nygaard realized that the concepts in SIMULA I could be applied to programming in general and as a result they designed SIMULA 67 – later on just called SIMULA.

The SIMULA I [3] report from 1965 opens with the following sentences:

> *The two main objects of the SIMULA language are:*
> - *To provide a language for a precise and standardised description of a wide class of phenomena, belonging to what we may call "discrete event systems".*
> - *To provide a programming language for an easy generation of simulation programs for "discrete event systems".*

---

[2] Free from Kristen Nygaard.
[3] Kristen Nygaard in his obituary for Dahl [20].

As it may be seen, SIMULA should support *system description* as well as *programming*. At that time the term system description was used in a way similar to the term modeling today.[4]

SIMULA contains many of the concepts (object, class, subclass, virtual method, etc.) that are now available in mainstream object-oriented languages including UML. An exception is the SIMULA notion of active object with its own action-sequence, which strangely enough has not been adopted by many other languages (one exception is UML). For Dahl and Nygaard it was essential to be able to model concurrent processes from the real world application domains.

SIMULA users often experienced that they learned more from creating a SIMULA description of their system than from the actual simulation results. Nygaard together with Erik Holbæk-Hanssen and Petter Håndlykken therefore decided to develop a language, DELTA [11], purely for system description.

DELTA was based on the essential mechanisms from SIMULA. In addition, it had mechanisms for expressing true concurrency – as opposed to the pseudo parallel processes (coroutines) in SIMULA, and so-called time-consuming actions for describing continuous state changes over time – as opposed to the discrete event mechanisms supported by SIMULA. DELTA contained most of the mechanisms found in SIMULA but non-executable mechanisms were added to higher the level of descriptions. DELTA thus provided mechanisms that are beyond programming in the sense that a DELTA description may in general not be executed. DELTA did not get widespread acceptance outside a small community in Scandinavia, but in many aspects it was ahead of its time compared to subsequent work on specification languages and modeling languages.

Based upon SIMULA and DELTA, BETA was designed to be a a language that could be used for design as well as for programming. BETA was, however, designed more than 25 years ago (first published paper was at POPL'83 [13]). Since the design of BETA, new requirements to modeling (and programming) have emerged, but we think that the experience from the design and use of BETA may be useful for a unified language approach.

A main contribution of BETA besides the language was the development of a conceptual framework for object-oriented programming, and such a conceptual framework is essential for modeling.

2.2   The Scandinavian Approach to Modeling

In BETA (and SIMULA and DELTA[5]) the *program execution* is considered to be a *(physical) model* of some *referent system* (part of the application domain). The *program text* is considered to be a *description* of the model (program execution) and thereby a description of the referent system. Note that the program execution (i.e. the dynamic process taking place during execution of the program) is considered to be the model. The program text is not a model but a description of the model. At the time of SIMULA this was a common interpretation of the

---

[4] In the following the two terms may thus be used interchangeably.

[5] Slightly differently formulated since DELTA is not executable.

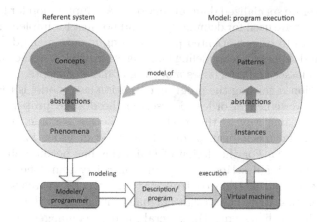

Fig. 1. Relationship between referent system, model and description

term *model*. This is in contrast to UML where the UML description is considered to be the model. The BETA model would in UML terms correspond to what would be generated at M0 (with executable UML), while a BETA program would correspond to a UML model at M1.

An analogy is a model train. The model of the real train station (or the one to be built) is the one consisting of tracks, switches, lights and small trains that move on these tracks. The model is not the description of how to build this train station.

At some point in time during the development of object-oriented methods and modeling languages, probably in connection with the introduction of graphical descriptions, model became the term used for the diagrams or descriptions. A box in a diagram representing really only a description of a part of a system may easily be confused with a model of the same part.

An essential part of the BETA project was the development of a conceptual framework for object-oriented programming. The purpose of the conceptual framework is to provide conceptual means for understanding and organizing knowledge about phenomena and concepts from the real world (application domain). And also to be explicit about the kind of properties of the real world that can be described in state-of-art object-oriented languages and in this way also serve as a driving force for the development of new abstraction mechanisms. Further development of a conceptual framework should be central in research on modeling. The reader is referred to [17,18,14] for a further elaboration of the modeling aspects of BETA.

2.3   Implications for Language Design

Apart from the direct support for active objects with their own action sequences, one of the main characteristics of the Scandinavian modeling approach to object-oriented modeling is that classes model application domain *concepts*, and subclasses therefore specialized domain concepts. An implication for language design is that classes are used for defining types and not just for implementing types. Other approaches to object-oriented programming maintain the distinction between classes and types, while modeling languages have followed the Scandinavian approach with classes and subclasses modeling domain concepts.

The implication regarding the program execution as a model is that language mechanisms are designed in order to describe the desired properties of model elements. In the same way as the mechanism of class is made in order to describe concepts, the mechanism of object is made in order for objects to be models of *phenomena*. For the design of DSLs this has become obvious. When making a language for describing e.g. train control systems one start by identifying the phenomena of train controls systems (tracks, switches, lights, etc.) and their properties, and then design language mechanisms that suits the purpose of describing such systems. For general purpose languages this will amount to identifying the desired properties of phenomena in general and then devise language mechanisms for this. As an example, when designing SIMULA it was important to describe phenomena with their own action sequence. Value properties of phenomena lead to attributes of objects (developed as part of the record concept prior to SIMULA), while potential behavior properties lead to procedures (methods) belonging to objects. Another example is that in BETA it was possible to describe that objects were parts of another object. For a programming language this is not needed (can be done by a const mechanism), while composition (as also found in UML) may be important for modeling.

3   Language Design Issues

As mentioned, modeling languages and programming languages have a common core of concepts, language constructs and other issues. In addition, there are a number of issues normally associated with modeling just as there are issues normally associated with programming. We believe that most of these issues apply just as well to modeling as to programming. In this section we discuss a number of general language design issues and in the next section we discuss concrete language constructs. We believe that research in modeling and programming languages will benefit from identifying theses issues and discuss them in a broader perspective. Issues like scope rules, type systems, semantics, etc. that obviously apply to both modeling and programming are not discussed in this paper.

3.1   Syntax

For mainstream languages, programming languages most often have a textual syntax while modeling languages have a graphical syntax. There is, however, no law or other justification for this. There are several examples of programming languages with a graphical syntax, and we shall later argue that a textual syntax may also be useful for a modeling language.

One may argue that a graphical syntax is better suited for communication than a textual syntax. Since modeling languages are primarily used in the initial phases of a project, the communication aspect is important. This is the case for communication in a team, between teams, with managers and perhaps also with customers. All of this argues for a graphical syntax. There is the well known phrase: *A picture says more than a thousand words*. There is, however, also a saying the other way around: *A word says more than a thousand pictures*.[6] As an example, the word "vehicle" communicates the concept in a much more efficient way than thousand pictures of vehicles. The point is that we use words to capture essential concepts and phenomena – as soon as we have identified a concept and found a word for it, this word is an efficient means for communication.

While the argument for graphical descriptions is that they are are good for providing overview, the fact is that graphical descriptions quickly become unmanageable when they get large. In addition when a model becomes stable and well understood, a textual description is more compact, and at that stage of a project there is no problem for the developers to work with at textual description of a model.

One of the benefits of object-oriented programming is that it has provided a common set of language constructs for programming as well as modeling. Objects, classes, subclasses, virtuals, etc. are core language elements in programming as well as modeling languages, and these are independent of what kind of syntax is used.

In our opinion text or graphics are just a matter of syntax, i.e. both types of language should/could have a textual as well as a graphical syntax. In addition, we find it useful to be able to mix textual and graphical descriptions in the same page/diagram/window. SDL [12] is an example of a language that has both a textual and a graphical syntax. In addition, it is possible to mix text and graphics in the same descriptions.

The original design of BETA was based on a textual notation, but later a graphical notation was added. The Mjølner tool [22] provided an integrated text, structure and graphical editor. The textual syntax and the graphical syntax were just different presentations of the same underlying abstract syntax tree, and the user could switch between these presentations. There was thus a one-to-one correspondence between the textual and the graphical syntax. This was the case for the abstraction mechanisms, but of course not for low-level control structures, assignments and expressions. Later, the graphical notation was changed into UML, the rationale being that this was a de facto standard graphical notation, but this created impedance problems. For a unified language this should not be an issue, and the one-to-one-correspondence principle is the only option.

As mentioned, SIMULA was designed as a modeling and a programing language, but based on a textual syntax. One may wonder whether or not a graphical notation was an issue. Graphical illustrations have been in common use since the early days of programming, for documenting programs. This was of course also the case for SIMULA. Such illustrations were informal and the intention

---

[6] Quote by Kristan Nygaard.

was to give the reader an idea about the structure of a given program. Current mainstream modeling languages have a formal graphical syntax and this is fundamentally different from using informal drawings for illustrating programs. We realize that some form of standardization of diagrams is necessary, but insisting on a formal graphical syntax for all usages of graphics may not be a good idea.

3.2   Constraints

Some of the elements of modeling languages impose constraints on the elements of the model. Constraints have also been an issue for programming languages for decades. At a general level, constraint languages impose structural relations or state changes by means of equations and/or relations. A language like Prolog may be seen as an example of a programming language based on equations. For object-oriented programming the work of Alan Borning, Bjorn Freman [5] and others are well-known examples of adding constraints to object-oriented languages. One of the first attempts was to use equations for stating the relations between graphical elements in a window. This is an example where equations often are easier to understand than a set of imperative statements.

Constraints have not made it into mainstream programming languages. The reason may be twofold: (1) it is in general not possible to solve arbitrary equations and/or relations – it is necessary to impose some kind of restrictions upon the kind of equations/relations that can be used, (2) constraints are rarely primitive language elements. They require a constraint solver that may be more or less complex. And since there is a broad variety of the kind of restrictions that can be imposed on the equations/relations, constraint mechanisms and their corresponding solver merely seems to belong to the library/framework level. The difficult part is to identify which primitive language elements to add to a given language in order to support constraints.

3.3   Domain Specific Languages

The notion of Domain Specific Language (DSL) is an issue often associated with modeling languages and therefore with graphical syntax. However, the idea of domain specific languages is orthogonal to programming and modeling languages. It has been an issue long before modeling languages were considered.

When SIMULA 67 was generalized (from the simulation language SIMULA I) to become a general purpose programming language, the simulation capabilities of SIMULA I were defined in a framework in terms of a predefined class `Simulation`. Class `Simulation` was the first example of an application framework and it is also considered an example of a DSL embedded within SIMULA. SIMULA actually has a special syntax that only applies together with class `Simulation`.

In general any application framework may be considered a DSL, and most often a DSL comes along with a framework. We do, however, not advocate defining a special syntax for each application framework. If several frameworks are used together, different syntaxes may be confusing. There are, however, cases for DSLs in very specific application domains where special syntax is required.

While DSLs started in languages with textual syntax (embedded or standalone languages), the syntax for DSLs within modeling is often graphical, the reason being that special kinds of well-established notations have to be supported. Examples are DSLs for feature modeling, where feature diagrams have to be supported, and TCL [24], a train control language, where the descriptions have to have the forms of tracks, switches, lights, etc.

For standalone languages, it is straightforward to associate a graphical syntax with the defining framework. For embedded DSLs we suggest that techniques for embedding a graphical language into a host (graphical) language be developed. This may also be used with complex language elements like state machines and associations which could then be defined as frameworks with an associated embeddable graphical syntax. We return to this in Sect. 4.

3.4   Object Models and Scenario Descriptions

Interaction diagrams like communication- and sequence diagrams in UML are useful for describing the essential scenarios of a given system. In a similar way, object models (instance specifications) in UML (at level M1) are useful for describing snapshots.

As mentioned, we consider the execution (level M0 in UML) to be the model, and therefore we think that language constructs for describing snapshots of the execution including objects and their relationships are important. Few programming languages include support for describing snapshots.

For the same reason it is a good idea to define a notation for describing snapshots/scenarios that is consistent with the language independent of whether it is a modeling or programming language or a combination. A tool may then check the consistency between scenario descriptions and the program/model just as the notation may be used in debuggers. Currently only modeling languages like UML seem to have this – few if no programming languages have an associated scenario notation. With the current use in UML, the language will have to have the notion of composite structure in order to provide a context for e.g. sequence diagrams with lifelines corresponding to the parts of such a composite structure.

3.5   Programming by Examples

When one or more scenarios have been made, one has to design a description of a model that covers the scenarios in the sense that the scenarios correspond to the model. In order to support this, it will of course be useful to be able to construct the model description more or less automatically from the scenarios. There are several authors that present techniques for deriving models from scenario descriptions. This includes techniques to construct state machines from sequence diagrams.

This is, however, not only an issue for modeling. It may be seen as analogous to programming by examples. The literature contains many examples of papers that present techniques for deriving programs from examples. One example is the paper by Henry Lieberman from 1982 [15].

3.6   Miscellaneous

UML has a number of mechanisms like *Components* and *Deployment* that we do not consider in this paper. Most of these are just as relevant for programming as for modeling. Components are just special objects (just like in UML), and programs also have to be deployed.

Use Cases appear to be quite separate from the rest of UML and they might just as well be used together with a programming language. There might, however, be a case for a tighter integration with sequence diagrams and thus with the execution, but for some reason this was not done when a major revision of UML (UML2) was made.

4   Language Concepts

4.1   State Machines

State machines are common for modeling, but have never become mainstream in programming languages. A common approach is to use the *design pattern* as described in [6]. In practice, however, it is necessary to be able to alternate between modeling and programming. When using the state-pattern it may be difficult to identify a given state machine in a program and good tools for code generation and reverse engineering are therefore required.

Another common approach is to define a state machine *abstraction* in a class library. This puts requirements on the programing language with regard to the ability to define a suitable abstraction for state machines. In order to support a graphical syntax for a state machine abstraction it is necessary to be able to associate such a syntax with the abstraction/library. As mentioned in Sect. 3.1, general support for embedding graphical syntax in a host language may be a solution.

Direct support by means of language constructs is of course a possibility. In [16] a mechanism for changing the virtual binding of a class is suggested as a means for supporting state machines. With direct language support it is of course straightforward to support a graphical syntax.

State machines are complex entities – this holds for simple state machines, but even more when composite states are included. This may imply that direct language support is not the the best solution – the language should be powerful enough to define the appropriate abstraction(s).

4.2   Associations

Associations are perhaps the modeling mechanism that is most often mentioned as lacking proper support in programming languages. In 1987 Rumbaugh [21] proposed programming language support for associations, and since then there have been several alternative proposals.

The reason that no mainstream programming language has direct support for associations may be due to the complexity of associations. Rumbaugh has a figure that shows the location of associations in the hierarchy of containers. This may be taken as an indication that associations should perhaps not be a built-in mechanism. It is, however, difficult to identify one or more less primitive mechanisms (besides references) that should be included instead. In addition to suggestions for language support, there are many examples of proposals for association libraries as in [26].

We are not aware of design patterns for supporting associations in general. There are specific design patterns for e.g. composite as in [6]. This may be an indication of the complexity of associations. There are in fact many ways to define such abstractions, i.e lack of standardization. The latter is perhaps due to the fact that UML is open for interpretation or perhaps that there is a need for variation here.

As for state machines we think that the best approach is to define abstractions (in class libraries) that support associations. This is not possible in most main-stream languages, so it is a challenge for programming language design. With respect to graphical syntax we again advocate to develop support for embedding a graphical syntax into a host language.

4.3   Asynchronous Events

Messages in mainstream object-oriented languages are synchronous in the sense that a method invocation blocks until the entire message has been executed and a possible value has been returned.

UML state machines have events that are both reception of asynchronous signals and methods calls. Most users of state machines in UML are using them in application domains where asynchronous signals are the means of communication, e.g. telecom or process control. fUML recognizes this by only supporting signals as events, while method calls are executed independently of the state of the object. This is in contrast to e.g. state patterns proposed for object-oriented programming languages, where method calls are the events.

In a unified language there seems to be two options: (a) support both kinds of events and make both of them controlled by states, (b) select one of them and provide the other as a framework on top of the language (not all modeling mechanisms have to be language mechanisms, in programming languages one is used to make frameworks instead of new language constructs). Starting with object-oriented programming (and not with executable UML), the most obvious choice is perhaps to have method calls as events, while for a unified language the choice may not be that obvious.

For many years the support for asynchronous method calls has been an is-sue for object-oriented programming platforms as well. There are numerous programming languages that support asynchronous method calls. Programming languages with asynchronous communication are often based on actors. Actors are objects with their own thread of control. They share no state with other actors; they communicate exclusively via asynchronous message passing.

Mapping of external events into synchronous or asynchronous method calls or more direct support in the language is also an independent issue.

4.4   Action Sequences

With respect to action sequences there is in general a major difference between programming languages and modeling languages. Programming languages are based on well established (sequential) statements such as assignments and control structures. For concurrent programming there is much less consensus – in fact concurrent object-oriented programming seems to be caught in a tar pit of low-level technical details of how to avoid locking problems, memory problems, and efficient use of thread-safe libraries. If one recalls the original goals of SIMULA as a modeling language that was also able to describe concurrent processes from the real-world, mainstream concurrent programming seems far away from supporting modeling.[7]

For modeling languages the picture seems pretty blurred in the sense that there are many suggestions for describing action sequences, including state machines, active objects, activity modeling, etc. Compared to programming languages, there is clearly an attempt to model action sequences at a higher level. This also holds for concurrent processes. UML 2 activities are typically used for business process modeling, for modeling the logic captured by a single use case or usage scenario, or for modeling the detailed logic of a business rule.

We do not think that the various proposals for modeling (sequential and concurrent) action sequences in say UML have matured to a point where they are usable in practice and can replace traditional programming language statements. We do, however, advocate that the same means for describing action sequences should be used for programming as well as modeling. We especially advocate a modeling approach to concurrency since we need more high-level concurrency abstractions in order to deal with the future of multi-core processors.

4.5   Other Language Constructs

In UML an object can be a member of several classes, which is not possible in mainstream programming languages. This is desirable for modeling as well as programming. In Chapter 18 in [18] we discuss a number of means for classification, including multiple classification and dynamic class membership.

We have mainly discussed language mechanisms that are often associated with modeling and argued that they are just as relevant for programming. In a similar way, there are a number of programming language mechanisms that have not found their way into modeling languages. These include statics, metaclasses

---

[7] We do not claim that SIMULA is the solution to concurrent programming – SIMULA may be able to describe real world processes, but has no support for synchronization of true parallel processes.

(reflection), generics, traits, (higher order) functions, general block-structure (arbitrary nesting of classes and methods), aspects, modules, and many more. If such mechanisms are useful for programming they are probably also useful for modeling. We do (of course) not argue that a unified language should contain the union of all possible language constructs. The point is that if a construct has proved useful for programming, it might as well be useful for modeling and vice versa.

5 Conclusion

We have argued for a unified approach to modeling and programming based on the fact that this was one of the strengths of object-orientation as provided by SIMULA. We think that the benefits of a unified approach are fading away since the design of programming languages and modeling languages seems to be more or less separate activities in different communities. If programming and modeling are separate activities, we will constantly be confronted with impedance mismatch between different representations just as programmers may not be concerned with modeling and vice versa. Eventually the code will win, either due to lack of time in a given project and/or because the code is the real thing.

We have also argued that programming is a modeling activity even in technical domains that are not related to the so-called real world. In our opinion any object-oriented program should reflect the concepts and phenomena in the given domain and the basic core of object-orientation includes a conceptual framework as well as a set of language constructs that facilitate modeling. We have also argued that further development of the conceptual framework for object-orientation is an important activity within modeling and programming.

The approach to modeling has implications for language design as well as for the design of notations for illustrating scenarios and including the model (program execution).

We have discussed a number of issues often associated with modeling and argued that most of these issues are relevant for programming as well. The other way around, most issues relevant for programming are also relevant for modeling. One conclusion is that programming and modeling may benefit from a unified approach.

For modeling there may be a need for concepts at a higher level than primitives in programming languages. Examples are state machines and associations. A programming language should support defining these concepts as abstractions (class libraries). We acknowledge that current state-of-art of language abstractions may not be sufficient to define such abstractions. This calls for further research in order to develop more powerful abstraction mechanisms.

We have argued that a textual or graphical syntax is relevant for modeling and programming, and we have argued for techniques to support embedding of graphical syntax within a host language. This is especially relevant to support graphical notations associated with abstractions for e.g. state machines and associations.

Modeling languages may contain non-executable parts that express constraints on the elements of the description. With a unified approach there is of course still a need for such non-executable elements, but these should be integrated with the language. There are programming languages that have support for non-executable elements like invariants, assertions, and pre- and postconditions just as there are so-called constraint-based languages. There is thus good reason to integrate non-executable parts into a unified modeling and programming language.

Finally, there are issues related to the model itself (where model is the program execution). Modeling languages include elements for describing scenarios and object models. Bearing in mind that the model is the program execution, it is of course important that language elements for describing the model in terms of scenarios and/or objects are treated as a first-class issue and not left to just be the design of a debugger. We need means for presenting the model.

References

1. Cook, S.: Object Technology – A Grand Narrative?. In: Thomas, D. (ed.) ECOOP 2006. LNCS, vol. 4067, pp. 174–179. Springer, Heidelberg (2006)
2. Cook, W.: Peek Objects. In: Thomas, D. (ed.) ECOOP 2006. LNCS, vol. 4067, pp. 180–185. Springer, Heidelberg (2006)
3. Dahl, O.-J., Nygaard, K.: SIMULA—a Language for Programming and Description of Discrete Event Systems. Technical report, Norwegian Computing Center (1965)
4. Dahl, O.-J., Nygaard, K.: SIMULA: an ALGOL-based Simulation Language. Communications of the ACM 9(9), 671–678 (1966)
5. Freeman-Benson, B.N., Borning, A.: Integrating Constraints with an Object-Oriented Language, June 29-July 3 (1992)
6. Gamma, E., Helm, R., Johnson, R., Vlissides, J.: Design Patterns: Elements of Reusable Object-Oriented Software. Addison-Wesley Professional Computing Series. Addison-Wesley, Reading (1995)
7. Gosling, J., Joy, B., Steele, G.: The Java (TM) Language Specification. Addison-Wesley, Reading (1999)
8. Object Management Group: Semantics of a Foundational Subset for Executable UML Models FTF Beta 2 (2009)
9. Object Management Group: OMG Unified Modeling Language (OMG UML), Superstructure Version 2.3 (2010)
10. Hejlsberg, A., Wiltamuth, S., Golde, P.: The C# Programming Language. Addison-Wesley, Reading (2003)
11. Holbæk-Hanssen, E., Håndlykken, P., Nygaard, K.: System Description and the DELTA Language. Technical Report Report No. 523, Norwegian Computing Center (1973)
12. ITU: Specification and Description Language (SDL), Recommendation Z.100, ITU T (1999)
13. Kristensen, B.B., Madsen, O.L., Møller-Pedersen, B., Nygaard, K.: Abstraction Mechanisms in the BETA Programming Language. In: Tenth ACM Symposium on Principles of Programming Languages, Austin, Texas (1983)
14. Kristensen, B.B., Madsen, O.L., Moller-Pedersen, B.: The When, Why and Why not of the BETA Programming Language. In: Hailpern, B., Ryder, B.G. (eds.) History of Progamming Languages III, San Diego, CA. SIGPLAN (2007)

15. Lieberman, H.: Designing Interactive Systems From The User's Viewpoint. In: Degano, P., Sandewall, E. (eds.) Integrated Interactive Computing Systems, Stresa. North-Holland, Amsterdam (1987)
16. Madsen, O.L.: Towards Integration of Object-Oriented Languages and State Machines. In: Technology of Object-Oriented Languages and Systems (TOOLS Europe 1999), Nancy (1999)
17. Lehrmann Madsen, O., Møller-Pedersen, B.: What object-oriented programming may be - and what it does not have to be. In: Gjessing, S., Nygaard, K. (eds.) ECOOP 1988. LNCS, vol. 322, pp. 1–20. Springer, Heidelberg (1988)
18. Madsen, O.L., Møller-Pedersen, B., Nygaard, K.: Object-Oriented Programming in the BETA Programming Language. Addison Wesley, Reading (1993)
19. Madsen, O.L.: ECOOP 1987 to ECOOP 2006 and Beyond. In: Thomas, D. (ed.) ECOOP 2006. LNCS, vol. 4067, pp. 186–191. Springer, Heidelberg (2006)
20. Nygaard, K.: Ole-Johan Dahl. Journal of Object Technology 1(4) (2002)
21. Rumbaugh, J.: Relations as Semantic Constructs in an Object-Oriented Language. In: Meyrowitz, N. (ed.) OOPSLA 1987 – Object-Oriented Programming, Systems Languages and Applications, Orlando, Florida, USA. Sigplan Notices, vol. 22. ACM Press, New York (1987)
22. Sandvad, E.: An Object-Oriented CASE Tool. In: Knudsen, J.L., Löfgren, M., Madsen, O.L., Magnusson, B. (eds.) Object-Oriented Environments—The Mjølner Approach, Prentice Hall, Englewood Cliffs (1994)
23. Stroustrup, B.: The C++ Programming Language. Addison-Wesley, Reading (1986)
24. Svendsen, A., Olsen, G.K., Endresen, J., Moen, T., Carlson, E., Alme, K.-J., Haugen, O.: The Future of Train Signaling. In: Czarnecki, K., Ober, I., Bruel, J.-M., Uhl, A., Völter, M. (eds.) MODELS 2008. LNCS, vol. 5301, pp. 128–142. Springer, Heidelberg (2008)
25. Yourdon, E., Constantine, L.L.: Structured Design: Fundamentals of a Discipline of Computer Program and Systems Design. Yourdon Press Computing Series (1979)
26. Østerbye, K.: Design of a Class Library for Association Relationships. In: LCSD 2007, Montréal, Canada (2007)

Generic Meta-modelling with Concepts, Templates and Mixin Layers

Juan de Lara[1] and Esther Guerra[2]

[1] Universidad Autónoma de Madrid, Spain
`Juan.deLara@uam.es`
[2] Universidad Carlos III de Madrid, Spain
`eguerra@inf.uc3m.es`

Abstract. Meta-modelling is a key technique in Model Driven Engineering, where it is used for language engineering and domain modelling. However, mainstream approaches like the OMG's Meta-Object Facility provide little support for abstraction, modularity, reusability and extendibility of (meta-)models, behaviours and transformations.

In order to alleviate this weakness, we bring three elements of *generic programming* into meta-modelling: *concepts*, *templates* and *mixin layers*. Concepts permit an additional typing for models, enabling the definition of behaviours and transformations independently of meta-models, making specifications reusable. Templates use concepts to express requirements on their generic parameters, and are applicable to models and meta-models. Finally, we define functional layers by means of *meta-model mixins* which can extend other meta-models.

As a proof of concept we also report on METADEPTH, a multi-level meta-modelling framework that implements these ideas.

1 Introduction

Meta-modelling is a core technique in Model Driven Engineering (MDE), where it is used for language engineering and domain modelling. The main approach to meta-modelling is the OMG's Meta-Object Facility (MOF) [11], which proposes a linear, strict meta-modelling architecture enabling the definition and instantiation of meta-models. MOF has a widespread use, and has been partially implemented in the Eclipse Modeling Framework (EMF) [13]. However, even though meta-modelling is becoming increasingly used on an industrial scale, current approaches and tools are scarcely ever concerned with scalability issues like reusability, abstraction, extendibility, modularity and compatibility (i.e. ease of composition) of models, meta-models and transformations.

Generic programming [5,14] is a style of programming in which types (typically classes) and functions are written in terms of parametric types that can be instantiated for specific types provided as parameters. This promotes the abstraction of algorithms and types by lifting their details from concrete examples to their most abstract form [14]. The advantage is that any type that fulfils the algorithm's requirements can reuse such a *generic* algorithm. Hence, generic

D.C. Petriu, N. Rouquette, Ø. Haugen (Eds.): MODELS 2010, Part I, LNCS 6394, pp. 16–30, 2010.

programming shifts the emphasis from type-centric to requirements-centric programming [9], enhancing generality and reusability.

In this paper we bring into meta-modelling and language engineering some of the successful, proven principles of generic programming. The goal is to solve some of the weaknesses of current approaches to meta-modelling, transformation and behaviour specification concerning reusability, modularity, genericity and extendibility. For example, current approaches to behaviour specification tend to define behaviour using types of one particular meta-model. However, as generic programming often does, one should be able to define generic behaviours applicable to several meta-models sharing some characteristics and without resorting to intrusive mechanisms. In this respect, we show that the use of *generic concepts* specifying requirements from parametric types permits defining behaviours in an abstract, non-intrusive way, being applicable to families of meta-models.

Furthermore, models often suffer from an early concretization of details which hinders their reusability. The use of model *templates* allows delaying some details on the model structure by defining model parameters. In this way, a model template could be instantiated with different parameters, allowing its reusability in different situations, and enhancing its compatibility and modularity. Model templates are also a mechanism to implement patterns for domain-specific languages and model component libraries.

Finally, *mixin layers* [12] allow defining meta-models with generic functional capabilities to be plugged into different meta-models. We found especially useful the definition of *semantic mixin layers* containing the necessary run-time infrastructure for the definition of semantics of meta-model families.

As a proof of concept, we have implemented these elements in a multi-level meta-modelling framework called METADEPTH [3]. However, our aim is not to describe an extension of METADEPTH's capabilities. We believe that *genericity* has a wide potential in meta-modelling, and hence what we describe here has immediate applicability to other frameworks, like the MOF. A prototype of the tool can be downloaded from `http://astreo.ii.uam.es/~jlara/metaDepth/`.

The paper is organized as follows. Section 2 reviews generic programming. Section 3 introduces METADEPTH so that its syntax is used in the rest of the paper. Section 4 presents generic concepts for meta-modelling, Section 5 presents model templates and Section 6 introduces semantic mixin layers. Section 7 discusses related research and Section 8 concludes.

2 Generic Programming

Genericity [5] is a programming paradigm found in many languages like C++, Haskell, Eiffel or Java. Its goal is to express algorithms and data structures in a broadly adaptable, interoperable form that allows their direct use in software construction. It involves expressing algorithms with minimal assumptions about data abstractions, as well as generalizing concrete algorithms without losing efficiency [5]. It promotes a paradigm shift from types to algorithms' requirements, so that even unrelated types may fulfil those requirements, hence making algorithms more general and reusable.

In its basic form, generic programming involves passing type parameters to functions or data types which are then called *templates*. In this way, template functions or classes require the parameter types to fulfil a number of requirements for a correct instantiation of the template. This set of requirements is usually expressed using a *concept* [9]. Typical requirements include, e.g., a type which must define a "<" binary relation, or a list of data objects with a first element, an iterator and a test to identify the end. Rudimentary concepts exist e.g. in Java, limited to express the requirements of a single type by demanding it to inherit from a specified class or to implement a set of interfaces.

As an example, Listing 1 shows a C++ template function *min* that returns the minimum of two elements of a parametric type T. The requirement for the type T is to define the "<" operator, specified by concept LessThanComp[1].

```
1  template <typename T> requires LessThanComp<T>
2     T min(T x, T y) { return y < x ? y : x; }
3  concept LessThanComp <typename T> { bool operator<(T, T); }
```

Listing 1. A template and a concept example in C++.

Mixins are classes designed to provide functionality to other classes, typically through parameterized inheritance, promoting code reuse and modularity. Mixin layers [12] extend mixins by encapsulating fragments of *multiple classes* to define a layer of functionality, which can be added to other sets of classes. They were proposed as a technique for implementing collaboration-based designs, where objects play different roles in different collaborations. In this context, mixin layers provide the needed functionality for each collaboration, so that the final system is obtained by composing layers.

3   METADEPTH

METADEPTH [3] is a new multi-level meta-modelling framework with support for multiple meta-levels at the same time using *potency* [1]. This approach is very useful to describe what we call *deep languages*, which are languages that involve two or more meta-levels at the user level. An example of a deep language is the combination of UML class and object diagrams, if one thinks of object diagrams as instances of class diagrams [3]. The framework uses a textual syntax and is integrated with the Epsilon family of languages[2], so that EOL [7] can be used to express constraints and behaviours. EOL extends OCL with imperative constructs to manipulate models.

---

[1] Concepts have been post-poned from C++0x, the last revision of C++.
[2] http://www.eclipse.org/gmt/epsilon/

```
 1  Model PetriNet {
 2    abstract Node NamedElement {
 3      name : String {id};
 4    }
 5    Node Place : NamedElement {
 6      outTr : Transition[*] {ordered,unique};
 7      inTr  : Transition[*] {ordered,unique};
 8      tokens: Token[*] {unique};
 9    }
10    Node Token {}
11    Node Transition : NamedElement {
12      inPl : Place[*] {ordered,unique};
13      outPl: Place[*] {ordered,unique};
14    }
15    Edge ArcPT(Place.outTr,Transition.inPl) {}
16    Edge ArcTP(Transition.outPl,Place.inTr) {}
17    minPlaces : $Place.allInstances()->size()>0$
18  }
```

Listing 2. Meta-model for Petri nets, in METADEPTH's syntax and UML.

Listing 2 shows a meta-model for Petri nets using METADEPTH's syntax to the left and a UML representation to the right. Petri nets are a kind of automaton with two kinds of vertices: *Places* and *Transitions*. Places contain tokens, and can be connected with transitions through arcs (and the other way round).

The listing declares an abstract node NamedElement owning a field name. The field's id modifier states that no two instances of NamedElement can have the same value for the field. Both Place and Transition inherit from NamedElement. The former declares three association ends (outTr, inTr and tokens) with cardinality 0..*. The modifier ordered keeps the collection elements in the order of assignment, while unique forbids duplicated elements. The opposite ends of outTr and inTr are declared by the edges ArcPT and ArcTP. Thus, in METADEPTH's syntax, Model is similar to a meta-model, Node to a meta-class, and Edge to a meta-association (in fact to an associative class).

METADEPTH supports the definition of constraints and derived attributes either in Java or in EOL. Constraints can be declared in the context of Models, Nodes or Edges. Line 17 in the listing declares an EOL constraint named minPlaces, which demands PetriNet models to have at least one Place. As METADEPTH allows specifying multiplicities in the definition of Nodes, the same effect can be obtained by replacing line 5 by "Node Place[1..*] : NamedElement {".

The defined meta-model can be instantiated as Listing 3 shows. This Petri net model represents a system with two processes (producer and consumer) communicating through a buffer of infinite capacity. The right of Listing 3 shows the system using the usual Petri nets visual notation, with places represented

```
1  PetriNet ProducerConsumer {
2    Place WP { name="waitProduce"; }
3    Place RP { name="ReadyProduce"; }
5    Transition ReadyP  { name="readyP"; }
4    Transition Produce { name="in"; }
6    ArcPT (RP, Produce);
7    ...
8    Place Buffer { name="Buffer"; }
9    ...
10   Place C  { name="Consume"; }
11   Place WC { name="waitConsume"; }
12   Transition Consume { name="out"; }
13   Transition ReadyC  { name="waitC"; }
14   ...
15 }
```

Listing 3. A Petri net with the Producer-Consumer example.

as circles, transitions as black rectangles, and tokens as black dots inside places. The dotted rectangles delimit the different conceptual components of the system.

Listing 3 makes use of the normal instantiation capabilities found in most meta-modelling frameworks (like EMF [13]). However, one soon notices that the definition of our model could be improved concerning abstraction, modularity and reusability. First, the user could have been offered higher-level modelling elements than places and transitions, like *Buffers* and *Processes*. Moreover, inspecting the model, one realizes that the two processes have exactly the same structure (two places connected by transitions). Therefore, it would have been useful to have a meta-modelling facility to define model components – similar to modelling patterns – that the user can instantiate and interconnect. Section 5 will demonstrate how the use of templates allows performing this *at the model level*, without any need to modify the meta-model.

Finally, METADEPTH allows defining behaviour for models using either Java or EOL. EOL is however very well suited for this purpose, as it permits defining methods on the meta-classes of the meta-models. Listing 4 shows an example simulator written in EOL to execute Petri net models. The entry point for its execution is the operation *main*, which is annotated with the required meta-models (PetriNet in our case). The listing declares the auxiliary operations enabled and fire on the context of the Transition meta-class. These are invoked in the loop of the main() operation, firing the enabled transitions.

This simulator works well for instances of the Petri net meta-model. However, there are many languages whose behaviour can be defined in terms of Petri nets. Therefore, couldn't we abstract the essential elements of Petri net-like languages and define such behaviour in a generic way? Next section will show that concepts are a solution to this issue.

```
1  @metamodel(name=PetriNet,file=PetriNet.mdepth)
2  operation main() {
3    while (Transition.allInstances()->exists(t | t.enabled() and
3                                              t.fire())) {}
4  }
5  operation Transition enabled() : Boolean {
6    return self.inP1->forAll(p | p.tokens.size()>0);
7  }
8  operation Transition fire() : Boolean {
9    for (p in self.outP1)
10     p.tokens.add(new Token);
11   for (p in self.inP1) {
12     var t : Token := p.tokens.random();
13     p.tokens.remove(t); delete t;
14   }
15   return true;
16 }
```

Listing 4. A simulator for Petri nets.

4   Concepts for Language Engineering

Now we are in the position to discuss how to bring elements of generic programming into meta-modelling. This section shows how to define *concepts*, and how to use them to define generic behaviours applicable to language families. The following two sections will discuss model and meta-model templates.

A *concept* in meta-modelling is a pattern specification that expresses requirements on models or meta-models. Concepts provide a dual typing in the context where they are used, which we use to define behaviour independently of specific meta-models. This is useful for reusability and composition of behaviours.

Let's start discussing an illustrative scenario. Assume one needs to describe the behaviour of two languages, one in the domain of Production Systems (where pieces are produced and consumed by machines) and the other for Communication Networks (where packets are produced and consumed by computers). Thus, one would define one program to simulate the first kind of models, and another different one to simulate the second kind of models. This situation is illustrated to the left of Fig. 1. In the figure we assume that behaviours are realized using EOL programs, but our approach is applicable to other means of specification of in-place model transformations, like e.g. graph transformation.

Analysing the semantics of these two languages reveals similarities between the two programs implementing them. Actually, this is due to the fact that both behaviours can be mapped into the standard semantics of Petri nets. Hence, instead of defining such similar behaviours twice, we can transform the models into a common language and define the behaviour for the common language only once. This situation is depicted to the right of Fig. 1, where Model 1 is transformed into Model 1' and Model 2 is transformed into Model 2', being

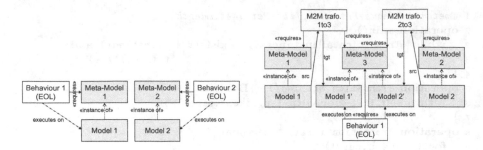

Fig. 1. Direct implementation of behaviours (left). Transformational approach (right).

both transformed models conformant to the same meta-model for which the behaviour is specified. However, this situation is not ideal either, as one has to define specific model-to-model transformations between each language and the common language. Moreover, after modifying the transformed model according to the behaviour, this has to be translated back to the original language.

An improvement that avoids transforming models is to use extension or inheritance mechanisms for meta-models (see the left of Fig. 2). In this case, the meta-models 1 and 2 extend a third meta-model for which the behaviour is defined. In particular, their classes extend (or subclass) the classes that participate in the defined behaviour for meta-model 3, so that this behaviour also applies to the classes in 1 and 2. However, this solution is intrusive as it requires that all defined meta-models for which we want to define the semantics to inherit or extend the same meta-model. This may become unfeasible if more than one semantics (e.g. timed and untimed) is to be defined for the same language.

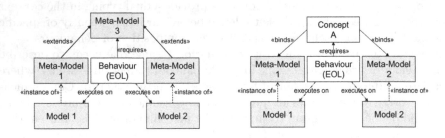

Fig. 2. Inheritance of behaviour (left). Approach based on concepts (right).

In this scenario, *concepts* can simplify the situation as they can express requirements on meta-models or models that some other elements (in this case the behaviour) needs. In our example, we can define a concept expressing the requirements that a simulator for Petri net-like languages needs. Such simulator abstracts from the specific details of the languages, and uses only the elements defined in the concept, hence being *independent of any meta-model* and therefore non-intrusive. Thus, if our two original languages satisfy the requirements of the concept, then the behaviour can be applied to their instances as shown to the right of Fig. 2. This scheme is the simplest and cleanest of the four, and its benefits increase as we find new meta-models in which the concept is applicable as we can reuse the defined behaviour for them. Moreover, the mechanism is non-intrusive: the meta-models for which we are defining the behaviour are not modified and are oblivious of the concepts.

In our approach a *concept* has a name and a number of parameters that represent generic types of models, nodes, edges or fields. Concepts can be bound against models and meta-models by a pattern-matching mechanism. In this way, a concept C defines a language $L(C)$ of all (meta-)models that satisfy the requirements imposed by the concept C. If C is defined at the meta-model level, $L(C)$ contains a family of meta-models sharing similar characteristics. We use concepts to define generic behaviours using their parameters as generic types, as well as to describe conditions to be fulfilled by template parameters. In contrast to generic programming, where concepts are used to restrict the allowed types to only those defining a certain set of operations, concepts in meta-modelling refer to structural features of (meta-)models, and thus they can impose a certain structure for their nodes, edges and fields, as well as define arbitrary constraints to restrict their applicability.

Listing 5 shows a concept, using METADEPTH's syntax. The concept characterises languages with similar structural features, enabling their simulation using the same semantics, which we call `Token-Holder`. The concept declares seven parameters, which are treated as variables and start by "&". The body of the concept requires &M to be a model with three nodes. Node &T plays the role of token. Node &H plays the role of a holder of tokens, as it is demanded to define an attribute of type &T. Node &P plays the role of a process or transition, and it must define two fields modelling the connection to input and output holders. The body of a concept may include extra conditions expressed in EOL, as well as constant elements as opposed to variables. For example, we could demand node &H to have an attribute `name:String`.

```
1  concept TokenHolder(&M, &H, &P,        6      Node &P {
1          &T, &tokens, &inHolders,       7          &inHolders : &H[*];
1          &outHolders) {                 8          &outHolders: &H[*];
2      Model &M {                         9      }
3          Node &H {                     10      Node &T {}
4              &tokens : &T[*];          11  }
5          }                             12  }
```

Listing 5. A concept expressing the requirements for `Token-Holder` semantics.

We use this concept to characterize the family of meta-models sharing the Token-Holder semantics. For example, it can be bound to the `PetriNet` meta-model of Listing 2, where &H is bound to `Place`, &P to `Transition`, and so on.

Nonetheless, the concept can be bound to other meta-models as well. For instance, Listing 6 defines a meta-model for Production Systems and its binding over the `TokenHolder` concept. The meta-model declares machines and conveyors, which can be connected to each other. Conveyors hold parts, which are fed into machines. Machines process parts, which are produced into conveyors. In this way, this working scheme is adequate for its simulation using Token-Holder semantics. Hence, we use the `TokenHolder` concept and bind it to the meta-model in line 21: conveyors act like places, machines as transitions, and parts as tokens. We explicitly pass concrete meta-model elements to the pattern matcher in the `bind` command. The binding process matches association ends with a more general cardinality (e.g. `inHolders` with cardinality "*") to association ends with more restricted cardinality (e.g. `inC` with cardinality "1..*"). This is so as all instances of the meta-model fulfil the cardinalities of the concept. The contrary is not allowed, as in that case some instances of the meta-model would not fulfil the cardinalities of the concept.

```
1   Model ProdSys {                 15      owner         : Conveyor[0..1];
2     Node Machine {                16    }
3       ref : String;               17    Edge PH(Machine.outC,Conveyor.inM);
4       type: String;               18    Edge HP(Conveyor.outM,Machine.inC);
5       inC : Conveyor[1..*];       19    Edge iP(Part.owner,Conveyor.parts);
6       outC: Conveyor[1..*];       20  }
7     }                             21  bind TokenHolder(ProdSys
8     Node Conveyor {               21                  ,ProdSys::Conveyor
9       outM : Machine[*];          21                  ,ProdSys::Machine
10      inM  : Machine[*];          21                  ,ProdSys::Part
11      parts: Part[*];             21                  ,ProdSys::Conveyor::parts
12    }                             21                  ,ProdSys::Machine::inC
13    Node Part {                   21                  ,ProdSys::Machine::outC)
14      creationTime: int;
```

Listing 6. Binding the `Token-Holder` concept.

We can define generic behavioural specifications for the concepts, applicable to instances of any meta-model that satisfies the concept's requirements. Listing 7 shows an excerpt of the EOL simulator for the `Token-Holder` concept. The program first states that it needs concept *TokenHolder* (line 1), and that it will be executed on instances of meta-models satisfying the concept. Then, the program uses the generic types and features defined by the concept, but nothing else. This program is actually an abstraction of that of Listing 4, because this one does not require concrete types. The working scheme is the same, but the operations *enabled* and *fire* are added to the class &P gets bound to. The simulator can be used to execute any instance of the `ProdSys` and `PetriNet` meta-models, hence being more reusable than the one in Listing 4.

```
1 @concept(name=TokenHolder,file=TokenHolder.mdepth)
2 operation main() {
3    while (&P.allInstances()->exists(t | t.enabled() and t.fire()))) {}
4 }
5 operation &P enabled() : Boolean {
6    return self.&inHolders->forAll(h | h.&tokens.size()>0);
7 }
8 operation &P fire() : Boolean {...}
```

Listing 7. Token-Holder behaviour expressed over concept TokenHolder.

5   Model Templates

Concepts express requirements of models and meta-models. By using such abstraction mechanism, behaviours and transformations can be expressed in a type independent way, becoming more reusable. In this section we show how *model templates* can be used to define models in a generic way.

Templates use concepts to express requirements on the type parameters they receive. They declare a number of variables which can be checked against concepts. In this way, when the templates are instantiated, an implicit binding process checks whether the actual parameters satisfy the concepts. A template T requiring concept C defines a language $L(T)$ of all its possible instantiations using as parameters any element of $L(C)$, the language defined by the concept. In this way, a template can actually be seen as a function $L(C) \xrightarrow{T} L(T)$.

The possibility of *instantiating* templates is very interesting for modelling, because we can express patterns and generic model components using templates, which we can later instantiate and combine. Consider again the Producer-Consumer Petri net model presented in Section 3. The model would benefit from a higher-level representation enabling the definition of processes (for the producer and the consumer) as well as of buffers. For this purpose we can define two model templates, acting like model components or modelling patterns that the modellers can use to construct their models.

Listing 8 shows how to specify the templates with METADEPTH. The first template Buff2 (lines 7–13) defines a generic buffer with one input and one output transitions. These two transitions (&Tri, &Tro), together with their owning models (&PNi, &PNo), are passed as parameters to the template. Then, the template simply imports both received models (line 9), declares one place (line 10) and connect it to the received transitions (lines 11–12). In addition, the template requires in line 8 that the input parameters satisfy the concept SimpleTrans. The concept, defined in lines 1–5, requires the transition to have one input and one output place, checked by the EOL constraint in line 5.

The second template, TwoStateProc (lines 15–22), defines a two-state process. In this case, the template has no parameters and acts like a pattern which can be instantiated by the modeller. In a realistic scenario, we may like to pass as parameters the names of the places, but currently METADEPTH does not support template parameters of basic data types, which is left for future work.

```
1  concept SimpleTrans(&M, &T) {      14  // --------------------------
2  PetriNet &M {                      15  template<>
3    Transition &T {}                 16  PetriNet TwoStateProc {
4  }                                   17    Place p1 {}
5  } where $&T.inP1.size()=1 and      18    Place p2 {}
5             &T.outP1.size()=1$      19    Transition t12 {}
6  // --------------------------       20    Transition t21 {}
7  template<&PNi,&Tri,&PNo,&Tro>      21    ...
8   requires SimpleTrans(&PNi,&Tri),  22  }
8            SimpleTrans(&PNo,&Tro)   23  // --------------------------
9  PetriNet Buff2 imports &PNi,&PNo{  24  TwoStateProc<> Producer;
10   Place Buffer {}                  25  TwoStateProc<> Consumer;
11   ArcPT (Buffer, &Tro);            26  Buff2<Producer,Producer::t12,
12   ArcTP (&Tri, Buffer);            26         Consumer,Consumer::t12>
13 }                                   26         ProducerConsumer;
```

Listing 8. Defining and using model templates.

Lines 24–26 instantiate the templates. The resulting model `ProducerConsumer` is equivalent to the one in Listing 3. However, the use of templates has risen the abstraction level of the model, which is now more concise, and we have reused the definition of the template `TwoStateProc`. Altogether, model templates help in defining component and pattern libraries for domain specific languages.

6   Meta-model Templates and Semantic Mixin Layers

Templates are not only useful to define generic models, but can be applied to meta-models to provide an extensible way of defining languages, similar to mixin layers [12]. In our context, a mixin layer is a set of functionalities added to a meta-model by extending the elements passed as parameters in the template that implements the functionalities. Here we explore *semantic mixin layers*, which are *meta-model templates* declaring functionality needed to express the behaviour of meta-models. These templates are complemented with behavioural specifications, defined over the generic types of the mixin.

In order to define the semantics of a language, it is often the case that its meta-model has to be extended with auxiliary classes and elements needed for the simulation. For example, when simulating an automaton, we need a pointer to the current state and the sequence of symbols to be parsed. When simulating an event system, we need a list of the scheduled events ordered by their simulation time. These extra elements are not part of the language, but of the simulation infrastructure. If the language for specifying the semantics is powerful enough, we can use it to create the required simulation infrastructure. For instance, EOL provides data structures like `Collections` or `Maps` that can be used for that purpose. However, some specification languages lack this expressivity (e.g. graph transformation), so that in general, a simulation infrastructure needs to be modelled and rendered.

The working scheme of semantic mixins is shown to the right of Fig. 3. It shows a mixin layer template T that is used to extend the meta-model members of a semantic family, characterized by concept C. $L(T)$ contains the meta-models in $L(C)$ once they have been extended with the execution infrastructure. In this way, T can be seen as a function with domain $L(C)$ which adds such infrastructure. Then, we can define a simulator for the mixin layer T, which will be applicable to instances of any meta-model in $L(T)$.

Assume we want to define a simulator for timed token-holder languages. These languages follow a token-holder semantics, but transitions fire after a given delay. The simulator would necessitate storing a list of the firings that are currently scheduled, together with the transition and tokens involved in each firing. These extra elements are not part of the timed token-holder language, but devices needed only for simulation. Hence, a separate mixin layer incorporates these elements into the language definition in a non-intrusive way.

Fig. 3 shows to the left the template implementing the mixin layer. It declares the necessary infrastructure to simulate instances of meta-models that satisfy the concept TTokHold, so that the template definition requires such a concept. This concept is similar to the concept TokenHolder in Listing 5, but in addition transitions (variable &P) are required to define a distinguished time field storing the firing delay. The template defines a family of meta-models which extend any meta-model &M satisfying concept TTokHold with the machinery needed for their simulation. For instance, assume we add an attribute delay to the Machine class in Listing 6. Then, the meta-model ProdSys is a valid binding for the concept TTokHold, and hence we can instantiate the mixin layer for the meta-model in order to incorporate it the simulation infrastructure. This is done by declaring TimedSched<ProdSys, ProdSys::Conveyor, ...> SimProdSys.

In particular, the template in Fig. 3 extends the received meta-model &M with a class Event to store the events, and a singleton class FEvtList to handle the event list. Moreover, the class with role &P (transition) is added a collection evts storing the scheduled events associated to the transition, and the class with role &T (token) is extended with the event in which the token is engaged, if any.

Behaviours associated to semantic mixin layers use the generic types of the template. Listing 9 shows an excerpt of the simulator associated to the TimedSched mixin layer. The simulator uses a FEvtList object (line 3) to keep the current simulation time and the list of scheduled events. The list of events is initialized with the set of active transitions (lines 5–6). The main simulation loop (lines 8–13) advances the simulation time to the time of the first event in the list, fires the transition associated to the event, and schedules new events (this latter is not shown in the listing).

Associating the simulator to the mixin layer has the advantage that the simulator can be reused with any meta-model to which this mixin layer has been applied (i.e. any meta-model fulfilling the TTokHold concept), like SimProdSys, hence obtaining highly reusable specifications.

```
1  template <&M,&H,&P,&T,&tok,&inH,&outH,&time>
2    requires TTokHold(&M,&H,&P,&T,&tok,&inH,&outH,&time)
3  Model TimedSched extends &M {
4    Node &P { evts: Event[*]; }
5    Node &T { evts: Event[0..1]; }
6    Node FEvtList[1] {
7      first: Event[0..1];
8      time : double;
9    }
10   Node Event {
11     time: double;
12     next: Event[0..1];
13     proc: &P;
14     toks: &T[*];
15   }
16   Edge ProcTm(&P.evts, Event.proc)
17   { t:double; }
18   Edge TokTm(&T.evts, Event.toks)
19   { t:double; }
20 }
```

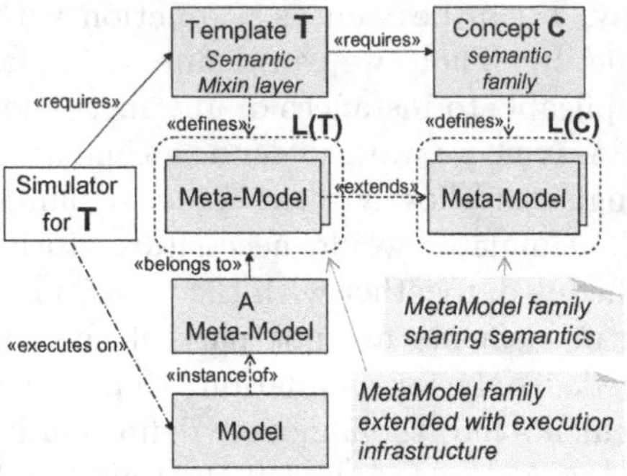

Fig. 3. Semantic mixin layer adding infrastructure to simulate `TTokHold` concepts (left). Working scheme of semantic mixin layers (right).

```
1  @template(name=TimedSched)          8   while (not finish) {
2  operation main() {                  9     FEL.time:= FEL.first.time;
3    var FEL   := new FEvtList;       10     var t: &P := FEL.first.proc;
4    FEL.time := 0;                   11     t.fire();
5    var enab: Set(&P):= getEnabled();12     ...
6    FEL.schedule(enab);              13   }
7    var finish: Boolean := false;    14 }
```

Listing 9. Excerpt of the simulator for the `TimedSched` mixin layer.

7 Related Work

The use of templates in modelling is not new, as they are already present in the UML 2.0 specification [10], as well as in previous approaches like Catalysis' model frameworks [4] and package templates, and the aspect-oriented meta-modelling approach of [2]. Interestingly, while all of them consider templates for meta-models (or class diagrams), none consider concepts or model templates.

Catalysis' model frameworks [4] are parameterized packages that can be instantiated by name substitution. Hence, they are similar to our meta-model templates. The package templates of [2] are based on those of Catalysis, and are used to define languages in a modular way. They are based on string substitution, as the parameters of the templates are strings that are substituted in the template definition. This approach is realized in the XMF tool [15]. Although package templates were incorporated into the UML 2.0 specification, the MOF does not consider genericity at the meta-model or model level.

Kermeta (`kermeta.org`) includes facilities for model typing [8], allowing establishing a subtyping relationship between meta-models. Hence, generic behaviours can be defined in a generic meta-model and applied to any subtype meta-model. This approach has been applied to generic refactorings [8].

Our work extends the mentioned approaches in several ways. First, we can apply templates not only to meta-models, but also to models, as seen in Section 5 (cf. Listing 8). Moreover, as our framework supports an arbitrary number of meta-models through potency [3], we can apply templates at any meta-level. Second, our approach is based on *concepts*, which helps in expressing requirements on template parameters. In addition, we can define behaviour for concepts and templates (in particular with semantic mixin layers), independently of meta-models. Third, our approach provides a stronger support for templates, as our template parameters are model elements whose requirements can be expressed by *concepts*. This permits type checking at the template level. Finally, whereas we consider the definition of behaviours, this is missing in other works [2,4,10].

Generic (meta-)modelling has fundamental differences with generic programming. The first refers to the level of granularity, as generic programming deals with generic classes or functions, whereas we consider generic (meta-)models which include several modelling elements, more similar to mixin layers. Second, while the purpose of programming concepts is to identify whether a class defines certain operations, modelling concepts check structural properties of models.

Another set of related research are the (meta-)model modularization approaches, like *Reuseware* [6]. In that approach, the authors develop a language-independent composition language, which can be used to define composition interfaces for models, in an intrusive way. While *Reuseware* solves the modularization of models, our templates provide in addition an instantiation mechanism, suitable to construct patterns and component libraries. Moreover, [6] does not consider behaviours and lacks abstraction mechanisms like concepts.

8   Conclusions and Future Work

In this paper we have shown the benefits of bringing concepts, templates and mixin layers into language engineering. Concepts allow expressing requirements of template parameters, and by themselves permit defining behaviours independently of meta-models, hence becoming more reusable. Templates can be applied to models or meta-models and promote extendibility, modularity and reusability. At the model level, they are useful to define patterns and model component libraries. We have seen that mixin layers, a kind of template meta-models, are especially useful to provide the necessary infrastructure to execute models. These elements have been realized in the METADEPTH tool (the examples and the tool are at `http://astreo.ii.uam.es/~jlara/metaDepth/Genericity.html`). However, the discussions are general and applicable to other contexts as well.

We are currently exploring the potential opened by genericity. We believe the semantics of modelling languages can be classified using concepts. Hence, we will define concepts for transition-based semantics, communication semantics, discrete-event semantics, and so on. The combination of concepts and semantic mixin layers will provide support for the rapid prototyping of language semantics. We are also exploring the construction of pattern libraries for domain-specific languages through model templates. We are working in improving the METADEPTH support for genericity, adding extension relations between concepts, to allow the incremental construction of concepts and concept libraries. Genericity is also applicable to the definition of generic model-to-model transformations. Finally, we are also working on an algebraic formalization, and a proof of type safety of specifications using concepts.

Acknowledgements. Work sponsored by the Spanish Ministry of Science, project TIN2008-02081 and mobility grants JC2009-00015 and PR2009-0019, and by the R&D programme of the Community of Madrid, project S2009/TIC-1650.

References

1. Atkinson, C., Kühne, T.: Rearchitecting the UML infrastructure. ACM Trans. Model. Comput. Simul. 12(4), 290–321 (2002)
2. Clark, T., Evans, A., Kent, S.: Aspect-oriented metamodelling. The Computer Journal 46, 566–577 (2003)
3. de Lara, J., Guerra, E.: Deep meta-modelling with METADEPTH. In: Vitek, J. (ed.) TOOLS 2010. LNCS, vol. 6141, pp. 1–20. Springer, Heidelberg (2010)
4. D'Souza, D.F., Wills, A.C.: Objects, components, and frameworks with UML: the catalysis approach. Addison-Wesley Longman Publishing Co., Inc., Amsterdam (1999)
5. García, R., Jarvi, J., Lumsdaine, A., Siek, J.G., Willcock, J.: A comparative study of language support for generic programming. SIGPLAN Not. 38(11), 115–134 (2003)
6. Heidenreich, F., Henriksson, J., Johannes, J., Zschaler, S.: On language-independent model modularisation. T. Asp.-Oriented Soft. Dev. VI 6, 39–82 (2009)
7. Kolovos, D.S., Paige, R.F., Polack, F.: The Epsilon Object Language (EOL). In: Rensink, A., Warmer, J. (eds.) ECMDA-FA 2006. LNCS, vol. 4066, pp. 128–142. Springer, Heidelberg (2006)
8. Moha, N., Mahé, V., Barais, O., Jézéquel, J.-M.: Generic model refactorings. In: Schürr, A., Selic, B. (eds.) MODELS 2009. LNCS, vol. 5795, pp. 628–643. Springer, Heidelberg (2009)
9. Musser, D.R., Schupp, S., Loos, R.: Requirement oriented programming. In: Jazayeri, M., Musser, D.R., Loos, R.G.K. (eds.) Dagstuhl Seminar 1998. LNCS, vol. 1766, pp. 12–24. Springer, Heidelberg (1998)
10. OMG: UML 2.2 specification, http://www.omg.org/spec/UML/2.2/
11. OMG: MOF 2.0. (2009), http://www.omg.org/spec/MOF/2.0/
12. Smaragdakis, Y., Batory, D.: Mixin layers: An object-oriented implementation technique for refinements and collaboration-based designs. ACM Trans. Softw. Eng. Methodol. 11(2), 215–255 (2002)
13. Steinberg, D., Budinsky, F., Paternostro, M., Merks, E.: EMF: Eclipse Modeling Framework, 2nd edn. Addison-Wesley Professional, Reading (2008)
14. Stepanov, A., McJones, P.: Elements of Programming. Addison Wesley, Reading (2009)
15. Tony Clark, J.W., Sammut, P.: Applied Metamodelling, a Foundation for Language Driven Development, 2nd edn., Ceteva (2008)

An Observer-Based Notion of Model Inheritance

Thomas Kühne

Victoria University of Wellington,
P.O. Box 600, Wellington 6140, New Zealand
Thomas.Kuehne@ecs.victoria.ac.nz

Abstract. A model-based engineering discipline presupposes that models are organised by creating relationships between them. While there has been considerable work on understanding what it means to instantiate one model from another, little is known about when a model should be considered to be a specialisation of another one. This paper motivates and discusses ways of defining specialisation relationships between models, languages, and transformations respectively. Several alternatives of defining a specialisation relationship are considered and discussed. The paper's main contribution is the introduction of the notions of an observer and a context in order to define and validate specialisation relationships. The ideas and discussions presented in this paper are meant to provide a stepping stone towards a systematic basis for organising models.

Keywords: model inheritance, model compatibility, language engineering, model evolution.

1   Introduction

As model-based engineering techniques gain traction it becomes increasingly important that the creation and handling of models is done with a "return on investment" perspective. A high frequency of model usage mandates that models are created and handled in a cost-effective manner. For instance, a model should not be created from scratch if another model exists that can be used to derive the new model from it. With models of substantial size, the derivation operation is typically cheaper than the creation operation and validation efforts performed on the existing model can partially be carried over to the derived model. Independently of whether or not two models were derived from each other, it pays off to avoid treating models in isolation from each other and capitalise on any relationships between them. Organising models in a network of relationships can aid model retrieval, support questions regarding model compatibility, and help to megamodel big systems [12].

Megamodels have models as their modelling elements and arrange them in a relationship graph. The meaning of an *instance-of* relationship between two models is well-understood but the same cannot be said for specialisation relationships between models [14]. In the following, I will often use the term "model inheritance" instead of "model specialisation" to avoid any connotation that the term "specialisation" carries. Just as "inheritance" between classes has many drastically differing interpretations [6,15], "inheritance" between models can also refer to a number of very different relationships between a supermodel and its submodels.

D.C. Petriu, N. Rouquette, Ø. Haugen (Eds.): MODELS 2010, Part I, LNCS 6394, pp. 31–45, 2010.

While it is possible to relate *token models* – models that only represent their subjects but are not types for any instances – to each other, this paper assumes that "model inheritance" implies that *type models* are related to each other. There is no need to distinguish between ontological or linguistic type models, as both have instances that *conform to* their respective type models [5]. A linguistic type model can be regarded as defining the syntax and static semantics of a language which is why the following discussion is relevant for language engineering just as well as for domain modelling, model evolution, and transformation definitions.

Language engineers can use model inheritance to derive one language definition from another. Such an approach does not only boost productivity but is also essential for creating *domain-customised languages*, i.e., domain-specific languages that aim to maintain compatibility to the general-purpose language they were derived from [3].

In domain modelling it also makes sense to identify commonalities between domain models, for instance in the form of *upper ontologies* [19]. An application of this type of domain model inheritance is the layered refinement of partial domain models within an ontological modelling level in the *"unified modelling library"* approach [2].

In the context of *model evolution*, models and their versions have a natural derivation relationship with each other and the main concern is to understand and optimise the degree of compatibility between model versions and their instances [9].

Finally, transformation definitions can also be regarded as models [4] and it is worthwhile attempting to define relationships between such transformation models.

One of the most valuable properties that a relationship between models can guarantee is a certain level of compatibility between the models. This is why this paper first discusses model compatibility (Sect. 2) and then looks at various ways to define model inheritance (Sect. 3), arguing that achieving model substitutability is the most valuable property to aim for. The paper then discusses a pragmatic way to extent the possibilities for defining model compatibility by using the notions of a model observer and a model context (Sect. 4). The discussion of related work (Sect. 5) precedes the conclusion (Sect. 6).

2   Model Compatibility

A very important criterion for judging the utility of model inheritance variants is the degree to which instances of a submodel $\mathcal{M}'$ are compatible with the supermodel $\mathcal{M}$ and vice versa. The direction of the specialisation relationship in Fig. 1 only signifies that $\mathcal{M}'$ is a new model that is derived from the old model $\mathcal{M}$. No other semantic constraints should be assumed since we want to consider any kind of derivation including those where $\mathcal{M}'$ is a reduced, less expressive version of $\mathcal{M}$.

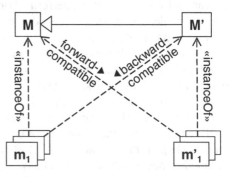

Fig. 1. Model Compatibility

Note that the terminology chosen for Fig. 1 uses the perspective of the type models. The diagonal dependencies can be read "conformsTo" upwards, while their labels indicate the respective type of compatibility regarding their downwards meaning. We would have to use the terminology in reverse, if we used the perspective of the instances.

Figure 1 makes the notions of forward- and backward-compatibility look more straightforward than they actually are. Before we can proceed to evaluate forms of model inheritance in Sect. 3, we need to gain a deeper understanding of these notions which involves to precisely define what a model is in this context.

2.1 Formal Foundation

I assume a model to be an instance of (i.e., a sentence in) some modelling language. A model is therefore just data. To turn that data into information, i.e., in order to be able to discuss properties of a model, we have to look at the meaning of a model. Formally, I regard the meaning of a model $\mu(\mathcal{M})$ to be a projection (π) of the subject $\mathcal{S}$ the model represents, i.e., $\mu(\mathcal{M}) = \pi(\mathcal{S})$.

The important part for the following discussion, though, is that we can associate both an intension and an extension [7] to the meaning of a type model. The intension $\iota(\mu(\mathcal{M}))$ of a model can be thought of to be a predicate that determines whether another model is to be considered an instance of $\mathcal{M}$ or not. If $\mathcal{M}$ represents a language definition then in practical terms a metamodel and its associated constraints fulfil the role of the intension. The intension $\iota(\mu(\mathcal{M}))$ thus is a characteristic predicate defining the extension $\varepsilon(\mu(\mathcal{M}))$ of the type model, i.e., the set of instances which conform to the type model: $\varepsilon(\mu(\mathcal{M})) = \{x \mid P(x)\}$, where $P = \iota(\mu(\mathcal{M}))$.

A supermodel $\mathcal{M}$ is *forward-compatible* with respect to a submodel $\mathcal{M}'$, if $\mathcal{M}'$-instances conform to $\mathcal{M}$. Likewise, a submodel $\mathcal{M}'$ is *backward-compatible* with respect to a supermodel $\mathcal{M}$, if $\mathcal{M}$-instances conform to $\mathcal{M}'$. It therefore stands to reason to establish the following formal definitions (using "$\rightarrow$" as logical implication):

Definition 1. *Given $\mathcal{M}' < \mathcal{M}$ (i.e., $\mathcal{M}'$ inherits from $\mathcal{M}$),*

$$forwardCompatible\,(\mathcal{M}, \mathcal{M}') \;\equiv\; \iota(\mu(\mathcal{M})) \leftarrow \iota(\mu(\mathcal{M}')) \tag{1}$$

$$backwardCompatible\,(\mathcal{M}, \mathcal{M}') \;\equiv\; \iota(\mu(\mathcal{M})) \rightarrow \iota(\mu(\mathcal{M}')) \tag{2}$$

Note that Def. 1 implies that the presence of both forward- and backward-compatibility means that the intensions of $\mathcal{M}$ and $\mathcal{M}'$ are equivalent, which in turn implies that there would be no point in deriving $\mathcal{M}'$ from $\mathcal{M}$. Yet, in practice we can achieve both forward- and backward-compatibility without requiring $\mathcal{M}$ and $\mathcal{M}'$ to be equivalent.

As a real world example, consider the upgrade from mono-FM to stereo-FM transmission. Old mono-receivers are agnostic of the presence of pilot signals and higher sidebands within stereo-signals. The baseband of a stereo-signal carries the sum of the left and right channels (L+R) and hence represents a proper mono-signal. Therefore, every stereo-signal is a proper mono-signal:

$$\iota(\mu(\mathcal{MO})) \leftarrow \iota(\mu(\mathcal{ST})),$$

or alternatively

$$\varepsilon(\mu(\mathcal{MO})) \supseteq \varepsilon(\mu(\mathcal{ST})).$$

This justifies deriving $\mathcal{ST}$ from $\mathcal{MO}$ and establishing the specialisation relationship $\mathcal{ST} < \mathcal{MO}$. As a result, $\mathcal{MO}$ is forward-compatible to $\mathcal{ST}$ (see Def. 1).

A new stereo-receiver ($\mathcal{ST}$) can reproduce old mono-signals (instances of $\mathcal{MO}$). In the absence of a pilot signal, stereo-receivers do not attempt to use the L-R information from the higher sideband of a stereo-signal and thus simply emit the L+R mono-signal of the baseband on both channels. $\mathcal{ST}$ is therefore backward-compatible to $\mathcal{MO}$. Yet, Def. 1.2 does not hold since the specification of a mono-signal does not imply the specification of a stereo-signal, i.e.,

$$\iota(\mu(\mathcal{MO})) \nrightarrow \iota(\mu(\mathcal{ST})).$$

In other words, there are elements in the extension of $\mathcal{MO}$ that do not conform to $\mathcal{ST}$:

$$\neg\forall x : \ x \in \varepsilon(\mu(\mathcal{MO})) \ \rightarrow \ \iota(\mu(\mathcal{ST}))(x).$$

Here is why: A mono-signal with an accidentally present pilot signal but garbage L-R information in the higher sideband conforms to the mono-signal specification but does not conform to the stereo-signal specification since the latter requires a proper L-R signal in the higher sideband. So, we do not seem able to affirm backward-compatibility. Yet, we know that stereo-receivers accept and properly process all signals emitted from mono-signal transmitters. So how can we reconcile the fact that a stereo-receiver ($\mathcal{ST}$) has higher requirements than the mono-signal specification ($\mathcal{MO}$) guarantees with our knowledge that any instance generated from $\mathcal{MO}$ will conform to the $\mathcal{ST}$ specification?

The above formulation of the question practically contains the answer: We have to distinguish between the instances that a model $\mathcal{M}$ *accepts* and the instances that $\mathcal{M}$ *generates*. In other words, we have to acknowledge that a type model $\mathcal{M}$ has two roles. The only role we have explicitly considered so far is that of a characteristic predicate, i.e., as a test to check whether an instance conforms to the respective type model. The other role of a type model is that of a generator of model instances. The set of the latter – I will refer to it as $\varepsilon_0(\mu(\mathcal{M}))$ – is a subset of the set of instances that the model accepts, i.e., $\varepsilon_0(\mu(\mathcal{M})) \subseteq \varepsilon(\mu(\mathcal{M}))$. Now we can state a relaxed, yet practical, definition of backward-compatibility:

Definition 2. *Given* $\mathcal{M}' < \mathcal{M}$,

$$backwardCompatible_r(\mathcal{M}, \mathcal{M}') \ \equiv \ \varepsilon_0(\mu(\mathcal{M})) \subseteq \varepsilon(\mu(\mathcal{M}')) \tag{3}$$

Figure 2(a) illustrates how simultaneous strong forward- and backward-compatibility implies that $\mathcal{M}$ is equivalent to $\mathcal{M}'$. Figure 2(b) shows that using a relaxed notion of backward-compatibility based on generated $\mathcal{M}$-instances, as opposed to accepted $\mathcal{M}$-instances, allows both forward- and relaxed backward-compatibility to co-exist.

Summarising, regarding forward-compatibility, for any instance that is accepted but not generated by $\mathcal{M}$, i.e., $m \in (\varepsilon(\mu(\mathcal{M})) \setminus \varepsilon_0(\mu(\mathcal{M})))$, there is an implied information loss when it is viewed through $\mathcal{M}$. In our example, mono-receivers cannot make use of the two channel information in a stereo-signal. Nevertheless, from the perspective of the mono-receiver all required information is available and this is all one can hope for regarding forward-compatibility.

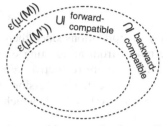

(a) Accepted instances imply equality

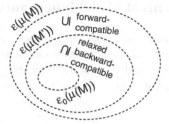

(b) Generated instances enable compatibility

Fig. 2. Strong vs Relaxed Backward-Compatibility

In modelling practice, often the intension of derived models is stronger than that of the base model and one can thus expect strong forward-compatibility (Def. 1.1), albeit with information loss. While it is not possible for a strong notion of backward-compatibility (Def. 1.2) to hold at the same time, in practice, we only need a relaxed notion of backward-compatibility (Def. 2).

The relaxed notion of backward-compatibility may still be too strong if $\mathcal{M}'$ requires properties not guaranteed by $\mathcal{M}$-generated instances, but it at least opens up the potential of an automatic upgrade of $\mathcal{M}$-generated instances to $\mathcal{M}'$-instances. Section 3 discusses derivation strategies which ensure that $\mathcal{M}'$ is not too demanding. I conclude this section by observing that different stakeholders require different forms of model compatibility:

Within "model evolution", backward-compatibility is one of the main concerns. One assumes that type models change and a large number of model instances is considered to be an asset that deserves protection. Hence, one either strives to change type models in a way that achieves backward-compatibility or seeks ways to automatically upgrade old model instances so that they conform to the new type model.

In contrast, programmers or modellers are typically far more concerned with forward-compatibility. Model instances are created programmatically and are therefore dispensable. However, (parts of) programs or models represent a high investment and one aims to obtain their forward-compatibility with new model instances. Additionally, new program/model parts are also required to exhibit some level of backward-compatibility if only to support the manipulation of new instances by old program/model parts. Unless the new program/model parts can accept the thus modified instances, the utility of the old program/model parts is heavily compromised.

Language engineers have the highest requirements. They are interested in maximising the backward-compatibility of a new language with respect to the base language it was derived from in order to be able to use old programs / models written in the base language. However, they are also interested in maximising the forward-compatibility of the base language since this will allow new programs / models to be used with old tools. Furthermore, the higher the degree of forward-compatibility, the quicker one expects programmers / modellers to learn the new language on the basis of the old base language. A strong degree of forward-compatibility means that the new language adds new features but does not unnecessarily destroy similarities to the old base language.

3 Forms of Model Inheritance

The meaning of "model inheritance" is open to many interpretations since there are many motivations as to why one would derive one model from an existing one. A submodel could be, among other things, a specialisation, a more restrictive version, a realisation, a part of a partitioning, an implementation, or an extended version of its supermodel. In the following, I concentrate on three main derivation kinds which can be used to understand and classify the above mentioned interpretations.

3.1 Specification Import

Two type models $\mathcal{M}$ and $\mathcal{M}'$ can be thought of to be in a *specification import* relationship if the construction of $\mathcal{M}'$ is based on (parts of) the construction of $\mathcal{M}$. In the context of class inheritance, specification import is referred to as "*subclassing*" [15]. This derivation strategy opportunistically tries to maximise the usage of existing (intensional) specification. No consideration is given to the (extensional) implications on model compatibility. For example, one could derive a simple language from a complex one by just pruning the metamodel of the former. This typically prohibits forward-compatibility, since the assumptions that can be made with regard to the presence of elements in $\mathcal{M}$ and their respective navigability often do not hold anymore in a pruned version. Backward-compatibility would not necessarily be affected in this case but then specification import does not impose any restrictions on how $\mathcal{M}'$ may tighten up requirements for $\mathcal{M}$-instances.

Therefore, in general, specification import does not make any guarantees about compatibilities of any kind. The above considerations, however, give rise to two classes of model derivations which guarantee forward-compatibility even though they involve the removal of elements:

1. *Compatible pruning* removes only strictly optional elements (with multiplicities that include zero) from $\mathcal{M}$.
2. *Compatible coarsening* removes non-optional elements in $\mathcal{M}$ but with the requirement that these elements must not be relied on by elements in $\mathcal{M}$ that remain part of $\mathcal{M}'$. In other words, no element in $\mathcal{M}'$ that can be observed through an $\mathcal{M}$-view must require any removed element through this $\mathcal{M}$-view. A typical example for elements that may safely be removed are subtypes that are not specifically referred to and whose instances can be replaced by supertype instances without loss of generality. Note that no operation on $\mathcal{M}$ must rely on the removed elements either. The coarsened version must not be distinguishable from a complete version under an $\mathcal{M}$-operation.

3.2 Conceptual Containment

Two type models can be thought of to be in a *conceptual containment* (also referred to as "*is-a*" [6]) relationship if the submodel $\mathcal{M}'$ puts stronger constraints on its instances. In other words, the intension of the submodel is stronger than that of the supermodel.

Definition 3. $\mathcal{M}' <_{\text{is-a}} \mathcal{M} \quad \rightarrow \quad (\iota(\mu(\mathcal{M}')) \rightarrow \iota(\mu(\mathcal{M})))$

Examples for such a strengthening are the specialisation of individual model elements such as replacing Rectangle with Square or the introduction of covariant relationships. In the UML, both association specialisation and association end redefinition can be used to introduce relationships that have stronger requirements than the ones they redefine [13]. For example, consider M to contain the elements Worker and Task connected by a worksOn association. Also, Worker and Task are specialised by SpecialisedWorker and SpecialTask respectively. If M' now adds a worksOn association between SpecialisedWorker and SpecialTask and furthermore demands that special tasks are only worked on by specialised workers then some valid M-instances are not valid M'-instances.

Note that according to Def. 1, the strengthening of the intension from M to M' means that conceptual containment guarantees forward-compatibility. This is desirable as it allows old tools to be used on new instances. However, note that in general there is a strong limitation to this advantage. As soon as old tools go beyond reading instances, e.g., for analysis or transformation, i.e., as soon as they start to modify instances, these modified instances are unlikely to be compatible to the new specification they once conformed to. The old tools do not know the new constraints introduced by the new specification and will typically not respect them. Forward-compatibility, while desirable, must thus in general be acknowledged as enabling non-mutating access to new model instances only.

The above observation implies a class of model derivations, though, which guarantees *mutator forward-compatibility* in the sense that any change that can be applied to M'-instances through an M-view will never make them invalid M'-instances: An *orthogonal extension* may introduce further constraints but only on new elements which must be optional. For this derivation class, conceptual containment maintains relaxed backward-compatibility.

3.3 Subtyping

Two type models M and M' can be thought of to be in a *subtyping* relationship if instances of M' behave exactly like instances of M; in other words, it is always possible to substitute instances of M with instances by M'. This defining property of subtyping is known as the *Liskov substitution principle* [16].

A subtype relationship $M' <_{\text{subt}} M$ provides us with

$$\forall x : \ x \in \varepsilon(\mu(M')) \ \rightarrow \ x \in \varepsilon(\mu(M)),$$

which is equivalent to $\varepsilon(\mu(M')) \subseteq \varepsilon(\mu(M))$. While this tells us that subtyping guarantees forward-compatibility, there does not seem to be a difference to conceptual containment which guarantees the same (cf. Def. 3). Yet, intuitively it is clear that subtyping is a stronger requirement then conceptual containment because an instance from a conceptually contained model M' is only known to conform to M but not required to be substitutable for an M-instance. Here is an example that illustrates this difference: Let us consider the "SpecialisedWorker worksOn SpecialTask" model from Sect. 3.2 again. An instance of this model conforms to the respective M model but if we then use the M-view to manipulate this instance we can violate its constraints.

In general, there are three outcomes such an $\mathcal{M}$-view manipulation attempt may have:

1. The model instance does not support the $\mathcal{M}$-view operation. For example, a square element may not be able to respond to a stretchVertically operation which would not have been a problem for a rectangle element.
2. The model instance supports the $\mathcal{M}$-view operation but does not conform to $\mathcal{M}'$ anymore after the operation has been performed. For example, in the above scenario assigning a normal Worker to a SpecialTask will create a model instance which does not conform to $\mathcal{M}'$.
3. The model instance supports the $\mathcal{M}$-view operation and remains an $\mathcal{M}'$-instance.

Clearly, from a model instance that can substitute an $\mathcal{M}$-instance we do not expect the first case. Furthermore, with respect to the second case, while the notion of substitutability does not express it explicitly, we expect subtype instances to keep respecting their constraints even under $\mathcal{M}$-view operations (see also Sect. 5). Using $f_{\mathcal{M}}$ as an operation available on $\mathcal{M}$-instances, we can thus define a necessary condition for subtyping:

Definition 4

$$\mathcal{M}' <_{\text{subt}} \mathcal{M} \rightarrow ((\iota(\mu(\mathcal{M}')) \rightarrow \iota(\mu(\mathcal{M}))) \wedge \forall f_{\mathcal{M}}, x : (x \in \mathcal{M}' \rightarrow f_{\mathcal{M}}(x) \in \mathcal{M}')).$$

Figure 3 illustrates that conceptual containment and subtyping are both defining subsets of $\mathcal{M}$'s extension but differ in how they may respond to $\mathcal{M}$-view operations.

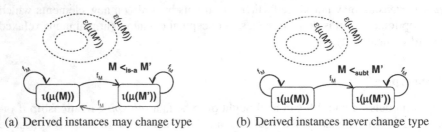

(a) Derived instances may change type   (b) Derived instances never change type

Fig. 3. Conceptual Containment vs Subtyping

Despite the property defined in Def. 4, subtyping does not imply backward-compatibility, not even the relaxed form of Def. 2. Not every $\mathcal{M}$-generated instance needs to conform to $\mathcal{M}'$. For example, $\mathcal{M}'$ may require additional mandatory navigability to a Company instance from each Worker instance. Nevertheless, the property defined in Def. 4 guarantees an important type of backward-compatibility in the form of *mutator forward-compatibility* (see Sect. 3.2) for $\mathcal{M}'$-instances. If the latter holds, $\mathcal{M}'$ is backward-compatible with $\mathcal{M}$ with respect to any $\mathcal{M}'$-instance no matter which change the latter is subjected to by $\mathcal{M}$-view operations. Consequently, subtyping guarantees the desirable mutator forward-compatibility beyond orthogonal extensions to all extensions that adhere to subtyping. The corresponding class of derivations, which can be aptly referred to as *conservative extensions*, is larger than the class of orthogonal extensions since now the tightening of requirements need not be confined to optional new elements, but can be extended to new mandatory elements. These elements might even be observable through an $\mathcal{M}$-view, albeit with information loss. For example, an additionally introduced SpecialisedWorker instance will be observable as a Worker instance, yet its mandatory link to a Company instance will not.

Obviously, a round-trip starting with the creation of an $\mathcal{M}'$-instance to the acceptance as an $\mathcal{M}$-instance, with subsequent modifications through $\mathcal{M}$-view operations, and the final re-adoption as an $\mathcal{M}'$-instance requires $\mathcal{M}$-view operations to preserve $\mathcal{M}'$-features. In practice, tools associated with $\mathcal{M}$ are not required to properly interpret all $\mathcal{M}'$-features but need to keep them intact while applying $\mathcal{M}$-view operations. Naturally, not every tool has this capability but open meta-formats can certainly support this and at least subtyping potentially allows the round-trip whereas conceptual containment does not. Note that object-oriented languages naturally support mutator forward-compatibility if inheritance is used according to the subtyping principle.

3.4   Making a Choice

Interestingly, the derivation classes identified in the previous sections are related to each other. Table 1 shows how the derivation classes extend each other and what their duals are. The notion of "duality" is based on the symmetry of $\mathcal{M}$ and $\mathcal{M}'$ to each other with respect to the changes and their implications on compatibility which can occur between them. Figure 1 shows this symmetry if one ignores the direction of the specialisation relationship. For the sake of the symmetry argument, let us assume $\mathcal{M}'$ to be the original and perform a *compatible pruning* to derive $\mathcal{M}$. This is equivalent to assuming $\mathcal{M}$ to be the original and performing an *orthogonal extension* to derive $\mathcal{M}'$.

The above implies a duality for the notions of forward- and backward-compatibility and indeed the guarantees that, e.g., a *conservative extension* makes about forward-compatibility (with information loss) translate to guarantees for *compatible coarsening* with respect to backward-compatibility (with information loss). With the above additional knowledge about compatibility in mind, given a choice of model inheritance variants, a natural question to ask is which one should be preferred.

Specification Import is to preferred when the emphasis is on *ease of construction*. Being able to chose a starting point $\mathcal{M}$, which makes it easiest to derive a new $\mathcal{M}'$ from it without compatibility concerns, makes the life of $\mathcal{M}'$'s developer easier.

Subtyping, the most constrained relationship, supports *ease of use*. Any person or tool being competent about $\mathcal{M}$ will be competent about large parts of $\mathcal{M}'$ since its instances are required to appear like $\mathcal{M}$-instances. Subtyping thus makes the life of $\mathcal{M}'$'s users easier. Moreover, it guarantees mutator forward-compatibility, i.e., supports a round-trip from new instances to old tools and back again.

Table 1. Dual Derivation Classes

		dual	
extends	Compatible Pruning	↔	Orthogonal Extension
	∨		∨
	Compatible Coarsening	↔	Conservative Extension

Conceptual Containment represents a useful middle ground if the strong requirements of subtyping cannot be imposed but one nevertheless wants to achieve some level of compatibility.

Note that the above variants are not mutually exclusive. If the cheapest option of specification import is performed with considerations for compatibility in mind, it can result in a conceptual containment or subtyping relationship. A simple strategy therefore is to aim for subtyping and settle for anything below it that is viable to produce within a given economic context. It will pay off, however, to make a return-on-investment analysis; the increased effort to create an $\mathcal{M}'$ that adheres to subtyping may often be amortised by the resulting advantages of increased compatibility and ease of use.

4   Observer-Based Notion of Substitutability

Section 2 introduced the important notion of model compatibility and Sect. 3 discussed the degree to which certain forms of model inheritance guarantee compatibility. It became clear that the most desirable derivation classes impose the most restrictions on how new models may be derived from existing ones and therefore are the most difficult to achieve in practice.

Subtyping, for example, is already no longer achievable if one wants to redefine the argument type of an equals method along with the concept that provides it. There are also many examples where instances in an collaborative ensemble depend on other participating instances to have certain upper type bounds [11]. Such ensembles cannot be introduced in a subtype model since modifications through a supertype-view would not respect the type bound constraints. In practice, it will therefore be hard to achieve compatibilities of the form

$$\varepsilon(\mu(\mathcal{M}')) \subseteq \varepsilon(\mu(\mathcal{M})),$$

and one will more often than not have to settle with

$$\exists \mathcal{M}_{\mathcal{N}} : (\varepsilon(\mu(\mathcal{M}')) \setminus \mathcal{M}_{\mathcal{N}}) \subseteq \varepsilon(\mu(\mathcal{M})),$$

i.e., only a subset of $\mathcal{M}'$-instances conform to the $\mathcal{M}$ specification. This is an example of compromised forward-compatibility but of course the symmetric situation exists for compromised backward-compatibility as well.

Observers

In practice, it is often not necessary to insist on uncompromised compatibility. For example, old tools can still be useful for new models if one is only interested in applying them to certain model instances that do not exploit compatibility-compromising language features. Currently, there are two unsatisfactory alternatives for dealing with such situations:

1. The compromised compatibility is incorrectly documented as an uncompromised compatibility, i.e., one chooses to indicate a subtyping relationship between two models even though it does not hold in general. Obviously, this creates incorrect expectations and should be avoided.

2. The compromised compatibility is not documented at all or with an unspecified meaning for model inheritance. Hence it could be easily broken with subsequent changes to tools and/or model instances.

Therefore, I introduce a specialisation relationship between two models that is based on the notion of an observer. Figure 4 illustrates how one could index a specialisation relationship (here with an *o* next to the specialisation arrowhead; the corresponding observer instance "o" to the right only being included for illustrative purposes) and thus refer to an entity that decides whether the two models are in the relationship it specifies or not. In Fig. 4, the specialisation relationship is not meant to be an instance of the observer, rather its meaning depends on the observer.

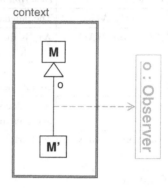

Fig. 4. Observer-Based Specialisation

There are many ways in which an observer could be defined and applied in practice. For example, an existing tool could be used as an acceptance checker in analogy to how programming languages used to be defined by their compiler implementations. Among many alternative ways to define observers, a natural alternative is to use a type model and require certain conformance criteria of the derived model.

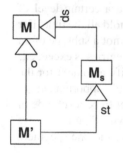

Fig. 5. Language-Based Observer

Figure 5 shows one approach that demands the derived model to be a subtype of the observer specification[1]. Table 2 lists a number of choices for ds (derivation strategy) and $\mathcal{M}_s$. Note how an observer defines a family of models/languages $\mathcal{M}'_i$ that share a commonality. Unlike with conventional specialisation, however, the commonality is not defined by the supermodel $\mathcal{M}$ only. Instead, an observer defines a tolerance for deviations against a standard subtyping interpretation. With a language-based observer, the choices for ds and $\mathcal{M}_s$ (see Tab. 2) determine the nature and the extend of this tolerance. The particular choices can, e.g., be motivated by the properties of legacy tools.

In the above, I referred to a *derivation strategy ds* in order to avoid a recursive definition of an observer-based specialisation. However, it is entirely possible to use another *o' observer* in place of the ds derivation strategy shown in Fig. 5, giving rise to meta-observers, i.e., observers that are used to define observers.

For models that define transformations, observers could be defined that focus on (parts of) the input/output relation. Specialisation relationships between transformation definitions could therefore be based on (partial) behavioural equivalence, rather than on any structural similarities between the definitions. Over and above defining an output-oriented view on transformations, observers could focus on certain parts of transformed models and/or certain transformation properties.

---

[1] Note that $\mathcal{M}_s$ is rendered as a type model but according to Fig. 4 also is an instance of an Observer (meta-)model.

Table 2. Choices for Language-Based Observers

Choices	Description
$ds = st^*$, $\mathcal{M}_s = M$	The language-based observer is used to define standard subtying (st).
$\mathcal{M}_s = mcc^\dagger(M)$	$\mathcal{M}_s$ is the root of a family of $\mathcal{M}'_i$ that share a common conformance level to $\mathcal{M}$. The nature of the latter is determined by the choice for ds.
$ds = cc^\ddagger$	$\mathcal{M}_s$ is the root of a family of $\mathcal{M}'_i$ that share a common conceptual containment of $\mathcal{M}$.
$ds = $ selection	$\mathcal{M}_s$ selects only parts of $\mathcal{M}$, e.g., a subnotation of a language definition, and thus the family of $\mathcal{M}'_i$ is only required to conform to parts of $\mathcal{M}$.

*subtyping †maximum compatible coarsening ‡conceptual containment

Contexts

The idea of using an observer to mask out model parts and/or operations so that the remaining parts allow a model $\mathcal{M}'$ to be substituted for a model $\mathcal{M}$, adds a large degree of flexibility for specifying relationships between models. Designers can now be explicit about which parts of models need to be focused on in order to establish conceptual containment or even subtyping. Designers no longer need to leave this information undocumented, document it ambiguously, or overstate the case by using specialisation relationships that are too strong in general.

Sometimes, however, even observers cannot help to go beyond a certain level of compatibility between two models because some properties do not hold all the time. For example, a database model handling a limited amount of entries is not a subtype of an unlimited database in situations in which the maximum number of entries is exceeded.

This gives rise to the idea of a usage *context*. If we could specify a context for the limited database model that guarantees that the maximum number of supported entries will never be reached, we could specify the limited database model to be a subtype of the unlimited version *with respect to the chosen context*. This is why Figure 4 shows a context around a specialisation relationship. Only in contexts like the one specified, does the specialisation relationship apply.

Contexts should not be confused with another observer layer. A context rather confines changes to a model to ones that respect the constraints observed by the observer. Contexts hence dramatically increase the potential to specify strong specialisation relationships. Consider the "SpecialisedWorker/SpecialTask" refinement from Sect. 3.3. If we can provide contexts in which only valid work assignments are created then we can strengthen the refinement relationship from *conceptual containment* to *subtyping*! While a supertype-view operation may still potentially violate subtype requirements, the context prohibits such operations.

Summarising, often models are in a relationship that is not strong enough to allow the use of any of the standard conceptual containment or subtyping relationships. Observers then allow to introduce tolerance against the latter and hence enable specialisation relationships which otherwise would have been inappropriate.

Contexts, on the other hand, establish constraints that enable the use of less tolerant observers and thus stronger specialisation relationships.

5 Related Work

Inheritance has been suggested to be one of the basic relationships (next to instantiation and representation) between models in [14]. However this work only considered subtype specialisations.

The distinction made in Sect. 2.1, between the set of elements a type model accepts $(\varepsilon(\mu(\mathcal{M})))$ and the set of model instances the former can generate $(\varepsilon_0(\mu(\mathcal{M})))$, echoes the fact that classes in object-oriented programming languages are often assumed to play both roles at the same time [17]. Only a few programming languages explicitly separate these two discriminator and generator roles [18].

Liskov and Wing introduced the substitution principle for subtypes in the context of object-oriented programming languages [16]. Their discussion of subtypes include constrained subtypes that tighten constraints. Interestingly, the necessary precondition for these – the supertype view does not allow the manipulation of the further constrained variables in the subtype – is not explicitly mentioned. Another implicit assumption made in [16] is that subtype instances never need to change their type. On the one hand, this is surprising since supertype instances will have a supertype type after being manipulated, so the latter seems to be admissible behaviour for subtype instances as well. On the other hand, one can argue that subtype instances should not add any potential of invariant violations while being manipulated through supertype interfaces and that the migration of a subtype instance to become a supertype instance would represent such an invariant violation. Note that the *necessary* condition given in Def. 4 of Sect. 3.3 is not *sufficient* for subtyping; it allows subtype instances to behaviourally deviate from supertype instances. The notion of mutator forward-compatibility thus represents a weaker requirement than subtyping. This is useful if the emphasis is on guaranteeing backward-compatibility, i.e., safe manipulation round-trips for instances, but full behaviour conformance is considered to be too restrictive.

Interfaces in JAVA [1] can be regarded as a certain form of a language-based observer. Like observers, interfaces introduce tolerance against any features which are not mentioned by the interface. Two classes that implement the same interface might be declared to be subtypes through an observer-based specialisation relationship even though they are not subtypes regarding features not specified by the interface.

Dependent types, as provided by GBETA [10], can be regarded as a means to establish contexts as discussed in Sect. 4. They allow programs to specify safe application contexts for object ensembles that require family polymorphism [11]. The same mechanisms could, and should, be made available for models.

UML profiles, as long as they do not introduce constraints that are incompatible with subtyping or use subsetting of base metamodels, produce *conservative extensions* because they cannot introduce changes that are observable through an $\mathcal{M}$-view. Such UML profiles therefore guarantee mutator forward-compatibility and can be used to create families of models/languages [8].

6   Conclusion

This paper explored "model inheritance" with an emphasis on compatibility considerations. I regarded the submodel as being derived from the supermodel and used a formal approach to analyse what kind of compatibility guarantees can be made for various forms of model inheritance.

I treated forward- and backward-compatibility symmetrically which allowed me to identify dual derivation classes which are symmetric regarding their compatibility properties. Although space limitations did not permit explicitly analysing all compatibility cases, the symmetries between forward- and backward-compatibility and the four identified derivation strategies respectively, allow the straightforward transfer of the discussions to the dual scenarios.

In order to understand *simultaneous* forward- and backward-compatibility, I had to introduce the notion of a set of generated instances, $\varepsilon_0(\mu(\mathcal{M}))$, i.e., a subset of the full model extension. Such ε_0-sets do not only allow the definition of the practical notion of relaxed backward-compatibility, they can also be used to relax mutator forward-compatibility by restricting the considered instances to $\mathcal{M}'$-*generated* instances.

To the best of my knowledge, this paper is the first to establish that subtyping can be regarded as a strengthened form of conceptual containment that, among further constraints, adds a backward-compatibility requirement for subtype instances which have been modified under a supermodel view. I introduced the new term *mutator forward-compatibility* to characterise the ability of instances to survive a "round-trip" of casting, manipulation, and re-casting. Interestingly, mutator forward-compatibility neither implies backward-compatibility nor full behavioural compatibility for submodel instances, and thus defines a useful class of submodels that is larger than that of subtypes. This is a useful result as it ensures a safe manipulation round-trip, without requiring the strict behaviour conformance of subtypes if the latter is considered to be too restrictive.

In the same vein – recognising that uncompromised subtying is difficult to obtain in practice – I proposed *observers* to define custom relaxation criteria for specialisation relationships, thus allowing the establishment and precise documentation of relationships between models that are weaker than subtyping. Using a language-based observer approach, I showed that the Liskov-Substitution Principle can be obtained by using the strongest observer possible. Relaxations of this form are available through reducing the amount of observable differences, thus giving rise to a family of models/languages.

Finally, I proposed *contexts* to allow stronger observers to be used whenever a usage context can guarantee that otherwise observable violations of specialisation requirements cannot occur. If a context, for example, can restrict old tools that they only modify new instances in a way that keeps them compatible with new tools then a specialisation relationship based on a correspondingly strong observer can document this level of compatibility. A context that ensures immutability for a subset of model instances can lift a conceptual containment relationship to mutator forward-compatibility or potentially an even stronger subtyping relationship.

Summarising, the introduction of ε_0-sets, observers, and contexts makes it possible to properly document safe round-trip scenarios and thus protect their future integrity. The author hopes that the ideas and discussions presented in this paper represent a stepping stone towards a systematic basis for organising models.

References

1. Arnold, K., Gosling, J., Holmes, D.: The Java Programming Language, 3rd edn. Addison-Wesley, Reading (2000)
2. Atkinson, C., Kühne, T.: Rearchitecting the UML infrastructure. ACM Transactions on Modeling and Computer Simulation 12(4), 290–321 (2003)
3. Atkinson, C., Kühne, T.: A tour of language customization concepts. In: Zelkowitz, M. (ed.) Advances in Computers, vol. 70, ch. 3, pp. 105–161. Academic Press, Elsevier (June 2007)
4. Bézivin, J., Büttner, F., Gogolla, M., Jouault, F., Kurtev, I., Lindow, A.: Model transformations? Transformation models! In: Nierstrasz, O., Whittle, J., Harel, D., Reggio, G. (eds.) MoDELS 2006. LNCS, vol. 4199, pp. 440–453. Springer, Heidelberg (2006)
5. Bézivin, J.: In search of a basic principle for model driven engineering. Special Novática Issue "UML and Model Engineering" V(2), 21–24 (2004)
6. Brachman, R.: What is-a is and isn't: An analysis of taxonomic links in semantic networks. Computer 16(10), 30–36 (1983)
7. Carnap, R.: Meaning and Necessity: A Study in Semantics and Modal Logic. University of Chicago Press, Chicago (1947)
8. Cook, S., Kleppe, A., Mitchell, R., Rumpe, B., Warmer, J., Wills, A.: Defining UML family members using prefaces. In: Mingins, C., Meyer, B. (eds.) Proceedings of Technology of Object-Oriented Languages and Systems, TOOLS 1999, Pacific. IEEE Computer Society, Los Alamitos (1999)
9. Engels, G., Küster, J.M., Heckel, R., Groenewegen, L.: Towards consistency-preserving model evolution. In: IWPSE 2002: Proceedings of the International Workshop on Principles of Software Evolution, pp. 129–132. ACM, New York (2002)
10. Ernst, E.: gbeta – A Language with Virtual Attributes, Block Structure, and Propagating, Dynamic Inheritance. Ph.D. thesis, DEVISE, Department of Computer Science, University of Aarhus, Aarhus, Denmark (June 1999)
11. Ernst, E.: Family polymorphism. In: Knudsen, J.L. (ed.) ECOOP 2001. LNCS, vol. 2072, pp. 303–326. Springer, Heidelberg (2001)
12. Favre, J.M.: Foundations of meta-pyramids: Languages vs. metamodels - episode ii: Story of thotus the baboon. In: Language Engineering for Model-Driven Software Development. Dagstuhl Seminar Proceedings 04101. Internationales Begegnungs- und Forschungszentrum für Informatik (IBFI), Schloss Dagstuhl (2004)
13. Håvaldsrud, T.V., Møller-Pedersen, B.: Nested and specialized associations. In: RAOOL 2009: Proceedings of the Workshop on Relationships and Associations in Object-Oriented Languages, pp. 25–31. ACM, New York (2009)
14. Kühne, T.: Matters of (meta-) modeling. Software and Systems Modeling 5(4), 369–385 (2006)
15. LaLonde, W., Pugh, J.: Subclassing $\neq$ Subtyping $\neq$ Is-a. Journal of Object-Oriented Programming 3(5), 57–62 (1991)
16. Liskov, B.H., Wing, J.M.: A behavioral notion of subtyping. ACM Transactions on Programming Languages and Systems 16(6), 1811–1841 (1994)
17. Meyer, B.: EIFFEL the language. Object-Oriented Series. Prentice Hall, Englewood Cliffs (1992)
18. Murer, S., Omohundro, S., Szyperski, C.: Engineering a programming language: The type and class system of Sather. In: Gutknecht, J. (ed.) Programming Languages and System Architectures. LNCS, vol. 782, pp. 208–227. Springer, Heidelberg (1993)
19. Wang, X.H., Gu, T., Zhang, D.Q., Pung, H.K.: Ontology based context modeling and reasoning using owl. In: IEEE International Conference on Pervasive Computing and Communication (PerCom 2004), pp. 18–22 (2004)

MDE-Based Approach for Generalizing Design Space Exploration

Tripti Saxena* and Gabor Karsai

Department of Electrical Engineering and
Computer Science,
Vanderbilt University,
Nashville, TN 37205
{tsaxena,gabor}@isis.vanderbilt.edu

Abstract. Design Space Exploration (DSE) is the exploration of design alternatives before the implementation. Existing DSE frameworks are domain-specific where the representation, evaluation method as well as exploration algorithm are tightly coupled with domain-dependent assumptions. Although the tasks involved in DSE are similar, the inflexibility of the existing frameworks restricts their reuse for solving DSE problems from other domains.

This paper presents an MDE-based approach for generalizing DSE techniques. The framework supports a reconfigurable representation of a design space, which is decoupled from exploration algorithm. The framework can be configured to solve DSE problems from different domains and enables the designer to experiment with different approaches to solve the same problem with minimum effort. The main contributions of this framework are: (1) rapid modeling of DSE problems, (2) reuse of previously defined artifacts, (3) multiple solver support and (4) a tool for scalability study.

Keywords: Design Space Exploration, Domain-Specific Modeling Languages.

1 Introduction

A *design space* is a product of possible design choices, and *design space exploration* (DSE) is the process of searching through the design space to find specific design alternatives that satisfy the various design constraints and are "best" with respect to one or more objective functions. DSE problems exist in different domains like signal processing [1], software product lines [2], hardware-software codesign [3], etc. However, modeling and solving a DSE problem from scratch is complicated. The main challenge is to deal with the combinations of design choices that can yield an exponential number of design alternatives. This task is further complicated by the various functional and non-functional requirements which often conflict with each other. A design choice made for one set of requirements can have an impact on multiple sets of requirements.

---

* Corresponding author.

D.C. Petriu, N. Rouquette, Ø. Haugen (Eds.): MODELS 2010, Part I, LNCS 6394, pp. 46–60, 2010.

Existing DSE frameworks are configured to model and explore one or a set of DSE problems in a given domain only. For example, frameworks [4] and [5] are used for synthesis of embedded systems, while [6] and [7] are used for configuration of software product-lines. At the highest level, these DSE frameworks perform similar process steps: (1) model the design space, (2) evaluate design alternatives and (3) use exploration algorithms to traverse the design space and find feasible, satisfactory, and possibly optimized designs. Even though the underlying steps are similar, the representation, evaluation methods and exploration techniques supported by the frameworks are tightly coupled to domain-specific details, therefore they cannot be reconfigured to specify and solve other DSE problems within or across domains. This forces the domain-experts to either extend the existing framework or use another framework more suited to solve the DSE problem.

Current frameworks solve DSE problems by automatically refining the problem specification to a concrete model as a constraint problem, such as integer-linear programming (ILP) [8] and then feed it to an appropriate constraint solver, which checks whether the encoding has a satisfying solution. The efficiency of a solver to solve a DSE depends on the types of constraints, exploration objective and the size of the problem. For example, a SAT [9] solver can efficiently extract a set of valid configurations for a software product-line satisfying boolean constraints (inclusion/exclusion), but will perform poorly when the objective is to an optimal configuration that satisfies numerical resource constraints, where ILP solvers will perform better. Moreover, literature survey reveals that the same DSE problem can be solved using different solvers and techniques. For example, software product-line configuration problems have been solved using CSP [2] and SAT [10] solvers. At present there are no frameworks that provide the flexibility to select a solver to solve a given problem or use number of solvers on the same problem to compare their efficiency.

In this paper, we present the Generic Design Space Exploration (GDSE) framework, a *meta-programmable* tool that can be configured to model DSE problems from any domain and provides the flexibility to use different solvers and techniques to perform DSE. The GDSE Framework is based on Model-Driven Engineering (MDE) [11] approach that enables modeling on a higher level of abstraction, reuse of previously defined artifacts and provides mechanisms to transform models into various other forms. The MDE-based approach facilitates reuse of common DSE elements and enables association of DSE characteristics to the objects of any DSML. The framework also provides abstractions that decouple the representation of design space from the exploration algorithm, thereby enabling the flexibility to choose from different solvers and techniques to perform exploration.

The paper describes in detail the GDSE framework, which comprises of the Abstract Design Space Exploration language (ADSEL) , the Constraint Specification Language (CSL) to support writing constraints and a set interpreters that enable integration of a set of exploration solvers and techniques. The main contributions of this framework are: (1) tool for rapid modeling of DSE problems,

(2) reuse of previously defined artifacts, (3) multiple solver support and (4) a tool for scalability study.

The remainder of the paper is organized as follows: Section 2 presents an overview of the GDSE framework. Section 3 describes the languages and translators used in the framework in detail. Section 4 describes the use of the proposed approach to model a case study. Section 5 discusses the related works and finally Section 6 presents concluding remarks and future work.

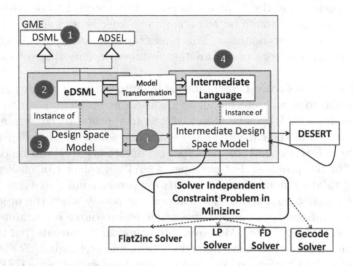

Fig. 1. Generic Design Space Exploration Framework

2   Overview of GDSE Framework

Figure 1 gives an overview of the GDSE framework and the steps performed to use it. The GDSE framework adopts Model Integrated Computing (MIC) as the core technology. MIC is based on the use of domain-specific modeling languages, model transformations, model analysis, and synthesis; and it is supported by a suite of meta-programmable tools, including Generic Modeling Environment (GME) [12]. GME allows the language designer to capture the syntactic and semantic aspects of a domain in a stereotyped UML-style class diagram (metamodel). This metamodel is instantiated into a graphical language, and metamodel class stereotypes and attributes determine how the elements are presented and used by modelers.

There are four steps involved in using the framework, where steps (1) and (2) are executed once per domain, while steps (3) and (4) are executed, iteratively, when a system is being designed. By following these steps DSE problems in any domain can be solved. We examine each of the steps in more detail:

1. **Design a Domain Specific Modeling Language (DSML)**: This step is specific to each individual domain (see [12] for details). A domain expert builds the DSML metamodel which captures entities in the domain and their relationships. The same DSML metamodel can be reused for solving different DSE problems within a domain.

2. **Extend the DSML**: The original DSML is then extended to capture the elements (constraints, objectives, metrics) of a particular DSE problem in the domain . This extension is performed using *Template Instantiation* technique of metamodel composition [13]. Using this technique, we record the common DSE metamodeling pattern as an abstract metamodel template, then instantiate its elements by inheriting pre-existing elements in the original DSML from the template elements. This enables the DSML elements to play the roles of corresponding template elements in the target metamodel. In GDSE framework, we call this generic language template as Abstract Design Space Exploration Language (ADSEL) and extended language resulting from the composition as eDSML, where 'e' stands for 'extended'. The composition is dependent on the nature of the DSE problem and has to be performed once for each kind of design space exploration in a given domain.

3. **Create a domain specific design space model**: The eDSML specification is used to configure the framework so that domain-engineers can use this version of the tool to create an instance(s) of the design space with constraints.

4. **Perform DSE**: The framework employs a two-stage transformation to automatically translate the design space model created in the previous step, first to a model in Intermediate Language (IRL), and then to a Minizinc [14] model, a solver-independent medium-level language used to express combinatorial search problems. The Minizinc model can be mapped to different solving techniques and solvers like constraint programming, mathematical modeling, etc. The Minizinc tool distribution includes a pre-defined translator which converts the Minizinc model to a low-level format (Flatzinc). It also provides translators to transform Flatzinc model to different solver specific languages. Moreover, Flatzinc is also supported by other external solvers like Gecode [15] and Eclipse [16].

3   Languages and Translators Supporting GDSE Framework

This section presents the languages and translators which form the framework. The language metamodels use GME metamodeling syntax which is well documented in [17]. Concepts like inheritance and containment are similar to those in UML. The stereotypes (ex: <<Model>>, <<Atom>>, <<Connection>>) express the binding of the abstract syntax to the concrete syntax implemented by the GME environment.

3.1   Abstract Design Space Exploration Language (ADSEL)

Abstract Design Space Exploration Language is the core of design space representation in the GDSE framework. ADSEL enables reuse of common DSE elements while modeling different DSE problems. Moreover, the metamodel composition enables association of DSE characteristics to objects of any underlying DSML. All the elements in the ADSEL metamodel are abstract and can be replicated and concretized in the target eDSML metamodel after composition with a DSML.

The ADSEL Metamodel consists of (i) *Component Types*, which provide a generic representation to hierarchically structure the design alternatives at any abstraction level, (ii) *Constraints*, which model the interactions between the design alternatives, (iii) *Function*, which captures the goal of the exploration and (iv) *Metrics*, which capture the metrics (for example, `totalcost`) required to compare the different design alternative during the exploration process. In the following, we describe each of category in detail.

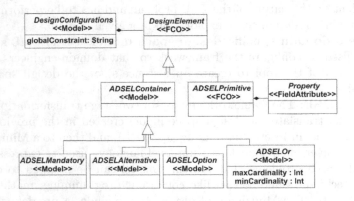

Fig. 2. Component Types in Abstract Design Space Exploration Language

Component Types: The design variants are structured hierarchically using Component classes: *Primitive, Mandatory, Alternative, Option* and *Or*. The *Primitive* class is a fundamental unit of composition. The *Mandatory* class models composition, which means all the child objects are included if the parent is included in a configuration. The *Alternative* class models a choice point where exactly one child object is included. The *Option* class models a choice point where one or none of the child objects is included. Finally, the *Or* class models a choice point where any number of child objects between the `minCardinality` and `maxCardinality` can be included if the parent is included in a configuration. The component types structure the design space in form of a tree where *Primitives* represent the leaf nodes. The design space is contained in *Design-Configurations* class.

This part of the metamodel has been influenced by *feature models* [18], which capture variability in a configurable application with set of features arranged in a tree structure. ADSEL uses a subset of the feature set types which are sufficient to capture generic structure of design spaces.

Properties: ADSEL allows associating a set of DSE properties to the *Primitive* components. The container components aggregate the properties of the contained objects using a composition function. A property specification includes the following parts:

- `PropertyType`, which specifies if a property is set before the exploration process (i.e. a parameter) or as a result of it (i.e. decision).
- `ValueType`, which can be {`INT`, `BOOL`, `CUSTOM`}, where `CUSTOM` is used when domain of the variable is restricted to instance id's of a metamodel element. (for example, `CUSTOM`: `Task` means that the variable domain consists of id's of the instances of Task).
- `Domain`, which can be a single value or set or range of values that the variable can take and depends on the `ValueType`.
- `Composition`, represents a recursive formula used to calculate property values of container components depending on its type. For example, if composition is ADD, then property value of a *Mandatory* object is given by

$$\sum_{c \in chil(m)} c.property$$

where child(m) returns the child objects. Currently, only {`ADD`, `MULT`, `MIN`, `MAX`, `MEAN`} are supported.

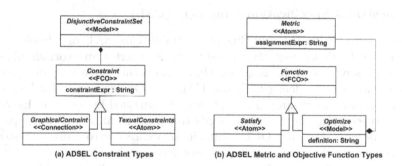

(a) ADSEL Constraint Types   (b) ADSEL Metric and Objective Function Types

Fig. 3. Constraints and Objectives in ADSEL

Constraints: ADSEL captures the constraints on the design space using the two constraint classes (shown in Figure 3): (1) *GraphicalConstraint*, which models dual context constraint used to impose a relation between two objects in the design space tree (for example, A requires B) and (2) *TextualConstraints*, which models a single context constraint (for example, `A.memory` ≤ `128`). These are explicitly instantiated in the design space model. By default a valid configuration should satisfy all constraints. Disjunctive constraints can be modeled using *DisjunctiveConstraintSet*, which can contain a set of (1) and (2) constraints, such that exactly one constraint in the set should be true. Besides these constraints ADSEL also supports *GlobalConstraint*, which is applied to the entire design space (for example, `forall(m in Module) (m.resourcetype != 0)`). It is modeled as an attribute of *DesignConfigurations* (shown in Figure 2). All constraint objects have an `expression` attribute, which captures the constraint definition specified using Constraint Specification Language (CSL), a simple language developed to facilitate user friendly syntax for writing constraints on elements of the design space.

Metric: This captures the temporary values required to compare the different design alternatives during the exploration. The value of the metric is calculated according to the `assignmentExpr` attribute. For example, utilization is a metric which is calculated depending on the WCET and Period of the tasks mapped on to the processor.

Function: This captures the goal of the exploration process. There are two kinds of functions(shown in Figure 3): (i) *Satisfy* objective is used to perform constraint-based DSE where the goal is to find design alternatives that satisfy all constraints, and (ii) *Optimize* provides a placeholder for specifying the cost functions used to compare the alternatives in the design space. Currently, the framework supports only single goal optimization. The *Optimize* objective uses metrics as parameters. Multiple objectives can be combined together using the function `definition` attribute.

3.2   Constraint Specification Language (CSL)

Existing approaches like ILP (only linear constraints) and SAT (only boolean constraint) support only a subset of the constraints. A generic framework should support an expressive constraint language that can capture all arithmetic, boolean and set constraints. Modeling tools like GME use Object Constraint Language (OCL) to specify the *requirements* that must be satisfied by a design. However, for DSE we need a language that can specify *constraints* which restrict the space of admissible designs. Although OCL is sufficiently expressive to capture these constraints, the expressions can sometimes become verbose and hard to read [19]. We need a more specialized constraint specification language that is easy to use with the representation. Our initial attempt was to use an extended subset of OCL (add traversal functions: `children`, `implementedby`). This extended subset was useful for expressing single context constraints but not for multi-context constraints, because by default OCL expressions are single context expressions which can become very complex when used to express constraints with multiple contexts.

   In order to overcome the limitations OCL, we developed Constraint Specification Language (CSL), a simple language to specify constraint expressions in the GDSE framework. The main goal was to overcome the verbosity of OCL expressions without compromising the expressiveness. At present, CSL consists of only the most essential elements needed to express constraints (property variables, relational, logical and set operators). A collection of operations are applied to the property variables and constants to form an expression. At the highest level an expression is a logical expression. There are two main differences between OCL and CSL:

(1) CSL supports dual-context expressions, where the two contexts are referenced by keywords $src and $dst. This allows us to write succinct cross-tree constraints. For example, constraint A1 requires B2 can be written in extended OCL and CSL as follows:

```
OCL context: R
OCL expression:
    children(A).implementedBy=children(A).children(A1) Implies
    children(B).implementedBy()=children(B).children(B2)

where R is the least common ancestor of A1 and B2.

CSL context: $src-A1 , $dst-B2
CSL expression: $src -> $dst
```

(2) OCL is a general expression language where expressions are tied to the classes, associations and attributes whereas CSL is more specialized, where expressions are algebraic relationship between attributes of the classes.

```
CSL expression:  $src.Cost < 100
```

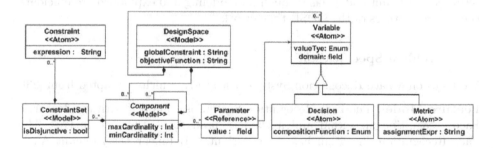

Fig. 4. Metamodel of IRL

3.3 Intermediate Language (IRL)

The GDSE Framework supports multiple solvers in the backend by the use of two solver independent formats: Intermediate Language (IRL) and Minizinc. IRL has been developed to simplify the transformation process from a domain specific design model to solver-independent model in Minizinc. IRL distills all visual and other details not related to DSE and captures design space and constraints in a form closer to one required by solver languages. Another advantage of IRL is that it allows use of symbolic constraint satisfaction tools like DESERT [20] that work at a higher abstraction level as compared to Finite Domain, SAT and ILP solvers. Figure 4 shows the metamodel of IRL.

3.4 Translators

The refinement of design space model to a concrete model in Minizinc is a two-stage process. The stage-1 transformation from eDSML model to IRL model is performed using domain independent transformation written in the Graph Rewriting and Transformation tool (GReAT) [21]. The stage-2 transformation from the IRL model to a model in Minizinc creates data structures for the design space tree and parses the CSL constraints to Minizinc constraint. This translator is written in C++. Currently, the framework enables the designer to choose the solver from {Flatzinc, LazyFD, Gecode} solvers, where LazyFd is a hybrid SAT-CSP solver based on [22]. Other solvers like MiniSAT [9] solver etc. can also be used but have not been tested yet. The solutions obtained from the selected solver can be visualized using Gecode GIST [15], a graphical tool used to interactively search the design space. The designer can also choose to feed back the solution models into the design space model.

4 Motivating Example: Software Product-Line Configuration

This section describes a simple software product-line configuration problem with resource constraint and walks through its modeling and exploration to elucidate the salient features of the GDSE Framework.

4.1 Problem Specification

We focus on a Face Recognition System case study, which is adapted from [23].

Feature Model: The Face Recognition System is equipped with two features: Face recognition algorithm and a Camera used to capture the images. The Face Recognition algorithm has three variants: (i) Linear Discriminant Analysis (LDA), (ii) Principal Component Analysis (PCA) and (iii) Bayesian. Each of these variants has two versions of implementations each. The camera generates images in two formats: (i) JPEG, (ii) TIFF. Each feature has set of parameters $\{memory_i, accuracy_i, cost_i\}$which specify the memory, accuracy and cost characteristics of the feature.

Constraints: (1) PCA requires the image in JPEG format, (2) Face Recognition algorithm must satisfy the upper bounds on memory, Memory $\leq$ 2048.

Problem Objective: The design space consists of 16 possible configurations and the goal is to find a configuration that satisfies all constraints, and minimizes cost.

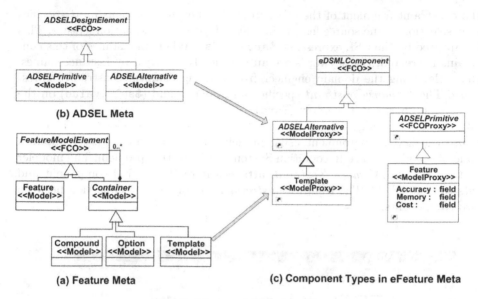

Fig. 5. Metamodel Composition

4.2 Step by Step Modeling of the Problem

(1) Create DSML: The first step mentioned in Section 2 is to create the DSML. Figure 5a shows the Feature metamodel sufficient for creating feature models. It consists of primitive element, *Feature* and container elements *Compound, Template* and *Option*.

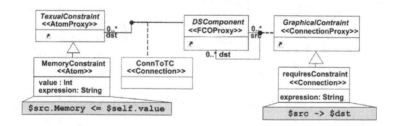

Fig. 6. Constraints in eFeature Metamodel

(2) Extending the DSML to model DSE problem: The domain expert extends the Feature metamodel to capture the feature configuration DSE problem. Figure 5c shows part of the extended-Feature (eFeature) metamodel, created for our example problem. The component entities (Feature, Alternative) of Feature meta are derived from ADSEL component(*ADSELPrimitive, ADSELAlternative*), thereby inheriting their properties. New DSE attributes (accuracy, memory and cost) are added to *Feature* class in eFeature metamodel. Figure 6 shows the constraint fragment of the eFeature meta. The *requiresConstraint* specifies that selection of the source feature implies selection of destination feature. This is captured by the CSL expression: $src → $dst. When an instance of this constraint is created, the keywords are automatically replaced by instance names, thus alleviating the domain engineer from writing complex constraint expressions. The *MemoryConstraint* specifies an upper bound ($self.value) on the memory property of its context ($src).

(3) Create a design space model: The eFeature metamodel is used to configure the GME environment using predefined interpreters. Figure 7 shows a concrete model of Face Recognition System configuration problem. The modeler instantiates the *MemoryConstraint*, attaches it to the desired component and sets the value field. The *requiresConstraint* is simply a line connection between two components.

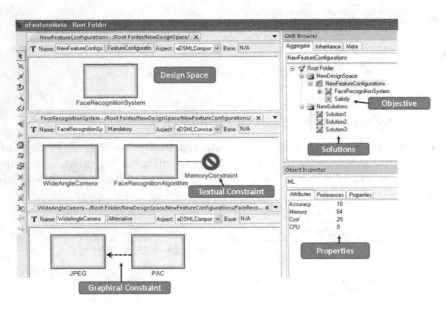

Fig. 7. Design Space Model and Feedback

(4) Exploration of design space model: After the model has been created the domain-engineer selects a solver to perform exploration and the solutions (if any) are appended in the design space model. Figure 7 shows the solutions obtained from the Flatzinc solver.

Table 1 shows time (in seconds) taken to compute all valid configurations for scaled up versions of our example problem. The goal of this exercise was just to compare the time taken by two different solvers to solve our product-line configuration problem and get an idea of what characteristics affect solver efficiency.

Table 1. Evaluation Result

Problem	No. of features	Flatzinc	LazyFD
test_1	14	0.079	2.017
test_2	25	0.1723	3.799
test_3	40	0.541	8.531
test_4	78	1.720	22.36

5 Related Works

A large body of work exists on representation and solution of DSE problems, especially in embedded systems and software product line domains. We sample a few domain specific and generic exploration frameworks and compares their capabilities with our framework.

DSE Frameworks for embedded systems design: Within the embedded systems domain, DSE frameworks are used for component selection, resource allocation, routing and scheduling.

Metropolis [4] is an integrated design environment for development of embedded systems. The framework uses an algebraic approach for DSE where each design alternative is a dataflow and exploration is performed using graph rewrite rules to generate alternatives that preserve the scheduling constraints. Metropolis uses representation and exploration algorithms which works well for the given problem, but can not be reused.

PISA [24] is a framework that uses an evolutionary multi-objective search algorithm to perform DSE. The search algorithm is implemented as a set of communicating processes. PISA is better than other frameworks in terms of flexibility since it separates the problem specification from the exploration algorithm.

Many other techniques and frameworks exist that focus on finding design alternatives that satisfy global constraints, and have been surveyed in [25]. Most of these frameworks are tightly coupled with the evaluation methods and are neither reusable (to solve a new DSE problem in the same domain), nor flexible (to support different solvers in the backend). Unlike these frameworks, the GDSE Framework decouples the representation and exploration algorithms from the evaluation methods, thereby enabling both reusability and flexibility.

DSE Frameworks for Software Product-line: Within software product-line domain, DSE frameworks are used to retrieve configurations that satisfy certain constraints. These frameworks use *feature models* to structure design variants in a tree like structure.

Feature Modeling Analyzer (FAMA) [6] is a framework for automated analysis of feature models integrating logic representation and off the shelf solvers. FAMA automatically selects the most suitable solver to perform an operation on the feature models. For example, OBDD solver counts the number of valid configurations, SAT solver selects a particular configuration. At present CSP, SAT and OBDD solvers are integrated in the framework.

Software Product Lines Online Tools (S.P.L.O.T) [7] is a Web-based framework similar to FAMA. It enables interactive analysis and configuration of software product lines and supports multiple solvers in the backend.

The goals of GDSE Framework are in sync with the goals of FAMA and SPLOT. These frameworks also support flexibility and extensibility for solving DSE problems in software product-line domain. The proposed framework can be viewed as a generalization of these frameworks and can be used to handle DSE problems from other domains as well.

Generic Frameworks: DESERT [20] is a generic DSE framework that has been used to perform coarse-grained DSE. The design alternatives are structured hierarchically in an AND-OR-LEAF tree with boolean constraints. The design tree and constraints are symbolically encoded, using Ordered Binary Decision Diagrams (OBDD)s [26]. The user interactively selects the hard constraints to prune the design space in a single step. Although this DSE approach is exhaustive, it does not scale well in the presence of continuous finite domain variables. DESERT-FD [27] is a DSE framework developed to overcome the limitations of DESERT. It uses a combination of OBDD and FD solver to perform DSE. Both frameworks are domain independent frameworks and can be used to represent and explore design spaces in any domain. Unlike the proposed framework, they use a single encoding mechanism to perform exploration and lack the flexibility of experimenting different solvers to explore the same space.

EXPLORA [28] is a Java based tool which enables generic DSE by providing support to integrate different optimization algorithms, cost functions and synthesis tools. This tool supports DSE at different abstraction levels but the reconfiguration has to be done programatically.

6   Conclusion and Future Work

In this paper, we presented a *meta-programmable* tool for representation and solution of DSE problems. The proposed approach has four main benefits. Firstly, the framework provides tooling for rapid modeling of DSE problems. The domain-experts can easily *meta-program* it to work for a DSE problem in any domain (using metamodel composition). Once this is done, the domain-engineers can use this version of the tool to create an instance of design space with constraint instances and can select a solver to perform DSE. Secondly, the framework supports reuse of the DSE metamodeling pattern (ADSEL) across domains so that the domain experts can just focus on the unique domain-constraints rather than re-implementing similar functionality. Within a domain, the same DSML metamodel can be reused to specify DSE problems at different abstraction levels. Thirdly, the proposed framework provides the flexibility to solve a given DSE problem using any solver supported in the backend. The framework can also used as a hybrid DSE tool where the solvers are used in series, each reducing the size of design space. Finally, the framework can be used as a scalability analysis tool to compare the efficiency of different solvers in solving a given exploration problem. This leads to a huge reduction in efforts as compared to the current techniques that require the designer to manually reformulate the problem in order to compare the efficiency of different solvers in solving the same DSE.

There are several research directions where development can further enhance the usability of the GDSE framework. Currently, the framework supports only hierarchical representation of design alternatives and exact solver techniques (FD, ILP) in the backend. In future we plan to extend the framework to support parametric representation and search-based techniques which work better on large design space. At present a domain expert manually creates extended-DSML by metamodel composition, which is simple but time consuming task. In future, we plan to semi-automate this process to ease reconfiguration of the framework.

Acknowledgments. This work was sponsored by DARPA, under its Software Producibility Program. The views and conclusions presented are those of the authors and should not be interpreted as representing official policies or endorsements of DARPA or the US government.

References

1. Hourani, R., Jenkal, R., Davis, W.R., Alexander, W.: Automated Design Space Exploration for DSP Applications. J. Signal Process. Syst. 56(2-3), 199–216 (2009)
2. Benavides, D., Trinidad, P., Ruiz-Cortés, A.: Automated Reasoning on Feature Models. In: Pastor, Ó., Falcão e Cunha, J. (eds.) CAiSE 2005. LNCS, vol. 3520, pp. 491–503. Springer, Heidelberg (2005)
3. Oh, H., Ha, S.: Hardware-Software Cosynthesis of Multi-Mode Multi-Task Embedded Systems with Real-Time Constraints. In: CODES 2002, pp. 133–138 (2002)
4. Balarin, F., Watanabe, Y., Hsieh, H., Lavagno, L., Passerone, C., Sangiovanni-Vincentelli, A.: Metropolis: An Integrated Electronic System Design Environment. Computer 36, 45–52 (2003)
5. Bakshi, A., Prasanna, V.K., Ledeczi, A.: MILAN: A Model Based Integrated Simulation Framework for Design of Embedded Systems. In: LCTES 2001: Proceedings of the ACM SIGPLAN workshop on Languages, compilers and tools for embedded systems, pp. 82–93. ACM, New York (2001)
6. Benavides, D., Segura, S., Trinidad, P., Ruiz-cortés, A.: FAMA: Tooling a framework for the automated analysis of feature models. In: Proceeding of the First International Workshop on Variability Modelling of Softwareintensive Systems (VAMOS), pp. 129–134 (2007)
7. Mendonca, M., Branco, M., Cowan, D.: S.P.L.O.T.: software product lines online tools. In: OOPSLA 2009: Proceeding of the 24th ACM SIGPLAN conference companion on Object oriented programming systems languages and applications, pp. 761–762. ACM, New York (2009)
8. Schrijver, A.: 15.1 : Karmarkar's polynomial–time algorithm for linear programming. In: Theory of Linear and Integer Programming, pp. 190–194. John Wiley & Sons, New York (1986)
9. En, N., Srensson, N.: An Extensible SAT-solver. In: Giunchiglia, E., Tacchella, A. (eds.) SAT 2003. LNCS, vol. 2919, pp. 502–518. Springer, Heidelberg (2003)
10. Janota, M.: Do SAT Solvers Make Good Configurators? In: Thiel, S., Pohl, K. (eds.) SPLC (2), Lero Int. Science Centre, pp. 191–195. University of Limerick, Ireland (2008)

11. Schmidt, D.C.: Model-Driven Engineering. IEEE Computer 39(2) (February 2006)
12. Sztipanovits, J., Karsai, G.: Model-Integrated Computing. Computer 30(4), 110–111 (1997)
13. Emerson, M., Sztipanovits, J.: Techniques for Metamodel Composition. In: OOP-SLA 6th Workshop on Domain Specific Modeling, pp. 123–139 (2006)
14. Nethercote, N., Stuckey, P.J., Becket, R., Brand, S., Duck, G.J., Tack, G.: MiniZinc: Towards a standard CP modelling language. In: Bessière, C. (ed.) CP 2007. LNCS, vol. 4741, pp. 529–543. Springer, Heidelberg (2007)
15. Tack, G.: Constraint Propagation - Models, Techniques, Implementation. phd. thesis, Saarland University, Germany (2009)
16. Apt, K.R., Wallace, M.: Constraint Logic Programming using Eclipse. Cambridge University Press, New York (2007)
17. Karsai, G., Sztipanovits, J., Ledeczi, A., Bapty, T.: Model-Integrated Development of Embedded Software. Proceedings of the IEEE, 145–164 (2003)
18. Kang, K.C., Kim, S., Lee, J., Kim, K., Shin, E., Huh, M.: FORM: A feature-oriented reuse method with domain-specific reference architectures. Ann. Softw. Eng. 5, 143–168 (1998)
19. Vaziri, M., Vaziri, A., Jackson, D.: Some Shortcomings of OCL, the Object Constraint Language of UML
20. Neema, S.: System-Level Synthesis of Adaptive Computing Systems. PhD thesis, Vanderbilt University (May 2001)
21. Agrawal, A.: Graph Rewriting And Transformation (GReAT): A Solution For The Model Integrated Computing (MIC) Bottleneck. In: International Conference on Automated Software Engineering, p. 364 (2003)
22. Feydy, T., Stuckey, P.: Lazy clause generation reengineered. In: Gent, I.P. (ed.) CP 2009. LNCS, vol. 5732, pp. 352–366. Springer, Heidelberg (2009)
23. White, J., Dougherty, B., Schmidt, D.C.: Selecting highly optimal architectural feature sets with Filtered Cartesian Flattening. J. Syst. Softw. 82(8), 1268–1284 (2009)
24. Bleuler, S., Laumanns, M., Thiele, L., Zitzler, E.: PISA - A Platform and Programming Language Independent Interface for Search Algorithms, pp. 494–508. Springer, Heidelberg (2003)
25. Gries, M.: Methods for evaluating and covering the design space during early design development. Integr. VLSI J. 38(2), 131–183 (2004)
26. Bryant, R.: Graph-Based Algorithms for Boolean Function Manipulation. IEEE Transactions on Computers 35, 677–691 (1986)
27. Eames, B.K., Neema, S.K., Saraswat, R.: DesertFD: A Finite-Domain Constraint based tool for Design Space Exploration. Design Automation for Embedded Systems (2009)
28. Cieslok, F., Esau, H., Teich, J.: EXPLORA - Generic Design Space Exploration during Embedded System Synthesis. In: DIPES 2000: Proceedings of the IFIP WG10.3/WG10.4/WG10.5 International Workshop on Distributed and Parallel Embedded Systems, pp. 215–226. Kluwer, B.V, Deventer (2001)

A Comparison of Model Migration Tools

Louis M. Rose[1], Markus Herrmannsdoerfer[2], James R. Williams[1],
Dimitrios S. Kolovos[1], Kelly Garcés[3,4], Richard F. Paige[1],
and Fiona A.C. Polack[1]

[1] Department of Computer Science,
University of York, UK
{louis,jw,dkolovos,paige,fiona}@cs.york.ac.uk
[2] Institut für Informatik,
Technische Universität München, Germany
herrmama@in.tum.de
[3] AtlanMod (EMN-INRIA)
Nantes, France
[4] ASCOLA (LINA-INRIA)
Nantes, France
kelly.garces@mines-nantes.fr

Abstract. Modelling languages and thus their metamodels are subject to change. When a metamodel evolves, existing models may no
longer conform to the evolved metamodel. To avoid rebuilding them from
scratch, existing models must be migrated to conform to the evolved
metamodel. Manually migrating existing models is tedious and error-
prone. To alleviate this, several tools have been proposed to build a migration strategy that automates the migration of existing models. Little
is known about the advantages and disadvantages of the tools in different situations. In this paper, we thus compare a representative sample of
migration tools – AML, COPE, Ecore2Ecore and Epsilon Flock – using
common migration examples. The criteria used in the comparison aim to
support users in selecting the most appropriate tool for their situation.

1 Introduction

When a metamodel evolves, existing models may no longer conform to the structures and rules of the metamodel [4]. To avoid rebuilding existing models from
scratch, these models are migrated to conform to the evolved metamodel. Manual migration is tedious and error-prone, and so migration needs to be automated [11]. Building an automated migration strategy (even if desirable in practice) is non-trivial, as it has to correctly migrate an arbitrary set of models.

Recently, many different tools for building a migration strategy have become
available. Each tool has strengths and weaknesses. However, little is known about
how the tools compare in practice and so tool selection is difficult.

In this paper, we compare four model migration tools, selected from those
described in Section 2. Following the systematic process outlined in Section 3,
the tools are applied to two examples to facilitate their comparison. Section 4

D.C. Petriu, N. Rouquette, Ø. Haugen (Eds.): MODELS 2010, Part I, LNCS 6394, pp. 61–75, 2010.
© Springer-Verlag Berlin Heidelberg 2010

reports our experiences in using each of the tools, highlighting their strengths and weaknesses using nine criteria that we deem important for model migration. From this comparison, Section 5 synthesises advice and guidelines to help users in identifying the most appropriate model migration tool for their situation.

2   Related Work

Model transformation. Model migration can be implemented in a general-purpose programming language (such as Java), or in a model-to-model (M2M) transformation language, such as QVT [19] (the current OMG standard), ATL [15] or Xtend (of the popular openArchitectureWare framework[1]).

[17] identifies different kinds of model transformations, and in particular two categories of relationship between source and target metamodel: *exogenous* and *endogenous*. In the former, the source and target metamodels differ, and the target model is constructed entirely by the transformation. In the latter, source and target metamodels are the same, and so the target model can be initialised to be the same as source model before the transformation. In model migration, source and target metamodels differ, and hence endogenous transformations cannot be used. Consequently, model migration strategies are often specified with exogenous model-to-model transformation languages, and must contain sections for copying from original to migrated model those model elements that have not been affected by metamodel evolution.

Model migration. As was first argued by Sprinkle [22], model migration is best served by a language that combines properties of exogenous and endogenous model transformation: we need to be able to specify the transformation from a source metamodel to a different target metamodel, but only for the metamodel elements for which a migration is required. Rose et al. [20] classify model migration approaches into the following categories:

Manual specification approaches provide transformation languages to manually specify the model migration. These transformation languages try to reduce the effort for building a migration strategy by providing mechanisms that are specific for model migration. For instance, the approaches described in [18,21,23] extend an exogenous transformation language to automatically copy model elements whose metamodel definition has not changed. While manual specification fosters correctness of the model migration, it also requires the most effort to build a migration strategy.

Operator-based approaches, such as [12,25], provide coupled operators that allow metamodel changes and model migration strategies to be specified together. By capturing recurring co-evolution patterns as operators, these approaches avoid the need to specify identity rules, reusing recurring combinations of metamodel evolution and model migration through coupled operations.

Metamodel matching approaches automatically generate an exogenous model transformation from the difference between two metamodel versions. Because

---

[1] http://www.openarchitectureware.org/

an exogenous transformation is generated, model elements that have not been affected by co-evolution must be considered. Unlike manual specification, boilerplate code for automatic copying is automatically generated. Cicchetti [1] was the first to report a metamodel matching approach, noting that some categories of change cannot be automatically migrated. Garcés et al. [7] provide a potentially more expressive approach that allows the matching strategy to be parameterised.

Comparison. Apart from the above categorisation based on theoretical aspects of existing model migration approaches, no work compares model migration tools. However, several papers compare model transformation languages. Czarnecki and Helsen [2] present a feature model to classify transformation languages according to their technical properties. Mens and van Gorp [17] present functional and non-functional requirements for transformation languages. Taentzer et al. [24] compare the graph transformation languages AGG, TGG, VIATRA, and VMTS using the well-known object to relational transformation example. Gronmo et al. [9] compare the transformation languages CGT, AGG, and ATL using a complex refactoring example. These comparisons are used here to derive criteria for the comparison of model migration tools.

3   Comparison Method

In this section, we present the approach used to compare the model migration tools. The comparison is based on practical application of the tools to the co-evolution examples presented in Section 3.1. The selection of tools for the comparison is described in Section 3.2. To contextualise the conclusions drawn in this paper, Section 3.3 describes the process used to carry out the comparison.

3.1   Co-evolution Examples

To compare migration tools, two examples of co-evolution were used. The first is a well-known problem in the model migration literature and was used to test the comparison process, as discussed in Section 3.3. The second is a larger example taken from a real-world model-driven development project, and was identified as a potentially useful example for co-evolution case studies in [13].

Petri Nets. The first example is an evolution of a Petri net metamodel, previously used in [1,7,21,25] to discuss co-evolution and model migration.

In Figure 1(a), a Petri Net comprises Places and Transitions. A Place has any number of src or dst Transitions. Similarly, a Transition has at least one src and dst Place. In this example, the metamodel in Figure 1(a) is to be evolved to support weighted connections between Places and Transitions and between Transitions and Places.

The evolved metamodel is shown in Figure 1(b). Places are connected to Transitions via instances of PTArc. Likewise, Transitions are connected to Places via TPArc. Both PTArc and TPArc inherit from Arc, and therefore can be used to specify a weight.

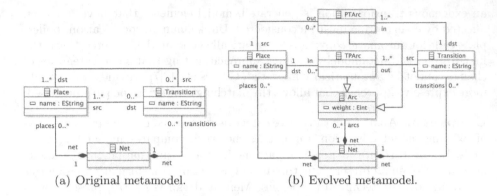

(a) Original metamodel.   (b) Evolved metamodel.

Fig. 1. Petri nets metamodel evolution (taken from [21]). Shading is irrelevant.

GMF. The second example is taken from the Graphical Modeling Framework (GMF) [8], an Eclipse project for generating graphical editors for models. The development of GMF is model-driven and utilises four domain-specific metamodels. Here, we consider one of those metamodels, GMF Graph, and its evolution between GMF versions 1.0 and 2.0.

The GMF Graph metamodel (not illustrated) describes the appearance of the generated graphical model editor. The metaclasses Canvas, Figure, Node, DiagramLabel, Connection, and Compartment are used to represent components of the graphical model editor to be generated. The evolution in the GMF Graph metamodel was driven by analysing the usage of the Figure#referencingElements reference, which relates Figures to the DiagramElements that use them. As described in the GMF Graph documentation[2], the referencingElements reference increased the effort required to re-use figures, a common activity for users of GMF. Furthermore, referencingElements was used only by the GMF code generator to determine whether an accessor should be generated for nested Figures.

In GMF 2.0, the Graph metamodel was evolved to make re-using figures more straightforward by introducing a proxy [5] for Figure, termed FigureDescriptor. The original referencingElements reference was removed, and an extra metaclass, ChildAccess, was added to make more explicit the original purpose of referencingElements (accessing nested Figures).

GMF provides a migrating algorithm that produces a model conforming to the evolved Graph metamodel from a model conforming to the original Graph metamodel. In GMF, migration is implemented using Java. The GMF source code includes two example editors, for which the source code management system contains versions conforming to GMF 1.0 and GMF 2.0. For the comparison of migration tools described in this paper, the migrating algorithm and example editors provided by GMF were used to determine the correctness of the migration strategies produced by using each model migration tool.

---

[2] http://wiki.eclipse.org/GMFGraph_Hints

3.2   Compared Tools

For the comparison in this paper, we selected one tool from each of the three categories – *manual specification, operator-based* and *metamodel matching* approaches – described in Section 2. We included a further tool from the manual specification category, Ecore2Ecore, as it is distributed with the Eclipse Modeling Framework, arguably the most widely used modelling framework. Each of these tools is discussed briefly below. Section 4 describes each tool in more detail.

AtlanMod Matching Language (AML) [7,6] is a model matching tool, which can be used as a *metamodel matching* migration tool. AML provides heuristics that the user combines to specify a metamodel matching strategy. A migrating ATL transformation is automatically generated by matching original and evolved metamodels.

COPE [12] is an *operator-based* migration tool. COPE provides a library of *co-evolutionary operators*. Each co-evolutionary operator specifies both a metamodel evolution and a corresponding model migration strategy. For example, the "Introduce Reference Class" operator from COPE evolves the metamodel such that a reference is replaced by a class and migrates models such that links conforming to the reference are replaced by instances of the reference class.

Ecore2Ecore [14] is a *manual specification* migration tool that is part of the Eclipse Modeling Framework (EMF). Migration is specified with a mapping model and hand-written Java code. Ecore2Ecore has been used in real-world projects, such as the Eclipse MDT UML2 project [3], to manage co-evolution.

Epsilon Flock [21] (subsequently referred to as Flock) is a *manual specification* migration tool. Flock is a domain-specific transformation language tailored for model migration. In particular, Flock automatically copies from original to migrated model all model elements that have not been affected by metamodel evolution. Flock is built atop Epsilon[3] [16], an extensible platform providing inter-operable programming languages for model-driven development.

3.3   Comparison Process

The comparison of migration tools was conducted by applying each of the four tools (Ecore2Ecore, AML, COPE and Flock) to the two examples of co-evolution (Petri nets and GMF). The developers of each tool were invited to participate in the comparison. The authors of COPE and Flock were able to participate fully, while the authors of Ecore2Ecore and AML were available for guidance, advice, and to comment on preliminary results.

We began the comparison by allocating responsibility for using each tool on the examples to a different person. Because the authors of Ecore2Ecore and AML were not able to participate fully in the comparison, two colleagues experienced in model transformation and migration stood in. To improve the validity of the comparison, each tool was used by someone other than its developer. Other than this restriction, the tools were allocated arbitrarily.

---

[3] http://www.eclipse.org/gmt/epsilon

Table 1. Summary of comparison criteria

Name	Description
Construction	Ways in which tool supports the development of migration strategies
Change	Ways in which tool supports change to migration strategies
Extensibility	Extent to which user-defined extensions are supported
Re-use	Mechanisms for re-using migration patterns and logic
Conciseness	Size of migration strategies produced with tool
Clarity	Understandability of migration strategies produced with tool
Expressiveness	Extent to which migration problems can be codified with tool
Interoperability	Technical dependencies and procedural assumptions of tool
Performance	Time taken to execute migration

The comparison was conducted in three phases. In the first phase, we identified criteria against which the tools would be compared. In the second phase, we used the first example of co-evolution (Petri nets) to familiarise ourselves with the migration tools and to assess the suitability of the comparison criteria. In the third phase, the tools were applied to the larger example of co-evolution (GMF) and conclusions were drawn from our experiences. Table 1 summarises the comparison criteria used in this paper. Further criteria could develop as a result of further experimentation in the future. The next section presents, for each criterion, observations from applying the migration tools to the co-evolution examples.

4   Comparison Results

By applying the method described in Section 3, four model migration tools were compared. This section reports similarities and differences of each tool, using nine criteria. Each subsection considers one criterion. The complete solutions are available online[4].

4.1   Constructing the Migration Strategy

Facilitating the specification and execution of migration strategies is the primary function of model migration tools. This section reports the process for and challenges faced in constructing migration strategies with each tool.

AML. An AML user specifies a combination of match heuristics from which AML infers a migrating transformation by comparing original and evolved metamodels. Matching strategies are written in a textual syntax, which AML compiles to produce an executable workflow. The workflow is invoked to generate the migrating transformation, codified in the Atlas Transformation Language (ATL) [15]. Devising correct matching strategies was difficult, as AML lacks documentation that describes the input, output and effects of each heuristic. Papers

---

[4] http://github.com/louismrose/migration_comparison

describing AML (such as [7,6]) discuss each heuristic, but mostly in a high-level manner. A semantically invalid combination of heuristics can cause a runtime error, while an incorrect combination results in the generation of an incorrect migration transformation. However, once a matching strategy is specified, it can be re-used for similar cases of metamodel evolution. To devise the matching strategies used in this paper, AML's author provided considerable guidance.

COPE. A COPE user applies *coupled operations* to the original metamodel to form the evolved metamodel. Each coupled operation specifies a metamodel evolution along with a corresponding fragment of the model migration strategy. A history of applied operations is later used to generate a complete migration strategy. As COPE is meant for co-evolution of models and metamodels, reverse engineering a large metamodel can be difficult. Determining which sequence of operations will produce a correct migration is not always straightforward. To aid the user, COPE allows operations to be undone. To help with the migration process, COPE offers the *Convergence View* which utilises EMF Compare to display the differences between two metamodels. While this was useful, it can, understandably, only provide a list of explicit differences and not the semantics of a metamodel change. Consequently, reverse-engineering a large and unfamiliar metamodel is challenging, and migration for the GMF Graph example could only be completed with considerable guidance from the author of COPE.

Ecore2Ecore. In Ecore2Ecore model migration is specified in two steps. In the first step, a graphical mapping editor is used to construct a model that declares basic migrations. In this step only very simple migrations such as class and feature renaming can be declared. In the next step, the developer needs to use Java to specify a customised parser (resource handler, in EMF terminology) that can parse models that conform to the original metamodel and migrate them so that they conform to the new metamodel. This customised parser exploits the basic migration information specified in the first step and delegates any changes that it cannot recognise to a particular Java method in the parser for the developer to handle. Handling such changes is tedious as the developer is only provided with the string contents of the unrecognised features and then needs to use low-level techniques – such as data-type checking and conversion, string splitting and concatenation – to address them. Here it is worth mentioning that Ecore2Ecore cannot handle all migration scenarios and is limited to cases where only a certain degree of structural change has been introduced between the original and the evolved metamodel. For cases which Ecore2Ecore cannot handle, developers need to specify a custom parser without any support for automated element copying.

Flock. In Flock, model migration is specified manually. Flock automatically copies only those model elements which still conform to the evolved metamodel. Hence, the user specifies migration only for model elements which no longer conform to the evolved metamodel. Due to the automatic copying algorithm, an empty Flock migration strategy always yields a model conforming to the evolved metamodel. Consequently, a user typically starts with an empty migration strategy and iteratively refines it to migrate non-conforming elements.

However, there is no support to ensure that all non-conforming elements are migrated. In the GMF Graph example, completeness could only be ensured by testing with numerous models. Using this method, a migration strategy can be easily encoded for the Petri net example. For the GMF Graph example whose metamodels are larger, it was more difficult, since there is no tool support for analysing the changes between original and evolved metamodel.

4.2   Changing the Migration Strategy

Migration strategies can change in at least two ways. Firstly, as a migration strategy is developed, testing might reveal errors which need to be corrected. Secondly, further metamodel changes might require changes to an existing migration strategy.

AML. Because AML automatically generates migrating transformations, changing the transformation, for example after discovering an error in the matching strategy, is trivial. To migrate models over several versions of a metamodel at once, the migrating transformations generated by AML can be composed by the user. AML provides no tool support for composing transformations.

COPE. As mentioned previously, COPE provides an undo feature, meaning that any incorrect migrations can be easily fixed. COPE stores a history of *releases* – a set of operations that has been applied between versions of the metamodel. Because the migration code generated from the release history can migrate models conforming to any previous metamodel release, COPE provides a comprehensive means for chaining migration strategies.

Ecore2Ecore. Migrations specified using Ecore2Ecore can be modified via the graphical mapping editor and the Java code in the custom model parser. Therefore, developers can use the features of the Eclipse Java IDE to modify and debug migrations. Ecore2Ecore provides no tool support for composing migrations, but composition can be achieved by modifying the resource handler.

Flock. There is comprehensive support for fixing errors. A migration strategy can easily be re-executed using a launch configuration, and migration errors are linked to the line in the migration strategy that caused the error to occur. If the metamodel is further evolved, the original migration strategy has to be extended, since there is no explicit support to chain migration strategies. The full migration strategy may need to be read to know where to extend it.

4.3   Extensibility

The fundamental constructs used for specifying migration in COPE and AML (operators and match heuristics, respectively) are extensible. Flock and Ecore2Ecore use a more imperative (rather than declarative) approach, and as such do not provide extensible constructs.

AML. An AML user can specify additional matching heuristics. This requires understanding of AML's domain-specific language for manipulating the data structures from which migrating transformations are generated.

COPE provides the user with a large number of operations. If there is no applicable operation, a COPE user can write their own operations using an in-place transformation language embedded into Groovy[5].

4.4   Re-use

Each migration tool capture patterns that commonly occur in model migration. This section considers the extent to which the patterns captured by each tool facilitate re-use between migration strategies.

AML. Once a matching strategy is specified, it can potentially be re-used for further cases of metamodel evolution. Match heuristics provide a re-usable and extensible mechanism for capturing metamodel change and model migration patterns.

COPE. An operation in COPE represents a commonly occurring pattern in metamodel migration. Each operation captures the metamodel evolution and model migration steps. Custom operations can be written and re-used.

Ecore2Ecore. Mapping models cannot be reused or extended in Ecore2Ecore but as the custom model parser is specified in Java, developers can decompose it into reusable parts some of which can potentially be reused in other migrations.

Flock. A migration strategy encoded in Flock is modularised according to the classes whose instances need migration. There is support to reuse code within a strategy by means of operations with parameters and across strategies by means of imports. Re-use in Flock captures only migration patterns, and not the higher level co-evolution patterns captured in COPE or AML.

4.5   Conciseness

A concise migration strategy is arguably more readable and requires less effort to write than a verbose migration strategy. This section comments on the conciseness of migration strategies produced with each tool, and reports the lines of code (without comments and blank lines) used.

AML. 117 lines were automatically generated for the Petri nets example. 563 lines were automatically generated for the GMF Graph example, and a further 63 lines of code were added by hand to complete the transformation. Approximately 10 lines of the user-defined code could be removed by restructuring the generated transformation.

COPE requires the user to apply operations. Each operation application generates one line of code. The user may also write additional migration code. For the Petri net example, 11 operations were required to create the migrator and no additional code. The author of COPE migrated the GMF Graph example using 76 operations and 73 lines of additional code.

Ecore2Ecore. As discussed above, handling changes that cannot be declared in the mapping model is a tedious task and involves a significant amount of low level code. For the PetriNets example, the Ecore2Ecore solution involved

---

[5] http://groovy.codehaus.org/

a mapping model containing 57 lines of (automatically generated) XMI and a custom hand-written resource handler containing 78 lines of Java code.

Flock. 16 lines of code were necessary to encode the Petri nets example, and 140 lines of code were necessary to encode the GMF Graph example. In the GMF Graph example, approximately 60 lines of code implement missing built-in support for rule inheritance, even after duplication was removed by extracting and re-using a subroutine.

4.6   Clarity

Because migration strategies can change and might serve as documentation for the history of a metamodel, their clarity is important. This section reports on aspects of each tool that might affect the clarity of migration strategies.

AML. The AML code generator takes a conservative approach to naming variables, to minimise the chances of duplicate variable names. Hence, some of the generated code can be difficult to read and hard to re-use if the generated transformation has to be completed by hand. When a complete transformation can be generated by AML, clarity is not as important.

COPE. Migration strategies in COPE are defined as a sequence of operations. The release history stores the set of operations that have been applied, so the user is clearly able to see the changes they have made, and find where any issues may have been introduced.

Ecore2Ecore. The graphical mapping editor provided by Ecore2Ecore allows developers to have a high-level visual overview of the simple mappings involved in the migration. However, migrations expressed in the Java part of the solution can be far more obscure and difficult to understand as they mix high-level intention with low-level string management operations.

Flock clearly states the migration strategy from the source to the target meta-model. However, the boilerplate code necessary to implement rule inheritance slightly obfuscates the real migration code.

4.7   Expressiveness

Migration strategies are easier to infer for some categories of metamodel change than others [10]. This section reports on the ability of each tool to migrate the examples considered in this comparison.

AML. A complete migrating transformation could be generated for the Petri nets example, but not for the GMF Graph example. The latter contains examples of two complex changes that AML does not currently support[6]. Successfully expressing the GMF Graph example in AML would require changes to at least one of AML's heuristics. However, AML provided an initial migration transformation that was completed by hand. In general, AML cannot be used to generate

---

[6] http://www.eclipse.org/forums/index.php?t=rview&goto=526894#
msg_526894If

complete migration strategies for co-evolution examples that contain *breaking and non-resolvable changes*, according to the categorisation proposed in [10].

COPE. The expressiveness of COPE is defined by the set of operations available. The Petri net example was migrated using only built-in operations. The GMF Graph example was migrated using 76 built-in operations and 2 user-defined migration actions. Custom migration actions allow users to specify any migration strategy.

Ecore2Ecore. A complete migration strategy could be generated for the Petri nets example, but not for the GMF Graph example. The developers of Ecore2Ecore have advised that the latter involves significant structural changes between the two versions and recommended implementing a custom model parser from scratch.

Flock. Since Flock extends EOL, it is expressive enough to encode both examples. However, Flock does not provide an explicit construct to copy model elements and thus it was necessary to call Java code from within Flock for the GMF Graph example.

4.8   Interoperability

Migration occurs in a variety of settings with differing requirements. This section considers the technical dependencies and procedural assumptions of each tool, and seeks to answer questions such as: "Which modelling technologies can be used?" and "What assumptions does the tool make on the migration process?"

AML depends only on ATL, while its development tools also require Eclipse. AML assumes that the original and target metamodels are available for comparison, and does not require a record of metamodel changes. AML can be used with either Ecore (EMF) or KM3 metamodels.

COPE depends on EMF and Groovy, while its development tools also require Eclipse and EMF Compare. COPE does not require both the original and target metamodels to be available. When COPE is used to create a migration strategy after metamodel evolution has already occurred, the metamodel changes must be reverse-engineered. To facilitate this, the target metamodel can be used with the Convergence View, as discussed in Section 4.1. COPE targets EMF, and does not support other modelling technologies.

Ecore2Ecore depends only on EMF. Both the original and the evolved versions of the metamodel are required to specify the mapping model with the Ecore2Ecore development tools. Alternatively, the Ecore2Ecore mapping model can be constructed programmatically and without using the original metamodel[7]. Unlike the other tools considered, Ecore2Ecore does not require the original metamodel to be available in the workspace of the metamodel user.

Flock depends on Epsilon and its development tools also require Eclipse. Flock assumes that the original and target metamodels are available for encoding the migration strategy, and does not require a record of metamodel changes. Flock can be be used to migrate models represented in EMF, MDR, XML and

---

[7] Private communication with Marcelo Paternostro, an Ecore2Ecore developers.

Z (CZT), although we only encoded a migration strategy for EMF metamodels
in the presented examples.

4.9   Performance

The time taken to execute model migration is important, particularly once a
migration strategy has been distributed to metamodel users. Ideally, migration
tools will produce migration strategies whose execution time is quick and scales
well with large models.

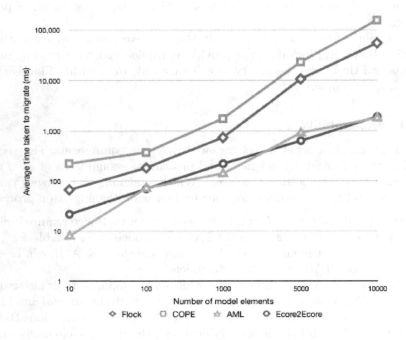

Fig. 2. Migration tool performance comparison

To measure performance, we produced Petri net models with a random generator, varying their size. Figure 2 shows the average time taken by each tool to
execute migration across 10 repetitions for models of different sizes. Note that
the Y axis has a logarithmic scale. The results indicate that, for the Petri nets co-
evolution example, AML and Ecore2Ecore execute migration significantly more
quickly than COPE and Flock, particularly when the model to be migrated contains more than 1,000 model elements. Figure 2 indicates that, for the Petri nets
co-evolution example, Flock executes migration between two and three times
faster than COPE, although the author of COPE reports that turning off validation causes COPE to perform similarly to Flock.

5   Discussion and Conclusions

The comparison results highlight the similarities and differences between a representative sample of model migration approaches. In this section, the differences are used to consider which tools are better suited to particular model migration situations.

COPE captures co-evolution patterns (which apply to both model and metamodel), while Ecore2Ecore, AML and Flock capture only model migration patterns (which apply just to models). Because of this, COPE facilitates a greater degree of re-use in model migration than other approaches. However, the order in which the user applies patterns with COPE impacts on both metamodel evolution and model migration, which can complicate pattern selection particularly when a large amount of evolution occurs at once. The re-usable co-evolution patterns in COPE make it well suited to migration problems in which metamodel evolution is frequent and in small steps.

Flock, AML and Ecore2Ecore are preferable to COPE when metamodel evolution has occurred before the selection of a migration approach. Because of its use of co-evolution patterns, we conclude that COPE is better suited to forward-rather than reverse-engineering.

Through its Convergence View and integration with the EMF metamodel editor, COPE facilitates metamodel analysis that is not possible with the other approaches considered in this paper. COPE is well-suited to situations in which measuring and reasoning about co-evolution is important.

In situations where migration involves modelling technologies other than EMF, AML and Flock are preferable to COPE and Ecore2Ecore. AML can be used with models represented in KM3, while Flock can be used with models represented in MDR, XML and CZT. Via the connectivity layer of Epsilon, Flock can be extended to support further modelling technologies.

There are situations in which Ecore2Ecore or AML might be preferable to Flock and COPE. For large models, Ecore2Ecore and AML might execute migration significantly more quickly than Flock and COPE. Ecore2Ecore is the only tool that has no technical dependencies (other than a modelling framework). In situations where migration must be embedded in another tool, Ecore2Ecore offers a smaller footprint than other migration approaches. Compared to the other approaches considered in this paper, AML automatically generates migration strategies with the least guidance from the user.

Despite these advantages, Ecore2Ecore and AML are unsuitable for some types of migration problem, because they are less expressive than Flock and COPE. Specifically, changes to the containment of model elements typically cannot be expressed with Ecore2Ecore and changes that are classified by [11] as *metamodel-specific* cannot be expressed with AML. Because of this, it is important to investigate metamodel changes before selecting a migration tool. Furthermore, it might be necessary to anticipate which types of metamodel change are likely to arise before selecting a migration tool. Investing in one tool to discover later that it is no longer suitable causes wasted effort.

Conclusions. This paper has compared a representative sample of approaches to automating model migration, an activity crucial for supporting software evolution in MDE. The comparison was performed by following a methodical process and used an example from a real-world MDE project. Some preliminary recommendations and guidelines in choosing a migration tool were synthesised from the presented results and are summarised in Table 2.

The criteria considered in this paper provide a foundation for further comparisons. For example, we recognise the importance of the usability and learnability of migration tools, and envisage a comprehensive user study (with 100s of users) for assessing these criteria. Future work will identify further comparison criteria and conduct further experimentation. In particular, we plan to investigate memory usage and forward-compatibility of tools.

Table 2. Summary of tool selection advice. (Tools are ordered alphabetically).

Requirement	Recommended Tools
Frequent, incremental co-evolution	COPE
Reverse-engineering	AML, Ecore2Ecore, Flock
Modelling technology diversity	Flock
Quicker migration for larger models	AML, Ecore2Ecore
Minimal dependencies	Ecore2Ecore
Minimal hand-written code	AML, COPE
Minimal guidance from user	AML
Support for metamodel-specific migrations	COPE, Flock

Acknowledgement. The work in this paper was supported by the European Commission via the MADES project, co-funded under the "Information Society Technologies" 7th Framework Programme (2009-2012). The work of the second author was funded by the German Federal Ministry of Education and Research (BMBF), grants "SPES2020, 01IS08045A" and "Quamoco, 01IS08023B". The work of the third author was supported by the EPSRC, through the Large-Scale Complex IT Systems project, "EP/F001096/1". The authors thank Kenn Hussey and Marcelo Paternostro for reviewing a draft of this paper.

References

1. Cicchetti, A., Di Ruscio, D., Eramo, R., Pierantonio, A.: Automating co-evolution in MDE. In: Proc. EDOC, pp. 222–231. IEEE Computer Society, Los Alamitos (2008)
2. Czarnecki, K., Helsen, S.: Feature-based survey of model transformation approaches. IBM Syst. J. 45(3), 621–645 (2006)
3. Eclipse. UML2 Model Development Tools project [online] (2009), http://www.eclipse.org/modeling/mdt/uml2 (Accessed September 7, 2009)
4. Favre, J.: Meta-model and model co-evolution within the 3d software space. In: Proc. ELISA Workshop, pp. 98–109 (September 2003)
5. Gamma, E., Helm, R., Johnson, R., Vlissides, J.: Design patterns: elements of reusable object-oriented software. Addison-Wesley, Reading (1995)
6. Garcés, K., Jouault, F., Cointe, P., Bézivin, J.: A Domain Specific Language for Expressing Model Matching. In: Proc. IDM, Nancy, France (2009)

7. Garcés, K., Jouault, F., Cointe, P., Bézivin, J.: Managing model adaptation by precise detection of metamodel changes. In: Paige, R.F., Hartman, A., Rensink, A. (eds.) ECMDA-FA 2009. LNCS, vol. 5562, pp. 34–49. Springer, Heidelberg (2009)
8. Gronback, R.C.: Eclipse Modeling Project: A Domain-Specific Language (DSL) Toolkit. Addison-Wesley Professional, Reading (2009)
9. Grønmo, R., Møller-Pedersen, B., Olsen, G.K.: Comparison of three model transformation languages. In: Paige, R.F., Hartman, A., Rensink, A. (eds.) ECMDA-FA 2009. LNCS, vol. 5562, pp. 2–17. Springer, Heidelberg (2009)
10. Gruschko, B., Kolovos, D.S., Paige, R.F.: Towards synchronizing models with evolving metamodels. In: Workshop on Model-Driven Software Evolution (2007)
11. Herrmannsdoerfer, M., Benz, S., Juergens, E.: Automatability of coupled evolution of metamodels and models in practice. In: Czarnecki, K., Ober, I., Bruel, J.-M., Uhl, A., Völter, M. (eds.) MODELS 2008. LNCS, vol. 5301, pp. 645–659. Springer, Heidelberg (2008)
12. Herrmannsdoerfer, M., Benz, S., Juergens, E.: COPE - automating coupled evolution of metamodels and models. In: Drossopoulou, S. (ed.) ECOOP 2009. LNCS, vol. 5653, pp. 52–76. Springer, Heidelberg (2009)
13. Herrmannsdoerfer, M., Ratiu, D., Wachsmuth, G.: Language evolution in practice. In: van den Brand, M., Gašević, D., Gray, J. (eds.) SLE 2009. LNCS, vol. 5969, pp. 3–22. Springer, Heidelberg (2009)
14. Hussey, K., Paternostro, M.: Advanced features of EMF. In: Tutorial at EclipseCon 2006, California, USA (2006), http://www.eclipsecon.org/2006/Sub.do?id=171 (Accessed September 07, 2009)
15. Jouault, F., Kurtev, I.: Transforming models with ATL. In: Bruel, J.-M. (ed.) MoDELS 2005. LNCS, vol. 3844, pp. 128–138. Springer, Heidelberg (2005)
16. Kolovos, D.S.: An Extensible Platform for Specification of Integrated Languages for Model Management. PhD thesis, University of York, United Kingdom (2009)
17. Mens, T., Van Gorp, P.: A taxonomy of model transformation. Electron. Notes Theor. Comput. Sci. 152, 125–142 (2006)
18. Narayanan, A., Levendovszky, T., Balasubramanian, D., Karsai, G.: Automatic domain model migration to manage metamodel evolution. In: Schürr, A., Selic, B. (eds.) MODELS 2009. LNCS, vol. 5795, pp. 706–711. Springer, Heidelberg (2009)
19. OMG. Query/View/Transformation 1.0 Specification [online] (2008), http://www.omg.org/spec/QVT/1.0/ (Accessed April 26, 2010)
20. Rose, L.M., Kolovos, D.S., Paige, R.F., Polack, F.A.C.: An analysis of approaches to model migration. In: Proc. Joint MoDSE-MCCM Workshop (2009)
21. Rose, L.M., Kolovos, D.S., Paige, R.F., Polack, F.A.C.: Model migration with Epsilon Flock. In: Tratt, L., Gogolla, M. (eds.) ICMT 2010. LNCS, vol. 6142, pp. 184–198. Springer, Heidelberg (2010)
22. Sprinkle, J.: Metamodel Driven Model Migration. PhD thesis, Vanderbilt University, TN, USA (2003)
23. Sprinkle, J., Agrawal, A., Levendovszky, T., Shi, F., Karsai, G.: Domain model evolution in visual languages using graph transformations. In: Proc. Workshop on Domain-Specific Visual Languages (2002)
24. Taentzer, G., Ehrig, K., Guerra, E., De Lara, J., Levendovszky, T., Prange, U., Varro, D.: Model transformations by graph transformations: A comparative study. In: Model Transformations in Practice Workshop at MoDELS 2005, Montego, 5p. (2005)
25. Wachsmuth, G.: Metamodel adaptation and model co-adaptation. In: Ernst, E. (ed.) ECOOP 2007. LNCS, vol. 4609, pp. 600–624. Springer, Heidelberg (2007)

Incremental Evaluation of Model Queries over EMF Models*

Gábor Bergmann[1], Ákos Horváth[1], István Ráth[1], Dániel Varró[1],
András Balogh[2], Zoltán Balogh[2], and András Ökrös[2]

[1] Budapest University of Technology and Economics,
Department of Measurement and Information Systems,
H-1117 Magyar tudósok krt. 2, Budapest, Hungary
{bergmann,ahorvath,rath,varro}@mit.bme.hu
[2] OptxWare Research and Development LLC,
H-1137 Katona J. u. 39
{andras.balogh,zoltan.balogh,andras.okros}@optxware.com

Abstract. Model-driven development tools built on industry standard platforms, such as the Eclipse Modeling Framework (EMF), heavily utilize model queries in model transformation, well-formedness constraint validation and domain-specific model execution. As these queries are executed rather frequently in interactive modeling applications, they have a significant impact on runtime performance and end user experience. However, due to their complexity, these queries can be time consuming to implement and optimize on a case-by-case basis. Consequently, there is a need for a model query framework that combines an easy-to-use and concise declarative query formalism with high runtime performance.

In this paper, we propose a declarative EMF model query framework using the graph pattern formalism as the query specification language. These graph patterns describe the arrangement and properties of model elements that correspond to, e.g. a well-formedness constraint, or an application context of a model transformation rule.

For improved runtime performance, we employ incremental pattern matching techniques: matches of patterns are stored and incrementally maintained upon model manipulation. As a result, query operations can be executed instantly, independently of the complexity of the constraint and the size of the model. We demonstrate our approach in an industrial (AUTOSAR) model validation context and compare it against other solutions.

Keywords: EMF, model query, incremental pattern matching, model validation.

1 Introduction

As model management platforms are gaining more and more industrial attraction, the importance of automated model querying techniques is also increasing. Queries form

---

* This work was partially supported by EU projects SENSORIA (IST-3-016004), SecureChange (ICT-FET-231101), INDEXYS (ARTEMIS-2008-1-100021), the Hungarian CERTIMOT (ERC_HU_09) project, and the János Bolyai Scholarship.

D.C. Petriu, N. Rouquette, Ø. Haugen (Eds.): MODELS 2010, Part I, LNCS 6394, pp. 76–90, 2010.

the underpinning of various technologies such as model transformation, code generation, domain specific behaviour simulation and model validation. In their most direct application, model queries may help find violations of well-formedness constraints of a domain-specific modeling language. Query evaluation entails a matching process, where an automated mechanism searches for model elements conforming to the structural pattern and attribute constraints imposed by the given query.

The leading industrial modeling ecosystem, the Eclipse Modeling Framework (EMF [1]), provides different ways to query the contents of models. These approaches range from (1) the use of high-level declarative constraint languages (like OCL [2]) to (2) a dedicated query language [3] resembling SQL, or, in the most basic case, (3) manually programmed model traversal using the generic model manipulation API of EMF. However, industrial experience (including those of the authors) shows scalability problems of complex query evaluation over large EMF models, taken e.g. from the automotive domain. Current practice for improving performance is manual query optimization, which is time consuming to implement on a case-by-case basis.

A promising way to address the performance problem is *incremental pattern matching* (INC) [4]. This technique relies on a *cache* which stores the results of a query explicitly. The result set is readily available from the cache at any time without additional search, and the cache is incrementally updated whenever (elementary or transactional) changes are made to the model. As results are stored, they can be retrieved in constant time, making query evaluation extremely fast. The trade-off is increased memory consumption, and increased update costs (due to continuous cache updates).

In the current paper, we propose EMF-INCQUERY, a framework for defining declarative queries over EMF models, and executing them efficiently *without manual coding*. For the query language, we reuse the concepts of graph patterns (which is a key concept in many graph transformation tools) as a concise and easy way to specify complex structural model queries. High runtime performance is achieved by adapting incremental graph pattern matching techniques.

The benefits of EMF-INCQUERY with respect to the state-of-the-art of querying EMF models include: (i) a significant performance boost when frequently querying complex structural patterns with a moderate amount of modifications in-between, (ii) efficient enumeration of all instances of a class regardless of location, and (iii) simple backwards navigation along references (these latter features address frequently encountered shortcomings of EMF's programming interfaces). We demonstrate the advantages of our approach over existing EMF query alternatives by conducting measurements on a model validation case study in the context of AUTOSAR [5], an industrial standard design platform for automotive embedded systems.

The paper is structured as follows: Section 2 introduces EMF and metamodeling, the mathematical formalism of graph patterns and AUTOSAR. Section 3 presents our declarative approach for queries over EMF. Section 4 elaborates the on-the-fly model validation case study in the domain of AUTOSAR, and Section 5 conducts benchmark measurements to assess the performance. A survey of similar tools and research is presented in Section 6. Finally, Section 7 summarizes the important points of the paper, draws conclusions and plots some future plans.

2   Background

In order to introduce our approach, this section briefly outlines the basics of the Eclipse Modeling Framework, graph patterns and gives a motivating example from the automotive domain based on the AUTOSAR framework.

2.1   Running Example: Constraint Checking in AUTOSAR Models

We demonstrate our model query technique by checking well-formedness constraints over AUTOSAR models. AUTOSAR (short for Automotive Open System Architecture, [5]) is an open and standardized automotive software architecture, jointly developed by automobile manufacturers, suppliers and tool developers. The objectives of the AUTOSAR partnership include the implementation and standardization of basic system functions while providing a highly customizable platform which continues to encourage competition on innovative functions. The common standard should help the integration of functional modules from multiple suppliers and increase scalability to different vehicle and platform variants. It aims to be prepared for the upcoming technologies and to improve cost-efficiency without making any compromise with respect to quality.

To improve quality and reliability of electrical/electronic systems, the validation of AUTOSAR models should be carried out in the early stages of the development process. The standard specifies a multitude of constraints, which should be satisfied to ensure proper functionality in this diverse environment. In this paper, we present three of these constraints, and define validators for each of them.

2.2   EMF and Ecore Metamodeling

The Eclipse Modeling Framework (EMF [1]) provides automated code generation and tooling (e.g. notification, persistence, editor) for Java representation of models. EMF models consist of an (acyclic) containment hierarchy of model elements (*EObjects*) with crossreferences – some of which may only be traversed by programs in one direction (unidirectional references). Additionally, each object has a number of attributes (primitive data values). Models are stored in *EResources* (e.g. files), and interrelated resources are grouped into *EResourceSets*.

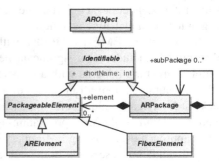

Fig. 1. AUTOSAR metamodel

EMF uses *Ecore* metamodels to describe the abstract syntax of a modeling language. The main elements of Ecore are the following: *EClass* (represented graphically by a rectangle in Fig. 1), *EAttribute* (entries in the rectangle) and *EReference* (depicted as edges). EClasses define the types of EObjects, enumerating EAttributes to specify attribute types of class instances and EReferences to define association types to other EObjects. Some EReferences additionally imply containment (graphically represented by a diamond). Unidirectional references are represented by arrows. Both ends of an association may have a multiplicity constraint attached to them, which declares the number of objects that, at run-time, may participate in an association. The most typical multiplicity constraints are i) the at-most-one (0..1), and (ii) the arbitrary (denoted by *). Inheritance may be defined between classes (depicted by a hollow arrow), which means that the inherited class has all the properties its parent has, and its instances are also instances of the ancestor class, but it may further define some extra features.

These concepts are illustrated by a simplified core part of the AUTOSAR [5] meta-model (Fig. 1). Note that in all metamodel figures of the paper, only relevant attributes are depicted, but no elements are omitted from the inheritance hierarchy. Every object in AUTOSAR inherits from the common ARObject class. If an element has to be identified, it has to inherit from the Identifiable class, and the shortName attribute has to be set. ARElement is a common base class for stand-alone elements, while specializations of FibexElement represent elementary building blocks within the FIBEX package. Instances of ARPackage class are arranged in a strict containment hierarchy by the sub-Package association, and every PackageableElement can be aggregated by one of the ARPackages using the element association.

2.3 Graph Patterns

Graph patterns [6] constitute an expressive formalism used for various purposes in Model Driven Development, such as defining declarative model transformation rules, defining the behavioral semantics of dynamic domain specific languages, or capturing general purpose model queries including model validation constraints. A graph pattern (GP) represents conditions (or constraints) that have to be fulfilled by a part of the instance model. A basic graph pattern consists of *structural constraints* prescribing the existence of nodes and edges of a given type (or subtypes, subject to polymorphism). Lan-

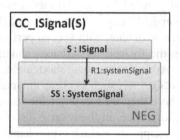

Fig. 2. Graph Pattern for the ISignal consistency check

guages usually include a way to express *attribute constraints*. A *negative application condition* (NAC) defines cases when the original pattern is *not* valid (even if all other constraints are met), in form of a negative sub-pattern. With NACs nested in arbitrary depth, the expressive power of graph patterns is equivalent to first order logic [7]. A match of a graph pattern is a group of model elements that have the exact same configuration as the pattern, satisfying all the constraints (except for NACs, which must be made unsatisfiable).

Fig. 2 depicts a sample graph pattern CC_ISignal. The structural part contains only a single node of type ISignal, but the NAC subpattern connects this node to a SystemSignal instance via an ISignal.systemSignal edge (note that some edges of that type may connect to a SystemSignalGroup instead of a SystemSignal, so the type assertion is relevant). Thus this graph pattern matches ISignal instances that are not connected to a SystemSignal. This graph pattern can be used as a declarative model query, in order to validate the model against a structural well-formedness constraint that requires each ISignal to be connected to a SystemSignal. See Section 4 for further examples.

Model queries with graph patterns. For readers with a strong EMF background, the idea of querying models by specifying graph patterns might not be straightforward. The key step in understanding the concept is that graph patterns declare *what* arrangement of elements is sought after, not *how* or *where* to find them. Each node in the pattern represents an EObject (EMF instance object), and the type of the node identifies the EClass of the object. This feature is useful to select only those model elements that conform to a certain type. Furthermore, the pattern nodes are connected by directed edges, annotated by an EReference type (or *containment*), to express how these elements reference each other. Finally, attribute constraints filtering and comparing the attributes of these elements can also be added.

3   Incremental Pattern Matching over EMF Models

3.1   Benefits

The aim of the EMF-INCQUERY approach is to bring the benefits of graph pattern based declarative queries and incremental pattern matching to the EMF domain. The advantage of declarative query specification is that it achieves (efficient) pattern matching without time-consuming, manual coding effort associated to ad-hoc model traversal. While EMF-INCQUERY is not the only technology for defining declarative queries over EMF (e.g. EMF Query or MDT-OCL), its distinctive feature is *incremental pattern matching*, with special performance characteristics suitable for scenarios such as on-the-fly well-formedness validation.

Additionally, some shortcomings of EMF are mitigated by the capabilities of EMF-INCQUERY, such as cheap enumeration of all instances of a certain type, regardless of where they are located in the resource tree. Another such use is the fast navigation of EReferences in the reverse direction, without having to augment the metamodel with an EOpposite (which is problematic if the metamodel is fixed, or beyond the control of the developer).

3.2   Usage

EMF-INCQUERY provides an interface for each declared pattern for (i) retrieving all matches of the pattern, or (ii) retrieving only a restricted set of matches, by binding (a-priori fixing) the value of one or more pattern elements (parameters).

In both cases, the query can be considered instantaneous, since the set of matches of the queried patterns (and certain subpatterns) are automatically cached, and remain available for immediate retrieval throughout the lifetime of the EMF ResourceSet. Even when the EMF model is modified, these caches are continuously and automatically kept up-to-date using the EMF Notification API. This maintenance happens without additional coding, and works regardless how the model was modified (graphical editor, programmatic manipulation, loading a new EMF resource, etc.).

3.3   Algorithm for Incremental Pattern Matching

EMF-INCQUERY achieves incremental pattern matching by adapting the RETE algorithm, well-known in the field of rule-based systems (see [4] for our first work on the application of RETE in graph patterns of a model transformation context). The following paragraphs give an overview of the EMF specific behaviour of RETE.

RETE network for graph pattern matching. RETE-based pattern matching relies on a network of nodes storing *partial matches* of a graph pattern. A partial match enumerates those model elements which satisfy a subset of the constraints described by the graph pattern. In a relational database analogy, each node stores a *view*. Partial matches of a pattern are readily available at any time, and they will be incrementally updated whenever model changes occur.

Input nodes serve as the underlying knowledge base representing a model. A RETE input node is introduced for each EClass, to contain the instances of the class (and subclasses), wrapped into unary tuples. The input nodes for EReferences and EAttributes contain all concrete occurrences of the structural feature as binary tuples *(source, target)*. Finally, the EMF notion of containment is also represented by binary tuples in an input node, and usable in pattern definitions.

At each *intermediate node*, set operations (e.g. filtering, projection, join, etc.) can be executed on the match sets stored at input nodes to compute the match set which is stored at the intermediate node. Finally, the match set for the entire pattern can be retrieved from the output *production node*. An important kind of intermediate node is the *join node*, which performs a natural join on its parent nodes in terms of relational algebra; whereas a *anti-join node* contains the set of tuples stored at

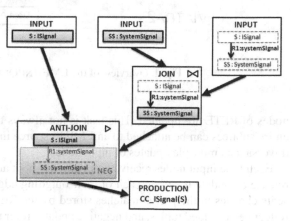

Fig. 3. RETE matcher of CC_ISignal

the primary input which do *not* match any tuple from the secondary input.

Fig. 3 shows a simplified RETE network matcher built for the CC_ISignal pattern (see Fig. 2) illustrating the use of join nodes. It uses three input nodes, for instances of EClass ISignal, EClass SystemSignal and EReference ISignal.systemSignal, respectively. The first join node connects the latter two to find ISignal.systemSignal edges that actually end in objects of type SystemSignal. The second intermediate node performs an anti-join of the first input node and the previous join node, therefore containing instances of ISignal that are *not* connected to a SystemSignal via ISignal.systemSignal. This is exactly the match set of pattern CC_ISignal, which is stored in the production node.

Updates after model changes. Upon creation, the RETE net is registered to receive notifications about all changes affecting an EMF ResourceSet, such as creation or deletion of model elements, via a service called EContentAdapter (or similar services provided by a transactional editing domain). Whenever receiving a notification, the input

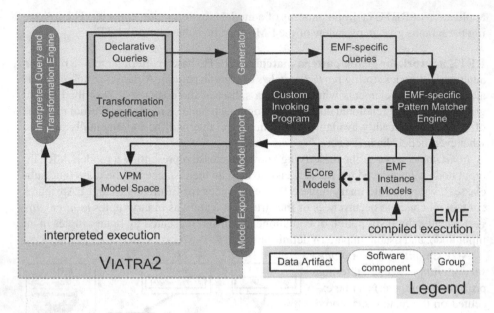

Fig. 4. Overview of the EMF-INCQUERY approach

nodes of RETE are updated. This task is not always trivial: along containment edges, entire subtrees can be attached to an EMF Resource in one step, which requires careful traversal and multiple updates of input nodes.

Each time input nodes receive notifications about an elementary model change, they release an update token on each of their outgoing edges. Such an update token represents changes in the partial matches stored by the RETE node. Positive update tokens reflect newly added tuples, and negative updates refer to tuples being removed from the set. Upon receiving an update token, a RETE node determines how the set of stored tuples will change, and release update tokens of its own to signal these changes to its child nodes. This way, the effects of an update will propagate through the network, eventually influencing the result sets stored in production nodes.

3.4   Architectural Overview of EMF-INCQUERY

Both the query language and the implementation of EMF-INCQUERY are adapted from the model transformation framework VIATRA2 [6]. However, the role of VIATRA2 is limited to the development phase, as the runtime module of EMF-INCQUERY is not dependent on it. Queries in EMF-INCQUERY can be defined by graph patterns in the transformation language [6] of VIATRA2. A *generator component* can be invoked to translate them to the *EMF-specific query* formthat serves as the input for the *EMF-based Pattern Matcher Engine*. The latter is responsible for evaluating queries over EMF ResourceSets, and is intended to be invoked from any Java program.

Graph patterns suitable for the EMF conversion have to refer to the metamodel elements of the relevant EMF format. Therefore VIATRA2 first needs to be aware of the

EMF metamodel (the *Ecore model*), which can be ensured by importing it into VIA-TRA2's (meta-)model representation, the VPM model space. As an additional benefit, the development of graph pattern based queries can be eased by taking advantage of the VIATRA2 framework. The VIATRA2 transformation interpreter shares identical functional behavior with EMF-INCQUERY. Therefore VIATRA2 serves as a faithful prototyping environment for graph patterns, capable of experimenting on EMF instance models imported into its model space. See Fig. 4 for a graphical overview of the various artifacts, software modules and their relations.

4   Benchmark Case Study

This section presents three well-formedness constraints from the AUTOSAR standard, which form the basis of our measurements in Section 5.

4.1   ISignal Constraint Check

The two metamodel elements for this constraint (SystemSignal and ISignal) are illustrated in Fig. 5, extending Fig. 1. A SystemSignal is the smallest unit of data (it is unique per System) and it is characterized by its length (in bits). (Also two optional elements can be specified, Datatypes and DataPrototype constants, but they are not used in this example.) An ISignal must be created for each SystemSignal (these will be the signals of the Interaction Layer). The graph pattern representation is explained in Section 2.3.

4.2   Signal Group Mapping Constraint Check

Related AUTOSAR elements.
The required metamodel elements for this constraint check are illustrated in Fig. 5. A PDU (Protocol data unit) is the smallest information which is delivered through a network layer. It is an abstract element in AUTOSAR, and has multiple different subtypes according to the available network layers. In this

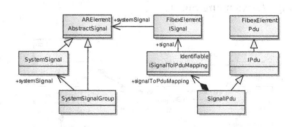

Fig. 5. AUTOSAR metamodel (ISignal)

case study, we will only examine IPdus (Interaction Layer PDU), and more precisely SignalIPdus. These SignalIPdus used to transfer ISignals. The positions of these ISignals are defined by the ISignalToIPduMappings. The ISignal can be a SystemSignal and a SystemSignalGroup as well. A signal group refers to a set of signals that must always be kept together to ensure the atomic transfer of the information in them.

Constraint check for signal group mapping. To ensure the atomic transfer of a SystemSignalGroup, they have to be packed properly into SignalIPdus. This means that if a SignalGroup is referenced from a SignalIPdu (with an ISignalToIPduMapping), then every Signal in it should be referenced as well from that SignalIPdu (note that an ISignalToIPduMapping references ISignals, but as every SystemSignal and SystemSignalGroup must have an ISignal, this is not a problem – the parent-child relationship is thus expressed between the SystemSignal and SystemSignalGroup instances). This constraint formulated as a graph pattern, matching a possible case of violation where the mapping element corresponding to the SystemSignalGroup is missing (as indicated by the NEG condition), can be seen in Fig. 6(a).

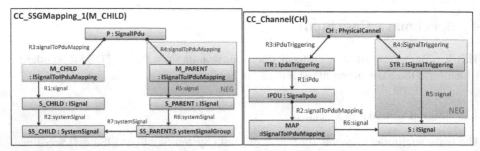

(a) Pattern to find invalid mappings   (b) Pattern to find invalid physical channels

Fig. 6. Consistency check patterns

4.3   Simple PhysicalChannel Consistency Check

Related AUTOSAR elements. To demonstrate the chosen consistency check, some additional AUTOSAR elements have to be described. These elements are illustrated by Fig. 7, extending Fig. 1.

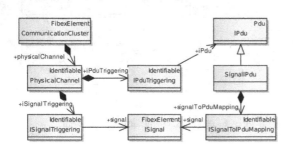

Fig. 7. AUTOSAR metamodel (Channel)

In AUTOSAR, *ECU (Electronic Control Unit)* instances can communicate with each other through a communication medium represented by a **PhysicalChannel**. Physical Channels are aggregated by a **CommunicationCluster**, which is the main element to describe the topological connection of communicating ECUs. A Physical Channel can contain **ISignalTriggering** and **IPduTriggering** elements. The **IPduTriggering** and **ISignalTriggering** describe the usage of IPdus and Signals on physical channels. ISignalTriggering defines the manner of triggering of an ISignal on the channel, on which it is sent. IPduTriggering describes on which channel the IPdu is transmitted.

Consistency check for physical channels. The following constraint has to be satisfied for a physical channel: if a CH PhysicalChannel contains an IPDU SignalIPdu (through an IPduTriggering), then all of the S ISignal, contained by IPDU (through an ISignal-ToIPduMapping), must have a related STR ISignalTriggering in the CH channel. In other words the channel is invalid if there is at least one S ISignal that has no related ISignalTriggering in the channel. This informal definition is formalized in Fig. 6(b) as a form of graph pattern. If the CC_Channel(CH) pattern can be matched for a Physical channel CH, then it is considered to be invalid.

5   Benchmarking and Evaluation

5.1   Generating Sample Models for Benchmarking

For a benchmarking evaluation, we designed a randomized model generator to create sample models of increasing size. For the three constraint cases, we used two different model families: (*A*) for ISignal and SSG and (*B*) for Channel. Both families contain an approximately equal number of valid and invalid model elements. The size of the sample model families ranges from a few thousand elements up to 600.000 (A) and 1.500.000 (B). See the appendix[1] for a detailed description of the generation algorithm.

5.2   Benchmarking

The benchmark simulates the typical scenario of model validation. The user is working with a large model, the modifications are small and local, but the result of the validation needs to be computed as fast as possible. To emulate this, the benchmark sequence consists of the following sequence of operations:

(1) First, the model is *loaded into memory*. In the case of EMF-INCQUERY, most of the overhead is expected to be registered in this phase, as the pattern matching cache needs to be constructed. Note however, that this is a *one-time* penalty, meaning that the cache will be maintained incrementally as long as the model is kept in memory. To highlight this effect, we recorded the times for the loading phase separately.

(2) Next, in the *first query phase*, the entire matching set of the constraints is queried. This means that a complete validation is performed on the model, looking for all elements for which the constraint is violated.

(3) After the first query, *model manipulations* are executed. These operations only affect a small fixed subset of elements, and change the constraint's validity (see the appendix[1]).

(4) Finally, in the *second query phase*, the complete validation is performed again, to check the net effect of the manipulation operations on the model.

Benchmark implementations. In addition to our EMF-INCQUERY-based implementation, we created two separate prototypes: a plain Java variant and an OCL variant that uses MDT-OCL [2]. The exact versions of EMF and MDT-OCL were 2.5.0 and 1.2.0 respectively, running on Eclipse Galileo SR1 20090920-1017. We ran the benchmarks

---

[1] All appendices, along with the complete source code and all test cases can be found at http://viatra.inf.mit.bme.hu/models10

SSG and iSignal validation pattern in model family A		EMF/Java			MDT-OCL			INCQuery			
Model Elements #	Model size [MB]	Res [s]	iSignal [s]	SSG [s]	Res [s]	iSignal [s]	SSG [s]	Res [s]	iSignal [s]	SSG [s]	Mem OH [MB]
2 373	30	0.06	0.00	0.25	0.13	0.16	3.58	0.17	0.00	0.00	3
4 748	31	0.08	0.00	0.94	0.16	0.17	13.53	0.22	0.00	0.00	6
9 449	32	0.13	0.01	3.67	0.20	0.19	52.48	0.30	0.00	0.00	12
18 850	33	0.22	0.01	14.52	0.30	0.22	210.48	0.45	0.01	0.00	22
37 721	37	0.42	0.01	58.56	0.47	0.27		0.75	0.01	0.01	45
75 692	43	0.78	0.02	239.53	0.86	0.33		1.58	0.01	0.01	92
151 359	55	1.81	0.03		1.84	0.53		3.22	0.02	0.02	187
302 778	81	3.63	0.06		3.64	0.88		6.19	0.02	0.02	373
605 402	135	7.14	0.09		7.48	1.63		12.00	0.02	0.03	746

Channel validation pattern in model family B		EMF/Java		MDT-OCL		INCQuery		
Model Elements #	Model size [MB]	Res [s]	Channel [s]	Res [s]	Channel [s]	Res [s]	Channel [s]	Mem OH [MB]
2 972	30	0.06	0.00	0.14	0.17	0.19	0.00	2
6 237	31	0.09	0.02	0.16	0.22	0.27	0.00	4
12 708	32	0.16	0.00	0.25	0.31	0.38	0.00	8
24 885	34	0.28	0.03	0.34	0.33	0.89	0.00	14
47 228	38	0.49	0.06	0.53	0.48	1.28	0.00	28
90 586	44	1.13	0.09	1.20	0.80	2.41	0.00	55
180 389	58	1.94	0.19	2.05	1.41	4.56	0.00	111
370 660	91	4.06	0.39	4.08	2.50	9.00	0.00	225
752 172	156	8.09	0.80	8.11	5.00	20.38	0.00	456
1 558 100	295	17.28	1.59	17.39	10.13	40.22	0.00	943

Legend: Res – resource loading time
           Mem OH – memory overhead

Fig. 8. Results overview

on an Intel Core2 E8400-based PC clocked at 3.00GHz with 3.25GBs of RAM on Windows XP SP3 (32 bit), using the Sun JDK version 1.6.0_17 (with a maximum heap size of 1536 MBs). Execution times were recorded using the java.lang.System class, while memory usage data has been recorded in separate runs using the java.lang.Runtime class (with several garbage collector invocations to minimize the transient effects of Java memory management). The data shown in the results correspond to the averages of 10 runs each.

All implementations share the same code for model manipulation (implementing the specification in the appendix[1]). They differ only in the query phases:

- The EMF-INCQUERY variant uses our API for reading the matching set of the graph patterns corresponding to constraints. These operations are only dependent on the size of the graph pattern and the size of the matching set itself (this is empirically confirmed by the results, see Section 5.3). To better reflect memory consumption, the RETE nets for all three constraints were built in each case.
- The plain Java variant performs model traversal using the generated model API of EMF. This approach is not naive, but intuitively manually optimized based on the constraint itself (but *not* on the actual structure of the model [8]).
- The OCL variant has been created by systematically mapping the contents of the graph patterns to OCL concepts, to ensure equivalence. We did not perform any OCL-specific optimization. The exact OCL expressions are in the appendix[1].

To ensure the correctness of the Java implementation, we created a set of small test models and verified the results manually. The rest of the implementations have been checked against the Java variant as the reference, by comparing the number of valid and invalid matches found in each round.

5.3 Analysis of the Results

Based on the results (Fig. 8), we have made the following observations:

(1) As expected, query operations with EMF-INCQUERY are nearly instantaneous, they are only measurable for larger models (where the matching set itself is large). In contrast, both Java and OCL variants exhibit a polynomially increasing characteristic, with respect to model size. The optimized Java implementation outperforms OCL, but only by a constant multiplier.

(2) Although not shown in Fig. 8, the times for model manipulation operations were also measured for all variants, and found to be uniformly negligible. This is expected since very few elements are affected by these operations, therefore the update overhead induced by the RETE network is negligible.

(3) The major overhead of EMF-INCQUERY is registered in the resource loading times (shown in the *Res* column in Fig. 8). It is important to note that the loading times for EMF itself is *included* in the values for EMF-INCQUERY. By looking at the values for loading times and their trends, it can be concluded that EMF-INCQUERY exhibits a linear time increase in both benchmark types, with a factor of approximately 2 compared to the pure EMF implementation. MDT-OCL does not cause a significant increase.

(4) The memory overhead also grows linearly with the model size, but depends on the complexity of the constraint too. More precisely, it depends on the size of the match sets of patterns and that of some sub-patterns depending on the structure of the constructed RETE network. (Actually, the memory overhead is sub-additive with respect to patterns, due to a varying degree of RETE node-sharing.)

It has to be emphasized that in practical operations, the resource loading time increase may not be important as it occurs only once during a model editing session. So, as long as there is enough memory, EMF-INCQUERY provides nearly instantaneous query performance, independently of the complexity of the query and the contents of the model. In certain cases, like for the SSG and ISignal benchmarks, EMF-INCQUERY is the only variant where the query can be executed in the acceptable time range for large models above 500000 elements, even when we take the combined times for resource loading and query execution into consideration. The performance advantage is less apparent for simple queries, as indicated by the figures for the Channel benchmark, where the difference remains in the range of a few seconds even for large models.

Overall, EMF-INCQUERY suits application scenarios with complex queries, which are invoked many times, with relatively small model manipulations in-between. Even though the memory consumption overhead is acceptable even for large models on today's PCs, the optimization techniques (based on combining various pattern matching techniques [8]) previously presented for VIATRA2 apply to EMF-INCQUERY too (even if their implementation will on EMF-level require some future work).

6 Related Work

Model queries over EMF. There are numerous technologies for providing declarative model queries over EMF. Here we give a brief summary of the mainstream techniques, none of which support incremental behavior.

The project EMF Model Query [3] provides query primitives for selecting model elements that satisfy a set of conditions; these conditions range from type and attribute checks to enforcing similar condition checks on model elements reachable through references. The query formalism has several important restrictions: (i) it can only describe tree-like patterns (as opposed to graph patterns); (ii) nodes cannot be captured in variables to be referenced elsewhere in the query; and (iii) the query can only traverse unidirectional relations in their natural direction. Indeed, the expressive power of Model Query is intuitively similar to a formal logic belonging to a class of languages called description logics [9], and weaker than first order logic. Therefore more complex patterns involving circles of references or attribute comparisons between nodes cannot be detected by EMF Model Query without additional coding.

EMF Search [10] is a framework for searching over EMF resources, with controllable scope, several extension facilities, and GUI integration. Unfortunately, only simple textual search (for model element name/label) is available by default; advanced search engines can be provided manually in a metamodel-specific way.

EMF-INCQUERY is not the first tool to apply graph pattern based techniques to EMF [11, 12], but its incremental pattern matching feature is unique.

Incremental OCL evaluation approaches. OCL [13] is a standardized navigation-based query language, applicable over a range of modeling formalisms. Taking advantage of the expressive features and wide-spread adoption of OCL, the project MDT OCL [2] provides a powerful query interface that evaluates OCL expressions over EMF models. However, backwards navigation along references can still have low performance, and there is no support for incrementality.

Cabot et al. [14] present an advanced three step optimization algorithm for incremental runtime validation of OCL constraints that ensures that constraints are reevaluated only if changes may induce their violation and only on elements that caused this violation. The approach uses promising optimizations, however, it works only on boolean constraints, therefore it is less expressive than our technique.

An interesting model validator over UML models [15] incrementally re-evaluates constraint instances (defined in OCL or by an arbitrary validator program) whenever they are affected by changes. During evaluation of the constraint instance, each model access is recorded, triggering a re-evaluation when the recorded parts are changed. This is also an important weakness: the approach is only applicable in environments where read-only access to the model can be easily recorded, unlike EMF. Additionally, the approach is tailored for model validation, and only permits constraints that have a single free variable; therefore general-purpose model querying is not viable.

Incremental Model Transformation approaches. The model transformation tool TefKat includes an incremental transformation engine [16] that also achieves incremental pattern matching over the factbase-like model representation of the system. The algorithm constructs and preserves a Prolog-like resolution tree for patterns, which is incrementally maintained upon model changes and pattern (rule) changes as well.

As a new effort for the EMF-based model transformation framework ATL [17], incremental transformation execution is supported, including a version of incremental pattern matching that incrementally re-evaluates OCL expressions whose dependencies have been affected by the changes. The approach specifically focuses on transformations, and provides no incremental query interface as of now.

VMTS [18] uses an off-line optimization technique to define (partially) overlapping graph patterns that can share result sets (with caching) during transformation execution. Compared to our approach, it focuses on simple caching of matching result with a small overhead rather than complete caching of patterns.

Giese et al. [19] present a triple graph grammar (TGG) based model synchronization approach, which incrementally updates reference (correspondence) nodes of TGG rules, based on notifications triggered by modified model elements. Their approach share similarities with our RETE based algorithm, in terms of notification observing, however, it does not provide support for explicit querying of (triple) graph patterns.

7   Conclusion and Future Work

In this paper, we presented EMF-INCQUERY as the next evolutionary step in efficiently executing complex queries over EMF models by adapting incremental graph pattern matching technology [4]. It is important to point out that, due to significant differences between EMF and VPM model representation and management - such as unidirectionally navigable graph models stored in multiple files in the case of EMF, vs. bidirectionally navigable graph models with multiple typing stored in a single modelspace in VIATRA2), we could actually reuse only the core concepts of RETE networks from our previous results [4, 8]. In essence, we built an incremental pattern matching solution specific to EMF technology, which is the scope of our paper.

The main lesson we learned from our experiments is that query evaluation should be tailored to the designated application scenario. We have specifically targeted EMF-INCQUERY to support the fast evaluation of complex model queries. Due to the fundamentals of the technology, this works best in the case of interactive applications, where the model modification operations are small (with respect to the size of the entire model). Our results have confirmed the high performance of our implementation, but also the fact that the designer needs to keep the memory impact in mind. Practical applications of this technology include on-the-fly model validation, interactive execution of domain-specific behavior languages, incremental model synchronization, model based monitoring and management, design space exploration and incremental maintenance of (aggregated) model views for development tool environments.

As future work, we intend to work on further automatic optimization, since, as with every declarative query formalism, there is always room for improvement. In the case of our RETE engine, this optimization targets the construction of the cache network, based on the pattern and the contents of the model itself. Additionally, we plan to work on integration with OCL as a query specification language. As it has been shown [20], a significant subsection of OCL can be mapped to the graph pattern formalism, especially if the pattern language is augmented with cardinality expressions.

References

1. The Eclipse Project: Eclipse Modeling Framework, http://www.eclipse.org/emf
2. The Eclipse Project: MDT OCL,
   http://www.eclipse.org/modeling/mdt/?project=ocl

3. The Eclipse Project: EMF Model Query,
   http://www.eclipse.org/modeling/emf/?project=query
4. Bergmann, G., Ökrös, A., Ráth, I., Varró, D., Varró, G.: Incremental pattern matching in the VIATRA model transformation system. In: Karsai, G., Taentzer, G. (eds.) Graph and Model Transformation (GraMoT 2008). ACM, New York (2008)
5. AUTOSAR Consortium: The AUTOSAR Standard, http://www.autosar.org/
6. Varró, D., Balogh, A.: The Model Transformation Language of the VIATRA2 Framework. Science of Computer Programming 68(3), 214–234 (2007)
7. Rensink, A.: Representing first-order logic using graphs. In: Ehrig, H., Engels, G., Parisi-Presicce, F., Rozenberg, G. (eds.) ICGT 2004. LNCS, vol. 3256, pp. 319–335. Springer, Heidelberg (2004)
8. Bergmann, G., Horváth, A., Ráth, I., Varró, D.: Efficient model transformations by combining pattern matching strategies. In: Paige, R.F. (ed.) ICMT 2009. LNCS, vol. 5563, pp. 20–34. Springer, Heidelberg (2009)
9. Baader, F., Calvanese, D., McGuinness, D.L., Nardi, D., Patel-Schneider, P.F. (eds.): The description logic handbook: theory, implementation, and applications. Cambridge University Press, New York (2003)
10. The Eclipse Project: EMFT Search,
    http://www.eclipse.org/modeling/emft/?project=search
11. Biermann, E., Ermel, C., Taentzer, G.: Precise semantics of emf model transformations by graph transformation. In: Czarnecki, K., Ober, I., Bruel, J.-M., Uhl, A., Völter, M. (eds.) MODELS 2008. LNCS, vol. 5301, pp. 53–67. Springer, Heidelberg (2008)
12. Giese, H., Hildebrandt, S., Seibel, A.: Improved flexibility and scalability by interpreting story diagrams. In: Magaria, T., Padberg, J., Taentzer, G. (eds.) Proceedings of GT-VMT 2009. Electronic Communications of the EASST, vol. 18 (2009)
13. The Object Management Group: Object Constraint Language, v2.0 (May 2006),
    http://www.omg.org/spec/OCL/2.0/
14. Cabot, J., Teniente, E.: Incremental integrity checking of UML/OCL conceptual schemas. J. Syst. Softw. 82(9), 1459–1478 (2009)
15. Groher, I., Reder, A., Egyed, A.: Incremental consistency checking of dynamic constraints. In: Rosenblum, D.S., Taentzer, G. (eds.) FASE 2009. LNCS, vol. 6013, pp. 203–217. Springer, Heidelberg (2010)
16. Hearnden, D., Lawley, M., Raymond, K.: Incremental model transformation for the evolution of model-driven systems. In: Nierstrasz, O., Whittle, J., Harel, D., Reggio, G. (eds.) MoDELS 2006. LNCS, vol. 4199, pp. 321–335. Springer, Heidelberg (2006)
17. Jouault, F., Tisi, M.: Towards incremental execution of ATL transformations. In: Tratt, L., Gogolla, M. (eds.) ICMT 2010. LNCS, vol. 6142, pp. 123–137. Springer, Heidelberg (2010)
18. Mészáros, T., et al.: Manual and automated performance optimization of model transformation systems. Software Tools for Technology Transfer (2010) (to appear)
19. Giese, H., Wagner, R.: From model transformation to incremental bidirectional model synchronization. Software and Systems Modeling (SoSyM) 8(1) (March 2009)
20. Winkelmann, J., Taentzer, G., Ehrig, K., Küster, J.M.: Translation of restricted OCL constraints into graph constraints for generating meta model instances by graph grammars. Electron. Notes Theor. Comput. Sci. 211, 159–170 (2008)

Active Operations on Collections

Olivier Beaudoux[1], Arnaud Blouin[2], Olivier Barais[3], and Jean-Marc Jézéquel[3]

[1] ESEO Group, Angers - GRI Team
`olivier.beaudoux@eseo.fr`
[2] INRIA Rennes - Triskell Team
`arnaud.blouin@inria.fr`
[3] University of Rennes 1 - Triskell Team
`{barais,jezequel}@irisa.fr`

Abstract. Collections are omnipresent within models: collections of references can represent relations between objects, and collections of values can represent object attributes. Consequently, manipulating models often consists of performing operations on collections. For example, transformations create target collections from given source collections. Similarly, constraint evaluations perform computation on collections. Recent research works focus on making such transformations or constraint evaluations active (*i.e.* incremental, or live). However, they propose their own solutions to the issue by the introduction of specific languages and/or systems. This paper proposes a mathematical formalism, centered on collections and independent of languages and systems, that describes how the implementation of standard operations on collections can be made active. The formalism also introduces a reversed active assignment dedicated to bidirectional operations. A case study illustrates how to use the formalism and its Active Kermeta implementation for creating an active transformation.

1 Introduction

The promise of model-driven engineering (MDE) is that the development and maintenance effort can be reduced by working at the model instead of the code level. Models define what is valuable in a system, and code generators produce the functionality that is common in the application domain. One of the main current issue for the MDE community is to support evolution in the stage of the software development process (*e.g.* to support incremental code generation). To address this issue, this paper works on formalizing operation on collections to support incremental models manipulation. Indeed, collections are omnipresent in the Model Driven Engineering field: collections of references can represent relations between objects, and collections of values can represent object attributes. Consequently, manipulating models often consists of performing operations on collections. Two essential model manipulations are constraint checking and model transformation: the former often uses (OCL) iterators to traverse collections, and the later generates target from source collections. This illustrates the importance of collections in Model Driven Engineering. However, whenever a model is *modified*, these operations are not efficient since they require a full

D.C. Petriu, N. Rouquette, Ø. Haugen (Eds.): MODELS 2010, Part I, LNCS 6394, pp. 91–105, 2010.
© Springer-Verlag Berlin Heidelberg 2010

re-execution as if the model was newly created. Many different solutions have been proposed to solve such an issue; they are all based on the concept of incremental [1], live [2] or active [3] model manipulation. Despite their omnipresence, collections are not the central piece of these approaches that are often tied to a specific language and/or system [4,5], or use usual manipulations combined with merge strategies [6].

This paper proposes a formalism that makes standard operations on collections active, independently from languages and systems. It shows how active transformations can be reduced to active operations on collections, thus underlining the interest of collections as first class objects for model manipulation. It evaluates the approach by studying complexities of active operations, and by explaining how active operations can be written with Active Kermeta, an implementation of our formalism on top of Kermeta [7].

The remainder of this paper is structured as follows. Section 2 explains how standard operations on collections can be made active through active loops, thus showing the foundation of our proposal. Section 3 illustrates the use of the formalism and its Active Kermeta implementation for writing active transformations. Section 4 evaluates complexities of active operations, discusses the possible optimizations, and compares the approach with related works. Finally, section 5 concludes on our contribution and its perspective.

2   From Standard to Active Operations

This section explains the semantics of active operations by describing their active loops: usual binary operations, application, selection, sort, and reversed assignment. Such a set of operations has been mainly inspired by OCL [8].

2.1   Preliminary: Definitions

The set of all collections is noted $\mathbb{C}$. Its subsets $\mathbb{U}$ and $\mathbb{O}$ define collections that respectively manage *uniqueness* and *order*. The four combinations define usual collection types: order set ($oset = \mathbb{U} \cap \mathbb{O}$), set ($set = \mathbb{U} - \mathbb{O}$), sequence ($seq = \mathbb{O} - \mathbb{U}$), and bag ($bag = \mathbb{C} - \mathbb{U} - \mathbb{O}$).

The following table introduces the minimal set of operations that is sufficient to express any other operation:

Operation	$C \notin \mathbb{O}$	$C \in \mathbb{O}$
$\lvert C \rvert$	cardinality of C	
$e \in C$	presence of e in C	
$e \in_i C$	n/a	presence of e in C at position $i \in [0..\lvert C \rvert[$
$C[i]$	n/a	element in C at position $i \in [0..\lvert C \rvert[$
$C[i..j]$	n/a	sub-collection of C from pos. i to pos. j
$C + e$	adds e into C	appends e at the end of C
$C +_i e$	n/a	inserts e into C at position $i \in [0..\lvert C \rvert]$
$C - e$	removes the first occurrence of e from C	
$C -_i$	n/a	removes from C the element at pos. $i \in [0..\lvert C \rvert[$

If $C \in \mathbb{U}$, operations $C + e$ and $C +_i e$ check the uniqueness of e within C: if $e \in C$ before the insertion, operations have no effect. The following table gives the notation used to iterate on collections:

Iteration	$C \notin \mathbb{O}$	$C \in \mathbb{O}$
$\forall e \in C,\, p(e)$	calls $p(e)$ for each element e of C	
$\forall e \in_i C,\, p(e, i)$	n/a	calls $p(e, i)$ for each element e at position i in C
$\forall' e \in C,\, p_a(e)$	calls $p_a(e)$ each time an element e is added into C	
$\forall' e \notin C,\, p_r(e)$	calls $p_r(e)$ each time an element e is removed from C	
$\forall' e \in_i C,\, p_a(e, i)$	n/a	calls $p_a(e, i)$ each time e is inserted at position i
$\forall' e \notin_i C,\, p_r(e, i)$	n/a	calls $p_r(e, i)$ each time e is removed from position i

The first two rows represent usual iterations throughout loops (symbol $\forall$): the iteration is performed once for all elements of the collection. The next two rows define an iteration throughout an *active loop* (symbol $\forall'$) that is composed of two *rules*: the *addition* rule ($\forall' ... \in ...$) *immediately* invokes procedure p_a for each element e of C (similar to usual loops), and *subsequently* invokes p_a each time a new element e is added into C; the *removal* rule ($\forall' ... \notin ...$) *subsequently* invokes procedure p_r each time element e is removed from C. The last two rows define the *indexed active loop* dedicated to ordered collections; such a loop can also be used in some situations with unordered collections (*e.g.* selection and sort, see sections 2.4 and 2.5). Active loops thus observe additions and removals performed on collections; they also observe replacements since a replacement is considered as a removal+addition pair (see section 4.2). Usual and active loops can use a predicate; for example, $\forall e \in C \,|\, e \neq 1,\, p(e)$ calls p for each e different from 1.

Usually operation $B = op(A_1, ..., A_n)$ computes the resulting collection B from the source collections A_i. The computation is based on a usual loop: changing A_i collections afterward does not change B. Conversely, an *active operation* is based on an active loop, and thus reevaluates B each time an addition or a removal occurs on A_i. One may find that using operator $=$ is ambiguous since it suggests bidirectionality; however, a change on B does *not* affect A_i. For this reason, operator $:=$ is used so that expression $B := op(A_1, ..., A_n)$ becomes unambiguous.

2.2   Union, Intersection and Difference

Usual binary operations, such as union, intersection and difference, have simple active loops. For example with operation $C := A \cup B$, each time an element e is added into A or B, it is also added into C; conversely, each time e is removed for A or B, it is also removed from C:

Operation	Order	Active loop		
$C := A \cup B$	$(A, B) \notin \mathbb{O}^2$	$\forall' e \in A,\, C + e$		$\forall' e \notin A,\, C - e$
		$\forall' e \in B,\, C + e$		$\forall' e \notin B,\, C - e$
	$(A, B) \in \mathbb{O}^2$	$\forall' e \in_i A,\, C +_i e$		$\forall' e \notin_i A,\, C -_i$
		$\forall' e \in_i B,\, C +_{|A|+i} e$		$\forall' e \notin_i B,\, C -_{|A|+i}$

Union preserves uniqueness, $i.e.$ $(A, B) \in \mathbb{U}^2 \Rightarrow C \in \mathbb{U}$, and order, $i.e.$ $(A, B) \in \mathbb{O}^2 \Rightarrow C \in \mathbb{O}$. Active loops for intersection and difference have been defined similarly.

2.3   Application

Application $B := A(f)$ consists of applying f on each element of A. It preserves the order and guarantees $|A| = |B|$; it cannot preserve uniqueness since f may have introduced pairs.

Application allows the definition of navigation *paths*. For example, if elements e of A define property[1] p, path $B := A.p$ is equivalent to $B := A(e \rightarrow e.p)$. However, the result must be flattened since $A(e \rightarrow e.p)$ returns a collection of properties, $i.e.$ a collection of collections. The following table gives the active loops for applications and paths:

Operation	Order	Active loop	
$B := A(f)$	$A \notin \mathbb{O}$	$\forall' e \in A,\ B + f(e)$	$\forall' e \notin A,\ B - f(e)$
	$A \in \mathbb{O}$	$\forall' e \in_i A,\ B +_i f(e)$	$\forall' e \notin_i A,\ B -_i$
$B := A.p$	$A \notin \mathbb{O}$	$\forall' e \in A,$	$\forall' e \notin A,$
		$\quad \forall' e' \in e.p,\ B + e'$	$\quad$ stop observation of $e.p$
		$\quad \forall' e' \notin e.p,\ B - e'$	$\quad \forall' e' \in e.p,\ B - e'$
	$A \in \mathbb{O}$	$\forall' e \in_i A,$	$\forall' e \notin_i A,$
		$\quad \forall' e' \in_j e.p,\ B +_k e'$	$\quad$ stop observation of $e.p$
		$\quad \forall' e' \notin_j e.p,\ B -_k$	$\quad \forall' e' \in_j e.p,\ B -_k$
		where $k = j + \sum_{n=0}^{n=i-1} |e[n].p|$	

2.4   Selection

Selection $B := A[f]$ consists of selecting elements of A that match predicate f. It preserves uniqueness and order since it filters A. Other operations can be derived from selection, such as operations *reject*, *detect*, *exists* and *forAll* defined by OCL [8], or operation $B := toUnique(A)$ that converts $A \in \mathbb{C}$ into $B \in \mathbb{U}$.

Operation	Order	Active loop	
$B := A[f]$	$A \notin \mathbb{O}$	$\forall' e \in A \mid f(e),\ B + e$	$\forall' e \notin A \mid f(e),\ B - e$
	$A \in \mathbb{O}$	$\forall' e \in_i A \mid f(e, i),\ B +_j e$	$\forall' e \notin_i A \mid f(e, i),\ B -_j$
		where $j =\mid A[0..i][f] \mid$	

As one can note, the previous active loops do not take into account any reevaluation of f required in some situations. For example, selection $persons[p \rightarrow p.age < 18]$ returns a collection of persons under 18. The active loop works fine whenever a person is added or removed from the collection; however, it fails whenever the age of a person goes above 18.

---

[1] A property is either a relation or an attribute. As explained in section 3.1, all properties are considered as collections.

Thus, we propose to *reify* (symbol $'$) predicate f into a *predicate collection* represented as a sequence of booleans. Let us consider that collection *persons* contains three people with ages 16, 42 and 12. Expression $persons.age\,[a \to a < 18]'$ returns predicate collection ($true$, $false$, $true$) indicating that $persons[0]$ and $persons[2]$ are below 18. Here we assume that all collections, including unordered ones, store their elements in an array (see section 4.1), thus allowing the use of the indexed accessor $C[i]$ and indexed loops $\forall'e \in_i C$. By *overriding* operation $B :=$ $A[f]$ with $B := A[P]$ where $P = A[f]'$, the desired selection can be performed: $persons[persons.age[a \to a < 18]']$.

Operation	Order	Active loop		
$P := A[f]'$		$\forall'e \in_i A,\ P +_i f(e)$		$\forall'e \notin_i A,\ P-_i$
$B := A[P]$	$A \notin \mathbb{O}$	$\forall'p \in_i P\,\lvert p,\ B + A[i]$		$\forall'e \notin_i A \mid e \in B,\ B - e$
		$\forall'p \in_i P\,\lvert \neg p,\ B - A[i]$		
	$A \in \mathbb{O}$	$\forall'p \in_i P\,\lvert p,\ B +_j A[i]$		$\forall'e \notin_i A \mid e \in_j B,\ B-_j$
		$\forall'p \in_i P\,\lvert \neg p,\ B-_j$		
		where $j = \lvert\, P[0..i][p \to p]\,\rvert$		

The addition rule of $B := A[P]$ is based on observing P but not A, which implies that $P := A[f]'$ must be computed *before* $B := A[P]$. The removal rule is based on observing A but not P, which allows retrieving element e of A that must be removed from B. Predicate collections can be combined through usual boolean operators:

Operation	Active loop	
$P' := \neg P$	$\forall'p \in_i P,\ P' +_i \neg p$	$\forall'p \in_i P,\ P'-_i$
$P := P_1 \wedge P_2$	$\forall'p_2 \in_i P_2,\ P +_i (P_1[i] \wedge p_2)$	$\forall'p_2 \notin_i P_2,\ P-_i$
$P := P_1 \vee P_2$	$\forall'p_2 \in_i P_2,\ P +_i (P_1[i] \vee p_2)$	$\forall'p_2 \notin_i P_2,\ P-_i$

These active loops are simple. However, it is necessary to decide which collection P_1 or P_2 must be observed for operators $\wedge$ and $\vee$. By convention, we fix that P_1 is defined *before* P_2 so that a change on P_1 is followed by a change on P_2; rules are thus based on observing P_2, which guaranties that $\lvert P_1 \rvert = \lvert P_2 \rvert$ when the rule is called ($P_1[i]$ can thus be used).

2.5   Sort

Sort $B := A\{f\}$ consists of sorting A accordingly to the value returned by f assuming that its type defines operator $<$. The sort operation preserves uniqueness but, naturally, not the order.

Operation	Order	Active loop	
$B := A\{f\}$	$A \notin \mathbb{O}$	$\forall'e \in A,\ B +_j e$	$\forall'e \notin A,\ B-_j$
	$A \in \mathbb{O}$	$\forall'e \in_i A,\ B +_j e$	$\forall'e \notin_i A,\ B-_j$
		where $j = \lvert A[e' \to f(e') < f(e)]\,\rvert$	

As for selection, the previous active loops do not take into account any reevaluation required if f uses paths on e. For example, sort $persons\{p \to p.name\}$ returns a collection of persons sorted by their name. This works fine whenever a person is added or removed from the collection but fails whenever the name of a person changes.

Thus, we propose again to *reify* (symbol $'$) function f into an *order collection* represented as a sequence of integers that gives positions after the sort. Let us consider that collection $persons$ contains three persons named "Emma", "Oliver" and "Alice". Expression $persons.name\{n \to n\}'$, abbreviated on $\{persons.name\}'$, returns order collection $(1, 2, 0)$, which means that $persons[0]$ representing "Emma" will occupy position $\{persons.name\}'[0] = 1$ after sorting. The order can then be used for sorting the collection:$persons\{\{persons.\,name\}'\}$. The following table *overrides* the previous one where $O := \{A\}'$ returns an order collection and $B := A\{O\}$ sorts A according to order O:

Operation	Active loop	
$O := \{A\}'$	$\forall' e \in_i A, O +_i j$ where $j = \|A[e' \to e' < e]\|$	$\forall' e \notin_i A, O -_i$
$B := A\{O\}$	$\forall' j \in_i O, B +_j A[i]$	$\forall' j \notin O, B -_j$

The active loop of $O := \{A\}'$ consists of adding or removing order j at/from position i. However, operation $+$ and $-$ must be refined for order collections to manage resulting positions correctly. For example, $O +_i j$ requires to increment (silently) all orders greater than j.

Moreover, the previous active loops do not allow sorting on multiple criteria. The full version is based on *partial order collections* that specify all *possible* positions; a partial order collection is represented by a sequence of sequences of integers. The previous example can be extended so that the persons are sorted by their last names and then by their first names: $persons\{\{persons.lastName\}' \wedge \{persons.firstName\}'\}$. Let us now consider that collection $persons$ contains three persons named "Emma G.", "Oliver B." and "Alice B.". We now have $\{person.\,lastName\}'$ that returns $((2), (0, 1), (0, 1))$ and $\{person.firstName\}'$ that returns $((1), (2), (0))$: "Oliver B." and "Alice B." have the same possible positions (0 or 1) represented by the two sequences $(0, 1)$, and final positions are given by combining the two partial order collections: $\{persons.lastName\}' \wedge \{persons.firstName\}' = ((2), (1), (0))$.

2.6   Reversed Assignment

Previous operations are unidirectional: in operation $B := op\,A$, modifying A induces a change on B, but modifying B does not induce any change on A, thus motivating the use of operator $:=$ instead of $=$. Bidirectionality implies that op is reversible, *i.e.* $A := op^{-1}B$, so that a change on B impacts collection A. Union, intersection, difference, selection and sort are not reversible; the only operation that can be reverted is the application: $B := A(f)$ can be reverted as long as f^{-1} exists.

However, application $B := A(f)$ and its reversed version $A := B(f^{-1})$ cannot be defined together since they both create a *new* resulting collection (respectively B and A). We thus introduce the *reversed assignment* operator (symbol $=:$) that can only be used on applications: application $B := A(f)$ creates B from A, while its reversed version $B =: A(f)$ (also written $B(f^{-1}) =: A$) allows the reverse *update*. Since A is always initialized before the reversed assignment, its addition rule *must only* be called subsequently to additions. Having $B =: A(f)$ implies that $B := A(f)$: we use operator $=$ so that $B = A(f)$ defines a *bidirectional application*. Active loops for reversed applications are defined as follows:

Operation	Order	Active loop	
$B =: A(f)$	$(A,B) \notin \mathbb{O}^2$	$\forall' e \in B,\ A + f^{-1}(e)$	$\forall' e \notin B,\ A - f^{-1}(e)$
	$(A,B) \in \mathbb{O}^2$	$\forall' e \in_i B,\ A +_i f^{-1}(e)$	$\forall' e \notin_i B,\ A-_i$

Navigation throughout collections is based on the flattening version of the application. In order to preserve the semantics of the active loop of path $B := A.p$ (see section 2.3), the active loop of the reverse path assignment $B =: A.p$ should define the following addition rule: $\forall' e' \in B,\ A + e_n,\ e_n.p + e'$ where e_n is the owner element of property p that contains e'. Figure 1 helps in understanding this rule.

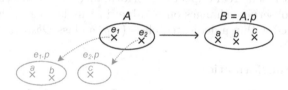

Fig. 1. Path principle

Such a definition has no general meaning: if e_n is already contained in A, which one is it (*e.g.* e_1 or e_2 of figure 1)? if not, to what corresponds e_n? This demonstrates that the path operation is not reversible since the transformation loses the required information due to the flattening. However, if $|A| = 1$ at any time, $e_n = A[0]$ necessarily: in this specific case, operations $B := A.p$ and $B =: A.p$, written $B = A.p$, mean that property p of singleton A equals B at any time. Operation $B = A.p$ is very useful to "bind" a property to another property. Reversed path assignment is defined as follows:

Operation	Order	Active loop	
$B =: A.p$	$(A,B) \notin \mathbb{O}^2$	$\forall' e \in B,\ A[0].p + e$	$\forall' e \notin B,\ A[0].p - e$
with $|A| = 1$	$(A,B) \in \mathbb{O}^2$	$\forall' e \in_i B,\ A[0].p +_i e$	$\forall' e \notin_i B,\ A[0].p-_i$

The following case study includes such a reversed path assignment.

3   Case Study

This section illustrates how previous active operations can be used for implementing active transformations. We first motivate the use of collections for representing any object property. We then give the active operations required for implementing an active transformation in the context of a user interface. We finally explains how the active transformation has been successfully implemented within Kermeta using our *Active Kermeta* framework.

3.1   Requirement: All Properties Are Collections

An object property can be either a relation or an attribute, and is *always* represented by a collection. This means that, if the property has a cardinality 0..1 or 1..1, its representing collection is a *singleton*. In such a case, an empty collection represents a null property value.

This requirement is implied by the use of paths that extends the dotted notation of OOP. For example, in expression $B := o.p_1.p_2$ where $|p_1| \leq 1$, $o.p_1$ represents the dotted notation of OOP while $p_1.p_2$ represents a path (see section 2.3). If p_1 is not considered as a singleton but as a value, the property value $o.p_1$ can be *null*, thus resulting in a null reference error within expression $o.p_1.p_2$. This requirement has no real impact on performance since observing a singleton is equivalent to observing changes on a value: in this last case, the value needs to be encapsulated within a dedicated class (*e.g.* a class *ObservableValue<T>*).

3.2   Active Transformation

Figure 2 gives the outline of the sample transformation: the left part represents source domain data, a directory of contacts; the right part represents the associated user interface (UI) that displays the contacts within a list widget, and allows editing contact properties throughout three text fields[2].

Linking domain data to UI is usually performed using "UI bindings" that are platform dependent and offer limited features. Using active operations avoids such drawbacks, and addresses a more general problem than UI binding [9]. A comparison between UI bindings and active operations is however beyond the scope of this paper. A complex example is provided within the Active Kermeta framework.

In the example of figure 2, *D2L* transforms directory d into list l that displays the contacts sorted by their last name and first name:

$$l.items := d.contacts\{\{d.contacts.lastName\}' \wedge \{d.contacts.firstName\}'\}(C2I)$$

C2I transforms each contact c into an item i that displays his/her first and last name, and also saves the link between c and i in reversed relation *contact*:

---

[2] UI objects are rendered through a graphical server not represented in the figure. Adding a contact is achieved through the button "Add" of the user interface: clicking on the button creates a new contact in the source data directly.

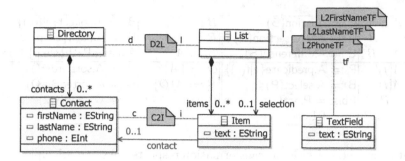

Fig. 2. Transformation outline

$$i.text := c.firstName + "\,"\," + c.lastName$$
$$i.contact := c$$

Operation $+$, not presented in this paper, is also active for a *String* singleton (see section 3.3). Relation *contact* allows a *reversible navigation* from the transformation target of the transformation source: $i = C2I(c)$ and $c = C2I^{-1}(i) = i.contact$. Such a relation is called a *trace*.

L2FirstNameTF (respectively *L2LastNameTF*) transforms the first name (respectively the last name) of the selected contact (relation *l.selection.contact*) into text-field *tf* in a bidirectional way:

$$tf.text = selection.contact.firstName$$

Finally, *L2PhoneTF* performs the same transformation but adds a bidirectional conversion between the *phone* number (an *Integer*) and the text field content (a *String*):

$$tf.text := selection.contact.phone(IntegerToString)$$
$$tf.text(StringToInteger) =: selection.contact.phone$$

3.3   Kermeta Implementation

Active operations have been implemented on top of Kermeta by the *Active Kermeta* framework, freely available at `http://gri.eseo.fr/software/activekermeta`. The framework proposes two packages dedicated to the four collection classes *Set*, *OrderedSet*, *Bag* and *Sequence*. Package *kermeta::observable* defines the minimal set of operations and active loops for these classes; the following table gives the syntax of Kermeta active loops:

$\forall' e \in C, ...$	C.eachAdded{e|...}	$\forall' e \in_i C, ...$	C.eachAddedAt{e,i|...}
$\forall' e \notin C, ...$	C.eachRemoved{e|...}	$\forall' e \notin_i C, ...$	C.eachRemovedAt{e,i|...}

Package *kermeta::active* implements active operations based on the active loops presented in section 2; the following table gives the syntax of Kermeta active operations:

$C := A \cup B$	C := A.union(B)	$B := A(f)$	B := A.collect$\{e\|f(e)\}$
$C := A \cap B$	C := A.intersection(B)	$B := A.p$	B := A.path$\{e\|e.p\}$
$C := A - B$	C := A.difference(B)	$B =: A.p$	A.assignPath$\{e\|e.p\}$.from(B)
$P := A[f]'$	P := A.predicate$\{e\|f(e)\}$	$O := \{A\}'$	O := A.sortOrder()
$B := A[P]$	B := A.select(P)	$B := A\{O\}$	B := A.sortedBy(O)
$P' := \neg P$	Pbis := P.not()	$O := O_1 \wedge O_2$	O := O1.and(O2)
$P := P_1 \wedge P_2$	P := P1.and(P2)	$P := P_1 \vee P_2$	P := P1.or(P2)

Writing an active Kermeta transformation respects the same principle as writing a usual Kermeta transformation: aspects are used to add new transformation operations on Ecore models [7]. The transformation of figure 2 has been implemented with active operations as follows:

```
1   aspect class Directory {
2       operation D2L(): List is do
3           result := List.new
4           result.items := contacts.sortedBy(
5               contacts.path{c|c.lastName}.sortOrder().and(
6                   contacts.path{c|c.firstName}.sortOrder())
7               ).collect {c|c.C2I()}
8       end
9   }
10
11  aspect class Contact {
12      operation C2I(): Item is do
13          result := Item.new
14          result.text := firstName.plusValue("␣").plus(lastName)
15          result.contact.add(self)
16      end
17  }
18
19  aspect class List {
20      operation L2PhoneTF(): TextField is do
21          result := TextField.new
22          var contact: Set<Contact> init selection.path{i|i.contact}
23          result.text := contact.path{c|c.phone}.collect (a|a.toString())
24          contact.assignPath{c|c.phone}.from(result.text.collect {t|t.toInteger()})
25      end
26
27      // ...
28  }
```

Operation *plus* (line 15), not described in this paper, is an active operation that concatenates two string singletons; its companion operation *plusValue* concatenates the literal string with the string singleton. Relation *contact* is added through an aspect of class *Item*.

As one may note, such a Kermeta code can be easily generated from the formal specification given in the previous section.

4   Evaluation

This section evaluates the worst case complexities of active loop rules, discusses the resulting performance in the contexts of both constraint evaluation and model transformation, and then compares the approach with related works.

4.1   Worst Case Complexities

The following table gives the *worst* case complexities of elementary operations on collections implemented as *array lists*:

Operation	$C \notin \mathbb{U}$	$C \in \mathbb{U}$
$|C|,\ e \in_i C,\ C[i]$	\multicolumn{2}{c}{$\mathcal{O}(1)$}	
$C + e$	$\mathcal{O}(1)$	$\mathcal{O}(n)$
$e \in C,\ C +_i e,\ C - e,\ C -_i$	\multicolumn{2}{c}{$\mathcal{O}(n)$}	

Due to the choice of the elementary operations, these complexities cannot be better for linked lists, nor for sorted sets ($C + e$ is even worse). Moreover, using hash sets should only improve the *average*-case complexities (*e.g.* $e \in C$ is $\mathcal{O}(1)$ in average). We can thus infer *worst*-case complexities of active loops from the previous table.

Since active loops of ordered collections differ from those of unordered collections, we must study complexities for each of the four collection types (*bag, seq, set* and *oset*). Moreover, we distinguish three cases of the active construction of collections: the initialization ("i.") that invokes the addition rule n times; the addition ("a.") that invokes the addition rule on each addition performed in the source collection; and the removal ("r.") that invokes the removal rule on each removal performed in the source collection. The following table synthesizes complexities for each rule of action loops:

Operation	bag i.	bag a.	bag r.	seq i.	seq a./r.	set i.	set a.	set r.	oset i.	oset a./r.
$A \cup B,\ A(f),\ A.p$	n	1	n	n	n	n	1	n	n	n
$A\{O\},\ A[f]',\ A[P]$	n	1	n	n	n	$n^2\ (n)$	$n\ (1)$	n	$n^2\ (n)$	n
$B =: A.p$	-	1	n	-	n	-	1	n	-	n
$\neg P,\ P_1 \wedge P_2,\ P_1 \vee P_2,\ O_1 \wedge O_2$	-	-	-	n	n	-	-	-	-	-
$A \cap B,\ A - B,\ \{A\}'$	n^2	n	n	n^2	n	n^2	n	n	n^2	n

Complexity for an initialization is not necessarily equal to $n \times c$ where c is the complexity of its addition rule. For example, the addition rule of $A \cup B$ where $(A, B) \in seq^2$ is based on operation $C +_i e$ that costs $\mathcal{O}(n)$: the initialization would thus cost $\mathcal{O}(n^2)$; however, operation $C +_i e$ here appends e at the *end* of C, which costs only $\mathcal{O}(1)$: the initialization phase thus costs $\mathcal{O}(n)$.

Operations in the first four rows are mainly $\mathcal{O}(n)$: additions cost $\mathcal{O}(1)$ for unordered collections, but cost $\mathcal{O}(n)$ for ordered ones because of the required shifting; removals always cost $\mathcal{O}(n)$ since they require a search in unordered collections, or a shifting of ordered collections. Note that the complexity of operation $A.p$ is given considering $|A.p| = n$, but not $|A| = n$. Collections with uniqueness have $\mathcal{O}(n^2)$ operations because $C + e$ must ensure the uniqueness. However, operations on row 2 do not require uniqueness from operation $+$: for example, selection $B := A[f]$ guaranties that $B \in \mathbb{U}$ if $A \in \mathbb{U}$ since it filters A; these operations can thus reduce their complexities (values surrounded by parenthesis). The last row has $\mathcal{O}(n^2)$ complexities: $A \cap B$ and $A - B$ require presence tests that cost $\mathcal{O}(n)$, and $\{A\}$ naturally requires two loops.

4.2 Discussion

The previous table illustrates that complexities for removals are always $O(n)$. Consequently, replacing element e_a by element e_b in collection C costs $O(n)$ since it performs a removal of e_a and an addition of e_b. This might be optimized for ordered collections since replacing one of its element only costs $O(1)$. This optimization requires the introduction of a *replace rule* within active loops. Moreover, replace rule can be mandatory in some circumstances; for example, replacing the value of a property with cardinality 1..1 violates the minimal cardinality constraint if a removal if performed. The replace rules can be easily inferred from addition and removal rules; they have not been considered in this paper for clarity.

An active transformation that counts m operations constructs its initial result in between $\mathcal{O}(m \times n)$ and $\mathcal{O}(m \times n^2)$, and subsequently updates each *individual* resulting collection in between $\mathcal{O}(1)$ and $\mathcal{O}(n)$. However, operations are not independent: modifying one source collection can result in multiple chained updates. A simplified view of such dependencies consists of representing the operations in a two dimensioned space where height h counts the independent chains of operations, and w counts the operations involved in a chain: $\mathcal{O}(m) = \mathcal{O}(h \times w)$. The number of operations Δw required to reify functions involved in selections and sorts (see sections 2.4 and 2.5) is included in number w. For example, single selection $persons[p \rightarrow p.age < 18]$ must be rewritten in active selection $persons[persons.age[a \rightarrow a < 18]']$ that counts $\Delta w = 2$ (path + predicate collection), *i.e.* $w = 3$.

Complexity of the initial construction varies from $\mathcal{O}(h \times w \times n)$ to $\mathcal{O}(h \times w \times n^2)$, and complexity of the subsequent chained updates varies from $\mathcal{O}(w)$ to $\mathcal{O}(w \times n)$: their ratio λ thus varies from $\mathcal{O}(h)$ to $\mathcal{O}(h \times n^2)$. This result illustrates the interest of active operations, especially for large models ($n \gg 1$) and/or complex transformations ($h \gg 1$).

The active loops proposed in section 2 should be implemented in a way that depends on the *context of use*, thus allowing possible optimizations that would increase λ by reducing width w of the dependency chains. In the context of incremental constraint evaluation, Cabot and Teniente [4] propose to take into account *only* changes that can induce constraint violation, thus defining a new specific context of use. Such a specific context requires that our model for observing collections should be refined so that addition and removal rules does not systematically invoke their associated procedures. Section 3 has presented the specific context of active transformations for user interfaces: the transformation binds the domain objects to their presentation. In such a context, the user works on a presentation that represents a (small) part of the full application model: this typically means that the transformation starts by a *selection* that filters the full model. Such a selection thus naturally "optimizes" the transformation by pre-filtering changes that do not impact the presentation. Moreover, the user can perform many changes on a single object in a short time-slot, thus resulting in many reevaluations of active operations. Once again, the observability model can be refined by using an asynchronous invocation of addition and removal rules, as done within Viatra [10]. This would improve performances by filtering any redundant modifications, such as multiple intermediate changes of a single property (only the last change should be considered).

Since it is centered on operations on collections, our approach is more suited to imperative transformations (*e.g.* Kermeta) than to declarative ones (*e.g.* ATL [11]). However, we think that our formalism can *help* in making declarative transformations active. Moreover, mappings expressed with higher level languages, such as Malan [12], should be automatically converted into active operations.

4.3 Related Work

Many research have been done on incremental evaluation of constraints and incremental transformations. We herein only cite some of the most recent ones.

Blanc *et al.* propose an original approach for detecting model inconsistency (constraint violation): the detection is performed on the model considered as a sequence of elementary construction operations, rather than a model considered as a set of elements [13]. The approach is thus naturally incremental. It shares some similarities with active operations: their elementary construction operations match the elementary rules (addition and removal) of active loops, and our addition rules are also used to initially build the content of collections. However, their approach is dedicated to constraint evaluation only, and the implementation is based on Prolog which is not widely used and not well adapted to MDE.

Cabot et Teniente optimize OCL constraint evaluation by considering only constraint violations: model changes that cannot violate constraints are filtered [4]. They also translate OCL contexts to better contexts. The proposed optimization is interesting and forms a specific context of use, as previously explained. However, users often temporally violate constraints when editing models (*e.g.* a user omits the type of a class attribute within an Ecore diagram): transition from state *violated* to state *respected* should not be ignored. The optimization, specific to constraint checking, cannot be used in the context of incremental transformation.

XSLT is probably the best known transformation language. Villard and Layaïda have developed incXLST, an incremental XSLT processor, thus showing the broader interest of incremental transformation [5]. The processor is based on re-instantiating transformation rules and merging the resulting fragments within the target document, and has limited featured. Framework eXAcT allows the transformation of DOM documents into DOM presentations (*e.g.* SVG presentations) [14]. However, eXAcT transformations are complex Java programs with limited features. Moreover, both incXSLT and eXAcT are not MDE tools.

QVT has established that incremental transformation is an important issue of MDE [15], but no incremental QVT-based transformation engine has been implemented yet. Xiong *et al.* proposed SyncATL, an incremental ATL processor [6], on the same principle as incXSLT: elicited ATL rules are re-executed and their results are merged with the target. As for incXSLT with XSLT, the processor is dedicated to ATL only. Hearnden *et al.* propose an original approach based on the use of SLD resolution, where SLD trees store the transformation context and dependency tables record dependencies between the transformation and the source model [2]. The drawback of the approach is the maintenance cost of the SLD trees and dependency tables.

The previous works make *declarative* transformations incremental by implementing new processors and/or algorithms tied to specific languages and/or systems. Using active operations on collections allows their direct execution on model instances, without requiring any specific processor or complex algorithm: *definition* of operations are directly *executable* in an active manner. We have shown that active operation can be easily used to implement Kermeta *imperative* transformations. We think that our formalism can *help* in making declarative transformation languages active, such as ATL [11], by generating the active operations for a given "passive" transformation. Some authors considered that declarative transformations should be expressed as mappings [3,1,12]. Here again, we think that active implementations of mappings, as defined by Akehurst [3], can be achieved by active operations.

5   Conclusion and Perspective

This paper proposes a formalism, based on active loops, for implementing active operations on collections. The standard set of operations, mainly inspired by OCL [8], is supplemented by a reversed assignment that allows the definition of bidirectional operations. A case study, fully implemented in Kermeta, illustrates that making a transformation active by using such a formalism does not require to change much the usual (*i.e.* passive) transformation; it also gives a specific context that requires active transformations with bidirectionality features: user interfaces. The complexity study shows that running active operations results in an interesting gain when compared to running all the "passive" operations. Moreover, such a gain can be increased by reducing operation dependencies with optimization strategies that can be implemented depending of the contexts of use (*e.g.* transformation within UI or evaluation of constraint violation).

We first plan to create an active implementation of the Malan language [12] based on *Active Kermeta*, thus showing the ability of active operations to implement *declarative* mappings and transformations. We will secondly focus on the use of active operations for incremental constraint validation by extending the proposed set of active operations , and by defining active class invariants through

Kermeta aspects. We thirdly plan to optimize the collection observability model of *Active Kermeta* with filtering and asynchronous treatment capabilities. Finally, we will use active operations in the context of user interfaces to link each of their components [16,17].

References

1. Giese, H., Wagner, R.: From model transformation to incremental bidirectional model synchronization. Software and Systems Modeling 8(1), 21–43 (2008)
2. Hearnden, D., Lawley, M., Raymond, K.: Incremental model transformation for the evolution of model-driven systems. In: Nierstrasz, O., Whittle, J., Harel, D., Reggio, G. (eds.) MoDELS 2006. LNCS, vol. 4199, pp. 321–335. Springer, Heidelberg (2006)
3. Akehurst, D.H.: Model Translation: A UML-based specification technique and active implementation approach. PhD thesis, University of Kent (2000)
4. Cabot, J., Teniente, E.: Incremental evaluation of OCL constraints. In: Dubois, E., Pohl, K. (eds.) CAiSE 2006. LNCS, vol. 4001, pp. 81–95. Springer, Heidelberg (2006)
5. Villard, L., Layaïda, N.: An incremental XSLT transformation processor for XML document manipulation. In: Proc. of WWW 2002, pp. 474–485. ACM, New York (2002)
6. Xiong, Y., Liu, D., Hu, Z., Zhao, H., Takeichi, M., Mei, H.: Towards automatic model synchronization from model transformations. In: Proc. of ASE 2007, pp. 164–173. ACM, New York (2007)
7. Muller, P.A., Fleurey, F., Jézéquel, J.M.: Weaving executability into object-oriented meta-languages. In: Briand, L.C., Williams, C. (eds.) MoDELS 2005. LNCS, vol. 3713, pp. 264–278. Springer, Heidelberg (2005)
8. Warmer, J.B., Kleppe, A.G.: The object constraint language: getting your models ready for MDA. Addison-Wesley, Reading
9. Beaudoux, O., Blouin, A.: Linking data and presentations: from mapping to active transformations. In: Proc. of DocEng 2010. ACM, New York (2010) (in press)
10. Varró, D., Balogh, A.: The model transformation language of the viatra2 framework. Sci. Comput. Program. 68(3), 187–207 (2007)
11. Jouault, F., Kurtev, I.: Transforming models with ATL. In: Bruel, J.-M. (ed.) MoDELS 2005. LNCS, vol. 3844, pp. 128–138. Springer, Heidelberg (2006)
12. Blouin, A., Beaudoux, O., Loiseau, S.: Malan: A mapping language for the data manipulation. In: Proc. of DocEng 2008, pp. 66–75. ACM, New York (2008)
13. Blanc, X., Mounier, I., Mougenot, A., Mens, T.: Detecting model inconsistency through operation-based model construction. In: Proc. of ICSE 2008, pp. 511–520. ACM, New York (2008)
14. Beaudoux, O.: XML active transformation (eXAcT): transforming documents within interactive systems. In: Proc. of DocEng 2005, pp. 146–148. ACM, New York (2005)
15. OMG: MOF QVT final adopted specification. OMG document, OMG (2005)
16. Blouin, A., Beaudoux, O.: Improving modularity and usability of interactive systems with Malai. In: Proc. of EICS 2010, pp. 115–124. ACM, New York (2010)
17. Beaudoux, O., Beaudouin-Lafon, M.: OpenDPI: A toolkit for developing document-centered environments. In: Enterprise Information Systems VII, pp. 231–239. Springer, Heidelberg (2006)

*trans*ML: A Family of Languages to Model Model Transformations

Esther Guerra[1], Juan de Lara[2], Dimitrios S. Kolovos[3],
Richard F. Paige[3], and Osmar Marchi dos Santos[3]

[1] Universidad Carlos III de Madrid, Spain
eguerra@inf.uc3m.es
[2] Universidad Autónoma de Madrid, Spain
Juan.deLara@uam.es
[3] University of York, UK
{dkolovos,paige,osantos}@cs.york.ac.uk

Abstract. Model transformation is one of the pillars of Model-Driven Engineering (MDE). The increasing complexity of systems and modelling languages has dramatically raised the complexity and size of model transformations. Even though many transformation languages and tools have been proposed in the last few years, most of them are directed to the *implementation* phase of transformation development. However, there is a lack of cohesive support for the other phases of the transformation development, like requirements, analysis, design and testing.

In this paper, we propose a unified family of languages to cover the life-cycle of transformation development. Moreover, following an MDE approach, we provide tools to partially automate the progressive refinement of models between the different phases and the generation of code for specific transformation implementation languages.

1 Introduction

Model-Driven Engineering (MDE) relies on models to conduct the software development process. In this way, high-level models are refined using automated transformations until the code of the final application is obtained. A key aspect in MDE is automation of operations applied to models (i.e. model management). In particular, there is a recurring need to transform models between different languages and levels of abstraction, e.g. to migrate between language versions, to translate models into semantic domains for analysis, to generate platform-dependent from platform-independent models, or to refine and abstract models. This kind of transformation is called Model-to-Model (M2M) transformation.

In MDE, transformations are seldom specified with general-purpose programming languages (e.g. Java) but with M2M transformation languages specially tailored for the task of transforming models [3]. Prominent examples of such languages are QVT [12], ATL [1], Triple Graph Grammars [15] and ETL [10].

M2M transformations are deployed as software and, like any other software, they need to be analysed, designed, implemented and tested. Therefore, their development requires systematic engineering processes, notations, methods and

D.C. Petriu, N. Rouquette, Ø. Haugen (Eds.): MODELS 2010, Part I, LNCS 6394, pp. 106–120, 2010.
© Springer-Verlag Berlin Heidelberg 2010

tools. This need is more acute in industrial projects, where the complexity of models and modelling languages makes necessary large and complex transformations. Surprisingly, most transformation languages proposed by the MDE community are either directed towards the *implementation* phase of transformations or are not integrated in a unified engineering process. As a consequence, there is a lack of cohesive support for transformations – involving notations, methods and tools – across all development phases. This makes more difficult the design of large-scale transformations, hinders the standardization and codification of best practices (e.g. patterns analogous to design patterns in UML), and complicates the maintenance and understandability of the transformation code.

In this paper we present a family of modelling languages, called *trans*ML, which covers the whole life-cycle of transformation development: requirements, analysis, design and testing. It can be used together with any transformation implementation language. Moreover, following an MDE approach to the construction of transformations, we provide partial automation for the refinement of *trans*ML models and the generation of code for specific transformation implementation languages. We also provide support for reengineering transformation code by its parsing into *trans*ML models, and facilitating platform migration.

Paper organization. §2 discusses previous attempts to model M2M transformations, pointing out limitations. Next, §3 proposes a set of languages that cover the identified needs to build transformations in the large. §4 presents tool support for forward and reverse transformation engineering, followed by §5, which evaluates the approach with an industrial case study. Finally, §6 concludes.

2   Related Work

Most recent research in M2M transformation has focused on the implementation phase, either to develop new implementation languages, or to test final implementations. This is likely due to the infancy of M2M transformation research, and is analogous to early research on software engineering languages where the focus was directed to implementation languages. There, analysis and design notations came later, when issues of system scale became a concern.

Only a few proposals for design notations for transformations can be found in the literature. For example, [13] presents a language to design transformations, but focusing only on their implementation. Another example is [4], which covers the low-level design of transformations, being able to represent the structure of rules using diagrams similar to UML class diagrams.

Closer to our engineering view of building transformations are the works that consider several phases of development. For example, [16] identifies a transformation development life-cycle and proposes describing transformations incrementally, starting from transformational patterns and partial specifications of transformations, which are gradually refined. However, no concrete notation or tool is proposed. The position paper [11] envisages a mapping and a transformation view for transformations. Its aim is providing a precise semantics for mappings in terms of Petri nets so that the transformation view can be generated from the mappings view. Still, the framework is ad-hoc for their particular transformation approach and cannot be applied to other implementation languages.

Finally, there is limited work on languages to express composition of transformations; this can be viewed as a kind of architectural design [14,18] through the definition of new architectural languages. Whereas [14] is a specific language for composing ATL transformations, in [18] the approach is more platform independent. In both cases, other phases of transformation development are neglected.

In summary, we observe a lack of modelling notations and tools to cover the complete life-cycle of transformation development in a cohesive way. Transformation developers should be able to use such notations with their favourite transformation implementation languages, in the same way as the UML can be used with any object-oriented programming language. Having available such transformation modelling notations would make possible to apply systematic engineering principles to transformation development, to trace the models in the different stages of the development (in a non ad-hoc way), as well as to apply MDE techniques to obtain transformation code from high-level models. Such notations are urgently needed in order to be able to benefit from proven software engineering principles, like design patterns [2,8] for model transformations.

3   A Family of Languages to Model Transformations

How are transformations developed? The answer is too frequently *"in an ad-hoc manner"*. Jumping directly to an implementation language may be sufficient for simple transformations, but this approach is challenging in the large. If transformation technology is to be used in industry, transformations must be constructed using engineering principles. Hence, the process of transformation development should include other phases, in addition to coding and testing, namely: requirements, analysis, architectural design, high-level design and detailed design.

The notations to be used in these phases have to consider the specificities of model transformation development. Fig. 1 gives an overview of *trans*ML, the family of languages we propose, and shows how they are interrelated. In the upper part, the figure shows the family of proposed languages, made of a requirements diagram, formal specification diagrams and simple scenarios to cover the transformation analysis, architecture diagram, high-level design view of the transformation specified as a mapping diagram, and rule diagrams for the low-level design. The figure also shows relations to trace elements across diagrams (e.g. to discover the requirements each rule is addressing). The objective of these diagrams is guiding the construction of the software artifacts shown on the bottom of the figure: the transformation code (in any implementation language such as QVT or ETL), the generation of test cases, the run-time verification of transformation code and the orchestration of transformations.

We do not prescribe a particular process in which these phases should occur, but in our experience, transformations are often built in an iterative, incremental way. We also do not suggest that *all* diagrams have to be used when building any transformation (just like when building object-oriented systems it is not mandatory to use all UML diagram types). Depending on the project characteristics,

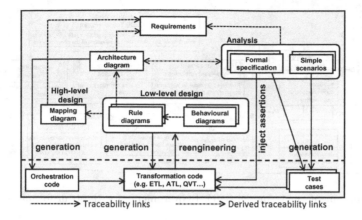

Fig. 1. Model transformation framework

we may emphasize the use of the formal specification language (e.g. for complex transformations that should preserve behaviour), or just use the high-level design diagrams but not the low-level ones for small, one-to-one transformations. However, the full power of *trans*ML comes by using its diagrams in combination.

Next we present *trans*ML in detail. We will use as an example the classical class-to-relational transformation to ease understanding, and provide evaluation of its use with a complex transformation in an industrial project in §5.

3.1 Requirements Elicitation

Just like any other software, transformation developers need to record the transformation rationale, identifying functional and non-functional requirements. Therefore, notations helping the hierarchical decomposition of requirements and permitting traccability to further models are especially useful. Here we could use any technique and notation from the Requirements Engineering community. However, in order to trace requirements into subsequent phases, *trans*ML includes a representation of requirements in the form of diagrams, similar to SySML requirements diagrams[1]. The meta-model for this representation is shown to the left of Fig. 2, and enables hierarchical decomposition, classification, refinement and traceability of requirements. Requirements are classified in a dual way: attending to whether they are functional or not, and to whether their source is an input model, an output model or the transformation itself.

As an example, the right of Fig. 2 shows the requirements diagram for the class-to-relational transformation. Requirements for the input model are annotated with a right arrow in the upper right corner, whereas requirements of the transformation are annotated with dented wheels. Thus, requirement 0.1 restricts input models to have no redefined attributes. On the other hand, requirement 0.3.1 derives from requirements 0.3.2 and 0.3.3.

---

[1] http://www.omg.org/spec/SysML/1.1/

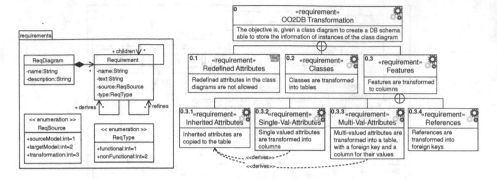

Fig. 2. Requirements meta-model (left). Requirements for the transformation (right).

3.2   Analysis

Software engineers use a variety of mechanisms to analyse, understand and reason about requirements. We have identified techniques based on scenarios and on formal specification languages, which we have adapted for *trans*ML.

First, once some requirements are fixed, engineers can write scenarios, which are examples of the transformation (similar to the role of uses cases in UML). We call these examples *transformation cases*, which describe how concrete source models are transformed into target ones. The examples may contain either full-fledged models or model fragments. As an example, the left of Fig. 3 shows a transformation case that explains the transformation of a multi-valued attribute into a table and a foreign key from the table associated to its owner class.

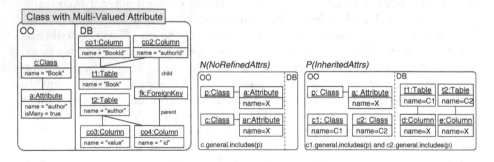

Fig. 3. Transformation case (left). Restriction on the input model (center). Verification property (right).

The purpose of *transformation cases* is twofold. First, they are used to understand and reason about what the transformation has to do. Second, they can be used as input to model transformation-by-example techniques [19] which derive a rough sketch of the transformation, and can also be used as test cases for the transformation implementation.

The second notation we use in this phase is a visual, formal *specification* language [7]. Similar to the role of Z [17] or Alloy for general software engineering, this language is used to: (i) describe in an abstract manner what the transformation has to do without stating how to do it, (ii) specify correctness properties that the implementation should satisfy, and (iii) specify restrictions on the input or output models. These specifications can be used later for formal reasoning of transformation requirements, and for specification-driven testing of transformations through the generation of an oracle function to test the transformation.

Our specification language abstracts from concrete examples, and is based on declarative patterns that express *allowed* or *forbidden* relations between two models [7]. Patterns have a graphical part, and can include constraints (we use EOL [9] for this). Patterns expressing allowed relations are called positive, while those expressing forbidden relations are called negative. Thus, the language supports constructive and non-constructive specification styles (in contrast to scenarios, which are always constructive). Moreover, patterns are bi-directional, so that they can be interpreted both source-to-target and target-to-source. This allows the specification of uni-directional and bi-directional transformations.

Since *trans*ML has been designed to be independent of the language used to implement the transformation, our specification language supports the two usual styles for M2M transformation: trace-based and traceless, depending on whether explicit traces are given between source and target elements or not. In the latter case, patterns are similar to QVT relations [12] and can include positive and negative graph pre- and post-conditions (*when* and *where* clauses respectively). Trace-based and traceless patterns have a formal semantics which allows answering correctness questions about specifications (e.g. whether there are conflicts between patterns). The details of the semantics of this language and its compilation into OCL for testing are available in [7].

As an example, the center of Fig. 3 shows a negative pattern (indicated by the N(...)) used to express a restriction on the input models. It *refines* requirement 0.1 in Fig. 2. The pattern checks the existence of two classes c and p such that p is an ancestor of c, having both an attribute with same name (represented by variable X). As the pattern is negative, models in which such pattern occurs are invalid. As we will see latter, code will be injected in the transformation to test whether a given input model qualifies for the transformation.

The right of the figure shows a pattern expressing a property of the transformation itself. The pattern is positive (indicated by the P(...)) and expresses that if a class p has two children classes c1 and c2, then each attribute in the ancestor class p has to be replicated as a column in the tables associated to c1 and c2. The tables in which the classes are transformed are located by equality of names (variables C1 and C2), but any formula relating their names would also be allowed. This kind of patterns will be used for the run-time verification of the transformation code, in order to check whether the implementation generates target models satisfying these properties.

3.3   Architecture

Large software is seldom monolithic, but is decomposed into interacting blocks. Hence engineers have to design its architecture. We have included a modelling language for architectural design which permits the modular decomposition of functional units. This is very useful in large-scale transformations, which need to be split in different units and orchestrated. Moreover, it is often the case that the transformation has to be integrated with further software components providing extra functionality, such as code generators. For the design of this language we have taken some ideas from works dealing with orchestration of transformations [14,18], as well as from architectural description languages [6].

Our architectural language is made of *components* and connectors. Components interact through directional interfaces with a type given by meta-models, event types, actors or other components (to allow higher-order transformations). They can have a set of constraints, can be arranged hierarchically, and may represent transformations (model-to-model, model-to-text, text-to-model or in-place), software (a black-box) or actors (to model human intervention).

The left of Fig. 4 shows a simple architectural diagram for our example. The model depicts a chain of transformations: the first takes an OO model and transforms it into a DB model, the second optimises this DB model, and the third generates textual code for a particular platform. The diagram shows the transformations as components with typed, directional interfaces. The type of the interfaces is given by one or more meta-models, together with extra (OCL) constraints to rule out models which conform to the meta-model but are not handled by the transformation. Models conforming to those interfaces can be the input/output of the transformations. The type also allows checking compatibility when connecting two transformation components. The right of the figure shows a type-centric view of the same model. This view is similar to a mega-model [5], where transformation components are visualized as arrows connecting interface types. This architectural view can bridge modelware and grammarware technical spaces by including model-to-text and text-to-model transformations.

Fig. 4. Architectural diagram: transformation-centric and type-centric views

3.4   High-Level Design: Mappings

The design of a transformation benefits from proceeding from a high to a lower level of abstraction, and therefore we provide different notations for them. The high-level design of a transformation is given by a *mapping diagram* that defines the mappings between the elements of the arbitrary number of languages involved in the transformation. This diagram provides an intuition of which is transformed into what, without giving details on the how, thus enabling the transition between analysis and design. This is similar to Triple Graph Grammar schemas [15], however our mappings are not intended to be used as an auxiliary tracing mechanism to guide the actual execution of the transformation code.

Fig. 5 shows to the left an extract of the mappings meta-model. A *mapping model* is established between several languages, each one defined by a meta-model. Mapping models can define the directionality of the transformation using the *navigable* attribute in *ModelEnds*. Models are structured in packages, each one containing mappings, which can also be organized hierarchically. Mappings connect elements in the meta-models of the involved languages through *MappingEnds*. Mappings are provided with constraints, given either in uninterpreted text or in some language like OCL, expressing when mappings between elements should hold. The mapping meta-model refers to the meta-models of the languages involved in the transformation. We use an abstract class *ModellingElement*, which can be replaced by any concrete meta-modelling infrastructure.

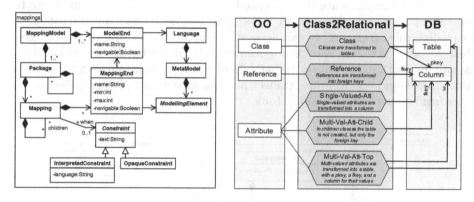

Fig. 5. Excerpt of mapping meta-model (left). Mapping diagram example (right).

The right of Fig. 5 shows a mapping diagram. It has one block for each language, containing the relevant elements of their meta-model. Another block includes mappings connecting some of these elements to indicate a causal relation between them. The links from the mappings to the language elements have a role name (e.g. fkey, pkey), a multiplicity (1 is assumed if it is empty) and a direction (to denote either access or creation of elements). As our transformation is unidirectional, mapping ends are depicted with arrows on the side of the DB.

Mapping diagrams can be used with different levels of detail. One can start with a rough sketch of the mappings and add details as the transformation is better understood. For example, in Fig. 5 we have omitted element `ForeignKey` of the DB meta-model. The mapping diagram is a high-level design notation, independent of the transformation implementation language. Moreover, it is not necessarily the case that a mapping has to be implemented by a unique rule and vice-versa. As we show next, we can use rule diagrams as a way to design the implementation of mappings if more details are needed before coding.

3.5   Low-Level Design: Rule Structure and Rule Behaviour

Low-level detailed design diagrams indicate *how* the transformation has to be implemented. Here we separate the description of the rule structure from its behaviour. Hence, one or several *rule structure diagrams* may describe the structure of the rules in the transformation, and several *rule behaviour diagrams* attached to the rules can be used to specify what these rules should do. These notations will help in describing good practices and transformation patterns, in the same way as UML helps to record object-oriented patterns. Rule diagrams are also useful to generate code for different platforms, and reengineering of existing code.

Fig. 6 shows part of the meta-model of the rule structure diagrams. This kind of diagram depicts the structure (input/output parameters) of each rule, their execution flow, and data dependencies (e.g. parameter passing) between them. Rule diagrams refine mapping diagrams by giving the low-level design of how the specified mappings are to be realized. In this way, a rule can contribute to implement several mappings, and a mapping can be realized by several rules. Regarding rule structure, we can declare uni-directional or bi-directional rules, their involved domains and their parameters. Concerning the execution flow, we support both explicit flows (subclasses of `Flow`) as well as non-deterministic constructs found e.g. in graph transformation, as one can place a collection of rules inside a non-deterministic `Block`.

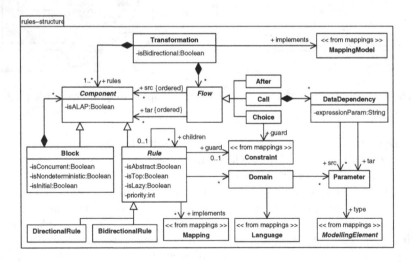

Fig. 6. Excerpt of the meta-model of the rule structure diagram

Fig. 7 shows to the left a rule structure diagram with four rules. The diagram is semi-collapsed, as it only shows the parameters of the OO domain. The diagram shows the rule execution flow by means of rounded rectangles (`Block` objects), in a notation similar to activity diagrams. Hence, the starting point is the block containing rule *Class2Table*, which implements the *Class* mapping. After executing this rule, the control passes to another block with three rules, to be executed in arbitrary order. In particular, rule *MultiValuedAtt2Table* has been designed to implement two mappings: *Multi-Val-Att-Child* and *Multi-Val-Att-Top*. In all cases, rules are applied at all matches of the input parameters.

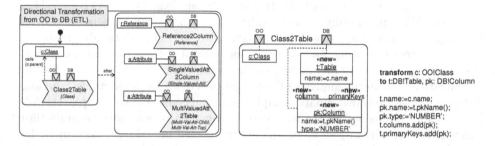

Fig. 7. Rule structure diagram for ETL (left). A behavioural rule diagram in visual (center) and textual (right) notation.

Our rule language captures the main features of transformation languages. However, a particular rule diagram has to consider the specific implementation platform. For example, rules can have an arbitrary number of input parameters if we use ATL as the implementation language, whereas rules have only one input parameter if we use ETL, and we have patterns if using QVT-R. Also, platforms differ in the execution control of their rules. While in graph transformation the execution scheme is "as long as possible" (ALAP) and we can have rule priorities or layers, in ETL rules are executed once at each instance of the input parameter type. Hence, even though the language covers the most widely used styles of transformation, for its use with particular platforms we define *platform models* for different transformation languages. These models contain the features allowed in each languages, and can be used to check whether a rule model is compliant with an execution platform when code is generated, as well as by editors to guide the user in building compliant models with the platform. Nonetheless, we believe that a general design language will enable platform interoperability.

From the point of view of the rule structure diagrams, rules are black-boxes: their behaviour is still missing, in particular, attribute computations and object and link creations are not specified. We use *rule behaviour diagrams* to specify the actions each rule performs. We have identified three ways of expressing behaviour: (i) action languages, (ii) declarative, graphical pre- and post-conditions, and (iii) object diagrams annotated with operations like *new*, *delete* or *forbidden*.

In the case of an action language, one can use the concrete syntax of existing transformation implementation languages such as ATL or ETL. The case of pre-

and post-conditions follows the style of graph transformation [15]. The third option is present in Fujaba (http://fujaba.de). The center of Fig. 7 shows a behavioural diagram using this third type of syntax where created elements are annotated with the *new* keyword. The right of the figure shows the same rule using an action language with ETL syntax.

3.6   Implementation and Testing

*trans*ML does not include any implementation language, but we use existing target languages to implement the transformations (e.g. QVT, ATL or ETL). Using the MDE philosophy, code for different platforms can be generated from the diagrams, specifically from the rule (structure and behaviour) diagrams.

With respect to testing, test cases can be generated from the *transformation cases*, and assertions can be injected in the transformation code from the formal specification built in the analysis phase. This injected code is an *oracle function*, independent of the transformation implementation code. As an example, the following listing shows part of the EOL code automatically generated from pattern N(NoRefinedAttrs) in Fig. 3, which can be injected into the *pre* section of the transformation code to discard non supported input models:

```
operation sat_NoRefinedAttrs () : Boolean {
  return not OO!Class.allInstances().exists(p |
              OO!Class.allInstances().exists(c | c <> p and
                OO!Attribute.allInstances().exists(a |
                  p.features.includes(a) and
                  OO!Attribute.allInstances().exists(ar |
                    ar <> a and c.features.includes(ar) and
                    checkatt_NoRefinedAttrs(p, c, a, ar)))));
}
operation checkatt_NoRefinedAttrs
    (p:OO!Class,c:OO!Class,a:OO!Attribute, ar:OO!Attribute) : Boolean {
    var X:=a.name;     var Xar:=ar.name;
    return c.general.includes(p) and X=Xar;
}
```

3.7   Traceability

Even though the different *trans*ML diagrams can be used in isolation, their power comes from their combined use. This is so, as one can trace requirements into the code and build the final transformation by the progressive refinement of models. In this way, we have defined traceability relations between the different diagrams as shown to the left of Fig. 8. These relations correspond to the dotted arrows in Fig. 1. Thus, it is possible to trace which requirements are considered by a given scenario, specification property, architectural component or mapping. We can also trace the mappings and components a rule implements, and the behavioural diagram that refines a rule. Therefore, we can trace which requirements each rule addresses and vice-versa.

4   Tool Support

We have developed Ecore meta-models for the presented languages, together with several model transformations and code generators that allow automating the conversion between diagrams, as shown to the right of Fig. 8. The purpose of these transformations is to provide partial automation for model refinement from requirements to code generation. For example, given a mapping diagram we can generate a skeleton of a rule diagram, which has to be completed with the behaviour model by the transformation developer. All model transformations have been implemented with ETL, and all code generators with EGL.

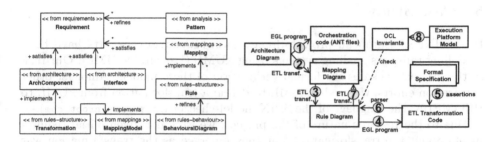

Fig. 8. Traceability links (left). Tool support (right).

The code generator with label "1" takes as input the architecture diagram, and generates ANT files that orchestrate the execution of the transformation chain specified in the architecture (i.e. it will ask the user the models to transform and pass them to the appropriate transformations). This generator also produces one additional ANT file for each transformation in the architecture, which defines tasks to automate the other labelled activities in the figure.

Transformation "2" generates one mapping diagram for each transformation in the architecture. These mapping diagrams are added a mapping for each concrete class defined by the input ports types. Transformation "3" generates a simple rule diagram from a mapping diagram that contains one rule for each mapping. Each rule stores a trace pointing to the mapping it implements. The opposite transformation is also possible for reengineering (label "7").

As stated before, one may use features of rule diagrams that are not available in the specific platform. In order to check whether a certain set of rule diagrams fits a particular execution platform, we have created an OCL code generator (label "8") that, given a platform model (ETL in our case), synthesizes OCL constraints. These constraints are checked on the rule diagrams, discovering whether they conform to the features of the platform.

In "4", ETL code is generated from the structural rule diagram, taking into account the flow directives. A parser for reverse engineering (label "6") generates the diagram from ETL code. Finally, the generator in "5" produces OCL code from the properties defined with the specification language. There are two ways to inject this code into ETL transformations. Firstly, code generated from patterns specifying restrictions on the input model is included in the *pre* section of the transformation, and checked on the input model before the transformation starts. If the model violates these constraints, a pop-up window informs the user of the unsatisfied properties. Secondly, code generated from patterns specifying properties of the transformation or of the expected output models is injected in the *post* section of the transformation, and checked when the transformation ends. This is used to perform run-time verification of the transformation. The user is informed of any violated property and of the rules that are responsible for the error. An example screenshot is shown in Fig. 10.

5   Case Study

In the INESS European project (http://www.iness.eu), experts have been modelling railway signalling systems using xUML (Executable UML). Our task in this project includes the formal verification of these models. Amongst other verification efforts, we used *trans*ML to define a transformation from xUML to PROMELA, the language of the SPIN model-checker (http://spinroot.com).

Due to the research nature of the project, we were not given initial requirements about the transformation, but they emerged as the transformation was better understood. Examples of requirements for the input models include: (i) classes always have an associated state machine; (ii) multiple-inheritance is not allowed; (iii) a special class is used to instantiate a scenario (representing a railway track layout) for the execution (analysis) of the model; (iv) objects can only be created in the state-machine of the "application" class. Fig. 9 shows to the left a specification pattern expressing the restriction (ii) of no multiple inheritance.

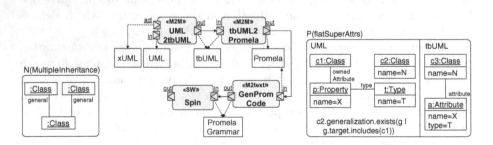

Fig. 9. A restriction on the input model (left). Architecture of the project (center). A verification property for transformation *UML2tbUML* (right).

This transformation poses many challenges, mostly concerned with handling the action language in its full generality. For this purpose, we split the transformation in several steps that could be handled more efficiently. The architecture of the final system is shown in the center of Fig. 9. It makes use of an intermediate meta-model, called (transition-based) tbUML, which is a simplified UML meta-model that only considers the structure of class diagrams and the possible set of transitions of the state-machines. Thus, the first transformation performs a flattening of the classes and states machines. This transformation makes use of the xUML meta-model for handling the action language. Then, the tbUML model is transformed into a PROMELA model, from which code conforming to the PROMELA grammar is generated as input to SPIN.

Splitting the transformation facilitates the elicitation of requirements. For instance, requirements related to the flattening of classes in the first transformation include copying attributes, associations and states for each class and its generalizations (a pattern specifying the requirement on attributes is to the right of Fig. 9). Requirements related to the flattening of state machines include aggregating and creating transitions depending on concurrent events of orthogonal states and of state machines associated to super-classes, as well as on exit actions in composite states.

Fig. 10. Testing the implementation

We used the mapping diagrams of *trans*ML to understand and reason about corresponding elements in the two M2M transformations, and to generate skeleton rule structure diagrams from them. We also generated assertion code for the run-time verification of the transformations. Fig. 10 shows a moment in the execution of the first transformation (more than 1600 LOC), where a violation of the verification property `flatSuperAttrs` occurs. By having traceability from the models into the code, we were able to identify the erroneous rule.

6   Conclusions and Lines of Future Work

Transformations should be engineered, not hacked. For this purpose we have presented *trans*ML, a family of languages to help building transformations using well-founded engineering principles. The languages cover the life-cycle of the transformation development including requirements, analysis, architecture, design and testing. We have provided partial tool support and automation for the MDE of transformations, and evaluated the approach using an industrial project, which showed the benefits of *modelling* transformations.

We are currently working in improving the tool support for our approach, in particular the usability of the visual editors and the integration of the different languages. We are also planning the use of *trans*ML in further case studies, and investigating *processes* for transformation development.

Acknowledgements. Work funded by the Spanish Ministry of Science (project TIN2008-02081 and grants JC2009-00015, PR2009-0019), the R&D programme of the Madrid Region (project S2009/TIC-1650), and the European Commission's 7th Framework programme (grants #218575 (INESS), #248864 (MADES)).

References

1. ATL, http://www.sciences.univ-nantes.fr/lina/atl/
2. Bézivin, J., Jouault, F., Paliès, J.: Towards model transformation design patterns. In: EWMT 2005 (2005)
3. Czarnecki, K., Helsen, S.: Feature-based survey of model transformation approaches. IBM Systems Journal 45(3), 621–646 (2006)
4. Etien, A., Dumoulin, C., Renaux, E.: Towards a unified notation to represent model transformation. Technical Report RR-6187, INRIA (2007)
5. Favre, J.-M., Nguyen, T.: Towards a megamodel to model software evolution through transformations. Electr. Notes Theor. Comput. Sci. 127(3), 59–74 (2005)
6. Garlan, D., Monroe, R.T., Wile, D.: Acme: Architectural description of component-based systems. In: Foundations of Component-Based Systems, pp. 47–68. Cambridge University Press, Cambridge (2000)
7. Guerra, E., de Lara, J., Kolovos, D.S., Paige, R.F.: A visual specification language for model-to-model transformations. In: VLHCC 2010. IEEE CS, Los Alamitos (2010)
8. Iacob, M., Steen, M., Heerink, L.: Reusable model transformation patterns. In: 3M4EC 2008, pp. 1–10 (2008)
9. Kolovos, D.S., Paige, R.F., Polack, F.: The Epsilon Object Language (EOL). In: Rensink, A., Warmer, J. (eds.) ECMDA-FA 2006. LNCS, vol. 4066, pp. 128–142. Springer, Heidelberg (2006)
10. Kolovos, D.S., Paige, R.F., Polack, F.: The Epsilon Transformation Language. In: Vallecillo, A., Gray, J., Pierantonio, A. (eds.) ICMT 2008. LNCS, vol. 5063, pp. 46–60. Springer, Heidelberg (2008)
11. Kusel, A.: TROPIC - a framework for building reusable transformation components. In: Doctoral Symposium at MODELS (2009)
12. QVT, http://www.omg.org/docs/ptc/05-11-01.pdf
13. Rahim, L.A., Mansoor, S.B.R.S.: Proposed design notation for model transformation. In: ASWEC 2008, pp. 589–598. IEEE CS, Los Alamitos (2008)
14. Rivera, J.E., Ruiz-Gonzalez, D., Lopez-Romero, F., Bautista, J., Vallecillo, A.: Orchestrating ATL model transformations. In: MtATL 2009, pp. 34–46 (2009)
15. Schürr, A.: Specification of graph translators with triple graph grammars. In: Mayr, E.W., Schmidt, G., Tinhofer, G. (eds.) WG 1994. LNCS, vol. 903, pp. 151–163. Springer, Heidelberg (1994)
16. Siikarla, M., Laitkorpi, M., Selonen, P., Systä, T.: Transformations have to be developed ReST assured. In: Vallecillo, A., Gray, J., Pierantonio, A. (eds.) ICMT 2008. LNCS, vol. 5063, pp. 1–15. Springer, Heidelberg (2008)
17. Spivey, J.M.: An introduction to Z and formal specifications. Softw. Eng. J. 4(1), 40–50 (1989)
18. Vanhooff, B., Ayed, D., Baelen, S.V., Joosen, W., Berbers, Y.: Uniti: A unified transformation infrastructure. In: Engels, G., Opdyke, B., Schmidt, D.C., Weil, F. (eds.) MODELS 2007. LNCS, vol. 4735, pp. 31–45. Springer, Heidelberg (2007)
19. Varró, D.: Model transformation by example. In: Nierstrasz, O., Whittle, J., Harel, D., Reggio, G. (eds.) MoDELS 2006. LNCS, vol. 4199, pp. 410–424. Springer, Heidelberg (2006)

Henshin: Advanced Concepts and Tools for In-Place EMF Model Transformations

Thorsten Arendt[1], Enrico Biermann[2], Stefan Jurack[1],
Christian Krause[3,*], Gabriele Taentzer[1]

[1] Philipps-Universität Marburg, Germany
{arendt,sjurack,taentzer}@mathematik.uni-marburg.de
[2] Technische Universität Berlin, Germany
enrico@cs.tu-berlin.de
[3] CWI Amsterdam, The Netherlands
c.krause@cwi.nl

Abstract. The Eclipse Modeling Framework (EMF) provides modeling and code generation facilities for Java applications based on structured data models. Henshin is a new language and associated tool set for in-place transformations of EMF models. The Henshin transformation language uses pattern-based rules on the lowest level, which can be structured into nested transformation units with well-defined operational semantics. So-called amalgamation units are a special type of transformation units that provide a forall-operator for pattern replacement. For all of these concepts, Henshin offers a visual syntax, sophisticated editing functionalities, execution and analysis tools. The Henshin transformation language has its roots in attributed graph transformations, which offer a formal foundation for validation of EMF model transformations. The transformation concepts are demonstrated using two case studies: EMF model refactoring and meta-model evolution.

1 Introduction

Model-driven software development (MDD) is considered as a promising paradigm in software engineering. Models are ideal means for abstraction and enable developers to master the increasing complexity of software systems.

In model-driven development, the transformation of models belongs to the essential activities. Since models become the central artifacts in MDD, they are subject to direct model modifications, translated to intermediate models, and finally code is generated. While direct model modifications are usually performed in-place, i.e. directly on the model without creating copies, model translations usually keep source models untouched and produce new models or code. These transformations are called out-place.

Another crucial concept for MDD are domain-specific modeling languages which allow the definition of models on an adequate abstraction level with all

---

* Supported by the NWO GLANCE project WoMaLaPaDiA.

D.C. Petriu, N. Rouquette, Ø. Haugen (Eds.): MODELS 2010, Part I, LNCS 6394, pp. 121–135, 2010.

information needed to generate the right models or code. A promising approach to define domain-specific modeling languages is the Eclipse Modeling Framework (EMF) [1,2] which has evolved to a well-known and widely used technology. EMF provides modeling and code generation capabilities based on so-called structural data models. As they describe structural aspects only, they are mainly used to specify domain-specific languages. EMF complies with Essential MOF (EMOF) as part of OMG's Meta Object Facility (MOF) 2.0 specification [3].

For various kinds of EMF model modifications such as refactorings, introduction of design patterns and other modeling patterns, we need a powerful in-place transformation approach, operating directly on EMF models. There are several in-place model transformations approaches which can transform EMF models directly, e.g. Kermeta [4], EWL [5], EMF Tiger [6], and Moment2 [7]. The corresponding transformation languages are either rather simple or in case the of Kermeta, not declarative enough to offer the opportunity for formal reasoning on model transformations.

To fill this gap, we have developed the transformation language and tool environment Henshin, operating directly on EMF models. Henshin is a successor of EMF Tiger in the sense that it is also based on graph transformation concepts but extends the transformation language of EMF Tiger considerably. Henshin comes along with a powerful, yet declarative model transformation language, offering the possibility for formal reasoning. Its basic concept of transformation rules is enriched by powerful application conditions and flexible attribute computations based on Java or JavaScript. Furthermore, it provides the concept of transformation units defining control structures for rule applications in a modular way. A special kind of transformation unit are amalgamation units which offer a forall-operator for applying transformation rules in parallel. For further flexibility, special units for code execution can be added.

The Henshin tool environment consists primarily of a fast transformation engine, several editors, and a state space generator to support reasoning by model checking based on state space generation from transformation systems, useful for model checking transformations. Since these transformation concepts are close to graph transformation concepts, it is possible to translate the rules to AGG [8], a tool environment for algebraic graph transformation where they might be further analyzed concerning conflicts and dependencies of rule applications as well as their termination.

Two example applications of Henshin are considered: (1) refactoring of EMF models [9], more precisely refactoring *Pull Up Attribute* and (2) a simple form of meta-model evolution [10] where two evolution steps of a Petri net model are reflected on instance models being concrete Petri nets in abstract syntax.

The paper is organized as follows: Section 2 introduces the Henshin transformation language and describes its most important concepts. In Section 3 and 4, we present two case studies on refactoring and meta-model evolution. The Henshin tool environment is presented in Section 5. A discussion of related work can be found in Section 6 and concluding remarks in Section 7.

2   The Henshin Transformation Meta-model

In the following, we describe informally our transformation language using the Henshin transformation meta-model, which is also an EMF meta-model and moreover uses the Ecore meta-model for typing purposes. The Henshin transformation language is based on graph transformation concepts [11,12,13] and therefore offers a visual syntax and means for formal reasoning about transformations.

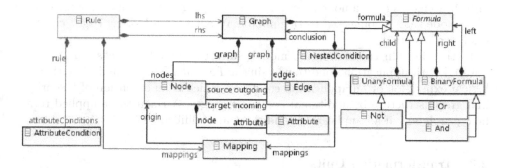

Fig. 1. Rules with application conditions

2.1   Rules and Matching

A transformation rule consists of left and right-hand side graphs (respectively LHS and RHS) which describe model patterns by their underlying (graph) structure (cf. Fig. 1). Furthermore, attribute conditions can be defined for rules. Nodes refer to objects while edges refer to references between objects. Nodes, edges and attributes refer to *EClass*, *EReference*, and *EAttribute* via references called *type* (not shown in Fig. 1) which are classes of the Ecore meta-model. These type references are used as an explicit typing, e.g. a node connected to a certain *EClass* will will match only to objects of this type. *Mappings* between LHS and RHS can be defined between nodes. Since EMF models cannot contain parallel edges of the same type between the same nodes, edge mappings are implicitly given if both, their source and target nodes are mapped. For clarity, we omit the explicit notation of multiplicities in all figures. As a general guideline, all reference types using names in plural have 0..* multiplicity. All others have upper bound 1. Note that we concentrate on the structure of the transformation meta-model and neglect the properties of model elements such as their names.

Rules can be applied to a construct called *EmfGraph* that serves as an aggregation of *EObjects*. Only the *EObjects* within an *EmfGraph* will be considered for matching. Therefore, deleting *EObjects* removes them from the underlying *EmfGraph* representation only. The EObject might still be used in another context but it is no longer visible for further rule applications.

2.2   Application Conditions

To conveniently determine where a specified rule should be applied, application conditions can be defined. An important subset of application conditions are negative application conditions (NACs) which specify the non-existence of model patterns in certain contexts.

Application conditions allow the definition of first order logical formulas over graph conditions, being atomic conditions that enforce the existence or non-existence of model patterns, as well as further conditions over conditions (nesting). Statements like "a node must have an incoming edge or an outgoing edge" or "a node that is connected to this node may not have a looping edge" can be easily expressed.

In the Henshin transformation model, shown in Fig. 1, *Graphs* can be annotated with application conditions using a *Formula*. This formula is either a logical expression or an application condition which is an extension of the original graph structure by additional nodes and edges. A rule can be applied to a host graph only if all application conditions are fullfilled.

2.3   Transformation Units

To control the order of rule applications, it is possible to define control structures over rules called *TransformationUnits*. The most basic transformation unit is a rule itself which corresponds to a single application of that rule. All available transformation units are depicted in Fig. 2. For example, there are constructs for non-deterministic rule choices (*IndependentUnit*) and rule priority (*PriorityUnit*). Except for *Rules* and *AmalgamationUnits*, transformation units can have one or more subunits which are executed according to the semantics of its parent unit. For instance, subunits of an *IndependentUnit* will be executed in random order.

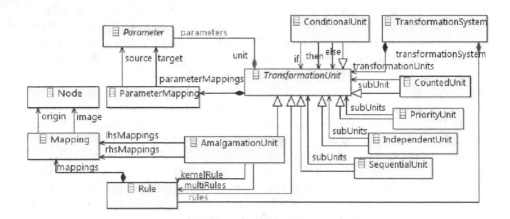

Fig. 2. Transformation units and parameters

Furthermore, it is possible to pass objects and values from one unit to another one via parameters. In this way, the object flow between different rules and units can be controlled and complex transformations can be parameterized. Each transformation unit can have an arbitrary number of *Parameters* which can either refer to a specific EObject or contain a specific value. *ParameterMappings* define how parameters of transformation units are passed to their subunits.

Applicability. A unit is applicable if it can be successfully executed. Applicability is defined differently for different transformation units. For example, *PriorityUnits* or *IndependentUnits* are always applicable while a *SequentialUnit* is applicable only if all of its subunits are applicable in the given order.

Termination. A unit terminates if it is successfully executed or if no rule was applied in the context of that unit. *ConditionalUnits* or *SequentialUnits* terminate if their subunits terminate. However, subunits of *PriorityUnits* and *IndependentUnits* may be applied repeatedly. This can easily result in infinite loops when nesting units of those kinds. *IndependentUnits* and *PriorityUnits* terminate if their subunits do not contain any applicable rule.

2.4   Amalgamation

A special kind of transformation units are *AmalgamationUnits* which are useful to specify forall operations on recurring model patterns. An amalgamation unit contains an interaction scheme consisting of one *Rule* which acts as a kernel rule and multiple rules which act as multi rules. The embedding of a kernel rule into a multi rule are defined by *Mappings* between nodes of the LHS of the kernel and the multi rule. The semantics of such an interaction scheme is that the kernel rule is matched exactly once. This match is used as a common partial match for each multi rule which are matched as often as possible. The effect is that the modification defined in the kernel rule is applied only once while modifications defined in the multi rules are applied a certain number of times depending on the number of matches. For a detailed presentation of amalgamation concepts, see [12]. An amalgamation unit is applicable if its kernel rule is applicable. It terminates after one application.

2.5   Relation to Algebraic Graph Transformation

The presented language concepts of Henshin have their origin in algebraic graph transformation [11]. This concerns the syntactical structure of rules and transformation units as well as their semantics wrt. *EMFGraphs*. While an *EMFGraph* corresponds to a typed, attributed graphs, the given EMF model represents the type graph. Nodes and edges in rules are related to EObjects and EReferences which are typed over the same given EMF model. Formulas relate to graph conditions [11] over typed, attributed graphs. The amalgamation concept is formulated for typed graphs with node type inheritance and containment in [12]. Finally, transformation units are defined in [13] using an approach-independent form. However, parameters have not been considered yet in the formal setting, but will be in future work.

To summarize, our general aim is to give a formal semantics to the full transformation language as solid basis for further validations. A large foundation is already available and will be completed in the near future.

3   EMF Model Refactoring

In this section we present an example refactoring for EMF based models [1] using the advanced concepts of Henshin.

3.1   DSL *SimplifiedClassModel (SCM)*

Figure 3 shows the meta-model of DSL *SimplifiedClassModel (SCM)* for modeling simplified class diagrams being useful in an early stage of the software development process to formulate analysis models. SCM can be considered as simplification of the UML superstructure [14]. Meta-attributes and references *name, qualifiedName, visibility,* and *redefinedAttribute,* as well as well-formedness rules correspond to those known from UML and are not explained in detail here.

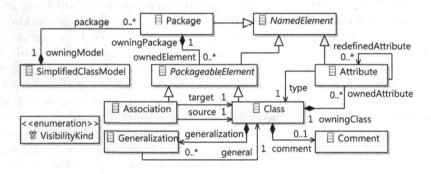

Fig. 3. DSL *SimplifiedClassModel (SCM)* - meta-model

3.2   Model Refactoring *Pull Up Attribute*

SCM refactoring *Pull Up Attribute* moves a common attribute from all direct subclasses of a given class to this class. The name of the attribute to be moved is given by parameter `attributename` while parameter `superclassname` specifies the qualified name of the class the attribute has to be pulled up to. In order to apply *Pull Up Attribute*, the following preconditions (**PC**) have to be checked:

- The class with qualified name `superclassname` does not already have an attribute named `attributename` (**PC1**).

 – For each direct subclass of the class with qualified name `superclassname`:
  • There is an attribute named `attributename` (**PC2**).
  • Visibility (**PC3**) and type (**PC4**) of the attribute named `attributename` are the same.
  • If the attribute named `attributename` redefines another attribute each attribute named `attributename` in each other subclass of the class with qualified name `superclassname` has to redefine the same attribute (**PC5**). Furthermore, the redefined attribute must have visibility *private*, i.e. it must not be visible in class with qualified name `superclassname` (**PC6**).

If each precondition is fulfilled, the class with qualified name `superclassname` gets a new attribute named `attributename`. Corresponding attributes are removed from all subclasses. The new attribute gets the same visibility as before, except that visibility *private* has to be set to *protected* since a subclass must have access to the new attribute as well. Moreover, already redefined attributes have to be referenced by the new attribute.

3.3 Implementation Using Henshin

The Henshin implementation of *Pull Up Attribute* uses a *SequentialUnit* which in turn uses three *IndependentUnits* as subunits. The first *IndependentUnit* is responsible for preconditions checking and contains six rules. Each rule is specified in a way that the class with qualified name `superclassname` gets a comment 'ERROR' if a certain precondition is violated.

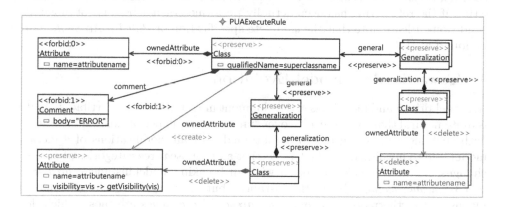

Fig. 4. Rule *PullUpAttributeRule*

The second *IndependentUnit* performs the transformation using an *AmalgamationUnit*. Figure 4 shows two rules (the *kernel* and a *multi rule*) of the *AmalgamationUnit* as well as their LHS, RHS, and two NACs in an integrated view. LHS objects (nodes and edges) can be identified by tags ⟨⟨*preserve*⟩⟩ or ⟨⟨*delete*⟩⟩, objects tagged by ⟨⟨*preserve*⟩⟩ or ⟨⟨*create*⟩⟩ form the RHS of the rule. Kernel rule nodes are bordered by a single line, whereas the multi rule contains all those of the kernel rule and those objects bordered by two lines. They represent so-called multi-objects.

The kernel rule moves the attribute from a class to its superclass. In its LHS we are looking for an attribute named `attributename` contained in a subclass of the class with qualified name `superclassname`. A condition on attribute *visibility* changes its value to *protected* only if its previous value was *private*. This is done by invoking Java method `getVisibility()` where the previous visibility is given by variable *vis*. There are two NACs which have to be checked before executing the specified transformation ($\langle\!\langle forbid:0\rangle\!\rangle$ and $\langle\!\langle forbid:1\rangle\!\rangle$). The first NAC checks whether the superclass has not been annotated by comment 'ERROR', whereas the second one checks whether the superclass does not already own an attribute named `attributename`. After rule application the class with qualified name `superclassname` owns the attribute named `attributename`.

The multi rule deletes the corresponding attribute from each further subclass. Its LHS corresponds to the kernel rule LHS enriched by a sub-pattern for possibly other subclasses of the class with qualified name `superclassname` that own an attribute named `attributename`. This additional pattern is matched into the model graph as often as different further subclasses exist. According to the $\langle\!\langle delete\rangle\!\rangle$ tagged multi-object the corresponding attribute will be removed from each further subclass.

The third *IndependentUnit* consists of one single rule that removes comment 'ERROR' possibly inserted before. Each part of the refactoring (checking, performing, and cleaning) has to be encapsulated by an *IndependentUnit* in order to assure a successful execution of *Pull Up Attribute*, i.e. the target model is valid either if the refactoring has been actually performed or not because of violated conditions. Please note that the complete specification of *Pull Up Attribute* can be found at [15].

4   Towards Meta-model Evolution

In model-driven and model-based development models are the key artifacts. As it is quite natural that models evolve over time the compliance of existing instances with such meta-models needs to be obtained. Not all modifications of a meta-model lead to invalidity. In [10], Cicchetti et al. propose three categories of model changes: *Not breaking changes* occur without breaking model instances, *breaking and resolvable changes* break the instances but can be resolved by automatic means and furthermore, *breaking and unresolvable changes* are those which do break the instances and which cannot be resolved automatically.

In our case study below, we follow the *manual specification* approach, i.e. we encode meta-model and instance model changes manually since currently there does not exist a meta-model evolution framework based on Henshin. Nevertheless, we give a practical idea how (semi-) automatic meta-model evolution can be realized with Henshin leading to an *operator-based co-evolution* approach.

Henshin is able to handle any Ecore-based model, thus we can create transformation rules for both, meta-models and its instances. In general, meta-models may occur in form of an Eclipse plug-in with generated model classes or standalone as *.ecore* file. The latter is more flexible and since Henshin supports Dynamic EMF, we use such Ecore files in our approach. In the following case study, the control flow is currently implemented in form of a simple Java class which loads related models and transformation rules and which triggers the transformation performed by the Henshin interpreter. This implementation as well as corresponding models and rules are part of our Henshin examples plug-in [16].

Our case study is dealing with the evolution of a Petri net meta-model. Figure 5 shows a simple Petri net meta-model on the left while an evolved one is shown on the right. A simple Petri net contains `Places` and `Transitions` which can be interconnected by dedicated references. `Net` serves as root node. The enhanced meta-model provides further nodes, `ArcPT` and `ArcTP`, serving as connection entries between `Places` and `Transitions` or `Transitions` and `Places`, respectively. Since `ArcPT` and `ArcTP` inherit from abstract `Arc`, it can be used to specify a weight. Complying Petri net instances can be deduced easily and are not shown due to space constraints.

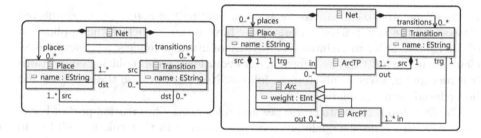

Fig. 5. Evolving Petri net meta-models. The original model is shown on the left while the evolved model is shown on the right.

In order to perform an evolution as shown in Fig. 5, the utilization of a set of general rules is conceivable being applied in a certain order. For example, the first iteration step may be a replacement of a connection between two classes by a connection class. The next iteration step may be to *extract a super-class* analog to the well-known corresponding refactoring. Afterwards the attribute could be introduced into the super-class. Each meta-model modification comes with an adaption of its instance models. In the following we concentrate on the replacement of connections only to demonstrate meta-model evolution with Henshin. Such a replacement rule may be modeled in a very general way as shown in Fig. 6. While two classes with given names and their container package are *preserved*, two references shown in the upper area are *deleted* and another four references and one class are *created*. Two *eOpposite* references between each two *EReferences* are omitted to keep the rule compact here. A negative application condition checks for the existence of a class named equally to the introduced class since doublets are *forbidden*. Note that *srcName*, *trgName* and

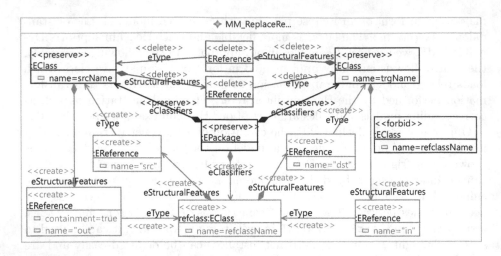

Fig. 6. General rule for replacing a connection by a connection class

refclassName are so-called *parameters* representing the names of the connected classes and the new reference class. They have to be set before the application of the rule. In order to maintain compliance of instance models, e.g. meta-model elements in use must not be removed, our evolution step of replacing connections is structured in several sub-steps as follows. Note, in our case these steps could be deduced even automatically.

The first step is to create new types and references. The creation part of Fig. 6 leads to such a rule. The deletion part has to occur in that rule as well but in terms of a preserved part. Having match and co-match, this allows to maintain information about concrete classes and references to be replaced. For the following

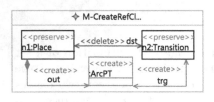

Fig. 7. Rule for replacing a connection by a connection class

we assume the parameters are set as follows: *srcName*="Place", *trgName*="Transition" and *refclassName*="ArcPT". The second step is to modify all instance models such that old direct references are deleted and replaced by instances of the new class, each referred to by an instance of the source and target class. With the previous rule, its match and its co-match at hand, the generation of a rule as depicted in Fig. 7 targeting instance model changes is quite conceivable. The rule may be embedded into an independent unit additionally. In this case it is applied as often as possible, i.e. the replacement takes place sequentially. A parallel replacement would be possible as well by utilizing an amalgamation unit. In that case the kernel rule would be empty and the rule in Fig. 7 would be the multi rule.

In the third step we remove a direct reference from the meta-model. This rule corresponds to the *preserve* and *delete* parts of Fig. 6. In addition, the rule is equipped with a partial match by the references matched in the first step.

5   Tool Environment

Henshin [16] is developed in a joint effort of the Technische Univerität Marburg, the Technische Univerität Berlin and the CWI Amsterdam. The tool set is implemented in the context of the Eclipse Modeling Framework Technology (EMFT) [17] project, which in turn serves as an incubation project for the top-level project Eclipse Modeling. Henshin is currently comprised of three modules:

1. a tree-based and a graphical editor for defining transformation systems,
2. a runtime component, currently consisting of an interpreter engine, and
3. a state space generator and an extension point for analysis tools.

In the following, we briefly describe the state of the art of the Henshin tool set.

5.1   Editors

There are currently two editors available for defining model transformations in Henshin: i) a tree-based editor, generated by EMF itself, and extended with additional notation and tools to ease the editing of transformations, and ii) a graphical editor, implemented using GMF. Multi-panel editors, such as the one of EMF Tiger [6] and AGG [8], separate the editing of respectively left-hand side, right-hand side, and negative application conditions into multiple views. We chose an integrated view on transformation rules, similar to the Fujaba [18], GReAT [19], and GROOVE [20] editors. Examples of integrated transformation rules in the graphical editor are depicted in Figs. 4, 6 and 7.

5.2   Runtime

The Henshin runtime currently consists of an efficient interpreter engine. Given a transformation system and an EMF model as input, the transformation is performed directly, i.e., in-place, on the given model. For exogenous transformations, it further produces an additional output model instance. Note that endogenous transformations are particularly well-supported by the interpreter, since they are always executed in-place without the need of deep-copying model instances. The interpreter supports the full expressiveness nested conditions and transformation units, including amalgamations. Like EMF itself, the interpreter is independent of the Eclipse Platform and can be used in non-Eclipse applications as well.

5.3   Validation of Model Transformations

In Henshin, we currently provide the following validation support: To analyze in-place model transformations, we have developed a state space generation tool, which allows to simulate all possible executions of a transformation for a given input model, and to apply model checking, similar to the GROOVE [20] tool. Fig. 8 depicts the graphical state space explorer for the academic dining philosophers example. Here, the state space is finite, there exists one initial state (green, on the left) and two deadlock states (red, on the right), in which none of the

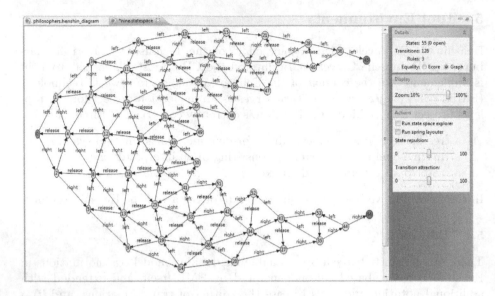

Fig. 8. State space generation tool

rules is applicable anymore. Large state spaces can also be generated and analyzed outside of the graphical tool. We use parallel algorithms for the state space exploration and can therefore benefit from modern multi-core processors. In its current version, our tool is able to handle state spaces with millions of states.

Our state space generator supports two different equalities for objects: i) the basic one defined by EMF itself (implemented in `EcoreUtil.equals()`), and ii) an equality based on graph isomorphisms. The latter abstracts from the order of elements in multi-valued references. In particular for highly symmetric models, such as the simple dining philosophers example, the use of graph equality reduces the size of the state space significantly. Note that Henshin currently does not provide means for recognizing the order of elements in multi-valued references. Therefore, the more compact state space induced by graph equality can be shown to be formally equivalent to the one generated using the basic EMF equality.

The state space tool set further provides an extension point for model checkers. We have integrated the third-party model checker CADP [21], which allows to verify temporal properties, specified as modal μ-calculus formulas. Moreover, we have integrated an existing OCL [22] validator for invariant checking. Found counter examples for both validation tools are shown as traces in the graphical state space explorer.

6   Related Work

Since model transformation is a key concept of model-driven development, a number of model transformation approaches have been developed. Especially two kinds of model transformations are distinguished in MDD: (1) in-place model modification within the same language and (2) out-place translation of models to models of other languages or to code. Model transformation approaches supporting exogenous out-place transformations well are e.g. QVT, ATL, and Tefkat. We do not relate Henshin closer to these approaches due to space limitations. In the following, we consider EMF model transformations approaches for endogenous in-place transformations like Kermeta [4], EWL [5], Mola [23], Fujaba [18], EMF Tiger [6], and Moment2 [7] which we want to compare closer with Henshin.

Kermeta is an EMOF compliant textual approach to support behavior definition based on an action language which is imperative and object-oriented. Thus, Kermeta transformations are not rule-based and do not a formal foundation. Its tool environment includes a parser, a type-checker and an interpreter. The Epsilon Wizard Language is used to write small in-place transformations within the Epsilon project. The central concept are wizards which can be compared to rules. A wizard consists of a guard, a title and a do-section where the update is programmed in an imperative, object-oriented style. A formal foundation of the Epsilon Wizard Language is not mentioned. *EMF Tiger* is the predecessor of Henshin basing on graph transformation concepts as well. However, its transformation language is rather simple in the sense that it is purely rule-based and allows simple attribute changes only. Application conditions of rules are just sets of negative patterns. *Moment2* supports transformations of EMF models based on rewriting logic, as implemented in Maude. Its transformation language provides the concept of rewrites similar to graph transformation rules. Rewrites can be equipped with complex conditions expressed as OCL [22] constraints. However, rewrites cannot be composed to larger transformation modules. Due to its formalization based on rewrite logic, some static analysis and formal verification based on model checking are possible. *MOLA* supports transformations on EMF models where transformations are specified by MOLA diagrams consisting of graphical statements such as rules, loops, and calls to subprograms. An interpreter for Fujaba's story diagrams working on EMF models is presented in [18]. Both tools work directly on EMF models and offer similar language concepts as Henshin, namely rules based on patterns, and control constructs such as sequences and loops. However, a concept such as amalgamation is not offered by these tools. Furthermore, both MOLA and the story diagram interpreter do not have a formal basis for further validations of model transformations. *Viatra* [24] provides a rule and pattern-based transformation language combining graph transformation and abstract state machine (ASM) concepts. Modeling languages are defined by a proprietary meta modeling approach covering all main meta modeling concepts. The import of models in standard meta modeling formats such as EMF is supported as well. Based on graph patterns and rules, the Viatra transformation language offers advanced transformation features [24] including recursive graph patterns, generic and meta-transformations as well as control structures based on ASMs. Henshin's transformation features differ from these especially concerning the execution of rules which might also be in parallel, as in amalgamated units.

Henshin is the only in-place transformation approach which comes along with a powerful transformation language being executed by a transformation engine that operates directly on EMF models. Moreover, its transformation features are all based on algebraic graph transformation [11,12,13].

Comparing Henshin's transformation language and tool set with the one of GROOVE [20], we can state that both are based on graph transformation and support nested application conditions as well as universal quantification using amalgamation. The use of regular expressions for matching is supported by GROOVE, but not by Henshin. Model checking in GROOVE is done using LTL or CTL formulas, whereas Henshin supports the more expressive modal μ-calculus through the CADP [21] model checker, as well as validation of OCL [22] invariants. To the best of our knowledge, GROOVE cannot handle EMF models yet.

7   Conclusion

In this paper, we present the Henshin transformation model for in-place transformations of EMF models. It builds up on graph transformation concepts such as rule-based transformation, nested and pattern-based application conditions for rules, and a variety of transformation units to define control structures for rule applications. To summarize, the Henshin transformation concepts rely basically on rules and patterns which can lead to a high amount of non-determinism when executing transformations. This amount can be reduced by the use of rule parameters, conditions and transformation units.

The direct execution of Henshin transformations allows a tight integration of transformations on inter-related EMF models as shown in the simple meta-model evolution example. Typing information can be dynamically loaded and re-loaded such that instance models can be re-typed over a modified meta-model. In the future, we intend to elaborate the translation of meta-model transformations to instance transformations further.

Although not addressed in this paper, Henshin can also be used for exogenous transformations such that source and target meta-model are integrated into correspondence meta-model in between. The transformation is formulated over this integrated meta-model. To view the target model only, we plan to extend Henshin by model operations such as projection operations restricting an instance model to the target domain.

References

1. EMF: Eclipse Modeling Framework, http://www.eclipse.org/emf
2. Steinberg, D., Budinsky, F., Patenostro, M., Merks, E.: EMF: Eclipse Modeling Framework, 2nd edn. Addison Wesley, Reading (2008)
3. MOF: Meta Object Facility (MOF) Core, http://www.omg.org/spec/MOF

4. Kermeta: http://www.kermeta.org
5. Kolovos, D.S., Paige, R.F., Polack, F., Rose, L.M.: Update transformations in the small with the Epsilon Wizard Language. Journal of Obj. Tech. 6(9), 53–69 (2007)
6. Biermann, E., Ehrig, K., Köhler, C., Kuhns, G., Taentzer, G., Weiss, E.: Graphical Definition of Rule-Based Transformation in the Eclipse Modeling Framework. In: Nierstrasz, O., Whittle, J., Harel, D., Reggio, G. (eds.) MoDELS 2006. LNCS, vol. 4199, pp. 425–439. Springer, Heidelberg (2006)
7. Boronat, A.: MOMENT: A Formal Framework for Model Management. PhD thesis, Universitat Politècnica de València (2007)
8. AGG: Attributed Graph Grammar System, http://tfs.cs.tu-berlin.de/agg
9. Biermann, E., Ehrig, K., Köhler, C., Kuhns, G., Taentzer, G., Weiss, E.: EMF Model Refactoring based on Graph Transformation Concepts. ECEASST 3 (2006), http://easst.org/eceasst
10. Cicchetti, A., Ruscio, D.D., Eramo, R., Pierantonio, A.: Automating co-evolution in model-driven engineering. In: 12th International IEEE Enterprise Distributed Object Computing Conference, pp. 222–231. IEEE Computer Society, Los Alamitos (2008)
11. Ehrig, H., Ehrig, K., Prange, U., Taentzer, G.: Fundamentals of Algebraic Graph Transformation. Monographs in Theoretical Computer Science. Springer, Heidelberg (2006)
12. Biermann, E., Ermel, C., Taentzer, G.: Lifting Parallel Graph Transformation Concepts to Model Transformation based on the Eclipse Modeling Framework. ECEASST 26 (2010), http://easst.org/eceasst
13. Kuske, S.: Transformation Units-A structuring Principle for Graph Transformation Systems. PhD thesis, University of Bremen (2000)
14. UML: Unified Modeling Language, http://www.uml.org
15. EMF Refactor, http://www.mathematik.uni-marburg.de/~swt/modref
16. Henshin, http://www.eclipse.org/modeling/emft/henshin
17. EMFT: Eclipse Modeling Framework Technology, http://www.eclipse.org/modeling/emft
18. Giese, H., Hildebrandt, S., Seibel, A.: Improved flexibility and scalability by interpreting story diagrams. ECEASST 18 (2009), http://easst.org/eceasst
19. GReAT: Graph Rewriting and Transformation, http://www.isis.vanderbilt.edu/tools/GReAT
20. Kastenberg, H., Rensink, A.: Model checking dynamic states in GROOVE. In: Valmari, A. (ed.) SPIN 2006. LNCS, vol. 3925, pp. 299–305. Springer, Heidelberg (2006)
21. Garavel, H., Mateescu, R., Lang, F., Serwe, W.: CADP 2006: A toolbox for the construction and analysis of distributed processes. In: Damm, W., Hermanns, H. (eds.) CAV 2007. LNCS, vol. 4590, pp. 158–163. Springer, Heidelberg (2007)
22. OCL: The Object Constraint Language, http://www.omg.org/technology/documents/formal/ocl.htm
23. MOLA: MOdel transformation LAnguage, http://mola.mi.lu.lv
24. Balogh, A., Varró, D.: Advanced model transformation language constructs in the VIATRA2 framework. In: SAC 2006: Proceedings of the 2006 ACM Symposium on Applied Computing, pp. 1280–1287. ACM, New York (2006), http://eclipse.org/gmt/VIATRA2

A Technique for Automatic Validation of Model Transformations

Levi Lúcio, Bruno Barroca, and Vasco Amaral

Departamento de Informática, Faculdade de Ciências e Tecnologia
Universidade Nova de Lisboa, Portugal*
{Levi.Lucio,Bruno.Barroca,Vasco.Amaral}@di.fct.unl.pt

Abstract. We present in this paper a technique for proving properties about model transformations. The properties we are concerned about relate the structure of an input model with the structure of the transformed model. The main highlight of our approach is that we are able to prove the properties for all models, i.e. the transformation designer may be certain about the structural soundness of the results of his/her transformations. In order to achieve this we have designed and experimented with a transformation model checker, which builds what we call a state space for a transformation. That state space is then used as in classical model checking to prove the property or, in case the property does not hold to produce a counterexample. If the property holds this information can be used as a certification for the transformation, otherwise the counterexample can be used as debug information during the transformation design process.

1 Introduction

Nowadays model transformation tools [9,11] have become the topic of intensive research due to their importance in Model Driven Development (MDD). In the MDD context, these tools are used for several activities such as model refinement, refactoring, translation, validation or operational semantics. These activities can turn out to complex and error prone. This said, automatic validation techniques for model transformations are of the utmost importance.

In our laboratory, we have developed a new tool named DSLTrans [3] to assist the software engineer while specifying model transformations. DSLTrans aims at overcoming the flaws of state of the art model transformation tools — most importantly lack of confluence and termination guarantees — by proposing a simple visual language with basic primitives. The main idea behind DSLTrans is that, due to its simplicity, we can assure these features by construction.

---

* The presented work has been developed in the context of project BATIC3S partially funded by the Portuguese foundation FCT/MCTES ref. PTDC/EIA/65798/2006, the doctoral grant ref. SFRH/BD/38123/2007 and the post doctoral grant ref. SFRH/BPD/65394/2009. We would also like to thank Vasco Sousa and Carla Ferreira for the fruitful discussions.

D.C. Petriu, N. Rouquette, Ø. Haugen (Eds.): MODELS 2010, Part I, LNCS 6394, pp. 136–150, 2010.

In this paper, we present a technique for automatic validation of model transformations expressed in DSLTrans. We will describe a symbolic model checker which was built to guarantee transformation properties expressed in the form of an implication: 'if a structural relation between some elements of the source model holds, then another structural relation between some elements of the target model should also hold'. Our symbolic model checker computes for each possible execution of a transformation, an equivalence class representing a set of source models and their corresponding transformations. We can then validate that transformation by checking if our transformation property holds for every computed equivalence class.

1.1   Related Work

In order to aid the construction of the proof of semantic preservation along a set of transformation rules [2] introduced a language to anotate those rules with assertions. The idea is to then pass these annotations to a reasoning framework that will derive, at the meta level, conclusions about the overall transformation. The work presented in [1] aims at validating a model transformation by using the Alloy tool. In this case, Alloy simulates the transformation by generating a model example of the source language and then analyzing the results of the transformation.

The authors of [5] present a constructive fashion to automatically generate a valid transformation (the authors refers to transformations as ontology alignment) which in principle would preserve the semantic properties of the input and output models. This generation is done by using the Similarity Flooding algorithm which is based on the calculus of a distance measurement between source and target languages.

Similarly to our approach, the authors of [10] enable the declaration of a syntactic structural correspondence between terms in source and target languages. However, they use this structural correspondence to automatically verify the results at the end of each transformation. With this approach, the quality engineer will only realize that the transformation is invalid when some pair of models input/output violates the declared structural correspondence.

1.2   Structure of the Paper

This paper is organized as follows. In section 2, we introduce the DSLTrans language by providing a transformation which we use as running example throughout this paper. We then present how the state space is built for the transformation and how that state space is used to prove some properties; In section 3 we introduce the formalization of our approach with the aim of having a precise description of the transformation model checker and a base for its implementation; In section 4, we will describe how we have implemented the transformation model checker using SWI-Prolog and provide a notion of the space complexity of our algorithm; finally, in section 5, we finish with some technical directions on how to improve the space and time complexities of our transformation model checker.

2 Motivating Example

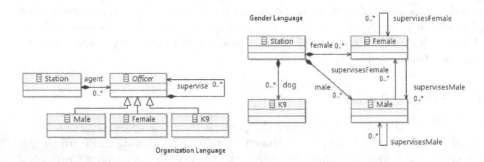

Fig. 1. Metamodels of a squad of agents(left) and a squad organized by gender(right)

2.1 The Transformation Language

The transformation language we use as a base for this work is called DSLTrans [3] and was developed in our laboratory. DSLTrans is a relatively simple transformation language having a reduced number of primitives. In order to introduce DSLTrans let us first present the running example we will use throughout this paper. Fig. 1 presents two metamodels of languages for describing views over the organization of a police station. The metamodel annotated with 'Organization Language' represents a language for describing the chain of command in a police station, which includes male officers (*Male* class), female officers (*Female* class), and dogs (*K9* class). The officer chain of command is expressed using the EMF's containment named 'supervise'. The metamodel annotated with 'Gender Language' represents a language for describing a different view over the chain of command, where the officers working at the police station are classified by gender. In Fig. 2 we present a transformation written in DSLTrans between models of both languages. The purpose of this transformation is to flatten a chain of command given in language 'Organization Language' into two sets of male and female officers. Within each of those sets the command relations are kept, i.e. a female officer will be directly related to all her female subordinates and likewise for male officers. An example of one such transformation can be observed in Fig. 3, where the original model is on the left and the transformed one on the right. Notice that in the figure the boxes represent instances of the classes in the metamodels of Fig. 1. In particular, the elements s, m_k and f_k in the figure on the left are instances of the source metamodel elements *Station*, *Male* and *Female* respectively. The primed elements in the figure on the right are their instance counterparts in the target metamodel.

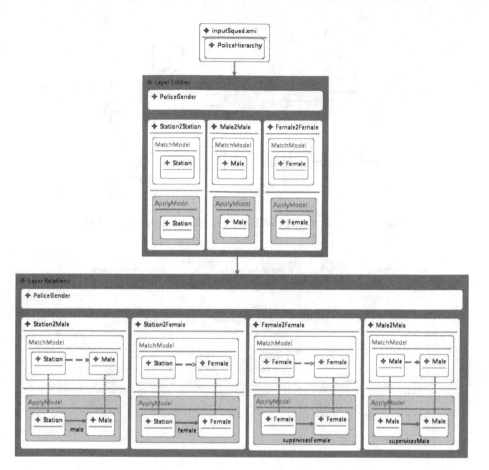

Fig. 2. A model transformation expressed in DSLTrans

We can identify in the transformation in Fig. 2 several components. Firstly, the transformation is divided into two steps, formally called *layers*. Each layer defines a set of transformation rules and a transformation rule is a pair ⟨*match, apply*⟩, where both *match* and *apply* are patterns holding elements of the metamodel of language 'Squad Organization Language' — the source language — and of language 'Squad Gender Language' — the target language — respectively. Layer 1 (named 'Layer Entities') of the transformation includes three simple transformation rules to translate elements of a model of language 'Organization Language' into their counterparts in language 'Gender Language'. Layer 2 (named 'Layer Relations') includes four transformations that give structure to the elements built in the previous layer. The transformation rules in layer 2 reveal two interesting features of DSLTrans:

- *Indirect links*: these links can be observed in the *match* pattern of all the transformations of layer 2 and are noted as a dashed arrow. A model matches

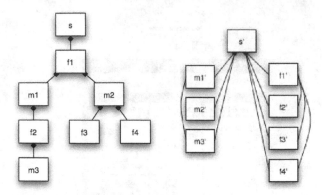

Fig. 3. Original model (left) and transformed model (right)

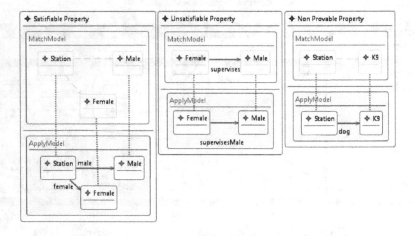

Fig. 4. Validation properties over a DSLTrans model

such an indirect link if there exists a path of containment associations between instances of the two connected metamodel elements;

– *Backward links*: backward links connect elements of the *match* and the *apply* patterns and are noted as dashed (vertical) lines. They can also be observed in all the transformation rules of layer 2. Backward links are used to refer to elements created in a previous layer in order to use them in the current one. For example, the leftmost transformation rule of layer 2 in Fig. 2 takes instances of *Station* and *Male* (of the 'Gender Language' metamodel) which were created in a previous layer from instances of *Station* and *Male* (of the 'Organization Language' metamodel), and creates an association 'male' between them.

A particular characteristic of DSLTrans as a transformation language is that throughout all the layers the source model remains intact as a match source.

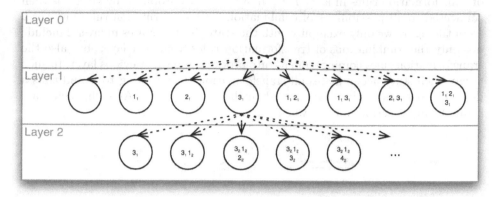

Fig. 5. Partial state space for the transformation in Fig. 2

The *match* pattern of a transformation rule can match multiple times the source model and per each of those matches an instance of the *apply* pattern is created. Each layer thus creates a set of target metamodel instances and relations between those instances. In order to refer to elements created in a previous layer in a transformation rule, backward links have to be used. A complete description of the DSLTrans language including its formal syntax and semantics can be found in [3]. An example of a complex transformation of UML to Java using DSLTrans can be found in [8].

2.2 Properties and Their Proof

Now that the transformation language has been defined we can move on to describe the properties we wish to prove about our transformations. Examples of these properties can be observed in Fig. 4. In natural language the property named 'Satisfiable Property' reads as follows: 'Any model which includes a police station that has both a male and female chief officers will be transformed into a model where the male chief officer will exist in the male set and the female chief officer will exist in the female set'. The primary goal of our model checker is to prove that, given a transformation, such a property will hold for all models given as inputs to that transformation.

   Practically, this proof is achieved by building what we call the state space of a transformation. Each state of the transformation state space corresponds to a possible combination of the transformation rules of a given layer, combined with all states of the previous layer. Using the example of the transformation given in Fig. 2 we can build a rough sketch of such a state space which we present in Fig.5. In the figure we identify each transformation rule in each layer by a number with an index. For example transformation 1_1 corresponds to the first transformation — e.g. left to right in Fig. 2 — in layer one. The state space starts with the initial state— which in the figure belongs to layer 0 — where no transformation has been applied. The initial state then connects to all possibilities of combinations of transformation rules in layer 1. Each of the states produced by layer 1 is then connected to all possibilities of combinations of transformation rules in layer 2 — in the figure we only exemplify with the state 3_1. The states in layer 2 include not only the combinations of transformation rules from that layer, but also the transformation rules coming from a state produced by the previous layer. In such a way each state accumulates all transformation rules leading to it and thus a describes pattern(s) that should exist in the source model. As such, each state symbolically describes an equivalence class of input models.

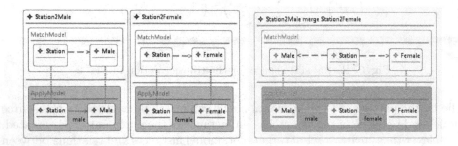

Fig. 6. Original transformations rules (left) and a possible collapse of those rules (right)

We can be more precise while building such equivalence classes. In Fig. 6 we exemplify what we call the *collapse* of two of the rules of the transformation in Fig. 2. Due to the semantics of DSLTrans it may occur that, for example, if we have the two transformations on the left of Fig. 6 applied to a model, the instance of *Station* used by the match pattern of the two rules is the same. This comes from the fact that, in DSLTrans, the same input can consumed by several transformation rules within the same layer. In this case we can collapse the two classes in one in the state we are building. In fact, we can even go further and collapse the *Station* classes in the apply pattern of the two rules which would mean that both *Station* instances previously created in layer 1 (notice the backward link) are actually the same. This leads to the state shown in Fig. 6 on the right. In fact this state is required to prove the 'Satisfiable Property' in Fig. 4.

More generally, *collapsing* transformation rules is used to add more defini-tion to the equivalence classes represented by each state than the simple union of transformations as can be seen in Fig. 2. In this union, all elements of the same type in the disjoint graphs of the united transformation are seen as refer-ring to different objects in the input model — i.e. several elements of the same type within a transformation necessarily refer to different objects in a model. By adding the collapsed transformation rule states to the state space, the proofs of our properties become complete given we are covering more models in our symbolic states.

The proof of a property is then achieved by walking through the state space and checking every complete transformation state space path (starting from the initial state): if there is a state that satisfies the *match* pattern of the property, then there must exist a subsequent state for which the *apply* pattern satisfies the *apply* pattern of the property.

In Fig.4, the property named 'Unsatisfiable Property' represents a property that is not true for the transformation in Fig. 2. In natural language the property states the following: 'If a male officer commands a female officer in the original model, then that relation will be preserved in the transformed mode'. In our simple example, this is clearly not true given that the point of our transformation is to build separate lists of male and female officers. That said, in order to be proved, the property should hold on all paths of the state space, therefore it is sufficient to find one path where the property does not hold to render the property false. Such a path can then be used as a counterexample and may be useful for the transformation designer in the sense that it may point out a sequence of transformation rules leading to a wrong transformation result.

It may also happen that a property is non provable. In Fig. 4, the property named 'Non Provable' refers to dogs in the *match* pattern, a situation which is never contemplated by the transformation rules in Fig. 2. As such, the only possible statement about this property is that, although the source metamodel would allow such *match* patterns, the transformation does not implement them. This situation may point out to the transformation designer that (s)he is missing transformation rules to address certain patterns of the input models.

3 Formalization

In this section we will present the detailed theory for our transformation symbolic model checker. The theory is introduced incrementally and it formalizes the informal description given in section 2. The goal of such a formalization is to provide a precise definition of our symbolic model checker, to abstractly build the algorithms to perform the proofs and to provide a base for the study of the complexity of such algorithms. The formalization we provide tackles the core syntax and semantics of our symbolic model checker, but for tractability reasons leaves out: negative conditions in transformation rules; dealing with class attributes; inheritance and other complex relations in metamodels and their instances. Moreover, the proofs for the propositions stated during the formalization can be found at [6].

3.1 Graph Definitions

Definition 1. *Typed Graph*
A typed graph is a triple $\langle V, E, \tau \rangle$ where V is a finite set of vertices, $E \subseteq V \times V$ is a set of edges connecting the vertices and $\tau : V \to Type$ is a typing function for the elements of V, where $Type$ is a set of type names. Edges $(v, v') \in E$ are noted $v \to v'$. The set of all typed graphs is called TG.

Definition 2. *Typed Graph Union*
Let $\langle V, E, \tau \rangle, \langle V', E', \tau' \rangle \in TG$ be typed graphs. The typed graph union is the function $\sqcup : TG \times TG \to TG$ defined as:

$$\langle V, E, \tau \rangle \sqcup \langle V', E', \tau' \rangle = \langle V \cup V', E \cup E', \tau \cup \tau' \rangle$$

Definition 3. *Typed Subgraph*
Let $\langle V, E, \tau \rangle = g, \langle V', E', \tau' \rangle = g' \in TG$ be typed graphs. g' is a typed subgraph of g, written $g' \blacktriangleleft g$ iff for all $v_1' \to v_2' \in E'$ there is a $v_1 \to v_2 \in E$ such that $\tau'(v_1') = \tau(v_1)$ and $\tau'(v_2') = \tau(v_2)$.

Notice that the notion of subgraph in the context of typed graphs is not directly concerned with the topology of the involved graphs, but rather with the topology of the nodes having the same type.

3.2   Metamodel, Model and Transformation Definitions

We start by defining the notion of metamodel. A couple of metamodels were introduced in Fig. 1 and can be seen as typed graphs where the nodes are classes and the edges are associations.

Definition 4. *Metamodel*
A metamodel $\langle V, E, \tau \rangle \in TG$ is a typed graph where τ is a bijective typing function. The set of all metamodels is called META.

Formally, a metamodel corresponds to a graph of typed elements where only one element for each type is represented.

Let us now define the notion of model. Two models can be observed in Fig. 3 and can also be seen as typed graphs, instances of a given metamodel. Only, as can be observed in Fig. 3, models can have several instances of the same type.

Definition 5. *Model*
A model is a 4-tuple $\langle V, E, \tau, M \rangle$ where $\langle V, E, \tau \rangle$ is a typed graph. Moreover $M = \langle V', E', \tau' \rangle \in META$ is a Metamodel and the codomain of τ equals the codomain of τ'. Finally $\langle V, E, \tau \rangle \blacktriangleleft M$, which means $\langle V, E, \tau \rangle$ is an instance of a metamodel M. The set of all models for a metamodel M is called $MODEL^M$.

Definition 6. *Match-Apply Model*
A Match-Apply Model is a 6-tuple $\langle V, E, \tau, Match, Apply, Bl \rangle$, where $Match = \langle V', E', \tau', s \rangle$ and $Apply = \langle V'', E'', \tau'', t \rangle$ are models, $V = V' \cup V''$, $E = E' \cup E'' \cup Bl$ and $\tau = \tau' \cup \tau''$. Edges $Bl \subseteq V' \times V''$ are called backward links. s is called the source metamodel and t the target metamodel. The set of all Match-Apply models for a source metamodel s and a target metamodel t is called MAM_t^s.

A match-apply model is an extended definition of a model which is suited to define the semantics of a model transformation. Given the semantics of DSLTrans which keeps the source model unchanged and modifies the apply model as several transformations are applied, a match-apply model is a suitable formalism to store the intermediate steps of a transformation. In particular, the *backward links* allow keeping a history of which elements in the match model created which elements in the apply model.

Definition 7. *Transformation Rule*
A *Transformation Rule* is a 7-tuple $\langle V, E \cup Il, \tau, Match, Apply, Bl, Il \rangle$, where $\langle V, E, \tau, Match, Apply, Bl \rangle \in MAM_t^s$ is a match-apply model. $Match = \langle V', E', \tau', s \rangle$ and the edges $Il \subseteq V' \times V'$ are called indirect links. The set of all transformation rules having source metamodel s and target metamodel t is called TR_t^s.

We define a *transformation rule* as a particular kind of match-apply model which allows *indirect links* in the *match* pattern, but not in the *apply* one. The reason for this is that *match* patterns can be more abstract than models, but *apply* patterns define — in fact build — instances of models. In Fig. 2, we have presented several examples of transformation rules.

Definition 8. *Property*
A *Property* is a 7-tuple $\langle V, E \cup Il, \tau, Match, Apply, Bl, Il \rangle$,
where $\langle V, E, \tau, Match, Apply, Bl \rangle \in MAM_t^s$ is a match-apply model. $Match = \langle V', E', \tau', s \rangle$, $Apply = \langle V'', E'', \tau'', t \rangle$ and the edges $Il \subseteq (V' \times V') \cup (V'' \times V'')$ are called indirect links. The set of all properties having source metamodel s and target metamodel t is called $Property_t^s$.

The language to describe properties is in fact very similar to the language to express transformations, with the additional possibility of expressing indirect links in the *apply* pattern — thus allowing more abstract patterns than the ones expressed in transformations. This is natural given that the properties of a transformation can be more abstract than the rules implementing them.

Finally, we define *layers* as sets of transformation rules and *transformations* as lists of layers.

Definition 9. *Layer, Transformation*
A *layer* is a finite set of transformation rules $tr \subseteq TR_t^s$. The set of all layers for a source metamodel s and a target metamodel t is called $Layer_t^s$. A *transformation* is a finite list of layers denoted $[l_1 :: l_2 :: \ldots :: l_n]$ where $l_k \in Layer_t^s$ and $1 \leq k \leq n$. The set of all transformations for a source metamodel s and a target metamodel t is called $Transformation_t^s$.

We naturally extend the notion of union in definition 2 to models (definition 5), match-apply models (definition 6) and transformation rules (definition 7).

3.3 Transformation Collapse Definitions

Let us now define some useful functions for the construction of a transformation's state space. The Graph Node Collapse function allows merging two nodes of a graph having the same type. This function is subsequently used by the Graph

Collapse Function that recursively builds a set of all the possible collapsed graphs from a graph.

Definition 10. *Graph Node Collapse*
Let $\langle V, E, \tau \rangle \in TG$ be a typed graph. A graph node collapse is a function χ : $TG \to \mathcal{P}(TG)$ such that:

$$\chi_{\langle V,E,\tau \rangle} = \big\{ \langle V \backslash \{y\}, E', \tau \backslash (y, \tau(y)) \rangle \mid$$
$$x, y \in V \wedge \tau(x) = \tau(y) \wedge$$
$$E' = \{(x, z) \mid (y, z) \in E\} \cup$$
$$\{(z, x) \mid (z, y) \in E\} \cup$$
$$\{(w, z) \mid (w, z) \in E \wedge w \neq y \wedge z \neq y\}\big\}$$

This definition is naturally extended to transformations TR_t^s by limiting the two elements x and y that are collapsed to be either members of the Match pattern of the transformation or elements that are connected by a backward link.

Definition 11. *Graph Collapse Function*
Let $g \in TG$ be a typed graph. The graph collapse function collapse : $TG \to \mathcal{P}(TG)$ is recursively defined as:

$$collapse(g) = \begin{cases} \{g\} & \text{if } \chi_g = \emptyset \\ \chi_g \cup \{g\} \cup \bigcup_{g' \in \chi_g} collapse(g') & \text{if } \chi_g \neq \emptyset \end{cases}$$

This definition is also naturally extended to transformation rules TR_t^s.

Proposition 1. *Finiteness of the result of the graph collapse function*
Let $\langle V, E, \tau \rangle \in TG$ be a typed graph. The collapsed graph set collapse($\langle V, E, \tau \rangle$) is a finite set of graphs, each graph in that set having a finite set of nodes.

3.4   State Space

In order to define the state space for a transformation let us start by defining the possible combinations of transformations within a layer. More than that, we also define a label for each of those combinations of transformation which is used as label for the transitions in the transformation state space we build. These labels hold the identifiers of the transformations leading to a state and will be subsequently used to build counterexamples for properties that are unsatisfiable.

Definition 12. *Layer combinations*
Let $l \in Layer_t^s$ be a layer. The set of layer combinations CL_l is obtained as follows:

$$CL_l = \bigcup_{tc \in \mathcal{P}(l)} (tc, \bigsqcup_{t \in tc} t)$$

Definition 13. *Transformation state space*
Let $tr = [l_1 :: \ldots :: l_n] \in Transformation_t^s$ be a transformation. The transformation state space $SP_{tr} \subseteq TR_t^s \times (\mathcal{P}(TR_t^s) \times \mathbb{N}) \times TR_t^s$ is the least set that satisfies the following rules:

$$\frac{(tc, ut) \in CL_{l1}, tr = [l_1 :: R] \in Transformation_t^s, st \in collapse(ut)}{\langle \emptyset, \emptyset, \emptyset, \emptyset, \emptyset, \emptyset \rangle \xrightarrow{tc_1} st \in SP_{tr}}$$

$$\frac{\begin{array}{c} tr = [H :: l_k :: l_{k+1} :: R] \in Transformation_t^s, st \xrightarrow{tc_k} st' \in SP_{tr} \\ tc \in \mathcal{P}(l_k), (tc', ut) \in CL_{l_{k+1}}, st'' \in collapse(st' \sqcup ut) \mid st' \end{array}}{st' \xrightarrow{tc'_{k+1}} st'' \in SP_{tr}}$$

Notice that H and R are lists. We also define SP_{tr}^* as the transitive closure of SP_{tr}. The $\mid : \mathcal{P}(TR_t^s) \times TR_t^s \to \mathcal{P}(TR_t^s)$ operator enforces that the backward links existing in the second parameter transformation also exist in the transformations of the first parameter.

We now build the state space for a transformation by gathering all the combinations of transformations for each layer, the result of collapsing them, and building the state space as shown in Fig. 5. Notice in particular that the second inference rule in definition 13 merges the states from a previous layer k and from the current layer $k + 1$. Notice also that all transitions in the transition state space are labeled with the transformations tc_k from the previous k layer that caused it.

Proposition 2. *Finiteness of the transformation state space*
Let $[l_1 \ldots l_n] \in Transformation_t^s$ be a transformation. The transformation state space $SP_{[l_1 \ldots l_n]}$ is finite.

The result in proposition 2 is crucial since by definition model checking can only be performed on finite state spaces.

3.5   Property Semantics

Let us now proceed to formally define the semantics of our properties in the state space generated by the rules of definition 13. As we have stated in section 2, a property can be *satisfiable, unsatisfiable* or *non provable*. We start with the definition of a state in a state space (formally defined as a transformation) being model of a property. As a reminder, each state of the state space is a symbolic representation of a set of models given as input to the transformation being validated and their corresponding transformations. In fact, a state holds a set of patterns that should be instantiated in the input model — the *match* part of the state — as well as in the output model — the *apply* part of the state. By validating a property at the level of the symbolic states, we validate it for the whole set of input and output models of a given transformation.

Definition 14. *Model of a Property*
A transformation rule $\langle V_r, E_r, \tau_r, Match_r, Apply_r, Il_r \rangle = T \in TR_t^s$ *is a model of a property* $\langle V_p, E_p, \tau_p, Match_p, Apply_p, Il_p \rangle = P \in Property_t^s$, *written* $T \vDash^s P$ *if:*

1. $\langle V_p, E_p \setminus Il_p, \tau_p \rangle$ *is a typed subgraph of* $\langle V_r, E_r, \tau_r \rangle$
2. *if* $v_p \to v_p' \in Il_p$ *then there exists* $v_r \to v_r' \in E_r^*$ *where* $\tau(v_p) = \tau(v_r)$, $\tau(v_p') = \tau(v_r')$ *and* E_r^* *is obtained by the transitive closure of* E_r.

Definition 15. *Satisfiable Property*
Let $tr = [l_1 :: \ldots :: l_n] \in Transformation_t^s$ *be a transformation.* tr *satisfies property* $P \in Property_t^s$, *written* $tr \vDash P$, *where:*

$$tr \vDash P \Leftrightarrow \forall s_0 \xrightarrow{lb_0} \ldots \xrightarrow{lb_n} s_n \in SP_{tr}^* . (\exists i . s_i \vDash^s match(P)) \Rightarrow (\exists j \geq i . s_j \vDash^s P)$$

where $s_0 = \langle \emptyset, \emptyset, \emptyset, \emptyset, \emptyset, \emptyset \rangle$ and $0 \leq i \leq j \leq n$.

Informally, for all paths belonging to tr's state space, if the property's *match* pattern is found in a given state, then a subsequent state in that path is model of the property. Note that the projection function *match* returns the match pattern of a property.

Definition 16. *Unsatisfiable Property*
Let $tr = [l_1 :: \ldots :: l_n] \in Transformation_t^s$ *be a transformation.* $tr \in TR$ *does not satisfy property* $P \in Property_t^s$, *written* $tr \nvDash P$, *where:*

$$tr \nvDash P \Leftrightarrow \exists s_0 \xrightarrow{lb_0} \ldots \xrightarrow{lb_n} s_n \in SP_{tr}^* . (\exists i . s_i \vDash^s match(P)) \Rightarrow (\nexists j \geq i . s_j \vDash^s P)$$

where $s_0 = \langle \emptyset, \emptyset, \emptyset, \emptyset, \emptyset, \emptyset \rangle$ and $0 \leq i \leq j \leq n$.

The sequence $lb_0, \ldots, lb_n$ *is called a* counterexample *for property* P *in transformation* tr.

Informally, there exists a path belonging to tr's state space where the property's *match* pattern is found in a given state, but no subsequent state in that path is model of the property.

Definition 17. *Non Provable Property*
Let $tr = [l_1 :: \ldots :: l_n] \in Transformation_t^s$ *be a transformation. A property* $P \in Property_t^s$ *is not provable for* tr, *written* $tr \nVdash P$, *where:*

$$tr \nVdash P \Leftrightarrow \forall s_0 \xrightarrow{lb_0} \ldots \xrightarrow{lb_n} s_n \in SP_{tr}^* . (\nexists i . s_i) \vDash^s match(P)$$

where $s_0 = \langle \emptyset, \emptyset, \emptyset, \emptyset, \emptyset, \emptyset \rangle$ and $0 \leq i \leq n$.

Again informally, the *match* pattern can never be found in any state of the state space of tr.

4   Experimentation and Results

Using our implementation — downloadable at [7] — in SWI-Prolog, we have generated a state space for the the presented police station transformation, resulting in a state space with an order of magnitude of 10^4 states. Our implementation reflects the formalization in section 3. The transformation description in DSLTrans is represented as a set of facts in a entity/relationship schema, and the generated state space is represented as a list of transition predicates $t(LayerId,SquareGraphComb, Label, SquareGraphComb')$. The layer identifier $LayerId$ precisely identifies the depth position of each of the transition's states, in the overall state space. Each state $SquareGraphComb$ and $SquareGraphComb'$ is represented as predicate $graph(match(Match),apply(Apply),blinks(BLinks))$, where $Match$, $Apply$ and $BLinks$ are lists of entities and relations which were merged and combined from the given transformation description.

5   Conclusions and Future Work

In this paper we have presented a model checker for model transformations expressed in the DSLTrans language. The transformations in DSLTrans are by construction confluent and terminating [3]. We have added to the language the possibility to establish syntactic structural correspondences between patterns in the source language and patterns in the target language of the transformation. This correspondence, which we call properties, is checked in a finite state space which is generated by all the possible combinations of applications of the rules specified in the transformation. Once one such property is validated for the transformation at the meta level, we can certify that it holds for all input instances of that transformation. As future work, we will perform experiments on larger transformation and address spatial and time complexities in our state space generation algorithm. Given that, on average, many states for a given state space share the same structure, we are considering using BDD-like structures [4] to compact space and accelerate state space calculation and property proof. Another possibility is to use available model checkers as interpreters for our algorithm. In this fashion we could benefit from already studied state space explosion control mechanisms. Finally, the study presented in this paper needs to be extended to structures with more semantic content than the one that can be represented by plain typed graphs. With this work we have made significant progress in understanding the fundamental issues in building a model checker for model transformations. However, a more detailed understanding and formalization of the semantics of metamodels, models and properties is needed in order to build proofs at the level of abstraction a transformation engineer would require.

References

1. Anastasakis, K., Bordbar, B., Küster, J.: Analysis of model transformations via alloy. In: Baudry, B., Faivre, A., Ghosh, S., Pretschner, A. (eds.) Proceedings of the workshop on Model-Driven Engineering, Verification and Validation (MoDeVVA 2007), Nashville, TN, USA, pp. 47–56. Springer, Heidelberg (October 2007)

2. Asztalos, M., Lengyel, L., Levendovszky, T.: Towards automated, formal verification of model transformations. In: ICST 2010: Proceedings of the 3rd International Conference on Software Testing, Verification and Validation, pp. 15–24. IEEE Computer Society, Los Alamitos (2010)
3. Barroca, B., Lucio, L., Amaral, V., Felix, R., Sousa, V.: A visual language for model transformations. Technical report, UNL-DI-2-2010, University Nova de Lisboa, Portugal (2010), http://solar.di.fct.unl.pt/twiki/pub/BATICCCS/ModelTransformationPapers/vltechrep.pdf
4. Bryant, R.E.: Graph-based algorithms for boolean function manipulation. IEEE Trans. Computers 35(8), 677–691 (1986)
5. Falleri, J.-R., Huchard, M., Lafourcade, M., Nebut, C.: Metamodel matching for automatic model transformation generation. In: Czarnecki, K., Ober, I., Bruel, J.-M., Uhl, A., Völter, M. (eds.) MODELS 2008. LNCS, vol. 5301, pp. 326–340. Springer, Heidelberg (2008)
6. SOLAR Group. Detailed proofs for the paper: a technique for automatic validation of model transformations, http://solar.di.fct.unl.pt/twiki/pub/BATICCCS/ModelTransformationPapers/detailed_proofs.pdf
7. SOLAR Group. Transformation model checker, http://solar.di.fct.unl.pt/twiki/pub/BATICCCS/ReleaseFiles/transmc.zip
8. SOLAR Group. Transforming uml to java using dsltrans, http://solar.di.fct.unl.pt/twiki/pub/BATICCCS/ModelTransformationPapers/UML2Java.zip
9. Jouault, F., Kurtev, I.: Transforming models with atl. In: Bruel, J.-M. (ed.) MoDELS 2005. LNCS, vol. 3844, pp. 128–138. Springer, Heidelberg (2005)
10. Narayanan, A., Karsai, G.: Verifying model transformations by structural correspondence. ECEASST, 10 (2008)
11. Object Management Group. Query/view/specification (December 2005), http://www.omg.org/cgi-bin/apps/doc?ptc/05-11-01.pdf

Static- and Dynamic Consistency Analysis of UML State Chart Models

Christian Schwarzl[1] and Bernhard Peischl[2]

[1] Virtual Vehicle, Vehicle Electrics/Electronics and Software,
8010 Graz, Austria
christian.schwarzl@v2c2.at
[2] Graz University of Technology, Institute for Software Technology,
8010 Graz, Austria
bernhard.peischl@ist.tugraz.at

Abstract. UML state chart models describing the behavior of a system can be used as a formal specification thereof. The existence of advanced modeling tools allows for model simulation and enables the execution of manually created tests on the models. In this work the usage of static and dynamic model analysis techniques is proposed to reveal errors in these models. The static analysis focuses on the syntax, communication structure and non-determinism. The dynamic analysis is based on a random test approach and can reveal bugs like deadlocks and inter-model loops. Further the data generated during the dynamic analysis allows for additional correctness checks such as e.g. the number or lengths of paths. The presented approach is implemented in a prototype and revealed several bugs in an industrial case study not found during simulation and manual model testing.

1 Introduction

Model development in an industrial setting is a challenging task due to the large size and the number of interacting models. These models can also be used as a formal specification for suppliers delivering the actual implementation of an e.g. electronic control unit (ECU). Particularly in such scenarios the presence of bugs in the model is critical due to the high cost, caused if the bug is found at a late stage of the development process like integration testing. The existence of a formal specification of the system behavior also suggests the automatic generation of test cases based on these models. For this reason the correctness of the model is key to enable a model based development and test process.

The existence of advanced modeling tools like Rhapsody [1] allows the generation of executable code from behavioral UML state chart models [2]. This code can be executed and used to exercise the models in a simulation. Due to the simulation it is possible to test the developed models manually, which is necessary to reveal possible bugs. Although various industrial tools [3,4] and research prototypes [5,6,7] for test generation exist, they rely on a correct specification of the system.

D.C. Petriu, N. Rouquette, Ø. Haugen (Eds.): MODELS 2010, Part I, LNCS 6394, pp. 151–165, 2010.

The current approach suggests the usage of static model analysis and techniques used for test case generation to enhance the model correctness of UML state chart models. During static model inspection the model structure as well as the contained code is automatically checked against common errors listed below. Although static analysis methods are already implemented in various tools, a more complete set is provided in this approach:

- **Syntax:** The code on the model contained in the actions of transitions and states as well as the transition guards are examined with respect to the defined grammar.
- **Existence:** A check is performed whether all variables and attributes used in guards and actions are defined on the model.
- **Data type:** The data types occurring within an assignment have to have the same data type. This prevents for example the assignment of incompatible types like floating point values to integer variables.
- **Communication:** In particular the possibility of a message reception in the target model of a send command is considered. A model has to have at least one transition triggered by a message sent by another model.
- **Non determinism:** The existence of non deterministic behavior caused by overlapping parameter ranges is verified. An overlapping parameter range can occur if a state has multiple outgoing transitions triggered by the same event, which has at least one parameter. The value range of each event parameter is defined by the guard of its according transition. An overlap causing non determinism exists if an intersection between any pair of value ranges is not empty.
- **Transition hiding:** During this test the traversability of all transitions is checked. A transition cannot be traversed if a transition with the same input message and higher priority exists, which covers the same or a larger parameter range.

Given syntactically correct state chart models their described behavior can still have inconsistencies, which can not be detected during a static analysis. For this reason suitable test suites are required to ensure the intended behavior of the system models. The preparation of such test suites is a tedious task and is usually performed manually. Another approach is the usage of automatic white-box testing techniques like random testing. These techniques allow the automatic execution of the models by using random input parameters. Although this methods can drive models into failure situations, the automatic failure detection is hard to achieve. The reason is that the reactions of a given input can not be checked due to the missing oracle.

In contrast a random walk, which is introduced in this work, enables the automatic detection of such situations whereby a failure trace is provided. This is achieved by the usage of a different concept where the input needed to achieve a certain reaction is calculated. In particular the following model failures can be revealed:

- **Deadlock:** A model reaches a state including the valuation of its attributes prohibiting the traversal of every outgoing transition.

- **Infeasible transitions:** A transition is infeasible if it is triggered by a sent message of another model and no path on any of these sender model exists, which can fulfill its guard.
- **Inter-model loops:** Inter-model loops are circular dependencies in the model communication structure. For example a message reception m_r in model $M1$ depends on model $M2$ whereby $M2$ depends on $M1$ to be able to send the desired message m_r.

In addition to the static and dynamic model analysis the usage of assertions on the models is proposed. These checks can take place at two different stages during the analysis process:

1. **Model:** Assertions on the model contain usually conditions on message variables and attributes, which have to be fulfilled during the simulation.
2. **Dynamic analysis:** This type of assertions performs checks, which allows to state necessary conditions on the generated paths during the message resolution (see Section 5). This can for example contain the number of generated paths or its visited states.

The concepts already efficiently used in software development can also improve the model development quality. The main advantages of the presented approach are its automatism and the incorporation of multiple strategies to ensure the syntactical and enhance the semantic correctness. Further it generates failure traces. A failure trace describes the path through the model, which leads to the found failure and can be extremely helpful for debugging.

Section 2 gives an overview of the used UML elements and introduces an example containing several modeling flaws. In Section 3 and 4 the static and dynamic consistency checks are presented. The algorithms used for handling the communication dependencies between the models is described in Section 5. The obtained results from an industrial case study are shown in Section 6 and Section 7 discusses related work. Finally a conclusion is given in Section 8.

2   Example Model

A UML state chart consists of states, transitions, variables and their according values. Thereby a transition consists of an event, which can be created by an according message reception of the model, a guard and an action. The guard defines a condition, which must be satisfied to enable the traversal. Finally actions can be specified on each transition to assign values to variables or to send messages to other models. UML also allows to model transitions without an event. These transitions are called *completion transitions* and are traversed as soon their guard evaluates to true.

In addition to these basic elements, a state chart can also have pseudo states, entry- and exit-actions on states, sub states and nested state charts, which simplifies the modeling process. Pseudo states are special states, which do not describe

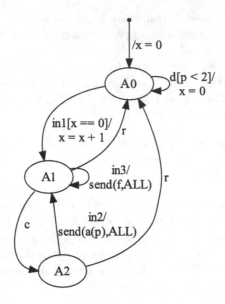

Fig. 1. Model A

a system state but provide various functionalities to simplify modeling. The presented approach can handle *condition states, junction states, deep history, entry-* and *exit points* and *diagram connectors*.

Condition states have at least one incoming and several outgoing transitions where the outgoing transition guards must differ. The usage of junction states allows the reduction of the number of transitions by merging multiple incoming transitions into one outgoing. Entry- and exit states are always used in pairs, because they establish interfaces between nested state chart models and other states. A nested state chart model (NSCM) is an additional SCM, which is embedded in a state. Transitions into deep history states behave like they were linked to the deepest, last visited sub state of the state, in which the history state lies. A sub state lies within another state and can also have sub states or an NSCM. Diagram connectors allow the direct connection of two states beyond the borders of nested state charts.

In the remainder a transition is given as an arrow connecting a source- (S_s) and target-state (S_t) following the syntax $S_s \xrightarrow{event[guard]/action} S_t$. The initial state is defined through a default transition, which starts from a point instead of a state and can only have actions. The Figures 1,2 and 3 show the behavior description of an illustrative example. These models contain the following bugs, inefficiencies and assertions described in Section 3 and 4.

1. **Inter-model loop:** $A1 \xrightarrow{c} A2$ is part of an inter-model loop between *Model A* and *Model B*.
2. **Deadlock:** On $A1, A2 \xrightarrow{r} A0$ the assignment $x = 0$ is missing, which leads to a deadlock. This cannot be found by random testing, because during a

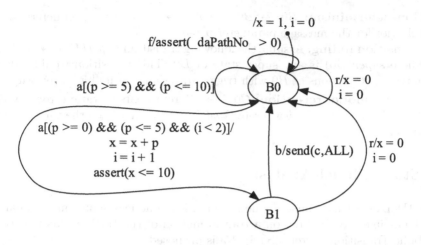

Fig. 2. Model B

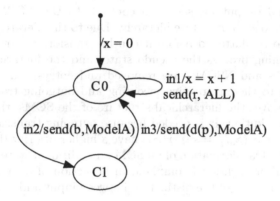

Fig. 3. Model C

random test it is impossible to distinguish, whether the message reception is required for a correct behavior. The reason is that both behaviors are valid scenarios in UML. In contrast a random walk can detect the dead-lock, because it will not find a valid path during communication dependency resolution. This results from the fact that no traversable transition in this system state exists.

3. **Code level Assertion:** $B0 \xrightarrow{a} B1$ shows an example of code level assertion. The default transition $\bullet \xrightarrow{/x=1, i=0} B0$ with the incorrect assignment $x = 1$ instead of $x = 0$ enables this code level assertion to fail, if the transitions $B0 \xrightarrow{a((p \geq 0) \&\& (p \leq 5) \&\& (i \leq 2))} B1 \xrightarrow{b} B0$ are traversed twice.

4. **Dynamic analysis assertion:** In $B0 \xrightarrow{f} B0$ an example of dynamic analysis assertion is given.

5. **Non-determinism:** $B0 \xrightarrow{a} B0$ and $B0 \xrightarrow{a} B1$ allow a non-deterministic behavior for the message parameter $p = 5$.

6. **Transition hiding:** Assume the following transition $super(B0) \xrightarrow{a} B^*$ exists where $super(B0)$ is any super state of $B0$. This transition would hide all outgoing transitions of $B0$ with trigger a, because of its higher priority.

7. **Missing model reception:** $C0 \xrightarrow{in1} C1$ represents a static error, because *ModelA* cannot receive b whereby *ModelB* would have been the correct target model.

3   Static Model Analysis

Since UML SCMs have an ambiguous semantic a unique dynamic model analysis is not possible. For this reason a transformation of the UML SCMs into the a Symbolic Transition System (STS) [15] is proposed.

An STS has a similar but reduced set of modeling elements. It also consists of states, variables and transitions, whereby a transition distinguishes clearly between input and output messages. In contrast to UML SCMs it does not facilitate any pseudo state nor state hierarchy. Due to the hierarchical structure, every SCM has to be flattened before it can be transformed into an STS [10]. During the flattening process the pseudo states and the hierarchy, introduced through sub states and NSCMs, are removed and entry- and exit-actions on states are moved to their respective incoming and outgoing transitions. Since the flattening removes the hierarchical structure of the SCMs, this information has to be kept in addition. It is needed because outgoing transitions of a super state S_{sup} of a state S ($S_{sup} = super(S)$) have a higher priority than transitions from S. During the transformation of an SCM an additional state and transition has to be created for each send command in an action of an UML transition. This is necessary because of the distinction between input and output messages.

Model Structure: Initially the model structure is checked against some defined rules. These rules state in general the structural requirements, which have to be fulfilled by the model. For example the number of incoming and outgoing transitions needed for a certain pseudo state can be defined. In addition checks on events, guards and actions can be performed. Default transitions for example must not have a guard or an event at all whereas every outgoing transition of a condition state must have a guard and again no event is allowed. Also the existence of elements like default transitions in a state, if multiple sub states exist, can be verified.

Textual Model Parts: During parsing of each assignment or condition a tree containing all operators and operands is built. Each element contains the variable name or the static value given in the model allowing for a data type check. The data types are defined through the attributes and message parameters, which have to be defined on the UML model in advance. The data types of constant values in the actions or guard are identified through their syntax; e.g. using points for float which are not found in integer values. In addition the syntax of the whole statement or condition, respectively, is checked during parsing. Also the existence of attributes to which values are assigned or which are used in conditions can be checked, because they have to be modeled in the SCM.

Model Message Reception: While building the communication structure containing all message dependencies between the models, a possible reception can be found easily. A failure is found if a message is sent to a model, which cannot receive the message at all. This is likely to be an error in the model. If a message is broad-casted to all available models this checks loose detail, because it can only be verified if any model can receive the message. In addition a warning is given if only one receiver is found, which could be an actual model error, but is at least a source for future complications.

Transition Hiding: This checks the message parameter ranges of equal messages on transitions leaving the same state or a super state of a state. UML defines that a transition leaving a super state has a higher priority than transitions from a sub state. Therefore it is possible that a transition cannot be executed at all because no according parameter value exists. For this reason it has to be ensured that parameter values exist, which allow only guards of transitions with a lower priority evaluating to true. This can be achieved by iterating through every outgoing input transition of every state in the STS and by calculating a parameter valuation for the respective extended guards. These extended guards consist of the condition initially defined on the transition and the inversed guards of all transitions with the same input message with a higher or equal priority. If the extended guard cannot be solved then no valuation exists, which allows the transition to be traversed. This makes the transition obsolete and indicates a modeling error.

Non-determinism: The detection of non-determinism based on overlapping parameter ranges is similar to the detection of hidden transitions. Both have a condition in common, which contains multiple guards. The difference is, that the condition is constructed for every transition pair triggered by the same message. This condition is a conjunction of the two guards. If the condition can be solved then an overlapping parameter range is detected and a non-deterministic behavior is found.

4 Dynamic Model Analysis

The dynamic model analysis focuses on modeling errors, which are syntactically correct but lead to unexpected or unwanted behavior commonly known as bugs. Since testing is a time consuming process, a fully automatic technique for consistency analysis is proposed. It is based on a random walk through the model and uses structural communication dependency resolution methods to find possible paths through the concurrent models.

An exhaustive model analysis would require the execution of the possibly infinite number of paths caused by e.g. loops. This situation is intensified by the usage of data causing a state space explosion, which makes the use of e.g. model checkers impossible. The random walk approach needs only to consider a fraction of the state space at a time, because the models are traversed stepwise. A step in this context means the random selection of a transition and the generation of paths allowing its traversal. In each step the concrete values of the previous step can be used to reduce the size of the state space. Although the presented message dependency resolution algorithm can – in the worst case – lead to an exponential path growth, the absolute number of possibilities is vastly reduced. Due to the loss of exhaustiveness the absence of bugs cannot be guaranteed, but the detection power increases with the number of performed steps during a random walk.

Deadlocks: During a random walk a transition is randomly selected, its communication dependencies are resolved as described in Section 5 and then traversed. A deadlock occurs if a state in the model is reached, which does not have any traversable outgoing transitions. There are basically two possibilities how the deadlock can occur:

First it can be a modeling error, which leads to the deadlock if the model is exercised in a certain way. A typical example is given in Figure 1. In this example the outgoing transition $A0 \xrightarrow{in1[x==0]/x=x+1} A1$ has a condition on attributes in the guard, which were not set accordingly to $x = 0$ in $A1, A2 \xrightarrow{r}$ $A0$ before entering the state. This leads to a deadlock after two traversals of $A0 \xrightarrow{d[p<2]/x=0} A0$, because this transition becomes infeasible. The reason is its dependency on $Model\ C$ (see Figure 3) where the sent parameter increases with every traversal.

The second possibility is that the used path generation algorithms failed to create a valid path. This can be a result of the needed restrictions on the generation technique to be able to handle the possibly infinite number of paths. However, the restrictions can be chosen by the model developer and therefore the requirements given by the model can be taken into account to circumvent this situation.

Infeasible transitions: Assume the path generation techniques described in Section 5 are chosen appropriate to suffice the model requirements. This means that if no valid path can be created then there exists no path at all allowing the selected transition to be traversed for the current system state. Since in general the guard of the selected transition allows the traversal, the fact that it cannot be triggered by any path implies that this transition or its guard, respectively, must be infeasible. This is illustrated in the following example consisting of two transitions where p is the input parameter, which can be chosen for the message im in the given range: $D0 \xrightarrow{im[0 \leq p \leq 10]/send(g(p), ALL)} D1, E0 \xrightarrow{g[20 \leq p \leq 30]} E1$. In this example a correct message is sent but the required input parameter range for a is disjunct from the parameters possible for im. For this reason no input value can be generated leading to an infeasible transition.

If the stated assumption does not hold false positives are likely to be created. However, in this case the false positives can be seen as warning, because the behavior differs from the model developer conception, which leads to the inappropriate chosen restrictions.

Inter-model loops: Inter-model loops occur, if the model communication has a circular dependency. This means that a reception of a message in one model depends on a second one, which depends on the first model to create the particular message (see messages c and a in Figures 1 and 2). Such model constructs are erroneous, because – as shown in the given example – the circular dependent transition can never be traversed. The reason is that due to the circular dependency a transition has to be traversed before the desired transition. In the special case where the circular dependent transition is part of a loop this behavior could be correct – assuming the model attributes still have values so that the guard of the desired transition remains true – but is still bad modeling practice and could lead to false positives during a static analysis. Usually such transitions lead to another state prohibiting the traversal of the initial desired transition traversal.

Failure trace: The creation of traces through the models revealing errors in the model are particularly useful for debugging and bug fixing. Due to the usage of a random walk such a failure trace can be created by recording the selected transitions including the used parameter values. These traces can also be stored and replayed for e.g. regression testing.

Assertions: Assertions can be used to define additional checks during the model simulation. They can check the system state or use data available during the dynamic analysis in the presented approach and are given by the keyword *assert*. An example of both assertion types is given in Figure 2 where transition $B0 \xrightarrow{f} B0$ uses a condition on data of the dynamic analysis ($\_daPathNo\_$) and $B0 \xrightarrow{a[(p \geq 0)\&\&(p \leq 5)\&\&(i<2)]} B1$ defines a check on the system state.

The first assertion uses information only available during the random walk. In particular it is possible to check data like the number of valid paths created for a given transition as presented in the example. In addition various parameters can be checked like the length of the paths, visited states or transitions or the sender models of required messages. These kind of assertion generally allows for expressing the model developer's intention of the behavior and provides warnings and error messages if conflicts occur.

The second assertion type allows for additional checks on the model by incorporating the structure and the parameter values. They are equal to assertions used in code in software development and are a helpful extension to identify inconsistencies. The example given above can reveal the incorrect assignment of $x = 1$ on the default transition in *Model B* after traversing the transition $B0 \xrightarrow{a[(p \geq 0)\&\&(p \leq 5)\&\&(i<2)]} B1$ if no intermediate reset r is received.

5 Message Dependency Resolution

Due to the communication among the models their dependencies, which are defined through their input-/output behavior, have to be incorporated in the input generation. In general this means that the reactions on a message reception sent by another model as well as the detection of paths ensuring the dispatch of a wanted message have to be taken into account. This approach uses path search algorithms on the basis of STS and symbolic execution techniques to guarantee their validity. The path validity can be ensured by building and solving its path constraint, which is built bottom up and contains all guards and actions needed to uniquely traverse the whole path. A path is only valid if its path constraint can be solved by a constraint solver like GNU Prolog, meaning that a valuation for all involved attributes and message parameters exists, which fulfills all conditions on the path.

Possible non deterministic behavior depending on the occurring parameter values can be eliminated during the path constraint creation. This is achieved by incorporating the inversed guards of all transitions, which have the same message as trigger. The same is true for completion transitions where also a deterministic behavior can be guaranteed. Since it is possible that a parameter range of one guard is a full subset of the parameter range of another transition guard, no valid path containing these transitions having the parameter subset as guard will be found.

The path generation algorithms use depth first search (DFS), which can return multiple potential candidates. A selection from the obtained candidates based on criteria like length or coverage is possible to reduce the overall path number and therefore enhance scalability.

5.1 Input Message Creation

The directed creation of an input message reception is performed if the traversal of a designated transition is desired. In the simplest case – meaning the required message is not part of any model communication – this can be achieved by creating the message including the according parameter values. If the message is sent by at least one other model the arising dependencies have to be resolved. I.e. the required precondition for sending this particular message has to be determined. This procedure ensures that every involved model is in the same state as it would be if the message dispatch was initiated by itself.

Before the search for paths sending the desired message all possible models, which are capable of sending this message at all have to be identified. After the application of the path search algorithms on the identified models a selection algorithm is used to determine the paths for further processing.

Since these paths can also communicate with other models, which must be resolved before the path validity can be checked, the same technique as described in this section is used for every input message sent by another model on the paths. Due to the fact that these created paths can also send messages along the path, which are not the desired message for which the path was created initially, their influence on the receiving models has to be incorporated as described in the next section.

5.2 Output Message Execution

Whenever a message is sent between models the possible reactions of the receiving models have to be taken into account. These reactions range from no influence at all – if the receiver model is in a state where the message is not accepted – to multiple different, possibly non deterministic behaviors depending on the message parameters. This stems from the fact that the current state of a model may have multiple outgoing transitions with the same input message. In this case a path for every reception possibility, including the situation where no transition can be traversed, because none of their guards evaluates to true for specific message parameter values, has to be created.

The number of possibilities is also extended by completion transitions after the receiving transition where each assigned guard can evaluate to true or false. Again, non deterministic behavior can occur if guards have overlapping parameter ranges. However this can be prevented, if the inversed guard is taken into account during the path constraint construction.

6   Results

The presented results were obtained from a prototype based on an UML state chart model depicting an industrial case study. The model consists of six communicating models containing 33 states and 154 transitions. To show the applicability of this approach eleven mutants were placed manually in the case study whereby the length of the random walk needed for the detection is presented. The following mutants were used:

1. Changed compare operators in guards: e.g. $\geq$ instead of $<$.
2. Incorrect or missing assignments of attributes: e.g. $x = y$; instead of $x = z$;
3. Missing send commands: a message sending was intended by the modeler but actually not performed in the model

These mutants are a selection of faults often introduced during software development, whereas the presented approach is not limited to them. The results are focused on the infeasible transitions during the dynamic analysis. The reason is that no inter-model loops or deadlocks occur in the used model structure.

The used prototype was able to identify eight out of the eleven seeded faults whereby a found fault was removed immediately after its exposure, because its influence on the model communication. The three missed mutants could not be found by this algorithm, because – although the behavior was flawed – the model consistency was maintained. The results are presented in more detail in Table 1 and Figure 4 where the mean and standard deviation of the length l of the random walk for 50 independent runs for each number of alive mutants n are shown.

Table 1. Lengths (l) of random walks needed to detect one of the n faults

n	l	n	l
11	38 ± 24	7	154 ± 95
10	57 ± 41	6	164 ± 136
9	89 ± 78	5	544 ± 486
8	94 ± 59	4	676 ± 506

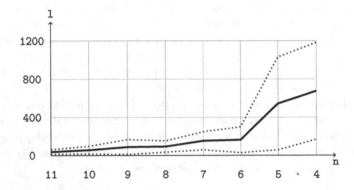

Fig. 4. Random walk lengths until a fault detection. The black line is the mean and the dotted lines represent the standard deviation of 50 runs.

The given mean reflects the fact that it is harder to find one bug out of few than of many. The simulations also clearly showed that the mutants directly influencing the consistency like incorrect message parameters were found first. The high standard deviation indicates a high variability in the detection time, which is directly influenced by the transition selection strategy used during the random walk.

The undetected three mutants could be revealed using the proposed code assertions by ensuring that the attribute values are consistent to the current state in the state chart model. In summary the presented approach was able to reveal all faults and is a useful technique to enhance the model consistency of communicating state chart models. The static analysis ensures a certain formalism of the model, which is then used to detect inconsistencies. While the dynamic analysis can be used without manual interaction, its detection power can be extended by the use of assertions added by the model developer.

7   Related Work

Model consistency is an increasing topic of interest due to the manifold applications in which models are used. This is reflected in the literature where various approaches were studied including different views on this complex topic. An overview of existing approaches and a brief glossary is given in [12].

Techniques like the data-flow testing [14] and constraint logic programming (CLP) have been proposed for consistency checks of class diagrams.

In [8,9] an assessment framework is proposed to check the consistency and semantic quality of models. The syntactical consistency is ensured by checking the model against a defined meta model and is performed fully automatically during the model development. In addition the semantic quality is improved by using queries and human domain knowledge. A query in this approach consists of a set of constraints, which have to be fulfilled by the model.

The usage of model checkers like Spin and UPPAAL to verify the behavioral model specification is proposed in [13] and [11]. Although good results have been achieved with these approaches the scalability – especially in the presence of data like attributes and message parameters – remains an open issue.

Random walks on behavioral models were performed by the test case generation tool TorX [6]. Since it is based on Labeled Transition Systems (LTS) [17] a transformation of the UML state chart models is needed. This can be achieved by using the process algebra LOTOS [20] as intermediate format and has been proposed in [19]. Again this approach suffers from the state space explosion problem due to the enumerative nature of LTS.

To overcome the state space explosion the usage of symbolic representations – where data is stored in variables – has been proposed in [7,15]. Both approaches use a symbolic transition system (STS) and perform random walks on the model. However, these approaches are limited to a single model and therefore cannot handle inter-model communication.

Symbolic execution was used for random white-box testing in the tool SAGE [18]. It is based on the code of the implementation under test (IUT) and uses symbolic techniques to trace the execution of random inputs. SAGE uses inverted constraints of the trace and code coverage heuristics to create new input data for enhancing code coverage capabilities. Although there are similarities in the input data generation between SAGE and the presented approach, SAGE is not able to handle changing communication structures depending on the system state.

8 Conclusion

Static and dynamic analysis methods have been proposed in this work to enhance the consistency of concurrent communicating state chart models. During the static analysis structural and syntactical failures on the model are detected and presented. Based on the syntactical correct model checks additional checks are performed to ensure model determinism, which could be violated by e.g. overlapping message parameter ranges. The static analysis is a simple to use straightforward technique and is a sound basis for model formalization.

Based on the formalized model dynamic analysis methods were performed to reveal behavioral bugs. This is done by a random walk, which traverses a model and resolves the model communication dependencies to create valid input sequences. Due to this methodology bugs like deadlocks and infeasible transitions can be revealed and according results were presented from an industrial case study. The empirical results show that the induced bugs could be found during the mutation test as long as they altered the consistency, which makes transitions infeasible. Changes in the behavior being correct by means of consistency can be revealed by the usage of assertions as proposed in this approach. They can – as known from software development – perform checks on the valuation of message parameters and attributes. In addition the data available during the resolution of the model communication dependencies can be verified. This allows for additional checks on the intended model behavior by incorporating its structure depending on the variable system state.

This approach can be extended in a future work by using the assertions not only for checks but include them explicitly during the communication dependency resolution to generate failure traces exploiting their condition. Also transition selection control methods for the random walk could improve the overall performance of this approach.

Acknowledgement

The authors wish to thank the "COMET K2 Forschungsförderungs-Programm" of the Austrian Federal Ministry for Transport, Innovation and Technology (BMVIT), the Austrian Federal Ministry of Economics and Labour (BMWA), Österreichische Forschungsförderungsgesellschaft mbH (FFG), Das Land Steiermark and Steirische Wirtschaftsförderung (SFG) for their financial support.

References

1. IBM: Rational   Rhapsody,   http://www-01.ibm.com/software/rational/products/rhapsody/developer/ (last visited July 2010)
2. OMG: UML Superstructure reference, http://www.omg.org/spec/UML/2.1.2/Superstructure/PDF/ (last visited April 2010)
3. Conformiq: Qtronic, http://www.conformiq.com/products.php (last visited April 2010)
4. Smartesting: Test Designer, http://www.smartesting.com/index.php/cms/en/explore/products (last visited April 2010)
5. Jard, C., Jéron, T.: TGV: theory, principles and algorithms: A tool for the automatic synthesis of conformance test cases for non-deterministic reactive systems. Int. J. Softw. Tools Technol. Transf., 297–315 (2005)
6. Tretmans, J., Brinksma, E.: TorX: Automated Model Based Testing. Cte de Resyste (2003)
7. Clarke, D., Jéron, T., Rusu, V., Zinovieva, E.: STG: A Symbolic Test Generation Tool. In: Katoen, J.P., Stevens, P. (eds.) TACAS/ETAPS 2002. LNCS, vol. 2280, pp. 470–475. Springer, Heidelberg (2002)
8. Chimiak-Opoka, J., Lenz, C.: Use of OCL in a model assessment framework: An experience report. Electronic Communications of the EASST 5 (2006)
9. Chimia-Opoka, J., Felderer, M., Lenz, C., Lange, C.: Querying UML Models using OCL and Prolog: A Performance Study. In: Software Testing Verification and Validation Workshop, ICSTW 2008, pp. 81–88 (2008)

10. Schwarzl, C., Peischl, B.: Test Sequence Generation from Communicating UML State Charts: An Industrial Application of Symbolic Transition Systems. In: QSIC 2010: Proceedings of the International Conference on Quality Software (2010) (to be published)
11. Diethers, K., Huhn, M.: Vooduu: Verification of Object-Oriented Designs Using UPPAAL. In: Jensen, K., Podelski, A. (eds.) TACAS 2004. LNCS, vol. 2988, pp. 139–143. Springer, Heidelberg (2004)
12. Malgouyres, H., Motet, G.: A UML Model Consistency Verification Approach Based on Metamodeling Formalization. In: SAC 2006: Proceedings of the 2006 ACM Symposium on Applied Computing, pp. 1804–1809 (2006)
13. Zhao, X., Long, Q., Qiu, Z.: Model Checking Dynamic UML Consistency. In: Liu, Z., He, J. (eds.) ICFEM 2006. LNCS, vol. 4260, pp. 440–459. Springer, Heidelberg (2006)
14. Wang, C., Cavarra, A.: Checking Model Consistency using Data-Flow Testing. In: APSEC 2009, pp. 414–421 (2009)
15. Frantzen, L., Tretmans, J., Willemse, T.: Test generation based on symbolic specifications. In: Grabowski, J., Nielsen, B. (eds.) FATES 2004. LNCS, vol. 3395, pp. 1–15. Springer, Heidelberg (2005)
16. Duale, A., Uyar, M.: A Method Enabling Feasible Conformance Test Sequence Generation for EFSM Models. IEEE Trans. Comput. 53, 614–627 (2004)
17. Tretmans, J.: Test generation with inputs, outputs, and quiescence. LNCS, pp. 127–146. Springer, Heidelberg (1996)
18. Godefroid, P., Levin, M., Molnar, D.: Automated Whitebox Fuzz Testing. In: Proceedings of NDSS 2008 (Network and Distributed Systems Security), pp. 151–166 (2008)
19. Chimisliu, V., Schwarzl, C., Peischl, B.: From UML Statecharts to LOTOS: A Semantics Preserving Model Transformation. In: QSIC 2009: Proceedings of the 2009 Ninth International Conference on Quality Software, pp. 173–178 (2009)
20. International Organisation for Standardization: ISO 8807: LOTOS – A formal description technique based on the temporal ordering of observational behaviour (1989)

Verifying Semantic Conformance of State Machine-to-Java Code Generators

Lukman Ab Rahim and Jon Whittle

School of Computing and Communications, InfoLab21,
Lancaster University, Lancaster LA1 4WA, UK
{abrahim,whittle}@comp.lancs.ac.uk

Abstract. When applying model-driven engineering to safety-critical systems, the correctness of model transformations is crucial. In this paper, we investigate a novel approach to verifying the conformance to source language semantics of model-to-code transformations that uses annotations in the generated code. These annotations are inserted by the transformation and are used to guide a model checker to verify that the generated code satisfies the semantics of the source language – UML state machines in this paper. Verifying the generated output in this way is more efficient than formally verifying the transformation's definition. The verification is performed using Java Pathfinder (JPF) [1], a model checker for Java source code. The approach has been applied to verify three UML state machine to Java code generators: one developed by us and two commercial generators (Rhapsody and Visual Paradigm). We were able to detect non-conformance in both commercial tools, which failed some semantic properties extracted from the UML specification.

1 Introduction

In the development of safety- or mission-critical systems, the success of a model-driven engineering (MDE) project depends heavily on the correctness of model transformations. This includes verifying whether the code generator preserves the source language semantics – i.e., whether the generator has the property of *semantic conformance* to the source language semantics[1]. This paper presents our work in verifying the semantic conformance of code generators for one of the most common modeling notations used in the development of safety- or mission-critical systems, the UML state machine.

Verifying code generators is an arduous task because of their complexity. We argue, therefore, that it is more practical to verify semantic conformance of a code generator indirectly by verifying the generated code rather than attempting to verify the definition of the generator – an approach also taken in Proof-Carrying Code [2,3] and in [4,5,6]. In this case, semantic conformance is verified every time a program is generated. There are two advantages to this approach: (1) as noted earlier, verifying a generated program is likely to be much

---

[1] Henceforth, we use the term *semantic conformance* as shorthand to mean semantic conformance to source language semantics.

D.C. Petriu, N. Rouquette, Ø. Haugen (Eds.): MODELS 2010, Part I, LNCS 6394, pp. 166–180, 2010.

simpler than verifying a transformation's definition, and (2) it is the code that will be deployed; therefore, greater confidence may be achieved by verifying the generated code itself. There are disadvantages, of course: (1) verification is only carried out for programs generated and deployed, not all possible generated programs, and (2) verification effort is required from the consumer of the generated code since the verification cannot be applied *a priori* on the transformation's definition. Disadvantage (1) is not an issue because if code can be generated but will not be deployed, it matters little whether it is correct. Disadvantage (2) is more problematic and it is this which we address in this paper. We present an approach for automating the verification of semantic conformance for each generated program and call this approach Annotation-Driven Model Checking (ADMC).

ADMC verifies the semantic conformance of code generators by model checking the generated code every time a program is generated. The novelty of the approach is the adaptation of the code generator to insert annotations into the generated code. One type of annotation is Java assertions, which represent the properties to be verified and are used by the Java Pathfinder (JPF) tool [1] to model check the generated code. Therefore, the properties that can be checked using ADMC are properties that can be translated into Java boolean statements (statements that return true or false). Furthermore, JPF is built on top of the standard Java JVM; ADMC can only verify properties of Java programs that run on the standard Java JVM.

ADMC can be used by tool developers to assess whether their code generator conforms to the UML semantics or by tool users to ensure that they select a code generator meeting the UML semantics. ADMC is based on two key principles: (1) verification is on the generated code rather than on the code generator; this reduces the complexity, and (2) it does not assume access to the source code of the generator; that is, ADMC may be applied by tool vendors, who do have such access, or by tool users, who may not. With regards to (2), the architecture of ADMC uses an additional model transformation to generate a component, containing the annotations, that is an extension to the generated code.

The reader should note that ADMC does not attempt to prove full behavioural correctness of the generated code nor does it prove complete semantics preservation of the model-to-code transformation. Rather, ADMC focuses only on checking semantic conformance in the sense defined earlier. This allows ADMC to scale without requiring a labour-intensive formal proof process; indeed, all verification in this paper is performed fully automatically.

We have applied ADMC to verify three code generators including two commercial tools – Rhapsody [7] and Visual Paradigm [8]. ADMC showed that neither of the commercial tools conform fully to the UML state machine semantics; there are some properties that fail the verification and there are some that cannot be verified because UML notations are not supported by the tools.

This paper is organized as follows. Section 2 gives a description of the UML state machine semantics and the JPF tool. Section 3 illustrates the ADMC approach using our own code generator and Section 4 evaluates the approach by verifying two commercial code generators, Rhapsody and Visual Paradigm. Section 5 discusses existing work in verifying semantic conformance and semantic preservation. Section 6 concludes this paper and discusses future work.

2   Background

This section describes the UML 2.1.1 state machine semantics [9] and captures them as a list of properties. We restrict discussion to semantics explicitly specified in the UML specification. This section also describes JPF.

2.1   UML State Machine Semantics

We consider the following subset of the UML state machine notation in this paper. A state machine consists of vertices that can be either a state or pseudostate, and transitions that connect two vertices. There are three types of state: simple state, composite state and submachine state. A composite state is used to compose a complex state and can be orthogonal (the composite state has multiple independent regions) or non-orthogonal (the composite state has only one region). An orthogonal composite state can have many active sub-states (one for each region). A submachine state allows a state machine to be part of another state machine and encourages reusable state machines. A state may have entry, exit and do behaviours. An entry behaviour executes when a state is entered and the exit behaviour executes on exit. The do behaviour is executed after the execution of the entry behaviour and continues whilst the state remains active.

Various types of pseudo-states also exist for indicating the start of a state machine, terminating a state machine and creating compound transitions. Four

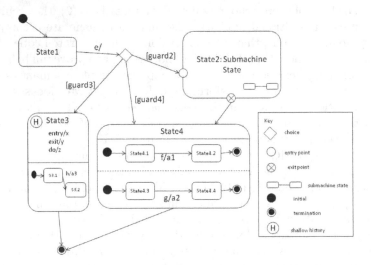

Fig. 1. UML State Machine Notation

pseudo-states of particular interest (because of the semantics) are choice, history, entry point and exit point pseudo-states. A choice pseudo-state is used as a selection mechanism: the outgoing transition selected depends on the guard of the transition. A history pseudo-state is used to enter a composite state and continue from the most recently active sub-state. There are two types of history pseudo-state: shallow history and deep history. Shallow history only records the history of the outermost composite state while deep history also records the history of nested composite states inside the parent composite state. Entry and exit points are used as an alternative entry and exit to composite and submachine states. The UML notation for these concepts is shown in Figure 1.

A state machine has at least one region. Syntactically, all vertices and transitions are located in regions. A region is active when one state in this region is active (has been entered) and becomes inactive when the region is exited through the final state or the exit point.

When created, a state machine starts with an initial pseudo-state and automatically transitions to the first state. A transition may have triggers, a guard and an effect. Certain transitions have well-formedness constraints: e.g., an outgoing transition from an initial pseudo-state cannot have triggers or guards. A state machine changes state through the firing of transitions, which are triggered by dispatching events from an event pool. After being dispatched, if an event causes a transition to be fired, the event is said to be consumed and if not the event is discarded. Furthermore, an event can be deferred by the current active state and when deferred, the event is inserted back into the event pool.

Transitions are executed by computing a set of enabled transitions and by firing a subset of these such that there are no conflicts between the enabled transitions in this subset. A transition is enabled when the event that triggers the transition is dispatched, the transition's source is the current active state and the transition's guard is true. Two enabled transitions may be in conflict in a number of ways. If one transition originates from a composite state and the other originates from a direct/indirect substate, the transitions are in conflict and the transition that fires is the transition in the innermost region. Two transitions in the same region are also in conflict if they both originate from the same state. In this case, a nondeterministic choice is made.

Below, we capture the UML state machine semantics as a list of properties. These properties have been defined based on an analysis of the UML 2.1.1 specification [9]. Not all properties are shown here. Where UML is incomplete or ambiguous, we make no attempt to choose a semantics. We therefore only check conformance with respect to well-defined semantics in UML 2.1.1. For ease of reference in the rest of the paper, each semantic property is named (in bold, italic and square parentheses).

- **Run-to-completion** *[R2C]*: An event will only be dispatched from the event pool when the state machine is in a stable configuration. A stable configuration means that all transitions and behaviours have finished executing and the state machine is in one of its states and not a pseudo-state.

- **Entry order** *[EnO]*: When entering a composite/submachine state, the state's entry behaviour must be executed before that of the sub-states.
- **Exit order** *[ExO]*: When exiting a composite/submachine state, the exit behaviours of the currently active sub-states are executed before the composite/submachine state's exit behaviour.
- **Entry via entry points** *[EnEP]*: When entering via an entry point, the effect behaviour of the transition outgoing from the entry point is executed after the composite/submachine state's entry behaviour.
- **Exit via exit points** *[ExEP]*: When exiting via an exit point, the effect behaviour of the transition incoming to the exit point is executed before the composite/submachine state's exit behaviour.
- **Entry via history pseudo-state** *[EHP]*: When entering a composite state through a history pseudo-state, the current active sub-state will be the last active sub-state from the previous entry. If the composite state is entered for the first time through a history pseudo-state, the initial state of the composite is entered.
- **Ill-formed choice transition** *[ICT]*: When a transition ends at a choice pseudo-state and none of the choice pseudo-state's outgoing transitions can be fired the whole compound transition is said to be ill-formed. UML does not define a repair action in this case.
- **Transition enablement rules** *[TER]*: The rules to enable a transition for firing are: 1) the source of the transition is an active state, 2) the event that triggers the transition was dispatched and 3) the guard is true.
- **Transition firing rules** *[TFR]*: The rules to fire a transition are: 1) the transition must be enabled and 2) the transition has the highest priority to fire among the enabled transitions. In [9], firing priority rules are specified only for the case of conflicting transitions.
- **Conflicting transitions** *[CT]*: Conflicting transitions occur when an event causes a transition to fire in an active region and in one or more of its active subregions. In this case, firing priority is given to the transition in the innermost active subregion.
- **Number of fired transitions** *[NFT]*: The number of transitions fired should equal the number of fireable transitions. Normally, at most one transition is fired per active region. In the case of conflicts, only one transition is selected among the conflicting transitions.
- **Order of transitions execution steps** *[OTES]*: When a transition is fired, the following steps are taken in sequence: 1) the source state of the transition is exited, 2) the effect behaviour of the transition is executed and 3) the target state of the transition is entered.
- **Conflicting deferred events** *[CDE]*: Conflicting deferred events occur when 1) a composite state defers an event while one or more of its sub-states do not defer the event or vice versa, and 2) the current active state in an orthogonal region defers the event while another region's current active state does not. In the first case, the conflict is resolved depending on what the sub-states do with the event. In the second case, the event is always consumed.

There are other semantic properties that are not mentioned explicitly above because they are associated to notation that is syntactic sugar and hence they can be reduced to one of the properties above.

2.2 Java Path Finder (JPF)

JPF is a model checker for Java which uses a special purpose Java Virtual Machine (JVM) and a Depth-First Search (DFS) module that traverses the Java program's state graph [1]. Using the DFS module, JPF traverses a program's state graph and checks if any of the properties to be verified are violated.

JPF has two methods for users to specify the properties to be checked. One method is to extend a general *Property* class provided by JPF and the second method is to use Java assertions. The general *Property* class is a template for JPF users to define the properties they want JPF to check. JPF also comes with two standard properties to check deadlocks and uncaught exceptions, which are both implemented as a subclass of the general *Property* class. The uncaught exception property is also used to check failing assertions (in Java, failing an assertion is treated as an exception).

The tool also provides a class containing methods to define atomic blocks, produce random boolean and integer values, and reduce the state graph by specifying certain paths to ignore. These methods can be used to help model check the Java program. To use these methods, the user needs to insert them into the program being verified. JPF generates a counter-example if the model checking result is negative.

3   Annotation-Driven Model Checking

ADMC verifies semantic conformance of UML state machine to Java code generators to the UML state machine semantics. The verification is conducted by model checking the generated code. Figure 2 demonstrates the approach. We identify two roles in this process: the *producer*, responsible for developing annotations for the code generator and developing a transformation to insert these annotations into generated code; and the *consumer*, who wishes to develop a state machine model and verify the generated code. As an example, the producer role could be played by a tool vendor and the consumer role by a tool user. Alternatively, the producer role could be played by an organisation purchasing a tool but wishing to carry out its own verification activities.

The producer carries out activities for each code generator, *CG*, of interest. As a prerequisite, s/he needs to understand the nature of code generated by *CG*. Given this, the producer's role is to develop the annotation transformation, *AT*. *AT* is a model-to-code transformation that generates components for verification. These components represent the UML state machine semantic properties as Java assertions and link these with code generated by *CG* by extension of the generated code.

The consumer simply wishes to use ADMC to verify a particular program generated by *CG*. The consumer needs no knowledge of the properties or Java

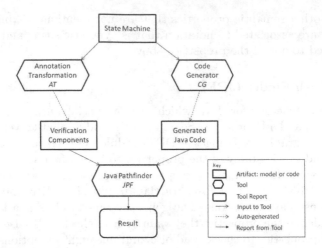

Fig. 2. Annotation-Driven Model Checking

assertions. S/he merely applies the tool chain on the right-hand-side of Figure 2 and this process is fully automatic. The consumer's main role, therefore, is to construct the state machine model.

Note that the construction of AT is done only once for a particular code generator. AT, however, is dependent on CG because the formalisation of the properties as Java assertions depends on the way that the Java code is generated. For example, there are different ways to implement a state. The code generator can use the State design pattern and create objects for each state, or create a unique integer constant to represent individual state. When using the State design pattern approach, AT can extend the State class and add boolean attributes to represent the successful entry and exit of states. These boolean attributes/flags can be used in asserting properties associated to the entry and exit of states. Representing states as unique integer constants does not permit this method of annotating.

The following subsections explain ADMC in detail, using our own code generator to illustrate.

3.1   Understanding the Code Generator (Producer)

The objective of this task is to understand how the code generator translates the UML state machine notation into Java. The result of this task helps in completing the second task, Defining the Assertions. This task can be skipped if the producers are tool vendors because they should already understand the code generator.

Understanding how the code generator translates a state machine can be carried out by studying the transformation rules or the generated code. While trying to understand the code generator, the producers need to find answers to questions such as how the generated code receives and dispatches events, how

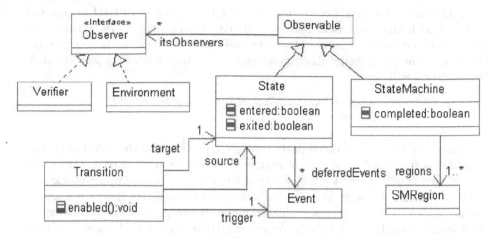

Fig. 3. The Code Pattern

run-to-completion is implemented, how transitions are selected for firing and how states handle deferred events.

To illustrate how this task is carried out, we will use the *SimGen* code generator as an example and answer the questions that we listed above. The *SimGen* code generator is a simple state machine-to-Java generator that was used to develop and test ADMC. SimGen generates code based on the code pattern shown in Figure 3[2]. The answers to the questions above are:

The *Environment* class in the code pattern will dispatch events when notified by the *State Machine* class. The *State Machine* class will only notify the *Environment* when it is in a stable configuration. Selecting transitions for firing is carried out by the *SMRegion* class. After receiving an event from the *Environment*, the *State Machine* will pass the event to all its regions. Each region will check if the event is deferred by its current active state. If not, the region will check if the event triggers a transition originating from its current active state. A transition triggered by the event is enabled for firing if the guard method returns true.

3.2   Defining the Assertions (Producer)

After understanding the code generator, the producer can start to define the assertions. Assertions are written in Java in the following form:

$$assert\ <boolean\ statement>:<error\ message>$$

Thus, the producers need to translate the properties into boolean statements and identify: 1) what information is needed to specify the assertions, 2) how to acces this information, and 3) where to add these assertions.

---

[2] Due to the size of the code pattern, Figure 3 only shows the elements discussed in this section.

To illustrate this task we will use the *[TER]* property. *[TER]* is asserted by checking if the event being dispatched triggers transitions originating from the current active state, and if these transitions' guard methods return true. Given *e* as the event being dispatched and *t* as a transition that was enabled, the assertion will be:

assert t.getSource().equals(region.getCurrentActiveState())
&& t.getTrigger().equals(e) && t.guard():"Fail TER";

The assertion consists of three parts that are connected by the AND operator. The first part checks if the current active state is the source of transition *t*, the second part checks if event *e* triggers transition *t*, and the third part checks the guard condition. Looking at this assertion, we use auxiliary methods such as *equals*, *getSource* and *getTrigger*. These methods are part of the code pattern used by *SimGen*. If such methods are not available, they must be added as part of the annotations.

Some assertions use boolean flags to check certain properties. For example, the flag *completed* in the *State Machine* class. This flag is used to show the state machine is in a stable configuration. The flag is set to *false* each time a transition is fired and set back to *true* after the run-to-completion step has finished. Similar to the auxiliary methods, flags and the commands to set their value need to be added as part of the annotations, if they are not already part of the generated code.

After defining the assertions, the producer needs to decide where to insert the assertions. For *SimGen*, all the assertions are grouped into the verification components (VC), which is a subclass of the Verifier class. As a consequence, the generated code will be extended with calls to notify VC. Using this approach has the advantage of putting all the assertions into one place. Going back to the *[TER]* example, a call to the *enabled* method is followed by a notification to VC to check the assertion.

3.3   Developing the Transformation *AT* (Producer)

Transformation *AT* is used to generate the verification components. The transformation rules in *AT* should generate the verification components that contain the assertions and extend the generated code with auxiliary methods and boolean flags where necessary. Transformation *AT* is written in Epsilon Generation Language (EGL). Note, however, that ADMC does not mandate the use of a particular transformation language; we used EGL because of familiarity.

We highlight once more that the boolean flags, assertions and auxiliary methods depend greatly on the code generator. As a result, the complexity of the assertions and auxiliary methods – and, hence, the complexity of *AT* – may vary significantly between code generators. We stress once more that this procedure need only be undertaken once for each generator.

3.4 Verifying the Generated Code (Consumer)

Once the previous steps have been carried out by the producer, the consumer's task – to verify semantic conformance for code generated from a state machine – is relatively straightforward and automatic. We have implemented a tool which automates the process: the state machine is passed to *SimGen*, which generates code, and to *AT*, which generates verification components. The combined generated code is then passed to JPF, which exhaustively searches the state space, starting from the *main* method in a *main* class passed as a parameter to JPF. JPF checks the properties each time it encounters an assertion. To ensure complete coverage of the execution flow, the *Environment* simulates all possible externally injected events.

JPF returns, for each state machine, either with *success* or with a counter-example that violates a property. If there is a failure, it is the consumer's decision how to address it: either by contacting the tool vendor, modifying the state machine to avoid the error, or fixing the generated code manually.

4 Evaluation

To evaluate ADMC, we applied the approach to two commercial code generators: Rhapsody [7] and Visual Paradigm [8]. We report on the application of ADMC to verifying Rhapsody. The case with Visual Paradigm was similar. As noted in the previous section, to apply ADMC to Rhapsody requires the producer to: understand the generated code, identify the assertions and where to insert them, and generate transformation *AT*.

Every commercial tool generates code differently and this must be understood before assertions can be properly formulated. The Rhapsody tool does not follow the State pattern as with *SimGen*. Rather, it generates a class with integer variables to represent states in the state machine. This class also contains methods that represent the transitions. Checking the guards of these transitions is performed using *select* statements and the selection of which transitions to fire is carried out using switch-case statements. Each event is translated into an instance of an *Event* class. Events are dispatched using the *takeEvent* method that is part of the Rhapsody state machine execution framework accessed by the generated code.

The code generated by Rhapsody is not difficult to understand and, in fact, knowing the UML semantics helps in performing this task. By understanding the semantics, we are able to understand the purpose of methods in the generated code and identify where we should add the assertions.

Due to the differences between the code generated by *SimGen* and Rhapsody, the assertions for Rhapsody are syntactically different than those for *SimGen*. For example, in Rhapsody's case, we require a different set of boolean flags: e.g., boolean flags to represent the entry and exit of the current active state of each region. The assertions are added in methods associated to the properties: e.g., assertion for *[EnO]* is added after the call to a composite state's entry behaviour.

We developed AT for Rhapsody using EGL. The verification components generated by AT are implemented using extension of Rhapsody classes.

4.1   Verification Result

Table 1 shows the verification result of Rhapsody and Visual Paradigm. Rhapsody fails two properties, which are ill-formed choice transition *[ICT]* and entry via entry points *[EnEP]*.

Rhapsody fails the *[ICT]* property because it translates a choice pseudo-state in the same way it translates a junction pseudo-state. In UML, the choice and junction pseudo-states have different semantics. Guards of transitions connected to a junction pseudo-state are evaluated before the transitions are fired. On the other hand, for a choice pseudo-state, the guards are evaluated dynamically during the firing of the transition.

Rhapsody fails *[EnEP]* because the entry point's outgoing transition's effect behaviour is not executed after entering the submachine state.

Table 1. Verification Result

	Rhapsody	Visual Paradigm
Successful Property	*[R2C] [EnO] [ExO] [ExEP]* *[TER] [OTES]*	*[OTES]*
Failed Property	*[ICT] [EnEP]*	*[EnO] [ExO]*
Unverifiable Property	*[EHP] [CDE] [TFR] [CT]*	*[R2C] [EnEP] [ExEP] [CDE]* *[ICT] [CT] [EHP] [TER]*

There are certain properties that ADMC cannot verify because there are state machine notations that Rhapsody does not support. Rhapsody does not support the shallow history pseudo-state nor does it support deferred events. Hence, *[EHP]* and *[CDE]* do not hold.

The *[CT]* property is not verified because we could not determine where to insert the assertion. This is due to the complexity of the generated code. Of course, with unlimited resources, a better understanding of the generated code could be achieved which would allow us to check *[CT]*. However, when verifying Rhapsody, we attempted to take into account practical considerations that might be associated with the producer and dropped properties if the code could not be sufficiently understood within a reasonable timeframe. The *[TFR]* property could not be verified because it is dependent on the *[CT]* property. We encountered similar problems with Visual Paradigm.

The *[NFT]* property is problematic in general. It is typically very hard, and may be impossible, to determine the expected number of fired transitions by examining the code alone and without modifying the code. This is because the generated code simply may not contain this information. However, this information can be obtained by examining the input state machine. As a result, there needs to be a separate translation of the state machine that can identify which transitions are enabled, can assess whether there are any conflicts between the enabled transitions and can calculate the number of transitions expected to fire. Furthermore, this new translation must be accessible by the *Verifier*. We have not yet implemented this and hence were unable to verify *[NFT]* for either of the two commercial generators.

Visual Paradigm's code generator performs worse than Rhapsody's. There are many properties which cannot be verified at all because many of the state machine notations are not supported in the generator. For example, Visual Paradigm cannot generate code for state machines containing pseudo-states other than the initial pseudo-state. Events and deferred events are also not translated into code. Therefore, we cannot determine where to add the assertions for the *[R2C]*, *[CDE]*, *[TER]* and *[NFT]*. The only properties we can verify are *[EnO]*, *[ExO]*, and *[OTES]*.

Visual Paradigm fails the *[EnO]* property because, when entering a composite state, the sub-states are not entered afterwards. Similarly, Visual Paradigm fails the *[ExO]* property because the sub-states are not exited before the composite state. Visual Paradigm only conforms to the *[OTES]* property.

From the result of these verifications, ADMC has successfully verified two commercial code generators and clearly highlights the conformance level of these tools. These verifications also prove that ADMC can be used in situations where the transformation rules are not accessible by the producers and can only rely on the generated code to create and add the assertions. It is important to note that the large number of unverifiable properties does not negate the applicability of ADMC itself; rather, it makes clear the lack of support that even well-known commercial generators provide for the UML state machine semantics.

5   Related Work

There has been a wide body of work on verifying that model transformations are semantics-preserving – in the sense that the application-specific model semantics hold in the generated model (or code). For example, Varro and Pataricza [10] use model checking to check properties in both source and target models. If both models have the intended properties, the transformation is said to be semantically correct. Staats and Heimdahl [11] use a similar approach when verifying semantic correctness of a Simulink-to-C code generator. Chaki et al. [12] and Pnueli et al. [13] propose the use of an approach based on proof-carrying code (PCC) [2,3] but where model checking is combined with the use of a theorem prover, which is normally used in PCC.

To ensure semantic preservation, Barbosa et al. [14] propose an extension to the MDA four layered architecture. They propose the addition of a semantic metamodel and model into the architecture. The approach uses a formal checker to verify the conformance of both static and dynamic semantics based on the semantic metamodel. This approach requires a lot of effort because the semantic models need to be created for each source and target model.

All of these works focus on verifying semantic preservation in general. The scope of ADMC, however, is much narrower as it focuses only on semantic conformance to the source language semantics. Whilst this makes ADMC less general, it also makes it more practical: there is no need for the consumer to formulate properties to prove and a background in formal methods is not required because the process is fully automated (at least in our examples so far).

ADMC is, in essence, a simplified form of PCC for model transformation. A number of authors have investigated applying the principles of PCC to model-based transformations. Autofilter [15], AutoBayes [4], and AutoCert [6] are three tools that use theorem provers guided by annotations to verify the preservation of certain semantic properties. Autofilter and AutoBayes are restricted to the domain of geometric state estimation and data analysis problems respectively. AutoCert improves on Autofilter and AutoBayes by being a domain independent tool and provides a model-driven mechanism to generate the annotations. ADMC differs from these approaches in two ways. Firstly, it verifies source language semantic properties, whereas Auto* focus on domain-specific properties in the given domain. Secondly, Auto* use an automated theorem prover to prove properties of the generated code, using annotations as a guide. Whereas this process can be automated for certain domain-specific properties, a great deal of effort is required by the producer to set up the infrastructure so that the proofs will go through automatically. Based on our experience, the level of effort required by ADMC is greatly reduced and, in particular, is practical for those with only limited training in formal methods.

More lightweight approaches have also been proposed to check semantic preservation. For example, Baar and Marković [16] verify semantic preservation of a transformation that refactors UML class diagram and OCL constraints. The verification is performed by evaluating the conformance of source and target models to their OCL constraints. The evaluator is implemented as a graph transformation. A similar approach is discussed by Whittle and Gajanovic [17]. More generally, semantic conformance has also been defined as whether a model conforms to the semantics of its metamodel. Egea and Rusu [18] check for this notion of semantic conformance using the ITP/OCL tool. This concept, however, is different from the notion of semantic conformance used in this paper.

6   Conclusion and Future Work

This paper presented a verification approach, ADMC, for verifying the conformance of state machine to Java code generators to the UML state machine semantics. ADMC is based on inserting assertions into the generated code, which are then checked by the Java Pathfinder model checker. The code for verification is maintained separately from the code generated from the input model. The novelty of the approach is in using an annotation transformation, AT, to annotate the generated code with assertions that are added based on information in the source model. The approach was evaluated by applying it to two commercial code generators, Rhapsody and Visual Paradigm. Both generators failed to satisfy some properties.

ADMC can be used in a number of ways. Tool vendors may develop AT themselves and then ship this transformation with the tool so that tool users can check code generated on a case-by-case basis. Alternatively, since ADMC requires no access to the source code of the generator, tool users themselves can develop AT to ensure that code generated for use in safety-critical applications conforms to the UML semantics. One appealing use case is as follows. Tool vendors could develop AT, ship it with the product, and offer it as a certificate which the tool user can then use to check the semantics. It is also important to note that, in practice, many companies use home-grown code generators, modify commercial generators, or extend generated code with hand-written code. ADMC supports all of these use cases. Traditional *a priori* verification of a transformation's definition does not support them.

So far, the input state machine models we use have been of medium size. As a result, Java Pathfinder has been able to check the semantic properties automatically. However, we would anticipate that for very large models, this may not be the case. To address this, we are investigating whether it is possible to represent state reduction strategies (such as abstract interpretations) as annotations and generate them using AT.

One outstanding issue is how to prove that the assertions have been defined correctly and are inserted at the correct locations. This is a non-trivial problem. Note, however, that, depending on how ADMC is used, such a proof may not be necessary. We advocate that ADMC is used more as a debugging aid rather than to attempt to provide a fully rigorous proof. In the former case, it is not crucial to prove the assertions themselves because if an assertion cannot be proven, it either points to a bug or the assertion needs to be fixed. Used in this way, however, ADMC will not necessarily find all bugs.

In addition, ADMC, as presented in this paper, is specific to state machine-to-Java generators and to state machine semantics. However, the ideas transfer easily to other model transformations and other properties. Common properties specific to a domain (e.g., security properties) can be encoded in AT and ADMC could potentially be extended to check domain-specific properties of an input model. We will tackle these issues in future work.

References

1. Visser, W., Havelund, K., Brat, G., Park, S.J., Lerda, F.: Model checking programs. Automated Software Engineering Journal 10(2), 203–232 (2003)
2. Necula, G.C.: Proof-carrying Code. In: Proceedings of the 24th ACM SIGPLAN-SIGACT symposium on Principles of programming languages (POPL 1997), pp. 106–119. ACM, New York (1997)
3. Colby, C., Lee, P., Necula, G.C.: A Proof-Carrying Code Architecture for Java. In: Emerson, E.A., Sistla, A.P. (eds.) CAV 2000. LNCS, vol. 1855, pp. 557–560. Springer, Heidelberg (2000)
4. Schumann, J., Fischer, B., Whalen, M., Whittle, J.: Certification Support for Automatically Generated Programs. In: Proceedings of the 36th Annual Hawaii International Conference on System Sciences, pp. 1–10. IEEE, Los Alamitos (2003)

5. Denney, E., Fischer, B.: Extending Source Code Generators for Evidence-Based Software Certification. In: 2nd International Symposium on Leveraging Applications of Formal Methods, Verification and Validation (ISoLA 2006), pp. 138–145. ACM, New York (2006)
6. Denney, E., Fischer, B.: Generating Customized Verifiers for Automatically Generated Code. In: Proceedings of the 7th International Conference on Generative Programming and Component Engineering (GPCE 2008), pp. 77–88. ACM, New York (2008)
7. IBM: Rational   Rhapsody,   http://www-01.ibm.com/software/rational/products/rhapsody/developer/
8. Visual Paradigm International: Visual paradigm, http://www.visual-paradigm.com/
9. OMG: Unified Modeling Language: Superstructure version 2.1.1. OMG (February 2007)
10. Varró, D., Pataricza, A.: Automated formal verification of model transformations. In: Jürjens, J., Rumpe, B., France, R., Fernandez, E.B. (eds.) CSDUML 2003: Critical Systems Development in UML; Proceedings of the UML 2003 Workshop. Number TUM-I0323 in Technical Report, Technische Universität München, pp. 63–78 (September 2003)
11. Staats, M., Heimdahl, M.: Partial Translation Verification for Untrusted Code-Generators. In: Liu, S., Maibaum, T., Araki, K. (eds.) ICFEM 2008. LNCS, vol. 5256, pp. 226–237. Springer, Heidelberg (2008)
12. Chaki, S., Ivers, J., Lee, P., Wallnau, K., Zeillberger, N.: Model-Driven Construction of Certified Binaries. In: Engels, G., Opdyke, B., Schmidt, D.C., Weil, F. (eds.) MODELS 2007. LNCS, vol. 4735, pp. 666–681. Springer, Heidelberg (2007)
13. Pnueli, A., Shtrichman, O., Siegel, M.: The Code Validation Tool CVT: Automatic Verification of a Compilation Process. Software Tools for Technology Transfer 2, 192–201 (1998)
14. Barbosa, P.E.S., Ramalho, F., de Figueiredo, J.C.A., dos Jr., A.D.S.: An extended MDA architecture for ensuring semantics-preserving transformations. In: 32nd Annual IEEE Software Engineering Workshop, pp. 33–42 (October 2008)
15. Denney, E., Fischer, B., Schumann, J., Richardson, J.: Automatic Certification of Kalman Filters for Reliable Code Generation. In: IEEE Aerospace Conference, pp. 1–10. IEEE, Los Alamitos (2005)
16. Baar, T., Marković, S.: A graphical approach to prove the semantic preservation of UML/OCL refactoring rules. In: Virbitskaite, I., Voronkov, A. (eds.) PSI 2006. LNCS, vol. 4378, pp. 70–83. Springer, Heidelberg (2007)
17. Whittle, J., Gajanovic, B.: Model transformations should be more than just model generators. In: Briand, L.C., Williams, C. (eds.) MoDELS 2005. LNCS, vol. 3713, pp. 32–38. Springer, Heidelberg (2005)
18. Egea, M., Rusu, V.: Formal executable semantics for conformance in the MDE framework. Innovations System Software Engineering 6(1-2), 73–81 (2010)

A Dynamic-Priority Based Approach to Fixing Inconsistent Feature Models

Bo Wang[1,2], Yingfei Xiong[3], Zhenjiang Hu[4], Haiyan Zhao[1,2,*],
Wei Zhang[1,2], and Hong Mei[1,2]

[1] Key Laboratory of High Confidence Software Technologies,
Ministry of Education, China
[2] Institute of Software, School of EECS, Peking University, Beijing, 100871, China
{wangbo07,zhhy,zhangw}@sei.pku.edu.cn, meih@pku.edu.cn
[3] Generative Software Development Lab, The University of Waterloo, Canada
yingfei@swen.uwaterloo.ca
[4] GRACE Center, National Institute of Informatics, Japan
hu@nii.ac.jp

Abstract. In feature models' construction, one basic task is to ensure the consistency of feature models, which often involves detecting and fixing of inconsistencies in feature models. Several approaches have been proposed to detect inconsistencies, but few focus on the problem of fixing inconsistent feature models. In this paper, we propose a dynamic-priority based approach to fixing inconsistent feature models, with the purpose of helping domain analysts find solutions to inconsistencies efficiently. The basic idea of our approach is to first recommend a solution automatically, then gradually reach the desirable solution by dynamically adjusting priorities of constraints. To this end, we adopt the constraint hierarchy theory to express the degree of domain analysts' confidence on constraints (i.e. the priorities of constraints) and resolve inconsistencies among constraints. Two case studies have been conducted to demonstrate the usability and scalability of our approach.

Keywords: Feature Model, Priority, Inconsistency Fixing.

1 Introduction

Feature models [1,2] have been widely adopted to reuse the requirements of a set of similar products in a domain. During the process of requirements reuse, specific products that satisfy all the constraints are derived from feature models. However, inconsistent feature models (called IFMs) contain contradictory constraints that cannot be satisfied at the same time, leading to no valid products derivable from IFMs [3]. Therefore, in the construction of feature models, one basic task is to ensure the consistency of feature models, which often involves the detecting and fixing of inconsistencies in feature models.

---

* Corresponding author.

D.C. Petriu, N. Rouquette, Ø. Haugen (Eds.): MODELS 2010, Part I, LNCS 6394, pp. 181–195, 2010.

Although several approaches have been proposed to detect inconsistencies, there lacks an effective approach to aiding domain analysts to fix the inconsistencies of feature models. Finding a solution to fix inconsistencies requires quantitative analysis of certain parts of the IFMs. Even if one solution is found, it is still unclear whether there exist alternative or better solutions. Moreover, finding solutions becomes more and more difficult when feature models grow large. The largest feature model [4] reported in academy has more than 5000 features. In industry, feature models often grow up to thousands of features [5].

In this paper, we propose a dynamic-priority based approach to the interactive fixing of inconsistencies in feature models, and report an implementation of a system that not only automatically recommends a solution to fixing inconsistencies, but also supports domain analysts to gradually reach the desirable solution by dynamically adjusting priorities of constraints. To this end, we adopt the *constraint hierarchy theory* [6], a known practical theory in user interface construction [7], to express the degree of domain analysts' confidence on constraints (i.e. the priorities of constraints) and resolve inconsistencies by deleting one or more weaker constraints.

The main contributions of our paper are summarized as follows:

- We show the importance of the constraint hierarchy theory in fixing IFMs, and implement an efficient constraint hierarchy system[1] for fixing IFMs by adapting and extending an existing incremental algorithm, SkyBlue [7,8].
- We extend the constraint hierarchy theory with a dynamic-priority based mechanism to help domain analysts find the desirable solution; if domain analysts are not satisfied with the solution the system recommends, they can declaratively adjust the priorities of weaker constraints so that a new solution can be produced.
- We successfully apply our system to check and fix the feature model of the web store domain and the randomly generated feature models, which indicates that our approach is promising and potentially useful in practice.

The rest of this paper is organized as follows. Section 2 introduces some preliminary knowledge. Section 3 gives an overview of our approach and illustrates it with an example. Section 4 amplifies the whole process of our approach. Section 5 illustrates usability and scalability of our approach through case studies. Section 6 describes the related work, and Section 7 concludes the paper and highlights the future work.

2   Preliminaries

In this section, we first give a short introduction to feature models, and then introduce the theory of constraint hierarchies and a constraint solver-SkyBlue. The three above are the fundamentals for fixing inconsistencies in feature models.

---

[1] See http://sei.pku.edu.cn/~wangbo07/ for more detail

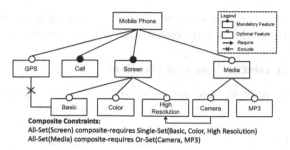

Fig. 1. A simplified feature model of the mobile phone domain

2.1 Feature Model

A feature model defines a set of possible products of a domain, in terms of features and the relationships between them. Fig. 1 shows a simplified feature model of the mobile phone domain (used in [9]), which adopts our meta-model of feature models [10].

A feature model is hierarchically organized. Features with different abstract levels and granularities form a hierarchy structure through *refinement relationships* between them. Refinements relationships bring constraints on features. The root feature should be bound in all products. In feature models, if a feature is bound (i.e. selected in a specific product), so it is parent. A *mandatory* feature means that it should be bound, if its parent is bound. An *optional* feature indicates that it can be unbound (i.e. deselected in a specific product), even if its parent is bound.

There are three kinds of *simple constraints* on two features, namely *require*, *m-requires*, and *excludes*. If feature A *requires* feature B, it means that B cannot be unbound when A is bound. If feature A *m-requires* feature B, it means that A and B should be bound or unbound at the same time. If feature A *excludes* feature B, it indicates that at most one of them can be bound. A mandatory feature or optional feature brings constraints with their parents, *m-requires* and *requires*, respectively.

There are three kinds of *predicates* on a set of features, namely *All*, *Alternative* and *Or*. Predicates *All*, *Alternative*, and *Or* mean these predicates are true only if all, one, and at least one features are bound in their feature sets, respectively. For example, *Or-Set(Camera, MP3)* indicates that the *Or* predicate is true when at least one features from this set are bound.

Based on predicates, there are three kinds of *composite constraints* on two feature sets, *composite-requires*, *composite-m-requires*, and *composite-excludes*. For example, *All-Set(Screen) composite-requires Single-Set(Basic, Color, High Resolution)* means if *Screen* is bound, one feature of the single feature set should be bound. For the details of the composite constraints, see Section 4.1.

Inconsistent Feature Models. A feature model is *inconsistent* if it cannot produce any valid product that satisfies all the constraints of the feature model [3]. Inconsistency is a severe problem, since we reuse feature models by deriving products from them. The inconsistencies in feature models happen when some elements of feature models are overconstrainted by contradictory constraints.

2.2   Constraint Hierarchies and SkyBlue

When overconstrainted models are checked by a constraint solver, it is not enough for the solver to signal an inconsistency and wait the modeler to fix the detected inconsistency. The *constraint hierarchy theory* [6] provides a way to specify how the overconstrainted model should be handled by maintaining constraint hierarchies. A constraint hierarchy contains a set of constraints, each assigned with a priority, indicating the importance of the constraint. Given an overconstrainted model, the constraint solver can leave weaker constraints unsatisfied in order to satisfy stronger constraints.

SkyBlue is an incremental, scalable, and efficient constraint solver that uses local propagation to maintain the constraints hierarchy. The input of SkyBlue is a set of variables and constraints on these variables. The output of SkyBlue is a set of values that satisfy stronger constraints and leave contradictory weaker constraints unsatisfied.

In SkyBlue, each constraint is equipped with one or more *methods*; SkyBlue satisfies a constraint by selecting and executing one of its methods. For example, "feature B *excludes* feature C" has two methods: 1) Unbind(B); 2) Unbind(C)(see Fig. 2(b)). This constraint can be satisfied by executing any one of these two methods. A constraint is *enforced* if it has a selected method, otherwise, it is unenforced. Choosing one method for a constraint is known as *enforcing*. Choosing no methods for a constraint is known as *revoking*. The variables and constraints form the *constraint graph*. The constraint graph, together with the selected methods, form the *method graph*.

The output of SkyBlue, the value set for constraints, is calculated through constructing and executing a *locally-graph-better* (called LGB) method graph. A method graph is LGB if there are no method conflicts and there are no unenforced constraints that could be enforced by revoking one or more weaker constraints (and possibly changing the selected methods for other enforced constraints with the same or stronger strength) [8].

As a simple example, consider the IFM (in Fig. 2(a)) and its corresponding constraint graph (in Fig. 2 (c)). Each constraint in the feature model (*C1-C4*)

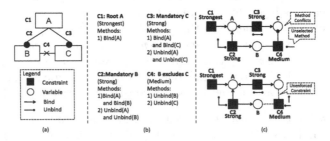

Fig. 2. A simple example for SkyBlue

has one or more methods to make the constraint hold. (in Fig. 2 (b)). To satisfy every constraint, SkyBlue tries to select a method from each constraint, as shown in the upper of Fig. 2 (c), but there is a method conflict: variable C is determined by two methods (i.e. Bind(C) and Unbind(C)) and determined to different value, from $C3$ and $C4$, respectively. To resolve this conflicts, SkyBlue finds the stronger constraints that can be enforced, while leaving the weaker constraints unenforced by constructing LGB method graph. The LGB method graph of this example is shown in the lower of Fig. 2 (c), in which $C4$ is revoked. After executing the selected methods in the LGB method graph, A, B and C equal bound (selected in the product), which satisfy the three stronger constraints, namely $C1$, $C2$ and $C3$.

3   Approach Overview

In this section, we give an overview of our approach, before using an example to illustrate how to fix inconsistencies.

3.1   Dynamic-Priority Based IFM Fixing Process

In our approach, we detect and fix inconsistencies of feature models incrementally; we start with an empty feature model and then add constraints one by one. Every time a constraint is added into the feature model, we check inconsistencies, recommend a solution and help domain analysts find a more desirable solution. An overview of our approach is shown in Fig. 3.

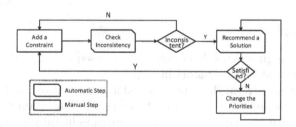

Fig. 3. The dynamic-priority based IFM fixing process

After a constraint is added to the feature model, the feature model may become overconstrainted because of the newly-added constraint. We check the inconsistency by first mapping the newly-added constraint to a SkyBlue constraint (called SBC), then trying to enforce the SBC through constructing a LGB method graph. If the constructed LGB method graph does not contain any unenforced constraints, the feature model is consistent.

If the constructed LGB method graph contains unenforced constraints and the newly-added SBC is enforced in this LGB, the feature model becomes inconsistent because of the newly-added SBC. We recommend a solution to domain analysts to fix the inconsistent feature model. This solution is composed of the

unenforced constraints in the LGB method graph, and can be executed to fix
the inconsistencies by deleting the unenforced constraints.

Domain analysts can examine the recommended solution. If they do not want
some unenforced constraints deleted because of the newly added constraint, they
can raise the priorities of these unenforced constraints, with the help of the
dynamic-priority mechanism provided in our approach. We will recommend another solution according to the new priorities. When domain analysts are satisfied with the solution, the solution is performed, and the feature model becomes
consistent again.

If the newly-added SBC is unenforced in the constructed LGB method graph,
the newly-added SBC conflicts with some same or stronger constraint in the feature model. Our approach will recommend dropping this newly-added constraint.

For all the unenforced constraints in the LGB, we provide constraints with the
same or higher priorities as potential conflict information to domain analysts,
with the purpose of aiding them find desirable solutions.

Note that our approach not only supports the checking and fixing of feature
models from scratch, but also supports these of a feature model that has already
been constructed. Given a constructed feature model, we extract all its constraints, and map them to the SBCs. We first add and enforce the root feature
to the constraint graph and then the other SBCs, according to their priorities,
from weaker constraints to stronger constraints. After each SBC is added, we
recommend solutions when inconsistencies detected, help domain analyst find
desirable solutions according to their feedback, perform the solutions to fix inconsistencies. After all the SBCs are added, the feature model is checked and
fixed completely.

3.2   An Example

To demonstrate the process of dynamic-priority based IFM fixing, let us see how
to fix the inconsistent feature model in Fig. 4.

Suppose all the constraints have been added into the feature model except "feature *C excludes* feature *D*" (the red part in Fig. 4). These constraints are first
transformed into SBCs, according to the concrete rules in Tables 1 and 2. They are

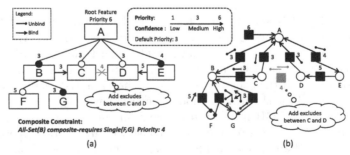

Fig. 4. An example of dynamic-priority based IFM fixing

then added to the constraint graph by enforcing themselves and construing LGB method graph one by one. The feature model is consistent before adding "feature *C excludes* feature *D*", since the LGB method graph shown in Fig. 4(b) contains no unenforced constraints. Note that even some variables are determined by more than one method in the LGB method, there is no conflicts, because these variables are set to a same value (see Section 4.2 for our definition for method conflicts in feature models).

After the *"exclude"* constraint is added, the feature model become inconsistent. In the generated LGB method graph, constraint "feature *B requires* feature *C"* is unenforced. We recommend deleting this constraint to fix inconsistencies.

If domain analysts are not satisfied with the recommended solution, they adjust priorities of the unenforced constraints to find the desirable solution with the help of the potential conflict information, and then we recommend other solutions according to the new priorities. For example, if the domain analysts think the *"require"* constraint should not be deleted, they raise the priority of it to 4, then we recommend another solution by constructing a new LGB method graph, in which the *"Mandatory* feature *B"* is unenforced. Therefore this constraint is recommended to be deleted.

4   Fix IFM with Dynamic Priority

In this section, we first describe how we implement the constraint hierarchy theory in fixing IFMs, through revising and extending SkyBlue. Then we show how to reach the desirable solution by adjusting priorities.

4.1   Map Feature Models to Constraint Graphs

To use SkyBlue to detect and fix inconsistencies, the first thing is to map the elements of feature models to the elements of SkyBlue constraint graphs.

Generally speaking, the mapping consists of two steps: 1) each feature of the feature model is mapped to a variable of the SkyBlue constraint graph; 2) each constraint of the feature model is mapped to a SkyBlue constraint (called SBC) that is represented by a set of methods. In feature models, each feature can have only two states: 1) bound; 2) unbound. Therefore, it is possible to derive methods from the constraints through combinations of the states of features. Concrete rules for the mapping from constraints of feature models to SBCs are listed in Tables 1 and 2.

Bind(feature) means the bind state of the feature is *bound*, and *Unbind(feature)* means the bind state of the feature is *unbound*. *Predicate(feature-set)* represents the value (*True* or *False*) of the predicate on the feature set.

In our approach, a simple constraint (i.e., *require* and *exclude*) can be represented by a composite constraint. For example, "feature *A requires* feature *B"* can be represented as "*All-Set(A) composite-requires All-Set(B)*". Therefore, we can map simple constraints to SBCs according to these rules.

Table 1. Methods for constraints

Relationship		Number of Methods	Methods
Mandatory A B		2	{Bind(A), Bind(B)} or {Unbind(A), Unbind(B)}
Optional A B		2	{Bind(A)} or {Unbind(B)}
Composite-Requires Predicate Predicate Set-A → Set-B		2	{Predicate(Set-A) = False} or {Predicate(Set-B) = True}
Composite-M-requires Predicate Predicate Set-A ↔ Set-B		2	{Predicate(Set-A) = False, Predicate(Set-B) = False} or {Predicate(Set-A) = True, Predicate(Set-B) = True}
Composite-Excludes Predicate Predicate Set-A ⟶✕⟶ Set-B		2	{Predicate(Set-A)= False} or {Predicate(Set-B)= False}

Table 2. Methods to determine the values of predicates

Predicate	Value	Number Of Methods	Methods
All Set-A $\{A_1, A_2 ... A_n\}$	True	1	{Bind(A_1),Bind(A_2) ...Bind(A_n)}
	False	n	{Unbind(A_1)} or {Unbind(A_2)} or ... {Unbind(A_n)}
Alternative Set-A $\{A_1, A_2 ... A_n\}$	True	n	{Bind(A_1),Unbind(A_2),Unbind(A_3)...Unbind(A_n)} {Bind(A_2),Unbind(A_1),Unbind(A_3)...Unbind(A_n)} or ... {Bind(A_n),Unbind(A_1),Unbind(A_2)...Unbind(A_{n-1})}
	False	$1+(n^2-n)/2$	{Unbind(A_1),Unbind(A_2)...Unbind(A_n)} or Any two of the features in the group are bound
Or Set-A $\{A_1, A_2 ... A_n\}$	True	n	{Bind(A_1)} or {Bind(A_2)} or ... {Bind(A_n)}
	False	1	{Unbind(A_1), Unbind(A_2) ...Unbind(A_n)}

In order to derive combinations of the states of a composite constraint's features(i.e. methods), our system 1) finds the combinations of values of the composite constraint's predicates according to the last three rows of Table 1; 2) derive the combinations of the bind states of each predicate's features to hold the predicate value determined in the first step, according to Table 2.

For example, given *"All-Set(A) composite-m-requires Alternative-Set(B,C)"*, first two combination of predicates, namely, {*All-Set(A) = True, Alternative-Set(B,C) = True*}, {*All-Set(A) = False, Alternative-Set(B,C) = False*}, are generated. Then the combinations to hold the values of these predicates are generated. After that, the derived methods for this composite constraint are: {*Bind(A), Bind(B), Unbind(C)*}, {*Bind(A), Unbind(B), Bind(C)*}, {*Unbind(A), Bind(B), Bind(C)*}, {*Unbind(A), Unbind(B), Unbind(C)*}.

4.2   Recommend a Solution to Fix IFM

After one constraint is added to the feature model and in turn added to the SkyBlue constraint graph by mapping it to a SBC, our system detect inconsistencies and recommend a solution by two steps: 1) constructing a new LGB method graph through enforcing the newly-added SBC and other SBCs; 2) using the LGB to recommend a solution. Our system uses SkyBlue's LGB construction algorithm, and we extend SkyBlue by redefining method conflicts and specializing the method execution process.

Constructing a LGB method graph involves enforcing the constraints in the constraint graph. To enforce a constraint, SkyBlue selects a method for it, change the methods of same and stronger constraints, or revoke one or more weaker constraints. This process is called constructing a *method vine* or *mvine*. When an mvine for a SBC is build, they are successfully enforced.

Note that each time a constraint is successfully enforced (i.e. an mvine is constructed), one or more weaker constraints may be revoked. To construct a LGB method graph, these revoked constraints are added to the unenforced constraint set. Then our algorithm repeatedly tries to enforce all of them by constructing mvines for these constraints, until none of the constraints can be enforced. This process terminates because of the finite number of constraints. The pseudo code of constructing a LGB method graph is shown below.

Construct a LGB method graph

```
constructLGB(Constraint SBC){
    //clean the unenforced constraint set
    clearUnenforcedCnSet();
    addToUnenforcedCnSet(SBC);
    While(UnenforcedCntSet != null){
        unenforcedCn = UnenforcedCnSet.get();
    //enforce the unenforced constraint,
    //add the revoked constraints to the unenforced constraint set
        buildMvine(unenforcedCn, unenforcedCnSet);
    }
}
```

SkyBlue uses a backtracking depth-first search to build mvines. The pseudo code of building an mvine is shown as follows:

Build an Mvine for a unenforced constraint

```
buildMvine(Constraint root){
    While (root has methods){
        Method m = getMethodFromConstraint(root);
        If(!checkConflicts()){
            return true;
        }Else{
            Constrint cn = getConflictsConstraint();
            If(cn weaker than root){
                revokeConstring(cn);
                return true;
            }Else{
                buildMvine(cn);
            }
        }
    }
    return false; //start backtrack
}
```

The process of building an mvine for an unenforced constraint (called root constraint in the building process) is actually a local propagation process, the building process will end in the following situations:

- if this selected method does not conflict with other methods, this branch of the depth-first search mvine does not extend any further;
- if this selected method conflicts with the selected methods of weaker enforced constraints, SkyBlue just revokes these weaker constraints and adds them

into the unenforced constraints set and this branch of the mvine does not extend any further;

- if this selected method conflicts with the selected methods of the same or stronger enforced constraint, SkyBlue selects other methods of these constraints; if these selected methods conflict with yet other constraints, choose other methods.

Our system redefines *method conflicts* and revises the corresponding part of the SkyBlue algorithm for building mvines. In SkyBlue, method conflicts happen when a variable is determined by more than one methods. However, in method graphs of feature models, the variables in constraint graphs can only be *bound* and *unbound*. Therefore, even if a variable is determined by more than one methods, it may not cause a conflict (e.g. see variable B in Fig. 4 (b)). Conflicts happens only when a variable is set to different values.

Our algorithm can also handle graphs that contain directed cycles, when executing methods to satisfy the constraints in the cycle. In SkyBlue, it is not possible to find an execution sort to satisfy the constraints in a cycle. In our system, however, methods that determine a variable set the variable to one fixed value. Therefore, our system can just execute all the methods to satisfy all the constraints.

SkeBlue provides two techniques [8], namely, *Local Collection* and *Walkabout Strength* to optimize the performance when constructing LGB method graphs. Our system successfully implement the *Local Collection* technique based on the new definition of method conflicts. The *Walkabout Strength* technique for feature models is still under construction. However, our scalability case study in Section 5.2 shows that our system can scale up to large feature models without the *Walkabout Strength* technique.

After a LGB method graph is constructed, we recommend a solution to domain analysts. How to analyze the LGB method graph to find a solution is described in Section 3.1.

4.3   Choose other Solutions through Dynamic-Priority

After a solution is recommended to fix inconsistencies, domain analysts may not be satisfied with this solution. In our approach, they can choose other solutions to fix the inconsistencies, by raising the priorities of the constraints in the solution.

The recommended solution consists of a set of weaker unenforced constraints to be deleted. These constraints conflict with some enforced constraints that have the same or higher priorities. Provided with the solution, domain analysts may not want some of the constraints in the solution to be deleted. To get a solution that does contain this constraint, domain analysts should increase the priority of the constraint. After the priority is adjusted, we construct a new LGB method graph, with the hope of re-enforcing the raised constraint and recommending a new solution based on this new LGB method graph. This process continues until domain analysts are satisfied with the solution. The pseudo code of changing priorities is listed as follows:

Changing a constriaint's prioritiy

```
changePriority(Constraint SBC, Priority p){
    oldPriority = SBC.priority;
    SBC.priority = p;
    If (oldPriority<p){
        If (!SBC.isEnforced())
            ConstructLGB(SBC);
    }
    Else If(oldPriority>p){
        If (SBC.isEnforced())
            ConstructLGB(SBC);
    }
}
```

5 Case Studies

To investigate whether our approach is useful to fix inconsistencies in feature models, we undertook two case studies. The first one is a preliminary case study that focused on whether our approach helps domain analysts fix IFMs efficiently. The second case study investigated whether our approach is scalable to large feature models.

5.1 Usability

In the following, we first describe the process of the usability case study, then give an analysis to the results.

Study setup. In this case study, five participants were asked to build a feature model of the web store domain using our system, which is integrated into a Feature Model Graphical Editor we developed before. These participants have diverse backgrounds: two of them are senior undergraduate students who have little experience with domain engineering. The other three are graduate students whose research interests are software reuse. None of them know the approach until the case study and they are familiar with web store systems.

The five participants took the role of domain analysts to identify main features, refinements, simple constraints, composite constraints of the web store feature model. During the case study, our system recorded usage logs that include the scale of feature models, the number of the detected inconsistencies and the number of the recommended solutions. After the case study, the efficiency of our system is investigated through questionnaires.

Results. The usage log is summarized in Table 3. (The constraints showed in the results are the constraints explicitly modeled into the feature model, they do not contain the simple constraints that are brought with the *Mandatory* and *Optional* features.)

Most of the participants built the web store domain feature model containing about 50 features. For all the constructed feature models, there are few composite constraints. On average, when an inconsistency is detected, about 2 recommendations are needed to find the desirable solution, except for participant 4. The

Table 3. Usage log of the usability case study

Particip ants	Features	Simple Constraints	Composite Constrains	Number of Inconsist encies	Average Recommend ation times	Max Recommend ation times	Average Deleted Constraints	Max Deleted Constraints
P1	53	17	0	7	2.57	6	1.71	2
P2	50	6	1	5	1.4	2	1.8	3
P3	57	7	3	6	2.5	3	1.5	2
P4	34	8	3	6	3.17	6	1.83	4
P5	50	6	3	3	1.33	2	1.67	2

relatively small feature model conducted by participant 4 has more constraints. More recommendations are needed to find the desirable solution when inconsistencies detected.

The concerns of the questionnaires are classified into three categories: 1) whether the participants need recommended solutions when fixing inconsistencies; 2) whether our system can help the participants fix inconsistencies; 3) whether assigning priorities to constraints bring a lot of burden. Based on the answers to these concerns, we conclude as follows:

- Three graduate students have experience with feature model construction before. They pointed out that they often did not know how to fix the inconsistencies in relatively large and complex feature models. According to their understanding, two factors lead to this difficulty. The first one is that they have to first find out the meaning of the constraints, then analyze the inconsistencies and finally figure out how to fix them. The second factor is that when analyzing the inconsistencies, some irrelevant features and constraints disturb the domain analysts.
- Four out of five participants think our system is very helpful when fixing inconsistencies, the rest one cannot be sure whether it is helpful. The participants reported that our system helped them focus on where the inconsistencies are and how to solve them, by providing recommendations. Adjusting priorities can help them find alternative or better solutions. The time needed to fix an inconsistency is also reduced greatly.
- All the participants think assigning priorities bring them trouble when constructing constraints, due to the lack of the standards for the priorities of constraints. They think the default priority is rather helpful. They also point out that adjusting priorities is relatively much easier, because they can adjust priorities through comparing constraints.

5.2 Scalability

In this case study, we investigate the scalability of our system. To evaluate the scalability, we randomly generate feature models and fix the inconsistencies in the generated feature models. We use generated models because it is very difficult

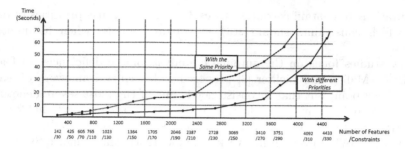

Fig. 5. Experiments results for fixing randomly generated feature models with the same and different priorities, respectively

to get real world large feature models. Although there are publications about large models, none of these models are publicly available. On the other hand, industrial feature models are always confidential.

We implement an algorithm to generate feature models randomly[2]. Each generated feature model contains a root feature. We can specify the number of the subtrees that are connected to the root feature, the height of the subtrees, the number of the chid features for each non-leaf feature in the subtrees, the number of the constraints. The percentage of the variability of features are: Mandatory (25%) and Optional (75%).

To make the study reflects the scalability of our system, we generate two groups of feature model, with the same and different (randomly between 1 and 5) priorities. In our case study, we adopt the first recommended solution to fix inconsistencies.

The environment for our experiments is a Win 7 PC with a 2.66GHz CPU, 2GB memory and the result is shown in Fig. 5. (The constraints showed in the results are the constraints explicitly modeled into the feature model, they do not contain the simple constraints that are brought with the *Mandatory* and *Optional* feature.) Our system checks and fixes inconsistencies incrementally. For example, in the second case, 425 mandatory or optional features are added (each bring a constraint), and 50 constraints are explicitly modeled, we check 475 times in total and cost 0.8s in all.

From the result, we can see that, our system can handle feature models with more than 4000 features and 300 constraints, which is a good support for domain analysts when they fix inconsistencies in feature models.

6   Related Work

Feature models are first proposed by Kang et al. [1] in the feature-oriented domain analysis (FODA) method. Czarnecki et al. [11] proposed probabilistic feature models, in which soft constraints express the conditional probability of

---

[2] See http://sei.pku.edu.cn/~wangbo07/ for the source code.

configurations to contain certain features. Our approach use priorities to determine which constraints should stay in feature models, when inconsistency happens.

Many studies focus on the automatic analysis of the deficiencies of feature models [9]. Maßen and Lichter [3] proposed a deficiency framework of feature model. They point out that inconsistency is one of the most severe deficiencies in feature models. Mannion et al. [12] was the first to use propositional formulas to analyze feature models. Batory [13] proposed an approach to detecting deficiencies with SAT Solver. In his work, a Logic Truth Maintenance System was designed to analyze feature models. Benavides et al. [14] were the first to use constraint programming for analysis on feature models. Our previous work [15] focused on how to analyze feature models using BDD.

However, all these works only focus on the detection of deficiencies. Egyed [16] proposed an approach to fixing inconsistencies in UML models. Trinidad et al. [17] focus on the explanation of deficiencies in feature models based on constraint programming, but they do not give a solution to the deficiencies and the scalability of his approach is also not clear. White et al. [18] focus on detect errors on the configuration of a feature model, and propose changes in the configuration in terms of features to be selected or deselected to correct the error. Our approach focuses on the feature model itself, not the configuration of feature models.

7   Conclusion and Future Work

In this paper, we adopt the constraint hierarchy theory and extend the constraint solver-SkyBlue to implement a system that can help domain analysts fix inconsistent feature models effectively. When a constraint is added to the feature model, we automatically check the inconsistencies by constructing a LGB method graph, and recommend domain analysts a solution for fixing the inconsistencies by analyzing the constructed LGB method graph. Furthermore, we can recommend other solutions so that a more desirable solution can be obtained based on the feedback of domain analysts. The feedback is expressed declaratively through the adjustment to the priorities of constraints. Our future work will focus on working on more practical examples, and investigating applicability of our approach to inconsistency fixing of other models such as UML models.

Acknowledgments. The authors would like to thank Shin Nakajima (NII, Japan) and Lu Zhang (Peking University, China) for discussing with us on model inconsistency detection and fixing, and to Hiroshi Hosobe (NII, Japan) for introducing Delta/Skyblue to us. This work is supported by the National Basic Research Program of China (973) under Grant No. 2009CB320701, the Science Fund for Creative Research Groups of China under Grant No. 60821003, the Natural Science Foundation of China under Grant No. 60703065, 60873059 and the National Institute of Informatics (Japan) Internship Program.

References

1. Kang, K.C., Cohen, S.G., Hess, J.A., Novak, W.E., Peterson, A.S.: Feature-oriented domain analysis (FODA) feasibility study. Technical report, CMU-SEI (1990)
2. Czarnecki, K., Helsen, S., Eisenecker, U.W.: Formalizing cardinality-based feature models and their specialization. Software Process: Improvement and Practice 10, 7–29 (2005)
3. von der Maßen, T., Lichter, H.: Deficiencies in feature models. In: Workshop on Software Variability Management for Product Derivation, in Conjunction with SPLC (2004)
4. She, S., Lotufo, R., Berger, T., Wasowski, A., Czarnecki, K.: The variability model of the Linux kernel. In: VaMoS, pp. 45–51 (2010)
5. Batory, D.S., Benavides, D., Cortés, A.R.: Automated analysis of feature models: challenges ahead. Commun. ACM 49, 45–47 (2006)
6. Borning, A., Freeman-Benson, B.N., Wilson, M.: Constraint hierarchies. Lisp and Symbolic Computation 5, 223–270 (1992)
7. Sannella, M.: SkyBlue: A multi-way local propagation constraint solver for user interface construction. In: ACM Symposium on User Interface Software and Technology, pp. 137–146 (1994)
8. Sannella, M.: The SkyBlue constraint solver and its applications. In: PPCP, pp. 258–268 (1993)
9. Benavides, D., Segura, S., Cortés, A.R.R.: Automated analysis of feature models 20 years later: a literature review. Information Systems (2010)
10. Zhang, W., Mei, H., Zhao, H.: Feature-driven requirement dependency analysis and high-level software design. Requir. Eng., 205–220 (2006)
11. Czarnecki, K., She, S., Wasowski, A.: Sample spaces and feature models: There and back again. In: SPLC, pp. 22–31 (2008)
12. Mannion, M.: Using first-order logic for product line model validation. In: Chastek, G.J. (ed.) SPLC 2002. LNCS, vol. 2379, pp. 176–187. Springer, Heidelberg (2002)
13. Batory, D.S.: Feature models, grammars, and propositional formulas. In: Obbink, H., Pohl, K. (eds.) SPLC 2005. LNCS, vol. 3714, pp. 7–20. Springer, Heidelberg (2005)
14. Benavides, D., Trinidad, P., Cortés, A.R.: Using constraint programming to reason on feature models. In: SEKE, pp. 677–682 (2005)
15. Zhang, W., Yan, H., Zhao, H., Jin, Z.: A BDD-based approach to verifying clone-enabled feature models' constraints and customization. In: Mei, H. (ed.) ICSR 2008. LNCS, vol. 5030, pp. 186–199. Springer, Heidelberg (2008)
16. Egyed, A.: Fixing inconsistencies in uml design models. In: ICSE, pp. 292–301 (2007)
17. Trinidad, P., Benavides, D., Durán, A., Ruiz-Cortés, A., Toro, M.: Automated error analysis for the agilization of feature modeling. J. Syst. Softw. 81, 883–896 (2008)
18. White, J., Schmidt, D.C., Benavides, D., Trinidad, P., Cortés, A.R.: Automated diagnosis of product-line configuration errors in feature models. In: SPLC, pp. 225–234 (2008)

Taming Graphical Modeling

Hauke Fuhrmann and Reinhard von Hanxleden

Real-Time and Embedded Systems Group, Department of Computer Science
Christian-Albrechts-Universität zu Kiel, Olshausenstr. 40, 24118 Kiel, Germany
{haf,rvh}@informatik.uni-kiel.de
www.informatik.uni-kiel.de/rtsys/

Abstract. Visual models help to understand complex systems. However, with the user interaction paradigms established today, activities
such as creating, maintaining or browsing visual models can be very tedious. Valuable engineering time is wasted with archaic activities such as
manual placement and routing of nodes and edges. This paper presents
an approach to enhance productivity by focusing on the *pragmatics* of
model-based design.

Our contribution is twofold: First, the concept of *meta layout* enables
the synthesis of different diagrammatic views on graphical models. This
modularly employs sophisticated layout algorithms, closing the gap between MDE and graph drawing theory. Second, a *view management* logic
harnesses this auto-layout to present customized views on models.

These concepts have been implemented in the open source Kiel Integrated Environment for Layout Eclipse Rich Client (KIELER). Two
applications—editing and simulation—illustrate how view management
helps to increase developer productivity and tame model complexity.

1 Introduction

Simply put, the main task of a programmer is to command the computer to do the
right thing. The programming mechanics of computers has undergone quite an
evolution: From manually stamping programs on punch cards over non-reversible
type writers to the main method still used today—text editor and keyboard. While
different IDEs might offer various support levels for large software artifacts, the
basic mechanics of writing or changing a line of code is rather standard and efficient. Hence, editing text has been established for many decades.

The introduction of graphical models has added the second dimension to one-
dimensional text. However, this new freedom comes at a heavy price: We are
back to the early times of mechanical typewriters with rather archaic user interactions. Graphical layout has to be manually defined by placing and routing of
nodes and edges. Deleting graphical objects, like using white-out on a typewriter,
creates new white-space that might not be large enough to insert new expressions, i. e. new graphical constructs. Manually creating more space in a complex
diagram is like using scissors and glue. In fact, in large industrial projects it is
not uncommon that highly-paid engineers use scissors and glue to create large
hand-crafted posters from print-outs to help navigate through complex models.

D.C. Petriu, N. Rouquette, Ø. Haugen (Eds.): MODELS 2010, Part I, LNCS 6394, pp. 196–210, 2010.

Graphical views on models are manually defined and hence static like a type-written piece of paper. Creating multiple different views, e. g., for different levels of abstraction, onto the same model requires much manual editing work. Often one ends up working with one single abstraction level or changing syntax from graphical to structural to get more detailed or more abstract representations. Although abstraction might play an important role for MDE, so far, graphical aspects of models certainly do not. Instead of unfolding their potential as a vivid means of communication they remain no more than syntactic sugar. When trying to communicate with the computer through graphical models, the computer will not answer in the same language. For example, model transformations typically lose the graphical information and result in a model without a graphical view, which is like typing in text and getting a punch card as an answer. Even graphical means like graph grammars do not produce proper layouts for newly introduced items. If one believes that a diagram communicates the meaning of a model better than another representation, and if one wants this to be widely accepted by domain users that are not necessarily computer scientists, then one has to teach computers to truly master this language.

This paper presents an approach to bridge the gap between MDE and graph drawing theory to enable the automatic processing of graphical models and fundamentally enhance the user interaction mechanisms—also for rich diagram notations. After the related work in Sec. 2, Sec. 3 gives the required terminology and defines the focus of our approach—*pragmatics*. Sec. 4 introduces the central contributions: First, Sec. 4.1 explicates how *meta layout* enables the synthesis of different diagrammatic views on graphical models. Meta layout offers interfaces to plug in sophisticated layout algorithms and to utilize them according to higher-level optimization criteria. Second, Sec. 4.2 presents how *view management* logic employs this auto-layout to dynamically and interactively present custom views on models. Sec. 5 illustrates these concepts with the open source Kiel Integrated Environment for Layout Eclipse Rich Client (KIELER). Sec. 5.2 discusses two fields of application—model editing and simulation. Sec. 6 presents an experimental evaluation, the paper concludes in Sec. 7.

For a more detailed presentation than space permits here, we refer to another report [1] that includes a further discussion of the layout parametrization (Sec. 4.1) and structure-based editing (Sec. 5.2).

2   Related Work

This work is an interdisciplinary task and hence there is a large body of related work emerging from related communities.

The MDE community employs means of user experience enhancements orthogonal to ours [2]. There are multiple recent approaches on creating model-to-model transformations not by complex transformation languages, but *from examples* [3] or *by demonstration* [4]. It would be interesting to combine such approaches with the structure-based editing framework presented in Sec. 5.2 to give the user very natural ways to define custom editing operations him- or herself. Also, transformation languages based on triple graph grammars [5] could augment structure-based editing by graphical views on the transformations themselves.

The field of *Human Centred Software Engineering* [6] also addresses usability and productivity. However, these approaches mainly focus on the question of how to make the best user experience with a given product. In contrast, we try to enhance the development process itself with novel tool support.

Another related community focuses on software visualization [7], which mainly presents what we call *effects* on graphical views (cf. Sec. 4.2). We also employ the notion of *focus & context* by Card et al. [8], see Sec. 5.2. Musiel and Jacobs [9] apply this technique to UML class diagrams, using notions of *level of detail* and a rudimentary specialized automatic layout algorithm. In our approach to view management we try to generalize such ideas by orchestration of software visualization concepts (effects) with the context (triggers) in which they should be applied to dynamically synthesize graphical views on models.

Automatic layout problems for arbitrary diagrams are often NP-complete, and diagram quality is difficult to measure [10]. However, the graph drawing theory community emerged with sophisticated algorithms that solve single layout problems efficiently with appealing results [11,12]. There exist open layout library projects with multiple sophisticated algorithms such as the Open Graph Drawing Framework (OGDF) [13], Graphviz [14] and Zest[1]. There are also commercial tools such as yFiles (yWorks GmbH) and ILOG JViews [15]. Demirezen et al. use automatic layout in Eclipse with the GraphViz tool as an example of reusing tools employing model transformations [16].

The KIEL project [17] evaluated the usage of automatic layout and structure-based editing in the context of *Statecharts*. It provided a platform for exploring layout alternatives and has been used for cognitive experiments evaluating established and novel modeling paradigms. However, it was rather limited in its scope and applicability, hence it has been succeeded by the KIELER project, which is the context of the work presented here.

3   Pragmatics

In linguistics the study of how the meaning of languages is constructed and understood is referred to as *semiotics*. It divides into the disciplines of syntax, semantics and pragmatics [18]. These categories can be applied both to natural as well as artificial languages, for programming or modeling. In the context of artificial languages, *syntax* is determined by formal rules defining expressions of the language and *semantics* determines the meaning of syntactic constructs [19]. "Linguistic *pragmatics* can, very roughly and rather broadly, be described as *the science of language use*" [20]. This also holds for MDE with its artificial languages, as discussed in the following. However, first we clarify some more terminology specific to MDE according to the modeling linguists Atkinson and Kühne [21].

The main artifacts in MDE are *models* with two main concepts: A model *represents* some software artifact or real-world domain and *conforms* to a *metamodel*,

---

[1] http://www.eclipse.org/gef/zest/

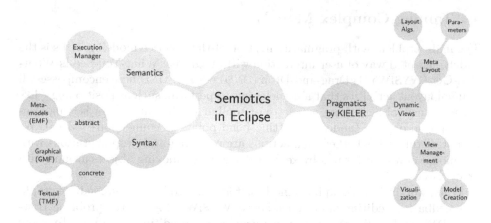

Fig. 1. KIELER focuses on *pragmatics* and enhances the use of syntax and semantics of models which are defined by modeling platforms such as Eclipse

defining its *abstract syntax*. Additionally, the *concrete syntax* is the concrete rendering of the abstract concepts. Concrete syntax can be textual or displayed in a structured way, for example a tree view. To be comprehensible, also a graphical syntax is very often used, the Unified Modeling Language (UML) is one example.

A *graphical model* is a model that *can* have a graphical representation, e. g., a UML class model. A *view* onto the model is a concrete drawing of the model, sometimes also *diagram* or *notation model*, e. g., a class diagram. The abstract structure of the model leaving all graphical information behind is the *semantical* or *domain model*, or just *model* in short. Hence, the *model* conforms to the abstract syntax, while the *view* conforms to the concrete syntax. A view can represent any subset of the model, which in some frameworks is used to break up complex models into multiple manageable views. Hence, there is no fixed one-to-one relationship between model and view.

State-of-the-practice approaches still lack generic answers on how to specify *semantics* [22], but handle *syntax* of models very well, both abstract and concrete. They provide code generators to easily provide model implementations, syntax parsers and textual and graphical editors with common features like the Eclipse Graphical Modeling Framework (GMF)[2].

The third field of linguistics, *pragmatics*, traditionally refers to how elements of a language should be used, e. g., for what purposes a certain statement should be used, or under what circumstances a level of hierarchy should be introduced in a model. We slightly extend this traditional interpretation of pragmatics to all practical aspects of handling a model in its design process [23]. This includes practical design activities themselves such as editing and browsing of graphical models in order to construct, analyze and effectively communicate a model's meaning.

---

[2] http://www.eclipse.org/modeling/gmf/

4   Taming Complex Models

The main problem with pragmatics in state-of-the-practice modeling IDEs is the widely accepted way of user interaction with diagrams: What-You-See-Is-What-You-Get (WYSIWYG) Drag-and-Drop (DND) editing. DND here encompasses all manual layout activities that a modeler has to perform, such as positioning—like dragging new objects from a palette or toolbar to the canvas—or setting sizes of graphical objects (nodes) or setting bend points of connections (edges). We do not distinguish whether such actions are real drag-and-drop operations with the mouse or are performed by keyboard, e.g. when moving objects around with arrow keys.

When working with graphical models, it is useful to have an immediate graphical feedback on editing operations, hence, WYSIWYG is not the problem. However, DND adds a lot of extra mechanical effort on editing diagrams. To quote a professional developer [24]: "I quite often spend an hour or two just moving boxes and wires around, with no change in functionality, to make it that much more comprehensible when I come back to it."

With such a standard editing paradigm one often ends up with exactly one static view for a subset of a model where the developer once has decided the abstraction level—e. g., level of detail or subset of displayed nodes. To get a different view requires to start the editing process all-over.

4.1   Meta Layout

The idea of *meta layout* is to synthesize views automatically, thus freeing the user to focus on the model itself. As discussed further in Sec. 4.2, this not only saves time formerly spent on manual drawing activities, but yields completely new possibilities for user interaction. The meta layout framework consists of two main parts: (1) A bridge between layout algorithm libraries and diagram editors and (2) parametrization possibilities to get the desired layout result of available algorithms, see also Fig. 2.

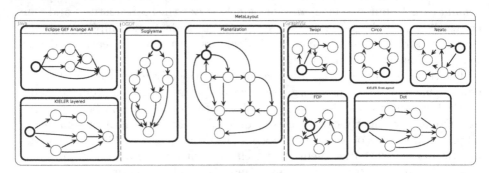

Fig. 2. Meta layout in KIELER: Employ different layout algorithms in one diagram

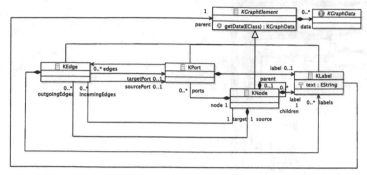

Fig. 3. The KGraph: An Ecore class diagram with mixed upward planarization

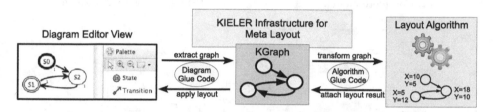

Fig. 4. Overview of the Kieler Infrastructure for Meta Layout (KIML)

The layout bridge connects a range of layout algorithms with established graphical model diagram editors. Fig. 3, with a class diagram of the KGraph, shows an example layout/editor combination.

As illustrated in Fig. 4, the meta layout framework contains a basic graph data structure, the *KGraph*, for exchanging data between a concrete diagram editor and a layout algorithm. To achieve genericity, this does not assume any specific format of either of the two worlds. Glue code that translates between used data structures in both domains allows to use any diagram editor with any layout algorithm. The KGraph is used as an intermediate format to (1) formulate the layout problem and to (2) store the layout result, i. e. the concrete coordinates and sizes. The KGraph follows the ideas of GraphML[3] but is simplified to the needs in this context.

Meta layout not only bridges between diagrams and layouters, it also tries to do this in a smart customizable way. It provides an extensible layout option system with priorities to specify which layouter types fit best to which diagram kinds. Parameters provided by the algorithms can be made available in the framework. Additionally, layouters get called recursively if the algorithms themselves do not handle nested graphs. Furthermore, meta layout allows to use multiple different layout algorithms for different parts of one and the same view as shown in Fig. 2, which is well suited for nested models. More details on these features are given elsewhere [1].

---

[3] http://graphml.graphdrawing.org/

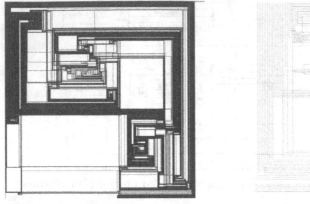

(a) Complete model.

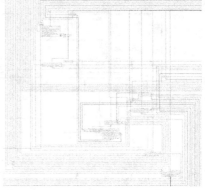

(b) Cutout with 20x zoom.

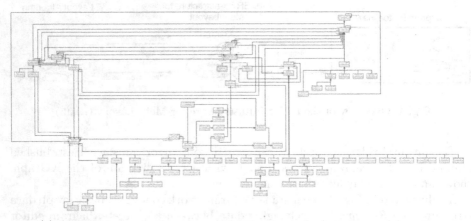

(c) A filtered view to the same model showing only Activity model parts.

Fig. 5. Class diagram of the UML 2.1 metamodel in Eclipse. Standard navigation techniques come to their limits. Views become unusable. Filtering in view management can synthesize a feasible view.

In summary, meta layout bundles a set of layout algorithms and matches them with concrete diagram syntaxes. It lets the user mix parameters and layouters to find the optimal layout result for custom model views.

However, there are limits of automatic layout of views when models become too complex. Consider for example the current UML2 Metamodel, which consists of 263 types with no nested structuring and thousands of relations and inheritances between the classes. This metamodel is available as an EMF Ecore model in the Eclipse Model Development Tools (MDT)[4], as a semantical model augmented with some very small manually placed views, but due to the model's complexity, there is no complete view available [25]. With meta layout, it is

---

[4] http://www.eclipse.org/modeling/mdt

possible to synthesize such a view; Fig. 5a shows the layout generated by KIML using the Mixed-Upward-Planarization algorithm [26], which is optimized for class diagrams and respects the different types of edges. However, the result looks more like a VLSI integrated-circuit die and is hardly usable. Especially the numerous relations make the diagram unreadable. Standard navigation techniques like manual zooming and panning come to their limits; see also Fig. 5b. This limitation of plain layout application prompts the need for *view management*, discussed next.

4.2 View Management

When models and their corresponding views become too complex, it is time for abstraction. *View management* is inter alia a means to automate the choice of right abstraction levels. For a given model, view management chooses the subset of the model that should be presented in a view. It decides the *level of detail* [9] for all graphical elements and adds other graphical effects to views. This automatic synthesis of views is only possible due to the automatic layout service offered by meta layout. Hence, in different words, meta layout provides model views as a service which view management uses. The idea of view management is to focus automatically to the parts of the model that are "currently interesting."

Obviously the context in which the user employs the model is important for this task. For example, to learn only about a smaller subset of the UML, e.g., Activity models, one may create a customized view on the UML metamodel that only contains elements immediately relevant to Activity models. Fig. 5c shows such a view that is again automatically synthesized with meta layout. However, this limited set of only 79 classes with much less edges presents a view that actually can be used very well to browse Activity models.

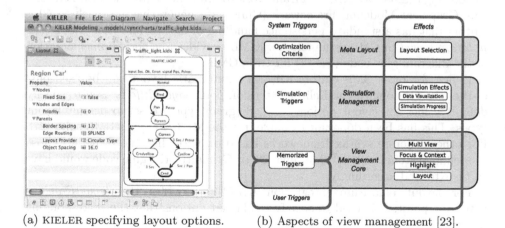

(a) KIELER specifying layout options.   (b) Aspects of view management [23].

Fig. 6. Meta layout and view management

To make view management context sensitive requires a generic architecture that allows to define conditions under which certain views shall be synthesized. View management listens to *triggers* or *events* under which certain graphical *effects* should be executed on the view. The orchestration of a set of triggers and effects forms a *view management scheme* (VMS), see also Fig. 6b. Triggers are categorized in user triggers—e. g., manual selection of elements—and system triggers—e. g., an event during a simulation run. Effects range from highlighting elements, configuring levels of details, filtering graphical objects to visualizing simulation data. An important effect uses the meta layout to rearrange the view that might have been changed by other effects like filters. As space here is limited, our following examples concentrate on the filtering mechanism. The next section presents an implementation of view management and discusses two applications.

5   Kiel Integrated Environment for Layout Eclipse Rich Client (KIELER)

The approaches presented in this paper are implemented and evaluated in the project KIELER, the Kiel Integrated Environment for Layout Eclipse Rich Client.[5] In the spirit of genericity, KIELER builds on the plug-in concept provided by Eclipse and especially its modeling projects.[6] As illustrated in Fig. 1, KIELER provides enhancements for pragmatics, to be combined with syntax and semantics defined by other projects.

5.1   Kieler Infrastructure for Meta Layout (KIML)

KIML uses the Eclipse Modeling Framework (EMF) to specify abstract syntax. For concrete syntax KIML supports graphical editors generated with the Graphical Editing Framework (GEF), a framework to implement graphical DSL editors. The Graphical Modeling Framework (GMF) is a generative approach to GEF editors that has a standard persistence handling of models and their views (the *notation model* in GMF terminology). KIML provides a generic implementation of the diagram glue code (Fig. 4) for GEF/GMF.

Hence, for most GMF editors KIELER's automatic layout can be used out-of-the-box. Optionally, the Eclipse extension point *layoutInfo* is used to specify default values for layout options, e. g., diagram types to setup default layout types. This has been done, for example, for the MDT/Papyrus UML suite [27]. For other concrete syntax frameworks based on GEF, like the Generic Eclipse Modeling System (GEMS)[7], Marama [28] or Graphiti[8], the glue code would have to be extended accordingly.

For layout algorithm integration KIELER provides the *layoutProvider* extension point. It is used to specify the layout options that the corresponding

---

[5] http://www.informatik.uni-kiel.de/rtsys/kieler

[6] http://www.eclipse.org/modeling/

[7] http://www.eclipse.org/gmt/gems/

[8] http://www.eclipse.org/modeling/gmp

algorithm accepts and priorities for diagram types that it supports. The algorithm itself has to be implemented following a simple abstract class.

How rich a diagram notation may be is determined by the diagram editor and the supported features of the concrete layout algorithm. Currently it supports many rich notations like nesting, hyperedges, multiple edge types, unconnected boxes (e. g., orthogonal regions, swimlanes), port constraints, flow direction, which can be extended in order not to limit the concrete syntax of models and gets elaborated in [1]. It explicitly focuses not only on popular current Eclipse-based editors, but also on widely accepted notations like Matlab/Simulink or Labview.

5.2   Applications for View Management

As an example, the following illustrates how view management in KIELER augments the editing and simulation of *SyncCharts* [29].

Simulation with Focus & Context. One means to learn about the behavior of a SyncChart is to execute it stepwise while the simulation browser highlights active states. This paradigm is used by most state machine based tools like Matlab/Simulink/Stateflow or Rhapsody. The usual means for navigation are panning, zooming and opening different parts of the model in different windows or canvases. However, for complex models it becomes difficult and effort prone to manually navigate through a model. Figs. 7a/b demonstrate this with an avionics application [30].

To alleviate this problem, the view management service can synthesize a new view on the model dynamically. The idea is to use *focus and context* methods to present only the "interesting" parts of the model [17]. For SyncCharts, a natural definition of "interesting" considers the currently *active* states, as illustrated in Figs. 7c/d. In KIELER, a specific trigger for the simulation notifies the view management about changes in state activity. A simple effect then highlights active states. An additional effect changes the level of detail at which the model objects get displayed in the view. In KIELER this is implemented by using GEF's methods to collapse or expand compartments, which comprise the contents of states and parallel regions. Afterwards view management uses KIML to rearrange all elements and zooms-to-fit to make best use of the given space. This unfolds the potentials of focus & context, as it presents all required details in the *focus* while still showing the direct neighbor inactive states collapsed with reduced detail level as the *context*. An animated morphing between the different views is provided to match the mental map of the user. For an impression of this, the reader is referred to example videos on-line (or the KIELER tool itself).

Structure-Based Editing. Another task in an MDE design process is to create or modify models. One approach to harness view management is to go back to textual editing. A textual editing framework like Xtext[9] can be enriched with graphical views synthesized on-the-fly to get full round-trip engineering.

---

[9] http://www.eclipse.org/Xtext/

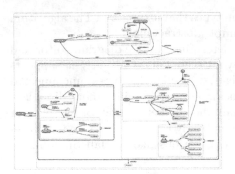

(a) The whole SyncCharts model.

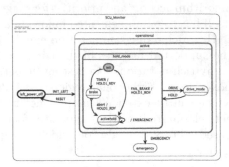

(b) Even in deep hierarchy usually the full complexity of the model is hidden.

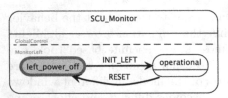

(c) Focus & Context (1): Starting a simulation collapses all inactive states and manually collapsed regions.

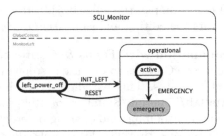

(d) Focus & Context (2): Advancing a simulation will always expand only active states with their full hierarchy.

Fig. 7. Focus & Context in a SyncChart

An alternative approach that stays in the graphical domain and keeps the direct visual feedback like WYSIWYG is *structure-based editing*. It employs model-to-model (M2M) transformations on the semantic model—its structure. It is an interactive approach where the user can work on the model view. The workflow for editing a model reduces to the following steps: (1) Focus a graphical model object for modification and (2) apply an editing transformation operation. View management with KIML applies the transformation, creates new graphical elements, and rearranges the resulting view.

The general implementation scope is shown in Fig. 9a. Again, to be generic, it allows any M2M transformation framework to be used with KIELER Structure-Based Editing (KSBasE). To integrate with the user interface, KIELER connects to the Eclipse Textual Modeling Framework (TMF) Xtend transformation system and all graphical GMF editors.

6   Evaluation

To assess the benefits of view management for model editing, we have conducted a study using KIELER. The hypothesis to be evaluated was that structure-based

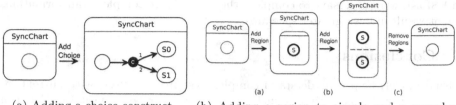

(a) Adding a choice construct.   (b) Adding a region to simple and a complex
                                          state, followed by removal of all regions.

Fig. 8. Example transformations for SyncCharts

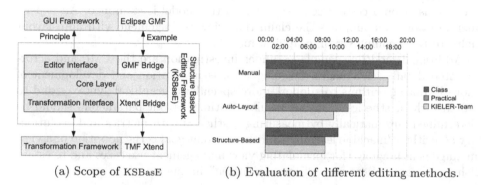

(a) Scope of KSBasE   (b) Evaluation of different editing methods.

Fig. 9. KIELER Structure-Based Editing (KSBasE)

editing reduces the development times for creation and modification of graphical
models significantly compared to usual WYSIWYG Drag-and-Drop (DND) editing. The 30 subjects divided into three different categories: The *class* group was
familiar with the syntax of SyncCharts but not with modeling editors. The *practical* group took part in a practical course and had some experience already with
Eclipse GMF editors. The last group comprised developers of the *KIELER team*,
combining experiences with SyncCharts and the Eclipse SyncCharts editor.

The task was to create three different SyncCharts, using a different input
method in random order for each: (1) standard Drag-and-Drop editing, (2) DND
editing with manually triggered automatic layout and (3) structure-based editing
as presented above. The models were provided in a comprehensible but formal
textual notation. The experiment and its outcome are described in detail elsewhere [31], but Fig. 9b summarizes the results.

Editing with automatic layout decreased the necessary modeling times in
average by nearly 33%. Full KSBasE reduced the times by another 15% compared
to DND. From auto-layout to KSBasE the difference was mainly influenced by
the earlier experience, e. g., how well keyboard shortcuts could be employed.

The SyncCharts in the tasks were of rather simple structure, and only creation was required, no modifications. Hence, only rather plain transformations

in KSBasE were necessary to complete the tasks. More complex transformations might result in even greater speedups.

7   Conclusions

Visual models help to understand complex systems. However, with current interaction paradigms, activities such as creating or browsing visual models can be very tedious. We presented an approach on enhancing the *pragmatics* of model-based design—the way a user interacts with models. The concept of *meta layout* enables the dynamic synthesis of different diagrammatic views on graphical models. *View management* builds upon automatic layout to configure views on models given a certain context in which the model is examined. An experimental evaluation supports the claim that view management with auto-layout helps to tame complexity in graphical modeling.

Additional modeling languages under investigation are the UML and actor-oriented dataflow languages. Ongoing work is integration and development of more layout algorithms to support more specialized graphical syntaxes and to enhance the aesthetics of layout results. Optimal layout parameters should be determined automatically by measuring aesthetics with metrics and evolutionary algorithms/machine learning. Another current goal is the adoption of a view management language for formulating view management use cases and to establish view management as a "first-class citizen" in modeling.

References

1. Fuhrmann, H., von Hanxleden, R.: Taming graphical modeling. Technical Report 1003, Christian-Albrechts-Universität zu Kiel, Department of Computer Science (May 2010)
2. Seffah, A., Gulliksen, J., Desmarais, M.C.: An introduction to human-centered software engineering. In: Human-Centered Software Engineering—Integrating Usability in the Software Development Lifecycle. Human-Computer Interaction Series, vol. 8, pp. 3–14. Springer, Netherlands (2005)
3. Brosch, P., Langer, P., Seidl, M., Wieland, K., Wimmer, M., Kappel, G., Retschitzegger, W., Schwinger, W.: An example is worth a thousand words: Composite operation modeling by-example. In: Schürr, A., Selic, B. (eds.) MODELS 2009. LNCS, vol. 5795, pp. 271–285. Springer, Heidelberg (2009)
4. Sun, Y., White, J., Gray, J.: Model transformation by demonstration. In: Schürr, A., Selic, B. (eds.) MODELS 2009. LNCS, vol. 5795, pp. 712–726. Springer, Heidelberg (2009)
5. Biermann, E., Ehrig, K., Köhler, C., Kuhns, G., Taentzer, G., Weiss, E.: Graphical Definition of In-Place Transformations in the Eclipse Modeling Framework. In: Nierstrasz, O., Whittle, J., Harel, D., Reggio, G. (eds.) MoDELS 2006. LNCS, vol. 4199, pp. 425–439. Springer, Heidelberg (2006)
6. Gulliksen, J., Göransson, B., Boivie, I., Persson, J., Blomkvist, S.: Åsa Cajander: Key principles for user-centred systems design. In: Human-Centered Software Engineering—Integrating Usability in the Software Development Lifecycle. Human-Computer Interaction Series, vol. 8, pp. 17–36. Springer, Netherlands (2005)

7. Diehl, S.: Software Visualization: Visualizing the Structure, Behavior and Evolution of Software. Springer, Heidelberg (2007)
8. Card, S.K., Mackinlay, J., Shneiderman, B.: Readings in Information Visualization: Using Vision to Think. Morgan Kaufmann, San Francisco (January 1999)
9. Musial, B., Jacobs, T.: Application of focus + context to UML. In: APVis 2003: Proceedings of the Asia-Pacific symposium on Information visualisation, pp. 75–80. Australian Computer Society, Inc., Darlinghurst (2003)
10. Purchase, H.C.: Metrics for graph drawing aesthetics. Journal of Visual Languages and Computing 13(5), 501–516 (2002)
11. Di Battista, G., Eades, P., Tamassia, R., Tollis, I.G.: Graph Drawing: Algorithms for the Visualization of Graphs. Prentice Hall, Englewood Cliffs (1999)
12. Jünger, M., Mutzel, P.: Graph Drawing Software. Springer, Heidelberg (October 2003)
13. Chimani, M., Gutwenger, C.: Algorithms for the hypergraph and the minor crossing number problems. In: Tokuyama, T. (ed.) ISAAC 2007. LNCS, vol. 4835, pp. 184–195. Springer, Heidelberg (2007)
14. Gansner, E.R., North, S.C.: An open graph visualization system and its applications to software engineering. Software—Practice and Experience 30(11), 1203–1234 (2000)
15. Sander, G., Vasiliu, A.: The ILOG JViews graph layout module. In: Mutzel, P., Jünger, M., Leipert, S. (eds.) GD 2001. LNCS, vol. 2265, pp. 469–475. Springer, Heidelberg (2002)
16. Demirezen, Z., Sun, Y., Gray, J., Jouault, F.: Supporting tool reuse with model transformation. In: 18th International Conference on Software Engineering and Data Engineering (SEDE 2009), pp. 119–125. ISCA, Las Vegas (June 2009)
17. Prochnow, S., von Hanxleden, R.: Statechart development beyond WYSIWYG. In: Engels, G., Opdyke, B., Schmidt, D.C., Weil, F. (eds.) MODELS 2007. LNCS, vol. 4735, pp. 635–649. Springer, Heidelberg (2007)
18. Morris, C.W.: Foundations of the theory of signs. International encyclopedia of unified science, vol. 1. The University of Chicago Press, Chicago (1938)
19. Gurr, C.A.: Effective diagrammatic communication: Syntactic, semantic and pragmatic issues. Journal of Visual Languages and Computing 10(4), 317–342 (1999)
20. Haberland, H., Mey, J.L.: Editorial: Linguistics and pragmatics. Journal of Pragmatics 1, 1–12 (1977)
21. Atkinson, C., Kühne, T.: Model-driven development: A metamodeling foundation. IEEE Software, 36–41 (2003)
22. Motika, C., Fuhrmann, H., von Hanxleden, R.: Semantics and execution of domain specific models. Technical Report 0923, Christian-Albrechts-Universität Kiel, Department of Computer Science (December 2009)
23. Fuhrmann, H., von Hanxleden, R.: On the pragmatics of model-based design. In: Choppy, C., Sokolsky, O. (eds.) Foundations of Computer Software. Future Trends and Techniques for Development. LNCS, vol. 6028, pp. 116–140. Springer, Heidelberg (2010)
24. Petre, M.: Why looking isn't always seeing: Readership skills and graphical programming. Communications of the ACM 38(6), 33–44 (1995)
25. Object Management Group: Unified Modeling Language: Superstructure, version 2.0 (August 2005), http://www.omg.org/docs/formal/05-07-04.pdf
26. Gutwenger, C., Jünger, M., Klein, K., Kupke, J., Leipert, S., Mutzel, P.: A new approach for visualizing UML class diagrams. In: SoftVis 2003: Proceedings of the 2003 ACM Symposium on Software Visualization, pp. 179–188. ACM, New York (2003)

27. Fuhrmann, H., Spönemann, M., Matzen, M., von Hanxleden, R.: Automatic layout and structure-based editing of UML diagrams. In: Proceedings of the 1st Workshop on Model Based Engineering for Embedded Systems Design (M-BED 2010), Dresden (March 2010)
28. Grundy, J., Hosking, J., Huh, J., Li, K.N.L.: Marama: an eclipse meta-toolset for generating multi-view environments. In: ICSE 2008: Proceedings of the 30th International Conference on Software Engineering, Leipzig, Germany, pp. 819–822. ACM, New York (2008)
29. André, C.: SyncCharts: A visual representation of reactive behaviors. Technical Report RR 95–52, rev. RR 96–56, I3S, Sophia-Antipolis, France (Rev. April 1996)
30. Fuhrmann, H., von Hanxleden, R.: Enhancing graphical model-based system design—an avionics case study. In: Conjoint workshop of the European Research Consortium for Informatics and Mathematics (ERCIM) and Dependable Embedded Components and Systems (DECOS) at SAFECOMP 2009, Hamburg, Germany (September 2009)
31. Matzen, M.: A generic framework for structure-based editing of graphical models in Eclipse. Diploma thesis, Christian-Albrechts-Universität zu Kiel, Department of Computer Science (March 2010), http://rtsys.informatik.uni-kiel.de/~biblio/downloads/theses/mim-dt.pdf

Taming EMF and GMF
Using Model Transformation

Dimitrios S. Kolovos[1], Louis M. Rose[1], Saad Bin Abid[2],
Richard F. Paige[1], Fiona A.C Polack[1], and Goetz Botterweck[2]

[1] Department of Computer Science,
University of York, YO10 5DD, York, UK
{dkolovos,louis,paige,fiona}@cs.york.ac.uk
[2] Lero - The Irish Software Engineering Research Centre,
Limerick, Ireland
{saad.binabid,goetz.botterweck}@lero.ie

Abstract. EMF and GMF are powerful frameworks for implementing tool support for modelling languages in Eclipse. However, with power comes complexity; implementing a graphical editor for a modelling language using EMF and GMF requires developers to hand craft and maintain several low-level interconnected models through a loosely-guided, labour-intensive and error-prone process. In this paper we demonstrate how the application of model transformation techniques can help with taming the complexity of GMF and EMF and deliver significant productivity, quality, and maintainability benefits. We also present EuGENia, an open-source tool that implements the proposed approach, illustrate its functionality through an example, and report on the community's response to the tool.

1   Introduction

The Eclipse Modelling Framework (EMF)[1] is a widely used model management framework implemented atop the Eclipse software development platform. Over the last few years, Eclipse and EMF have become the de facto standards in the MDE community; the majority of MDE tools (e.g. ATL, oAW, Kermeta, MOFScript, Epsilon) are seamlessly integrated with them. EMF provides flexible and powerful support for constructing models and defining modelling languages. To better support end-users that desire powerful graphical editors for constructing models, the Graphical Modelling Framework (GMF) has been developed: it is a powerful and widely-used framework for implementing graphical editors for EMF-based modelling languages.

Both EMF and GMF adopt a generative approach to achieving their objectives: starting from an Ecore[1] metamodel which specifies the abstract syntax of the modelling language, developers derive and maintain a set of more fine-grained, lower-level models that describe graphical syntax and implementation

---

[1] Ecore is the object-oriented metamodelling language of EMF.

D.C. Petriu, N. Rouquette, Ø. Haugen (Eds.): MODELS 2010, Part I, LNCS 6394, pp. 211–225, 2010.
© Springer-Verlag Berlin Heidelberg 2010

options, and which can be consumed by EMF and GMF code generators to re-alise the editor. EMF and GMF are particularly powerful and flexible, providing customization options for almost every aspect of the generated editor. However, the price to be paid for power and flexibility is increased complexity. As dis-cussed in the industrial experience report presented by Wienands and Golm [2], implementing a graphical editor for a modelling language using EMF and GMF is a loosely guided and error-prone process, mainly because it requires develop-ers to hand craft and maintain a number of low-level, complex interconnected models. Increased complexity in conjunction with sub-optimal tool support for creating and maintaining the required low-level models make implementing a graphical editor with GMF a painful experience, particularly for inexperienced developers.

In this paper we demonstrate how model transformation can help with taming the complexity of GMF and EMF, by raising the level of abstraction, lowering the entrance barrier for new developers, and delivering significant productivity and quality benefits to the process of constructing graphical editors for modelling languages. In particular we demonstrate EuGENia, a mature and widely used tool that adopts a single-sourcing approach based on metamodel annotation and model transformation techniques (both model-to-model and in-place model transformation) for automatically producing and maintaining all the low-level models required by the EMF and GMF code generators.

The paper is organized as follows. Section 2 outlines the process of devel-oping a graphical editor using EMF/GMF and highlights the error-prone and labour-intensive steps. Following this, Section 3 demonstrates how we have used metamodel annotation, model-to-model and in-place model transformation to automate these steps in the context of EuGENia. Section 4 evaluates the findings of this work and demonstrates the productivity and quality benefits delivered by model transformation in this practical problem. Section 5 provides an overview of related work, and Section 6 concludes the paper and provides directions for further work on the subject.

2   Motivation

In this section we outline the process of implementing a graphical editor for a modelling language using EMF and GMF and identify the labour-intensive, error-prone and maintenance-crippling steps it involves. Figure 1 provides a graphical overview of the process and the artefacts involved. The first part of the process involves specifying the abstract syntax of the language using Ecore and generating the respective Java code from it in two stages, using the EMF built-in code generator. The second part involves specifying the graphical syn-tax of the editor using a number of graphical syntax-specific GMF models in three stages, and then using the GMF code generator to generate the concrete graphical editor.

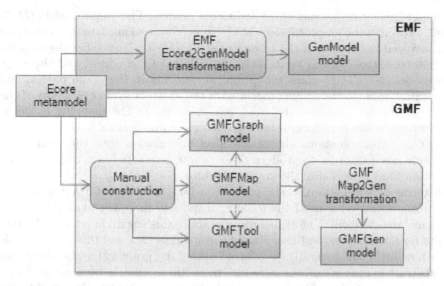

Fig. 1. EMF/GMF Process Overview

2.1 Specifying Abstract Syntax and Generating Code Using EMF

Firstly, the developer needs to define the abstract syntax of the language using Ecore. Following that, the developer can invoke the built-in EMF transformation to transform the Ecore metamodel into a *GenModel*. A *GenModel* is a model which captures lower-level information that specifies how the metamodel should be implemented in Java (e.g. the Java package under which the code will be generated, copyright information to be embedded in the generated files, whether certain UI elements will be generated or not, etc.). Once derived from the Ecore metamodel, a GenModel can be customised and fine-tuned manually. Finally, the GenModel is consumed by an EMF built-in code generator which produces all the necessary code and configuration files.

If the Ecore metamodel is subsequently modified, EMF provides a built-in reconciler that can detect changes in the metamodel and propagate them to the respective GenModel without overwriting the user-defined customisations. However, the reconciler is only effective for simple changes in the Ecore meta-model; for more complex changes the GenModel needs to be regenerated and customised from scratch. This introduces a significant maintenance overhead as it is not always clear to developers which changes in the metamodel can or can-not be reconciled automatically. Therefore, it is common practice to maintain documentation about all manual changes in a separate location (e.g. a text file) so that they can be reapplied (manually) when necessary.

2.2 Specifying Graphical Syntax and Generating Code with GMF

Once the metamodel has been defined and the respective EMF code has been generated, to implement a graphical editor for the language using GMF, the developer needs to construct three additional models. The *graph* model (*GMF-Graph*) specifies the graphical elements (shapes, connections, labels, decorations etc.) involved in the editor, the *tooling* model (*GMFTool*) specifies the element creation tools that will be available in the palette of the editor, and the *mapping* model (*GMFMap*) maps the graphical elements in the graph models and the creation tools in the tooling model with the abstract syntax elements of the Ecore metamodel (classes, attributes, references etc.). The mapping model is then automatically transformed into an even more fine-grained generator model (*GMFGen*) which contains all the low-level information that the GMF code generator needs in order to produce the concrete artefacts (Java code and configuration files) that realize the graphical editor.

In terms of automation, GMF provides a built-in wizard for automatically generating initial versions of the tooling, graph and mapping models from the Ecore metamodel itself. Unfortunately, in practice this wizard fails to yield useful results for anything beyond very simple metamodels [2] - and this is reasonable given how little can generally be inferred about the graphical syntax based on the abstract syntax alone. As a result, these three models need to be hand-crafted using a set of very basic tree-based editors provided by GMF, and this is widely-recognized to be a laborious and error-prone process, particularly given the complexity of the GMF metamodels, and the low-level error messages that GMF produces. Perhaps more challenging than constructing these GMF-specific models is maintaining them as, unlike in EMF, in GMF there is no reconciler that can update these models automatically (even for very simple changes) when the Ecore metamodel changes. Therefore, once customised in any way, these models need to be maintained manually.

As a result, implementing a graphical editor with EMF and GMF is a laborious and error prone task, particularly so for the inexperienced developer. Given that implementing a simple graphical editor is typically one of the first steps attempted by most of the newcomers in MDE [2], the risk of forming a negative impression about the quality of the MDE tool-chain from their interaction with GMF is considerable. Moreover, even for seasoned MDE developers[2], this predominately manual and repetitive process is clearly tedious.

3   EuGENia: Model Transformation to the Rescue

Having criticised some aspects of GMF in the previous section, it is worth stressing again that, despite its weaknesses, GMF still is one of the most powerful, flexible and widely used open-source graphical editor framework available today and when tuned appropriately it can achieve impressive results (the widely used IBM RSA UML modeller, as well as the open-source Topcased and Papyus modelling tools are all implemented atop GMF).

To shield developers from the complexity of GMF and address the highlighted challenges, in this work we adopt a *single-sourcing* approach, in which additional

---

[2] http://voelterblog.blogspot.com/2009/06/gmf-is-still-awful.
html

information necessary for implementing a graphical editor is captured by embedding high-level annotations in the Ecore metamodel. We then use automated model-to-model and in-place transformations to generate, in a consistent and repeatable manner, the platform-specific models required by the EMF and GMF code generators. In this section we demonstrate an implementation of our approach in the context of the EuGENia tool [3] and highlight the productivity, quality and maintainability benefits that our approach delivers.

3.1   Generating GenModels with EuGENia

The first challenge highlighted in Section 2 is to customise the EMF generator model (*GenModel*) produced automatically from an Ecore metamodel, and keep the two synchronized with minimal effort when the Ecore metamodel is subsequently modified. To address this challenge we annotate the Ecore model with GenModel-specific information. A model-to-model transformation (Ecore2GenModel) consumes the annotated Ecore metamodel and creates a GenModel, where in addition to the main Ecore elements (classes, features etc.), their annotation values are also transformed into respective GenModel feature values. As an example, in Figure 2 beyond creating the *Simplem2* GenPackage from the *simplem2* EPackage, the value of the *emf.gen basePackage* annotation of the *simplem2* EPackage has also been copied into the *basePackage* attribute of the respective GenPackage[3].

For more complex customizations which require creating or deleting elements in the GenModel, EuGENia supports user-defined *polishing transformations*. In this context we use the term *polishing transformation* to describe a user-defined

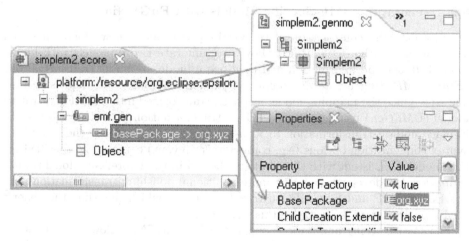

Fig. 2. Exemplar output of the Ecore2GenModel transformation

---

[3] The basePackage attribute specifies the base package under which all Java code will be generated.

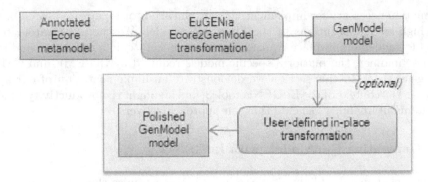

Fig. 3. The EuGENia Ecore2GenModel transformation workflow

in-place model transformation - with a predefined file-name and location relative
to the Ecore metamodel - which is executed by EuGENia after the built-in
Ecore2GenModel transformation and through which the developer can fine-tune
the produced GenModel in a programmatic, and thus repeatable, manner. This
is illustrated in Figure 3 and a concrete example of a polishing transformation
is provided in Listing 1.3 of Section 4.

Using the built-in Ecore2GenModel transformation and the optional user-
defined polishing transformation, the GenModel no longer needs to be maintained manually. It can be regenerated at any point from the Ecore metamodel.
A screencast that demonstrates the Ecore2GenModel transformation in action
is available at:

http://www.eclipse.org/gmt/epsilon/cinema/#eugenia-genmodel.

3.2   Generating GMF-Specific Models with EuGENia

To automate the construction of the GMF-specific models, we follow a similar approach to the one outlined above: we annotate Ecore models with high-
level GMF-specific information and then use a model-to-model transformation
(*Ecore2GMF*) to generate the tooling, graph and mapping GMF models - all in
one step. Once the mapping model has been transformed into a GMF generator
model (*GMFGen*) using the built-in GMF transformation, EuGENia applies an
in-place update transformation to it (*FixGMFGen*), as some of the graphical
syntax configuration options (e.g. compartment layout) can only be specified in
this model. Consistent with the practice followed in the Ecore2GenModel transformation, the developer can contribute additional polishing transformations for
the Ecore2GMF and FixGMFGen transformations, which fine-tune the generated models. Figure 4 illustrates this workflow.

The GMF-specific annotations supported by EuGENia allow developers to
specify a large proportion of the graphical syntax of the language including
node shapes, feature-based and static labels, class- and reference-based associations (links), affixed and phantom nodes, compartments (with a free or a list-
based layout), colours and borders. Section 4.1 provides a detailed example that

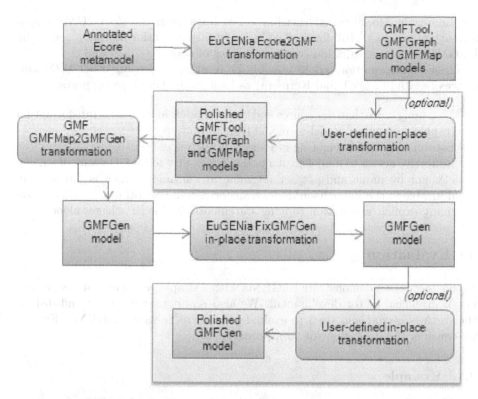

Fig. 4. The EuGENia Ecore2GMF and FixGMFGen transformation workflow

demonstrates a substantial subset of the supported annotations and a complete list of all the annotations supported by EuGENia is available in [4]. It is worth stressing that the annotations supported by EuGENia are not a 1-1 mapping with the features of GMF (otherwise it would be just as complex). GMF features that are not covered by the annotations that EuGENia provides (e.g. setting the font of particular types of nodes) can be managed using the polishing transformation mechanism. A screencast that demonstrates the GMF-model generation part of EuGENia is available at
http://www.eclipse.org/gmt/epsilon/cinema/#Eugenia

3.3 Implementation Notes

The EuGENia transformations are implemented using the Epsilon platform [5]. More specifically, the built-in *Ecore2GenModel* transformation has been implemented using the rule-based ETL [6] model-to-model transformation language, while the *Ecore2GMF* and *FixGMFGen* transformations have been implemented using the imperative EOL language [7]. The Ecore2GMF transformation is implemented with an imperative – and not a rule-based – language due to its high complexity and need for low-level control of the execution flow. In terms of size,

the Ecore2GenModel transformation is 264 lines long, the Ecore2GMF transformation contains 1167 lines of code (including operation libraries), and the
FixGMFGen transformation contains 91 lines of code.

These transformations could possibly be implemented using other M2M languages (e.g. ATL, QVT and Kermeta) as long as the language supports:

- Managing more than one source and target models in the same transformation
- In-place as well as model-to-model transformation
- Establishing and navigating cross-model references
- Reflective access to model elements (i.e. the ability to find a feature of a given
  element by name and get/set its value at runtime), which is particularly
  desirable in the Ecore2GenModel transformation that otherwise will contain
  many explicit annotation copying statements (76 for EPackages alone).

4   Evaluation

In this section we demonstrate EuGENia with a simple yet representative example of graphical editor development. We also report user feedback and discuss
the testing mechanisms used to evaluate the correctness of EuGENia. Finally,
we consider the limitations of our approach.

4.1   Example

In this section we present an example that demonstrates EuGENia for implementing the graphical editor of a Simple Component-connector Language (SCL)
using EMF and GMF. Firstly, we specify the abstract syntax of SCL using Ecore.
Briefly, an SCL model contains named components, which contain any number
of ports and subcomponents. Pairs of components can be linked through their
ports. The Ecore metamodel of SCL, expressed in the Emfatic textual notation
for Ecore is illustrated in Listing 1.1.

Listing 1.1. The SCL Ecore metamodel in Emfatic

```
1   @namespace(uri="scl", prefix="scl")
2   package scl;
3
4   class Component {
5     attr String name;
6     val Component[*] subcomponents;
7     val Port[*] ports;
8   }
9
10  class Connector {
11    attr String name;
12    ref Port#outgoing from;
13    ref Port#incoming to;
14  }
```

```
15
16  class Port {
17    attr String name;
18    val Connector#from outgoing;
19    ref Connector#to incoming;
20  }
```

For EuGENia to realize the graphical editor for SCL using EMF and GMF, we need to annotate the Ecore metamodel as shown in Listing 1.2. In particular, the annotations specify the following:

- Line 2: Source code should generated in the *org.eclipse.epsilon.eugenia.examples* Java package
- Line 5: Each diagram contains a top-level Component model element.
- Line 6: Each component is represented in the diagram as a light blue node labelled with the *name* of the component.
- Line 9: Each Component has a compartment in which sub-components are placed.
- Lines 15-16: Each Connector is represented as a link (association) between its *from* and *to* ports. The end attached to the *to* port is decorated with an arrow.
- Line 23: Each Port is represented as a 15x15 icon-less circle, attached to the border of the component to which it belongs (Line 11).
- Line 24: Each Port is labelled with its *name*. The label is located outside the circle.

Listing 1.2. The annotated SCL Ecore metamodel in Emfatic

```
1   @namespace(uri="scl", prefix="scl")
2   @emf.gen(basePackage="org.eclipse.epsilon.eugenia.examples")
3   package scl;
4
5   @gmf.diagram
6   @gmf.node(label="name", color="219,238,253")
7   class Component {
8     attr String name;
9     @gmf.compartment(layout="free")
10    val Component[*] subcomponents;
11    @gmf.affixed
12    val Port[*] ports;
13  }
14
15  @gmf.link(source="from", target="to",
16    label="name", target.decoration="arrow")
17  class Connector {
18    attr String name;
19    ref Port#outgoing from;
20    ref Port#incoming to;
21  }
```

```
22
23  @gmf.node(figure="ellipse", size="15,15", label.icon="false",
24     label.placement="external", label="name")
25  class Port {
26     attr String name;
27     val Connector#from outgoing;
28     ref Connector#to incoming;
29  }
```

From this annotated metamodel, EuGENia can automatically generate the
GMF editor that appears in Figure 5. While the generated editor is fully-functional,
we wish to further customise it to match our requirements (see Figure 6) .

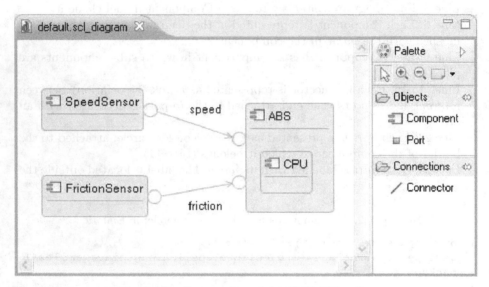

Fig. 5. The first version of the GMF SCL editor

To achieve this, we specify the polishing transformation shown in Listing 1.3
and place it in a predefined location (a file named Ecore2GMF.eol in the same
directory as SCL.ecore) so that EuGENia can locate and execute it it after the
built-in Ecore2GMF transformation every time it is invoked.

Listing 1.3. The polishing in-place transformation in EOL

```
1  // Add bold font to component label
2  var componentLabel = GmfGraph!Label.
3     selectOne(l|l.name="ComponentLabelFigure");
4  componentLabel.font = new GmfGraph!BasicFont;
5  componentLabel.font.style = GmfGraph!FontStyle#BOLD;
6
7  //Set background color and border
8  //of the component compartment
```

```
9  var componentCompartment = GmfGraph!Rectangle.
10 selectOne(r|r.name="ComponentSubcomponentsCompartmentFigure");
11 var lineBorder = new GmfGraph!LineBorder;
12 lineBorder.width = 1;
13 componentCompartment.backgroundColor =
14   createColor(255,255,255);
15 componentCompartment.border = lineBorder;
16
17 operation createColor(red : Integer, green : Integer,
18   blue : Integer) : GmfGraph!RGBColor {
19
20   var color = new GmfGraph!RGBColor;
21   color.red = red;
22   color.blue = blue;
23   color.green = green;
24   return color;
25 }
```

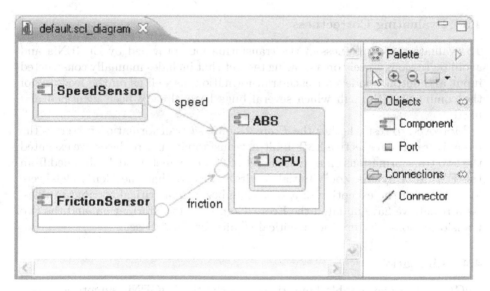

Fig. 6. The polished version of the GMF SCL editor

Specifying the graphical syntax information in the form of annotations in the SCL metamodel involved adding 7 lines of Emfatic code (excluding line-breaks for formatting reasons). From these 7 lines, 59 elements were produced by EuGENia in the graph, tooling and mapping models. The productivity benefits delivered by EuGENia increase alongside the size and complexity of the metamodel - mainly because the graph, mapping and tooling models do not support the notion of inheritance and therefore inheritance in the Ecore metamodel causes a significant amount of duplication in these models. For example, for the

FileSystem metamodel[4], 5 lines of Emfatic annotations result in 102 elements in the graph, tooling and mapping models.

Polishing transformations may not have similar productivity results in terms of the number of model elements they produce/modify (for example the polishing transformation in Listing 1.3 takes 25 lines of code to create 3 and modify 2 elements), however in our experience the effort spent for construcing them quickly pays off as graphical editor development is a highly iterative process [2].

4.2   Community Feedback

EuGENia is part of the Epsilon component of the Eclipse Modeling GMT project. Since it was first released in August 2008, it has been widely used in the Eclipse modelling community both by researchers (at Fraunhofer FOKUS, SINTEF and several universities) and practitioners (at IBM, Siemens and WesternGeco). Evidence for this exists among the large number of posts in the Epsilon forum[5] that refer to EuGENia. A long talk[6] on EuGENia was also delivered in the predominately industrially-oriented Eclipse Summit Europe 2009.

4.3   Evaluating Correctness

To evaluate the correctness of the transformations provided by EuGENia and avoid regressions we rely on a growing test set that includes manually constructed input and output models for each transformation, as well as on the feedback of the community (through which several bugs have already been identified and fixed[7]).

Moreover, to test whether the *Ecore2GenModel* transformation preserves the behaviour of the respective EMF built-in transformation it replaces, we executed the two transformations on a common set of 20 Ecore metamodels obtained from the EMFText Syntax Zoo[8]. Initial results indicated that the GenModels were identical with the exception of a small number of non-critical attribute values. As a result, we have updated the Ecore2GenModel transformation, and the two transformations now produce identical results for our test-set.

4.4   Limitations

EuGENia has two notable limitations. Firstly, the EuGENia annotations pollute metamodels with information irrelevant to their primary purpose (abstract syntax definition). User feedback indicates that this is a fair trade-off for the increased usability. To avoid metamodel pollution without sacrificing usability, we are experimenting with more modular concrete syntaxes for Ecore models.

---

[4] http://www.eclipse.org/gmt/epsilon/doc/articles/
   eugenia-gmf-tutorial/
[5] http://www.eclipse.org/gmt/epsilon/forum/
[6] http://www.eclipsecon.org/summiteurope2009/sessions?id=979
[7] http://bit.ly/bMOP6R
[8] http://www.emftext.org/index.php/EMFText_Concrete_Syntax_Zoo

More specifically, we are investigating the definition of a textual syntax based on Emfatic [8], which allows annotations to be specified in separate physical files and merged at runtime using name-based correspondences. Another option, suggested by EuGENia users, is to extract a standalone language from the annotations provided by EuGENia.

The second limitation of EuGENia is that, to compose polishing transformations, developers need to become familiar with both the transformation language (EOL) and the GMF-related metamodels. Having said this, extensive documentation and several concrete examples are publicly available for EOL; moreover its similarity to OCL helps to make familiarisation easier. Familiarisation with the EMF and GMF metamodels can be achieved in an incremental manner, using models produced by EuGENia as a foundation for incremental exploration.

5   Related Work

Similarly to EuGENia, GmfGen [9] also aims at simplifying the incremental development of GMF editors. The graph, mapping and tooling models depicted in Figure 1 typically contain some duplication of information. This duplication exasperates any inconsistency problems that may arise when changes are made to one of the models. GmfGen provides templates for generating the models needed to construct a GMF editor. The templates remove most of the duplication present in GMF models. However, GmfGen does not address the steep learning curve encountered when first using GMF to generate a visual editor. In fact, knowledge of GMF is required to understand the way in which GmfGens templates are constructed. Instead, EuGENia focuses on abstracting away from GMF.

Several graphical modelling frameworks of similar functionality to GMF are available, most notably MetaEdit+ [10], GME [11] (and its Eclipse-based GEMS branch), AToM^3 [12], and XMF-Mosaic [13]. A detailed analysis of their features appears in [14]. In this work we have concentrated on GMF only as it is increasingly gaining momentum, mainly due to its open-source nature, its extensive set of features, and the immense success of the underlying EMF framework which is widely accepted as the de-facto for modelling in the Java and Eclipse communities.

An early version of the work presented in this paper was presented in a workshop paper [15]. Since this publication, EuGENia has been extended significantly based on feedback from the community, and additional features such as the Ecore2GenModel transformation, and the support for polishing transformations have been realized.

6   Conclusions and Further Work

In this paper we have presented EuGENia, a tool that employs metamodel annotations as well as model-to-model and in-place model transformations to deliver productivity and consistency benefits to the process of developing graphical model editors with the EMF and GMF frameworks. EuGENia has been well-received from the Eclipse modelling community and there is strong evidence that it is extensively used by both researchers and practitioners.

While EuGENia already greatly improves the usability of GMF and lowers the entrance barrier for inexperienced developers, a significant amount of work remains including support for: sub-diagrams, multiple (non-hierarchical) diagrams in the same file, and advanced property editing. Ongoing research seeks to addresses some of these issues in the MOSKitt[9] and EEF[10] projects. We aim to converge with these projects and progressively extend EuGENia to support, in a usable and intuitive manner, all of the features discussed above.

An additional interesting direction for further research is to target alternative graphical editor frameworks such as the upcoming Graphiti framework[11] from SAP, or web-based frameworks such as UMLCanvas[12].

Acknowledgements

Parts of this work were supported by the European Commission's 7th Framework Programme, through grant #248864 (MADES), and by Science Foundation Ireland grant 03/CE2/I303_1 to Lero, http://www.lero.ie/.

References

1. Steinberg, D., Budinsky, F., Paternostro, M., Merks, E.: EMF: Eclipse Modelling Framework, 2nd edn. Eclipse Series. Addison-Wesley Professional, Reading (December 2008)
2. Wienands, C., Golm, M.: Anatomy of a Visual Domain-Specific Language Project in an Industrial Context. In: ACM/IEEE 12th International Conference on Model Driven Engineering Languages and Systems (MoDELS), Denver, Colorado, USA, pp. 453–467 (2009)
3. Epsilon Eclipse GMT Component: EuGENia, http://www.eclipse.org/gmt/epsilon/doc/eugenia
4. Epsilon Eclipse GMT Component: EuGENia GMF Tutorial, http://www.eclipse.org/gmt/epsilon/doc/articles/eugenia-gmf-tutorial/
5. Eclipse Foundation: Epsilon Modeling GMT component, http://www.eclipse.org/gmt/epsilon
6. Kolovos, D.S., Paige, R.F., Polack, F.A.C.: The Epsilon Transformation Language. In: Vallecillo, A., Gray, J., Pierantonio, A. (eds.) ICMT 2008. LNCS, vol. 5063, pp. 46–60. Springer, Heidelberg (2008)
7. Kolovos, D.S., Paige, R.F., Polack, F.A.C.: The Epsilon Object Language. In: Rensink, A., Warmer, J. (eds.) ECMDA-FA 2006. LNCS, vol. 4066, pp. 128–142. Springer, Heidelberg (2006)
8. IBM alphaWorks: Emfatic Language for EMF Development (February 2005), http://www.alphaworks.ibm.com/tech/emfatic
9. Schnepel, E.: GenGMF: Efficient editor development for large meta models using the Graphical Modelling Framework. In: Proc. Special Interest Group on Model-Driven Software Engineering (SIG-MDSE) (2008)

---

[9] http://www.moskitt.org
[10] http://www.eclipse.org/modeling/emft/?project=eef#eef
[11] http://www.eclipse.org/proposals/graphiti/
[12] http://umlcanvas.org/

10. MetaCase: Meta-Edit+, http://www.metacase.com
11. Generic Modeling Environment, http://www.isis.vanderbilt.edu/Projects/gme
12. De Lara, J., Vangheluwe, H.: Using AToM3 as a Meta-CASE Tool. In: Proc. 4th International Conference on Enterprise Information Systems, Ciudad Real, Spain, pp. 642–649 (April 2002)
13. Xactium: XMF-Mosaic, http://www.xactium.com
14. Amyot, D., Farah, H., Roy, J.-F.: Evaluation of Development Tools for Domain-Specific Modeling Languages. In: Gotzhein, R., Reed, R. (eds.) SAM 2006. LNCS, vol. 4320, pp. 183–197. Springer, Heidelberg (2006)
15. Kolovos, D.S., Rose, L.M., Paige, R.F., Polack, F.A.C.: Raising the Level of Abstraction in the Development of GMF-based Graphical Model Editors. In: Proc. 3rd Workshop on Modeling in Software Engineering (MISE), ACM/IEEE International Conference on Software Engineering (ICSE), Vancouver, Canada (May 2009)

A Visual Traceability Modeling Language

Patrick Mäder and Jane Cleland-Huang

DePaul University, Chicago, IL, USA
patrick.maeder@tu-ilmenau.de, jhuang@cs.depaul.edu

Abstract. Software traceability is effort intensive and must be applied strategically in order to maximize its benefits and justify its costs. Unfortunately, development tools provide only limited support for traceability, and as a result users often construct trace queries using generic query languages which require intensive knowledge of the data-structures in which artifacts are stored. In this paper, we propose a usage-centered traceability process that utilizes UML class diagrams to define traceability strategies for a project and then visually represents trace queries as constraints upon subsets of the model. The Visual Trace Modeling Language (VTML) allows users to model queries while hiding the underlying technical details and data structures. The approach has been demonstrated through a prototype system and and evaluated through a preliminary experiment to evaluate the expressiveness and readability of VTML in comparison to generic SQL queries.

1 Introduction

Software and systems level traceability is a well-known concept, supporting a number of software engineering tasks such as impact analysis, requirements validation, and coverage analysis. However, studies suggest that developers and other project stakeholders often create traceability links only because they are required to by external regulations or by process improvement initiatives. Although the required link creation process serves a useful purpose for helping to validate that the system being constructed meets its requirements, studies have shown that stakeholders rarely re-use traceability links during the long-term use and maintenance of the system [8,1,5]. This failure can be partially attributed to the fact that current tools make it difficult for project stakeholders to construct non-trivial, yet useful traceability queries.

In contrast to the recent research focus on decreasing the costs of trace creation, this paper introduces an expressive Visual Trace Modelling Language (VTML) designed to increase the benefits of tracing, through making it more accessible to software developers and other project stakeholders. This follows the approach taken in database research and practice to develop visual query methods that allow users to formulate database queries in a relatively simple and intuitive way [13]. Instead of creating an entirely new notation, our approach utilizes standard UML class diagrams to model trace queries as a set of constraints enforced onto a subset of a traceability meta-model. Taking this more conservative approach

D.C. Petriu, N. Rouquette, Ø. Haugen (Eds.): MODELS 2010, Part I, LNCS 6394, pp. 226–240, 2010.
© Springer-Verlag Berlin Heidelberg 2010

means that VTML can be adopted by any organization familiar with UML, and also that queries can be modeled and executed using standard tools available on most projects. VTML is implemented using a goal-oriented approach which enables project stakeholders to clearly define their traceability needs for the project, develop an associated strategy for capturing the necessary traceability links, and model complex traceability queries in a relatively intuitive way.

The remainder of the paper is structured as follows, Section 2 provides a brief overview of the relevant traceability features included in common development and requirements management tools. Section 3 reviews related work on modeling traceability queries. Section 4 describes an usage-centered traceability process and how traceability queries contribute to it. Section 5 discusses our visual traceability query language and its main concepts. Section 6 shows sample queries, and discusses the application of visual traceability queries, and their definition and validation. Section 7 then discusses an experiment to evaluate the ease of use and understandability of our modelling language.

2 State of Practice in Trace Query Modeling

Almost all leading requirements management tools provide support for common traceability tasks such as coverage and impact analysis based on traceability links created by the user. However this trace functionality is quite rudimentary. Coverage analysis is typically achieved through filtering out unrelated elements within a structural component of the model, while impact analysis is achieved through showing elements related through established traceability links. For example, IBM Rational RequisitePro/Systems Developer^{TM} provides a feature called a Traceability Query, which allows users to create a diagram of all elements dependent upon a selected one or all elements on which a selected element depends. IBM DOORS^{TM} provides a feature that visualizes chains of links across multiple types of artifacts. Similarly, Sparx Enterprise Architect^{TM} provides a feature for generating implementation reports based on user created traces of a specific, pre-defined type.

In most projects, support for more complex traceability queries is provided through a tool-specific API or by direct access to the underlying data structures. For example, Enterprise Architect allows user-defined queries to be modeled as SQL statements on the underlying database, but these queries require substantial knowledge of the tool's internal data structures or of its API. This type of approach does not make it easy for users to develop and use trace queries as an integral day-to-day component of their work.

3 Related Work

To address these limitations, several researchers have developed languages and notations for supporting trace queries, or of adopting standard query languages such as SQL or XQuery. One goal of any such query language is to allow users to specify their queries at an abstraction level that focuses on the purpose of the trace, as opposed to its underlying data representation. However, there are several specific challenges that make trace queries difficult to handle. Among other issues, traceable artifacts such as requirements, design, code, and test cases, are often represented in heterogeneous formats with different underlying data structures. Although ideally in the future the use of integrated case tools might lead to more standard representations, current traceability solutions must deal with an enormously broad representation of data types and formats.

Maletic and Collard [6] describe a Trace Query Language (TQL) which can be used to model trace queries for artifacts represented in XML format. TQL specifies queries on the abstraction level of artifacts and links and hides low-level details of the underlying XPath query language through the use of extension functions. Nevertheless, TQL queries are non-trivial for users without knowledge of XPath and XML to understand. Zhang et al. [12] describe an approach for the automated generation of traceability relations between source code and documentation. The authors use ontologies to create query-ready abstract representations of both models. The Racer query language (nRQL) is then used to retrieve traces; however nRQL's syntax requires users to have a relatively strong mathematical background.

Wieringa [11] discusses the use of Entity Relationship Models (ERM) to represent traceability links. He points out that "... an ER model of links can be implemented using any database technology" meaning that ad hoc queries can be easily constructed. As ERMs are now often represented as class diagrams, VTML extends this notion by utilizing class diagrams to visualize both the structure of the traceability information and the queries built upon it. Schwarz et al. [9] utilize a meta-model referred to as the Requirements Reference Model (RRM) to store artifacts and relations, and then issue queries using the Graph Repository Query Language (GReQL). The authors show two sample queries with syntax similar to SQL, but provide no further detail concerning the implementation of their approach nor its validation. Nevertheless, their use of a defined meta-model for representing the underlying data is very useful.

Sherba et al. [10] discuss the specification of a traceability system, called TraceM, based on information integration and open hypermedia. This work provides an interesting foundation for VTML, as it describes an optimal basis for our approach. The authors address the problem of heterogeneous artifact representations through proposing a service-based architecture with translators that normalize the heterogeneous data, and schedulers that allow the user to define when to update the normalized data. Among these services is also a query service that "allows filtering of relationships so that different views of the information space can be created based on the needs of various stakeholders." In related work, Lin et al. [3] implemented Poirot, a service-oriented approach for retrieving artifacts dynamically at runtime from a variety of requirements management tools such as RequisitePro^{TM} and DOORS^{TM}. Poirot retrieves data using adapters that interface with standard APIs provided by each case tool, and then transform the data into Poirot's XML schema. Our query language could be integrated with the query services of either TraceM or Poirot.

4   Defining the Traceability Information

VTML assumes the presence of an underlying meta-model, that we refer to as the Traceability Information Model (TIM). The TIM provides the context in which VTML queries can be specified and executed [8]. Our approach utilizes a goal-oriented method for identifying long-term strategic trace queries and the underlying data and traceability links needed to support them. This approach minimizes the effort involved in trace creation and maintenance while maximizing its value. The techniques used to identify traceability goals and to construct the TIM are founded in the systematic Goal-Question-Metric (GQM) approach proposed by Basili et al. [2]. There are three steps involved in the process and these are described in the following subsections.

Step 1: Identify tasks that require traceability. In this first step, specific tasks that are dependent upon traceability should be defined. For example, in a safety critical project a safety officer might need to retrieve all requirements that mitigate identified hazards in order to construct a safety case, or a developer might need to check whether the code she/he is editing either directly or indirectly impacts specific quality constraints captured in the software requirements specification. Such questions can be identified systematically through identifying project goals and then analyzing the project roles and their related tasks.

Step 2: Define traceability. Once trace related tasks have been identified, it is necessary to define a project level trace strategy to ensure that the necessary traceability links are created and maintained. Many researchers agree on the necessity of such a project-level definition as it facilitates a consistent and ready-to-analyze set of traceability relations for a project. This definition is commonly called a traceability information model or traceability meta-model and usually represented as a UML class diagram. Figure 1 shows an example of a traceability information model.

Such an information model is composed of two basic types of entities: traceable artifact types represented as classes, and the permitted traceability relations between the artifact types represented as associations. Traceable artifact types serve as the abstractions supporting the traceability perspective of a project, but they do not necessarily reflect concrete datasets that exist in the traced models. For example, a traceable artifact type might represent an abstraction of several different concrete artifact types existing in the related models, or conversely it could refer to a single artifact type in a tool. Figure 1 also shows the mapping of traceable artifact types to their source documents, each one stereotyped as a 'toolArtifact'. There are several reasons for distinguishing between tool artifact types and abstract traceable artifact types; however the pertinent issue here is that a tool artifact provides information about how a certain traceable artifact type is represented within a concrete tool or model. A more concrete discussion of the traceability information model is given in [4]. As trace creation and maintenance can be expensive, each proposed trace should be evaluated to ensure that it serves a useful purpose. It is also useful to define important properties for each of the traceable artifacts. For example, in Figure 1 the 'UseCase'

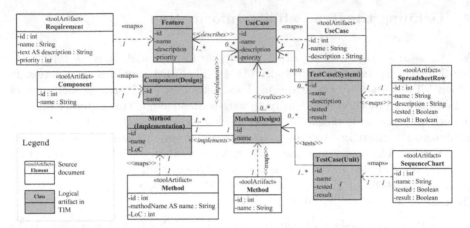

Fig. 1. Example of a project-specific traceability information model

artifact type includes 'id', 'name', and 'description' properties, all of which can be returned as trace query results or used to define constraints that filter out unwanted artifacts.

Step 3: Define traceability queries. Once traceability tasks have been identified (Step 1) and the TIM established (Step 2), it is necessary to define a set of trace queries that provide an efficient way of supporting the defined tasks. This step is largely ignored by current tools, which assume that trace queries will either be overly simple or that high-end users will export data and write customized scripts to support their more advanced trace queries.

As the TIM provides a graphical representation of logical dependencies between artifacts in a development project, it is natural to use it to specify traceability queries too. There are several benefits to this approach. First traceability queries can be constrained to act on the traceable artifacts and traceability relations defined in the TIM, with the underlying assumptions that associated data capture is integrated into the software development and management process. Second, visualizing trace queries in this way can make them more intuitive for typical project stakeholders. This conjecture is tested through the experiment described in Section 7 of this paper.

There are several well-established query languages such as SQL and XQuery which can provide the same results for a specific dataset as the method we propose in this paper; however there are two specific issues that we believe justify using VTML:

– Traceability queries deal to a large extent with the existence of relations between artifacts and with the count of those relations, although such queries can be specified in standard query languages such as SQL, they lead to rather complex, recurring constructs. For example, a simple query against the TIM in Figure 1, designed to identify implemented methods related to a given set of use cases, translates into the following SQL statement:

```
SELECT "UseCase".id, "Method(Implementation)".id
```

```
FROM "Method(Implementation)","LINKS_Method(Implementation)_Method(Design)",
"Method(Design)", "LINKS_Method(Design)_UseCase", "UseCase"
WHERE
"Method(Implementation)".id ="LINKS_Method(Implementation)_Method(Design)".sourceID AND
"LINKS_Method(Implementation)_Method(Design)".targetID = "Method(Design)".id
AND "Method(Design)".id = "LINKS_Method(Design)_UseCase".sourceID AND
"LINKS_Method(Design)_UseCase".targetID = "UseCase".id AND "UseCase".id
```

- A large part of a traceability query specified in a standard language refers to the underlying data structure. For traceability purposes this has already been described in the TIM, and redefining it in each trace query introduces unwanted redundancy.

By re-using information previously specified in the TIM, VTML hides most of the technical details and creates queries at the traceability perspective of a project.

5   Defining Visual Traceability Queries

This section describes the way in which VTML queries are modeled over the TIM. The discussion is separated into a specification of the general structure of a query, a specification of constraints on a query and finally the inclusion of aggregation functions as part of a query.

5.1   Query Structure

Class diagrams provide a convenient way of representing a query, which can be modeled as a structural subset of the traceability information model. This means that a query may be composed from all traceable artifact types across all permitted traceability relations defined within the current traceability information model of a project. This approach also has the significant benefit of utilizing a widely adopted modeling language, with all its associated tool support.

In addition to modeling traceable artifact types and their relationships, the TIM also associates a set of properties with each traceable artifact. These properties, which are defined as attributes for each artifact type, can be used to specify query constraints and can also be returned as results of a trace query. When these properties are used within a query, they are stereotyped to show whether they represent a 'result' or a 'filter constraint'. As depicted in Figure 2, each stereotype is associated with a graphical symbol placed in front of the property name. For example, attributes stereotyped as 'results' are represented by a bar graph symbol, while attributes used to filter the results are annotated with a filter symbol. Most UML modeling tools support the use of graphical symbols in place of stereotypes. An identifier property exists by default for each traceable artifact type and is used to join the underlying data structures (artifacts and traces) automatically. This property is only shown within a query if it is intended to be returned in the result set.

5.2   Defining Constraints

While structural elements support queries across traceable artifacts, more specific queries can only be obtained by specifying constraints. There are three kinds

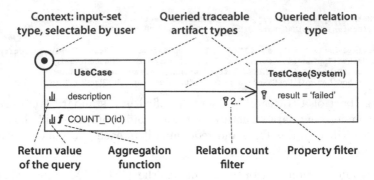

Fig. 2. Features of a visual traceability query

of constraints that can be specified in our notation: constraints to properties of traceable artifacts, constraints to the number of existing traceability relations between artifacts, and constraints on the scope which defines the user-selected input set of a query.

The first type of constraint refers to the properties of traceable artifacts. As previously discussed, these properties can become part of a query's result or may be used to filter out unwanted artifacts. In VTML the constraint is defined after the name of a property attribute within a traceable artifact type. A stereotype 'filter' is attached to the attribute and visually represented as the filter symbol (see Figure 2). The constraint is specified as a logical expression consisting of the property name, a logical comparison ($=, <, >, <=, >=, !=$) and a value or several values as boolean expression ($\&\&, \|, !$).

Multiplicity constraints refer to the number of existing traceability relations between two artifacts. By specifying multiplicities for a traceability relation between two traceable artifact types, it is possible to constrain the query results to only those artifacts that provide the specified number of traceability relations. Similar to property constraints, a stereotype 'filter' is attached to the multiplicity and visually represented as a symbol (see Figure 2). As standardized in UML class diagrams, multiplicities can be defined as a single number, a list of numbers, or as a range of numbers, and therefore provide significant flexibility in specifying constraints with respect to the number of existing traceability relations. For the current prototype implementation we decided to interpret an unspecified multiplicity as $1..*$. Multiplicity constraints facilitate a wide variety of trace queries, for example, to retrieve all requirements with no (zero) related acceptance tests, or conversely all requirements that fan-out to 2 or more design elements.

The final type of constraint refers to a so-called query scope which defines the traceable artifact type that a query can be applied to. While executing a query, the user may choose to perform the query on all artifacts of that type within a model or to constrain it to a subset of those. The scope is defined by attaching the stereotype 'scope' to one of the traceable artifact types of a query and is visually represented as an encircled dot (see Figure 2). The example in Figure 2 means that the query is applicable to use cases and the user may decide to provide a specific input-set of use cases to be queried or to perform the query on all use cases.

In order to increase readability of queries we apply directed associations starting from the scope element. Although, this is not required for the automated interpretation of the query by a tool, feedback from early user studies has shown that it can increase readability for human users.

5.3   Aggregation Functions

Some trace queries may require aggregation of the query results. For example, instead of requesting a list of concrete artifacts which fulfill a certain query, a user might require the trace query to return their count. For this purpose standard query languages provide a set of aggregation functions. VTML currently supports the same functions as SQL. These functions are defined as methods within traceable artifact types and a stereotype 'function', visually represented as a f symbol, is attached (see Figure 2).

5.4   Integrating Other Techniques

In addition to standard aggregation functions VTML supports an extended set of customized functions, implemented as code snippets. For example, a function could be developed to aggregate code metrics for all classes or methods that traced from a specified requirement. For evaluation purposes we developed two such functions and successfully incorporated them in the VTML and executed them as trace queries.

5.5   Limitations and Analysis of the Approach

It is important to observe that all defined constraints of a query apply in parallel. That means that for each artifact within the user-selected scope all defined constraints must be fulfilled in order to be part of the results. We found that limitation acceptable as we were able to express a broad range of desired queries during the development of VTML. However, the notation does not support some specific types of queries, for example, artifacts that either have a certain property value or a relation to another artifact. Such queries need currently to be performed separately, concatenating the results as an additional step. We could not find an appropriate visual way of representing those dependencies between constraints, while keeping the simplicity of the visual notation. We are currently evaluating the use of filter references that can be used to write complex boolean expression involving all filters as an additional text.

Moody [7] describes nine principles for designing cognitively effective visual notations against which we qualitatively validated our VTML approach. As advocated by Moody, our notation provides a 1:1 mapping between semantic constructs that we are aiming to express and the graphical symbols used to represent them (semiotic clarity). All our symbols are clearly distinguishable from each other (perceptual discriminability). The participants of our experiment reported no problems in identifying the meaning of our symbols (semantic

transparency). Visual traceability queries show only the actual queried part of
the available traceability information (complexity management). The representation of our queries builds upon the representation of the traceability information
model (cognitive integration). We apply a cognitively manageable number of visual symbols (graphic economy) where appropriate and use text to complement
these graphics (dual coding). Finally, we assumed that the traceability information model is represented as a UML class diagram and created our notation
accordingly; however if the traceability information model were to be represented
using a different notation the VTML notation should be updated accordingly
(cognitive fit).

6 Applying Visual Traceability Queries

This section provides examples of visual traceability queries and discusses different aspects of their application. Although we only depict a small sampling of
queries in this paper, we have used VTML to express a much wider variety of
useful trace queries in a mid-sized industrial project.

6.1 Example Queries

Figure 3 shows four query examples that demonstrate VTML's ability to express
a variety of traceability queries, including ones that could not easily be modeled
in existing requirements management tools.

The query shown in Figure 3a finds features that are implemented by more
than one component of the design model and so highlights possible deficiencies
in the design. Figure 3b depicts a query that returns all methods implementing
a 'failed' unit test case and so facilitates the analysis of the discovered problem
in the source code. The query in Figure 3c returns the description of all use
cases that are implemented by methods with more than 50 lines of code. The

(a) Query: Find features scattered
among multiple components

(b) Query: Find methods implementing
'failed' unit test cases

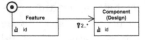

(c) Query: Show uses cases implemented
by methods with $> 50LoC$

(d) Query: Find redundant traces
between use cases and implementation

Fig. 3. Example queries

purpose of such a query could be to identify and review complex usage scenarios. Figure 3d shows a query, inspired by a real world example, that finds redundant traceability relations between use cases and implementation methods. While the traceability information model allows both routes, the idea is that either the one or the other should be chosen by the user in order to avoid conflicts during other analyses. Both routes could be allowed, because only some of the use cases are documented in the design model and can be traced via such artifacts.

6.2 Transformation Into Executable Queries

One of the major benefits of VTML is that trace queries are specified over the TIM, and do not need to reference the underlying data structures. This means that a user specifies and reads queries from the traceability perspective of a project. However, in order to execute these queries it is necessary to transform them into a query format that is supported by the actual data sources. Although VTML is not bound to any specific underlying query language, we demonstrate its feasibility through a transformation of visual traceability queries into SQL queries executable on the traceability repository of our *traceMaintainer* proto-type. The transformation is fully automated and converts the features of a visual traceability query step by step into an executable SQL query.

The VTML transformation is implemented using a XSLT script that translates queries in XMI format, exported from a compatible UML modeling tool, into SQL statements executable on *traceMaintainer's* database. The transformation is not only dependent upon the target query language, but also on the structure of the repository. For the prototype implementation we decided to store each traceable artifact type, defined with the traceability information model, as a separate table as well as each traceability relation defined among these types. This is one possi-ble way of implementing the data structure, but not the only one. The rationale behind our implementation decision was that different traceable artifact types as well as different defined traceability relations might have varying numbers and types of properties making it more difficult to store all in the same table.

6.3 Supporting the Creation and Validation of Queries

In order to execute the defined queries, our current prototype requires the user to export the created queries into XMI format, which is supported by all major modeling tools. Future iterations of our prototype tool could include a VTML wizard to provide interactive guidance on how to create queries for certain com-mon purposes (e.g., counting elements over several artifact levels). Furthermore, as all queries are subsets of the traceability information model, the TIM can be used to validate the structural correctness of each query. Additionally, defined constraints can be validated for their syntactical correctness by using regular expressions. While extensions to the traceability information model will have no effect on defined queries, deletions and modifications could invalidate a query if the required information becomes unavailable following the change. Our tool revalidates queries each time they are transformed into the executable format.

7   Evaluation

We designed a preliminary experiment to comparatively evaluate the understandability and the ease of use of VTML with respect to other query languages. However, the experiment reported in this paper, was limited to a comparison with SQL, which represents an expressive and broadly adopted query language used in industry. We formulated two research questions:

Q1 Reading: Does the use of Visual Traceability Queries result in a more accurate and faster understanding of a query's purpose compared to equivalent techniques?

Q2 Constructing: Does the use of Visual Traceability Queries result in a more accurate and faster construction of traceability queries compared to equivalent techniques?

Our experiment had one independent variable, the query notation, and two treatments: VTML and SQL. Our experiment aimed to find out whether there is a causal relationship between the treatment and the time and correctness for reading and constructing queries.

7.1   Experimental Set-up

In order to answer these two research questions, we designed a controlled experiment which included trace queries we had previously seen executed in actual industrial projects.

Subjects. The subjects comprised 18 practitioners and students with a basic knowledge of UML modeling and database engineering as well as writing and understanding SQL queries. Our participants had an average experience of 3.5 years in using SQL queries but only an average of 2.2 years with UML. This indicates that for many of the subjects we were evaluating a well-known technique against a relatively new approach.

Procedure and Tasks. All the data was gathered via questionnaires. In addition to providing actual answers to the questions in the questionnaire, the time it took to complete individual tasks was recorded. The experiment consisted of the following steps:

1. All subjects completed a series of questions to describe her/his background and experience in the field of software and data engineering.
2. All subjects read a tutorial about the general purpose of software traceability, the use of a traceability information model, and the purpose of traceability related queries. The material also contained a table comparing features of a query expressed in SQL and VTML. The subjects were allowed to use the tutorial material throughout the entire experiment.
3. All participants were given a set of nine different queries, each expressed in either SQL or VTML. For each query we provided four possible answers, and the participants were directed to select the answer which they felt most closely represented the meaning of the query. Each query was presented to 9 participants in SQL and 9 in VTML.

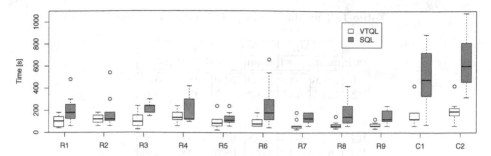

Fig. 4. Time required to understand (R1–R9) and construct queries (C1, C2)

4. All subjects were also asked to construct two queries, one written in SQL and one modeled in VTML. The assignment was random.
5. All subjects completed a questionnaire concerning their experience using both VTML and SQL to read and construct traceability queries.

7.2 Results

Q1 Reading queries. Table 1 shows that subjects viewing our visual notation responded on average (mean) 26% to 63% faster to the nine questions (R1–R9) than subjects viewing the same query in SQL notation, thereby reducing the time to understand a query by 45%. However the difference was statistically significant in only six of the nine queries (see p-values in column t-test) due to the high variability in the response time. Figure 4 visualizes response time and variability across all tasks. The variability could have been caused by different experience levels of the subjects; however this will be analyzed in a future experiment. Post experiment interviews also suggested that the multiple choice design allowed users to guess the answer without fully understanding the query, which certainly could have impacted the results of the query reading task. For reading visual queries, 14.9% of the given answers were incorrect using the visual notation, while only 10.5% were incorrect using SQL. However, half of the incorrect answers in both notations referred to the same query, suggesting that the answers we provided might have been misleading. Furthermore, two-thirds of the incorrect answers for visual queries were given for the first three questions, suggesting that comprehension of visual queries increased with experience.

Q2 Constructing queries. Table 1 shows that subjects constructed the same query in our visual notation on average 69% faster than in SQL. Despite the relatively large variability, especially in the time spent constructing SQL queries (see Figure 4), the differences for both construction tasks (C1, C2) are statistically significant. Again, this is likely due to differences in experience of our subjects. Only 6.7% of the constructed visual queries (one query) were partly incorrect, while 89.5% of the constructed SQL queries were at least partly incorrect. This suggests that our approach facilitates a significantly faster and more correct specification of traceability queries than SQL.

Table 1. Time differences [s] for performing tasks

task	VTML mean	sd	SQL mean	sd	diff VTML	t-test
R1	101.6	53.6	206.9	134.0	-51%	0.03
R2	121.1	45.5	178.2	153.5	-32%	0.16
R3	112.1	70.4	220.9	48.3	-49%	0.00
R4	145.0	55.0	210.3	123.2	-31%	0.09
R5	94.1	63.4	126.8	57.1	-26%	0.14
R6	95.1	42.3	257.9	208.3	-63%	0.02
R7	71.7	48.2	131.1	45.7	-45%	0.01
R8	68.8	34.5	171.2	113.3	-60%	0.01
R9	68.3	25.2	143.5	62.1	-52%	0.00
∅					**-45%**	
C1	153.0	100.4	500.5	276.6	-69%	0.00
C2	202.9	112.7	647.4	271.0	-69%	0.00
∅					**-69%**	

7.3   Threats to Validity

Important threats to the validity of the experiment are divided into four common categories.

External Validity. Our experiment shows results of subjects with a diverse background in the field of our experiment, from practitioners to students, with practical experience, for example, as product managers, developers, requirements engineers and designers. Nevertheless, the relatively small size of our sample does not allow us to draw general conclusions, we rather see our experiment as an initial validation which will now lead into an extended study. All of the presented queries had a realistic purpose and were determined based on our knowledge of traceability in industrial settings.

Internal Validity. To decrease variability in knowledge across participants we provided an introductory tutorial. The written form of the material minimized the possible influence of the experimenters on the results. The notation in which a query was represented was randomly assigned in order to balance learning effects. None of the participants provided more than two incorrect answers suggesting a sound understanding of the topic. Although, we improved the multiple-choice answers for the questions during pilot tests, some of the answers might still have been misleading as previously discussed.

Reliability. We expect that replications of the experiment will offer results similar to those presented here. Concrete measured results will differ from those presented here as they are specific to the subjects, but the underlying trends and implications should remain unchanged. Our participants had a large variety of experience regarding the topic of the experiment.

Construct Validity. Our experiment aimed at evaluating the understandability and the ease of use of our visual notation compared to existing techniques. We decided to focus on reading and constructing of traceability queries as we believe that those are the most important applications for a visual traceability modeling language. If a notation is easier to use and comprehend, then the measures of time and correctness should correspondingly show lower values. Our experiments therefore focused on these measures.

8   Conclusions and Future Work

This paper has presented a usage-centered traceability process that first defines the traceability strategies for a project and then models traceability queries visually using VTML. It introduces a novel way to specify traceability queries that utilizes the project's TIM and builds on UML concepts that are well known to most users. In this way users apply the same technique to describe and execute traceability queries as they use for modeling the overall project artifacts. Furthermore, the specification of queries is constrained to entities defined within the TIM, facilitating a consistent traceability view of a project as well as limiting possible choices in the specification of queries to the actual available ones.

The experiment we performed has demonstrated that users are able to read and construct traceability queries more quickly using VTML. This was especially marked following an initial learning curve. This curve appeared most evident for users with less prior UML experience. Our experiment further suggests that visually constructed traceability queries are substantially more correct compared to the same queries constructed with SQL. As a proof of concept and to gain more experience we developed a prototype implementation. Future work will involve augmenting the prototype to include more advanced features to guide the user through the task of creating and validating trace queries. Furthermore, although our current prototype uses XSLT to transform visual queries into executable ones, we are exploring more general transformations that can be customized to different underlying data schemes and various query languages such as SQL, XQuery, and LINQ. Finally, we intend to conduct a more comprehensive study that evaluates whether VTML can by used by stakeholders to create traceability links that help them perform useful tasks in an industrial settings.

Acknowledgments

This work was partially funded by the National Science Foundation grant #CCF: 0810924.

References

1. Arkley, P., Riddle, S.: Overcoming the traceability benefit problem. In: Proceedings 13th International Requirements Engineering Conference, pp. 385–389. IEEE Computer Society, Los Alamitos (2005) ISBN 0-7695-2425-7

2. Basili, V.R., Caldiera, G., Rombach, H.D.: Goal Question Metric Paradigm. In: Marciniak, J.J. (ed.) Encyclopedia of Software Engineering, vol. 1, pp. 528–532. John Wiley & Sons, Chichester (1994)
3. Lin, J., Lin, C.C., Cleland-Huang, J., Settimi, R., Amaya, J., Bedford, G., Berenbach, B., Khadra, O.B., Duan, C., Zou, X.: Poirot: A distributed tool supporting enterprise-wide automated traceability. In: RE, pp. 356–357. IEEE Computer Society, Los Alamitos (September 2006)
4. Mäder, P., Gotel, O., Philippow, I.: Getting Back to Basics: Promoting the Use of a Traceability Information Model in Practice. In: 5th Workshop on Traceability in Emerging Forms of Software Engineering (TEFSE 2009). In conjunction with ICSE 2009, Vancouver, Canada (May 2009)
5. Mäder, P., Gotel, O., Philippow, I.: Motivation Matters in the Traceability Trenches. In: Proceedings of 17th International Requirements Engineering Conference (RE 2009), Atlanta, Georgia, USA (August 2009)
6. Maletic, J.I., Collard, M.L.: Tql: A query language to support traceability. In: TEFSE 2009: Proceedings of the 2009 ICSE Workshop on Traceability in Emerging Forms of Software Engineering, pp. 16–20. IEEE Computer Society, Washington (2009)
7. Moody, D.L.: The 'physics' of notations: Toward a scientific basis for constructing visual notations in software engineering. IEEE Trans. Software Eng. 35(6), 756–779 (2009)
8. Ramesh, B., Jarke, M.: Toward reference models of requirements traceability. IEEE Transactions on Software Engineering 27(1), 58–93 (2001)
9. Schwarz, H., Ebert, J., Riediger, V., Winter, A.: Towards querying of traceability information in the context of software evolution. In: 10th Workshop Software Reengineering, Bad Honnef, May 5-7. LNI, vol. 126, pp. 144–148. GI (2008)
10. Sherba, S.A., Anderson, K.M., Faisal, M.: A framework for mapping traceability relationships. In: Second International Workshop on Traceability in Emerging Forms of Software Engineering (TEFSE 2003) (October 2003)
11. Wieringa, R.: An introduction to requirements traceability. Tech. Rep. IR-389, Faculty of Mathematics and Computer Science (November 1995)
12. Zhang, Y., Witte, R., Rilling, J., Haarslev, V.: An ontology-based approach for the recovery of traceability links. In: 3rd Int. Workshop on Metamodels, Schemas, Grammars, and Ontologies for Reverse Engineering (ATEM 2006), Genoa, Italy, October 1 (2006)
13. Zloof, M.: Query-by-example: A database language. IBM Systems Journal, 324–343 (1977)

Application Logic Patterns – Reusable Elements of User-System Interaction

Albert Ambroziewicz[1,2] and Michał Śmiałek[1]

[1] Warsaw University of Technology,
Warsaw, Poland
{ambrozia,smialek}@iem.pw.edu.pl
[2] Infovide-Matrix, Warsaw, Poland

Abstract. Patterns of various kind are commonly used to reduce costs and improve quality in software development. This paper introduces the concept of patterns at the level of detailed descriptions of the user-system dialogue. Application Logic Patterns define generalised sequences of interactions performed by the system and its users in the context of an abstract problem domain. The patterns are organised into a library. They are precisely described by a language which is defined through a strict meta-model. It extends the notation and semantics of the UML activities and use cases. Each of the patterns describing the visible system dynamics is linked to an abstract domain model central to all the patterns. The patterns can be easily instantiated by substituting abstract domain notions with the notions specific to a given domain. This ease of use and reduction in effort is validated in a controlled experiment using an open-source tool.

1 Introduction

Contemporary software systems present high repeatability in their structure and their logic (behaviour). It is an obvious desire of software developers to be able to reuse the reoccurring elements within the various artifacts they produce during the software lifecycle, following the idea of Alexander [1]: *to describe the core solution to problem, in such a way that you can use the solution a million times over, without ever doing it the same way twice.* Good quality systems have patterns applied consciously by the developers. Mainly, though, this application is performed at the levels of architecture, design and code structure, following (and extending) the classical GoF library of design patterns [2]. Some approaches follow Fowler's idea of analytical patterns [3] which are defined at the problem space (requirements), rather than the solution space (design).

Fowler's analytical patterns can be seen as an attempt to generalise the structure and logic of problem domains. This leads us to "domain patterns" introduced also by Fowler in [4]. It can be noted that describing the problem domain can be treated as a separate discipline within software engineering (see [5] for an excellent discussion). Domain engineering attempts to define the logic of a given problem domain (called also "business logic"). This logic is in general

D.C. Petriu, N. Rouquette, Ø. Haugen (Eds.): MODELS 2010, Part I, LNCS 6394, pp. 241–255, 2010.

independent of the ways software applications handle user-system interactions. We can thus try to separate this "application logic", also known as workflow logic [4] from the domain logic. The application logic would then contain pure flows of abstract user-system interactions. A complete software system would be a composition of application logic flows interwoven with the domain logic (and user interface) descriptions. This can be translated into a commonly used architectural pattern of Model-View-Controller (MVC, see [6]) where the application logic is equivalent to the controller layer.

This paper is an attempt to capture application logic flows that occur in repeatable form within various software systems. It can be noted that such flows of events are contained in the well-known use cases [7,8]. Use cases comprise scenarios that define the dialogue (interaction) between the user and the system, causing actions performed by the system, within a given problem domain. In order to be able to repeat such scenarios in various contexts we would need to abstract over any specific problem domain. We thus propose to extract pure application logic, taking away all the specifics of a problem domain. This way we introduce patterns that comprise generic application logic that can be used in many domain contexts. At the same time we propose to introduce mechanisms for fast application of such patterns. These mechanisms include a precisely defined application logic language where the links to an abstract domain can be easily substituted by the links to a specific domain. With the use of a dedicated tool, the developers can instantly instantiate the chosen patterns by "switching" from abstract notions to those from the current problem domain. We propose an initial library of such easily instantiable patterns. The library can be extended with additional variants of the proposed patterns. What is also important, the growing library can be searched through for the most relevant patterns, suitable for the given problem domain and its logic.

In the following sections we will introduce and define the Application Logic Patterns (ALP) and give an overview of the pattern library. We will also present the definition of the pattern language though a meta-model. This meta-model is implemented within a tool which will be also presented. The tool was used to perform an experiment to acknowledge applicability of the presented ALP concept.

2   Related Work

The idea of extracting abstract application logic can be seen as inspired by parameterised use cases, proposed by Cockburn in [8]. Cockburn gives an example of the "Find a whatever" use case, leaving the construction of other such use cases to the readers. Our approach is even closer to that proposed (but not elaborated in further literature) by Robertson [9]. Robertson proposes to connect requirements scenarios with "data patterns". Such scenarios contain references to data processing operations within the data models. This paves the way to constructing abstract application logic separated from the domain logic. A similar approach was described in [10] where natural language scenarios were analysed for regularities independent of problem domain which can lead to formulating patterns.

It is important that this last approach uses models in the form of a "lexicon" of domain elements independent of the scenario flows (see also [11]). The flows contain natural language sentences with "episodes" referring to the notions in the lexicon. The episodes are written in constrained natural language defined with a formal grammar. Another approach to scenario-based requirements patterns is introduced (but not elaborated further) in [12]. In this solution, an atomic reuse unit for composing scenario sentences is a case frame which forms a controlled grammar similar to the one of episodes. An even more precise specification of scenarios related to external domains is included in the Requirements Specification Language (RSL). An overview and the language reference can be found in [13] and [14] respectively. In RSL, the "lexicon" or "terminology" is additionally mapped onto individual domain models. This way, the various terms used within the scenarios can be related to a specific domain. Moreover, the individual interactions or system actions (scenario sentences) are written in a very simple language inspired by [15] and also similar to essential use cases (see [16]). The RSL constructs have been the basis for constructing the current ALP language. This is due to the existence of ready tool support and good acceptance of the language in the industrial contexts (see validation report in [17]).

The above (quite sparse throughout the past 15 years) approaches to formulate application logic patterns do not offer any systematic library of patterns in the form of reusable models. On the other hand, the idea of patterns within the requirements discipline is somewhat dominated by two prominent books in the area of use case patterns [18,19]. The first of these books still does not offer reusable models but rather best practices in writing use cases. The second book finally proposes a set of reusable models, but stops at the level of detail of what can be called the "use case interrelations". This evident gap has been recently filled by Langlands [20]. He proposes a systematic set of patterns that define detailed flows of interactions and system actions, and which he calls "patterns inside the use case oval". The flows are generalised and described using activity diagrams and simple natural language. Our approach is quite similar in this respect but we extend this significantly by proposing a systematic and unambiguous way to link an external abstract domain which enables semi-automated instantiation of patterns.

3   Introducing Application Logic Patterns

In summary, we would like our patterns to possess characteristics of Cockburn's parameterised use cases, defined both at the level of Overgaard&Palmkvist's high-level use case patterns and Langlands' use case content patterns. At the same time we want them to be associated with an abstract problem domain, easily substitutable by a concrete one. In this section we will give a definition of such patterns and substantiate it with simple examples.

Definition. *"An Application Logic Pattern (ALP) is one or more closely related use cases together with their representations describing the details of application logic (cf. controller in the MVC pattern). These representations are described*

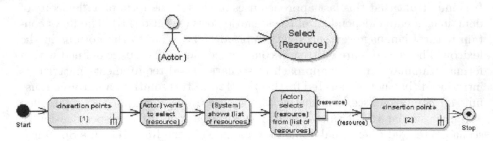

Fig. 1. "Select Resource" ALP - use case level and representation level

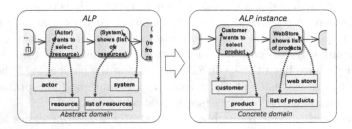

Fig. 2. Example of ALP Instantiation

by sequences of interactions between abstract actor(s) and a system and system actions defining an abstract observable behaviour of the system (abstract events). The sequences can have conditions determining the event flow. The events are defined with simple imperative sentences containing only references to an abstract problem domain. Instantiation of a pattern is performed by substituting references to the abstract domain with references to a specific one."

To illustrate the above definition we will now present a simple pattern shown in Figure 1. It is written in a strictly defined ALP language. The general notation is taken from UML's [21] use case and activity models. For the use case and action names it follows the notation of SVO (subject-verb-object) sentences found in RSL [14]. As pointed out in [15], this notation is satisfactory to describe unambiguously the atomic actor – system interactions and internal system actions. What is characteristic for the ALP notation, are the links to an abstract domain, central to all the patterns. These links are highlighted (here: by putting in brackets). Every subject and object in the use case name and scenario steps (actions in the activity) are linked to appropriate abstract notions. It can be noted that these highlighted links to the central abstract domain elements are the "parameters" of the pattern.

The parametrisation process consists in setting concrete "values" to the pattern "parameters". This is illustrated in Figure 2. In each of the ALP's actions we substitute abstract notions (e.g. "resource") with corresponding concrete notions from the problem domain at hand (e.g "product", for a WebStore system). It should be stressed that this substitution is performed only once for all the used patterns. In general, we substitute the whole abstract problem domain with a concrete one.

The activity diagram in Figure 1 contains also nodes that follow the UML's CallBehaviourAction notation (see [21]). These nodes are marked with a stereotype («insertion point») and denote possible inclusion of activities from other ALPs. The insertion points (cf. extension points in UML) are ordered and the ordering sequence is indicated by a number in brackets. An example for such interaction flow inclusion is shown in Figure 3 which presents another ALP. The "(Resource) Transfer" ALP utilises the previously introduced "Select (resource)" by inserting its activity into the first insertion point. This insertion is denoted through a new «invoke» relationship (a control flow in the activity diagram). It can be noted that for the purpose of defining ALPs unambiguously we do not follow the tangled semantics of UML use cases with the «include» and «extend» relationships. Instead we use semantics introduced already in 1999 by Berg&Simons [22]. Moreover we combine the two standard relationships into a single one which means conditional or unconditional inclusion of the activity of the invoked use case in the place of the insertion point. It can be noted that the patterns connected with a «utilize» relationship can pass domain elements as "parameters" (see Fig. 3 bottom). This can be also shown in the activity diagrams where data flows pass appropriate domain elements (e.g. "resource") and also certain conditions based on the status of these elements are possible (see Fig. 3 top). The invocation relationships can be also used at the level of use cases. This is shown in Figure 4 which depicts the "Manage (resource)" pattern (equivalent to the CRUD pattern from e.g. [19]).

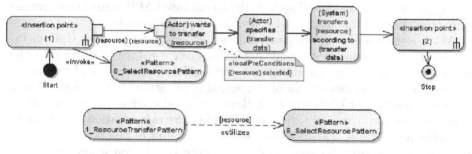

Fig. 3. "Transfer Resource" ALP - representation level and relation to another pattern

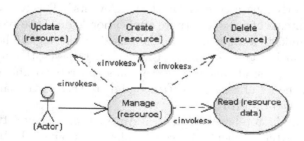

Fig. 4. Use case diagram for a complex ALP

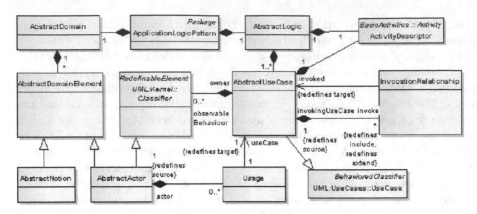

Fig. 5. Core part of the ALP metamodel

4 Metamodel of the ALP Language

When designing the ALP language we wanted to fulfill several requirements. First, we wanted its constructs to be as close to natural language as possible. Second, we wanted to reuse the commonly accepted use case notation. At the same time our aim was to clarify use cases and provide notation for the "abstract use case contents". Many of our requirements are met by the already mentioned RSL [14]. The metamodel presented in this section is thus an extension of the relevant parts of the RSL metamodel. An additional motivation for using the RSL metamodel was that it provides means to define automatic transformations to design and code (see [23]). This way, the instantiated ALPs can obtain runtime semantics through the introduced transformations up to code.

At the level of use cases, our metamodel significantly redefines the UML metamodel [21]. This is due to its many ambiguities (see e.g. [24]). We introduce the invocation relationship that substitutes the ambiguous include and extend relationships. For the description of the actual application logic we have chosen the basic notation of UML activities. However, we also advocate purely textual concrete notation (consistent with the presented abstract notation), as shown in the following sections. The basic idea is that every unit of functionality (here: a use case) has its logic represented by sets of sentences (action sentences, control sentences, conditions). These sentences point to elements of an abstract vocabulary, that is clearly separated from the flow of "events". This way we have easy access to the contents of a use case (pure application logic of the system) and, at the same time, links to a coherent vocabulary used by this logic. The vocabulary notions that occur in the logic can be easily parameterised – the links just have to be "rewired" to point at concrete concepts in a concrete vocabulary. Both the vocabulary and the set of use cases corresponding to that vocabulary are placed in a container called the ALP.

Figure 5 shows the top-level metamodel. An ApplicationLogicPattern is a container for other pattern elements (hence specialisation from the UML's Package). Every ALP contains one AbstractDomain and one AbstractLogic. The abstract

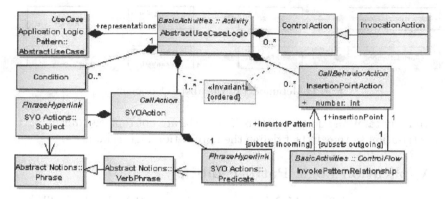

Fig. 6. Metamodel of the abstract application logic

logic is composed of one or more AbstractUseCases interrelated through InvocationRelationships (redefining use case inclusion and extension; for more details on invocation please refer to [25]). The abstract domain contains several AbstractDomainElements (AbstracNotions and AbstractActors). In addition to containing use cases, each abstract logic is represented by an ActivityDescriptor, a specialisation of the UML's Activity. Such descriptors can by used on diagrams like 3 (bottom part) to indicate relationships between pattern logics. The simple metamodel for these relationships was omitted for brevity.

The details of the AbstractUseCase representation are contained in AbstractUseCaseLogic as presented in Figure 6. Being a UML Activity, the AbstractUseCaseLogic contains actions and conditions. Condition and ControlAction sentences allow for branching the flow of control between scenarios within a single use case. A special case of ControlActions are InvocationActions expressing the passing of control to another, invoked use case. Every InvocationAction points to an InvocationRelationship (not shown in the diagram) between the current and the invoked use case. Regular scenario sentences expressing interactions between the system and an actor are SVOActions. The points of interaction in which other patterns' execution flows can be included by means of InvokePatternRelationships are indicated by InsertionPointActions.

The SVOActions are composed of two elements: a Subject and a Predicate. They point to appropriate elements of the abstract domain structured as in Figure 7. Every Phrase is connected to a proper AbstractDomainElement constituting its name. Phrases contain one or more Objects, each pointing to an AbstractNoun. This multiplicity is used to handle notions like "user account" or "application form", that are single domain elements from the point of view of an abstract domain, but are composed of more than one word. Treating separate words as single notions would disable the possibility of parameterising globally only parts of domain elements names (for example: "object1", "object1 form" → "application", "application form"). A special type of AbstractDomainElement is AbstractNotion. In addition to a naming Phrase, it can also contain any number of VerbPhrases as contained "statements". The difference between a Phrase and a VerbPhrase is that

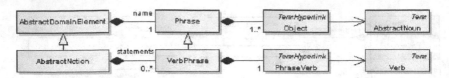

Fig. 7. Metamodel of the abstract domain

the latter, contains an additional Verb. The verbs are not replaced during pattern parametrisation as they in fact define the application logic semantics.

5   Application Logic Pattern Library

Having the above defined ALP language we have gathered a basic library of patterns. The individual patterns and their relationships were found during the analysis of a large collection of so-called "software cases" (see [23]). These cases had their requirements specifications prepared using RSL with constructs similar to that of the ALP language. There were analysed more than 50 software cases with more than 1000 use cases. The cases were prepared by the industrial and academic participants of the ReDSeeDS project (www.redseeds.eu, see [26]) and students during classes on model-driven software development (see [27]). Our analysis of this vast material showed recurring logic despite of the particular problem domains for the various systems (ranging from fitness club and theme park, through web stores, fire brigade support, procurement systems, up to several financial and banking systems). In summary, we have identified the following core patterns of application logic.

1. **(Resource) transfer.** Describes a user – system interaction in terms of a specification for a process of transferring a resource (see Figure 3). The abstract transfer data may characterise e.g. the delivery target, the way to relocate the resource and other transfer parameters.
2. **Share (resource).** Represents abstract functionality related to making a resource available to some other entity of a system (e.g. another actor). The main actor in this interaction specifies the other participating entity, to which the system makes the resource available.
3. **(Resource) partition.** Describes the logic related to dividing a resource into parts – both according to a relative and a nominal factors (the partitioning type is specified by the actor).
4. **Bind (resource).** The logic representing abstract functionality for binding of two resources. In the first interaction step both resources are selected by the main actor, and then the system binds them in the manner specified by the user.
5. **Manage (process).** This pattern contains a use case model for basic process management – its parametrisation, initiation and stopping.
6. **Manage (resource).** This patterns realises the typical create-read-update-delete (CRUD) cycle of a domain resource. Its top-level structure is presented in Figure 4.
7. **Search for (resource).** Defines a sequence of interactions performed during a typical "search" process based on parameterised search criteria. An actor is

presented a search criteria form, and the system looks for domain resources that match the criteria. Eventually a list of found elements is shown.

8. **Select (resource).** This sequence of interactions allows for selecting a resource from a list. Its details are shown in Figure 1. This simple ALP is the base for most of the patterns in the library, as the majority of them necessitate resource pre-selection.

9. **(Resource data) verification.** Describes the interactions related to verifying data entered by an actor to a system. The pattern does not depend on the data input method, only on the description of a resource for which the data is verified. When the verification fails, an appropriate message is shown.

10. **Manage (collection).** A pattern containing a use case model for basic collection management – adding, removing and listing elements.

These patterns form a coherent structure with some selected dependencies shown in Figure 8. It can be noted that this collection can be the starting point for specifying more detailed and more sophisticated ALPs. The patterns we propose contain just the most general functionality that can be easily extended by adding scenarios to the existing ones.

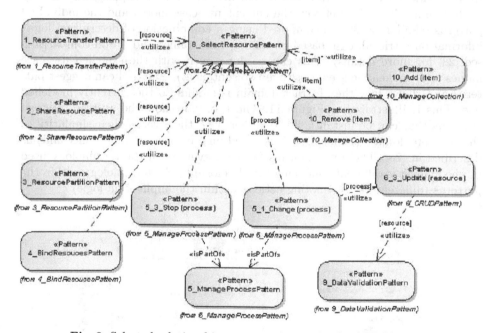

Fig. 8. Selected relationships among patterns in the ALP library

6   Tool Support for ALP Management and Instantiation

We have implemented the presented library of patterns within the ReDSeeDS tool (redseeds.sourceforge.net). The tool offers capabilities to define requirements specifications in RSL. We have adapted the tool so that the pattern library is now formulated as a separate reusable abstract "software case". This is illustrated in Figure 9. The left panel shows several packages, each denoting an individual pattern, specified within the right panel. As it can be seen, the ALP concrete notation has been adapted to the capabilities of the tool. The scenarios are written in purely textual format with clearly marked parts of the SVO sentences. These parts point to abstract domain elements (not shown in the Figure).

Whenever we want to reuse the patterns, we can refer to the pattern software case and import relevant patterns to our current workspace. This is illustrated in Figure 10. The first step is to create a new use case ("Selecting product"). The analyst now selects a relevant pattern ("Select (resource)") and imports it to the current concrete use case. The abstract scenario sentences fill-in the previously empty use case. Then, the analyst adapts the domain elements by changing their abstract names to concrete ones (e.g. "resource" to "product"). If this domain adaptation was done previously, the last step is performed automatically by the tool (adaptation needs to be done only once for all the reused patterns).

The above reuse scenario can be applied when the analyst already knows which pattern from the library is applicable to the specific concrete use case. In less evident cases, the ReDSeeDS tool provides search capabilities allowing to determine similarity between the current use case model and the individual patterns (similarity ratio is computed using a combination of description logic, information retrieval, case-based reasoning, taxonomies and graph comparison, see [28] for more details). This can be done even with the sketched use case names and/or skeleton scenarios (one-two sentences). The tool can suggest patterns and shows how the abstract domain is similar to the currently modelled one. This is illustrated in Figure 11. The tool can show the abstract domain elements that can be instantiated, together with the level of their similarity to the concrete domain elements. This is based on advanced matching mechanisms described in [28]. These mechanisms function even when the terminology used by the analyst is different (but semantically close) to the terminology within the patterns (different verbs denoting actions within the application logic).

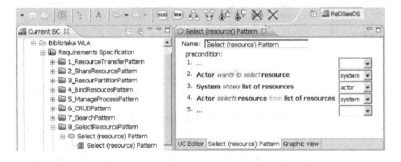

Fig. 9. Managing ALPs within the ReDSeeDS tool

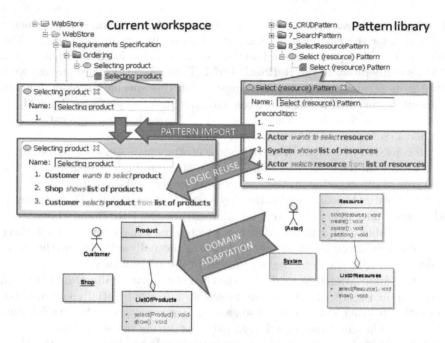

Fig. 10. Using the ReDSeeDS tools to instantiate an ALP

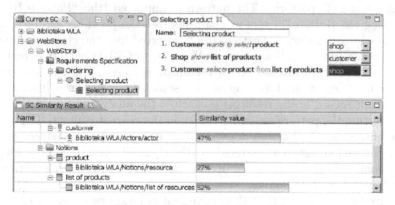

Fig. 11. Finding a similar ALP

7   ALP Validation Experiment

In [29] there was reported high reuse potential for use cases. It has been shown that in a typical system, the majority of use cases can be reused either within a given problem domain or independent of the domain. In the current study we wanted to acknowledge these levels of reuse for the ALPs. We also wanted to determine the gains in productivity when using ALPs with the tooling framework presented in the previous section. For this purpose we have arranged a simple experiment perfomed by one of the authors (analyst experienced in RSL).

The experiment was performed in two major steps. First, a simple requirements specification for the customer-related part of an on-line store was created. The requirements model (use cases and scenarios) was created in RSL without using the ALPs deliberately in the ReDSeeDS tool. Thus, the scenario sentences were written from scratch, using the RSL notation on this specific problem domain. The specification consisted of 11 use cases divided into two packages. Each of the use cases was described by at least one scenario. Altogether, the application logic contained 45 sentences (SVO, conditional and invocation). The final domain specification consisted of a single actor (the store customer), a single system element (the store system itself) and 14 domain elements containing 28 phrases. In the second step of the experiment, there were deliberately used the patterns from the library to create the same application logic as in the first step. Three patterns hand-picked from the library were used: Manage process, CRUD and Manage collection (see Table 1 for details). After the selected patterns were imported, there was made a decision on which pattern elements are actually suitable and they were complemented with the elements not present in the ALP library.

The ALP adaptation process during the the experiment, is illustrated through an example in Figure 12. The requirements specification initially contains the "Requesting re-stock notification" use case. Its scenario was written in full during the first step, and then reused from patterns during the second step. In this second step, there has been found a suitable pattern in the library (see the "Pattern Selection" arrow pointing at the "Start (process)" use case, being part of the "Manage (process)" pattern). The pattern is imported (the "Pattern Import" arrow) using the ReDSeeDS tool mechanisms (see the previous section). In the Figure, the dashed arrows indicate patterns inserted into the chain of imported logic ("Manage (process)/Start (process)" invokes "CRUD pattern/Create (resource)", which in turn invokes "Data validation pattern", ...). The solid arrows indicate reused sentences. Please note that some of the imported pattern sentences are not reused in the resulting scenario – the analyst has discarded them when importing the patters as not necessary in the current context. The bottom of the Figure shows a two-step domain adaptation. First, an abstract domain for the resource management pattern ("CRUD") is adapted to comply with the abstract domain of the "Manage (process)" pattern. Finally, it is instantiated to become the on-line store domain.

The experiment showed that the above instantiation procedure can be performed very quickly with the use of the ReDSeeDS tool. The most time consuming part is the instantiation of the problem domain. However, this is comparable to the time it took to introduce the problem domain from scratch (in the first step of the experiment). Having this task done, the instantiation process is as fast as selecting the pattern, importing all the included sentences (one click) and deleting the ones that are redundant or irrelevant. This was significantly faster than creating the same scenarios from scratch. It has to be noted that the first step was performed by a person that knows the patterns and they were in fact reused from his memory. For a less skilled analyst we could assume additional gains trough the possibility to reuse the logic itself which is not initially mastered by that analyst.

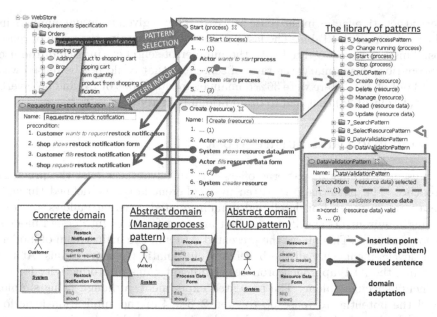

Fig. 12. Requirements model used in experiment with example APL reuse

Table 1. Use cases and patterns with their reuse ratios

Package	Use Case	Pattern used	Sentence reuse	Domain el. reuse	Discarded pattern sentences
Shopping	Browsing shopping cart Adding product to cart Changing item quantity Removing product from cart	Collection	79%	44%	0
Orders	Browsing order history	CRUD (Browse)	67%	50%	0
	Requesting re-stock notification	Manage process (Start process)	100%	100%	6
	Browsing products	CRUD (Browse)	60%	50%	0
	Reviewing order	CRUD (Read)	100%	100%	3
Weighted mean:			71%	64%	Sum: 9

In addition to the above qualitative analysis, we have also gathered quantitative data. We have counted the reused elements with the granularity of individual sentences (SVOs, conditions, invocations) and domain elements. The number of reused elements was compared with the size of the original specification (first step) giving the resulting "reuse ratio". For instance, in the example in Figure 12, all the sentences and domain elements were reused, so the reuse ratio is equal to 1. This result can be found in Table 1 (the 3 use cases for which no patterns were used are not included in the table, but wre taken into account for calculations). We have also counted the sentences that were discarded and not re-used from the patterns (negative factor in the reuse process). This is given in actual numbers in the last column of the Table. The last row in Table 1 contains the mean of reuse ratios. This has been weighted with the number of sentences in each of the use case scenarios. In summary, the ratio of sentences that could not be reused was 29% (13 out of 45). There were 36% domain elements (5 out of 14) and 36% verb phrases (10 out of 28) that had to be additionally introduced.

8 Conclusion and Future Work

The presented library of patterns offers certain advantages over the previous approaches. The patterns are written in a coherent language defined through a meta-model. Its level of detail and domain-related coherence allows for constructing requirements specifications that are transformable into design models (as shown in [23]). This places the presented ALPs in the mainstream of model-driven development with all the benefits of automatic transformations. At the same time, the ALP approach promises significant gains in productivity for requirements specifiers alone. The presented experiment, although being simple, showed the potential to reuse up to even 2/3-3/4 of the application logic for a typical business software system. We plan to extend this experiment by applying the ALPs to several business cases with more participants include less skilled ones (students). Moreover, this reuse can be automated to significant extend with the presented tooling. This gives a motivation to continue research in this direction. We plan to extend the current simple pattern library into an evolvable pattern repository. The patterns could be defined at various levels of detail and in various variants. This kind of repository could be searched through with queries based on partial use case models. The search engine would then offer several variant patterns that could be discussed with the client and applied instantly. The new solutions could be inserted back to the repository as additional variants of the existing patterns (including domain-specific variants).

References

1. Alexander, C., Ishikawa, S., Silverstein, M.: A Pattern Language: Towns, Buildings, Construction. Oxford University Press, Oxford (1977)
2. Gamma, E., Helm, R., Johnson, R., Vlissides, J.: Design Patterns. In: Elements of Reusable Object-Oriented Software. Addison Wesley, Reading (1995)
3. Fowler, M.: Analysis patterns: reusable objects models. Addison-Wesley Longman Publishing Co., Inc., Boston (1997)
4. Fowler, M.: Patterns of Enterprise Application Architecture. Addison-Wesley Longman Publishing Co., Inc., Boston (2002)
5. Bjørner, D.: Role of domain engineering in software development - why current requirements engineering is flawed! In: Pnueli, A., Virbitskaite, I., Voronkov, A. (eds.) PSI 2010. LNCS, vol. 5947, pp. 2–34. Springer, Heidelberg (2010)
6. Reenskaug, T.: Models-views-controllers. Technical note, Xerox PARC (1979)
7. Jacobson, I., Christerson, M., Jonsson, P., Overgaard, G.: Object-Oriented Software Engineering: A Use Case Driven Approach. Addison-Wesley, Reading (1992)
8. Cockburn, A.: Writing Effective Use Cases. Addison-Wesley, Reading (2000)

9. Robertson, S.: Requirements patterns via events/use cases. Technical report, Atlantic Systems Guild Ltd. (1996)
10. Ridao, M., Doorn, J., Leite, J.C.S.d.P.: Domain independent regularities in scenarios. In: Proceedings of the RE 2001, pp. 120–127 (2001)
11. Leite, J.C.S.d.P., Hadad, G.D.S., Doorn, J.H., Kaplan, G.N.: A scenario construction process. Requirements Engineering 5, 38–61 (2000)
12. Watahiki, K., Saeki, M.: Scenario patterns based on case grammar approach. In: Proceedings of the RE 2001, pp. 300–301 (2001)
13. Śmiałek, M., Ambroziewicz, A., Bojarski, J., Nowakowski, W., Straszak, T.: Introducing a unified requirements specification language. In: Proc. CEE-SET 2007, Software Engineering in Progress, Nakom, pp. 172–183 (2007)
14. Kaindl, H., Śmiałek, M., et al.: Requirements specification language definition. Project Deliverable D2.4.1, ReDSeeDS Project (2007), http://www.redseeds.eu
15. Graham, I.M.: Task scripts, use cases and scenarios in object-oriented analysis. Object-Oriented Systems 3(3), 123–142 (1996)
16. Constantine, L.L.: What do users want? Engineering usability into software. Windows Tech Journal (1995, rev. 2000)
17. Mukasa, K.S., et al.: Requirements specification language validation report. Project Deliverable D2.5.1, ReDSeeDS Project (2007)
18. Adolph, S., Bramble, P., Cockburn, A., Pols, A.: Patterns for Effective Use Cases. Addison Wesley, Reading (2002)
19. Overgaard, G., Palmkvist, K.: Use Cases: Patterns and Blueprints. Addison Wesley, Reading (2005)
20. Langlands, M.: Inside the oval: use case content patterns. Technical report, Planet Project (2010), http://planetproject.wikidot.com/use-case-content-patterns
21. Object Management Group: Unified Modeling Language: Superstructure, version 2.2, formal/09-02-02 (2009)
22. van den Berg, K.G., Simons, A.J.H.: Control flow semantics of use cases in UML. Information and Software Technology 41(10), 651–659 (1999)
23. Śmiałek, M., Kalnins, A., Ambroziewicz, A., Straszak, T., Wolter, K.: Comprehensive system for systematic case-driven software reuse. In: van Leeuwen, J., Muscholl, A., Peleg, D., Pokorný, J., Rumpe, B. (eds.) SOFSEM 2010. LNCS, vol. 5901, pp. 697–708. Springer, Heidelberg (2010)
24. Astudillo, H., Génova, G., Śmiałek, M., et al.: Use cases in model-driven software engineering. In: Bruel, J.-M. (ed.) MoDELS 2005. LNCS, vol. 3844, pp. 262–271. Springer, Heidelberg (2006)
25. Śmiałek, M., Bojarski, J., Nowakowski, W., Ambroziewicz, A., Straszak, T.: Complementary use case scenario representations based on domain vocabularies. In: Engels, G., Opdyke, B., Schmidt, D.C., Weil, F. (eds.) MODELS 2007. LNCS, vol. 4735, pp. 544–558. Springer, Heidelberg (2007)
26. Jedlitschka, A., Mukasa, K.S., Weber, S.: Case reuse verification and validation report. Project Deliverable D6.2, ReDSeeDS Project (2009), http://www.redseeds.eu
27. Szmurło, R., Śmiałek, M.: Teaching software modeling in a simulated project environment. In: Kühne, T. (ed.) MoDELS 2006. LNCS, vol. 4364, pp. 301–310. Springer, Heidelberg (2007)
28. Wolter, K., Śmiałek, M., Hotz, L., Knab, S., Bojarski, J., Nowakowski, W.: Mapping mof-based requirements representations to ontologies for software reuse. In: CEUR Workshop Proceedings (TWOMDE 2009), vol. 531 (2009)
29. Issa, A., Odeh, M., Coward, D.: Using use case patterns to estimate reusability in software systems. Information and Software Technology 48, 836–845 (2006)

A Metamodel-Based Approach for Automatic User Interface Generation

António Miguel Rosado da Cruz[1] and João Pascoal Faria[2]

[1] ESTG-Instituto Politécnico de Viana do Castelo, Av. do Atlântico, s/n 4900-348 Viana do Castelo, Portugal
miguel.cruz@estg.ipvc.pt
[2] Faculdade de Engenharia da Universidade do Porto / INESC Porto,
Rua Dr. Roberto Frias, s/n 4200-465 Porto, Portugal
jpf@fe.up.pt

Abstract. One of the advantages of following a MDA-based approach in the development of interactive applications is the possibility of generating multiple platform-specific user interfaces (UI) from the same platform independent UI model. However, the effort required to create the UI model may be significant. In the case of data-intensive applications, a large part of the UI structure and functionality is closely related with the structure and functionality of the domain entities described in the domain model, and the access rules specified in the use case model. This paper presents an approach to reduce the effort required to create platform independent UI models for data intensive applications, by automatically generating an initial UI model from domain and use case models. For that purpose, UML-aligned metamodels for domain and use case models are defined, together with a MOF-based metamodel for user interface models. The transformation rules that drive the UI model generation are introduced. It is also proposed a MDA-based process for the development of data intensive interactive applications based on the proposed model architecture and transformations.

Keywords: MDD, MDA, Metamodel, User Interface Automatic Generation, Model Transformation.

1 Introduction

Model-driven development (MDD) is mainly focused on platform independent modeling activities rather than programming activities. This allows software engineers to focus on concepts of the problem domain, and the way they shall be modeled in order to produce a software solution, rather than being distracted by technical issues of the solution domain. Within an MDD setting, code can be automatically generated from models to a great extension, dramatically reducing the most costly and error-prone aspects of software development [1].

Model-driven development of interactive applications enables the generation of multiple platform-specific user interfaces (UI) from the same platform independent UI model. However, the effort required to create the UI model may be significant. In

D.C. Petriu, N. Rouquette, Ø. Haugen (Eds.): MODELS 2010, Part I, LNCS 6394, pp. 256–270, 2010.

the case of data-intensive applications, a large part of the UI structure and functionality is closely related with the structure and functionality of the domain entities described in the domain model, and the access rules specified in the use case model. This paper presents an approach to reduce the effort required to create platform independent UI models for data intensive applications, by automatically generating an initial UI model from domain and use case models.

The approach presented is based on a well identified subset of UML that permits the construction of a complete and rigorous platform independent model (PIM) of a software system (including constraints and actions), and extends that UML subset with new metamodel elements, that turn possible the model-driven automatic generation, by model transformation, of a User Interface Model (UIM), and the model-to-code generation of a final application from the rigorous PIM. The generation of a PIM level UIM allows its configuration and/or modification prior to generating the final code. The main contributions of this paper are:

- the definition of a process for the automatic generation of user interface models and executable prototypes from domain and use case models;
- the definition of a UI metamodel that allows the platform independent modeling of the UI structure and of the bindings from the UI structure to the domain model, therefore providing a set of models that contains all the information for generating a fully executable prototype;
- extensions to the UML metamodel, that better enable taking profit of the model features when generating the UIM; and,
- the description of a set of transformation rules that allow the derivation of a default UIM from the Domain Model (DM) and Use Case Model (UCM).

In previous work [2, 3], we informally defined extensions to the DM and UCM to better support UI generation, and explained how DM and UCM features could be mapped into UI features. In this paper, we formalize the extensions to the DM and UCM by specifying the metamodels that they shall conform to, formalize the UIM metamodel, and define the transformation rules in terms of those meta-models.

Although not detailed in this paper, the research work that yielded the presented approach is supported by a proof of concept tool and has been validated through two case studies [4].

The proposed process is presented in the next section together with the contextualization of the presented metamodels within the UML metamodel. In the following sections, the metamodels for DM, UCM, and UIM are introduced. Section 6 presents the transformation rules for automatically obtaining a UIM from the DM and UCM. Section 7 briefly overviews related work. Finally, some conclusions are drawn together with some proposals for future work. A running example is used along the paper to illustrate the approach.

2 Proposed Generation Process and Model Architecture

The approach proposed in this paper comprises an iterative development process that enables the automatic generation of UI models from early, progressively enriched, platform independent system models, and a metamodel defining the concepts that allow a platform independent system modeling according to 3 views: a structural view, that is established through a DM; a functional view, defined by a UCM; and, a user interface view, defined through a UIM. After the modeling activity and the UIM generation step, in each iteration, the approach permits the generation of an executable user interface prototype (UIP), which enables the complete model validation by other stakeholders besides the modeler himself.

The DM represents the business entities and events of the problem domain, just like intended by the Unified Process [5].

The process, illustrated in Fig. 1, starts with the construction of a UCM and a DM that conform to a metamodel that specializes and extends UML [6, 7]. A simple UI can be automatically generated from the DM specification (by a model to model transformation process from DM to UIM, followed by a model to code transformation) supporting only the basic CRUD operations (Create, Retrieve, Update and Delete) and navigation along the associations defined. In subsequent iterations, the DM can be refined, and more information can be added to it, allowing the generation of richer user interfaces, and application prototypes.

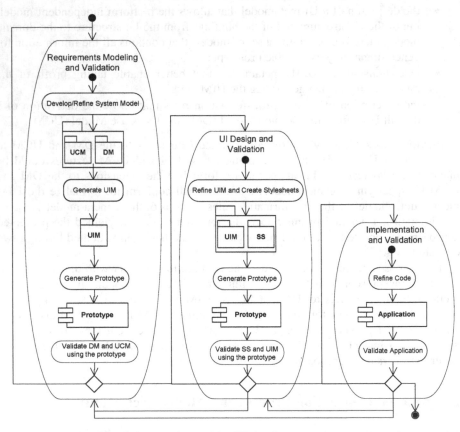

Fig. 1. Proposed generative UI development process

When desired, the modeler may develop a UCM. In the proposed approach, there is a full integration between the UCM and the DM, as use case specifications are established over the structural DM. The UCM enables the separation of functionality by actor, and its customization (e.g.: hiding functionality for some actors). A corresponding UIM and a UIP are then automatically generated from both the DM and the UCM.

Figure 2 contextualizes the metamodel defined for this approach by dividing it in three packages corresponding to the referred model views and relating them to the UML and MOF.

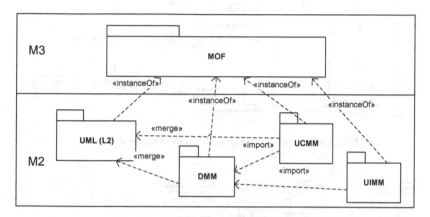

Fig. 2. Metamodel contextualization

MOF provides the concepts for defining the UML metamodel, which is stratified in language units used for defining compliance levels[6, 7]. Compliance level 0 (L0) has a single language unit that enables modeling of class-based structures, and is formally described as the UML Infrastructure, or package Core, which is shared between MOF and the UML. Level 1 (L1) adds language units and extends the capabilities of L0 for use cases, interactions, structures, activities and actions, and L2 adds language units and extends the capabilities of L1 for state machine modeling and profiles.

The Domain Metamodel (DMM) and the Use Case Metamodel (UCMM) are partially merged with UML L2, incrementally adding features to some of its elements, by specializing or redefining other metamodel elements [7].

The User Interface Metamodel (UIMM) is defined conforming to the MOF meta-metamodel and imports features from the DMM, which enable model integration.

3 Metamodel for Domain Models

The metamodel for domain models is depicted in Figures 3 and 4, and specializes and extends the UML language unit for class diagrams [6]. The reused UML elements are shaded and the ones that have been modified, either by adding or specializing features, have only the name compartment shaded. The modified UML elements are Class

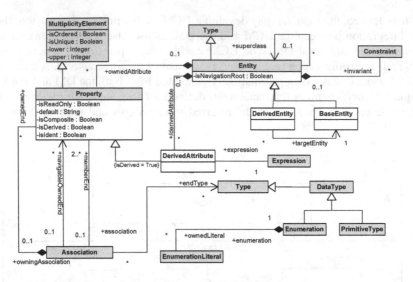

Fig. 3. Metamodel for Domain Models (structural features)

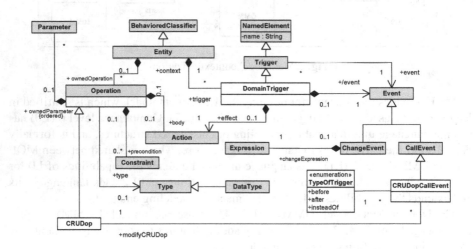

Fig. 4. Metamodel for Domain Models (behavioral features)

(with an alias "Entity"), Property and Operation. Entity (Class) has a new attribute, isNavigationRoot, that enables the identification of an entry point for navigating in the structure. This is useful when generating a UIM from the DM alone, without the development of a UCM. BaseEntity and DerivedEntitiy specialize the modified UML Class and inherit all its features, semantics and concrete notation. The BaseEntity models a problem domain persistable concept in a platform independent manner. Property has a new attribute, isIdent, which enables the identification of properties that are used by the business user as an instance identification or summarization structural feature. This is different from a unique identifier.

Operation is extended in order to comprise, besides operations that are user-defined in an Action Semantics-based language, the basic CRUD operations (CRUDop) that are considered to exist by default for instances of every BaseEntity (see Fig. 4).

The DM metamodel adds new model elements to the UML metamodel, easing the purpose of constructing a complete and rigorous PIM. DerivedEntity and Domain-Trigger deserve further explanation.

3.1 Derived Entities

A DerivedEntity models an interesting view in the problem domain (e.g. a business view). DerivedEntities are non-persistent domain entities with a structure closer to the business domain, like a business document, and so closer to the UI needs. A Derive-dEntity must target a BaseEntity that acts as the root for referencing derived attributes. It is treated essentially as a virtual specialization of the target BaseEntity, possibly restricted by a membership constraint and extended with derived attributes. It may also hide attributes from the target BaseEntity. A Derived Entity may be distinguished by having its name preceded by a slash in a concrete notation.

3.2 Domain Triggers

The DM metamodel includes constructs for defining domain triggers, which are used to capture generic business rules or to modify the default behavior of CRUD operations (CRUDop). Domain triggers are defined in the context of an Entity (see Fig. 4). A DomainTrigger inherits from the UML Trigger, but has only two possible kinds of associated events:

- **ChangeEvent:** It is the UML ChangeEvent class but with the changeExpression association end restricted to Expression type. In standard UML it can be a ValueSpecification, that includes the possibility of defining an OpaqueExpression, which promotes the definition of platform specific expressions (e.g. Java expressions) within a PIM, which is considered to be a bad modeling practice [1]. The ChangeEvent triggers a DomainTrigger when the condition defined in the changeExpression holds.
- **CRUDopCallEvent**. It is a specialization of UML's CallEvent, restricted to CRUD operations, and with the possibility to intercept the call to an operation before, after or instead of calling it. It provides a way of modifying the default behavior of CRUD operations. A CRUDopCallEvent triggers a DomainTrigger before, after or instead of an identified CRUD operation call, within the context of an instance of a class, enabling the reinforcement of business rules.

Fig. 5 shows the DM constructed for an example Library System that will help illustrate the approach along the paper. The DM has been developed in several iterations and, as defined in the process presented in section 2, an executable prototype has been automatically generated and tested at the end of each iteration.

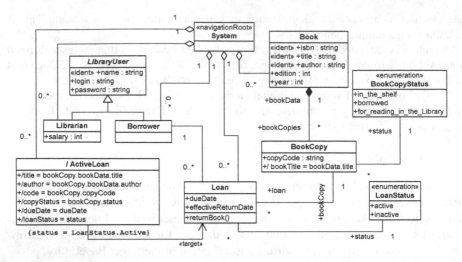

Fig. 5. Domain model (DM) for an example Library System

4 Metamodel for Use Case Models

The metamodel for use case models, shown in Figures 6 and 7, specializes and extends the UML language unit for use cases [7].

In the approach proposed, the UCM is defined in close connection with the DM, to specify and organize the CRUD, user-defined or navigational operations over Base or Derived Entities that are available for each actor. The definition of a UCM also enables the use of several features, such as task-model-like relations, that permit a fine tuning of the interaction within a use case [8, 9], if the modeler wants to go deep in detailing a use case: enable, deactivate and choice. The data manipulated in each use case is typically determined by the domain entity (base or derived) and/or operation associated with it. Several constraints limit the types of use cases and UC relationships that can be defined [4].

The UCM metamodel extends UML and modifies standard elements UseCase, Extend and Operation. The UML UseCase has been added attributes that enable a smooth integration between a UCM and the respective DM.

A UseCase may identify an entity class (BaseEntity or DerivedEntity) from the DM. If a BaseEntity is identified, then it is possible to restrict the CRUD operations available, by associating only the allowed CRUD operations to the UseCase.

It has been defined a merge increment to the UML Extend class, for being possible to associate to it a link name and an aggregation operation. The association of an aggregation operation to an Extend only makes sense when the Extend is about an entity collection use case, in which case the associated aggregation operation must belong to the operations associated to the extended use case. Operations may be user-defined in an Action Semantics-based action language, or may be the basic CRUD instance operations that are defined by default in every BaseEntity.

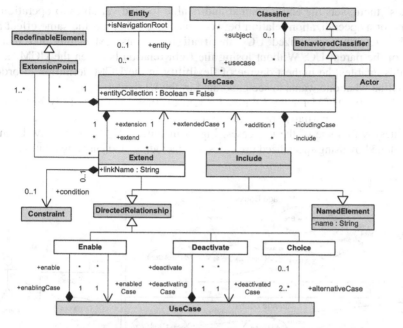

Fig. 6. Metamodel for Uose Case Models

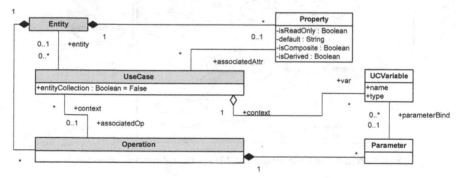

Fig. 7. Possible Use Case relations to Domain Model elements

One can distinguish two categories of use cases, which have been addressed in [2]:

- **Independent use cases**, that can be initiated directly, and so can be linked directly to actors (that initiate them) and appear as application entry points.
- **Dependent use cases**, that can only be initiated from within other use cases, called *source* use cases, because they depend on the context set by the source use cases; the dependent use cases extend or are included by the source ones, according to their optional or mandatory nature, respectively.

As can be seen in Fig. 7, a use case may be associated to an entity class in the DM.

If the modeler wants to reach a higher degree of detail, a use case may also be associated to an operation, entity attribute or a set of use case variables. This kind of use cases must be included in another use case, through an «include» relation, that "aggregates" them, sets the entity context and is able to bind variables to operations' parameters, or a specialization relation between use cases, that has the same effect as include, but lets the specialized UC inherit all inclusions, extensions and meta-attributes of the parent UC. Without losing the tight relation between the UCM and the DM, this enables the highest degree of flexibility in the UCM definition in order to better define what one wants to see generated in the UI model.

Fig. 8 shows the UCM for the Library System example, which is fully integrated with the DM. Table 1 partially shows the entity types and operations associated (via tagged values) with some of the use cases. Fig. 8 includes UC "Register New Loan", which is detailed by using specialized use cases and including, and enabling relations.

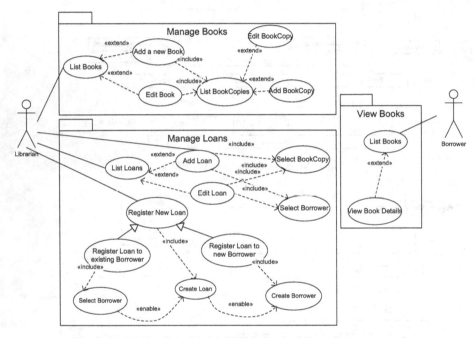

Fig. 8. Partial Use Case Model (UCM) for the LibrarySystem example

Table 1. Entities/operations associated (via tagged-values) with use cases in Fig. 8

Use case	entity	entity Collection	associatedOp
List Books	Book	True	
Add a new Book	Book	False	Create
Edit Book	Book	False	Update, Delete
List BookCopies	BookCopy	True	
Add BookCopy	BookCopy	False	Create
Edit BookCopy	BookCopy	False	Update, Delete
View Book Details	Book	False	Retrieve
Select Borrower	Borrower	False	Update (link)
Create Borrower	Borrower	False	Create
Create Loan	Loan	False	Create

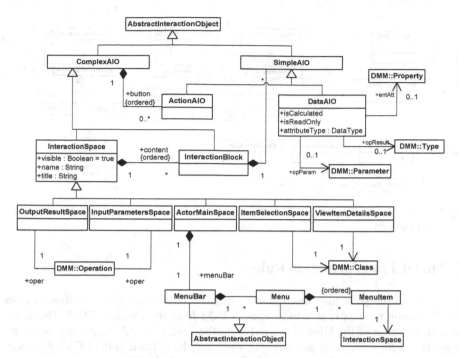

Fig. 9. Metamodel for User Interface Model

5 Metamodel for User Interface Models

The proposed metamodel for User Interface models (UIM) is depicted in Figs. 9 and 10. The proposal focus on forms-based data-intensive applications, so the developed UIM metamodel contains elements for modeling forms and lists, and navigating through them. The UIMM imports elements defined in the DMM, in order to guarantee the whole system model consistency, and together have all the information needed to generate an executable prototype.

The top level element from which every element in the UIMM inherits from is AbstractInteractionObject, or AIO. There are two types of AIO: ComplexAIO and SimpleAIO. The first models elements that contain other elements, and the latter models simple elementary objects used within complexAIO elements.

An InteractionSpace (IS) represents an abstract object that, at PIM level, is a UI container where interaction occurs. An IS is composed of InteractionBlocks, which, in turn, are made of SimpleAIOs, like DataAIOs, that are typically associated to entity properties in the DM, or ActionAIOs. These latter may be DomainOperations, like the call of a CRUD or user defined operation, operations for Navigation between InteractionSpaces, or UIOperations, that allow actions over UI elements.

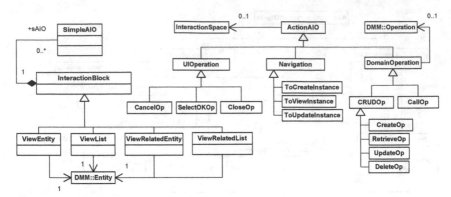

Fig. 10. UIM Metamodel parts for the InteractionBlock subtree, in the left, and the ActionAIO subtree, at the right

6 Model Transformation Rules

According to the presented development process (see section 2) an automatic model transformation process is able to generate a UIM from the DM and UCM. The structural information of the UIM is derived from the DM, although its presentation may be restricted for some users according to what may be defined in the UCM. Although implemented imperatively in the proof-of-concept tool, the transformation rules were defined declaratively through LHS-RHS relations, in which the RHS defines the elements being generated or modified in the target model when a pattern matching is verified in the LHS. Due to space limitations, the mapping rules that drive the transformation process from the DM and UCM to the UIM cannot be fully presented in this paper. A complete presentation can be found in [4].

In what respects to structural UI information, a base domain entity is by default mapped to an InteractionSpace with a ViewEntity block, with a DataAIO for each attribute and ActionAIOs for the CRUD operations, depending on the context (creating a new instance or editing an existing instance). Inheritance is treated by creating a DataAIO for each inherited attribute in the ViewEntity generated for the specialized entity.

To-many relations (associations, aggregations or compositions) are mapped to a ViewRelatedList block in the InteractionSpace generated for the source entity, with a list of DataAIOs, one for each identifying attribute of the related instances of the target class, and ActionAIOs for adding new instances and for editing or removing the currently selected instance.

To-one relations are mapped to a ViewRelatedEntity block in the interaction space generated for the source class, with a DataAIO for each identifying attribute of the related instance of the target class. If the UIM is being generated solely from the DM, and if the related instance is not fixed by the navigation path followed so forth, then a Navigation AIO is also generated for selecting the related instance.

Within ViewList and ViewRelatedList blocks, DataAIO objects will correspond to table columns in concrete representations, while in other kinds of interaction blocks they will correspond, for instance, to labels and text fields.

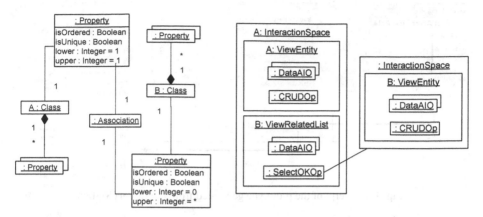

Fig. 11. A sample DM metamodel instance (abstract syntax), in the left, and a partial correspondence to a UIM metamodel instance.

Derived attributes map to output-only DataAIOs, and default values are mapped to initial values in DataAIOs. Each derived entity (view) is mapped to an interaction space with a ViewEntity having an input/output DataAIO for each attribute of the target class, an output-only DataAIO for each derived attribute, and ActionAIOs for the CRUD operations over the target class.

In what respects to UI-functionality related information, from the UCM, an actor is mapped into an ActorMainSpace, where the actor starts its application usage experience. A Use Case Package is mapped to a menu in the actor's main space, with a menu item for each UC within the package that is directly linked to the actor.

A use case (UC) with attribute entityCollection set to true (UC of type *List Entity* or *List Related Entity*) is mapped to an interaction space with a ViewList or a ViewRelatedList, depending if it is an independent or a dependent UC, displaying the full list of instances of the associated entity, with ActionAIOs for the allowed operations (according to the dependent use cases).

An extension UC associated to an entity that is the "many" side of a relation with the entity associated to the extended UC (UC of type *Select Related Entity*) is mapped to an interaction space with a ViewList displaying the list of candidate instances, with ActionAIOs for selecting one instance.

A UC with attribute entityCollection set to false (UC of type *CRUD Entity* or *CRUD Related Entity*) is mapped to an interaction space with a ViewEntity or a ViewRelatedEntity block displaying the object attribute values, through DataAIOs, with ActionAIOs corresponding to the CRUD operations allowed. In the case of a related instance, the showed «ident» attributes of the source object cannot be edited.

A UC associated to a user-defined operation (UC of type *Call User-Defined Operation*) generates a CallOp within the ViewEntity corresponding to the entity where the operation is defined. Blocks for entering the input parameters and displaying the result, in case they exist, are also generated.

A Navigation ActionAIO is typically generated from an Extend or an Include relationship.

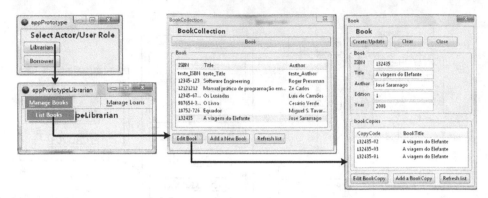

Fig. 12. Excerpt of the prototype generated from the LibrarySystem

Fig. 12 shows part of the prototype generated for the LibrarySystem, showing the UI flow of a Librarian actor executing use cases List Books → Edit Book.

7 Related Work

Few approaches in the literature allow a model-to-model generation of a UIM and prototype, within a MDD setting. The XIS method [10, 11], like the OO-Method [12] and the ZOOM approach [13] are able to produce a fully functional (executable) application, but the demanded input models are time consuming and arduous to build.

XIS allows two approaches to interactive systems generation: a dummy approach that demands the full specification of a DM, an actors' model, and a UIM; and a smart approach, which enables the derivation of the UIM by demanding the construction of two other models, a business entities model and a use case model. This approach to the UIM derivation is simpler than its full construction, but it comes with the cost of the inflexibility of the generated UI. XIS business entities select domain entities relations to provide a lookup or master/detail pattern to the UI needed for the interaction inside the context of a use case [10, 11]. Like in the XIS smart approach, in our approach the modeler must attach to each use case an Entity (base or derived) from the DM. The difference is that, in our approach, relations between entities are inferred from the DM, thus not being needed a separate business entities model to provide higher level entities to the UCM. The relation's selection provided by the XIS business entities model is done, within our approach, in the UCM by modeling or not related use cases associated to related entities for navigating through the relations.

Similarly to XIS and the OO-Method, in our approach CRUD operations are predefined, but their default behavior may be modified through domain triggers. User defined operations are not possible to specify in the XIS approach. In the OO-Method, user defined operations (services and transactions) can be specified by using formal language OASIS or, in a limited form, by specifying the way each service changes the object state, categorizing each attribute [12]. The OO-Method permits, as well, the specification of allowed states and state transitions within a class. Each state transition may have attached a control (guard) or triggering condition. In our approach user defined operations may be specified using an UML Action Semantics-based language.

The ZOOM approach models a system by building a graphical model, which is then translated to the ZOOM language [13]. The models that are demanded by the approach, in order to automatically generate an executable application, are: a structural model, which must contain all the classes of the application (including design classes); a finite state machine model that models the system behavior and is the central communication mechanism to connect the structural model to the UI model; and, a UI model, which models the UI screens by using predefined components that are organized according to a user defined layout.

Elkoutbi et al. [14] and Martinez et al. [15] approaches generate a UI from the structural, use case and UI behavioral models, but demand the attachment of UI related information (input/output fields and/or widgets) to collaboration diagrams or message sequence charts used to specify use case behavior. The generated output is only able to simulate the specified use cases through the generated UI, with no business level application behavior.

8 Conclusions and Future Work

This paper addresses an approach to MDD comprising a development process and a UML-aligned model architecture that enable a gradual approximation to the final application by deriving a default UIM from early DM and UCM and an application prototype from these three system model views. On each iteration the system models are further refined in order to accommodate all the requirements and to generate a suitable UIM. UI look&feel is achieved by modifying the UIM, without detaching it from the related DM, and by applying stylesheets to the generated UI code.

The approach proposed combines advantages of the state-of-art approaches and adds a few own contributions. The main distinguishing point is that it doesn't demand a UIM for UI generation; instead, it is able to generate a UIM and executable prototype from the DM alone or the UCM also. Other points are that it takes advantage of OCL invariants and preconditions to generate validation routines in the executable prototype; adds use case relations based on constructs typically found in task-models; allows defining triggers activated by CRUD-operations' invocation or by a state condition holding; makes use of an actions language to specify triggers and class operations [4].

The presented metamodels enable a complete and rigorous modeling of a data-intensive form-based system. Being this the case of most of the business applications, this approach enables full final-code generation, provided that target platforms and architecture may influence the selection of a model-to-code generator.

Future evolutions may include: the development of a complete support tool that may integrate with existing MDA or UML diagramming tools; or, the opportunity to specify the target architectures and feed them to a generic model-to-code generator.

References

1. Frankel, D.S.: Model Driven Architecture - Applying MDA to Enterprise Computing. Wiley Publishing, Inc., Indianapolis (2003)
2. Cruz, A.M.R., Faria, J.P.: Automatic generation of user interface models and prototypes from domain and use case models. In: Proceedings of the 4th ICSOFT (ICSoft 2009), Sofia, Bulgaria, vol. 1, pp. 169–176. INSTICC Press (July 2009)

3. Cruz, A.M.R., Faria, J.P.: Automatic Generation of Interactive Prototypes for Domain Model Validation. In: Proceedings of the 3rd ICSOFT (ICSoft 2008), Porto, Portugal, SE/GSDCA/MUSE, pp. 206–213. INSTICC Press (July 2008)
4. Cruz, A.M.R.: Automatic generation of user interfaces from rigorous domain and use case models. PhD thesis. F.E.U.P., University of Porto, Portugal (2010) (to be published)
5. Jacobson, I., Booch, G., Rumbaugh, J.: The Unified Software Development Process. Addison Wesley, Reading (1998)
6. OMG: Unified Modeling Language (OMG UML) Infrastructure (February 2009)
7. OMG: Unified Modeling Language (OMG UML) Superstructure (February 2009)
8. Paternó, F., Mancini, C., Meniconi, S.: ConcurTaskTrees: A Diagrammatic Notation for Specifying Task Models. In: Proceedings of the IFIP TC13 Int'l. Conf. on HCI, INTERACT 1997, pp. 362–369. Chapman & Hall, Ltd, Boca Raton (1997)
9. Paternó, F.: Task Models in Interactive Software Systems. In: Handbook of Software Engineering and Knowledge Engineering, vol. I, pp. 817–835. World Scientific Publ., Singapore (2001)
10. Silva, A.R.: The XIS approach and principles. In: Society, I.C. (ed.) Proceedings of the 29th EUROMICRO Conference, New Waves in System Architecture (2003)
11. Silva, A.R., Saraiva, J., Silva, R., Martins, C.: XIS - UML Profile for eXtreme Modeling Interactive Systems. In: 4th International Workshop on Model-based Methodologies for Pervasive and Embedded Software (MOMPES 2007). IEEE Computer Society, Los Alamitos (2007)
12. Pastor, O., Molina, J.C.: Model-Driven Architecture in Practice. Springer, Heidelberg (2007)
13. Jia, X., Steele, A., Qin, L., Liu, H., Jones, C.: Executable visual software modeling the ZOOM approach. Software Quality Control 15(1), 27–51 (2007)
14. Elkoutbi, M., Khriss, I., Keller, R.: Automated prototyping of user interfaces based on UML scenarios. Journal of Automated Software Engineering 13(1), 5–40 (2006)
15. Martinez, A., Estrada, H., Sanchez, J., Pastor, O.: From early requirements to user interface prototyping: A methodological approach. In: Proceedings of ASE 2002, pp. 257–260 (2002)

Rapid UI Development for Enterprise Applications: Combining Manual and Model-Driven Techniques

Arne Schramm, André Preußner, Matthias Heinrich, and Lars Vogel

SAP Research Center Dresden
{arne.schramm,andre.preussner,matthias.heinrich,lars.vogel}@sap.com

Abstract. UI development for enterprise applications is a time-consuming and error-prone task. In fact, approximately 50% of development resources are devoted to UI implementation tasks [1]. Model-driven UI development aims to reduce this effort. However, the quality of the final layout is a problem of this approach, especially when dealing with large and complex domain models. We share our experience in successfully using model-driven UI development in a large-scale enterprise project. Our approach mitigates the problems of model-driven UI development by combining manual layout with automatic inference of UI elements from a given domain model. Furthermore, we provide means to influence the UI generation at design time and to customize the UI at runtime. Thus, our approach significantly reduces the UI implementation effort while retaining control of the resulting UI.

Keywords: Model-Driven UI Development, UI Generation, UI Customisation.

1 Introduction

Enterprise applications, such as the SAP Enterprise Resource Planning or the SAP Transportation Management, are used by companies to execute and manage their business processes. One of their main tasks is to provide CRUD (Create, Read, Update, Delete) functionality for business objects, such as products, customers, business partners, etc. The properties and relations of these business objects are captured in *domain models*. Enterprise applications provide different views on the domain model of a company. Developers of user interfaces (UIs) for enterprise applications are facing a number of challenges.

1. **Development Costs:** Implementing user interfaces for enterprise applications is a labour-intensive and therefore costly task. Developers have to repeat similar working steps, such as choosing widgets and binding data to them, many times. To reduce the effort of UI creation, many model-driven approaches [2,3,4,5] have been proposed. They use several intermediate models to describe user interfaces at different layers of abstraction [6]. Given an appropriate tool support, developers can derive the UIs from models much

D.C. Petriu, N. Rouquette, Ø. Haugen (Eds.): MODELS 2010, Part I, LNCS 6394, pp. 271–285, 2010.

more efficiently and in a less error-prone way than implementing them from scratch. A drawback of this methodology with respect to the effort of UI creation is that every UI widget still has to be modelled manually. In particular, the mapping of data fields of the domain model to UI widgets is a recurring task that can be automated to a great extent. However, a fully automated UI generation based on a domain model produces significantly limited interfaces in terms of clarity, understandability, and usability [7], especially for complex models.

2. **Diversity of Users:** Users of an application can have different roles that may require role-specific views on the data they are working with. This forces software companies to develop diverse UIs for different groups of users, instead of providing one UI that satisfies the expectations of all users [2]. Furthermore, the users of an application may have different skills and experience levels, preferences, or cultural backgrounds, and therefore different expectations regarding a convenient UI. Thus, flexible mechanisms for UI adaptation, and customisation are needed.

3. **Software Evolution and Maintenance:** Companies need to be able to quickly respond to trends and changes in the market. Therefore, the IT landscape of an enterprise has to support constant evolution [8]. An example is a transportation company extending their services from nation-wide to international transports. This affects the company's domain model, since addresses of partners and customers now need a new attribute indicating their country. To support setting or reading this attribute, the company needs to change, re-compile and re-install the UI for its transportation management system.

In our approach we address the above mentioned challenges as follows.

1. We combine the benefits of model-driven UI development with automatic UI generation to create meaningful and user centric results with minimal effort. The UI designer creates the layout structure of the application which ensures the clarity, while the atomic UI widgets are automatically generated using information from a domain model.

2. We enable developers to rapidly create a business application for a certain domain, and adapt it to the needs of a specific user role. The user can individually customise the resulting UI.

3. Using our approach, minor changes in the domain model, such as adding or deleting an attribute, are automatically reflected in the UI after a restart of the application. Structural changes, such as adding or deleting business objects, can be incorporated in an application with little effort thanks to our tool support.

The remainder of this paper is organised as follows. Section 2 introduces a real-world example that is used to explain the challenges tackled by our approach. Section 3 describes our hybrid approach for UI development combining manual and model-driven techniques. Section 4 points out the advantages and disadvantages of our approach by means of two industrial use cases. Section 5 lists related work in the field of model-driven UI development and ad-hoc UI generation. Finally, Section 6 summarizes the paper and proposes ideas for future work.

The ideas presented in this paper were partly developed in the scope of the EU-funded ServFace project.[1]

2 Organisational Context and Running Example

This section gives an overview of our organizational context and its challenges from the UI development perspective. SAP Transportation Management (SAP TM) is a solution for transportation management. This includes applications for the management of transportation requests, which contain, e.g., the business partners, the source and destination locations, or the items to be transported. The customers of SAP TM, typically transportation companies, have very different business models. Some offer complex transports over various locations using diverse means of transportation, while others provide only limited transport services. The differences in the business models are reflected in different requirements for the software support. While the services offered by the SAP TM solution are suitable for most of the customers, and thus the underlying domain model is the same for all these customers, the UIs have to be adapted for each customer to match the needs imposed by the various business models. Until today more than one million UIs have been built on top of the transportation solution. For one customer even 1145 different UI screens have been developed. The development of each of these UIs is a tedious and expensive effort. This motivated us to find a solution for efficient UI creation and customisation. Existing UIs for the transportation management solution consist mainly of elements for editing data (approximately 80%) and only a minor part (approximately 20%) is used for navigation and administration. For this reason, we focus on the creation of form-based editors that provide CRUD functionality for DM elements.

Running Example. To better illustrate our approach, we introduce an example based on a simplified scenario. The application enables users to manage transportation requests. The domain model for this scenario is shown in Figure 1.

The model consists of eight classes containing in total 45 attributes. Creating a form-based editor manually would take some time even for such a small model. Assuming that each attribute needs at least a label and a widget for editing its value, a programmer has to define nearly 100 widgets and bind them to elements in the domain model. In the following section we introduce our UI development approach that reduces this effort significantly.

3 Our UI Design Methodology

In this section we describe how UIs are created following our approach. First, we briefly outline the steps needed to create a UI from an application designer's perspective. In the following subsections we explain in detail the important concepts and components of our approach.

---

[1] http://www.servface.eu, last visited July 9, 2010.

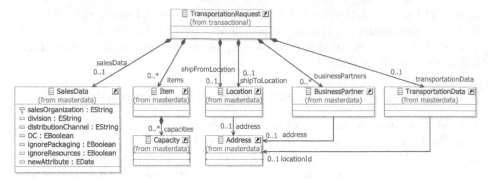

Fig. 1. Excerpt of the Simplified Domain Model for Transportation Requests

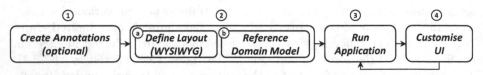

Fig. 2. Application design process

3.1 Application Design Process

Figure 2 gives an overview of the four steps in our application design process.

1. **Create Annotations:** As the starting point we assume that the domain model for the domain, for which an application shall be developed, is given as an EMF model (EMF = Eclipse Modeling Framework)[2]. The developer may add annotations to the model to influence the appearance of the generated UI. We do not have tool support for this step, since EMF provides excellent tools itself.

2. **Define Layout and Reference Domain Model:** To create the UI, the designer defines the layout (a), and sets references to elements of the domain model (b) using a WYSIWYG editor.

3. **Run Application:** Thanks to our interpretive approach the application can now be used without any additional generation or compilation steps. Besides the manipulation of domain model elements, the application provides persistency of data, and convenience features such as auto-completion.

4. **Customise UI:** The UI can be customised individually by the users to adapt it to their needs. After this customisation step the application can be used without a restart.

3.2 Model and Tool Overview

Figure 3 gives an overview of the models and tools that are used to create and customise applications. The numbers refer to the application development steps in Figure 2. The Final Application is generated using an interpretive approach.

---

[2] http://www.eclipse.org/modeling/emf, last visited May 2, 2010.

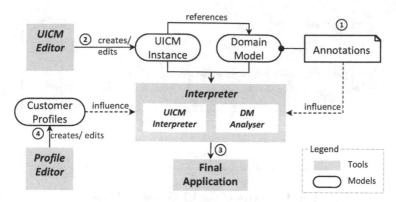

Fig. 3. Model and tool overview

Input for the Interpreter are two models, the UI Container Model (UICM) and the Domain Model (DM). While the UICM is different for each new application, the DM is created once by domain experts, and reused for all applications for that specific domain. The UICM is created using the UICM Editor, which is explained in Section 3.3. The UICM contains two kinds of information, the UI container structure, and the references to DM elements. The generation of the container structure is detailed in Section 3.4, and the generation of UI widgets based on the DM is explained in Section 3.5. To influence this generation, developers can enrich the DM with UI specific meta-data using annotations, which are described in Section 3.6. The resulting application can be customised individually using the Profile Editor as explained in Section 3.7.

3.3   Modelling the Application – The UICM Editor

The UI of an enterprise application must be well-structured to enable users to work efficiently. Automatic UI generation fails to create such well-structured UIs for large and complex domain models. Therefore, we decided to let the designer create the layout of an application's container structure by creating instances of the UICM.

Figure 4 shows an excerpt of the metamodel of the UICM, which we defined using EMF. Although the number of offered UI container elements is quite limited, it is our experience that the available elements are sufficiently powerful. Furthermore, it requires only a very low introductive training and can be used efficiently by designers.

Figure 5 shows the UICM Editor, a WYSIWYG editor for creating form-based applications. It consists of 5 parts: The Controls palette (1) providing the container elements, the Data Objects palette (2) offering the DM elements, the GUI outline containing a tree-view of the UI, the Properties view (4) for manipulating the properties of the currently selected UI element, and the Editor view (5) that provides the modelling area and displays the WYSIWYG representation of the application that is currently built.

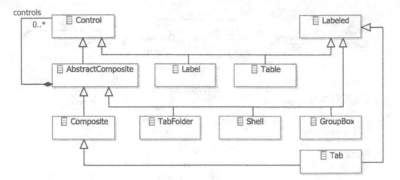

Fig. 4. Excerpt of the UI Container Model

Fig. 5. UICM Editor

To describe the container structure of an application, the designer drags and drops different container elements from the controls palette onto the modelling area (Step 2a in Figure 2). In this manner the designer creates a hierarchy of nested composites on different tabs[3], which can contain several sections. Then he drags and drops DM elements onto the containers. The DM elements are anaylsed and a suitable UI representation is generated and displayed inside the container (Step 2b in Figure 2).

The example application in the modeling area in Figure 5 contains such a container structure. Figure 6 shows an excerpt of the XML representation of the corresponding UICM. The application has three tabs, "Transportation Management" (Line 3), "Shipment Details", and "Route Details". The first tab contains

---

[3] Our interpreter displays tabs as pages in a multi-page editor.

```
1   <tm.widgets:Shell ...>
2     <controls xsi:type="tm.widgets:TabFolder">
3       <controls xsi:type="tm.widgets:Tab" text="Transportation Management" ...>
4         <controls xsi:type="tm.widgets:Composite" ...>
5           <controls xsi:type="tm.widgets:GroupBox" text="Sales Data" ...>
6             <dataObjects href=".../salesData" />
7           </controls>
8           ...
9         </controls>
10      </controls>
11    ...
12    </controls>
13  </tm.widgets:Shell>
```

Fig. 6. Excerpt of the example UICM

4 sections, "Sales Data" (Line 5), "Partners", "Items", and "Destination". The "Sales Data" section is bound to the "salesData" business object from the domain model (Line 6). The final application is shown in Figure 7.

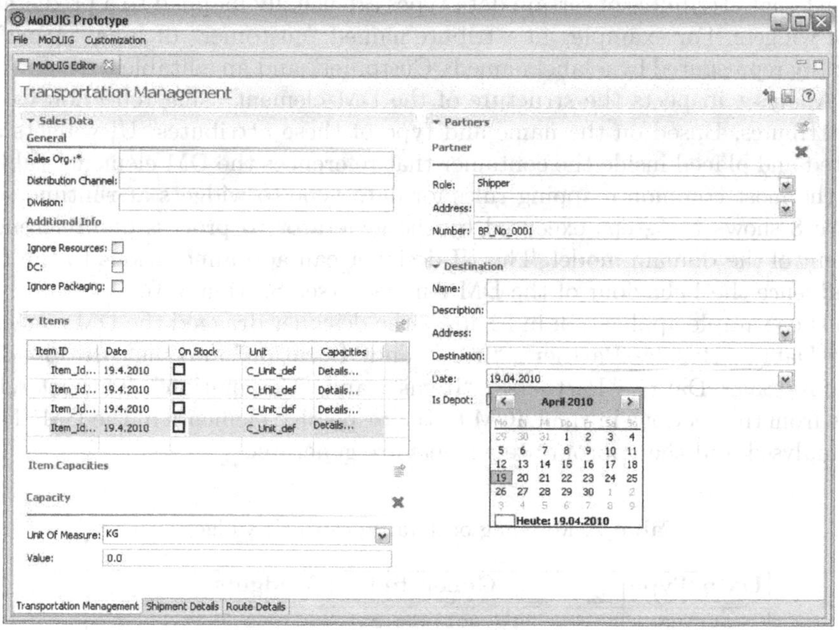

Fig. 7. Final application

3.4   Interpreting the Container Model – The UICM Interpreter

Due to the reasons discussed in Section 5 we decided to use an interpretive approach, and implemented a concrete interpreter using the Standard Widget

Toolkit (SWT).[4] The interpreter follows a strict set of rules to create widgets for the elements in the UICM. The UICM itself, however, is technology-agnostic, and different interpreters could create different UIs from it. The transformation rules applied by our interpreter are shown in Table 1.

Table 1. Mapping of UICM types to UI container widgets

UICM Element Type	UI Container Widget
Composite	org.eclipse.swt.widgets.Composite
TabFolder	org.eclipse.ui.part.MultiPageEditorPart
Tab	org.eclipse.ui.forms.widgets.ScrolledForm
GroupBox	org.eclipse.ui.forms.widgets.Section
Table	org.eclipse.jface.viewers.TableViewer

3.5   Inferring the UI Elements – The Domain Model Analyser

If the UICM interpreter finds a reference to a DM element in the UICM, the DM Analyser takes care of creating the atomic UI widgets. Here we take advantage of the fact that attributes of certain data types are usually mapped to a predictable set of widgets. For example, an attribute named "customer" of type "string" is typically represented by a label named "Customer" and an editable textbox. The DM Analyser inspects the structure of the DM element using reflection to get all attributes. Based on the name and type of these attributes, UI widgets are created and placed inside the container that references the DM element. Table 2 lists the most common mapping rules for data type to widgets at runtime, and Figure 8 shows the steps executed by the generator to process one referenced element of the domain model. The UI designer can add annotations to the DM to influence the behaviour of the DM Analyser (see Section 3.6).

In the example application in Figure 7 the designer dragged the DM elements "SalesData", "BusinessPartner", "Item", and "Location" into the corresponding sections "Sales Data", "Partners", "Items", and "Destination". This set references from the sections in the UICM to the respective elements in the DM. They are analysed and the appropriate widgets are generated.

Table 2. Mapping of data types to UI widgets

Data Type	Generated UI Widgets
string	org.eclipse.swt.widgets.Text
int	org.eclipse.swt.widgets.Text
double	org.eclipse.swt.widgets.Text
boolean	org.eclipse.swt.widgets.Button (SWT.CHECK)
date	org.eclipse.swt.widgets.DateTime
enumeration	org.eclipse.swt.custom.CCombo

---

[4] http://www.eclipse.org/swt/, last visited July 9, 2010.

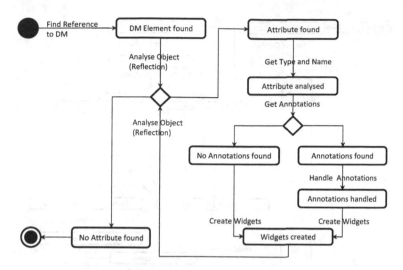

Fig. 8. Activity diagram of the UI generation

3.6   Influencing the Generated UI – Annotations

Annotations are one possible way of influencing the appearance of the generated UI. The annotations are created, stored, and passed to the DM Analyser
using the standard EMF annotation mechanism. Each DM element can have its
own annotations, which influence the appearance of the resulting UI element.
Currently, we support the following set of annotations.

Label. Defines the label for the UI element. Labels are displayed as read-only
textfields in front of the UI element.
Group. Defines a group of UI elements that are placed nearby together and
separated from other UI elements by a special separator, as can be seen e.g.
in Figure 7 for the UI elements grouped under "General" and "Additional
Info" in the "Sales Data" section. A group has a unique identifier and a
label.
GroupElement. Indicates that the UI element belongs to a certain group by
referring to its group identifier.
Ordering. Defines an order in which UI elements should be placed on the UI.
The order is given as an index. DM elements, which have no ordering annotation assigned, are placed below all ordered DM elements in the order of
their appearance in the EMF model.
Hide. Indicates that no UI element should be generated for this particular DM
element.
Default. Defines a default value that will be displayed in a new instance of the
corresponding UI element, and be used as value if the application user does
not specify another value.

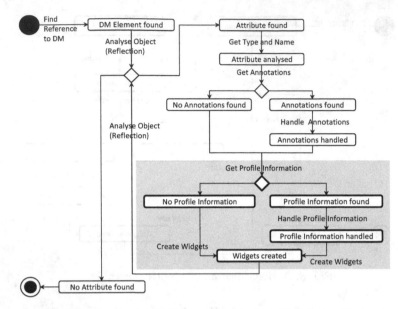

Fig. 9. Analysing DM elements using profile information

3.7   Customising the Resulting UI – The Profile Editor

The methodology described in the previous sections enables the application designer to quickly create and adapt UIs according to the needs of the customer. However, these UIs still have to be customisable on an individual basis, since users might have different roles in the company, and therefore may need different views on the domain data. Creating different UIs for each and every role would require significant effort for both development and maintenance. It is also desirable to have only one annotated instance of the domain model per customer, which eliminates the possibility of adding individual annotations per user. To enable individual customisation nonetheless, we introduced the concept of user profiles. The Profile Editor currently provides the following customisation possibilities to the user: Change layout, hide elements, change labels, and set individual default values.

The profiles influence the behaviour of the UICM Interpreter and the DM Analyser during the UI generation. They contain pieces of information that modify the appearance of UI elements. The effects of the profiles on the UI always overrride contradictory annotations. Figure 9 shows the activity diagram of the UI generation by the DM Analyser when taking profiles into consideration.

The Profile Editor uses a modified version of the Interpreter described in the previous subsection. This Interpreter generates a modified version of the application's UI with additional widgets, such as checkboxes to indicate whether a UI widget should be hidden, or textboxes to change labels. The benefit of that approach is the consistency of the look&feel.

4 Evaluation

In the project period of less than one year we have realised two different real-world scenarios. No extensive user study was available at the time of writing this paper, but the realisation of a larger evaluation involving customers is planned.

Development Costs and Productivity

As a very first evaluation of the productivity of our approach, we re-built a form-based editor for the creation of instances of the Universal Service Description Language (USDL) metamodel[5]. This metamodel consists of 46 classes with a total of 243 attributes. The manual implementation of the editor took 10 person days. It consists of four pages providing CRUD functionality for the elements of the four perspectives of USDL. Creating the same editor with our approach took less than two hours. One fact that speeded up the reimplementation is of course that the layout for the editor's UI was already given by the existing implementation. Taking this into account our approach needs approximately 1/10 of the time for the manual implementation.

Quality

The implementation of graphical UIs is usually the most error-prone part of the application development [9]. These implementation errors are completely eliminated as there is no implementation part in our UI creation process. The structure of our UI is modelled by defining instances of the UICM using a WYSI-WYG editor and the atomic UI widgets are generated automatically. However, from a design point of view, it is still possible to create disadvantageous UI layouts, which are misleading or badly structured. To mitigate that, we decided to provide a limited set of container elements in the UICM, so that the designer is also guided in the design choices up to a certain level.

Tool Support

Our approach allowed us to create a powerful tool support for the development of form-based CRUD applications. The UICM Editor enables the creation of applications in a WYSIWYG manner, and the Profile Editor provides an easy-to-use customisation of the final application. Both tools are integrated in a workbench that also runs the final application itself. In this way, the designer as well as a user can switch between the different tools and the final application, and thus immediately see and use the result of the design or customisation step. The tools and the final application use the UICM Interpreter and the DM Analyser as their foundation, which ensures a consistent look&feel of the UI.

Usability of the Final UI

The usability of UIs created with our approach is similar to the usability of manually created UIs for DMs with low to medium complexity. The DM Analyser

---

[5] http://www.internet-of-services.com/index.php?id=24, last visited May 2, 2010.

generates reasonable UI widgets that improve the usability, such as comboboxes
for enumerations, or calendar widgets for dates. Furthermore, the application provides convenience features such as autocompletion, and tab support (i.e. navigating to the next input field using the tabulator key). Of course, the clarity and
understandability of the UI depends to a great extent on layout created by the application designer, and the additional information available via annotations
during the UI generation, such as grouping and ordering.

For complex DMs with deeply nested or recursive data structures the restricted number of available structuring elements in the UICM currently hinders
the designer from creating clear UIs. One possible improvement is the usage of
the grouping and ordering annotation to enhance the visual structuring of the
generated UI elements. The available annotations as well as the UICM container
elements will be further evaluated and optimized.

Consistency

As mentioned in Section 2, roughly 80% of our UI elements are used to edit or
display data. The creation of these UIs in a predefined way leads to a consistent
look&feel of the different screens and applications. The look&feel of our generated UIs is defined by the different mapping rules applied by the interpreter.
Attributes of the same data type are always mapped to the same combination of
widgets, e.g., dates are always visualised in a calendar widget. Another benefit
of our approach is the consistency of error messages, hints or tooltips, as they
are also generated along with the widgets.

Customisability

One main requirement of our approach was that the resulting UI has to be
customisable individually, including the renaming and hiding of elements, setting
default values or changing the layout of the container structure. Providing these
possibilities allows the creation of one UI for a group of users, e.g., the employees
of one company, which can later be customized without implementation effort
by every user individually. Due to the interpretive approach the changes in the
UI are immediately reflected in the final application. The customisation can be
done by the user employing an adapted version of the interpreter. The benefit of
that is again a good usability and a consistent look&feel, also for the customise
view of the resulting application. The changes done by the user are stored in a
separate profile and taken into consideration by the interpreter and DM analyser
immediately.

Extensibility, Maintainability, and Flexibility

The flexibility of the created UI with regard to changes in the application's
requirements or the DM is improved. Small changes in the DM, e.g., adding or
deleting attributes or changing their data type do not even require the UI to
be modified, since the DM elements will be analysed using reflection every time

the application is run. For displaying new DM elements, the UICM has to be changed, so that it references the new model element. Again, there is no need for code generation or adaptation.

5   Related Work

Work from different fields of research was taken into account for our approach. The CAMELEON reference framework introduced by Calvary et al. [6] is the foundation for several works, e.g., by Vanderdockt [2] and Paternò [10], [11]. It defines several transient models, which are transformed into each other to create the final UI. Concept and task models are used to derive an abstract UI model (AUI), which is independent of any platform and implementation. A concrete UI (CUI) uses this information and turns it into an interactor-dependent UI description. In the last step, the runnable final UI is created.

There are two approaches to create the final UI. According to the methodology proposed in [6], the final UI code should be generated based on the CUI. This strong separation between the modelling and runtime environment however leads to insufficient support of evolution, especially in large-scale systems. The regeneration of complete systems is often not feasible and in some cases even not possible [12]. The second approach is to interpret the CUI instead of generating code. Interpretive model-driven approaches are discussed in [13], [14], and [15]. Meijler et al. [12] give a detailed comparison of generative and interpretive methods and present a hybrid approach supporting fine-grained changes in the model without re-generation of code. The main advantage of interpretation over code generation is flexibility. Because interpreters execute commands line by line, changes in any of these lines are directly reflected in the resulting application. There is no need for regeneration of code or model transformation. This allows for a fast adaptation of the UI to new tasks or focuses. The shortcomings of that are similar to our work, as they are bound to one preferred runtime and cannot generate different runtime platforms from one model according to MDA.

The aspect of automated UI generation is covered by Spillner et al. [16], [17]. The proposed methodology inspired us in developing the concepts of the DM Analyser. They retrieve their data model from WSDL files. The structure of the data model is then used to derive the UI elements from it. The mapping of data types to certain UI widgets is predefined to create highly usable UIs. We developed the annotation model based on the concept of additional UI hints introduced in this work.

6   Summary and Future Work

In this paper we presented our experience in the development of UIs for enterprise applications. The main challenge in this field are the high costs for development, customisation and maintenance. Our approach to reduce development effort combines explicit modelling of the UI's layout structure with automatic generation of the fine grained elements like labels and input fields based on a given domain model. The models are interpreted at runtime providing an increased flexibility. The interpreter and domain model analyser can be influenced by annotating the domain model at design time or creating custom profiles at runtime. We discussed the lessons learnt in detail. The benefits are a significantly reduced UI development effort, and the elimination of programming errors, since no manual implementation is required. Other enhancements are the consistency of the used UI elements and the flexibility of the resulting application. However, highly complex and deeply nested domain models can currently not be visualized in a satisfactory manner.

For future work we have a number of improvement ideas. The introduction of complex widgets like maps or graphs would improve the usability and efficiency of the UIs for end-users. The modelling of navigational elements has not been discussed in this work, but will be part of future work. Especially for UIs handling large parts of the DM, intuitive navigation between different screens and sections will improve the usability significantly. For very complex DMs, the usability of UIs created with our approach can be improved, as mentioned in the evaluation (Section 4). Different aspects of our methodology have to be reconsidered for that. One way would be the extension of the UICM, providing UI designers more possibilities for structuring the UI. An extended set of annotations could also help to accomplish that goal. Another idea to be further evaluated is the storage of the annotations separate from DM. This enables the provision of multiple annotation sets for the same model, or the separation of different annotation aspects, such as layout (e.g. Group and Order) from language (Label). In this way labels for different languages can be provided in separate files, one for each language, and separated from the language-independent annotations. Finally, the easy and fast adaptation of the UI's appearance and the application of corporate design to all screens of one customer could be enabled by supporting style sheets. For this we will investigate the possibilities provided by the Eclipse e4 project supporting CSS.

References

1. Myers, B.A., Rosson, M.B.: Survey on user interface programming. In: SIGCHI 1992: Human Factory in Computing Systems (1992)
2. Vanderdonckt, J.: A MDA-Compliant Environment for Developing User Interfaces of Information Systems. In: Proceedings of the 16th Conference on Advanced Information Systems Engineering (2005)
3. Sousa, K., Mendonça, H., Vanderdonkt, J.: Towards Method Engineering of Model-Driven User Interface Development. In: Winckler, M., Johnson, H., Palanque, P. (eds.) TAMODIA 2007. LNCS, vol. 4849, pp. 112–125. Springer, Heidelberg (2007)
4. Lu, X., Wan, J.: Model Driven Development of Complex User Interfaces. In: Proceedings of the MoDELS 2007 Workshop on Model Driven Development of Advanced User Interfaces (2007)
5. Ali Fatolahi, S.S.S., Lethbridge, T.C.: Towards a Semi-Automated Model-Driven Method for the Generation of Web-based Application from Use Cases. In: Proceedings of the 4th International Workshop on Model-Driven Web Engineering MDWE (2008)

6. Calvary, G., Coutaz, J., Bouillon, L., Florins, M., Limbourg, Q., Marucci, L., Paternó, F., Santoro, C., Souchon, N., Thevenin, D., Vanderdonckt, J.: The CAMELEON Reference Framework. Technical report (2002)
7. Myers, B., Hudson, S.E., Pausch, R.: Past, present, and future of user interface software tools. In: ACM Transactions on Computer-Human Interaction (TOCHI) (2000)
8. Lehmann, M., Ramil, J.: Evolution in Software and Related Areas. In: 4th International Workshop on Principles of Software Evolution (2001)
9. Mohan, R., Kulkarni, V.: Model Driven Development of Graphical User Interfaces for Enterprise Business Applications – Experience, Lessons Learnt and a Way Forward. In: Schürr, A., Selic, B. (eds.) MODELS 2009. LNCS, vol. 5795, pp. 307–321. Springer, Heidelberg (2009)
10. Paternò, F., Santoro, C., Scorcia, A.: Automatically adapting web sites for mobile access through logical descriptions and dynamic analysis of interaction resources. In: Proceedings of the Working Conference on Advanced Visual Interfaces (2008)
11. Paternò, F., Santoro, C., Spano, L.D.: Maria: A universal, declarative, multiple abstraction-level language for service-oriented applications in ubiquitous environments, vol. 16, pp. 1–30. ACM, New York (2009)
12. Meijler, T.D., Nytun, J.P., Prinz, A., Wortmann, H.: Supporting fine-grained generative model-driven evolution. Software and Systems Modeling (2010)
13. Atkinson, C., Kühne, T.: Rearchitecting the UML infrastructure. ACM Transactions on Modeling and Computer Simulation 12, 290–321 (2002)
14. Atkinson, C., Kühne, T.: Model-Driven Development: A Metamodeling Foundation. IEEE Software 50, 36–41 (2003)
15. Riehle, D., Fraleigh, S., Bucka-Lassen, D., Omorogbe, N.: The architecture of a UML virtual machine. In: 16th ACM SIGPLAN Conference on Object-oriented Programming, Systems, Languages, and Applications (2001)
16. Spillner, J., Braun, I., Schill, A.: Flexible Human Service Interfaces. In: Cardoso, J., Cordeiro, J., Filipe, J. (eds.) Proceedings of ICEIS (5), pp. 79–85 (2007)
17. Spillner, J., Feldmann, M., Braun, I., Springer, T., Schill, A.: Ad-Hoc Usage of Web Services with Dynvoker. In: Mähönen, P., Pohl, K., Priol, T. (eds.) ServiceWave 2008. LNCS, vol. 5377, pp. 208–219. Springer, Heidelberg (2008)

Environment Modeling with UML/MARTE to Support Black-Box System Testing for Real-Time Embedded Systems: Methodology and Industrial Case Studies

Muhammad Zohaib Iqbal[1,2], Andrea Arcuri[1], and Lionel Briand[1,2]

[1] Simula Research Laboratory, P.O. Box 134, Lysaker, Norway
[2] Department of Informatics, University of Oslo, Norway
{zohaib,arcuri,briand}@simula.no

Abstract. The behavior of real-time embedded systems (RTES) is driven by their environment. Independent system test teams normally focus on black-box testing as they have typically no easy access to precise design information. Black-box testing in this context is mostly about selecting test scenarios that are more likely to lead to unsafe situations in the environment. Our Model-Based Testing (MBT) methodology explicitly models key properties of the environment, its interactions with the RTES, and potentially unsafe situations triggered by failures of the RTES under test. Though environment modeling is not new, we propose a precise methodology fitting our specific purpose, based on a language that is familiar to software testers, that is the UML and its extensions, as opposed to technologies geared towards simulating natural phenomena. Furthermore, in our context, simulation should only be concerned with what is visible to the RTES under test. Our methodology, focused on black-box MBT, was assessed on two industrial case studies. We show how the models are used to fully automate black-box testing using search-based test case generation techniques and the generation of code simulating the environment.

1 Introduction

Real-Time Embedded Systems (RTES) are largely used in critical domains where high system dependability is required and expected. The basic characteristic of RTES is that they react to external events within certain time constraints. Extensive testing of such systems is important in order to verify their correct behavior under different timing constraints and adverse situations of the *environment* (or context). It is also important to verify that the system under test (SUT) does not lead the environment to a hazardous state. Testing RTES is particularly challenging since they operate in a physical environment composed of possibly large numbers of sensors and actuators. There is usually a great number and variety of stimuli with differing patterns of arrival times. Therefore, the number of possible test cases is usually very large if not infinite. Testing all possible sequences of stimuli/events is not feasible. Hence, systematic testing strategies that have high fault revealing power must be devised. Manually writing appropriate test cases for such complex systems would be a far too challenging and time consuming task. If any part of the specification of the RTES changes during its development, a very common occurrence in practice, then the

D.C. Petriu, N. Rouquette, Ø. Haugen (Eds.): MODELS 2010, Part I, LNCS 6394, pp. 286–300, 2010.

expected output of many test cases would potentially need to be recalculated manually. Automated test-generation and the use of an automated oracle are essential requirements when dealing with complex industrial RTES.

Moreover, testing the RTES in the real environment usually entail a very high cost and in some cases the consequences of failures would not be acceptable, for example when leading to serious equipment damages or safety concerns. In many cases the hardware, e.g., sensors and actuators, is not yet available at the time of testing as software and hardware are typically developed concurrently in RTES development. Since testing RTES on the real environment is not a viable solution, the use of a simulator is a common alternative.

In our work, we address the above issues by devising a comprehensive, practical methodology for black-box, model-based testing (MBT). The main contributions of this paper are as follows: It provides an environment modeling methodology based on industrial standards and targeted at MBT, and evaluates it on two industrial case studies. The models describe both the structural and behavioral properties of the environment. Given an appropriate level of detail, defined by our methodology, they enable the automatic generation of the environment simulator. The models can also be used to generate automated test oracles. These could, for example, be invariants and error states that should never be reached by the environment during the execution of a test case. Moreover, the models can further be used to automatically choose test cases. Sophisticated heuristics to choose appropriate test cases are automatically derived from the models without any intervention of the tester. To summarize, the only required artifacts to be developed by testers is the environment model and the rest of the process is expected to be fully automated. By using this automated MBT technology, one of our industrial partners was able to find new critical faults in their RTES. This paper focuses on how to make environment modeling as easy as possible for the purpose of supporting black-box, MBT, and shows its use for test automation. Due to space constraints, we only briefly discuss the details for code generation.

To support environment modeling in a practical fashion, we have selected standard and widely accepted notation for modeling software systems, the UML and its standard extensions. We use the MARTE [1] extensions for modeling real-time features and OCL for specifying constraints. We have also provided lightweight extension to UML to make it more useful in our context. As we will discuss later, environment modeling is not a new concept. But, most of the approaches use non-standardized notations or grammars for modeling, which makes them difficult to apply from a practical standpoint. To the best of our knowledge, modeling the environment of industrial RTES systems using a combination of UML, MARTE, and OCL has not been addressed in the literature. By using the proposed methodology, the software testers (who are primarily software engineers) can model the environment with a notation that they are familiar with and at a level of precision required to support automated MBT.

The importance of selecting standards for modeling was highlighted by the application of methodology on the two industrial case studies that belonged to completely different domains. An alternative to using standard notations for modeling could have been to create a Domain Specific Language (DSL) for environment modeling. Since the methodology needed to be generic for RTES irrespective of their application domain, making a DSL was not feasible. Making a DSL would have also reduced the benefits that we obtained from using standards and could have only been justified if existing standards did not fit our needs. Our case studies were developed using Enterprise Architect and IBM Rational Software Architect, though any of the widely available UML tools could have been used for this purpose.

The rest of the paper is organized as follow. Section 2 discusses the related work on environment modeling and testing based on environment models. The environment modeling methodology and simulation is discussed in Section 3. Section 4 describes the use of the environment modeling methodology for automated testing. Section 5 discusses the case studies on which the methodology was applied on and finally Section 6 concludes the paper.

2 Related Work

There are a few approaches reported in the literature for the environment modeling of embedded systems. Kishi and Noda [2] present an approach for modeling the environment of an embedded system using an aspect-oriented modeling technique. Karsai et al. [3] propose a new language for modeling the environment of an embedded system. Choi et al. [4] use annotated UML class and sequence diagrams for modeling and simulation of environment. Kreiner et al. [5] present a process to develop environment models for simulation of automatic logistic systems and its environment. Axelsson [6] evaluates how UML can be used to model real-time features and provides extension to UML for modeling of real-time systems and their environments. Gomaa [7] discusses the use of a context diagram for modeling the relationship between an RTES and its external entities. Friedentahl et al. use the concept of SysML block diagram and activity diagrams to represent the system and its interfaces with environment components [8].

There are a few works reported in literature that discuss testing based on the environment of a system. Auguston et al. [9] discuss the development of environment behavioral models using Attributed Event Grammar for testing of RTES. Bousquet et al. [10] present an approach for testing of synchronous reactive software by representing the environmental constraints using temporal logic. Larsen et al. [11] propose an approach for online testing of RTES based on time automata and environmental constraints. Heisel et al. [12] propose the use of a requirement model and an environment model using UML state machines along with the model of the SUT for testing. Adjir et al. [13] discuss a technique for testing RTES based on the model of the system and model of intended assumptions in the environment in Labeled Prioritized Timed Petri Nets.

As discussed above, there are approaches in literature that deal with modeling the environment of a system for various purposes. Most of these approaches are only limited to modeling the static structure of the environment, as they do not focus on test automation. The approaches that deal with modeling of behavioral aspects either use notations with which the software engineers are not familiar, or provide extensions for environment modeling that do not have well-defined semantics. Moreover, the properties of the environment, such as its timeliness and non-determinism, are not modeled in a standard way. The environment models should be compatible with other standard techniques available for model manipulation, e.g., model transformations, consistency checking. For this reason, the modeling language should have well-defined constructs. All environment modeling approaches aimed at supporting testing, except by Heisel et al. [12], use non-standard languages for modeling. Heisel et al. models both the SUT and the environment, which does not fit our purpose: black-box, system testing. Moreover, they model the concepts of probabilities and time using non-standard notations, without using the UML extension mechanisms. Last but not least, none of the relevant work assesses their environmental methodology on an actual RTES system, which we believe is a requirement to assess the credibility and applicability of any MBT approach.

3 Environment Modeling – Methodology

If environment models are to be used for RTES, they should not only be sufficiently detailed, but should also be easy to understand and modify as the environment and RTES evolve. To handle the complexity of realistic RTES environments, the modeling language should have provision for modeling at various levels of abstraction. The modeling language should also have well-defined syntax and semantics for the tools to analyze the models and for the humans to accurately understand them. The language should also provide features (or allow possible extensions) for modeling real world concepts, real-time features, and other concepts, such as non-determinism, required by the environment components. The UML, MARTE profile, and the OCL together fulfill the important requirements of an environment modeling language.

Even though we are using the same notations to model the environment that are used for modeling software systems, it is important to note that the methodology for environment modeling is significantly different from system modeling. While modeling for the industrial cases, we abstracted the functional details of the environment components to an extent that only the details visible to the SUT were included. For environment behavior modeling, non-determinism is widely used, which is not nearly as common when modeling the internal behavior of a system.

For testing the system based on its environment, the behavior details of the environment are as important as its structural details. Structural details of the RTES environment are important to understand the overall composition of the environment (e.g., number and configuration of sensors/actuators), the characteristics of various components, and their relationships. We choose to model these details in the form of a *Domain Model* developed using UML class diagrams. The behavioral details of environment components are required to specify the dynamic aspects of the environment, for example, to determine the possible environment states, before and after its interactions with the SUT, and to specify the possible interactions between the SUT and its environment. For behavioral details, we used the UML State Machines augmented with the MARTE profile.

In the following subsections, we discuss the methodology for modeling the environment of a RTES. We also discuss various guidelines based on our experience of applying the methodology on two industrial case studies.

3.1 Modeling Structural Details as Environment Domain Model

The environment domain model provides information of the components of the environment, their characteristics, their relationships with one another and the SUT, and information regarding signal sending and reception. The various components modeled in the domain model together form the overall environment of the SUT. This means that all these components (their instances) will run in parallel with each other. Each component in the domain model can have a number of instances in the RTES environment. The information about the number of possible instances of a component in the environment is modeled as cardinalities on the associations between different components in the domain model. Therefore, the domain model can be used to obtain a number of potential configurations of the environment. Fig. 1 shows the partial domain model for the environment of one of our industrial cases, the sorting machine (named as *SortingBoard* in the figure). The sorting machine is part of an automated bottle recycling system and further details of the case study can be found in Section 5. The model shows various motors, sensors, mechanical devices taking part in sorting, and other systems the *SortingBoard* communicates with.

Note that the domain model that we develop is different from the ones commonly discussed in literature (e.g., [14]). The components represented as classes in the environment domain model will not necessarily relate to software classes. They may correspond to systems, users and concepts related to various natural phenomena. Domain modeling here is not a starting point for software analysis. The identification of components in the domain model, their properties, and their relationships is also different from what is commonly done for software analysis. Following, we further discuss various guidelines for modeling the structural details of a RTES environment.

Environment Components to be Included. Initially, all the environment components that are directly interacting with the SUT are included in the domain model. Then, each of these components is further refined to a level where we are certain to cover the important details for simulating the environment needed to test the SUT. If at any time the behavior of an environment component was getting too complex, when possible, we decomposed the component and divided its behavior into multiple concurrent state machines. This is especially useful if a component can be divided into components that are similar to existing components, so that we can specialize existing state machines. We used the stereotype *<<context>>* to represent components of the environment in the domain model. The components of the environment are made to communicate with each other and the SUT through signals, and are modeled as active objects.

Relationships to be Included. All those associations representing the physical or logical relationships among various environment components, or that were needed for components to communicate, should be included. A number of components in the environment might be similar to each other (e.g., various types of sensors). It is useful to relate these components (and their behavior) using the generalization/specialization relationship for simplifying the model, as our experience shows that such domain models get highly complex. For example, in the sorting machine case study, we modeled the association of the *SortingBoard* with the *SortingArm*, which is controlled by the board, and the *ItemSensor* that reports arrival of an *Item* (e.g., bottle). We used generalization in multiple places, including motors and sensors as shown in Fig. 1.

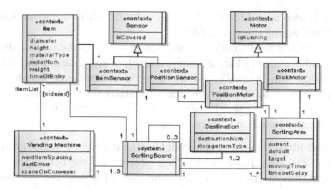

Fig. 1. Partial environment domain model showing properties and relationships of the sorting machine case study

Properties to be Included. From all properties that may characterize environment components, it is important to include only those properties that are visible to the SUT (or have an impact on a component that is visible to the SUT). These may include attributes that have a relationship to the inputs of the SUT, that constrain the behavior of a component with respect to the SUT, or that contribute to the state invariant of a component that is relevant to the SUT. In Fig. 1, all the modeled properties of *Item* are either visible to the *SortingBoard* or are used by other components. For example, the *serialNum* and *materialType* of *Item* is assigned by *VendingMachine* and is used by the *SortingBoard*.

Modeling the SUT. It is important to include the SUT in the environment domain model, so that its relationship with the other environment components can be specified. It is also useful to include the details of signal receptions by the SUT from other environment components. The SUT is stereotyped as *<<system>>*. The stereotype was used initially by Gomaa [7] to refer the system in a context diagram. The SUT modeled in the domain model should represent the SUT and its execution platform, as a single component.

3.2 Modeling Behavioral Details with UML State Machines and MARTE

For modeling the behavior details of the environment that have an impact on the SUT, we developed the UML State Machines with MARTE real-time extensions for various components in the environment. As discussed earlier, the environment components run in parallel to form the environment of the RTES. The components can send signals to each other and to the SUT. We can also view the environment as having one state machine with orthogonal regions, one for each component. Fig. 2 shows the state machine of a component for one of the industrial case studies. We have abstracted out the concepts for confidentiality reasons. Following, we discuss the details of the methodological guidelines we followed.

Identifying Stateful Components. Components whose states either affect the SUT or are affected by the SUT should be modeled with state machines. Apart from these components, it is also useful to model the behavior of other components on which we would like control during the simulation.

Overall, the environment should be modeled in a way that enables, after the initial configuration and provision of input data (parameters and guards), the full simulation of the interactions with the SUT. All the context components shown in Fig. 1 are stateful components of the sorting machine case study. For example, the *SortingArm* component was modeled as stateful since it receives signals from the *SortingBoard* and reacts differently based on its current state.

States to be Included. It is important to determine the right level of abstraction for a component state machine. If we want to precisely model the behavior of an environment component, this might lead to a large number of states. We are, however, only interested in state changes that have an impact on the SUT. A single state in an environment model state machine may correspond to a large number of concrete or physical states. For example, in the sorting machine, the Item states that were modeled were all related to its movement through the sorting machine whereas its other possible states were not of interest as an environment component of the *SortingBoard*.

Modeling Users in the Environment. Generally, for software system modeling users are only modeled as sources of inputs and data. The behaviors of users with respect to the system are mostly not considered. In the environment modeling methodology, it is useful to model the behavior of users in the environment to have a control over the inputs/outputs of the various components or the SUT. If a user participates in multiple roles, it is useful to model each role a user plays as a separate component. In the sorting machine case study, we modeled two different users (the operator and the persons who enter the items for sorting), each of them had considerable non-deterministic behavior. In certain cases it can be interesting to model both the expected and unexpected behavior of users using the proposed methodology.

Modeling Abstract Phenomena. Sometimes it is necessary to model abstract physical concepts, such as temperature, heat, voltage, and current. Mostly, information regarding these phenomena can be obtained and controlled through sensors and controllers, such as a temperature controller or sensor. Modeling of such concepts explicitly as environment components can be useful if a change in the state of these concepts impacts multiple components simultaneously, or if it is not possible to identify a related component in the environment that can act as a controller or sensor of this concept for simulation. As an example, consider a RTES on a vehicle that indicates its driver the time for a pit stop. The tires of a vehicle can burst when the temperature of the road gets too high. If there is no sensing mechanism available in the environment, then it is useful to make a state machine of temperature, with possibly two states representing below and above danger temperatures.

Modeling Transitions & Action Durations. Most of the transitions in the state machines of the components will either be based on signal events or time events. Timeout transitions are an important concept in RTES environment models. The MARTE *TimedEvent* concept is used to model timeout transitions, so that it is possible for them to explicitly specify a clock. Each environment component may have its own clock or multiple components may share the same clock for absolute timing. The clocks are modeled using the MARTE's concept of clocks. Specifying a threshold

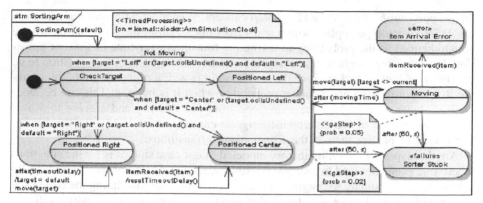

Fig. 2. State Machine of the *SortingArm* component in the sorting machine case study

time for an action execution or for a component to remain in a state is possible using the MARTE *TimedProcessing* concept. This is also a useful concept and can be used, for example, to model the behavior of an environment component when the RTES expects a response from it within a time threshold. When a *SortingArm* is signaled to move, after staying some time in the *Moving* state, it transitions to the *Not Moving* state (see Fig. 2).

Modeling Non-Determinism. Non-determinism is a particularly important concept for environment modeling and is one of the fundamental differences between models for system modeling and models for environment modeling. Following we discuss different types of non-determinism that we have modeled for our case studies.

Specifying exact value for timeout transitions might not always be possible for RTES environment components. To model their behavior in a realistic way, it is often more appropriate to specify a range of values for a possible timeout, rather than an exact value. Moreover, the behavior of humans interacting with the RTES is by definition non-deterministic. For modeling this behavior, we can add an attribute in the environment component and use OCL to constrain the possible set of values of the attribute and then use this attribute as a parameter of a timeout transition. In the sorting machine case study, the *SortingArm* may reach a sorting location from its center between 5 sec and 6 sec, depending on various physical conditions. This is modeled through the attribute *movingTime*, which is passed as a parameter to the change event on the transition from *Moving* to *Not Moving*. Legal values for the attributes are constrained using OCL.

Another important form of non-determinism is to assign probabilities to the transitions of state machines. In an RTES environment, we sometimes only know the probability of a component to go into a particular state over time and we are not sure about the exact occurrence of such conditions. For example, we can say that the probability of a car engine to overheat after running continuously for 10 hours is 0.05, but we cannot be certain about the exact instance in time when this situation will happen. We can model this in the engine state machine with a transition going from *Normal Temperature* state to *Overheated* state, during an interval of 10 hours, with probability of 0.05. For modeling these scenarios, we assigned a probability on the transitions using the property *prob* of the MARTE *GaStep* concept. Whenever a timeout transition has the *gaStep* stereotype applied with a non-zero value of *prob*, the combination will be comprehended as the probability of taking the transition over time of timeout transition. In the sorting machine case study, a *SortingArm* can get stuck in a position (e.g., because of a bottle blocking it or the arm jamming) with a probability 0.02 in a minute if it is not moving and a higher probability when it is moving. This can be modeled as shown in Fig. 2 by the transitions from *Not Moving* and *Moving* to *Sorter Stuck*. The sending of non-deterministic signals can also be modeled using this type of transitions, by placing them in the actions of such transitions.

Another type of probability that we modeled in our case studies is for the situations where one event can lead to multiple possible scenarios, but all of them are mutually exclusive. For example, we might want to represent the fact that during the communication with the SUT there is a chance that signals are received with or without distortion. To make the models more realistic, we assigned probabilities to each of such scenarios in the environment component. In terms of UML state machines, this means that multiple transitions are outgoing from one state based on the same event (maybe with identical guard). For modeling these scenarios, we assigned the MARTE *gaStep* stereotype to each of the multiple possible outgoing transitions. The example of communication with the SUT can be modeled by having two transitions going out of the environment component state on receiving of a signal, one labeled with a probability that the signal was corrupted and the other with the probability that the signal was fine. Modeling the distribution of event arrivals and timeout transitions can be useful for validation purposes, but is out of the scope of this paper, since our goal is verification of the SUT. Nevertheless, this type of information can be easily expressed in the model using the MARTE profile.

Modeling Error & Failure States. In the environment models, two types of states play a particularly important role: the error states and the failure states.

Environment error states are those states that the environment goes into because of unwanted response(s) (or lack of) from the SUT. Every component in the environment may have error states. If any component of the environment reaches one of these error states, then it means that the SUT is faulty. We use the stereotype <<*error*>> for such states in the environment model. For a *SortingArm*, an *Item* should not arrive while the arm is moving. This is an error state of the environment and can be caused if arm is not made to move on time by the *SortingBoard*. In Fig. 2, this has been modeled with the *Item Arrival Error* state.

Failure states model possible failures of environment components. A component may fail in several different ways with different consequences for the SUT. The SUT should appropriately behave under known, failing conditions. A failure can happen at any time during the execution of a component, e.g., a sensor may break at any time, and is modeled as non-deterministic behavior (as discussed). We use the stereotype <<*failure*>> for these failure states. The *Sorter Stuck* state discussed earlier, in which the *SortingArm* is stuck and cannot change its position, is a failure state of the environment.

3.3 Modeling the Constraints

To apply constraints on the relationships and restrictions on various value combinations (or state combinations) of objects, we have used the Object Constraint Language (OCL). We have also used OCL for representing the guards on the state machines, various state invariants and general constraints on the relationships of environment components.

RTES environment consists of a number of components including some real-world concepts (e.g., temperature, air pressure). If we consider all the various components of environment together, it is important to restrict the possible state combinations of these components to avoid infeasible situations (e.g., reverse and forward movement of motors is not possible at the same time). In our methodology, we have used OCL to specify constraints for such scenarios. For example, for the sorting machine, if a *SortingArm* is moving then only one *DiskMotor* and *PositionMotor* should be running at a given time. If the arm is not moving, both the motors should not be running. There can be a number of such constraints and it is important to model them to have a realistic simulation and testing based on the models. Otherwise, the models would end up in states that are not practically possible.

State invariants in the environment also play a significant role. Based on the values of the attributes of the component, the state invariants are used to evaluate the current state of the environment and derive state oracles (i.e., is the environment in the expected state?). We have used OCL to specify the state invariants. We also used OCL to specify the overall set of values that an attribute of an environment component can take. Last, the OCL constraints were also used for modeling non-determinism as discussed earlier.

3.4 Environment Modeling Profile

Our goal was to model the environment based only on the standard UML and its existing extensions as much as possible. We applied the standard notations and based on our needs for those case studies, where required, we provided light weight extensions to UML. In this section we will discuss the subsets of UML and MARTE that we used and the lightweight extensions that we have provided for environment modeling. From a practical standpoint, it was important to identify these subsets for the methodology, since the UML and MARTE standards are very large and most organizations would be reluctant to adopt such large notations.

We used the concept of Context, System, Error, and Failure under the form of UML stereotypes. Context is used to represent an environment component and is applied on the classes of the domain model. Similarly, System is also applied on the classes of the domain model and represents the SUT. Error represents the states of environment component that are only taken if there is an error in the SUT. Failure is also applied on the states and represents a failure in the environment. Within UML, we used the concept of Class diagram, State Machines. From MARTE, we only used the Time package and the GaStep concept from the GQAM package as shown in Fig. 3. This small subset of UML and MARTE was sufficient for modeling our two industrial case studies for the purpose of automated black-box testing.

3.5 Simulation of Environment Models

Due to size constraints, we cannot go into the details of the simulation and only briefly discuss it. The environment models developed using our methodology with UML and the MARTE profile are transformed into a RTES environment simulator in Java using a model to text transformation. The transformation was based on an extended version of the state pattern that accounts for asynchronous communication, time events, and change events. The simulator is used to test a RTES in conditions similar to its real environment. Since the standard for a concrete syntax of the UML Action Language is still not finalized, we made use of Java to specify actions. Once there is a standard UML Action Language, the actions can be written in that language and then translated into the target language of the RTES. For our case studies, the actions are written in Java and are converted into Java method calls.

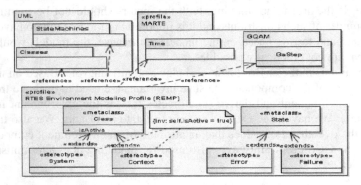

Fig. 3. Profile diagram showing various stereotypes and references

4 Model-Based Testing Based on Environment Models

In this section we briefly discuss how our modeling methodology is used to achieve automated system testing. Further details can be found in [15].

The UML/MARTE models of the environment are used to automatically generate a simulator for it. The simulator is used to test the RTES on the development platform. The information from the models is used to guide the generation of test cases and for generating automated oracles, which enable fully automated testing. Once test case and oracle generation is completely automated, it is possible to execute and evaluate a large number of test cases.

In our methodology, a test case is the setting used for the simulator. The information of what to configure in the simulator is automatically derived from the models and it is given as input to the test engine. Two types of setting are necessary:

-   Number and relations of the environmental components. For example, given a state machine representing a sensor, the Domain Model is used to determine how many sensors can be connected to the RTES (and so, we would know how many running instances we need for that state machine). Several different combinations are possible.

-   Each state machine can have non-deterministic events. The models are used to specify them and to provide details of their type. When the simulator is running, every time it requires a value to calculate a non-deterministic event, it then queries the test engine to obtain such values.

At the current moment, we have not investigated different configurations based on the Domain Models. We have focused on testing the behavior of the RTES given a single configuration. The goal of the testing is to provide a valid setting for the non-deterministic events such that an environmental error state (Section 3.2) is reached during the simulation, if any fault is present.

The simplest testing technique would be to provide (valid) random values each time the simulator queries the test engine for values to use in non-deterministic events. But more sophisticated techniques that exploit the information in the models can be used. For example, reaching the error state during simulation can be represented as a search/optimization problem, so Search Based Testing (SBT)[16] can be used. From the models we can automatically generate a *fitness function* to guide the search. Common heuristics such as *approximation level* and *branch distance* of the OCL constraints would be used for the fitness function. Due to size constraints, the investigated testing strategies are reported in [15], where we also proposed a *novel* fitness function that exploits the time properties of the UML/MARTE models.

The use of models for SBT in the case of RTES system testing is essential. In fact, to have effective heuristics (i.e., the fitness function) we need to have precise knowledge of the error states. This information is easily added in the models using stereotypes (Section 3.4). All the relevant states/transitions that lead to those error states can be exploited for the automatic derivation of the fitness function. On the other hand, if we have a simulator but no model, it is unlikely that it would be possible to automatically reverse-engineer all this necessary information from the code alone. Therefore, the fitness function would be necessarily written by hand, with all the related downsides that this choice brings.

In some relevant cases [15], it is possible to automatically derive very precise fitness functions. This happens when time constraints need to be satisfied (a typical case in RTES), e.g., a signal should be received within 10 milliseconds. A test case for which that signal is received after nine milliseconds gives more information than a test case in which the same signal is immediately received after one millisecond (notice that in both cases the constraint is satisfied). SBT can automatically exploit this information by focusing the search on simulator configurations that are more likely to yield a deadline miss. A tester does not need to write these heuristics, they are in fact automatically derived from the environment models. This is essential, because in general software testers do not have the expertise to write proper fitness functions for search algorithms.

The results in [15] show that our modeling methodology can be used for a fully automated system testing that is effective in revealing faults in industrial RTES. Although different testing strategies can be designed (e.g., Random Testing and SBT), the environment modeling methodology described here would still remain the same.

5 Case Studies

To evaluate the proposed methodology for environment modeling, we applied it on two industrial RTES. The application domains of the systems were entirely different. Because we cannot provide full details of the systems due to confidentiality restrictions, we are providing only a brief description. One of the RTES case studies (Case A) was a sorting system, which was part of an automated bottle recycling machine (developed by Tomra). The system communicated with a number of sensors and actuators to guide recycled items through the recycling machine to their appropriate destinations. The second RTES was a marine seismic acquisition system (Case B). One of the responsibilities of that system was to control the movement of seismic cables, where each cable had a large number of sensors and seismic vibrators, among other equipments. The system regularly communicated with these components and was responsible for managing the life cycle and connections for these components (among other things). We provide a summary of the environment models developed for both the case studies in Table 1.

For Case A, the RTES was configurable as three different types of systems; therefore the number of environment components was large. But most of the components' behavior could be modeled with a couple of states. The highest number of states was 18. Many components inherited a parent component behavior, i.e., its state machine. That was the case for example for *DiskMotor* and *Motor* in Fig. 1.

Though the number of components for Case B was more limited than for Case A, the number of instances for some of the components in the environment was very large (e.g., thousands of sensors of the same type communicating with the SUT), thus leading to many instances of executing state machines during simulation. The complexity of component state machines was also on average much higher than for Case A.

One important conclusion is that, in both cases, we were able to model the RTES environments with the subset of UML and MARTE that we identified and the lightweight extensions that we proposed. The models were sufficient to generate simulators that could be used to support large-scale test automation. In one of our industrial case study, using random testing and the SBST strategy described above, combined with using the environment model to identify error states (oracle), new critical faults were detected.

For both case studies, the number of components identified at the time of domain modeling was larger than what was finally required. During successive revisions and based on insight obtained through behavioral modeling, some components turned out to be unnecessary and were removed from the domain model. One practical challenge is that it was not easy in practice to identify the right level of abstraction to model the behavior of environment components. Sub-machines were widely used to incrementally refine the behavioral models until the right level of detail was achieved to simulate the behavior of component from the viewpoint of the SUT.

Table 1. Summary of the environment models of the two industrial RTES

Industry Case	# of env. components	Stateful components	Average # of states	Max states in a component	Max transitions in a component
Case A	55	43	~3	18	40
Case B	5	4	~12	19	29

6 Conclusion

In this paper, we have discussed a methodology for modeling the environment of a Real-Time Embedded System (RTES) in order to enable black-box, system test automation, which is usually performed by test engineers who are not informed of the design specifics of the RTES. For practical reasons and to facilitate its adoption, the methodology is based on standards: UML, MARTE profile, and OCL for modeling the structure, behavior, and constraints of the environment. We, and this is part of our methodology, made a conscious effort to minimize the notation subset used from these standards. We briefly discussed how the environment models are used to generate automated system test cases and a simulator of the environment to enable testing on the development platform. One advantage is that the methodology also allows more focus on the testing for critical and hazardous conditions in the RTES environment as environment failures and possible error states due to faults in the RTES implementation are explicitly modeled.

We modeled the environment of two industrial RTES in order to investigate whether our methodology and the notation subsets selected were sufficient to fully address the need for automated system testing. Our experience showed that was the case. In particular, by using our environment models to derive test cases and oracles, it was possible to automatically find new, critical faults in one of the industrial case studies using fully automated, large scale random and search-based testing.

Acknowledgements. The work presented in this paper was supported by Norwegian Research Council and was produced as part of the ITEA 2 VERDE project. We are thankful to Christine Husa, Tor Sjøwall, John Roger Johansen, Erling Marhussen, Dag Kristensen, and Anders Emil Olsen, all from Tomra, for their crucial support.

References

1. OMG: Modeling and Analysis of Real-time and Embedded systems (MARTE), Version 1.0 (2009), http://www.omg.org/spec/MARTE/1.0/
2. Kishi, T., Noda, N.: Aspect-oriented Context Modeling for Embedded Systems. In: Workshop on Early Aspects: Aspect-Oriented Requirements Engineering and Architecture Design, pp. 68–74 (2004)
3. Karsai, G., Neema, S., Sharp, D.: Model-driven architecture for embedded software: A synopsis and an example. Science of Computer Programming 73, 26–38 (2008)
4. Choi, K.S., Jung, S.C., Kim, H.J., Bae, D.H., Lee, D.H.: UML-based Modeling and Simulation Method for Mission-Critical Real-Time Embedded System Development. In: IASTED International Conference Proceedings pp. 160–165 (2006)
5. Kreiner, C., Steger, C., Weiss, R.: Improvement of Control Software for Automatic Logistic Systems Using Executable Environment Models. In: EUROMICRO 1998: Proceedings of the 24th Conference on EUROMICRO, pp. 20919–20923. IEEE Computer Society, Los Alamitos (1998)
6. Axelsson, J.: Unified Modeling of Real-Time Control Systems and Their Physical Environments Using UML. In: Eighth Annual IEEE International Conference and Workshop on the Engineering of Computer Based Systems (ECBS 2001), p. 18 (2001)
7. Gomaa, H.: Designing Concurrent, Distributed And Real-Time Applications With UML. Addison-Wesley Educational Publishers Inc., Reading (2000)

8. Friedenthal, S., Moore, A., Steiner, R.: A Practical Guide to SysML: The Systems Modeling Language. Elsevier, Amsterdam (2008)
9. Auguston, M., Michael, B., Shing, M.: Environment behavior models for automation of testing and assessment of system safety. Information and Software Technology 48, 971–980 (2006)
10. Du Bousquet, L., Ouabdesselam, F., Richier, J.L., Zuanon, N.: Lutess: a specification-driven testing environment for synchronous software. In: ICSE 1999: Proceedings of the 21st International Conference on Software Engineering, pp. 267–276. ACM, New York (1999)
11. Larsen, K.G., Mikucionis, M., Nielsen, B.: Online Testing of Real-time Systems Using Uppaal. In: Grabowski, J., Nielsen, B. (eds.) FATES 2004. LNCS, vol. 3395, pp. 79–94. Springer, Heidelberg (2005)
12. Heisel, M., Hatebur, D., Santen, T., Seifert, D.: Testing Against Requirements Using UML Environment Models. In: Fachgruppentreffen Requirements Engineering und Test, Analyse & Verifikation, pp. 28–31. GI (2008)
13. Adjir, N., Saqui-Sannes, P., Rahmouni, K.M.: Testing Real-Time Systems Using TINA. In: Núñez, M. (ed.) TESTCOM/FATES 2009. LNCS, vol. 5826, pp. 1–15. Springer, Heidelberg (2009)
14. Larman, C.: Applying UML and Patterns: An Introduction to Object-Oriented Analysis and Design and the Unified Process. Prentice Hall PTR, Upper Saddle River (2001)
15. Arcuri, A., Iqbal, M.Z., Briand, L.: Black-box System Testing of Real-Time Embedded Systems Using Random and Search-based Testing. Technical Report, Simula Research Laboratory (2010)
16. McMinn, P.: Search-based Software Test Data Generation: A Survey. Software Testing Verification and Reliability 14, 105–156 (2004)

Improving Test Models for Large Scale Industrial Systems: An Inquisitive Study

Andrew Diniz da Costa[1], Viviane Torres da Silva[2], Alessandro Garcia[1],
and Carlos José Pereira de Lucena[1]

[1] Laboratory of Software Engineering, Informatics Department
Pontifical Catholic University of Rio de Janeiro, Brazil
[2] Department of Computer Science,
Federal Fluminense University, Brazil
{acosta,afgarcia,lucena}@inf.puc-rio.br,
viviane.silva@ic.uff.br

Abstract. Although documentation of software tests is becoming increasingly important, there is little knowledge on whether modeling languages and tools are effective in industrial projects. Recent reports have pointed out that test modeling techniques might be barely used by software developers due to their inability to cover test concepts relevant in real-life large applications. This paper reports an inquisitive multi-phase study aimed at revealing test-relevant concepts not supported by modeling languages. The study encompassed several questionnaire responses and interviews with developers, and observational analyses run over two years in large-scale software projects. Various test concepts were brought forth and they fall in three categories: (i) test cases and software evolution, (ii) interdependencies between test cases, and (iii) categorization and grouping of test cases. Finally, the relevance of the identified test concepts is discussed in terms of an industrial system for inventory and supply control of petroleum products.

Keywords: Modeling, Software Testing, Industrial Applications.

1 Introduction

Documenting software tests is nearly as essential as documenting source code itself. Therefore, as the recognition on systematic software testing increases, there is a pressing need to conceive modeling techniques to explicitly document key concerns associated with test cases [11][12]. In fact, when software tests are not properly documented, their successful application is hindered, the investment to build and maintain them is not paid off, and they can even become the key reason for remaining faults in software projects [3][11][12]. Even though the number of test modeling languages (e.g. [16][18][19]) is growing, there is limited knowledge about the extent they are expressive enough for the documentation of test cases in large-scale industrial projects. One of the reasons is that different test cases have intricate relationships, and each of them plays different roles as a software project evolves.

D.C. Petriu, N. Rouquette, Ø. Haugen (Eds.): MODELS 2010, Part I, LNCS 6394, pp. 301–315, 2010.
© Springer-Verlag Berlin Heidelberg 2010

A test modeling language provides abstractions and a visual notation to represent testing-specific concerns and facilitate the communication of the project team. In general, the systematic evaluation of test modeling languages has been neglected in the literature. Their effectiveness is often assessed only by their own proponents [16][18][19]. In addition, there is growing evidence over the last decade that test modeling techniques are barely used by software developers due to their inability to cover test concepts relevant in evolving large systems [8][9]. On the other hand, identifying the effectiveness of test modeling languages in realistic projects is not trivial as project managers, developers and other stakeholders often do not have time to take part in controlled experiments.

In this context, this paper reports an inquisitive multi-phase study [21] aimed at revealing potential gaps or deficiencies of test modeling languages that are used in practice. In particular, we have conducted a questionnaire-based survey, interviews and retrospective analyses through several projects in order to identify test-relevant concepts not supported by existing modeling languages. Our study was conducted in a software engineering lab specialized in executing different types of software test, including performance, database and functional tests. The initial elicitation of test concepts was based on a retrospective analysis of tests carried out in a number of long-term software projects in such a lab.

Several participants were involved in the study, including fourteen developers with different testing skills that took part in the interviews and answered the questionnaire. The motivation for their participation is that over the last five years the testing team has faced numerous problems on documenting, maintaining and reusing test cases in various projects. After revealing a relevant set of test concepts, we analyzed their need and applicability in an industrial system for inventory and supply control of petroleum products. This system has a huge number of evolving requirements and business rules that must be tested with high frequency.

The paper is organized as follows. Section 2 presents the empirical procedures adopted to reveal a set of relevant test concepts that are not fully supported by existing modeling languages. This section also describes the results of a questionnaire applied to a set of subjects with different backgrounds and skills on testing complex systems. The goal was to receive their feedback about the relevance of explicating documenting certain testing concerns that are often neglected by modeling techniques. Section 3 highlights a retrospective analysis of documenting and explicitly reasoning about such testing concerns in the context of a large-scale petroleum control system. Section 4 discusses to what extent the available test modeling and management tools support testing activities by focusing on the identification of testing concepts explicitly captured by them. Section 5 presents the concluding remarks and future work.

2   Revealing Relevant Test Concepts: An Inquisitive Approach

We conducted an inquisitive study [21] to identify test concepts not supported by modeling languages proposed in the literature. We have relied on interviews, a questionnaire applied to developers in a lab, and the analysis of the testing process applied in large-scale software projects. We have opted for an inquisitive study, rather than running controlled experiments, as this empirical method allows us to reveal relevant testing concepts based on the experience of real developers, who worked in different software projects. Inquisitive analyses [21] are recommended for cases that require an exploratory investigation in a software engineering field and do not rely on well-defined hypotheses. In addition, controlled experiments would impose: (i) higher costs that are often impeditive to several real-life software projects, and (ii) additional time from the subjects who participated of the work.

Thus, the study was composed of two major complementary stages: (i) the identification of potential test concepts that need to be supported by test models (Sections 2.1 to 2.3), and (ii) an observational analysis of how such test concepts were important in a large-scale software project (Section 3). As stated, the former was mainly supported by the elaboration of interviews and a questionnaire distributed to several developers, which are discussed in the following subsections. The later relied on the outcome of the former, i.e. a list of recurring test concepts identified by developers and testers (Sections 2.2 and 2.3). This list was used to support a reflective analysis of how existing modeling languages could be enhanced while supporting testing in large-scale software projects (Sections 3 and 4).

2.1 Identifying Neglected Test Concepts: Empirical Procedures

The goal of the first stage was to detect testing concepts that were both considered useful in large-scale software projects and not fully (or partially) supported by existing modeling approaches. Therefore we derived a stepwise procedure to identify such a set of relevant concerns. Fig. 1 illustrates our steps, which are described below.

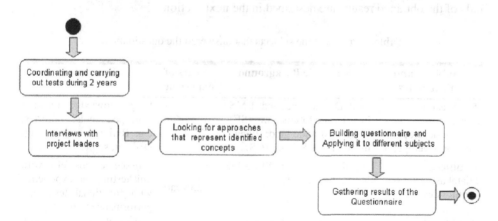

Fig. 1. Gathering candidate concepts for test modeling

The first step started three years ago, when we got involved in the analysis of testing activities in several long-term software projects in the domain of petroleum control (Section 3). Our aim was to carry out an initial identification of useful test concepts across these software projects. One of the paper authors was actually involved in the coordination and development of the testing activities in these projects. As the initial identification was exploratory, there was no specific constraint on the nature of testing concepts being gathered. This analytical work was performed during two years, and seven versions in three software projects were considered.

The initial analysis was followed by several interviews with test leaders. The goal of the interviews was to discuss with them to what extent those initially-elicited concepts were, according to their experience, potentially useful for test modeling and documentation. For some cases, they were able to pinpoint which of those concepts were not supported by either tools or modeling approaches for testing that they knew. The test leaders also explained in detail how the teams were handling or informally representing those testing concepts in their day-to-day testing activities. Our final list of elicited testing concepts is presented in the next subsection. Next, we decided to analyze to what extent a representative set of test modeling languages and management tools supported those concepts identified. Section 5 presents the key findings derived from this analysis.

The fourth step (Figure 1) involved the design of a questionnaire, which was applied to fourteen invited participants with different testing skills and experience. The goal of the questionnaire was to confirm (or not) the importance of the test concepts suggested by the test leaders. The subjects involved were members of the software projects mentioned above, and the main motivation of the participation was the improvement of the test process applied. Table 1 shows the profile of these participants. In order to remove or minimize the bias in the responses given by the subjects, the questionnaire design followed well-known recommendations [7] and was validated by two experts on testing modeling and experimental software engineering. In addition, a person was able to address emerging doubts or concerns about the questions when the questionnaire was applied. Finally, all the responses were gathered and analyzed in detail. The results were presented and discussed with the stakeholders involved. Details of the obtained results are described in the next section.

Table 1. Profile of the subjects that answered the questionnaire

Subjects and their Roles	Academic Background	Years of experience	Description
(5 subjects) 1 project leader 2 senior developers 1 junior developer	2 PhD candidates and 1 MSc in Software Engineering (SE), 1 grad., 1 undergrad. student in Computer Science (CS)	> 3 years	Large knowledge of testing concepts, tools, libraries, e.g. Rational tools, JUnit, DBUnit, so on.
(6 subjects) 2 database admins. 4 senior developers	1 PhD candidate in SE, 3 MSc in SE, 2 grad. in CS	1..3 years	Worked extensively with unit testing and experience with functional tests and performance tests.
(3 subjects) 2 senior developers 1 junior developer	2 undergrad. students in CS 1 undergrad. student in SE	< 1 year	Not much experience with tests, but knowledgeable of all test concepts.

2.2 Results of the Questionnaire

The questionnaire basically motivated each participant to answer if they agree or disagree, based on their own justifications, on the importance of each concept for test documentation. The identified testing concepts were classified in three categories: (i) test cases and software evolution, (ii) interdependences of test cases, and (iii) categorization and grouping of test cases. The first category is concerned with properties of test cases that usually change as the system evolves. The second category focuses on concepts that capture different types of relations between test cases, such as, dependencies between their executions. Finally, the third category captures different ways of organizing the test cases according to their key properties.

The most significant comments of the participants about the concepts falling in these three categories are discussed in the following. An overview of the results is illustrated in Fig. 2. For each concept, we described why the test leader initially suggested it and why the vast majority of the participants felt that it was, in fact, of relevance. Not by coincidence, all the subjects that have not agreed with the importance of one or more test concepts were the ones with less experience. Therefore, we do not detail in each test concept the reason for the disagreements.

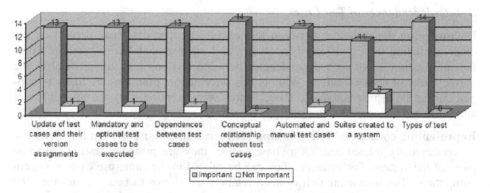

Fig. 2. Results of the Questionnaire: Important concepts for test modeling

A. Test Cases and Software Evolution

Documenting update of test cases and their version assignments: The test leaders stated that it is often needed to update test cases in order to reflect the modifications in requirements. Sometimes, the newest version of the test cases can only be used to test the latest version of the target software. The opposite may also be true, i.e., earlier system versions can only be tested by the older versions of the test cases. Thus, it is important to accurately document the association of the test cases with the corresponding version. Besides this, the participants felt that defining classifications of test cases are useful for test planning and for identifying their relative importance in particular software releases. An example of useful category mentioned is regression testing, which must be executed every time a new version of the system is defined.

Thirteen of fourteen subjects, which responded the questionnaire, agreed that the documentation of test case updates and respective version assignments were important. They mentioned that scenarios with several tests show with more evidence the need of identifying the system version applied to each test case. According to them, this concept is important in order to identify which are the requirements of a given version being tested by a particular test case. However, the subjects also mentioned that even in case of systems with a modest requirements base, to inform the version of the system tested by a given test case is a good practice. This is particularly important when the system has perspectives of growing and requires additional test cases. The control of updated tests for each version helps to organize the development process, especially if, for instance, regression tests are used.

Identifying mandatory and optional test cases: According to the test leader, the test team usually faces difficulties on the identification of the compulsory and optional tests to be executed for each software version. For instance, some of the tests do not have very high priority and can be executed if the test team will have enough time. Thirteen of fourteen people agreed that it is important to allow the identification of which test cases were created (or will be created) are mandatory or optional to be executed in the system under test (SUT). They mentioned that such an identification can define: (i) which tests can be executed (optional tests), and (ii) which tests are mandatory to be executed, regardless of the time of delivery of the system.

B. Interdependences of Test Cases

Documenting dependences between test cases: One test case may depend on another, including the provision of input data and environmental configuration. Thus, the information about such dependencies between test cases is fundamental to the correct order of tests execution. Without this information, problems are likely to happen during the testing activities. These factors were mentioned by the project leader and thirteen developers that considered this concept as important.

Representing conceptual relationships between test cases: Different test cases can be conceptually related and, as a consequence, they are probably testing the same parts of the system. For instance, they can be related to the same use case or system component. The documentation of such relationships helps to better understand the test coverage provided by those test cases according to a high-level point of view. Therefore, the visualization of the relationships between the test cases, according to a given requirement or design element, was considered useful by the test leader and all the fourteen subjects. According to them, the main reason was that it makes easier the identification of tests executed to validate a given requirement or functionality.

C. Categorizing and Grouping Test Cases

Documenting automated and manual test cases: Tests are either automatically or manually executed. The manual tests require to perform a set of actions manually. According to the test leader, when a large amount of tests are created, the identification of automated and manual tests is usually time-consuming. Besides this, such identification guides the tester to know which tool he/she should use to execute the test. Thirteen of fourteen participants thought it was important to identify which test cases are manual or automated, mainly with the purpose of better planning the tests. For instance, this explicit documentation would help the project leaders quickly pinpoint and locate project members with the required expertise depending on the manual or automated nature of the tests.

Documenting test suites created to a system: A test suite is a code component that executes a set of test cases automatically. Depending on the project, several suites can be defined. According to the test leader, it is important to represent these suits in order to facilitate the identification of the tests that will be executed by each suite and the identification of the order of such execution. Eleven people considered the documentation of suites very important. The other three considered that it is not really necessary to identify the suites of the test cases since, in general, only few suites are defined to test a given system and because suites are only considered facilitators to execute a set of test cases. It is important to note that the three people that found this concept not important have low experience with tests.

Identifying types of test: The identification of test types (e.g. functional, database, integration, security, etc.) helps to understand the purpose of each test. This was fully recognized by the test leader. Moreover, this information is useful on the delegation of tasks to members with expertise in running different test types. All the fourteen subjects agreed with the importance of such concepts due to the aforementioned reasons.

2.3 Proactive Proposal of Concepts by the Participants

Besides requiring the perception of subjects on testing concepts revealed upfront, the questionnaire also elicited the identification of other test concepts not mentioned in previous questions. Below, such concepts are mentioned with the most significant comments and justifications provided by the subjects.

- **Documenting testing-specific roles:** Two subjects mentioned that depending on the project, different roles can be played by individuals in the same test team, such as performance tester or tester of functional tests. Therefore, the documentation of testing-specific roles enables to quickly identify who worked at which test case. The subjects that highlighted the importance of documenting roles have large experience with management of projects. It is also important to highlight that our study was run in a lab specialized in software testing.
- **Identifying the priority of test execution in more detail:** This concept was recommended for two subjects that responded the questionnaire. According to them, depending on the available time to test some project, to define in more detail the priority of the tests can be useful, especially when the set of mandatory tests is large and the time to execute them is short. Thus, this representation can help to define orders of execution of the test cases.
- **Relating each test case with artifacts tested:** Three subjects informed that the documentation of which artifacts (e.g. class, component, etc) are being tested for each test case is important in two situations: (i) when it is needed to identify the artifact with problem, and (ii) when it is required to know the coverage of tests. Thus, the main focus of this concept is to allow the traceability of the artifacts tested by a given test.

3 Case Study: Inventory and Supply of Petroleum Products

This section presents a reflective analysis, based on a real software project, on how the explicit modeling of test concepts could potentially enhance a typical testing process. Even though a limited number of specific testing tools and notations were used in this project, we discuss in Section 4 to what extent they are representative of the state of the art. This project was carried out in a software engineering lab specialized on testing. In particular, this lab team has extensively worked on coordinating and carrying out tests of software systems developed for a Brazilian petroleum company. This team is already informally documenting the revealed testing concepts (Section 2) across several projects. However, due to space constraints, we decided to report the lessons learned observed in the largest and more complex system they have developed. This system controls the inventory and supply of petroleum and derived products (e.g. gasoline, kerosene, etc). During our reflective analysis process, we had several meetings with project members to discuss how the documentation of those identified testing concepts (Section 2.2) enhanced their day-to-day testing activities.

Some of the goals of the chosen system are to: (i) register routes (i.e. paths) based on ducts and ships that could be used to transport the derived products (e.g. gasoline, lubricating oil, kerosene, etc); (ii) predict when such products will arrive in terminals and refineries located in different places; (iii) plan the best routes to transport a particular product; (iv) register the real data that inform when and which products arrive in terminals and refineries; (v) compare real data with the predicted data; (vi) provide different types of reports and graphics to help on the analysis of different activities; and (vii) control when and which products are imported from or exported to other countries.

The system was developed by four teams responsible for the following elements: interface, database, requirements and test team. The test team was composed of seven people that executed functional, database and performance tests. Table 2 gives some details about the system characteristics, Table 3 relates the amount of use cases tested and the test types performed. Table 4 presents an overview of the solutions adopted by the testing team for each test concept identified (Section 2). Such solutions are described in detail in Section 3.1.

Table 2. Information about the petroleum control system

Project size	# of staffs	Test team	Status	Model size	Database	Test Cases
7 years	30 people	7 people	working	46 use cases 580 classes	283 tables	46 database tests 15 performance tests 100 automated functional tests 558 manual functional tests

Table 3. Relation between the test types and use cases tested

Types of test	Amount of Tests	Use Cases Tested	Amount of Use Cases Tested
Database Tests	46	4	11.5
Performance Tests	15	6	2.5
Automated Functional Tests	100	9	11.1
Manual Functional Tests	558	43	13.0

3.1 Test Concepts Documented in the Project

This section discusses how the identified test-specific concepts played an important role in our case study. All the solutions presented in this section were defined from meetings with the test team members that participated of the project. Each test in the project was classified as: regression, new or updated. The regression tests are those executed every time a new version of the system is defined. They do not depend on the new or updated requirements that have influenced the creation of the new system version. New tests are those created due to new system requirements or due to changes on the system functionalities. Updated tests are those tests that were modified due to the definition of a new requirement or the adaptation of a given requirement.

Table 4. Solution adopted for each test concept identified

Identified Concepts	Solution adopted
Update of test cases and their version assignments	An issue system is being used with an auxiliary document.
Mandatory and optional test cases	An issue system is being used with an auxiliary document.
Dependences between test cases	Description using the RTM tool.
Conceptual relationship between test cases	Use of the RTM tool.
Automated and manual test cases	Definition of the MTC and ATC acronyms.
Suites created to a system	Use of the RTM tool.
Identifying types of test	Definition of the GUI, DB and PER acronyms.

These classifications helped to perform the planning and the delegation of the tests for system version. An example of delegation is the execution of regression tests, which were usually performed by new members of the test team. Thus, these members were able to know the complexity and how to execute them. In a discussion with project members, they mentioned that if version-aware test cases were explicitly represented in a UML-based testing language, such as UML Testing Profile [16] and AGEDIS Modeling Language [18], it would motivate the use of those modeling languages. In this way, test classifications could be modeled without to affect the modeling of packages defined in the system.

In this project, the tests were already classified based on their priorities. There are both mandatory and optional tests. As explained in Section 2, mandatory tests are those ones considered essential, i.e., must be executed before the system is delivered to the customer. On other hand, optional tests are those with low priority and should only be executed if the test team has enough time to do so. This is a common scenario that happens in many software development companies.

Frequently, the subject that executes a given test is not necessarily the subject that has developed it. Thus, to have a documentation classifying the mandatory and optional tests is important to help the tester on choosing the tests with highest priorities. Besides using Atlassian JIRA [2], an issue system that controls the tests (tasks) created for a given version, the test team used an extra document composed of spreadsheets pointing out the mandatory and optional tests related to each system version updated. Thus, a modeling language that allows viewing these classifications would be effective to capture test compulsoriness. Another possible alternative is to adapt the notion of orthogonal variability models [17] to achieve the same purpose.

As stated in Section 2.2, to annotate if a test case is manual (MTC) or automated (ATC). Since the time spent to execute such tests are completely different, to know before hand the characteristics of the test that will be executed is fundamental to plan the time dedicated to such an activity. Therefore, the test team has included the MTC acronym in the names of the test cases when they are manual, and the ATC acronym when the tests are automated. The representation of manual and automated test cases in models might be not hard though. Thus, an approach that allows such modeling can help on the traceability between the tests with: (i) scripts that represent the code of the test (e.g. represented for classes or methods); (ii) documentation that describe the tests created; and (iii) documentation about artifacts tested (e.g. class and sequence diagrams).

Different functional, database or performance tests are usually executed by using different tools. In order to execute manual tests, the test team used Rational Manual Test tool (RTM) [15], while Rational Functional Tester [13] was used to automated functional tests, DBUnit [5] was used to automate database tests, and Rational Performance Tester [14] was applied to support performance tests. Since the test execution depends on particular tools and different testers usually have expertise in different test types, it is very important to classify the tests according to their types. A key benefit is that the test leader is able to better distribute them through test team members during the test planning. In this project, the test types were identified by the following key words: GUI (functional test), DB (database test) or PER (performance test). For instance, ATC_GUI_ReportRoutes and MTC_GUI_RegisterRoutes are examples of names given to an automated functional test name and a manual functional test name, respectively. This might be an indicator that the explicit classification of manual and automated tests should be supported by modeling languages. A simplistic approach could be through the use of stereotypes in UML.

The test team also agreed with the importance of documenting the relationships between the tests by identifying the different kinds of dependencies. This information helped the team to recognize the complexity related to the execution of a given test, and to better estimate the time to be spent in the test execution. If a test case depends on a large set of test cases to provide the input data, the tester will know that she/he will need to use the data provided by the suppliers to execute the client. Besides this, they will be able to estimate the time spent in the test activity based on the estimative of executing each test supplier. The use of dependencies between tests is particularly applied to avoid code duplication, i.e., common steps in different test cases and that need to be executed. The dependencies between the tests of this project were documented by associating a comment with the test. We found a substantial set of modeling languages (e.g. [16] [18] [19]) that represent the dependency concept. However, no one supported the representation of different kinds of dependencies (Section 4).

Thus, an approach that gets to support the modeling of the above test concepts would allow an easier documentation, avoiding workarounds (such as the creation of acronyms) or different tools and new patterns of documentation that companies eventually adopt and that often require a considerable learning curve. As discussed above, another advantage of the explicit modeling of the revealed test concepts is to allow a more efficient communication between the software testers and other stakeholders.

3.2 Additional Impact Analysis of the Test Concepts Documented

Due to the documentation of the test concepts following the approach mentioned in Section 3.1, the project team realized that the time spent in managing and executing the tests have drastically decreased. Before using such the tests acronyms (e.g. MTC, ATC, PER, DB, etc), the time spent in the test activity was higher than 16% of the planned time (see versions A and B in Table 4). However, when the test team started to explicitly document the newly-revealed testing concerns, a substantial improvement was observed. The first time the tests were documented following this approach was in version C. As illustrated in Table 5, the test team was able to finish the test activity in the expected time in the next two versions: D and E. The data presented in Table 4 were collected from the issue system [2] used in the project and that informs the time spent in each task of the project. In our discussions with the project members, all of them agreed that this time reduction was directly impacted by the explicit documentation of test concepts due to the reasons discussed in Section 3.1.

Table 5. Relation between the planned testing time and actual time spent in the project

Versions	Planned time (weeks)	Time used (weeks)	Time exceed (%)
Version A	6	7	16.7
Version B	7	8.5	21.4
Version C	6	6.5	8.3
Version D	7	7	0
Version E	8	8	0

3.3 Tool Support

After analyzing several available languages and tools dedicated to model the test activities, the project team has chosen the test management tool called Rational Test Manager (RTM) [15]. It provides state-of-the-art facilities to specify tests, such as allowing the grouping of tests based on a tree structure and the identification of the tests. This representation facilitates the understanding of the test coverage since we can see which test cases were created to a given requirement or functionality. Figure 3 illustrates an example where the test cases are related to use cases (approach used by our test team). In the example the use case UC01, which is related to the registration of routes, has two automated test cases, being one database (BD) test and one performance (PER) test in addition to a manual functional test case.

None of the analyzed modeling languages is able to define dependencies between tests, such as UML Testing Profile [16] and TTCN-3 [19] (Section 4). Thus, in order to have such an information documented we included it in the text fields provided by RTM. Suites were represented in RTM by using a tree structure where the nodes are other suites or test cases. This structure was also used to represent groups of tests, as explained before (see an example in Figure 4). Although other approaches, such as UML Testing Profile [16] and AGEDIS [18] that also represent the suite concept, we have chosen RTM since we were already using it to model other test characteristics and their approach is not better than the one presented by RTM. Details about the support provided by the available test modeling and management tools to model the mentioned concepts are presented in next Section 4.

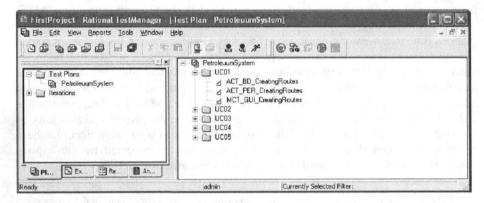

Fig. 3. Conceptual relation between test cases from RTM

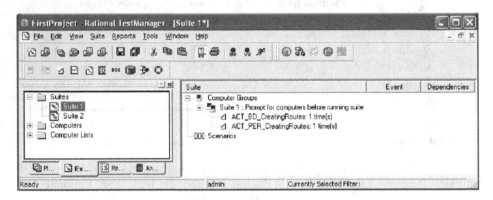

Fig. 4. Suites represented by RTM

4   Discussion

The UML Testing Profile [16] defines modeling means for designing, visualizing, and documenting the artifacts of test systems. Such approach extends UML 2.0 with test specific concepts like test components, verdicts, defaults, etc. These concepts are grouped into concepts for test architecture, test data, test behavior and time. Being a profile, the UML testing profile seamlessly integrates into UML: it is based on the UML meta-model and reuses UML syntax. Although the approach proposes interesting concepts of test systems, it does not provide important concepts that can be useful for test teams, such as the identification of (i) which system version each test is able to test, (ii) which tests are mandatory, (iii) which test types were created (e.g. functional, database, security and integration test), (iv) which types of dependences exist between tests (such as data dependence), and (v) which tests are automated and manual. On other hand, this approach provides some support to represent suites and a way to visualize the relationships between test cases according to a given requirement.

The Testing and Test Control Notation (TTCN-3) [19] is a modular language that has a similar look and feel to a typical programming language. This language is widely accepted as a standard for test system development in the telecommunication and data communication area. The main reason is that it comprises concepts suitable to all types of distributed system testing, such as important features necessary to specify test procedures and campaigns for functional, conformance, interoperability, load and scalability tests like test verdicts. Besides this, it matches mechanisms to compare the reactions of the system under test with the expected range of values, timer handling, distributed test components, ability to specify encoding information, synchronous and asynchronous communication, and monitoring. Similar to the UML Testing Profile, TTCN-3 also does not provide a set of useful concepts that test teams may need. All the concepts not included in the UML Testing Profile are also not contemplated on this work.

The testing language called AGEDIS modeling language (AML) [18] is based upon the UML (1.4) meta-model and enables the specification of tests for structural (static) and behavioral (dynamic) aspects of computational UML models. AML comes as part of the AGEDIS methodology [1] and has been designed with two main goals in mind: create a test adequate abstraction of the SUT that will be analyzed by the AGEDIS tools, which allows generating automatically suite tests, and set meaningful test directives for the testing process. AML presents the same problem mentioned for the UML Testing Profile and TTCN-3.

According to [20] the benefits of Model-Driven Engineering (MDE) for product software development have been demonstrated in numerous instances and could never be over-emphasized. Therefore, similar benefits can also be achieved in applying MDE to test software development. This form of Model-Based Testing (MBT) is called Model-Driven Test Engineering (MDTE) or simply Model-Driven Testing (MDT). However, to optimize the efficiency of MDT, good-practices and patterns specific to test development must be taken into account. Based on this idea, Feudjio [6] proposes a Unified Test Modeling Language (UTML) that is a test notation designed for pattern-oriented MDT. It provides the means for designing all aspects of a test system at a high level of abstraction and independent of any specific lower-level test infrastructure. Besides this, at the same time it provides a guidance in following test design patterns and avoids usual pitfalls of MDT. Such approach provides a tool called MDTester that allows modeling the concepts proposed by UTML. However, this tool does not allow to explicitly model the concepts described in Section III by using this approach.

Finally the authors in [15] propose an interesting test tool called Rational Test Manager (RTM). It is a central console for test activity management, execution and reporting. We are mentioning such a tool because it provides interesting test views from the interface that are not provided by the other mentioned approaches, such as the ability to group conceptually test cases. This grouping becomes easier their identification. Besides this, RTM allows viewing which suites are available, and which test cases each suite execute. On the other hand, the tool does not provide important test concepts, such as: (i) dependences between tests; (ii) the identification of which tests are mandatory and optional; (iii) which tests are automated and manual; (iv) the identification of test types; and (v) which tests are updated to a given version.

Table 6 summarizes how the approaches mentioned above represent the revealed test concepts (Section 2).

Table 6. Relation between test concepts and related work

Identified Concepts	UML Testing Profile	TTCN-3	AML	MDTester	RTM
Documenting update of test cases and their version assignments	No test classification	No test classification	No test classification	No test classification	No test classification
Mandatory and optional test cases to be executed	-	-	-	-	-
Automated and manual test cases	-	-	-	-	-
Dependences between test cases	Represented, except the types of test.	Represented, except the types of test.	Represented, except the types of test.	-	-
Conceptual relationship between test cases	-	-	-	-	It is possible to represent
Suites created to a system	Represented	-	Represented	-	Represented
Types of test	-	-	-	-	-

5 Conclusion and Future Works

This paper revealed a set of test concepts that can be useful while modeling test cases. Such concepts were identified from a inquisitive study that performed interviews and applied a questionnaire to subjects with different skills on software testing. Aiming to demonstrate the need for using such concepts while modeling the test cases of a system, Section 3 presents in detail the lessons learned from documenting (albeit informally) the new test concepts in the context of a large-scale system in the domain of petroleum inventory and supply. In the scenarios presented in Section 3, we described situations that emphasize the usefulness of such concepts.

As it is clearly stated in Section 4, the modeling approaches we have analyzed are only able to model a subset of the test concepts we have pointed out. Therefore, we are in the process of analyzing the availability of creating or extending a test modeling language in order to make it possible the modeling of the test concepts mentioned in Section 2. Possible alternatives are either the extension of an UML-compliant test modeling technique (e.g. UML Testing Profile) or the proposition of a new test profile that represents the test concepts via the use of new stereotypes. Besides, we are also investigating the need of modeling other test concepts that are mentioned in IEEE standards [10] and that have came to light due to our experience on testing systems in different domains.

References

1. AGEDIS - Automated Generation and Execution of Test Suites for DIstributed Component based Software, http://www.agedis.de
2. Atlassian JIRA, http://www.atlassian.com/software/jira/
3. Black, R.: Managing the Testing Process: Practical Tools and Techniques for Managing Hardware and Software Testing, 2nd edn. Wiley, Chichester (2002), ISBN: 0471223980
4. Booch, G., Rumbaugh, J., Jacobson, I.: Unified Modeling Language User Guide, 2nd edn. The Addison-Wesley Object Technology Series (2005)
5. DBUnit web site, http://www.dbunit.org/
6. Feudjio, A.V.: MDTester User Guide,
   http://www.fokus.fraunhofer.de/distrib/motion/utml/
7. Fink, A.: The Survey Kit: How to ask survey questions, vol. 2. Sage, Thousand Oaks (2003), ISBN 0761925791
8. Harrold, M.J.: Testing: A Roadmap. In: Proceedings of ICSE 2000, Future of Software Engineering, pp. 61–72 (2000)
9. Harrold, M.J.: Testing Evolving Software: Current Practice and Future Promise. In: Proceedings of ISEC 2008, pp. 3–4 (2008)
10. IEEE-SA Standards Board: IEEE Standard for Software Test Documentation, http://ieeexplore.ieee.org/stamp/stamp.jsp?tp=&arnumber=741968&userType=inst
11. Kaner, C., Bach, J., Pettichord, B.: Lessons Learned in Software Testing, 1st edn. Wiley, Chichester (2001), ISBN: 0471081124
12. Kaner, C., Falk, J., Nguyen, H.Q.: Testing Computer Software, 2nd edn. Wiley, Chichester (1999), ISBN: 0471358460
13. Rational Functional Tester, http://www-01.ibm.com/software/awdtools/tester/functional/
14. Rational Performance Tester, http://www.acutest.co.uk/acutest/testing-rational-ibm
15. Rational TestManager and Rational ManualTest, http://www-01.ibm.com/software/awdtools/test/manager/
16. OMG - Object Management Group, UML Testing Profile, version 1, http://www.omg.org/cgi-bin/doc?formal/05-07-07
17. Pohl, K., Bockle, G., Linden, F.: Software Product Line Engineering. Birkhauser, New York (2005), ISBN: 3540243720
18. Trost, J., Cavarra, A.: AGEDIS Language Specification, http://www.agedis.de/documents/d127_1/AGEDIS-ls-fpd.pdf
19. TTCN-3 web site, http://www.ttcn3.org/
20. UTML - The Unified Test Modeling Language for Pattern-Oriented Test Design, http://www.fokus.fraunhofer.de/en/motion/ueber_motion/technologien/utml/index.html21
21. Lethbridge, T., Sim, S., Singer, J.: Studying Software Engineers: Data Collection Methods for Software Field Studies. Empirical Software Engineering (Submitted May 2000)

Automatically Discovering Properties That Specify the Latent Behavior of UML Models*,**

Heather J. Goldsby and Betty H.C. Cheng

Department of Computer Science and Engineering
Michigan State University, 3115 Engineering Building
East Lansing, Michigan 48824 USA
{hjg,chengb}@cse.msu.edu

Abstract. Formal analysis can be used to verify that a model of the system adheres to its requirements. As such, traditional formal analysis focuses on whether known (desired) system properties are satisfied. In contrast, this paper proposes an automated approach to generating temporal logic properties that specify the *latent* behavior of existing UML models; these are unknown properties exhibited by the system that may or may not be desirable. A key component of our approach is MARPLE, a evolutionary-computation tool that leverages natural selection to discover a set of properties that cover different regions of the model state space. The MARPLE-discovered properties can be used to refine the models to either remove unwanted behavior or to explicitly document a desirable property as required system behavior. We use MARPLE to discover unwanted latent behavior in two applications: an autonomous robot navigation system and an automotive door locking control system obtained from one of our industrial collaborators.

1 Introduction

One approach to ensuring that models used for model-driven development provide the desired behavior is to analyze them for adherence to system requirements [1,2,3]. This analysis, however, does not detect errors in *latent behavior*, the unspecified and potentially unwanted behavior of the model; these errors could then be propagated to the implementation and even deployed. Uchitel et. al have proposed an approach for detecting one form of latent behavior called implied scenarios as part of the process of synthesizing a model from scenarios [4]. However, preexisting UML models cannot make use of this technique. Three broad categories of approaches have been developed to produce properties that could be used for analysis: *Requirements discovery approaches* (e.g., [5]) examine testing

---

* This work has been supported in part by NSF grants EIA-0000433, CNS-0551622, CCF-0541131, IIP-0700329, CCF-0750787, Department of the Navy, Office of Naval Research under Grant No. N00014-01-1-0744, Siemens Corporate Research, and a Quality Fund Program grant from Michigan State University.
** We gratefully acknowledge the feedback and insight provided by the reviewers of our earlier work.

D.C. Petriu, N. Rouquette, Ø. Haugen (Eds.): MODELS 2010, Part I, LNCS 6394, pp. 316–330, 2010.

and deployment artifacts to detect missing or erroneous properties; process improvements have been proposed as part of these approaches. *Refinement-based approaches* (e.g., [6]) infer properties from formally specified goals or requirements. Lastly, *specification generation techniques* (e.g., [7,8,9,10,11,12,13,14,15]) infer properties from a representation of a system (e.g., a model or code) or a derivative of the system (e.g., execution traces). Several previously developed specification generation approaches are able to infer temporal logic properties from a model [8,12], code [14], or execution traces [9,15]. For these approaches, the developer identifies a part of the system behavior to explore, either by restricting the exploration to a portion of the code [14], or by explicitly selecting the states, events, and variables that are of interest [8,9,12,15]. One ramification of having the developer guide the exploration is that the unexplored portions of the system may still conceal latent unwanted behavior. Ideally, developers would like to maximize both automation of property discovery and coverage, while minimizing the number of properties that must be examined.

In this paper, we propose an evolutionary-computation approach called MARPLE[1] to automatically generating properties that specify the latent behavior of UML models comprising an instance (class) diagram and multiple state diagrams. Evolutionary computation methods, such as genetic algorithms and genetic programming, have achieved considerable success, in some cases producing human-competitive designs [16]. Each evolutionary algorithm experiment comprises a population of individuals. Over the course of many generations, where each generation is subjected to natural selection, mutation, and crossover, the evolutionary algorithm seeks to optimize according to a *fitness function* that describes one or more objectives. For this approach, we use a recently developed technique called *novelty search*, where the objective is not to find one optimal solution, but rather to find a suite of sufficiently different solutions [17]. We use novelty search to enable MARPLE to produce properties that maximize coverage of the model's behavior, while minimizing human effort.

MARPLE uses novelty search to discover a set of properties that describe a UML model, where these properties describe behavior not explicitly stated in the requirements and may, in fact, be unacceptable latent behavior. Specifically, each individual within MARPLE represents a property created by instantiating one of the five most commonly occurring specification patterns [18] in the form of Linear Temporal Logic (LTL). Instantiating a pattern involves replacing the placeholders with evolved boolean propositions, where a proposition is created using attribute and operation information from a UML instance diagram of the system. Because the propositions can include conjunctives and disjunctives, the set of possible propositions is unlimited and too large for brute force search methods to explore. During the evolutionary process, mutations and crossover produce different LTL properties that may be satisfied by the UML model. The novelty of a property is assessed using the Spin model checker [19]. Specifically, the state space of the shortest *witness trace* (i.e., path that supports the property)

---

[1] MARPLE is named after Miss Marple, Agatha Christie's detective who was famous for detecting latent human behavior.

through the Spin representation of the model is compared to the state spaces of other properties. [2] If a *novel region* of the model state space is discovered (i.e., a region of the state space that has not been explored by previously evaluated properties), then the property is assigned a higher fitness value and MARPLE searches the new region more thoroughly. However, if a property explores a previously explored region of the state space, then it is assigned a low fitness value and MARPLE does not search the region as thoroughly. In this way, MARPLE discovers properties that cumulatively describe the behavior of the model. For readability purposes, the properties generated by MARPLE are presented to the developer in natural language [20] for assessment. The generated properties can be used by the developer to refine the requirements specifications (to explicitly sanction the latent behavior) or to modify the UML model (to remove unwanted latent behavior).

Overall, our approach enables developers to automatically explore UML models for properties representing potentially unwanted latent behavior. We illustrate our approach by using MARPLE to discover the unwanted latent behavior of models for an automobile door locking system obtained from one of our industrial collaborators. To further validate our approach, we have also applied it to a robot navigation system [21] and sought feedback from our industrial collaborators. The remainder of the paper is organized as follows. Section 2 presents relevant background information. Section 3 describes MARPLE. and describes results from our door locking case study. Section 4 describes how we validated the performance of MARPLE. Section 5 discusses related work. Finally, in Section 6, we present conclusions and discuss future work.

2   Background

In this section, we provide background information on the property specification patterns used for this approach, genetic programming, and novelty search.

2.1   Property Specification Patterns

Dwyer *et al.* identified several property specification patterns [18] that are commonly used to analyze systems for assurance needs. For our approach, we enable MARPLE to instantiate the five most common patterns (*Absence, Universality, Existence, Precedence,* and *Response*), using the global scope of applicability. [3] Additionally, to facilitate assessment by human developers, we use a previously developed structured English grammar [20] for the specification patterns to present relevant properties in natural language. Figure 1 depicts the natural language representations of these patterns, where p and q are placeholders for propositional expressions.

---

[2] Spin provides configuration options for generating the shortest path, which is how we produce the shortest witness trace.

[3] MARPLE can also be used to generate properties using other scopes. However, for brevity, we only present the global scope.

Pattern Name	Natural Language
Absence	Globally, it is never the case that **p** holds.
Existence	Globally, **p** eventually holds.
Universality	Globally, it is always the case that **p** holds.
Precedence	Globally, it is always the case that if **p** holds, then **q** previously held.
Response	Globally, it is always the case that if **p** holds, then **q** eventually holds.

Fig. 1. Global Specification Patterns

2.2 Genetic Programming

Genetic programming is an evolution-inspired approach to discovering computer programs that solve a problem. A genetic programming experiment comprises a *population* of individuals, where each individual is a program tree. Figure 2(a) depicts one such program tree that represents the function: x + (sin(x) * 5). Each node in the tree can be a *function* that takes one or more parameters that are represented as subtrees (e.g., +, *, sin), or a *terminal* that does not take any parameters and may represent either a variable or a constant (e.g., x, 5). At the start of the experiment, a population of individuals is created using a random assortment of the available functions and terminals. Each individual has an associated fitness that represents how closely it approximates the solution, e.g., the desired symbolic regression formula (x*x*x).

A genetic program consists of many generations of individuals. During each generation, the fitness of the individuals is evaluated. Then individuals with high fitness scores are selected to be used to create the subsequent generation. An individual may be selected for *mutation*, where one or more nodes within the program tree are changed to another node prior to being placed within the next generation. For example, Figure 2(b) depicts how the tree in (a) could have been mutated by replacing the multiply function (*) with the divide function (/) effectively changing the formula to be: x + (sin(x) / 5); shading denotes the point of change. An individual could also be selected for *crossover*, where a subtree is exchanged with a subtree from another selected individuals. For example, Figure 2(c) depicts how the tree in (a) could have been modified by crossover replacing the sin(x) subtree with the constant 7. Because the highly fit individuals are preferentially selected to be used as the raw material to create subsequent generations, over time, the solutions discovered by the genetic programming experiment optimize according to the fitness function.

In this paper, we use genetic programming as the basis for our representation of LTL properties, where each program tree represents one property and the terminals represent concepts defined by the UML model.

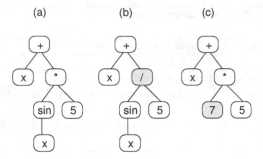

Fig. 2. Examples of a genetic program tree, where (a) is a tree, (b) is the same tree after a mutation, and (c) is the same tree after crossover. The shaded nodes represent the location of the change.

2.3   Evolutionary Computation and Novelty Search

In general, evolutionary computation is a search technique used to explore large and complex search spaces for solutions that optimize a fitness function. However, the application of a fitness function can sometimes be shortsighted leading to evolutionary computation approaches becoming "stuck" on sub-optimal solutions that represent local minima, rather than discovering the more complex and better solution. Lehman and Stanley originally developed novelty search, where fitness is a measure of how rare the behavior of an individual is, as a method for discovering more complex and better solutions [17]. Specifically, novelty search uses the following fitness formula:

$$\rho(x) = \frac{1}{k} \sum_{i=0}^{k} dist(x, u_i)$$

where $\rho(x)$ is the novelty measurement for individual x; k is the number of nearest neighbors used for the novelty calculation; and $dist(x, u_i)$ is the distance between individual x and its ith nearest neighbor, u_i. To calculate $\rho(x)$ the distance between x and all other individuals in the current population and the *archive* of previously discovered novel individuals is computed. The novelty metric is then computed by taking the mean of the distance to the k nearest neighbors. If the novelty value was greater than ρ_{min}, then the individual is entered into the archive. In this way, individuals that explored previously unseen areas of the search space were assigned a higher fitness. This technique has produced a neural net that enabled a robot to more effectively navigate the maze, as compared to neural nets created using evolutionary computation techniques that sought to maximize fitness, rather than novelty [17].

While in previous work novelty search was used to discover better solutions than other evolutionary computation techniques, in this paper, we use novelty search to discover a suite of properties that cumulatively attempt to cover the state space of a model.

3 Approach

At a high level, our approach uses novelty search to mine a model for properties that may represent either known sanctioned behavior or unknown latent behavior. Three steps are used for running MARPLE:

1. The developer configures MARPLE for a specific model.
2. The developer runs MARPLE to produce a set of properties.
3. The developer reviews the properties and uses the information to improve the model.

In this section, we provide further detail about this process using a door locking model obtained from industry as a running example.

3.1 Case Study

We illustrate our approach by applying it to an automobile door-locking system that was obtained from our industrial collaborators. Figure 3 depicts an object diagram for the system. The door-locking system is a distributed embedded system responsible for controlling the centralized door locks in a car. The door-locking system comprises two control units, placed in the driver and passenger doors, respectively. The units control the sensors and actuators located on the respective sides of the car. To lock and unlock the doors, the locks on the driver or passenger door may be used by inserting and turning a key in the key cylinder. All doors in the car will be locked or unlocked simultaneously. In addition, doors can be locked and unlocked from within the car, using a button located on each door. For safety reasons, unlocking always has priority over locking, so that in case of emergencies the car can be exited quickly.

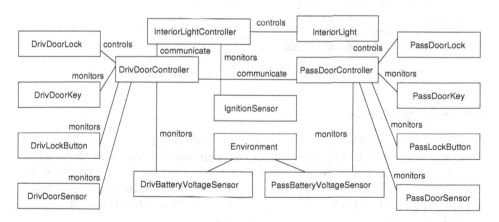

Fig. 3. Door Locking System Object Diagram

3.2 Step 1: Configuring Marple

To use MARPLE, a developer needs to provide: (1) a UML model that includes an object diagram and a set of state diagrams, where each state diagram describes the behavior of one object, and (2) a textual representation of the attributes and methods of the model. These attributes and methods are used as building blocks to create propositional expressions that replace the placeholders in the specification patterns. For example, Figure 4 depicts a snippet of the text file used to create the propositional expressions. For each operation, a propositional expression representing the operation being called is created. For each boolean attribute, a terminal where the attribute is true and another terminal where the attribute is false is created. For example, basic propositions **DrivDoorController.doorStatus == 0** and **DrivDoorController.doorStatus == 1** are among the propositions created for line 4. For each provided value of an integer, we create terminals where the attribute is equal to the value and when the attribute is not equal to the value. For example, basic propositions **DrivDoorController.batteryVoltage == 6** and **DrivDoorController. batteryVoltage != 6** are among the propositions created for line 2. The door locking system has 143 unique basic propositional expressions. Within MARPLE these basic expressions are then combined using conjunctives and disjunctives to form more complex propositional expressions.

```
1    classname DrivDoorController
2    attribute batteryVoltage int 6 9
3    attribute keyStatus int 0 1 2
4    attribute doorStatus boolean 0 1
5    attribute lockButtonStatus int 0 1 2
6    attribute iterations int 0 1 2 3 4
7    attribute initSuccess boolean 0 1
8    attribute voltageSuccess boolean 0 1
9    operation setBatteryVoltage
10   operation setKeyStatus
11   operation setDoorStatus
12   operation setLockButtonStatus
```

Fig. 4. An elided portion of the text file used to create model-specific terminals

3.3 Step 2: Marple

Given the inputs provided by the user as part of Step 1, MARPLE automatically produces a suite of LTL properties specified in natural language that cumulatively capture the requirements and latent behavior of the model. Here we describe: (1) how MARPLE internally represents properties, including how properties are mutated and crossed-over and (2) how the fitness function that governs the behavior of the evolutionary algorithm works.

Internal Property Representation. Essentially, each individual within a MARPLE experiment represents a property as a Genetic Program. When MARPLE starts, it randomly creates a population of these trees representing different properties.

Figure 5 depicts two such individuals and the natural-language representation of the property that they specify. To enable MARPLE to evolve such trees, we created a set of function nodes that are used to create properties for all possible models and a set of terminals that are propositional expressions and are model specific. Specifically, we provided function nodes for **Absence, Existence, Universality, Precedence,** and **Response** properties. Each tree had to be rooted with one of these nodes. Each of these nodes took a specific number of subtrees that correspond to the number of placeholders for propositional expressions. Next, we created two additional function nodes **and** and **or**, which are used to create more complex propositional expressions. For example, Figure 5(a) is an **Absence** property that contains a subtree with an **or** node.

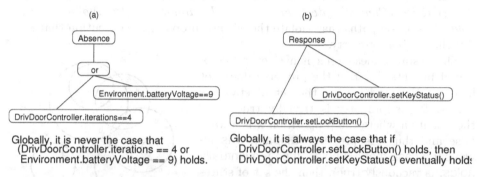

(a)

Absence

or

Environment.batteryVoltage==9

DrivDoorController.iterations==4

Globally, it is never the case that
(DrivDoorController.iterations == 4 or
Environment.batteryVoltage == 9) holds.

(b)

Response

DrivDoorController.setKeyStatus()

DrivDoorController.setLockButton()

Globally, it is always the case that if
DrivDoorController.setLockButton() holds, then
DrivDoorController.setKeyStatus() eventually holds

Fig. 5. Two properties generated by MARPLE. Property (a) represents unwanted latent behavior. Property (b) represents acceptable latent behavior.

If an individual property is selected for mutation, then one of its nodes or terminals is randomly exchanged with another node or terminal. Because MARPLE respects the type of a given node (e.g., a node representing an absence property will only be replaced with a node representing a different type of property), the produced property will always be syntactically correct. For example, after mutation, the property Figure 5 (a) may turn into property **Globally, it is never the case that DrivDoorController.batteryVoltage == 9 holds.**, which changes the boolean expression from a disjunctive expression to a basic proposition. Another possible property that could be constructed by mutating the property depicted in Figure 5 (a) is **Globally, it is always the case that DrivDoorController.iterations == 4 or Environment.batteryVoltage==9 holds**, which changes the type of property being specified from an absence property to a universality property.

If two properties are selected for crossover, then subtrees of the properties are exchanged. For example, if properties (a) and (b) in Figure 5 are selected for crossover, then the resulting properties might be:

- **Globally, it is never the case that DrivDoorController.setLockButton() holds.**
- **Globally, it is always the case that if (DrivDoorController.iterations == 4 or Environment.batteryVoltage == 9) holds, then DrivDoorController.setKeyStatus() eventually holds.**

where the underlined portions of the properties represent the parts that have been exchanged through crossover.

Fitness Function. The central aspect of measuring the novelty of a property is the distance metric that measures how similar (or different two properties) are. In this case, we use the novelty search function described in Section 2.3 and define distance as the difference between the state spaces covered by the *witness traces* of the respective properties, where a witness trace is the shortest path of execution through a model that satisfies a property. Specifically, first, we use the Spin model checker [19] to verify the property holds. Then, if it does, we invert the property to produce a witness property. For example, the witness property of the property described in Figure 5 is: *Globally, it is eventually the case that (DrivDoorController.iterations ==4 or Environment.battery Voltage == 9) holds.* Execution paths that violate the witness property are execution that satisfy the original property.

This distance measurement has several associated benefits. First, if the property does not hold for the model, then the set of states is empty. If the property is trivially true (e.g., the situation where the proposition **x** is always false and thus the property **Globally, it is always the case that if x holds, then y eventually holds.** is vacuously true), then the set of states is also empty. In this way, the distance metric compresses uninteresting properties together and enables us to discover more novel properties that explore different areas of the state space.

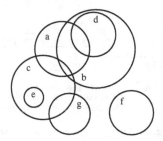

Fig. 6. Visualization of novelty metric

We then perform novelty search using the distance metric in order to discover latent model behavior. Figure 6 provides a graphical depiction of how novelty search works. For this example, we are assessing the novelty of property **a**. Each circle represents the state space of a property. If two circles overlap, then they share a common set of states (e.g., **c** and **e**, **a** and **c**). The distance between two circles is the set difference between their states. To compute the novelty of a property, we examine all possible pairs of properties both in the property and also in the archive of all previously generated properties. In this case, if k were equal to 2, then the nearest neighbors of property **d** would be properties **b** and **a**. The novelty of property **d** is the mean of the difference between **d** and **b** and the difference between **d** and **a**. Because we are interested in a suite of properties that cumulatively describe the behavior of the model, rather than a single penultimate property, each generated property is added to the archive.

3.4   Step 3: Assessing the Properties

At the end of a run, MARPLE returns the contents of the archive, which represents all of the generated properties, to the developer. These properties are provided in natural language, using Spider, a previously developed tool [20], to facilitate understanding. The properties may represent either requirements, latent acceptable behavior, or latent unacceptable behavior.

To assist the developer in analyzing the properties, we use a two-step approach to using the properties to uncover latent behavior:

1. Inspect and assess the absence, universality, and existence properties generated by MARPLE. These types of properties are able to detect subtle errors, such as whether or not an attribute ever changed values or a method was called. Within this step, we begin by assessing the properties with novelty values greater than zero, since these represent the minimal set of discovered properties that effectively explore the state space and as such provide an overview of the behavior of the model. If a property specifies potentially unwanted behavior, we then *zoom in* by looking at other properties that use the same attribute and class names, as these properties may specify the same behavior in a manner more intuitive to understand.
2. Inspect and assess the precedence and response properties generated by MARPLE. These properties are able to detect timing errors or unwanted relationships among model elements. We repeat the magnification process by first focusing on the novel properties and then zooming in on behaviors of interest.

To illustrate this approach, we use the results from one run of MARPLE, which produced 351 properties, 167 of which were verified as describing the model, of which 63 had a novelty value greater than zero.

Figure 7 depicts five absence and existence properties generated by MARPLE for the door-locking model. By visually inspecting these properties, we were able to classify properties 2 and 5 as representing acceptable model behavior. However, properties 1, 3, and 4 represent unwanted latent behavior – all of these properties specify that certain attribute values were never used.

1. **Absence Property:** Globally, it is never the case that (Environment.batteryVoltage==9 or DrivDoorController.iterations==4) holds.
2. **Existence Property:** Globally, (DrivDoorController.batteryVoltage != 9 or DrivDoorController.initSuccess==1) eventually holds .
3. **Absence Property:** Globally, it is never the case that DrivDoorController.initSuccess==1 holds.
4. **Absence Property:** Globally, it is never the case that DrivBatteryVoltageSensor.voltage==9 holds.
5. **Existence Property:** Globally, PassDoorController.setKeyStatus() eventually holds.

Fig. 7. Five absence and existence properties generated by MARPLE

Next, we visually inspected the model in an attempt to discover the source of the unwanted behavior. While examining the state diagram for the **DrivDoorController** we noted a subtle, but important error: The **DrivDoorController** was missing a transition that connected the start state to the initialization state Figure 8 depicts an elided version of the state diagram for the **DrivDoorController**.

Specifically, to illustrate the error, the elided diagram depicts only the initialization state and the compound states. The bolded transitions were included in the model. The dotted line transition represents the missing transition. Because the **DrivDoorController** was missing this transition, it did not initialize properly and thus did not initialize other components. The **PassDoorController** also contained this error. We consider this error to be subtle and difficult to detect, given it strongly influenced the behavior of the controllers and yet this model had been developed and analyzed by a member of our lab for adherence to requirements.

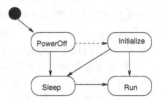

Fig. 8. The elided version of the DrivDoorController state diagram. The dotted line transition represents a missing transition that caused unwanted latent behavior.

Given serious unwanted latent behavior was detected early in the process, the model was corrected and the analyses rerun. However, if the absence, universality, and existence properties were acceptable, then we would expand our analysis to include the precedence and response properties.

4 Validation

While we have described the process of using MARPLE and have provided evidence that in one case MARPLE was able to detect unwanted latent behavior, To further validate our approach, we compare MARPLE's ability to discover properties that describe the door locking system to a control experiment that did not use novelty search.

The control version of MARPLE did not use novelty information for the evolutionary search process – properties were randomly selected for mutation, crossover, and survival. To ensure the generality of the control experiments, in addition to assessing MARPLE's performance on the door locking system, we also evaluated it on a model of an autonomous robot navigation case study, originally developed by Park et al. [21], and later revised and modeled by us [22]. To account for the stochastic nature of the evolutionary process, for each model, we ran 30 control runs and 30 MARPLE runs.

We then examined the central question of whether MARPLE is better able to identify novel properties than the control. Table 1 depicts the results. The first row is the total number of generated candidate properties, where these properties may have been either true or false for the model. For both systems, MARPLE generated over 35% more candidate properties than the control. The second row is the number of properties that were verified to describe the behavior of the model. Here, MARPLE produced more than twice as many properties that described the behavior of the model than the control. On average, over 45% of the properties generated by MARPLE were verified as describing the model. In contrast, less than 30% of the properties generated by the control were verified. The last row is the number of properties whose witness traces included at least one previously unvisited state. These properties represent 30-40% of the verified properties generated by MARPLE and indicate that MARPLE is exploring novel regions of the state space. Overall, these results demonstrate that MARPLE is an effective strategy for exploring the behavior of a model. In general, these runs took approximately 8 hours. This time period enables a developer to run MARPLE overnight and have results in the morning.

Table 1. The mean number of properties generated by the control and MARPLE runs for the door-locking system and robot navigation system

	Door-Locking System		Robot Navigation System	
	Control	Marple	Control	Marple
Candidate Properties	214.78	294.20	205.31	287.14
Properties	59	134	56	141
Novel Properties	-	43.27	-	59.27

We solicited feedback from our industrial collaborators regarding the properties identified and the overall process. First, they confirmed that the time frame for generating properties (essentially overnight) and the number of properties generated was reasonable. Second, the format in which the generated properties were presented (i.e., structured natural language) was an effective format for developers to review and determine whether the properties represented sanctioned or unwanted behavior. Third, the assessment process that we proposed was useful and viable. In general, the feedback was that MARPLE provided a much needed means for detecting unwanted behavior in models of high assurance systems.

5   Related Work

In general, specification generation techniques produce properties by instantiating property patterns that contain *placeholders* with propositions that specify valid properties. Three major categories of related work are: static inference, dynamic inference, and temporal logic query checking. *Static inference* approaches infer properties from code specifications by analyzing program text (e.g., [7,14]) or by analyzing the code using a modular model checker [11]. *Dynamic inference* approaches infer likely properties, called invariants, from execution traces generated by code specifications (e.g., [9,10,15]). *Temporal logic query checking* (e.g., [8,12]) finds the strongest formulae adhered to by the model that satisfy the *temporal logic query*, which is a temporal logic formula with placeholders.

Next, we discuss the specification generation techniques that generate temporal logic properties [8,9,12,14,15]. Perracotta [15], a dynamic inference approach, generates eight variations of the temporal logic response pattern from imperfect execution traces, where the developer instruments the program to monitor events and states of interest that constitute the possible propositions. Chang *et al.* [9] proposed a dynamic inference approach that generates temporal logic properties from a set of inference templates built using the Propel patterns [23]. Event traces are used to refine the inference templates to eliminate properties that are not satisfied by the program's event traces. Propositions based on developer-selected events are used to instantiate the property templates. Weimer and Necula proposed a static inference approach [14] to detecting bugs in source code. Their approach generates properties that specify the behavior of the error-handling code. Temporal logic query checking approaches [8,12] automatically find solutions to a temporal logic query. Specifically, to find the strongest formula, the query checker replaces the placeholders with combinations of developer-specified propositions.

In general, these approaches rely on developer knowledge (i.e., selected propositions to use and/or a selection of code) to determine the part of the system behavior to explore for properties. In essence, these approaches specify behavioral properties that refine the developer's understanding of a developer-specified segment of system behavior. Our approach can be used in a complementary fashion in that it identifies latent properties referring to propositions and/or properties *not explicitly* identified by the developer and that might otherwise remain concealed. For example, MARPLE could be used to identify unwanted latent behavior, and temporal logic query checking could be used to refine developer knowledge by identifying the strongest relationship among the MARPLE discovered propositions.

6   Conclusions and Future Work

In this paper, we have presented an approach to automatically generating properties that specify the unwanted behavior of UML models. Our approach relies on MARPLE, an evolutionary computation technique, to generate properties that are presented to the developer in natural language. Specifically, MARPLE generates properties by instantiating specification patterns with propositions developed using information in the UML class diagram. Regarding the scalability of this approach, as with most industrial uses of model checking and formal analysis, MARPLE is intended to be used on subsets of systems, particularly those of a critical nature. We have used MARPLE to detect latent properties of several models provided by our industrial partners in order to demonstrate its ability to work on models of industrial scale. Parallelizing the novelty search algorithm, changing the number of individuals within the population, or changing the number of generations that the algorithm runs could reduce the analysis time, and we will explore this optimization strategy in future work. Our approach is complementary to other specification generation techniques because it is able to identify unwanted latent behavior in portions of the model that may otherwise remain unexplored with the other approaches.

Our future work will explore extending Marple to use specification patterns that include additional scopes, as well as specification patterns for real-time properties and other types of properties [20,23]. These extensions will enable Marple to detect additional sources of latent behavior. Lastly, we are investigating using MARPLE to detect feature interaction properties and automatically generate test cases for the corresponding code [24].

References

1. McUmber, W.E., Cheng, B.H.C.: A general framework for formalizing UML with formal languages. In: Proceedings of the IEEE International Conference on Software Engineering (ICSE 2001), Toronto, Canada (May 2001)
2. Lilius, J., Paltor, I.P.: vUML: A tool for verifying UML models. In: Proceedings of the 14th IEEE International Conference on Automated Software Engineering, Washington, DC, USA, p. 255. IEEE Computer Society, Los Alamitos (1999)
3. Tanuan, M.C.: Automated Analysis of Unifed Modeling Language (UML) Specifications. Master's thesis, University of Waterloo, Canada (2001)
4. Uchitel, S., Kramer, J., Magee, J.: Detecting implied scenarios in message sequence chart specifications. SIGSOFT Softw. Eng. Notes 26(5), 74–82 (2001)
5. Lutz, R.R., Mikulski, I.C.: Requirements discovery during the testing of safety-critical software. In: ICSE 2003: Proceedings of the 25th International Conference on Software Engineering (2003)
6. Letier, E.: Reasoning about Agents in Goal-Oriented Requirements Engineering. PhD thesis, Louvain-la-Neuve, Belgium (2001)
7. Acharya, M., Xie, T., Pei, J., Xu, J.: Mining API patterns as partial orders from source code: from usage scenarios to specifications. In: ESEC-FSE 2007, pp. 25–34. ACM, New York (2007)
8. Chan, W.: Temporal-logic queries. In: Emerson, E.A., Sistla, A.P. (eds.) CAV 2000. LNCS, vol. 1855, pp. 450–463. Springer, Heidelberg (2000)
9. Chang, R.M., Avrunin, G.S., Clarke, L.A.: Property inference from program executions. Technical Report UM-CS-2006-26, University of Massachusetts (2006)
10. Ernst, M.D., Cockrell, J., Griswold, W.G., Notkin, D.: Dynamically discovering likely program invariants to support program evolution. IEEE Transactions on Software Engineering 27(2), 99–123 (2001)
11. Flanagan, C., Leino, K.R.M.: Houdini, an annotation assistant for ESC/Java. In: Oliveira, J.N., Zave, P. (eds.) FME 2001. LNCS, vol. 2021, pp. 500–517. Springer, Heidelberg (2001)
12. Gurfinkel, A., Chechik, M., Devereux, B.: Temporal logic query checking: A tool for model exploration. IEEE Transactions on Software Engineering 29(10), 898–914 (2003)
13. Jeffords, R., Heitmeyer, C.: Automatic generation of state invariants from requirements specifications. SIGSOFT Softw. Eng. Notes 23(6), 56–69 (1998)
14. Weimer, W., Necula, G.C.: Mining temporal specifications for error detection. In: Halbwachs, N., Zuck, L.D. (eds.) TACAS 2005. LNCS, vol. 3440, pp. 461–476. Springer, Heidelberg (2005)
15. Yang, J., Evans, D., Bhardwaj, D., Bhat, T., Das, M.: Perracotta: mining temporal API rules from imperfect traces. In: ICSE 2006: Proceedings of the 28th International Conference on Software Engineering, pp. 282–291. ACM, New York (2006)
16. Koza, J.R., Keane, M.A., Streeter, M.J., Mydlowec, M., Yu, J., Lanza, G.: Genetic Programming IV: Routine Human-Competitive Machine Intelligence. Springer, Heidelberg (2003)

17. Lehman, J., Stanley, K.: Exploiting open-endedness to solve problems through the search for novelty. In: Bullock, S., Noble, J., Watson, R., Bedau, M.A. (eds.) Artificial Life XI: Proceedings of the Eleventh International Conference on the Simulation and Synthesis of Living Systems, pp. 329–336. MIT Press, Cambridge (2008)
18. Dwyer, M.B., Avrunin, G.S., Corbett, J.C.: Patterns in property specifications for finite-state verification. In: Proceedings of the 21st International Conference on Software Engineering, pp. 411–420 (1999)
19. Holzmann, G.: The Spin Model Checker, Primer and Reference Manual. Addison-Wesley, Reading (2004)
20. Konrad, S., Cheng, B.H.C.: Real-time specification patterns. In: Proceedings of the International Conference on Software Engineering (ICSE 2005), St. Louis, MO, USA (May 2005)
21. Kim, M., Kim, S., Park, S., Choi, M.T., Kim, M., Gomaa, H.: UML-based service robot software development: a case study. In: ICSE 2006: Proceeding of the 28th International Conference on Software Engineering, pp. 534–543 (2006)
22. Goldsby, H.J., Cheng, B.H.C., McKinley, P.K., Knoester, D.B., Ofria, C.A.: Digital evolution of behavioral models for autonomic systems. In: Proceedings of the 5th International Conference on Autonomic Computing (ICAC 2008), Chicago, Illinois (June 2008)
23. Smith, R.L., Avrunin, G.S., Clarke, L.A., Osterweil, L.J.: Propel: an approach supporting property elucidation. In: ICSE 2002: Proceedings of the 24th International Conference on Software Engineering, pp. 11–21. ACM, New York (2002)
24. Cohen, M.B., Dwyer, M.B., Shi, J.: Coverage and adequacy in software product line testing. In: ROSATEA 2006: Proceedings of the ISSTA 2006 Workshop on Role of Software Architecture for Testing and Analysis, pp. 53–63. ACM, New York (2006)

Towards a Semantics of Activity Diagrams with Semantic Variation Points

Hans Grönniger[1], Dirk Reiß[2], and Bernhard Rumpe[1]

[1] Software Engineering, RWTH Aachen University, Germany
[2] Institut für Wirtschaftsinformatik, Abteilung Informationsmanagement
Technische Universität Braunschweig, Braunschweig, Germany

Abstract. UML activity diagrams have become an established notation to model control and data flow on various levels of abstraction,
ranging from fine-grained descriptions of algorithms to high-level workflow models in business applications. A formal semantics has to capture
the flexibility of the interpretation of activity diagrams in real systems,
which makes it inappropriate to define a fixed formal semantics. In this
paper, we define a semantics with semantic variation points that allow for
a customizable, application-specific interpretation of activity diagrams.
We examine concrete variants of the activity diagram semantics which
may also entail variants of the syntax reflecting the intended use at hand.

1 Introduction

Activity diagrams [1] are a widely accepted modeling language for representing
control and data flow within software systems. The notation is applicable to
various application domains and is useful on many levels of abstraction. To name
just a few forms of use, activity diagrams can be used for low-level descriptions
of algorithms similar to flow-charts [2], for modeling collaborating objects in an
object-based system, or for specifying simple web application page flows [3] and
high-level business application workflows [4].

The basic idea of activity diagrams is to model actions and their possible
orders of execution. Besides this common denominator, interpretation of what
constitutes an action and how to determine when and how an action is enabled or
when it finishes execution remains specific to the application area. Methodically,
the purpose of activity diagrams is also subject to project-specific interpretation:
it may be loosely used for documentation purposes, or formally employed for
analysis or code generation.

Formal semantics for activity diagrams helps to reduce misunderstandings between people and may enhance interoperability between tools. Because of the
flexibility of the notation regarding its possible forms of use, it turned out to
be inappropriate to use a single and fixed formal semantics. Instead, we define a semantics with semantic variation points which allow for a customizable,
application-specific interpretation of activity diagrams. Explicit semantic variation points help people to agree on the meaning of language constructs in a

D.C. Petriu, N. Rouquette, Ø. Haugen (Eds.): MODELS 2010, Part I, LNCS 6394, pp. 331–345, 2010.

certain project context. Invariant definitions constitute what we call the *inner semantics* of a notation. This separation helps to reduce the complexity of agreeing on a formal semantics. This paper concentrates on defining the inner semantics. Additionally, variants of activity diagrams, for example, to model low-level algorithms, are sketched.

The paper is structured as follows. In Section 2, we shortly describe the concrete and abstract syntax of activity diagrams. In Section 3, we define a formal inner semantics with variation points, which are interpreted in the different contexts in Section 4. In Section 5, we discuss related work and Section 6 concludes the paper.

2 Syntax of Activity Diagrams

Fig. 1 shows an example activity diagram. The workflow depicted therein describes an abstract view on a process for grading a thesis. It involves three roles (denoted on the left hand side): Student, Referee1 and Referee2. The workflow starts with a student who files a thesis. The action FileThesis has an output pin (Thesis t) that represents type and name of the outgoing data. The thesis is reviewed by Referee1 and Referee2 (fork to actions ReviewThesis1 *and* ReviewThesis2). Both actions have input and output pins – taking a Thesis t as input and passing on a Review r along the flow. When both actions have finished, the reviews are then evaluated by Referee1 (action Evaluate). Depending on the outcome of this action, either a certificate for the student is created (action CreateCert in case of passed) or note of the failure (action DetainFailure in case of failed) is taken. After either action, the activity is finished.

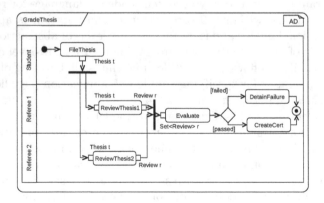

Fig. 1. Example activity "GradeThesis"

Please note that we currently do not consider constructs like hierarchical decomposition, interruptible activity regions or parameter sets which are present in the UML 2.2 [1] standard. Additional constructs can and will be handled in subsequent versions of the semantics. The focus of this work, however, is to show the handling of variants for the interpretation of activity diagrams.

2.1   Abstract Syntax

The abstract syntax of an activity diagram is given in Definition 1. An activity diagram has a name, a set of nodes and transitions. roleOf associates a role (being a name) to each node. A Node has a type, a name, a list of input and output pins, and some Effect when executed which remains unspecified for now. Transitions connect input and output pins of nodes. The names Src, Dst refer some node, the names InPin, OutPin refer to pins of the connected nodes. pinType yields the (data) type of the pin which also remains unspecified. Guards may be specified on outgoing transitions but actually belong to the source node. Therefore, we associate guards with output pins. These guards can be obtained by function guard. The exact structure of the language of guards is also not fixed in Definition 1.

Definition 1 (Abstract Syntax of Activity Diagrams).

$$
\begin{aligned}
\text{AD} \quad &= \text{Name} \times \wp(\text{Node}) \times \wp(\text{Transition}) \times \\
&\quad\; \text{roleOf} \times \text{pinType} \times \text{guard} \\
\text{Node} \quad &= \text{NType} \times \text{NName} \times \text{InPin}^* \times \text{OutPin}^* \times \text{Effect} \\
\text{roleOf} \quad &\in \text{Node} \rightarrow \text{Role} \\
\text{NType} \quad &= \{\text{action, initial, final, forkjoin, decisionmerge}\} \\
\text{Transition} \quad &= \text{Src} \times \text{OutPin} \times \text{Dst} \times \text{InPin} \\
\text{guard} \quad &\in \text{PName} \rightarrow \text{Guard} \\
\text{InPin, OutPin} \quad &= \text{PName} \\
\text{pinType} \quad &\in \text{PName} \rightarrow \text{PType} \\
\text{Src, Dst} \quad &= \text{NName} \\
\text{Role, NName, PName} &= \text{Name}
\end{aligned}
$$

As can be seen from Definition 1 the usually distinct node types for fork and join as well as decision and merge have been combined to more general nodes. A single fork, for example, is just a special case of a node of type forkjoin with exactly one input transition.

We introduce helper functions that operate on the abstract syntax for convenience.

- inT : AD × Node → $\wp$(Transition) yields all incoming transitions given a node.
- outT : AD × Node → $\wp$(Transition) returns all outgoing transitions of a node.
- Dot-notation is used to access parts of the abstract syntax. For instance, if $ad \in$ AD, then ad.Node denotes the set of nodes in ad.

Further, we assume that the following context conditions hold (among others). The diagram is complete in the sense that all nodes define pins when connected by a transition. Pins that are only control pins are given the (pseudo) type $\bot$. Pins with an underspecified data type are given the type $\top$ representing arbitrary values. Each transition references existing nodes and pins. In the concrete syntax (cf. Fig. 1), pins and their types may be left out but are assumed to be present in the abstract syntax.

As for the concrete syntax, we only consider a true subset of constructs compared to the UML standard. We also refrain from defining a simplified metamodel for the abstract syntax because our set-based notation is more succinct, precise, and convenient when defining the semantic mapping.

3   Inner Semantics of Activity Diagrams

We give a denotational semantics to activity diagrams. To do so, we precisely and explicitly define the (abstract) syntax (previous section), the semantic domain, and the semantic mapping [5].

3.1   System Model

The system model in the form of [6,7] serves as our semantic domain. It characterizes object-based systems by describing their structural, behavioral, and interaction aspects. The purpose of the system model is to have a common semantic domain for all kinds of UML diagram types. As described in [8] several UML sub-languages have already been mapped to the system model. A set-valued semantic mapping for individual diagram types allows for integrating multiple semantics: the integrated semantics of a set of models denotes all systems in the system model that fulfill all properties induced by the models. Object references are available as elements of a *universe of object identifiers* UOID[1]. Similarly, a universe of class names (UCLASS), variable names (UVAR), values (UVAL), methods (UMETH), threads (UTHREAD), and program counters (UPC) is part of each system in the system model providing static information. For each object oid, classOf(oid) $\in$ UCLASS determines its class. All methods m are defined in a class: definedIn(m) $\in$ UCLASS and there is a set of program counters for each method, i.e., pcOf(m) $\subseteq$ UPC.

From a global view-point, a system of the system model is a single non-deterministic state machine. The behavior is determined by a transition function of the form

$$\Delta : \text{STATE} \rightarrow \wp(\text{STATE})$$

where STATE is the set of global states. Each state $s \in$ STATE consists of three components. The data store dsOf(s) $\in$ UOID $\rightarrow$ (UVAR $\rightarrow$ UVAL) of a state s captures attribute values of all currently existing objects. The control store csOf(s) $\in$ UOID $\rightarrow$ UTHREAD $\rightarrow$ Stack(FRAME) saves computational states of methods in a stack of frames for each object and thread. A frame $f = (callee, mname, vars, pc, caller) \in$ FRAME stores the called object reference, the method name, current local variables, the current program counter, and the calling object. To access the program counter, we define $\pi_{pc}(f) = pc$. Finally, the event store esOf(s) holds unprocessed messages. As can be seen from the transition function above, we have a closed-world assumption. Inter-object

---

[1] All elements are defined in the context of a system $sm \in$ SystemModel. We write UOID but actually refer to a specific system's set of object identifiers UOID_{sm}.

communication is hidden in the global view since messages are sent directly to the receiving event stores. Concurrent activities are possible in one state transition because a global state as a whole captures the individual state of each object. A trace $t \in \text{TRACE}$ of a system in the system model is a finite or infinite sequence of states

$$t = s_1 \cdot s_2 \cdot s_3 \cdots \text{ such that } s_{i+1} \in \Delta(s_i)$$

For details regarding the rationale behind the system model and the actual definitions please consult [6,7].

3.2 Semantic Mapping

The basic idea of the semantic mapping, depicted in Fig. 2, is that an "instance" of the activity diagram is represented by some system model concepts such as objects, threads, etc. The abstract names e1, c1 and so on for these entities have been chosen deliberately to not suggest any specific choice. While Fig. 2 highlights only one instance, there may be multiple instances of the same diagram executing concurrently.

For an execution trace and a fixed instance it is then checked if all state transitions $s_{i+1} \in \Delta(s_i)$ conform to the behavior prescribed by the diagram. In Fig. 2, for example, the system model concept that represents action A has to be executed prior to the system model concepts that represent actions B and C. Thus, the inner semantics presented in this Section defines possible orders of executions of actions. How these actions manifest in a system is left open and can be detailed by "fixing" the variation points of the inner semantics.

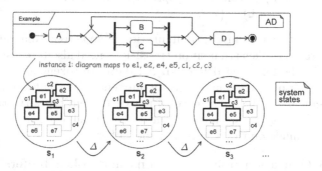

Fig. 2. Idea of mapping activity diagrams

The following definitions are given in standard maths. However, according to our approach presented in [8], all definitions (including abstract syntax) will be encoded in a theorem prover to obtain a machine-checkable language definition which is suitable for verification purposes.

In Definition 2, we introduce the set ADInst, i.e., the set of activity diagram instances. Depending on the intended interpretation of the activity diagram, it has to be possible to obtain, e.g., the representation of roles or actions as system model concepts. The exact definition is subject to specific interpretation and is consequently defined as a variation point.

Definition 2 (Variation point for activity diagram instances). ADInst *denotes a set of activity diagram instances for an activity diagram. Given an instance, we obtain the corresponding activity diagram by function* ad : ADInst → AD. *No further assumptions are made on the number and structure of elements of* ADInst *or on function* ad.

Our semantics is completely abstract in terms of how we represent an instance of an activity diagram as entities in the system. Establishing a connection between the *inner* semantics of the diagram and possible realizations is the aim of Sect. 4 where we discuss realization variants.

In each state of the system, information about the currently executing actions is required. Since the mapping of actions to system entities is not fixed, this also remains a variation point.

Definition 3 (Variation point of state of actions). *Function* executing : Node × ADInst × STATE → Bool *checks if a given node is currently executing for an instance in a system state.*

Pin types pose a restriction on what tokens may flow into or out of the nodes. This is defined in Definition 4.

Definition 4 (Variation point for assigning tokens to a pin type). *Function* elems : PType → $\wp$(Token) *yields a set of tokens that match the pin type. If the type is the special type* T, *then all tokens are valid (arbitrary data or just control), i.e.,* elems(T) = Token. *The special control token* ⊥ *is the only token matching* ⊥, *i.e.,* elems(⊥) = {⊥}.

To completely capture the current configuration of an activity diagram instance, control and data flow tokens that sit on transitions need also be considered. This is introduced in the following definition. All data are tokens as well. Function bufState in Definition 5 gives access to the current token buffer of a transition in a state. Elements in the buffer have to match the pin types the transition is connected to. These types are not necessarily equal but *compatible*. No further assumptions are made on the behavior of the buffer.

Definition 5 (Variation point on tokens and token buffers). Token *is a set of control and data tokens.* bufState : Transition × ADInst × STATE → Buffer(Token) *returns the current buffer of a transition in a state. Given a transition* t, *instance* inst, *and state* s, *the tokens in the buffer match the pin types of the transition:*

$$\forall e \in \text{bufState}(t, inst, s) :$$
$$e \in (\text{elems}(\text{ad}(inst).\text{pinType}(t.\text{InPin})) \cap \text{elems}(\text{ad}(inst).\text{pinType}(t.\text{OutPin})))$$

For convenience, we define bufEmpty$(t, inst, s) = ($bufState$(t, inst, s) = \epsilon)$ and bufNonEmpty$(t, inst, s) = ($bufState$(t, inst, s) \neq \epsilon)$.

Further, we determine the tokens produced and consumed on a transition in a system model step, $s' \in \Delta(s)$ in Definition 6.

Definition 6 (Consumption and production of tokens). *The function* cons : Transition $\times$ ADInst $\times$ STATE $\times$ STATE $\rightarrow$ Token* *returns tokens that have been consumed from a transition between to system states. Function* prod : Transition $\times$ ADInst $\times$ STATE $\times$ STATE $\rightarrow$ Token* *yields tokens that have been produced on a transition, respectively.*

Outputting a token may be guarded. We do not specify syntax nor semantics for the language Guard but, according to Definition 7, assume a function that evaluates guards given a context.

Definition 7 (Variation point on evaluation of guards). *Function* eval : Guard $\times$ ADInst $\times$ STATE $\rightarrow$ Bool *evaluates guards.*

isInitial in Definition 8 checks if a system state corresponds to an initial activity diagram configuration. A system state corresponds to an initial configuration if there are only tokens on the outgoing transitions of initial actions and no other action is currently executing.

Definition 8 (Initial states of a system). *For an instance inst $\in$ ADInst, the function* isInitial : ADInst $\times$ STATE $\rightarrow$ Bool *determines if a state $s \in$ STATE is an initial state:*

isInitial$(inst, s) =$
   $(\exists n \in$ ad$(inst)$.Node :
      $(n$.NType $=$ initial $\wedge \forall t \in$ outT$($ad$(inst), n) :$ bufNonEmpty$(t, inst, s)) \wedge$
   $(\forall n \in$ ad$(inst)$.Node :
      $(n$.NType $\neq$ initial $\implies \forall t \in$ outT$($ad$(inst), n) :$ bufEmpty$(t, inst, s) \wedge$
                                       $\neg$ executing$(n, inst, s)))$

A system state corresponds to a final configuration (Definition 9) if there are only tokens on the ingoing transitions of final actions and no other action is executing.

Definition 9 (Final states of a system). *For an instance inst $\in$ ADInst, the function* isFinal : ADInst $\times$ STATE $\rightarrow$ Bool *determines if a state $s \in$ STATE is a final state:*

isFinal$(inst, s) =$
   $(\exists n \in$ ad$(inst)$.Node :
      $(n$.NType $=$ final $\wedge \exists t \in$ inT$($ad$(inst), n) :$ bufNonEmpty$(t, inst, s)) \wedge$
   $(\forall n \in$ ad$(inst)$.Node :
      $(n$.NType $\neq$ final $\implies \forall t \in$ inT$($ad$(inst), n) :$ bufEmpty$(t, inst, s) \wedge$
                                    $\neg$ executing$(n, inst, s)))$

Two things may be noted here: a) Requiring that no other action is executing in an initial or final state results in unique, non-overlapping activity diagram instances with respect to system model entities. That means, changing the state in one instance does not affect any other instance. Currently, we still investigate under which conditions overlapping should be admissible since it enables interference between diagram instances which can be desired or unwanted. b) As an extension to Definition 9, we could define some pre-final state condition in that, although a final node was reached, other actions may still execute. Depending on the context, we could allow actions to carry on for some extra time to complete their tasks or kill them immediately.

We now define if a step in the system from state s to state s' with $s' \in \Delta(s)$ by an instance conforms to the behavior prescribed by the activity diagram. This definition may be extended if additional node types (such as hierarchical nodes) are defined.

Definition 10 (A well behaving system step). *The function* step *with signature* step : Node × ADInst × STATE × STATE → Bool *prescribes the allowed behavior in a system step w.r.t. an instance inst according to node n.*

$\text{step}(n, inst, s, s') =$
$((n.\text{NType} = \text{action} \implies$
$\quad (\text{startAct}(n, inst, s, s') \lor \text{finishAct}(n, inst, s, s') \lor \text{stepInst}(n, inst, s, s')))\land$
$(n.\text{NType} = \text{forkjoin} \implies \text{stepForkJoin}(n, inst, s, s'))\land$
$(n.\text{NType} = \text{decisionmerge} \implies \text{stepDecisionMerge}(n, inst, s, s'))$
$\lor \text{stutter}(n, inst, s, s'))$

The following function definitions all have the same signature like step.

Definition 11 (A stutter step). *The function* stutter *checks for a stutter step: The execution state (w.r.t. the instance inst) does not change and no tokens are consumed or produced.*

$\text{stutter}(n, inst, s, s') =$
$\quad (\text{executing}(n, inst, s) = \text{executing}(n, inst, s')\land$
$\quad \forall t \in \text{inT}(\text{ad}(inst), n) : \text{cons}(t, inst, s, s') = \epsilon\land$
$\quad \forall t \in \text{outT}(\text{ad}(inst), n) : \text{prod}(t, inst, s, s') = \epsilon)$

Definition 12 (Starting an action node). *The function* startAct *checks for a start of an action node: execution is started and the required token is consumed.*

$\text{startAct}(n, inst, s, s') =$
$\quad (\neg \text{executing}(n, inst, s) \land \text{executing}(n, inst, s')\land$
$\quad (\forall t \in \text{inT}(\text{ad}(inst), n) : \#(\text{cons}(1, t, inst, s, s')) = 1)\land$
$\quad (\forall t \in \text{outT}(\text{ad}(inst), n) : \text{prod}(t, inst, s, s') = \epsilon))$

Definition 13 (Finishing an action node). *The function* finishAct *checks for a finishing step of an action node: Execution is stopped and the required token is produced.*

$\text{finishAct}(n, inst, s, s') =$
$\quad (\text{executing}(n, inst, s) \land \neg \text{executing}(n, inst, s')\land$
$\quad (\forall t \in \text{outT}(\text{ad}(inst), n) : \#(\text{prod}(t, inst, s, s')) = 1)\land$
$\quad (\forall t \in \text{inT}(\text{ad}(inst), n) : \text{cons}(t, inst, s, s') = \epsilon))$

While startAct and finishAct allow for behavior of nodes that last longer than one system step, stepInst in Definition 14 is appropriate when the execution of a node can be finished in just one step.

Definition 14 (Instant reaction of an action node). *The function* stepInst *checks for a step of an action node that constitutes of executing the whole action.*

$$\text{stepInst}(n, inst, s, s') =$$
$$((\forall t \in \text{inT}(\text{ad}(inst), n) : \#(\text{cons}(t, inst, s, s')) = 1) \wedge$$
$$(\forall t \in \text{outT}(\text{ad}(inst), n) : \#(\text{prod}(t, inst, s, s')) = 1))$$

It is assumed that a node produces or consumes at most one token on each transition at a time. Definition 6 allows for a more general treatment where multiple tokens are considered. This can be exploited in future versions of the semantics when considering, for example, streams of tokens and parameter sets [1].

Definition 15 (Step on a fork/join node). *The function* stepForkJoin *checks for a step of a fork or join node (or a combination of both): On all input transitions a token is consumed while on all output transitions a token is produced.*

$$\text{stepForkJoin}(n, inst, s, s') =$$
$$((\forall t \in \text{inT}(\text{ad}(inst), n) : \#(\text{cons}(t, inst, s, s')) = 1) \wedge$$
$$(\forall t \in \text{outT}(\text{ad}(inst), n) : \#(\text{prod}(t, inst, s, s')) = 1))$$

Please note, according to Definition 15, the reaction of a fork/join node is instantaneous. While this may be adequate for many interpretations, it may be inappropriate for others. An alternative definition could introduce a two-phase behavior of fork/join similar to that of action nodes. Also a combined definition (instantaneous *or* delayed) is possible. The same holds for Definition 16.

Another interesting issue is the buffering of tokens. There is no need to produce all tokens in one go. What it means to store or retrieve a token depends on how the buffer is "implemented". A rather sophisticated but useful way would be to store arriving data values in attributes (one for each incoming pin) and use an intelligent controller that senses if all tokens arrived (i.e., all attributes are set). This would then be the instant in time at which all tokens are produced.

Definition 16 (Step on a decision/merge node). stepDecisionMerge *checks for a step of a decision or merge node (or a combination of both): There is exactly one input token consumed and exactly one output token produced on an output pin with its guard evaluated to true.*

$$\text{stepDecisionMerge}(n, inst, s, s') =$$
$$((\exists t \in \text{inT}(\text{ad}(inst), n) : \#(\text{cons}(t, inst, s, s')) = 1 \wedge$$
$$\forall t' \in \text{inT}(\text{ad}(inst), n) : t' \neq t \implies \text{cons}(t, inst, s, s') = \epsilon) \wedge$$
$$(\exists t \in \text{outT}(\text{ad}(inst), n) :$$
$$\#(\text{prod}(t, inst, s, s')) = 1 \wedge \text{eval}(\text{ad}(inst).\text{guard}(t.\text{OutPin}), inst, s') \wedge$$
$$\forall t' \in \text{outT}(\text{ad}(inst), n) : t' \neq t \implies \text{prod}(t, inst, s, s') = \epsilon))$$

The last definition of the inner semantics of activity diagrams now defines a satisfaction relation of a trace of the system with an activity diagram instance. The conditions that need to be fulfilled are: a) there is a state with an initial configuration (i-th state), and all subsequent steps b) behave according to function *step*, or c), if the execution reached a final configuration, it remains final.

Definition 17 (A trace that satisfies an activity diagram instance). *For a trace $t \in$ TRACE of a system in the system model and an activity diagram instance inst $\in$ ADInst, t satisfies inst, $t \models$ inst, exactly if*

$$(\exists i : \text{isInitial}(inst, t[i]) \land$$
$$(\forall j \geq i, n \in \text{ad}(inst).\text{Node} :$$
$$\text{step}(n, inst, t[j], t[j+1]) \land$$
$$(\text{isFinal}(inst, t[j]) \implies \text{isFinal}(inst, t[j+1])))))$$

Until now, we have not clarified how an activity diagram instance may look like under a specific interpretation. This is the aim of the next section.

4   Variants

In this section two variants of activity diagram interpretations are introduced. The degree of formality varies. A rather complete treatment of activity diagrams describing a single method execution which is made up of atomic actions is given. Activity diagrams in which actions are treated as complete methods are discussed informally. Further variants are briefly discussed in the conclusion.

4.1   Variant 1: Nodes as Atomic Actions

Consider the example in Fig. 3. The activity diagram describes an algorithm to compute the factorial of a number. Each action is assumed to be an atomic action. The whole activity is a method definition. The idea now is to specify variants of the definitions in Sect. 3 which are variation points to obtain a semantics in which we interpret an activity diagram as a single method. An instance of the activity diagram hence is a concrete single execution of that method. In this case, an activity diagram instance can be characterized by the following definition:

Definition 18 (Variant of Definition 2: Activity Diagram Instances). *An instance of an activity is a single method execution. The following functions constitute the context of the execution:*

- caller : ADInst $\rightarrow$ UOID *is the caller of the method.*
- meth : ADInst $\rightarrow$ UMETH *is the method described by the activity diagram.*
- params : ADInst $\rightarrow$ UVAR* *is the list of parameters of the method.*
- callee : ADInst $\rightarrow$ UOID *is the called object. It has to define the method, i.e., classOf(callee($inst$)) = definedIn(meth($inst$)).*
- pc : Node $\times$ ADInst $\rightarrow$ UPC *is a valid program counter value of the action for the specified method, i.e., pc($n, inst$) $\in$ pcOf(meth($inst$))*
- thread : ADInst $\rightarrow$ UTHREAD *is the thread executing the method.*

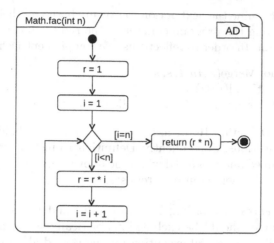

Fig. 3. Activity for method "fac"

Since all actions are atomic actions, we need not consider the execution state of a node. All executions are instantaneous and Definition 3 remains underspecified.

No data but only control flow is relevant in this variant, hence we set PType = $\{\bot\}$ and define elems($\bot$) = $\{\bot = \text{thread}(inst)\}$ for an instance $inst$. This is to model the fact that if there is a token in the buffer of a transition, then the target of the transition is the next action to execute. This is the case if the program counter of the current stack frame identified by some object and thread points to the node which is targeted. For some instance $inst$, transition t, and state s, this means

$$\text{bufState}(t, inst, s) = [\text{thread}(inst)]$$
$$\Leftrightarrow \text{pcOf}(\text{top}(\text{csOf}(s)(\text{callee}(inst))(\text{thread}(inst)))) = \text{pc}(t.\text{Dst}, inst)$$

where top is the first element of the stack. This fixes the variation points of Definitions 5 and 4.

We assume a given action language AL and set Effect = AL and Guard $\subseteq$ AL. Semantics is traditionally defined: An atomic action is evaluated in the context of an object and a thread that execute an action and it is checked whether the state s' mirrors the effect of executing the action in state s. Consider, for example, an action for setting an attribute SetAttr x y: the data store of the object is updated according to the given attribute x and value y. Also the program counter is advanced, i.e.,

$$\text{sem} : \text{AL} \times \text{UOID} \times \text{UTHREAD} \times \text{STATE} \times \text{STATE} \to \text{Bool}$$
$$\text{sem}(\text{SetAttr x y}, oid, th, s, s') =$$
$$(\text{dsOf}(s')(oid) = \text{dsOf}(s)(oid) \oplus [x \mapsto y] \wedge$$
$$\text{csOf}(s')(oid)(th) = \text{incPC}(\text{csOf}(s)(oid)(th)))$$

In order to make sure that actions are properly executed, we add the constraint that executing a node n in instance $inst$ corresponds to considering its effect:

$$\text{stepInst}(n, inst, s, s') \Leftrightarrow \text{sem}(n.\text{Effect}, \text{callee}(inst), \text{thread}(inst), s, s')$$

Decision nodes determine the next action to execute based on their guards. Since this is done by setting the program counter to the right value, guards have side effects in this variant. In order to reflect this, we complement Definition 16 with:

$$\text{stepDecisionMerge}(n, inst, s, s')$$
$$\Leftrightarrow \exists t \in \text{outT}(\text{ad}(inst), n) :$$
$$\text{sem}(\text{ad}(inst).\text{guard}(t.\text{OutPin}), \text{callee}(inst), \text{thread}(inst), s, s')$$

To not contradict Definition 16, we assume $\text{eval}(g, inst, s)$ to hold for all guards, instances, and transitions. Consequently, Definition 16 just ensures that exactly one token is consumed and produced while the above constraint ensures that the effect of a guard was observed in a system step.

Syntactic consequences: According to this variant and the semantics defined for it, fork/join nodes should be excluded syntactically since there is only one thread or token. The sequential execution by one thread also indicates that all nodes (except for decision nodes) may have only one output pin and that roles are excluded as well. Since only control flow between atomic actions is modeled, data types on pins are also disallowed.

4.2   Variant 2: Actions as Methods

In this variant, all actions are considered to be complete methods of some objects instead of atomic actions of one method. This might be a suitable interpretation of the activity diagram in Fig. 1.

Activity diagram instances can in this case be characterized as in Definition 19: Nodes correspond to methods, there is a set of threads executing these methods. A specific object on which the method is called is obtained by oid. Roles are represented as objects as well.

Definition 19 (Variant of Definition 2: Activity Diagram Instances). *An instance of an activity diagram in which actions denote methods is characterized by the following functions:*

- meth : Node × ADInst → UMETH *is the method referenced by the node.*
- threads : ADInst → ℘(UTHREAD) *is the set of threads in that instance.*
- oid : Node × ADInst → UOID *is an object that holds a method for the node.*
- rrep : Role × ADInst → UOID *is the object representing the role.*

Instances can be refined further by introducing sub-variants of Definition 19. For example, we may require that for an instance *inst*, the role of node n is defining the method, i.e.,

$$\text{definedIn}(\text{meth}(n, inst)) = \text{classOf}(\text{rrep}(\text{ad}(inst).\text{roleOf}(n), inst))$$
$$= \text{classOf}(\text{oid}(n, inst))$$

According to Fig. 1, for example,

$$\text{definedIn}(\text{meth}(\text{Evaluate}, inst)) = \text{classOf}(\text{rrep}(\text{Referee1}, inst))$$

So the method that implements action Evaluate is defined in a class that represents role Referee1. An interesting question in this context then is: Who is calling an action (i.e., method). Is it done by the role itself? Is there some additional control structure that checks if a role finished one of its methods and then calls (enables) the next one? Methods may, however, not be associated to roles at all. Instead, specific objects, structured roughly as in the *command* design pattern [9] could represent action nodes. To ensure data integrity, one has to be careful when allowing concurrent instances, i.e., concurrent executions of methods (or of a single method as in variant 1). Analysis of the activity diagrams would be required to proof or refute this property. At this state, we cannot faithfully give definite answers but will examine these questions in future work.

Executing a node (cf. Definition 3) means executing a method, so there has to be a stack frame $f = (\mathrm{oid}(n, inst), \mathrm{nameOf}(\mathrm{meth}(inst)), *, *, *)^2$ for a thread $th \in \mathrm{threads}(inst)$, i.e.,

$$\mathrm{executing}(n, inst, s) \Leftrightarrow f \in (\mathrm{csOf}(s)(\mathrm{oid}(n, inst)))(th))$$

Again, we could be more specific. For example, we could force the caller of the method to be the object that is representing the role, i.e., we have the last component of f equal to $\mathrm{rrep}(\mathrm{ad}(inst).\mathrm{roleOf}(n), inst)$. In this variant, a natural

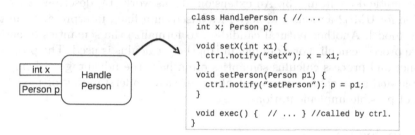

```
class HandlePerson { // ...
   int x; Person p;

   void setX(int x1) {
      ctrl.notify("setX"); x = x1;
   }
   void setPerson(Person p1) {
      ctrl.notify("setPerson"); p = p1;
   }

   void exec() { // ... } //called by ctrl.
}
```

int x
Person p
Handle Person

Fig. 4. Special buffering strategy for tokens as attributes

interpretation of tokens are method calls in the system. However, there is again more than one choice. A token may correspond to a call that is both carrying control and data. A single token could then correspond to a possibly complex parameter list for the method. In case of multiple incoming transitions to a node, we could also follow the idea discussed earlier that the actual method execution can only be started if all required input data has arrived on all input pins. The (incomplete) code snippet in Fig. 4 informally shows a possible implementation in which an action HandlePerson is mapped to a class which has attributes for all input pins. Setting the attribute also informs some controller that keeps track of the state of attributes. Once all attributes are set, the controller may call method exec that implements the actual behavior. Syntactically, all features introduced in Sect. 2 make sense in this variant, so there are no syntax restrictions as in the previous variant.

---

[2] Values we are not interested in can be marked as "wild card" by $*$.

5   Related Work

The common denominator of most works regarding the semantics of activity diagrams is the idea to define the possible orders of executions of actions. In that respect, our semantics is not different. The UML standard defines an informal token flow semantics with semantic variation points [1]. However, the standard provides no means to describe realizations. In our approach, we obtain realizations by stating variants of several function definitions. A formal approach uses procedural Petri-nets for the semantics of UML2 activity diagrams [10]. Here, only the control flow aspect of activity diagrams is covered (including concurrency and procedure calls), whereas data flow is covered in our approach as well. As an extension, the data flow in activity diagrams has been mapped to Colored Petri-nets [11]. Both works do not consider a specific application domain. Eshuis [4] develops a requirements-level and an implementation-level semantics for activity diagrams. Both semantics are fixed and focus on workflow management systems while we introduce an inner semantics from which variants can be developed. Another token-based approach in the application area of workflow management systems uses a virtual machine to execute activities [12]. Here, a fixed semantics is defined by mapping a model to its execution in said runtime engine. The semantics of UML actions is formally defined using the system model as a semantic domain in [13]. An extension of this work [14] describes a virtual machine for UML2 actions and activities based on a fixed interpretation in the system model. Another natural candidate to formalize the semantics of activities are process calculi. For example, in [15] the μ-calculus is used. The proposed Petri-net and process calculus semantics often have the advantage of being executable and analyzable but do not allow an easy understanding of models in terms of possible implementations.

6   Conclusion

We have defined a formal semantics for a subset of UML activity diagrams. The inner semantics was equipped with variation points that can be interpreted differently in specific application domains. Variants are obtained by deciding which system model entities make up a diagram instance and how their execution state and token flow is determined. This was sketched using two example variants.

Having clarified the inner semantics of activity diagrams in terms of the system model, we are now working towards formalizing different variants of activity diagram interpretations. In this paper, we were mainly concerned with rather low-level interpretations of activity diagrams as simple action or method executions. As discussed in [3], activity diagrams can be used to model simple web page flows but also complex collaborations in web information systems. Executing an action in this context means, for example, showing a web page to a user, waiting for a data update, and storing it in a session context or data base. Another interesting line of future work is to include further concepts from activity diagrams, for example, interruptible activity regions, parameter sets, etc. However, there is the danger of cluttering the notation with constructs which are only useful in very special situations. To avoid this, we will introduce these concepts as syntactic variants in addition to a relatively small language core as explained in [16]. Further, we are confident that it is possible to combine different interpretations of activity diagrams when considering hierarchical decomposition. For example, it is possible to model the content of nodes interpreted as methods by diagrams in which nodes are interpreted as basic actions and to adopt the diagram instance.

References

1. Object Management Group: Unified Modeling Language: Superstructure Version 2.2 (09-02-02) (2009), http://www.omg.org/spec/UML/2.2/Superstructure/PDF/
2. International Organization for Standardization (ISO): ISO 5807:1985 Information processing – Documentation symbols and conventions for data, program and system flowcharts, program network charts and system resources charts (1985)
3. Koch, N., Kraus, A., Cacharo, C., Meliá, S.: Integration of business processes in Web application models. Journal of Web Engineering 3(1), 22–49 (2004)
4. Eshuis, H.: Semantics and Verification of UML Activity Diagrams for Workflow Modelling. PhD thesis, Univ. of Twente (2002)
5. Harel, D., Rumpe, B.: Meaningful Modeling: What's the Semantics of "Semantics"? Computer 37(10), 64–72 (2004)
6. Broy, M., Cengarle, M.V., Grönniger, H., Rumpe, B.: Considerations and Rationale for a UML System Model. In: Lano, K. (ed.) UML 2 Semantics and Applications. Wiley, Chichester (2009)
7. Broy, M., Cengarle, M.V., Grönniger, H., Rumpe, B.: Definition of the System Model. In: Lano, K. (ed.) UML 2 Semantics and Applications. Wiley, Chichester (2009)
8. Grönniger, H., Ringert, J.O., Rumpe, B.: System Model-Based Definition of Modeling Language Semantics. In: Lee, D., Lopes, A., Poetzsch-Heffter, A. (eds.) FMOODS 2009. LNCS, vol. 5522, pp. 152–166. Springer, Heidelberg (2009)
9. Gamma, E., Helm, R., Johnson, R., Vlissides, J.: Design Patterns: Elements of Reusable Object-Oriented Software. Addison-Wesley Professional, Reading (1995)
10. Störrle, H.: Semantics of UML 2.0 Acitivities. In: Intl. Symp. Visual Languages/Human Computer Centered Systems, pp. 235–242 (2004)
11. Störrle, H.: Towards a Petri-net Semantics of Data Flow in UML 2.0 Activities. Technical Report TR 0504, University of Munich (2004)
12. Vitolins, V., Kalnins, A.: Semantics of UML 2.0 Activity Diagram for Business Modeling by Means of Virtual Machine. In: 9th IEEE International EDOC Enterprise Computing Conference, pp. 181–194. IEEE Computer Society, Los Alamitos (2005)
13. Crane, M.L., Dingel, J.: Towards a Formal Account of a Foundational Subset for Executable UML Models. In: Czarnecki, K., Ober, I., Bruel, J.-M., Uhl, A., Völter, M. (eds.) MODELS 2008. LNCS, vol. 5301, pp. 675–689. Springer, Heidelberg (2008)
14. Crane, M.L., Dingel, J.: Towards a UML virtual machine: implementing an interpreter for UML 2 actions and activities. In: Proceedings of Centrer for Advanced Studies on Collaborative Research (CASCON 2008), pp. 96–110. IBM (2008)
15. Küster, J., Koehler, J., Novatnack, J., Ryndina, K.: A Classification of UML2 Activity Diagrams. Technical report, IBM ZRL Technical Report 3673 (2006)
16. Cengarle, M.V., Grönniger, H., Rumpe, B.: Variability within Modeling Language Definitions. In: Schürr, A., Selic, B. (eds.) MODELS 2009. LNCS, vol. 5795, pp. 670–684. Springer, Heidelberg (2009)

An AADL-Based Approach to Variability Modeling of Automotive Control Systems

Shin'ichi Shiraishi

Toyota InfoTechnology Center Co., Ltd.
Akasaka 6-6-20, Minato-ku
Tokyo, Japan 107-0052

Abstract. While the complexity of automotive systems is increasing, nowadays, most of the newly developed functionalities are implemented by software. This implies that software plays an important role in the development of automotive systems. However, several inefficiency problems related to software remain unresolved. One problem is to find an effective way to handle a large-scale variation of automotive systems. Hence, this paper presents an AADL (Architecture Analysis & Design Language)-based approach to the variation-related problem. The proposed approach captures the variation of automotive systems and yields their variability models. The obtained models promote an efficient development that exploits system variation. In this paper, we explain the detailed procedure of AADL-based development with the help of an example of development of cruise control systems.

Keywords: ADL, architecture description language, AADL, architecture analysis & design language, variability modeling, automotive electronics systems.

1 Introduction

During the development of the latest automotive systems, new functionalities are generated by integrating independently developed systems. For example, navigation-cooperative systems such as shift control or suspension control systems are good examples of this kind of integration. However, such a systems integration can easily lead to a serious complication in automotive systems. Unfortunately, the complexity problem is especially severe in software development because software plays a leading role in the integration. Besides the complication, another problem is that the scale of software is being expanded rapidly; for example, one prediction [1] is that the scale will reach 100 million steps around the year 2015.

Although the complication and expansion of software are now actively in progress, unfortunately, some problems related to software development remain unresolved. For example, while an efficient systems integration requires fluent communication between engineers working in different technical areas, we do not have any effective communication basis on which engineers can share important information. This can be explained by the fact that each technical domain — e.g., body electronics, infotainment, powertrain, and so forth — has its own vocabulary that the others cannot easily recognize. Moreover, the fact that the development is widely distributed over several divisions, suppliers, and subcontractors makes this problem more severe.

Yet another problem is a large-scale variation of automotive systems. Several factors, e.g., car models, grades, classes, and markets, produce a large number of variants. Certainly, variability management for implementation codes is commonly employed in the

D.C. Petriu, N. Rouquette, Ø. Haugen (Eds.): MODELS 2010, Part I, LNCS 6394, pp. 346–360, 2010.
© Springer-Verlag Berlin Heidelberg 2010

practical field; however, we need high-level variability modeling of automotive systems that results in efficient variation handling and improved productivity.

Emerging technologies known as ADLs (architecture description languages) — e.g., AADL [2], AADL V2 [3], SysML [4], MARTE [5], EAST-ADL [6], and EAST-ADL 2 [7] — are recently drawing much attention from automotive engineers because of their potential to alleviate the abovementioned problems. These ADLs offer syntax that can capture the structure of software-centric systems at a high abstraction level. In other words, they can be possibly used as an information infrastructure for a wide variety of engineers working in different areas. This paper demonstrates how ADLs can be exploited in the development of automotive systems with detailed architecture descriptions. In particular, we focus on the variation handling problem and choose AADL[1] from among the abovementioned candidates. This is because AADL provides strong support for variation handling as is demonstrated in the following sections. In order to elucidate the concrete steps necessary for variability modeling, we utilize a case study of automotive systems: cruise control systems.

2 Architecture Analysis & Design Language (AADL)

AADL is derived from Honeywell's MetaH, which is a language for developing avionics system architectures. This implies that AADL inherently specializes in real-time system architectures (hardware and software) with respect to their design and analysis. AADL was originally standardized by SAE in 2004 [2], and then, the updated version (AADL V2) with new features—multi-layered architectures, virtual processors, and so on—was recently published in 2009 [3].

AADL descriptions consist of basic elements called *components*. A certain number of components connect each other and form an architecture of systems. AADL provides several types of components that compose a software architecture, such as *process*, *thread*, etc. In addition to the software architecture, we can use the following hardware components for describing an execution platform: *processor*, *device*, *bus*, and so forth. With regard to component interconnection, each component communicates via ports: *data port*, *event port*, etc. Furthermore, the software architecture is bound up with the execution platform by sharing a bus, e.g., a memory bus. A set of interconnected components composes a *system*. Figure 1 shows graphical notations of the aforementioned AADL components, system, and ports.

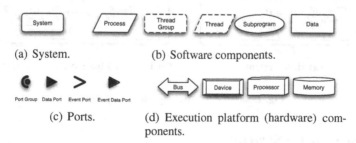

(a) System.   (b) Software components.

(c) Ports.   (d) Execution platform (hardware) components.

Fig. 1. Graphical notations of AADL

---

[1] It should be noted that we focus on AADL [2] rather than recently published AADL V2 [3].

An interface design (external specification) of components is given by a *type* definition in AADL. In contrast, an internal specification is specialized by an *implementation* of the type. It should be noted that the AADL allows a type definition to have multiple implementations. List 1 displays an excerpt of the AADL description of the sample system shown in Fig. 2(a). List 1 also explains that a type definition is implicitly described in contrast to the explicit description of an implementation.

List 1. Example of AADL description.

```
-- The following is an excerpt of the entire description.
system system1 -- Type Definition of Base System
-- No interface
end system1;
system implementation system1.impl -- Implementation Description
    subcomponents
        process1: process pr1.impl;
        process2: process pr2.impl;
    connections
        pr_com: data port process1.pr1_output -> process2.pr2_input;
end system1.impl;
```

In addition to the basic description strategy mentioned above, AADL is also equipped with the following vocabulary to deal with variants of components: *extends* and *refined to*. List 2 describes an extended base system shown in Fig. 2(b) that is a variant of the base system in Fig. 2(a). Later, in this paper, we discuss in detail how to exploit this extension mechanism for the purpose of variability modeling of automotive systems.

List 2. Example of description of variant: Fig. 2(b).

```
-- The following is an excerpt of the system variant.
thread th2_dash extends th2
    features
        th2_output: out data port; -- Additional Port
end th2_dash;
process implementation pr2.impl_dash extends pr2.impl
    subcomponents
        thread2_dash: thread th2_dash; -- Additional Thread
        -- Snip
end pr2.impl_dash;
system implementation system1.impl_dash extends system1.impl
    subcomponents -- pr2.impl_dash substitutes for pr2.impl
        process2: refined to process pr2.impl_dash;
        -- Snip
end system1.impl_dash;
```

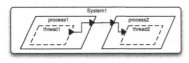

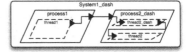

(a) Base system.   (b) Extended base system (a variant).

Fig. 2. Sample AADL diagrams of systems

3   Cruise Control Systems

This paper targets three types of cruise control systems, detailed explanations of which are provided below.

Cruise Control System: CC1. This cruise control system (hereafter referred to as CC1) is a base system on which the other two systems are developed. Its main function is constant-speed cruise control that renders the difference between the current vehicle speed and the target speed set by a driver to zero. In this system, the lower and upper speed limits for operation are 40 km/h and 100 km/h, respectively. This system controls the output torque of an engine via an external engine control computer. Figure 3(a) shows the hardware configuration of the cruise control system (CC1), including peripherals: switches, buses, ECUs, etc. The target application required to be developed in this study is software running on Driving Support Computer depicted in the center of Fig. 3(a).

Adaptive Cruise Control System: CC2. The adaptive cruise control system (hereafter refereed to as CC2) is an extended system derived from CC1. This system provides a new function of constant-distance cruise control that renders the difference between the target distance set by a driver and the current distance to a target vehicle traveling in front of the equipped vehicle to zero. In order to ensure constant-distance cruise control, this system includes a radar sensor that yields the following information: the distance from the equipped vehicle to the target vehicle and the relative speed between these two vehicles. The speed limits for operation are the same as CC1: 40 km/h – 100 km/h. The hardware configuration of this system is shown in Fig. 3(b); however, two gray boxes, Object Recognition Sensor and Front Controller, are excluded because they are dedicated to the full speed range adaptive cruise control system (see the next paragraph).

Full Speed Range Adaptive Cruise Control System: CC3. The full speed range adaptive cruise control system (hereafter referred to as CC3) is a further extended system derived from CC2. In addition to the radar sensor, this system includes an image sensor labeled Object Recognition Sensor in Fig. 3(b). The object recognition sensor captures the behavior of vehicles in front of the system-equipped vehicle. It works together with the radar sensor in a compensatory way to expand the effective range of sensing the distance and relative speed. This alleviates the speed limits for operation, such as 0 km/h–100 km/h. This wide-range sensing enables a stop-and-go function by following on the target vehicle. The hardware configuration of this systems has already been shown in Fig. 3(b).

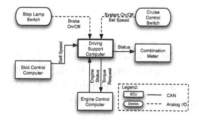
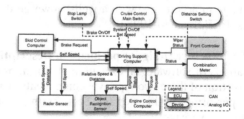

(a) Hardware configuration of the cruise control system: CC1.

(b) Hardware configurations of the adaptive cruise control systems: CC2 and CC3.

Fig. 3. Hardware configurations of cruise control systems

As shown above, this paper uses the following identifiers to distinguish one system from the others (CC1, CC2, and CC3).

4   AADL-Based Development of Automotive Control Systems

In this section, we choose the basic cruise control system (CC1) from the three types of systems mentioned in Sect. 3 and discuss in detail its development by using AADL.

4.1   Development Process

AADL does not depend on any development processes. In other words, we have to prepare a development process to which we can apply AADL. Thus, we assume the following steps of the development process [2].

1. Requirements Specification.
2. Architecture Design.
    (a) Specification Description (Type Definition): Functional Decomposition, Interface Design, Flow Design, etc.
    (b) Implementation Description & Analysis: Component Aggregation & Interconnection, Behavior Modeling, Flow Implementation, Flow Analysis, etc.
3. Code Implementation: Automatic Code Generation, Hand Coding, etc.

The above two steps, that is, *specification description* (*type definition*) and *implementation description*, are alternatively iterated along with delving deeper into an architecture hierarchy (see the next section for details).

4.2   AADL Descriptions of the Cruise Control System

In this section, we provide detailed AADL descriptions of the basic cruise control system (CC1) according to the development process explained in Sect. 4.1. Variability modeling, which is the focus of this paper, will be discussed in Sect. 5.

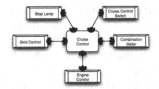

Fig. 4. Context diagram of CC1.

Requirements Specification. AADL does not provide any vocabulary for requirements specification. Thus, the requirements specification is written in a natural language in accordance with a well-known guideline such as IEEE Std. 830-1998 [8].

Architecture Design: Specification Description. This step describes external specifications of software, an execution platform, or subcomponents obtained by the decomposition of these two top-level components. That is to say, the type definition in AADL is performed in this step (cf. Sect. 2). In the subsequent discussion, we focus only on the software part.

First, on the basis of the information provided in Fig. 3(a), we prepare an initial diagram (context diagram) shown in Fig. 4. Our target is the software part of Cruise Control shown in Fig. 4. The context diagram allows us to describe some preliminary definitions, e.g., measurement units: km/h, Nm; data types: 32-bit long, 16-bit long; and so on.

---

[2] More precise explanations of each step will be given in the next section.

Second, by using these fundamental measurement units and data types, we describe the type definitions of software components and its peripherals. List 3 gives the type definitions of the top-level software component (*CruiseControlSoftwareCC1*) and the skid control computer (*skid_control_base*), which is a peripheral ECU from the viewpoint of the cruise control system and is a central component of a brake control system. Figure 5(a) shows the schematic type definition of *CruiseControlSoftwareCC1*. This figure also shows that the type definition in AADL yields the interface design between components.

List 3. Type definitions of the top-level software component and the skid control computer.

```
-- Top-level Component of Software
system CruiseControlSoftwareCC1
    features
        self_speed_in: in data port types::kph_type;
        can_bus_steering: requires bus access hardware::hs_can_bus;
        -- Snip
end CruiseControlSoftwareCC1;
-- Device: Skid Control Computer
device skid_control_base
    features
        self_speed: out data port types::kph_type;
        -- Requires CAN BUS
        hs_can_bus_self_speed: requires bus access hardware::hs_can_bus;
end skid_control_base;
```

Finally, we consider the functional decomposition such that a software component is split into some subcomponents. The external specifications (type definitions) of the obtained subcomponents are also determined. Furthermore, internal relationships among ports of each subcomponent are defined as flows (See *flows* in List 4).

The extracted subcomponents are connected to each other in the next step: the implementation description in Sect. 4.2 . As mentioned before, these two steps, i.e., the specification description (type definition) and the implementation description, are performed alternatively until leaf components of software architecture, such as processes or threads, are obtained.

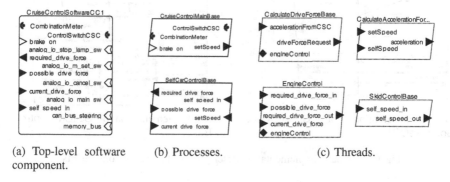

(a) Top-level software component.   (b) Processes.   (c) Threads.

Fig. 5. Schematic type definitions of software components

In the case of CC1, the top-level software component depicted in Fig. 5(a) consists of the following two processes: CruiseControlMainBase and SelfCarControlBase in Fig. 5(b). The former process CruiseControlMainBase is the manager of the entire system. The latter process SelfCarControlBase realizes a constant-speed cruise control algorithm. Moreover, SelfCarControlBase is composed of four types of threads depicted in Fig. 5(c). List 4 gives the type definitions of the process SelfCarControlBase in Fig. 5(b) and the thread SkidControlBase in Fig. 5(c).

List 4. Type definitions of a process and a thread.

```
process SelfCarControlBase
    features
        setSpeed: in data port types::kph_type;
        -- Snip
end SelfCarControlBase;
thread SkidControlBase
    features
        self_speed_in: in data port types::kph_type;
        self_speed_out: out data port types::kph_type;
    flows -- Flow Design
        FS0000: flow path self_speed_in -> self_speed_out;
end SkidControlBase;
```

Architecture Design: Implementation Description & Analysis. In this step, the internal specifications of software components whose external specifications have been defined previously are described. This procedure is called as *implementations* of the predefined *types* (cf. Sect. 2). More precisely, some subcomponents are aggregated and interconnected so as to form an upper-level component. List 5 presents the implementations of the system CruiseControlSoftwareCC1 shown in Fig. 5(a) and the process SelfCarControlBase shown in Fig. 5(b). The diagrams in Fig. 6 are the schematic descriptions of these implementations.

If further decomposition of the subcomponents is necessary, we will return to Sect. 4.2 and reconsider the functional decomposition at a sub-subcomponent level. As mentioned before, the decomposition is repeated until leaf components such as processes or threads are obtained. We can expect to obtain a hierarchical software architecture as a result of the iterative decomposition.

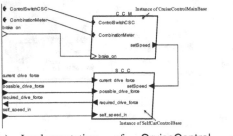

(a) Implementation of CruiseControl-SoftwareCC1 .

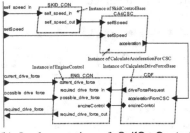

(b) Implementation of SelfCarControl-Base.

Fig. 6. Schematic implementation descriptions of software components

List 5. Implementation descriptions of a system and a process.

```
system implementation CruiseControlSoftwareCC1.impl
    subcomponents
        C_C_M: process CruiseControlMainBase.impl;
        S_C_C: process SelfCarControlBase.impl;
    connections
        -- Snip
end CruiseControlSoftwareCC1.impl
```

```
process implementation SelfCarControlBase.impl
    subcomponents
        CA4CSC: thread CalculateAccelerationForCSC.impl;
        CDF: thread CalculateDriveForceBase.impl;
        SKID_CON: thread SkidControlBase.impl;
        ENG_CON: thread EngineControl.impl;
    connections
        IC0007: data port SKID_CON.self_speed_out->CA4CSC.selfSpeed;
        -- Snip
end SelfCarControlBase.impl
```

In this step, predefined flows, e.g., *FS0000* in List 4, are also implemented as a multi-hop path from an input port to an output port via some internal subcomponents. On the basis of implemented flows, some analysis tools can enable quantitative analyses such as an end-to-end delay analysis and so forth.

After the iterative decomposition, the top-level software component *CruiseConrol-SoftwareCC1* is connected to its peripherals and the execution platform. List 6 shows that the execution platform *CCHardware*, peripheral ECUs such as *SKID_CONT*, devices such as *CMB_METER*, and *CCSoftware*, which is an instance of *CruiseControl-SoftwareCC1*, are interconnected via several buses such as a CAN bus and so on.

List 6. Implementation description of the cruise control system.

```
system implementation CruiseControlSystem.CC1
    subcomponents
        CCSoftware: system CruiseControlSoftwareCC1;
        CCHardware: system CruiseControlHardwarePlatformBase;
        SWITCH_CSC: system CruiseControlSwitchCSC;
        ENGINE: device devices::engine_control;
        SKID_CONT: device devices::skid_control_base;
        STOP: device devices::stop_lamp;
        CMB_METER: device devices::combination_meter;
    connections
        -- Backbone
        CC0000: bus access CCHardware.hs_can_bus_0000 -> CCSoftware.can_bus_steering;
        -- Others
        DC0010: data port SKID_CONT.self_speed -> CCSoftware.self_speed_in;
        -- CAN BUS
        can_msg_0010: bus access CCHardware.hs_can_bus_0000 -> SKID_CONT.
                      hs_can_bus_self_speed;
        -- Snip
end CruiseControlSystem.CC1;
```

Code Implementation. Now we can generate implementation codes from AADL descriptions derived in the previous steps. However, unfortunately, code implementation completely depends on the type of implementation languages used. Furthermore, even if we decide to use a certain language, e.g., the C language, we have to choose from several coding strategies depending on software platforms. This is because most languages, including the C language, do not provide any specific vocabulary that allows us to explicitly design software architectures such as processes or threads. For example, for the OSEK/VDX-C platform, we have to adopt a strategy that is different from that for the μITRON platform.

Let us consider the OSEK/VDX-C platform as an example. In this case, we can produce a configuration file in OIL (OSEK Implementation Language) and skeleton codes from AADL descriptions. An example of translation strategies from AADL into the C language on the OSEK/VDX-C platform is given below.

- Threads in AADL are converted into task definitions in an OIL configuration file. Then, skeleton codes corresponding to the task definitions are generated in a C code.
- Connections between threads in AADL are implemented as internal messages of OSEK/VDX-C. The definitions of the internal messages are prepared in the configuration file. However, function calls (message sending and receiving) are embedded into each task in the C code.
- Connections between processes in AADL that is bound to a CAN bus are implemented as CAN messages. In a similar way to the internal message, the CAN message definitions and function calls for message exchange are generated in the configuration file and the C code, respectively.

5 Variability Modeling of Cruise Control Systems Based on AADL

Next, we discuss the variability modeling of cruise control systems, i.e., CC1, CC2, and CC3. In these systems, there exit several kinds of variability at multiple levels. Thus, we explain detailed variability models on a level-by-level basis.

5.1 System Variant # 1: Adaptive Cruise Control System

We attempt to realize the adaptive cruise control system CC2 by extending the AADL descriptions of CC1 derived in Sect. 4.2. As seen in Sect. 3, CC2 differs from CC1 on the following points: an additional sensor (radar sensor), constant-distance cruise control, and brake control. Let us clarify how variability models are extracted from these differences at three different levels: *system*, *process*, and *thread* levels.

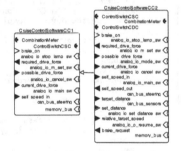

Fig. 7. Variability model diagram of the top-level software components

System Level. As shown in Fig. 3(b), a peripheral ECU (radar sensor) is newly installed in CC2. This implies that the external specification of the software component in Fig. 5(a) requires additional interfaces. On the other hand, the skid control computer needs to receive control commands for brake control. Hence, we discuss the variability modeling of these variations from two different viewpoints: *type definition* and *implementation description*, which are aligned with the linguistic structure of AADL.

Type Definition. Because of the newly installed radar sensor, the environment-system interaction varies from CC1. Moreover, the target system (adaptive cruise control system) needs to send control commands to the skid control computer in order to control the brakes. In addition to these variations, some new driver commands such as the desired distance must be recognized by the target system. For these reasons, the external specification of the top-level software component, namely, *type definition*, needs to be reconfigured.

List 7 defines the type of the top-level software component of CC2 as an extended type of CC1 (cf. List 3). List 7 also shows some additional ports for the target distance setting and brake control. Figure 7 demonstrates that the type definition of *Cruise-ControlSoftwareCC2* is expressed by extending *CruiseControlSoftwareCC1*.

List 7. Extension to type definitions (cf. List 3).

```
-- Top-level Software Component of CC2
system CruiseControlSoftwareCC2 extends CruiseControlSoftwareCC1
    features
        relative_target_speed: in data port types::kph_type; -- Radar Sensor
        target_distance: in data port types::m_type; -- Target Distance
        brake_request: out data port types::Nm_type; -- Brake Control
        -- Snip
end CruiseControlSoftwareCC2;
device skid_control_ext extends skid_control_base -- Device Extended for CC2
    features
            brake_request: in data port types::Nm_type; -- Additional Port for Brake
                        Control
end skid_control_ext;
```

Implementation Description. In addition to constant-speed cruise control, constant-distance cruise control is necessary for **CC2**. Moreover, input signals from the newly installed radar sensor need to be processed. Thus, the implementation of *Cruise-ControlSoftwareCC2* is varied as shown in List 8 and Fig. 8(a). In these descriptions, *F_C_R* is an instance of a new process that processes signals from the radar sensor and recognizes a vehicle traveling in front of the vehicle equipped with this system. On the other hand, *C_C_M* and *S_C_C* are instances of the processes *CruiseControlMainExt* and *SelfCarControlExt*, respectively. These two processes are variants of *Cruise-ControlMainBase* and *SelfCarControlBase*, respectively, used in **CC1**. The variation of these instances can be explained by comparing *C_C_M*s and *S_C_C*s shown in Figs. 8(a) and 6(a). The details of these variants are provided in the next paragraph.

List 8. Implementation description of *CruiseControlSoftwareCC2*.

```
system implementation CruiseControlSoftwareCC2.impl
    subcomponents
        C_C_M: process CruiseControlMainExt.impl; -- Variant
        S_C_C: process SelfCarControlExt.impl; -- Variant
        -- Additional Process
        F_C_R: process ForwardCarRecognitionBase.impl;
    connections
        -- Snip
end CruiseControlSoftwareCC2.impl;
```

Process Level. As shown in the previous section, the top-level software component *CruiseControlSoftwareCC2* consists of one new process and two variants of the processes used in **CC1**. We now consider an example of a variant of the process *Self-CarControlExt* so as to discuss variability modeling at the process level.

Type Description. The variant process *SelfCarControlExt* is defined by extending the process *SelfCarControlBase*. The variability of *SelfCarControlBase* and *SelfCarControlExt* is modeled as shown in List 9 and Fig. 9(a). The variability of the other process *CruiseControlMainBase* can be also described in a similar way.

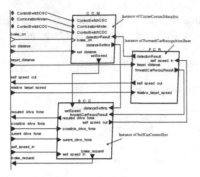
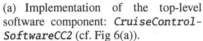

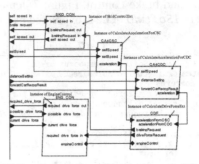
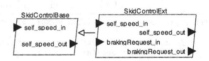

(a) Implementation of the top-level software component: *CruiseControl-SoftwareCC2* (cf. Fig 6(a)).

(b) Implementation of the process: *Self-CarControlExt* (cf. Fig. 6(b)).

Fig. 8. Schematic implementation descriptions of software components of the adaptive cruise control system

List 9. Extension to the type definition of *SelfCarControlBase* (cf. List 4).

```
process SelfCarControlExt extends SelfCarControlBase
  features
    -- Additional Ports
    forwardCarRecogResult: in data port types::FS_ForwardCarRecogResult;
    brake_request: out data port types::Nm_type;
    -- Snip
end SelfCarControlExt;
```

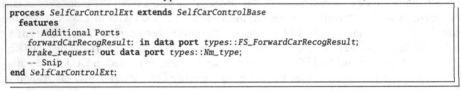

(a) Relation between the type definitions of the two processes: *SelfCarControl-Base* and *SelfCarControlExt*.

(b) Relation between the type definitions of the two threads: *SkidControlBase* and *SkidControlExt*.

Fig. 9. Variability model diagrams of processes and a threads

Implementation Description. As shown in the previous section, the external specification (type definition) of the process *SelfCarControlExt* is different from that of *SelfCarControlBase* in List 4. In other words, a new implementation description of *SelfCarControlExt* is necessary. Fortunately, we can borrow some threads that are used in the implementation of *SelfCarControlBase* (cf. List 5 and Fig. 6(b)).

The implementation of *SelfCarControlExt* by adopting the abovementioned strategy is described as shown in List 10 and Fig. 8(b). In these descriptions, *CA4CDC* is an instance of the thread *CalculateAccelerationForCDC* that is newly prepared and designated to constant-distance cruise control. Moreover, the instances *CA4-CSC* and *ENG_CON* are instantiated from the threads *CalculateAccelerationForCSC* and *EngineControl*. Fortunately, we can substitute these two instances for those in the implementation of *SelfCarControlBase* of CC1. The remaining instances *CDF* and *SKID_CON*, which are instantiated from *CalculateDriveForceExt* and *Skid-ControlExt*, can be prepared by extending the base threads used in *SelfCarControl-Base* (see the next section for details).

List 10. Implementation description of *SelfCarControlExt*.

```
process implementation SelfCarControlExt.impl
    subcomponents
        CA4CDC: thread CalculateAccelerationForCDC.impl; -- Additional thread
        CA4CSC: thread CalculateAccelerationForCSC.impl; -- Not varied
        ENG_CON: thread EngineControl.impl; -- Not varied
        CDF: thread CalculateDriveForceExt.impl; -- Variants
        SKID_CON: thread SkidControlExt.impl; -- Variants
    connections
        -- Snip
end SelfCarControlExt.impl;
```

Thread Level. The threads *CalculateDriveForceExt* and *SkidControlExt* of CC2 are realized by extending the threads *CalculateDriveForceBase* and *Skid-ControlBase* used in CC1. We consider the variant thread *SkidControlExt* for further discussion at the bottom level (thread level).

Type Description. The extended thread *SkidControlExt* can be generated by adding a new interface for sending control commands to the skid control computer. Therefore, *SkidControlExt* can be modeled as a variant of *SkidConntrolBase* as shown in List 11 and Fig. 9(b). We can apply the same discussion to the other thread *Calculate-DriveForceExt*. List 11 also gives the type definition of the newly prepared thread *CalculateAccelerationForCDC*.

List 11. Extension to the type definition of *SkidControlBase* (cf. List 4).

```
thread SkidControlExt extends SkidControlBase
        features -- Additional Ports
            brakingRequest_out: out data port types::Nm_type;
            brakingRequest_in: in data port types::Nm_type;
            -- Snip
end SkidControlExt
thread CalculateAccelerationForCDC
    features
        selfSpeed: in data port types::kph_type;
        distanceSetting: in data port types::m_type;
        forwardCarRecogResult: in data port types::FS_ForwardCarRecogResult;
        acceleration: out data port types::mpss_type;
    flows
        FS0000: flow path forwardCarRecogResult -> acceleration;
end CalculateAccelerationForCDC;
```

In the case of CC2, it is not necessary to consider the variability of implementations at the thread level. Thus, we shall return to this subject later.

We have seen that the adaptive cruise control system CC2 can be composed of new components, the same components as those of CC1, and variants of the base components used in CC1. These variants are generated by extending the type definitions of the base components. AADL can also handle the variability of implementation descriptions (see *refined to* in List 2). Hence, let us shift to the next topic: variability modeling of implementations.

5.2   Variant # 2: Full Speed Range Adaptive Cruise Control System

This section attempts to realize the full range adaptive cruise control system CC3 by further extending the AADL descriptions derived in Sect. 5.1. In particular, this section focuses on the variability of implementation descriptions because the variations of type definitions of CC3 are quite similar to those of CC2.

As explained in Sect. 3, CC3 is mainly different from the other systems in the following points: an additional sensor (object recognition sensor) and relaxation of the speed limits such that the lower limit is extended to 0 km/h.

System Level. The implementation of the top-level software component of CC3 is shown in List 12 and Fig. 10. The process S_C_C, which is an instance of *SelfCar-ControlExt*, has the same interfaces (same type) as S_C_C in Fig. 8(a); however, these two S_C_Cs have different implementations. This can be realized by comparing List 12 with List 8. The reason for this variation is that CC3 requires a new algorithm for the constant-distance cruise control with the wider speed range 0 km/h–100 km/h.

List 12. Implementation description of *CruiseControlSoftwareCC3*.

```
system implementation CruiseControlSoftwareCC3.impl
   subcomponents
      C_C_M: process CruiseControlMainExt.impl;
      S_C_C: process SelfCarControlExt.impl_ors; -- Variant
      F_C_R: process ForwardCarRecognitionExt.impl;
      -- Snip
end CruiseControlSoftwareCC3.impl;
```

Process Level. As shown in the previous section, the process *SelfCarControlExt* has two different implementations: *SelfCarControlExt.imp* and *Self-CarControlExt.imp_ors*. These relationships can be modeled as shown in Fig. 11(a).

List 13 gives the same implementation description *SelfCarControlExt.imp_ors*. As was the case with S_C_C in the previous section, the thread CA4CDC, which is an instance of *CalculateAccelerationForCDC*, has the same type as that shown in Fig. 8(b). However, these two CA4CDCs are implemented in different ways. On the other hand, the other threads comprising *SelfCarControlExt* are identical with those shown in Fig. 8(b). In this case, we can describe the implementation of *SelfCarControlExt* by extending the implementation *SelfCarControlExt.imp* in List 10. In List 13, *refined to* forms the variability model of *SelfCarControlExt.imp* and *SelfCarControlExt.imp_ors*.

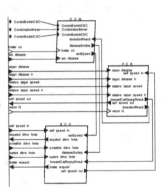

Fig. 10. Schematic implementation description of *Cruise-ControlSotwareCC3*

List 13. Extension to the implementation description of *SelfCarControlExt*.

```
process implementation SelfCarControlExt.impl_ors extends SelfCarControlExt.impl
   subcomponents
      CA4CDC: refined to thread CalculateAccelerationForCDC.impl_ors; -- Variant
end SelfCarControlExt.impl_ors
```

Thread Level. The thread *CalculateAccelerationForCDC* has two different kinds of implementations: *CalculateAccelerationForCDC.imp* and *CalculateAccel-erationForCDC.imp_ors*; these implementations are dedicated to CC2 and CC3, respectively. List 14 and Fig. 11(b) show the variability model of this thread-level variation.

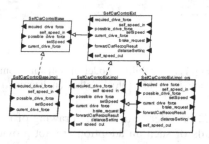 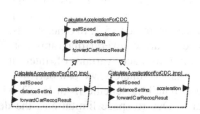

(a) Variability model of the implementations of *SelfCarControlBase* and *SelfCarControlExt*.

(b) Variability model of the implementations of *CalculateAccelerationForCDC*.

Fig. 11. Variability model diagrams of processes and threads

On the basis of what we discussed in Sects. 5.1 and 5.2, we can understand that AADL can provide models for capturing the variability of cruise control systems at multiple levels: system, process, and thread levels. Moreover, the *type–implementation* mechanism of AADL allows us to create models of minor variability with invariant interface specifications. Therefore, we can conclude that AADL is highly capable of variability modeling that is applicable to a complicated variation of real automotive systems.

List 14. The extension to the implementation description of *CalculateAccelerationForCDC*.

```
-- CalculateAccelerationForCDC for CC2
-- Base Description
thread implementation CalculateAccelerationForCDC.impl
end CalculateAccelerationForCDC.impl;
-- Variant
thread implementation CalculateAccelerationForCDC.impl_ors extends
        CalculateAccelerationForCDC.impl
end CalculateAccelerationForCDC.impl_ors;
```

In order for the characteristics of AADL to be enhanced, it needs to be precisely compared with other ADLs. Unfortunately, due to space limitations, we will present only a brief comparison between AADL and SysML in the next section.

5.3 Comparison with SysML

This section provides a qualitative comparison between AADL-based variability modeling and a SysML-based one. Similar to the *type definition* of AADL, the block definition diagram (BDD) of SysML defines an external specification (interface design) of blocks, which are the basic elements of SysML. SysML is derived from UML; therefore, the BDD is also inherently equipped with the inheritance mechanism. For example, Fig. 12 shows that the block *CruiseControlSoftwareCC2* is obtained by inheriting properties of the block *CruiseControlSoftwareCC1*. A comparison of Fig. 7 with Fig. 12

reveals that SysML provides variability modeling equivalent to AADL from the view-point of an external specification.

Furthermore, the internal block dia-gram (IBD) of SysML describes the func-tional decomposition of a block such as *implementation description* of AADL. However, SysML cannot describe the variability of an internal specification, which we saw in Sect. 5.2. In other words, we have to draw several diagrams cor-responding to each variant of internal sub-blocks. Fortunately, we can borrow a

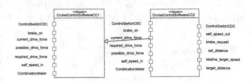

Fig. 12. Variability model of software compo-nents in SysML (block definition diagrams)

variation handling scheme from EAST-ADL2 in order to avoid the drawing of many diagrams. Due to space limitations, the details of such an adoption are not provided here.

6   Conclusion and Future Work

This paper presented the basic procedure for an AADL-based development of auto-motive control systems. We focused on software development and provided detailed AADL descriptions of cruise control systems. The discussion on the variability model-ing shows that AADL can efficiently deal with a variation of systems at multiple levels. We also found that the *type – implementation* structure of AADL brings high flexibil-ity to variability modeling. A brief comparison of AADL with SysML elucidated the characteristics of variability modeling in AADL.

In the future, it is necessary to consider an automatic code generator and a config-uration management technique based on variability modeling. It is also necessary to perform precise comparisons between AADL and other ADLs; this issue will be dis-cussed in a future study.

References

1. Interim report of the society for the study of reliability and security of information systems/-software in an advanced information society, tech. rep., the Ministry of Economy, Trade and Industry (June 2009),
   http://www.meti.go.jp/english/press/data/20090528_01.html
2. Architecture Analysis & Design Language (AADL). AS5506, SAE International (2004)
3. Architecture Analysis & Design Language (AADL). AS5506A, SAE International (2009)
4. OMG Systems Modeling Language (OMG SysML). Object Management Group (2007)
5. A UML Profile for Modeling and Analysis of Real-Time and Embedded Systems (MARTE). Object Management Group, http://www.omgmarte.org
6. EAST-ADL. ITEA EAST-EEA (Embedded Electronic Architecture)
7. EAST-ADL2. ATESST (Advancing Traffic Efficiency and Safety through Software Technol-ogy), http://www.atesst.org
8. IEEE Std. 830-1998 IEEE Recommended Practice for Software Requirements Specifications. IEEE (1998)

Extending Variability for OCL Interpretation

Claas Wilke, Michael Thiele, and Christian Wende

Technische Universität Dresden
Department of Computer Science
Institute for Software and Multimedia Technology
Software Technology Group
{claas.wilke,michael.thiele,christian.wende}@inf.tu-dresden.de

Abstract. In recent years, OCL advanced from a language used to constrain UML models to a constraint language that is applied to various modelling languages. This includes Domain Specific Languages (DSLs) and meta-modelling languages like MOF or Ecore. Consequently, it is rather common to provide variability for OCL parsers to work with different modelling languages. A second variability dimension relates to the technical space that models are realised in. Current OCL interpreters do not support such variability as their implementation is typically bound to a specific technical space like Java, Ecore, or a specific model repository. In this paper we propose a generic adaptation architecture for OCL that hides models and model instances behind well-defined interfaces. We present how the implementation of such an architecture for DresdenOCL enables reuse of the same OCL interpreter for various technical spaces and evaluate our approach in three case studies.

Keywords: OCL, OCL Infrastructure, OCL Tool, MDSD, Modelling, Constraint Interpretation, Technological Spaces, Variability, Adaptation.

1 Introduction

Model-driven software development (MDSD) aims to abstract from concrete software implementations and uses models to describe software systems. To ensure consistency of models, the Object Constraint Language (OCL) [1] has been developed as an extension of the Unified Modelling Language (UML) [2,3]. In recent years, OCL advanced to a constraint language used for various modelling and meta-modelling languages [4] like the Meta Object Facility (MOF) [5] or Ecore [6].

While OCL constraints are defined on models, they are evaluated on instances of these models. Besides instances of constrained models stored in various model repositories like MOFLON [7], Netbeans MDR [5], or EMF [6], they also can be realised using classic programming languages like Java [8], or C# [9], stored in database systems [10], or described with XML [11].

Several OCL tools support *variability at the model level* [12,13], i.e., constraint definition on different types of models. Yet, *variability at the model instance level*, i.e., constraint evaluation on different types of model instances, is not provided.

D.C. Petriu, N. Rouquette, Ø. Haugen (Eds.): MODELS 2010, Part I, LNCS 6394, pp. 361–375, 2010.

For OCL compilers as presented in [5,8,9,10] such variability is not possible, as the code generated from OCL constraints needs to be bound to the technical spaces used at model instance level. However, for OCL interpreters, we argue that a decoupling of the semantics evaluation from a concrete model instance type is possible. In this paper we propose a *generic adaptation architecture* for OCL interpreters that hides models and model instances behind well-defined interfaces. This enables reuse of the complete OCL infrastructure including the OCL parser, standard library and interpreter. We implemented such an infrastructure in *DresdenOCL* [14].

The remainder of this paper is structured as follows. In Sect. 2 we analyse diverse applications for OCL and motivate two variation points for OCL interpretation. In Sect. 3 we discuss the design and implementation of a *generic adaptation architecture* for OCL interpreters to realise the motivated variation points in DresdenOCL. In Sect. 4 we document the feasibility and benefits of our adaptation architecture by applying it to three case studies that use OCL with different combinations of models and model instances. In Sect. 5 we elaborate on lessons learnt during implementation and application of our approach. Finally, we present related work in Sect. 6 and conclude our contributions in Sect. 7.

2   Foundations

Originally, OCL was designed as a constraint language for UML. Recent work showed that OCL can be applied to various other modelling and meta-modelling languages. Thus, an abstract description of OCL and its relation to modelling languages is sensible.

2.1   The Generic Three Layer Architecture

As discussed in [8], OCL evaluation always involves three adjacent layers of the *MOF layered architecture* [15]. This leads to the notion of a *generic three layer architecture* for OCL as depicted in Fig. 1 (a). At layer Mn+1, OCL is bound to a concrete modelling language that has to provide concepts like types, navigable properties, and possibly operations. This binding allows the definition of OCL constraints on models that are described by the meta-model (Mn layer). During the evaluation of these constraints, an OCL interpreter has to query model instance elements for their properties or invoke operations on them (Mn-1 layer).

Model instances are often realised in a different *technological space* [16,17] than their model. Then, there are two model representations at the layer Mn (cf. Fig. 1 (a)): the original constrained *model* and a *model realisation* implementing the model in a specific technological space. The model realisation is typically derived by a transformation of the model (e.g., when using the *Eclipse Modeling Framework (EMF)* [18]). This leads to the problem that the connection between the different model representations at the Mn layer is hidden inside the transformation and may not be accessible from the OCL infrastructure. An

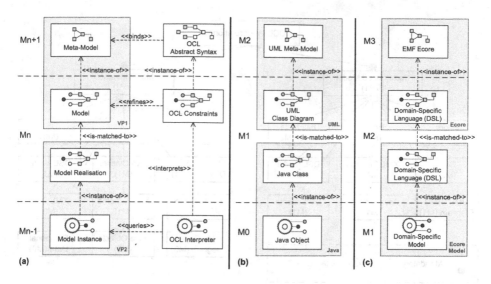

Fig. 1. The Generic Three Layer Architecture

algorithm matching the elements of the model realisation and the constrained model can re-establish this connection.

Instances of this generic three layer architecture are shown in Fig. 1 (b) and (c). Fig. 1 (b) exemplifies the application of OCL to constrain UML class diagrams. At M2 (Mn+1) the OCL abstract syntax is bound to the UML meta-model. At M1 (Mn) constraints are defined against UML class diagrams. At this layer the original UML model is transformed to a Java-based model representation where UML classes correspond to Java classes. At M0 (Mn-1) the OCL constraints are evaluated against Java objects.

The example in Fig. 1 (c) demonstrates the application of OCL constraints to define well-formedness rules (WFRs) for DSLs built with EMF Ecore. The generic three layer architecture is lifted one layer: At M3 (Mn+1) the OCL abstract syntax is bound to the Ecore meta-meta-model. At M2 (Mn) a new DSL is defined using Ecore and OCL-based WFRs. Since EMF contributes a runtime infrastructure for models and model instances no transformation is required at M2. The model and the model representation are identical. At M1 (Mn-1) the WFRs are evaluated against models built with the defined DSL.

2.2 Variation Points of OCL Interpretation

With instantiation of our generic three layer architecture for various OCL applications found in literature, we identified two variation points. The first variation point (VP1) describes variability at Mn+1 and Mn w.r.t. the modelling language used to specify constrained models. The second variation point (VP2) relates to variability at Mn and Mn-1 t w.r.t. the technological space model instances are realised and validated in (cf. Fig. 1 (a)).

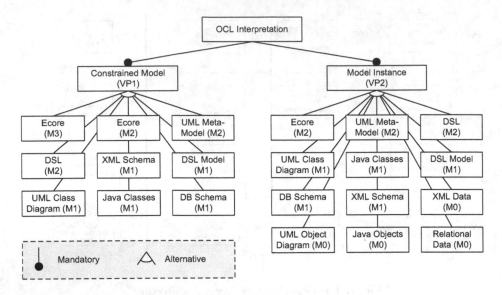

Fig. 2. Features of OCL interpretation

With the generic three layer architecture it is possible to vary several models and model instances independently. For example the same UML model can be combined with OCL evaluation on model instances realised in Java or a relational database, or the OCL evaluation on XML-based model instances can be used for models built with the UML or the Ecore meta-model. The feature model [19] depicted in Fig. 2 documents the variation space of OCL applications found in literature. The only constraint a variant configuration of the generic architecture has to satisfy is that the model instance bound to VP2 is located exactly one meta-layer below the model bound to VP1.

Several OCL tools provide support for variation on VP1 [6,13,14,20]. Yet, those tools do not address VP2 as their supported models require specific instances (typically both located in the same technological space). We argue that this tight coupling can be reduced to avoid the reimplementation of OCL interpreters for different technological spaces. In the following we contribute an implementation of the generic three layer architecture that supports VP1 and VP2.

3   Implementation

In this section we discuss the implementation of a generic adaptation architecture for DresdenOCL to realise the variation points identified in the previous section. First, we present *model adaptation* to address VP1. Afterwards, we discuss how *model instance adaptation* supports VP2.

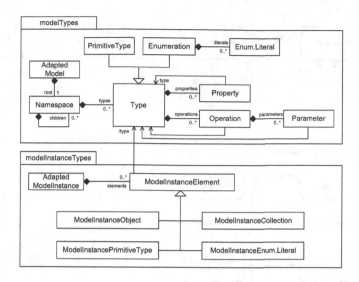

Fig. 3. Interfaces for model and model instance adaptation

3.1   Model Adaptation (VP1)

In order to define OCL constraints for various models, DresdenOCL requires a set of common interfaces defining structures that provide a dedicated abstraction to navigate and query models. Given this specific application purpose the interfaces – called `modelTypes` (or `pivotModel`) [12] – slightly differ from other generalisations of object-oriented metamodels like Ecore. They define the basic concepts such as `Type`, `Property`, `Operation` and `Parameter` that bind OCL constraints to a concrete model (cf. Fig. 3). DresdenOCL uses these concepts to parse and statically analyse OCL constraints, e.g., the OCL parser can determine the `Type` of OCL expressions.

For every model that shall be connected with DresdenOCL, a *model adapter* component has to be implemented (cf. Fig. 4, Mn+1 layer). It contains individual adapters that map concepts of the model's meta-model to corresponding concepts of the `modelTypes`. E.g., the UML meta-model concept `UMLClass` is adapted to the `modelTypes` concept `Type`. Furthermore, the model adapter component has to create instances of these adapters on demand resulting in an *adapted model* (cf. Fig. 4, Mn layer). The adapters are only created for model elements that are required and existing adapters are cached. Thus, unnecessary and expensive adaptation is avoided, especially when working on large models of which only parts are constrained.

3.2   Model Instance Adaptation (VP2)

In our generic adaptation architecture we applied the same principles for model instances as those are also hidden behind a set of common interfaces. This enables

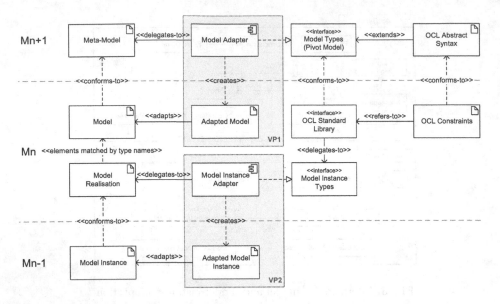

Fig. 4. The Generic Adaptation Architecture of DresdenOCL

the reuse of the same OCL interpreter and standard library for the dynamic evaluation of OCL constraints on model instances in various technical spaces.

To provide means for model instance adaptation, we introduced the `model-InstanceTypes`. The `modelInstanceTypes` are a set of `ModelInstanceElements` representing instances of primitive types, collections and objects defined in the model. Fig. 3 illustrates that `ModelInstanceElements` are typed. Since the model instance and the model can reside in different technological spaces, the types have to be computed in different ways for different model instances. E.g., a Java object's type in the model realisation is a Java class that can be matched to a UML class, as shown in Fig. 1 (b). This type computation is implemented by a specific *type matcher* component. For each element of a model instance the type matcher reflects the element's type in the model realisation and matches this type to a type in the model. Since the type matcher requires technical space specific information, each `modelInstanceTypes` implementation has to provide its own type matcher. On the other hand, model types are only accessed via standardised interfaces. Therefore, a type matcher can be reused in connection with all supported `modelTypes`. As a result, the interpreter can reason on the type of the `ModelInstanceElements` and thus, can select the constraints that have to be evaluated for these elements.

Additionally, the OCL interpreter needs to retrieve properties or invoke operations for which reflection capabilities are required. The `modelInstanceTypes` have to provide such capabilities. To ensure variability, reflection operations are part of the interfaces that have to be implemented by all `modelInstanceTypes`. This enables the model and model instance independent reuse of the OCL

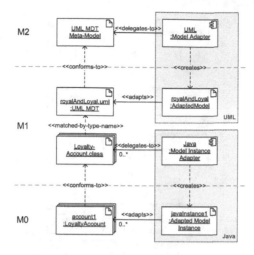

Fig. 5. Adapters used in the Royal and Loyal case study

interpreter and the OCL standard library, since type reasoning and reflective property and operation calls are hidden behind well-defined interfaces.

Like model elements, `ModelInstanceElements` are adapted on demand and adapted objects are cached to improve the performance and to avoid phenomena like *object schizophrenia* [21].

4   Case Studies

In this section we present three case studies to demonstrate the benefits of our generic adaptation architecture. The examples use different combinations of models and model instances located at different layers of the MOF layered architecture to illustrate the variability of our approach.

4.1   The Royal and Loyal System Example

As a first case study, we modelled and implemented the *royal and loyal system example* as defined in [3]. This example was designed by WARMER AND KLEPPE to teach the Object Constraint Language. It consists of 13 UML classes (including inheritance and enumeration types) and 130 constraints. We specified the royal and loyal system with a UML model (VP1) built with the *Eclipse Model Development Tools (MDT)* [6]. The model was implemented and instantiated in Java (VP2). Consequently, constraints were evaluated on Java objects.

The adapters required for the royal and loyal case study are shown in Fig. 5. To parse the royal and loyal constraints in DresdenOCL, a *UML model adapter* component was implemented. It adapts the required concepts of the UML meta-model to the `modelTypes` of DresdenOCL at the M2 layer. Hence, the royal and

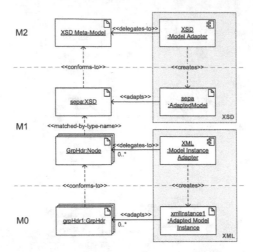

Fig. 6. Adapters used in the SEPA case study

loyal class diagram was adapted as a model at the M1 layer. For the Java implementation, a *Java model instance adapter* component was implemented that adapts the Java model elements (classes of the package `java.lang.reflect`) to the `modelInstanceTypes`. Thus, the objects of the royal and loyal Java implementation were adapted as a model instance in DresdenOCL at the M0 layer. Since the UML classes are transformed to Java classes, both are located at the M1 layer. Hence, the Java model realisation has to be matched with the UML model during interpretation.

The royal and loyal case study demonstrates that our generic adaptation architecture is able to support the common interpretation of OCL constraints defined on UML classes for Java objects.

4.2   SEPA Business Rules

In our second case study we interpreted OCL business rules defined on an XML schema (VP1) for XML documents (VP2) conforming to this schema. The NOMOS SOFTWARE company provides a service to check business rules on financial *Single Euro Payments Area (SEPA)* messages that are used in financial transactions of bank offices as defined by the *European Payment Council (EPC)*, *ISO20022*, and the *Euro Banking Association (EBA)* [22,23,24]. SEPA messages are described and shipped as XML documents. NOMOS SOFTWARE uses OCL constraints defined on XML schemas to validate XML documents against a set of business rules to ensure the consistency of SEPA messages. We evaluated about 120 constraints that are provided with the online demo.[1]

The adapters required for the SEPA case study are shown in Fig. 6. To parse the SEPA constraints into DresdenOCL, the *XSD model adapter* component

---

[1] http://www.nomos-software.com/demo.html

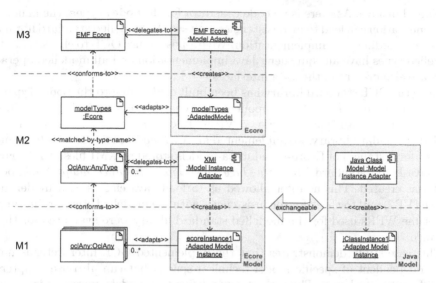

Fig. 7. Adapters used in the Standard Library case study

adapts required concepts of the XSD meta-model to the modelTypes of Dresden-OCL at the M2 layer. Consequently, the SEPA XML schema was adapted as a model at the M1 layer. The *XML instance adapter* component adapts the XML model elements (mainly the class org.w3c.dom.Node) to the modelInstance-Types. Thus, the nodes of the SEPA messages were adapted as model instances in DresdenOCL at the M0 layer.

The constraints were evaluated for three different XML files and the results have been successfully compared with the results of the NOMOS demo. This demonstrates that our model instance adaptation allows DresdenOCL to transparently interpret constraints on XML files as well, since the OCL interpreter had not to be modified for the SEPA case study.

4.3 The OCL2.2 Standard Library

The last case study depicts the ability to load different model instances of one model in order to check for inconsistencies between these instances. In this example we checked well-formedness rules (WFRs) for the OCL standard library of DresdenOCL. DresdenOCL's standard library is explicitly modelled as an instance of the modelTypes, describing predefined OCL types like Integer, OclAny or Sequence and their associated operations. Hence, accessing those types is reduced to a simple model import while the model can conveniently be queried, validated or altered [12]. The WFRs can be used to check whether all OCL types are declared and whether they support all operations that are defined by the current OCL specification [1].

Although modelling the standard library leads to great flexibility, an implementation that provides its dynamic semantics is still required. This implementation is realised in Java. As there is no code generator for the `modelTypes`, the manual implementation can lead to inconsistencies between the modelled standard library and the according Java implementation. We propose to use OCL to check that all modelled types have an equivalent Java implementation and all modelled operations are also present in the Java interfaces.

Since the OCL standard library has been built conforming to the `modelTypes`, an *EMF Ecore model adapter* component was required to parse OCL constraints defined on the `modelTypes` (cf. Fig. 7, VP1). To evaluate the constraints on the modelled standard library, we implemented an *XMI model instance adapter* component for instances of Ecore-based meta-models stored as XMI files (VP2). For the Java-based standard library a *Java class model instance adapter* component was created. This adapter allowed us to load Java classes as a model instance (VP2) and to check for inconsistencies with the modelled standard library. The same WFRs used for the modelled standard library were evaluated for this instance.

This case study demonstrates that the implemented OCL interpreter is not only independent of specific model technical spaces, but can also use adapters for different meta-layers. Thus, constraints defined on models, meta-models, and even meta-meta-models can be interpreted.

4.4   Future Case Studies

For future case studies we plan to implement new model adapters for VP1 including *WSDL* and *SQL-DDL* and further model instance adapters for VP2 including *C#* and *relational databases*.

5   Lessons Learnt

In this section we highlight some challenges we faced during the design and implementation of our generic adaptation architecture for DresdenOCL. We present solutions to these challenges and possible improvements.

Type Matching. Currently, type matching is realised by a simple type name match (including the names of their enclosing namespaces whenever possible). E.g., the Java class `LoyaltyAccount` is matched to the UML class `Loyalty-Account` in the royal and loyal case study. This matching algorithm can be rather complex and often information that could be used to improve the matching is hidden inside the adapters. E.g., when adapting an instance of an EMF Ecore model, one could use the *generator model* provided by Ecore to retrieve information used in the Ecore to Java transformation. We plan to improve this process by introducing type matching strategies that can be implemented using the *chain of responsibility* pattern [25]. The chain could start by trying to match the types using a model instance specific matcher that regards model transformation information whenever possible and ends by trying to simply match the type names as currently done.

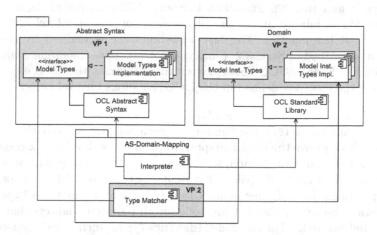

Fig. 8. Mapping the OCL abstract syntax and OCL domain; cf. [1, Sect. 10]

Element Unwrapping. Another problem when using adapters for `modelInstance-Types` is the unwrapping mechanism of adapted elements when invoking operations on the `ModelInstanceElements`. E.g., to invoke an operation of an adapted Java object we require `java.lang.Objects` as parameters instead of `Model-InstanceElements`. This unwrapping mechanism is easy for elements that have been adapted before as they simply can be unwrapped again. Unfortunately, during interpretation of OCL constraints, new instances of primitive types or new collections can be created by the standard library (e.g., when invoking the OCL operation `size()` on a collection that returns an `Integer` instance). Thus, a model instance adapter has to provide operations to reconvert primitive types and collections into elements of the adapted model instances. In some cases this can become rather complicated as the adaptation between types of the instance and the `modelInstanceTypes` interfaces has not to be bijective. For example, Java `ints` and `java.lang.Integers` are both mapped to `ModelInstaceIntegers`. During unwrapping, the Java model instance adapter component has to reflect whether the method to invoke requires an `int`, an `Integer` or another Java integer-like type instance. The unwrapping mechanism of an adapted instance can be considered as the most complicated and error-prone part of the complete model instance adaptation. Fortunately, model instances providing only structural information do not need this unwrapping mechanism as they provide no operations.

Comparision to Standard OCL Semantics Evaluation. The OCL specification [1, Sect. 10] defines three packages required for OCL evaluation: *Abstract syntax (AS)*, *Domain* and *AS-Domain-Mapping* (contributing *type-value mapping* and *expression-evaluation mapping*). Equivalent concepts can be identified in the presented approach as depicted in Fig. 8. The *Abstract Syntax* is defined by the `Model Types` and the `OCL Abstract Syntax`. In contrast to the OCL specification, different `Model Types Implementations` provide model variability and enable reuse of the `OCL Abstract Syntax`. The *Domain* is defined by the `Model`

Inst. Types and the OCL Standard Library. Different Model Inst. Types Impl. provide variability at the model instance (or domain) level and enable reusing the OCL semantics. The *type-value mapping* is realised by the Type Matcher as described in Sect. 3.2. Finally, the *expression-evaluation mapping* is realised by the DresdenOCL Interpreter that traverses the OCL expressions and invokes the methods defined in the OCL semantics for evaluation.

Automated Adapter Creation. The adaptation process of models and model instances contains parts that are similar for each adaptation and thus can be automated. To improve the model adaptation process, we developed a code generator for the creation of model adapter components. The code generator requires an annotated meta-model describing the relation of meta-model concepts to the modelTypes (e.g., the UML meta-class Classifier is annotated as a Type). The code generator generates the skeleton code for all required adapters that has to be completed manually. For the modelInstanceTypes, such a code generator is currently missing, but could be implemented as well.

Adaptation Testing. We developed two generic JUnit test suites that can be used to test the adaptation of a model or model instance, respectively. The test suites are initialised with a model or model instance that contains all the adapted concepts that shall be tested. The test suites then check whether all required methods to retrieve Types, Operations, Properties for the variation point VP1 are implemented or whether the reflection mechanism provided by VP2 is supported appropriately. These generic test suites helped us to ensure that all existing adaptations behave in the same expected manner and to easily detect wrong adaptations of elements. Furthermore, these test suites can be used to ensure the absence of specific bugs in *all* adaptations by adding new test cases if such a bug is detected in *one* of the adaptations.

6   Related Work

In the following we will discuss alternative tools to parse, interpret, or compile OCL constraints and the means they provide to support variability for models and model instances:

- The *USE* tool [26] contributes an OCL simulator that can evaluate OCL constraints against model snapshots. It is bound to UML class, UML object and UML sequence diagrams and does not provide means for model or model instance adaptations. Nevertheless, a case study proofed that it is possible to create snapshots from Java runtime objects that can be evaluated with USE [27].
- The *OCLE* tool [28] interprets OCL constraints on UML models. Furthermore, it provides a compiler to generate a Java implementation from a constrained UML model and the according OCL constraints. Model adaptation is not supported. Although OCLE does not allow for real model instance adaptation, XML files can be treated as model instances by transforming them into UML object diagrams.

- The *MIP OCL2 Parser* [29] is a Java library for parsing OCL constraints provided by the Institute for Defense Analyses. Constraints are checked syntactically and semantically against a UML class diagram. To use the parser, one must provide a Java implementation of the abstract UML model expected by the parser. Thus, the MIP parser provides very limited means for model adaptation. Since MIP does not contribute an interpreter or compiler for constraints, model instance adaptation is not relevant.
- The OCL interpreter and compiler provided by the *Kent Modeling Framework (KMF)* supports model adaptation via a central *Bridge* model [13]. Both, the compiler and the interpreter depend on a Java-based representation of model instances. Thus, model instance adaptation is not supported.
- The *Epsilon Validation Language (EVL)* introduced in [20] is quite similar to OCL. It comes with an interpreter that can be used for various EMF-based languages. Thus, model adaptation is possible. In [30], a first approach to reuse OCL semantics at the model instance level for various model realisations was proposed. This approach is limited to model instances defined at the same meta-layer as their models and operation calls are not supported.
- A standard OCL interpreter for EMF is provided by *MDT OCL* [6]. It is also tightly integrated with EMF and supports model adaptation for various EMF languages. The interpreter directly supports model instances represented in EMF. MDT OCL's architecture is highly extensible and could be adapted to other model instances using *Java Generics* [31]. However, we are not aware of any such adaptations.

This analysis of related work consolidates that variability at model level is considered useful and has already been implemented in various OCL tools. Supporting variability at model instance level – as suggested in this paper – is a consequent continuation of our previous and other's related work.

7 Conclusion

In this paper we presented a generic approach for OCL interpretation that addresses both model and model instance variability. Various OCL infrastructures support model variability, whereas – to the best of our knowledge – none of the existing OCL infrastructure supports complete model instance variability. Our approach addresses this problem by abstracting from domain-specific concepts and by introducing well-defined interfaces for models and their instances. With our implementation of such a generic adaptation architecture, the same OCL interpreter was applied to three case studies that are located at different modelling layers and use different combinations of models and model instances. We avoided new implementations of the OCL standard library for various different technical spaces and hence contribute a reusable OCL interpreter.

For future work, we plan to improve our approach by addressing the issues mentioned in Sect. 5. We are interested in evaluating the performance impact of our adapter-based approach for OCL interpretation. Therefore, we plan a benchmark comparing our interpreter with other interpreters and compilers, and a continuation of our previous work [10] on extensible OCL compilation.

Acknowledgements

We want to thank Tricia Balfe of NOMOS SOFTWARE for providing data for the XML case study and for continuous feedback during adaptation of the case study. Furthermore, we would like to thank all people that are or were involved in the DresdenOCL project.

References

1. OMG: Object Constraint Language, Version 2.2. Object Management Group (OMG), Needham (February 2010)
2. OMG: Unified Modeling Language^{TM}, OMG Available Specification, Version 2.2. Object Management Group (OMG), Needham (February 2009)
3. Warmer, J., Kleppe, A.: The Object Constraint Language - Getting Your Models Ready for MDA, 2nd edn. Pearson Education Inc., Boston (2003)
4. Akehurst, D., Howells, W., McDonald-Maier, K.: UML/OCL - Detaching the Standard Library
5. Loecher, S., Ocke, S.: A Metamodel-based OCL-compiler for UML and MOF. In: Stevens, P., Whittle, J., Booch, G. (eds.) UML 2003. LNCS, vol. 2863. Springer, Heidelberg (2003)
6. Eclipse Model Development Tools, http://www.eclipse.org/modeling/mdt/
7. Amelunxen, C., Königs, A., Rötschke, T., Schürr, A.: Metamodeling with MOFLON. In: Schürr, A., Nagl, M., Zündorf, A. (eds.) AGTIVE 2007. LNCS, vol. 5088, pp. 573–574. Springer, Heidelberg (2008)
8. Demuth, B., Wilke, C.: Model and Object Verification by Using Dresden OCL. In: Proceedings of the Russian-German Workshop Innovation Information Technologies: Theory and Practice, July 25-31. Ufa State Aviation Technical University, Ufa (2009)
9. Arnold, D.: C# Compiler Extension to Support the Object Constraint Language Version 2.0. Master Thesis, Carleton University, Ottawa, Ontario (2004)
10. Heidenreich, F., Wende, C., Demuth, B.: A Framework for Generating Query Language Code from OCL Invariants. In: Akehurst, D.H., Gogolla, M., Zschaler, S. (eds.) Ocl4All - Modelling Systems with OCL. ECEASST, vol. 9. Technische Universität, Berlin (2008)
11. Sakr, S., Gaafar, A.: Towards Complete Mapping between XML/XQuery and UML/OCL. In: Proceedings of the IADIS e-society 2004 conference (ES 2004), Avila, Spain. (2004)
12. Bräuer, M., Demuth, B.: Model-Level Integration of the OCL Standard Library Using a Pivot Model with Generics Support. In: Akehurst, D.H., Gogolla, M., Zschaler, S. (eds.) Ocl4All - Modelling Systems with OCL. ECEASST, vol. 9. Technische Universität, Berlin (2008)
13. Akehurst, D., Patrascoiu, O.: Ocl 2.0 - Implementing the Standard for Multiple Metamodels. In: OCL2.0 - Industry standard or scientific playground? - Proceedings of the UML 2003 Workshop, pp. 19–25 (2003) (Citeseer)
14. DresdenOCL, http://dresden-ocl.sourceforge.net/
15. OMG: Meta-Object Facility (MOF) Core Specification, Version 2.0. Object Management Group (OMG) (January 2006)
16. Kurtev, I., Bézivin, J., Aksit, M.: Technological spaces: An initial appraisal. In: CoopIS, DOA (2002)

17. Bézivin, J., Kurtev, I.: Model-based technology integration with the technical space concept. In: Metainformatics Symposium (2005) (Citeseer)
18. Eclipse Modeling Framework (EMF) Project, http://www.eclipse.org/modeling/emf/
19. Kang, K., Cohen, S., Hess, J., Novak, W., Peterson, A.: Feature-Oriented Domain Analysis (FODA) Feasibility Study. Technical Report CMU/SEI-90-TR-0211990, Software Engineering Institute (1990)
20. Kolovos, D., Paige, R., Polack, F.: Detecting and Repairing Inconsistencies across Heterogeneous Models. In: Proceedings of the 2008 International Conference on Software Testing, Verification, and Validation, pp. 356–364. IEEE Computer Society, Los Alamitos (2008)
21. Szyperski, C.: Component Software: Beyond Object-Oriented Programming. Addison-Wesley Longman Publishing Co., Inc., Boston (2002)
22. ISO: Payments Standards - Initiation - UNIFI (ISO 20022) Message Definition Report. International Organization for Standardization (ISO), Geneva (October 2006)
23. EPC: SEPA Business-To-Business Direct Debit Scheme Customer-To-Bank Implementation Guidelines, Version 1.3. Number EPC131-08. European Payments Council (EPC), Brussels (October 2009)
24. Euro Banking Association (EBA), https://www.abe-eba.eu/
25. Gamma, E., Helm, R., Johnson, R., Vlissides, J.: Design Patterns - Elements of Reusable Object-Oriented Software, 2nd edn. Addison-Wesley Professional, Indianapolis (1995)
26. Gogolla, M., Büttner, F., Richters, M.: USE: A UML-based Specification Environment for Validating UML and OCL. Science of Computer Programming 69(1-3), 27–34 (2007)
27. Occello, A., Dery-Pinna, A.M., Riveill, M.: Validation and Verification of an UML/OCL Model with USE and B: Case Study and Lessons Learnt. In: Proceedings of the Software Testing Verification and Validation Workshop, ICSTW 2008. IEEE International Conference on Software Testing, Verification, and Validation (ICST), Lillehammer, Norway, pp. 113–120. IEEE Digital Library (April 2008)
28. OCLE2.0 - Object Constraint Language Environment, http://lci.cs.ubbcluj.ro/ocle/
29. MIP OCL Parser (MIP MDA Tools), http://mda.cloudexp.com/
30. Kolovos, D.S., Paige, R.F., Polack, F.A.C.: Towards Using OCL for Instance-Level Queries in Domain Specific Languages. ECEASST, vol. 5. Technische Universität, Berlin (2006)
31. Damus, C.W.: MDT OCL Goes Generic - Introduction to OCL and Study of the Generic Metamodel and API. In: EclipseCon 2008, Slides of the presentation (2008)

Inter-modelling: From Theory to Practice

Esther Guerra[1], Juan de Lara[2], Dimitrios S. Kolovos[3], and Richard F. Paige[3]

[1] Universidad Carlos III de Madrid, Spain
eguerra@inf.uc3m.es
[2] Universidad Autónoma de Madrid, Spain
Juan.deLara@uam.es
[3] The University of York, UK
{dkolovos,paige}@cs.york.ac.uk

Abstract. We define inter-modelling as the activity of building models that describe how modelling languages should be related. This includes many common activities in Model Driven Engineering, like the specification of model-to-model transformations, the definition of model matching and model traceability constraints, the development of inter-model consistency maintainers and exogenous model management operators.

Recently, we proposed a formal approach to specify the allowed and forbidden relations between two modelling languages by means of bidirectional declarative patterns. Such specifications were used to generate graph rewriting rules able to enforce the relations in (forward and backward) model-to-model transformation scenarios. In this paper we extend the usage of patterns for two further inter-modelling scenarios – model matching and model traceability – and report on an EMF-based tool implementing them. The tool allows a high-level analysis of specifications based on the theory developed so far, as well as manipulation of traces by compilation of patterns into the Epsilon Object Language.

1 Introduction

Model Driven Engineering (MDE) attacks the accidental complexity in the software development process by increasing the abstraction level at which engineers work. Models (rather than code) are the core assets, and are used to generate code, validation and verification. Models are seldom oblivious of each other, and hence many activities in MDE involve building relations between two or more models either manually or (semi-)automatically. The development of systematic, well-founded techniques and tools for the creation and maintenance of inter-model relations is therefore at the core of MDE, and is especially critical in large-scale projects involving vast amounts of inter-related models [11].

The specifications of inter-model relations can be used in many ways. For instance, a model-to-model (M2M) transformation specification expresses how models of a language should be related with models of another one, and it is actually used to transform source models into target ones (or vice-versa). We call *inter-modelling* to the activity of specifying how two or more modelling languages have to be related. Further examples of inter-modelling include specifications for model matching and traceability, inter-model consistency, and synchronization.

D.C. Petriu, N. Rouquette, Ø. Haugen (Eds.): MODELS 2010, Part I, LNCS 6394, pp. 376–391, 2010.

Frequently, the specifications of different inter-modelling activities (e.g. M2M transformation and model matching) are built separately from each other – even if they relate *the same* modelling languages – and are written using different notations and tools. This produces scattered specifications that are prone to desynchronization and increase the maintenance effort. Moreover, all specifications that handle instances of the same meta-models need to be kept consistent, which is difficult to ensure if they lack formal semantics. Hence, a unified, formal notation able to specify different inter-modelling tasks would be very valuable.

Recently [6] we proposed a visual, declarative, bidirectional, formal language to describe M2M transformations. The language permits specifying allowed and forbidden relations between models of two modelling languages by means of patterns. Patterns have a formal semantics that enable checking whether two models are synchronized according to a pattern, and permitting static analysis. A synthesis procedure was developed in [6] to generate graph grammar rules solving two scenarios: source-to-target and target-to-source batch transformations.

In this paper we demonstrate that, in addition to transformation, our language can solve two further inter-modelling scenarios: model matching and model traceability. Hence, *the same* specification can solve different MDE tasks (transformation, matching and traceability) reducing the burden of developers. We also report on PAMOMO, an Eclipse tool that allows the definition of inter-modelling specifications, their analysis, and their operational use by compiling them into the Epsilon Object Language (EOL) [8]. The tool solves the following scenarios, for both model matching and model traceability:

1. Given two models M_1 and M_2, generate a trace model T relating both.
2. Given two models M_1 and M_2, and an existing trace model T,
   (a) verify whether T is valid (i.e. it has no missing or incorrect traces).
   (b) update T so that it becomes a valid trace model for M_1 and M_2.

The figure to the right shows the working scheme of our approach. An inter-modelling specification consists of a set of declarative triple patterns. This specification can be statically analysed (label 1) to check for conflicts between patterns, between patterns and the meta-models, and to assess meta-model coverage (i.e. check if all types are used by some pattern). Patterns can be used operationally

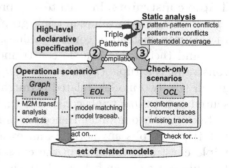

through their compilation into lower-level languages (label 2). In this paper, we compile them into EOL for model matching and model traceability, obtaining interoperability with EMF-based tools and an efficient implementation. Finally, patterns can be used for check-only scenarios (label 3) in order to find out whether two models are correctly traced and to detect incorrect or missing traces.

Paper organization. Section 2 presents our patterns for inter-modelling, which we use in Section 3 for model matching and traceability. Section 4 shows how to compile the patterns into OCL/EOL for these scenarios. Section 5 and Section 6 present tool support and a case study. We discuss related work in Section 7, and conclude in Section 8.

2   Our Pattern-Based Inter-modelling Language

In this section we briefly introduce our pattern-based language for inter-modelling. For technical details, the reader can consult [6].

Triple graphs. Our patterns are based on triple graphs [12], which are structures made of two graphs called source and target (S and T) related through a correspondence graph (C). Models can be represented as graphs with attributes in nodes and edges and with a type [4]. The correspondence graph is a graph in its own right, but we distinguish a special set of nodes M, called *mappings*. M is a subset of the set of nodes of the correspondence graph, $M \subseteq V^C$, and we define two functions $cs \colon M \to V^S$ and $ct \colon M \to V^T$ from M to the sets of nodes in the source and target graphs. These are called the correspondence functions, and are used to relate source and target nodes. Thus, we say that $x \in V^S$ is related to $y \in V^T$ iff $\exists m \in M$ s.t. $cs(m) = x$ and $ct(m) = y$. Altogether, a triple graph is a tuple $TrG = \langle S, C, T, M, cs, ct \rangle$.

We can relate two triple graphs through *triple morphisms*, e.g. when a triple graph represents a pattern that has to be found inside a bigger triple graph. A triple morphism $n \colon TrG_1 \to TrG_2$ is made of a triple of graph morphisms $n = \langle n^X \colon X_1 \to X_2 \rangle_{X \in \{S,C,T\}}$ relating the source, target and correspondence graphs of TrG_1 and TrG_2. In addition, the mappings of TrG_1 must be related to mappings of TrG_2, and the elements in TrG_1 that are not mappings cannot be identified to mappings of TrG_2 (i.e. $n^C(M_1) \subseteq M_2$ and $n^C(V_1^C \setminus M_1) \subseteq V_2^C \setminus M_2$).

Triple constraints. In order to interpret triple graphs as constraints, we substitute the set of data values in triple graphs by a finite set ν of sorted variables [6]. In this way, instead of concrete values, attributes point to variables of a given sort and their value can be constrained by a formula α. Altogether, a triple constraint is a tuple $CTrG = \langle TrG, \nu, \alpha \rangle$. It is important to note that a triple graph (i.e. two models related through a correspondence model) can be represented as a *ground* triple constraint where the formula α restricts the attributes to take exactly one value. Hence, we only need to consider triple constraints and not triple graphs anymore. As an example, the left of Fig. 1 shows a ground triple constraint taken from the class-to-relational example. The terms of the formula α are shown below, where the **and** connectives are omitted. Note that "=" denotes equality, not assignment.

Triple constraints can be related through *CTrG*-morphisms. A CTrG-morphism $a \colon CTrG_1 \to CTrG_2$ is made of a triple graph morphism with the following conditions: the formula α_2 of $CTrG_2$ must imply the formula α_1 of $CTrG_1$, and the same implication is demanded for the source and target restrictions of the formulae ($\alpha_2|_S \Rightarrow \alpha_1|_S$ and $\alpha_2|_T \Rightarrow \alpha_1|_T$). Roughly, the source $\alpha|_S$ (resp. target $\alpha|_T$) restriction of a formula α is the same formula but considering

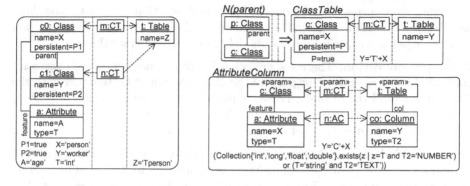

Fig. 1. Two related models as a ground triple constraint (left). Some P-patterns (right).

the variables of the source (resp. target) graph only [6]. In our current implementation, α can be any valid OCL expression given with EOL syntax.

Triple patterns. We use triple constraints as building blocks for triple patterns. A *triple pattern* describes in a declarative way a relation between two models. If the relation is allowed then we say the pattern is positive (P-pattern), whereas if the relation is forbidden then we say the pattern is negative (N-pattern). P-patterns are made of a *main constraint* Q declaring the allowed relation, an optional positive pre-condition (or parameter) C with CTrG-morphism $q: C \to Q$, and a set $N_{Pre} = \{Q \xrightarrow{c_i} C_i\}_{i \in Pre}$ of negative pre-conditions (which may be empty). N-patterns consist of just one constraint Q forbidden to occur.

The right of Fig. 1 shows two P-patterns. The upper one has a negative pre-condition (N(parent)) and demands persistent, top-level classes to be related with tables. Its formula constrains the names of the related class and table. The lower P-pattern has as parameter all elements tagged with <<param>>, which are shown together with the main constraint Q. It states that attributes and columns should be related, but only if their owning class and table are related.

3   Model Matching and Model Traceability

Patterns are interpreted differently depending on the scenario. The M2M transformation scenario looks at patterns either source-to-target or target-to-source, checking whether patterns are source- or target-enabled [6]. For instance, in forward transformation, pattern ClassTable in Fig. 1 is to be interpreted as "given a class without parents, there must be a table". Instead, model matching and model traceability consider the source and target of patterns *at the same time*. Thus, in these cases, the same pattern is interpreted as "given a class without parents and a table with suitable name, there should be a trace relating them". Hence, given a pattern, we define a suitable *directed pre-condition* for the scenario at hand, which in model matching and traceability is called *trace pre-condition*. Next, we define the notion of pattern *enabledness*, which consists on finding an occurrence of the directed pre-condition that does not violate any negative pre-condition of the pattern. Finally, we build the notion of *satisfaction* for the particular scenario (here for model matching and traceability)[1].

Trace pre-condition. The *trace pre-condition* of a P-pattern is the constraint made of the source and target parts of the main constraint Q, together with the parameter C and the formula. For example, the trace pre-condition of pattern ClassTable is made of objects c, t and *the complete formula*, while for pattern AttributeColumn it is made of objects c, t, a, co, m and the formula.

Trace enabledness. A P-pattern is *trace-enabled* in a triple constraint TrG if we find an occurrence of the pattern trace pre-condition in TrG, and none of its negative pre-conditions. In Fig. 1, ClassTable is enabled in the left constraint at objects {c0, t}, but not at objects {c1, t} as the latter belongs to an occurrence of the negative pre-condition (i.e. c1 has a parent). AttributeColumn is not trace-enabled because the table has no column.

Matched models. Two models are *matched* according to a specification, if each trace-enabled occurrence of every P-pattern in the specification belongs to an occurrence of the pattern's main constraint. This demands all suitable combinations of source and target elements to be traced. For N-patterns, we simply forbid their occurrence. The models to the left of Fig. 1 are correctly matched as the trace-enabled occurrence {c0, t} of pattern ClassTable is included in an occurrence of the main constraint (i.e. a mapping CT exists).

Traced models. Two models are *traced* according to a specification if, for each trace-enabled occurrence of every P-pattern in the specification, the source part is traced with *some* (in contrast to *all*) suitable occurrence of the target, or the other way round. Thus, model traceability does not require all combinations of source and target elements to be traced. Here, the rationale for the trace model is that it could have been generated from a forward or a backward transformation, hence we also demand a "uniform" distribution of traces. This means that it is not allowed to have one occurrence of the source to be traced twice, whereas another occurrence that could have been related with the same target elements as the first one is not traced at all (and similarly for the target). As an example, the models in Fig. 1 are correctly traced.

Fig. 2 illustrates the difference between model matching and model traceability, through an example of two models having two classes and two tables, equally named. Model matching gives a unique minimal solution (left), whereas traceability gives two minimal solutions (right). Connecting the two classes to the same table is not a valid traceability solution, as there would be an unconnected table, but enough classes in the source to be connected with. Whereas the model matching solution cannot be generated by forward or backward transformation (it contains redundant traces), any of the traceability solutions can. In fact, the matching solution is the union of all traceability solutions. While two matched models are always correctly traced, the converse is not true in general.

---

[1] The formalization can be found at: http://astreo.ii.uam.es/~jlara/PAMOMO.pdf

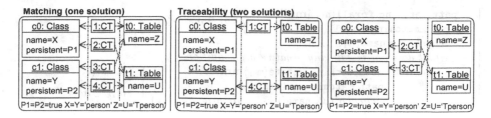

Fig. 2. Model matching vs. model traceability

4 Compilation of Patterns into OCL/EOL

We compile patterns into OCL/EOL to cover check-only and operational scenarios for model matching and traceability. In particular, we use OCL to check whether two models are correctly matched or traced, and EOL [8] to solve operational scenarios (i.e. to create a trace model from scratch so that two unrelated models become correctly matched or traced, and to recover the consistency of existing trace models by deleting incorrect traces and creating missing ones).

4.1 Check-Only Scenario: Satisfaction of Patterns by Models

Here the aim is, given two models and their traces, to identify whether the models are matched or traced according to a pattern specification. Thus, the OCL code synthesized from the specification has to verify that each occurrence of the trace-precondition of every P-pattern actually satisfies the pattern, and that the models do not contain occurrences of the N-patterns. In this scenario, the only difference between matching and traceability is that the former demands universal existence of traces (i.e. for all combinations of source and target elements) whereas traceability demands them existentially (i.e. for at least one of them if they involve the same source or target elements).

Thus, for each P-pattern p, we generate an operation sat_p that (a) seeks all trace-enabled occurrences of p and (b) checks if they are related by traces as specified by p. For (a), the operation iterates on the nodes of the trace precondition and checks if: (i) all node's edges in the trace pre-condition can be mapped to links in the models; (ii) all mappings in the trace pre-condition can be mapped to traces in the models; (iii) the attribute conditions evaluate to *true* when symbols are replaced by concrete attribute values from the models; and (iv) there are no occurrences of the negative pre-conditions in the models. For (b), we try to extend each occurrence of the trace pre-condition found in (a) to the full main constraint. Next we show the compilation of a P-pattern for model matching using the OCL-like syntax of EOL, which e.g. uses keyword **operation** instead of **query**:

```
operation sat_p.name() : Boolean {
  return
  -- (a) for each occurrence of the trace-enabling conditions...
```

$$\left.\begin{array}{l}\texttt{patt\_matching\_forall}\langle\texttt{n}_\texttt{i}\rangle \textbf{ implies}\dots \\ \texttt{patt\_matching\_forall}\langle\texttt{n}_\texttt{i}\rangle \\ \quad checkatt\_\texttt{p.name}(n_1,\dots,n_i)\end{array}\right\}\forall n_i \in nodes^p_{pre}$$

-- ... *that does not violate any negative pre-condition,*

$$\left.\begin{array}{l}\textbf{and not } \texttt{patt\_matching\_exists}\langle\texttt{m}_\texttt{i1}\rangle \textbf{ and}\dots \\ \quad\texttt{patt\_matching\_exists}\langle\texttt{m}_\texttt{ik}\rangle \\ \quad\quad checkatt\_\texttt{C}_\texttt{i}\texttt{.name}(n_1,\dots,n_i,m_{i1},\dots,m_{ik})\end{array}\right\}\begin{array}{l}\forall C_i \in N^p_{pre}, \\ \forall m_{ik} \in nodes^p_{C_i}\end{array}$$

-- *(b) check if it satisfies the main constraint*

$$\quad\textbf{implies}$$
$$\left.\begin{array}{l}\texttt{patt\_matching\_exists}\langle\texttt{n}_\texttt{i+1}\rangle \textbf{ and}\dots \\ \texttt{patt\_matching\_exists}\langle\texttt{n}_\texttt{j}\rangle \\ \quad checkatt\_\texttt{p.name}(n_1,\dots,n_i,n_{i+1},\dots,n_j);\end{array}\right\}\forall n_j \in nodes^p_{post}$$

}

where `p.name` and C_i`.name` are the names of the pattern and its negative pre-condition C_i; `patt_matching_forall<`n_i`>` and `patt_matching_exists<`n_i`>` are replaced by expressions seeking all or one occurrence of node n_i satisfying (i-ii) and the ground terms in the formula assigning a concrete value to its attributes; `checkatt_X` are operations that evaluate the non-ground terms of the formula in X; $nodes^p_{pre} = \{n_i | n_i \in V^S_Q \cup V^T_Q \cup q(V^C_Q)\}$ are the nodes in the pattern trace pre-condition, where V^X_Y contains the graph X's nodes of Y (e.g. V^S_Q contains the nodes of the source graph S in the main constraint Q) and $q(V^C_Q)$ contains the correspondence nodes in Q which are parameter of the pattern; $nodes^p_{post} = \{n_j | n_j \in V^C_Q \setminus q(V^C_Q)\}$ are the traces created by the pattern; $N^p_{Pre} = \{Q \xrightarrow{c_i} C_i\}$ are the pattern negative pre-conditions; and $nodes^p_{C_i} = \{m_{ik} | m_{ik} \in (V^S_{C_i} \cup V^T_{C_i} \cup V^C_{C_i}) \setminus c_i(nodes^p_{pre})\}$ are the nodes in the negative pre-condition that are not in the trace pre-condition.

In the operation, `patt_matching_forall<`n_i`>` collects all nodes in the model with same type, edges and attribute values as node n_i in the pattern. To improve performance, these checkings are evaluated before entering an inner loop. Thus, the code that replaces `patt_matching_forall<`n_i`>` is the following:

n_i`.type.`*allInstances().forAll*$(n_i \mid$
n_i`.nav(`n_j`) = `n_j **and** $\}\forall e \in edges^p_{pre} \vert src(e) = n_i,\ tar(e) = n_j,\ j \leq i$
n_k`.nav(`n_i`) = `n_i **and** $\}\forall e \in edges^p_{pre} \vert src(e) = n_k,\ tar(e) = n_i,\ k \leq i$
n_i`.nav(`n_l`) = `n_l **and** $\}n_i \in V^M_C, \forall n_l \in nodes^p_{pre} \vert cs(n_i) = n_l \text{ or } ct(n_i) = n_l,\ l \leq i$
n_m`.nav(`n_i`) = `n_i **and** $\}\forall n_m \in V^M_C \vert cs(n_m) = n_i \text{ or } ct(n_m) = n_i,\ m \leq i$
n_i`.att = `*value* **and** $\}\forall \text{ condition } v = value, \text{ where } v \text{ stores attribute } att \text{ of } n_i$

where n_i`.type` is replaced by n_i's type; $edges^p_{pre} = \{e | e \in E^S_Q \cup E^T_Q \cup q(E^C_Q)\}$ are the edges in the trace pre-condition; and $nav(n_j)$ in the expression n_i`.nav(`n_j`)` becomes the name of the association from node n_i to n_j. The generated pattern matching expressions are nested in operation `sat_p`, hence we implicitly order the nodes n_i. For efficiency we put first those nodes with higher number of links and ground constraints for their attributes. The code for `patt_matching_exists<`n_i`>` is similar but using *exists* instead of *forAll*.

After collecting the nodes, operation checkatt_X checks if they satisfy the non-ground part of the formula in X. The operation is generated for the trace-enabling condition of the pattern, its main constraint (both with same name but different parameters), and each negative pre-condition C_i. As an example, we show the operation generated for the trace-enabling condition:

operation $checkatt\_p.\mathbf{name}(n_1 : \mathbf{n_1.type}, \ldots, n_i : \mathbf{n_1.type}) : \mathbf{Boolean}$ {
  var $v := n_i.att;$ } $\forall$ *variable* v *storing an attribute of* $n_i \in nodes_{pre}^p$
  return $\alpha_{trace\_precondition};$
}

The operation sat_p for model traceability is similar, except that the expression that controls condition (b) (satisfaction of main constraint Q) just checks if the matched source elements satisfy Q with any combination of target elements, or if the target elements satisfy Q with any combination of the source ones.

Finally, from each N-pattern we generate one operation which checks the absence of occurrences of the N-pattern in the model. The operations are the same for model matching and traceability.

Example. Below we show part of the OCL code generated from ClassTable in Fig. 1, for the check-only model matching scenario:

```
operation sat_ClassTable() : Boolean {
  return  Class.allInstances().forAll(c | c.persistent=true implies
          Table.allInstances().forAll(t | checkatt_ClassTable(c, t)
  and not Class.allInstances().exists(p |
          c.parent.includes(p) and checkatt_ClassTable_parent(c, p))
  implies CT.allInstances().exists(m |
          m.source=c and m.target=t and checkatt_ClassTable(c, t, m))));
}
operation checkatt_ClassTable( c:Class, t:Table ) : Boolean
{ var X:=c.name;  var Y:=t.name; return Y='T'+X;  }
```

4.2 First Operational Scenario: Creation of Correct Traces

In operational scenarios we are given two models (already related or not) and the aim is to create missing traces and delete incorrect ones. For the former, from each P-pattern p we generate an EOL operation rule_p that (a) looks for a trace-enabled occurrence of the pattern and (b) creates the traces according to the pattern. Trace-enabledness is checked as in the check-only scenario, but includes two additional conditions: (v) the pattern must not have been applied to the same objects before (termination condition), and (vi) the result of applying the pattern must not violate any N-pattern in the specification.

Termination condition (v). In model matching we must ensure that the elements in the trace-enabled occurrence of a pattern are not related as specified by the pattern. Therefore, we generate an extra condition which is equal to that generated in the check-only scenario to check satisfaction of the main constraint (three last lines in the body of operation sat_p.name), but preceded by *not* instead of *implies*. This avoids enforcing a pattern twice for the same objects. In traceability we generate two stronger conditions checking that the source structure is not related to some occurrence of the target one, and vice-versa.

N-patterns (vi). In order to ensure that applying a P-pattern does not create occurrences of N-patterns, we encapsulate the creation actions into transactions which are rolled back if their execution results in an N-pattern violation. For efficiency reasons, after applying a P-pattern only those N-patterns which include elements created by the P-pattern are checked.

Creation of traces. If a set of objects satisfy all trace-enabling conditions, they are passed as parameters to operation `apply_p`, which creates all elements appearing in the correspondence graph of Q, but not in its positive pre-condition.

```
operation apply_p.name(n₁ : n₁.type,..., nᵢ : nᵢ.type) : Boolean {
  -- creation of new nodes
  var v.id : new v.type;  } ∀v ∈ nodes_post^p
  -- creation of new edges
  n_k.nav(n₁) := n_l;  } ∀e ∈ edges_post^p, with src(e) = n_k, tar(e) = n_l
  -- creation of new correspondence functions
  var n_c.nav(n_s) := n_s;  ⎫ ∀n_c ∈ V_Q^M ∩ nodes_post^p, with n_s ∈ V_Q^S,
  var n_c.nav(n_t) := n_t;  ⎭ n_t ∈ V_Q^T, cs(n_c) = n_s, ct(n_c) = n_t
  return true;
}
```

where `v.id` is replaced by a unique identifier for node v.

Example. Part of the generated matching code for pattern `ClassTable` is:

```
operation rule_ClassTable() : Boolean {
  return  Class.allInstances().exists(c | c.persistent=true and
          Table.allInstances().exists(t | checkatt_ClassTable(c, t)
  and not Class.allInstances().exists(p |
          c.parent.includes(p) and checkatt_ClassTable_parent(c, p))
  and not CT.allInstances().exists(m |
          m.source=c and m.target=t and checkatt_ClassTable(c, t, m))
  and apply_ClassTable(c, t))); }
operation apply_ClassTable( c:Class, t:Table ) : Boolean {
  var m:new CT;  m.source:=c;  m.target:=t;  return true; }
```

4.3   Second Operational Scenario: Deletion of Incorrect Traces

The previous operational mechanism ensures that the needed traces exist, but does not guarantee the absence of incorrect traces. This is so because it iterates on occurrences of the source and target nodes creating valid traces, but does not iterate on the occurrences of traces checking their correctness. Hence, two related models may have incorrect traces (apart from the correct ones) if somebody manually added an incorrect trace between them, or if the models evolved so that some traces became incorrect. Here we make a closed world assumption: only those traces that are correct according to the specification should exist.

In order to achieve this, we generate additional EOL operations that detect and delete incorrect traces. The operations check that, whenever there is a trace in the correspondence model, it is because some P-pattern demands its presence and it does not belong to an occurrence of any N-pattern.

We generate two types of operations, enforcing two levels of trace correctness. The first operation type is called *relaxed* and it does not take into account the negative pre-condition of patterns, since a pattern with negative pre-conditions specifies what should happen if the negative pre-conditions are not found but not if they are found. However the synthesized EOL code for trace creation does not enforce a pattern if its negative pre-conditions are found; therefore the second operation type checks that only those traces that our previous compilation is able to create actually exist. This second operation type is called *strict*. For space constraints we only show the compilation of the first operation.

$$
\begin{array}{l}
\textbf{operation } relaxed\_1\_t.\textbf{type } (t : \textbf{t.type}) \ \{ \\
\quad \textbf{if (not patt\_matching\_exists}\langle n_1 \rangle \ \textbf{and} \dots \\
\quad\quad\quad \textbf{patt\_matching\_exists}\langle n_i \rangle \\
\quad\quad\quad\quad checkatt\_p.\text{name}(n_1, \dots, n_i) \dots) \\
\quad\quad \{ \ \textbf{t.type}.allInstances().remove(t); \ \text{-- remove correspondence object} \\
\quad\quad\quad \textbf{delete } t; \ \} \\
\}
\end{array}
$$

with $\left. \begin{array}{l} \forall p \in enabling_t, \\ \forall n_i \in nodes^p_{pre} \cup nodes^p_{post} \setminus t \end{array} \right.$

where $enabling_t = \{p | p$ *is a P-pattern*, $\exists n \in nodes^p_{post}$ *with* $\overset{.}{n}.type = t\}$ is the set of P-patterns in the specification that create traces of type t.

Example. The first type of relaxed operation generated for trace CT is:

```
operation relaxed_1_CT( mt:CT ) {
  if (not Class.allInstances().exists(c |
         c.persistent=true and mt.source=c and
         Table.allInstances().exists(t |
         mt.target=t and checkatt_ClassTable(c, t, mt))))
       { CT.allInstances().remove(mt); delete mt; }
}
```

The generated EOL code for the operational scenarios works incrementally. Thus, given source and target models connected through an arbitrary trace model, the program invokes the deleting operations to delete the incorrect traces, and then the creation ones to reestablish trace correctness.

5   Tool Support

We have developed an Eclipse tool, called PAMOMO (http://astreo.ii.uam.es/~jlara/pamomo/main.htm), to build pattern specifications. It supports two modes of execution: *off-line* and *on-line*. In the former the designer can validate a specification or generate different files with EOL code to perform model matching, traceability, relaxed/strict deletion, or evaluate the satisfaction of a specification by models. In this execution mode the specification is compiled once and the result can be used afterwards for any incoming models, or be integrated in other tools and model driven tasks. In the *on-line* mode the designer selects the incoming source, correspondence and target models and the specification is applied to them for the chosen scenario. A ModeLink [9] file is generated showing the result in an Eclipse three-pane window, the one in the middle containing the generated trace model (see e.g. Fig. 6). The user can manipulate the result in order to e.g. annotate traces with additional information.

PAMOMO also supports analysis of meta-model coverage, identifying which types are included in each positive/negative pre-condition, main constraint or N-pattern. This has different interpretations depending on the scenario. For example, a P-pattern that defines as parameter a trace type that is not created by any other P-pattern in the specification may be useless.

Fig. 3 shows the PAMOMO meta-model used to define pattern specifications. It shows that *Specifications* are made of positive and negative patterns, both subclasses of *Pattern*. Patterns have a main constraint (role *constraint*), an optional positive pre-condition, and a set of negative pre-conditions, all modelled through class *ConstraintTripleGraph*. This class is made of three graphs with roles *source*, *target* and *correspondence*. The correspondence graph is a special kind of graph which may contain mappings that point to source and target objects.

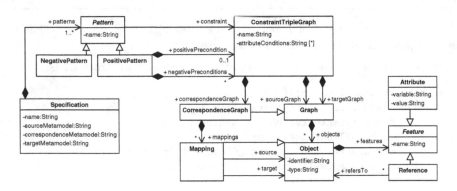

Fig. 3. Meta-model of PAMOMO

On top of this meta-model we have built a textual concrete syntax editor for PAMOMO with XText (http://eclipse.org/Xtext). This editor takes a textual representation of a specification like the one shown to the right of Fig. 5, and parses it to our model-based internal representation. Then, the code generators we have built synthesize EOL files for the chosen scenario, following the algorithms of previous section.

6   Example

In the literature, model matching has been mainly used to compare instances of the same meta-model. Here we show that it can be used for very different purposes, in particular to implement a GoF design pattern [5] discovery mechanism. On the one hand we have Ecore models where we want to identify instances of design patterns, and on the other hand a pattern design vocabulary with the definition of different design patterns and the roles participating in them. Fig. 4 shows part of the meta-model triple for this situation, which in the real case contains the complete Ecore meta-model to the left, and additional role specializations (apart from those for classes, operations and references) to the right. The correspondence meta-model binds roles to UML elements and groups the bindings of each pattern instance through class *Instance*.

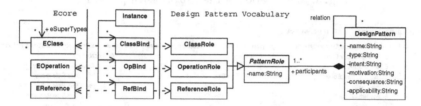

Fig. 4. Meta-model to annotate Ecore models with roles in a design pattern vocabulary

The meta-model permits annotating Ecore models with design pattern roles. Besides, we define a PAMOMO specification to automate the identification of design patterns in the Ecore models and annotate their elements with the roles they play in the design patterns. For instance, Fig. 5 shows the PAMOMO pattern for the *Proxy* design pattern. The pattern identifies occurrences of the proxy, and requires that the operations in *Subject*, *RealSubject* and *Proxy* have the same name, modelled with variables $n1$, $n2$ and $n3$, all having the same value (see condition). The pattern may define additional conditions, e.g. that the proxy defines one public operation for each public operation in the subject, and it does not define further public operations apart from these. We could also define another pattern to annotate all operations in a proxy instance, hence allowing variability on the number of operations that the *Proxy* wraps.

With our approach we formalize the structure of design patterns as an inter-modelling specification. If we apply this specification to an EMF model and a design pattern vocabulary model (instances of the meta-models in Fig. 4), we can identify instances of the patterns in the Ecore models, by using the mechanism for creation of traces in model matching. Fig. 6 shows the result provided by our tool in a simple example. The process identified one instance of the proxy in the model to the left. By selecting the created traces in the middle we can see the particular role assigned to each element in the EMF model. In the figure, the first trace binds role *Subject* to class *Graphic* in a proxy instance.

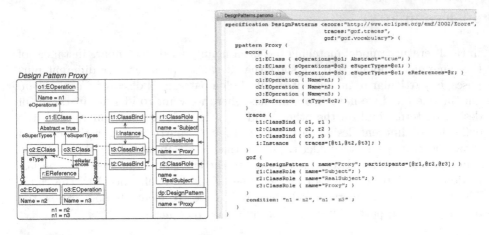

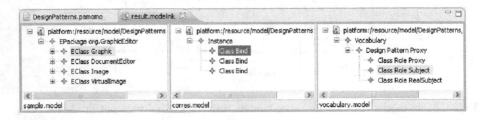

Fig. 5. Specification of the *Proxy* design pattern

Fig. 6. Model matching result: EMF model, trace model, design pattern vocabulary

The mechanism for trace manipulation is incremental: if we modify the EMF model after having identified design pattern instances, we can apply our operational mechanisms for deletion of incorrect traces (in case some instance was destroyed), as well as to identify new instances of patterns. Moreover, we plan to use PAMOMO for Ecore model completion w.r.t. design patterns by allowing users to manually annotate objects in the EMF model (i.e. assign them a role in the pattern vocabulary). We could then apply a backward transformation to create Ecore objects to obtain a correct instance of the design pattern.

7   Comparison with Related Work

Our long-term goal is providing a formal yet practical approach to integrate inter-modelling tasks. Whereas in [11] the focus is on representing sets of related models through macromodels (theoretically based on institutions), we provide a declarative, bidirectional language to describe inter-model relations, as well as a tool to enforce such relations. The goal in [2] is developing model management operators for schema mapping and data integration, while in [13] the authors use mega-models to distinguish between high- and low-level traceability models.

Among the existing traceability approaches, the Atlas Model Weaver (AMW) [1] supports the creation of weaving models (similar to our correspondence meta-model) establishing links between meta-model elements. This makes AMW usable only when the source and target meta-models are very similar, and just derives straight-forward source-to-target transformations. The specification of complex conditions enabling the creation of traces, like e.g. the one in Fig. 5, requires in addition specifying conditions *at the model level* by means of patterns of source and target instances, not supported in AMW. The work in [3] is based on a traceability meta-model in which OCL-like consistency conditions can be given. Note that both approaches are specific to traceability and are not formally founded, and therefore cannot be analysed. Finally, even though QVT-Relations [10] (QVT-R) allows setting all domains as check-only, specifications have a direction and relations have to be interpreted either source-to-target or target-to-source, being unsuitable for traceability.

Regarding model matching, existing approaches permit comparing models expressed in the same language, typically UML [14], and the customization of the comparisons is usually limited. However the advent of Domain Specific Languages makes evident the need for comparing heterogeneous models. In this respect, ECL is a dedicated language for model comparison [7] which supports heterogeneous models. However its rules are restricted to compare one source element with one target element, hence expressing a pattern like the one in Fig. 5 would require coding by hand the pattern-matching code that we generate automatically. Moreover, to the best of our knowledge, no model matching approach provides a formal foundation enabling the analysis of specifications. Regarding limitations, the advantages of formality with respect to analysis capabilities come to the price of less expressiveness than other low-level operational languages [7,8] (e.g. we do not provide primitives for creating elements in arbitrary loops).

Although TGGs can be used for model matching [12], their compilation into operational rules does not produce application conditions, and hence extra control mechanisms have to be designed ad-hoc. Using TGGs for check-only scenarios would require model parsing, and lacks an equivalent to our N-patterns. Regarding QVT-R, its semantics is not suitable for model matching because it is not possible to consider all domains at the same time, as our concept of trace-enabledness does. Moreover, the lack of an explicit concept of *trace* makes difficult its use for model matching.

Table 1 summarises the comparison of PAMOMO with the mentioned approaches. The symbols $\surd$ and $-$ indicate whether they support a given feature or not. The table shows whether the approaches can be used for traceability or matching (columns 2 and 3), if they admit an explicit trace meta-model (column 4), have a formal foundation (column 5), have a declarative style (column 6), admit non-constructive primitives similar to our N-patterns (column 7), whether the traces are defined at the meta-model level or if it is possible to define additional constraints at the model level as rules or patterns (*mm* vs. *m*, column 8),

Table 1. Comparison of different approaches for model traceability and matching

	Traceab.	Matching	Trace MM	Formal	Declarative	Non-constructive	m*	Heterogeneous
PAMOMO	√	√	√	√	√	√	m	√
AMW	–	–	√	–	√	–	mm	√
ECL	–	√	–	–	–	–	m	√
UMLDiff	–	√	–	–	–	–	–	–
QVT-R	–	–	–	–	√	–	m	√
TGGs	–	√	√	√	√	–	m	√

and if they permit relating heterogeneous languages (column 9). As it is apparent, PAMOMO is the only approach that supports both matching and traceability, under a unified formal semantics, making it suitable for inter-modelling tasks.

8 Conclusions and Future Work

This paper has shown the use of our pattern-based approach to specify model matching and model traceability conditions. For these scenarios, patterns can be used in check-only mode to test satisfiability, and in operational (incremental) mode to manipulate the trace model. We have shown realizations of these two activities using OCL and EOL respectively. Our patterns provide a unified, formal approach to inter-modelling, as pattern specifications can also be used to solve M2M transformation scenarios [6]. We have also introduced PAMOMO, an EMF-based tool that allows editing pattern-specifications, their static analysis, and their compilation into EOL for model matching and traceability.

On the practical side, we are working on optimizing the pattern matching algorithms, as well as in extending PAMOMO to solve M2M transformation scenarios. For this purpose we need to combine EOL with constraint solving techniques. On the theoretical side, we are currently working on new analysis techniques and on extending the expressivity of patterns.

Acknowledgements. Work funded by the Spanish Ministry of Science (project TIN2008-02081 and grants JC2009-00015, PR2009-0019), the R&D programme of the Madrid Region (project S2009/TIC-1650), the European Commission's 7th Framework programme (grant #248864 (MADES)), and the Engineering and Physical Sciences Research Council (EPSRC) (grant EP/E034853/1).

References

1. AMW: ATLAS Model Weaver, http://wiki.eclipse.org/AMW
2. Bernstein, P.A., Melnik, S.: Model management 2.0: manipulating richer mappings. In: SIGMOD, pp. 1–12. ACM, New York (2007)
3. Drivalos, N., Kolovos, D., Paige, R., Fernandes, K.: Engineering a dsl for software traceability. In: Gašević, D., Lämmel, R., Van Wyk, E. (eds.) SLE 2008. LNCS, vol. 5452, pp. 151–167. Springer, Heidelberg (2008)
4. Ehrig, H., Ehrig, K., Prange, U., Taentzer, G.: Fundamentals of algebraic graph transformation. Springer, Heidelberg (2006)

5. Gamma, E., Helm, R., Johnson, R., Vlissides, J.M.: Design Patterns. In: Elements of Reusable Object-Oriented Software. Addison Wesley, Reading (1994)
6. Guerra, E., de Lara, J., Orejas, F.: Pattern-based model-to-model transformation: Handling attribute conditions. In: Paige, R.F. (ed.) ICMT 2009. LNCS, vol. 5563, pp. 83–99. Springer, Heidelberg (2009)
7. Kolovos, D.S.: Establishing correspondences between models with the Epsilon Comparison Language. In: Paige, R.F., Hartman, A., Rensink, A. (eds.) ECMDA-FA 2009. LNCS, vol. 5562, pp. 146–157. Springer, Heidelberg (2009)
8. Kolovos, D.S., Paige, R.F., Polack, F.: The Epsilon Object Language (EOL). In: Rensink, A., Warmer, J. (eds.) ECMDA-FA 2006. LNCS, vol. 4066, pp. 128–142. Springer, Heidelberg (2006)
9. Modelink, http://www.eclipse.org/gmt/epsilon/doc/modelink/
10. QVT, http://www.omg.org/docs/ptc/05-11-01.pdf
11. Salay, R., Mylopoulos, J., Easterbrook, S.: Using macromodels to manage collections of related models. In: van Eck, P., Gordijn, J., Wieringa, R. (eds.) CAiSE 2009. LNCS, vol. 5565, pp. 141–155. Springer, Heidelberg (2009)
12. Schürr, A.: Specification of graph translators with triple graph grammars. In: Mayr, E.W., Schmidt, G., Tinhofer, G. (eds.) WG 1994. LNCS, vol. 903, pp. 151–163. Springer, Heidelberg (1994)
13. Seibel, A., Neumann, S., Giese, H.: Dynamic hierarchical mega models: comprehensive traceability and its efficient maintenance. In: SOSYM (2010) (in press)
14. Xing, Z., Stroulia, E.: UMLDiff: an algorithm for object oriented design differencing. In: ASE 2005, pp. 54–65. ACM, New York (2005)

Consistent Modeling Using Multiple UML Profiles

Florian Noyrit[1], Sébastien Gérard[1], François Terrier[1], and Bran Selic[2]

[1] CEA, LIST, Laboratory of model driven engineering for embedded systems,
Point Courrier 94, Gif-sur-Yvette, 91191, France
florian.noyrit@cea.fr, sebastien.gerard@cea.fr,
francois.terrier@cea.fr
[2] Malina Software Corp. Nepean, Ontario, Canada
selic@acm.org

Abstract. The design of complex technical system invariably involves multiple domain-specific languages to cover the many different facets of such systems. However, unless the languages are designed to be used in combination, this typically leads to conflicting specifications that are difficult to reconcile due to the ontological and other differences between the languages used. In this paper, we describe a pragmatic but systematic approach to resolving this problem for the special but common case in which the domain-specific languages are all defined as UML profiles.

1 Introduction

Complex embedded software systems generally involve many perspectives and domains. A number of standard approaches have been devised to help designers manage this complexity. Among the most effective is the use of model-based engineering (MBE) methods, which rely on the systemic use of models to reduce the apparent complexity of the system under development. These models typically abstract out much technological detail, while emphasizing those aspects that are of interest to stakeholders. However, given the heterogeneous nature of most complex systems, different categories of stakeholders will have different concerns and, therefore, focus on different aspects. This need is often met by providing different modeling languages, each suited to a particular domain (i.e., *domain-specific modeling languages* or *DSMLs*).

However, when multiple modeling languages are used to describe the different aspects of a given system, the problem of reconciling the corresponding language-specific models arises. Although each domain-specific model represents different concerns, given that they all deal with the same system, there is bound to be some overlap in these descriptions. Consequently, unless the individual DSMLs were explicitly designed to be mutually complementary, there is a high probability that they will be inconsistent. What is needed, then, is a way of facilitating the use of multiple languages such that the possibility of model conflicts is minimized.

This is the issue addressed in this paper. Specifically, we focus on the case where the DSMLs are defined in the form of UML profiles, although much of the work seems to be applicable more generally to DSMLs of all kinds. However, UML

D.C. Petriu, N. Rouquette, Ø. Haugen (Eds.): MODELS 2010, Part I, LNCS 6394, pp. 392–406, 2010.
© Springer-Verlag Berlin Heidelberg 2010

profiles, particularly ones that have been standardized, are of special interest, since they have the crucial benefits of familiarity (UML is the most widely used modeling language) and the ability to take advantage of standard UML tools. Also, given that all profiles share a common semantic foundation [1][2], the problem of reconciling the different languages is likely to be simpler. Of particular interest is the combined use of two standard profiles: SysML, a domain-specific profile for systems engineering, and MARTE, a profile for real-time and embedded systems development. This potent combination of DSMLs is likely to be used in numerous projects where MBE techniques are being used.

In the following section, we first introduce some useful terminology and concepts from the domains of ontology representation and semiotics (the study of symbols and their use in communications) to help us navigate the problems of combining multiple DSMLs. In first part of Section 3 we introduce the SysML/MARTE case study, which is used to illustrate both the main issues as well as key elements of our solution, and then we describe the proposed solution itself. This is followed by a discussion of its limitations and possible improvements (Section 4). Related work is reviewed and compared against our approach in Section 5, followed by a summary of the paper in Section 6.

2 Languages and Their Composition

The general problems of language and meaning have been studied since ancient times as have the problems of the relationships between different languages. It is helpful, therefore, to draw on this body of knowledge to provide a systematic framework for analyzing the issue of combining multiple DSMLs.

2.1 A Framework for Analysis

First, let us consider only one language. Aligned with Ullmann's triangle [3], we distinguish three basic conceptual layers:

— The *reality layer* consists of real world phenomena that are the subject of a language such as a DSML.
— The *conceptualization layer* contains abstractions that are, typically, internalized mental interpretations of elements of the real world. They are the mediators between real world phenomena and the symbols that represent them in the language layer.
— The *language layer* consists of a set of *symbols* that *represent* elements of the conceptualization layer.

The discipline of semiotics recognizes three distinct elements when considering these layers: syntax, semantics, and pragmatics. *Syntax* controls the manner in which symbols of a language are permitted to relate to each other. It defines the rules for constructing well-formed language statements (models) using a set of symbols. In case of modeling languages, syntax is usually defined by a metamodel supplemented by rules using some specialized language, such as OCL [4]. In MBE practice, syntax is typically refined further into *abstract syntax* and *concrete syntax* (i.e., the physical rendering of symbols). This refinement, which allows for multiple different concrete representations of a given symbol, inserts an extra layer into our framework.

The *semantics* of a language defines the relations between symbols and real-world phenomena by means of interpretation: assigning meanings to symbols and patterns of symbols. Most often, the semantics of computer languages, such as UML or C++, are defined informally, using a textual description in some natural language. UML, in particular, has been frequently criticized for its lack of formal semantics, so that various formalizations have been proposed for it. Notable among these is the Executable UML Foundation (fUML) specification, which provides a formal definition of the semantics of a subset of UML and which was recently standardized by the Object Management Group [1].

Fig. 1 depicts an example that illustrates the four layers in this framework: the concrete word «book» expresses an abstract symbol, the metaclass "Book", which represents the concept of book that someone has in mind, which, in turn, is an abstraction (conceptualization) of a real book.

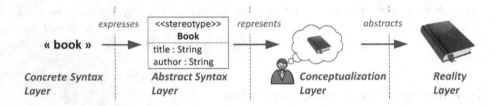

Fig. 1. Relations between concrete syntax, abstract syntax, conceptualization, and reality

To provide a full semiotic analysis, we should also consider the pragmatics: that is, the relation between symbols and the agents (e.g., people, computers) who use them, and how context impacts meaning. However, pragmatics is rarely formally defined and we shall not discuss it further in this paper.

2.2 Language Composition Issues

When combining multiple languages to describe a complex system, incompatibility issues can occur at different layers in our framework:

— *Expression issues*: These occur when two concrete representations are incompatible. For example, two different tools may use different concrete syntaxes to express the same abstraction (e.g., "book" in English and "livre" in French). This can lead to confusion and misunderstanding.

— *Syntax issues*: In this case, it is likely that the metamodels of the two languages are different or even incompatible, so that well-formed formulas according to one metamodel may not be well-formed according to the other. For example, in the context of a print shop, a book might be associated with the particular printing press on which it was created, whereas in a library or a bookstore such a relationship would be irrelevant.

— *Semantics issues*: This typically happens when two similar symbols from two different languages have different meanings. For example, in a travel agency, the term "book" signifies a type of transaction, whereas in a library the same word refers to a physical instance of a book.

Since we are focusing on computer languages, it is meaningful to consider how and to what extent automation can help in resolving these kinds of issues. Clearly, these problems require some form of understanding of the semantics of the languages involved. This means that it is necessary to go beyond mere metamodels, which only deal with syntax, and to analyze language conceptualizations.

In cases where language conceptualizations are defined implicitly (i.e., they are internalized in people's minds) or specified informally (e.g., via natural language), there is not much that can be done. Unfortunately, this is the most common method of specifying semantics in current MBE practice, leaving metamodels as the only formal entities open to computer treatment.

Although modeling language designers usually try to align their metamodels (abstract syntaxes) with corresponding conceptualizations, various pragmatic and implementation concerns, such as the idiosyncrasies of the UML profile mechanism, often break or obfuscate this correspondence. They introduce elements into the metamodel that can lead to incorrect inferences and confusion about the semantics of a language. This conflicts with the primary rationale behind DSMLs, which is to provide languages that express domain conceptualizations in the most direct and accurate way possible [5]. Consequently, we adhere to the view elaborated in [6], which proposes to systematically evaluate the suitability of a language by comparing its syntactical structure to the structure of its conceptualization.

Recent developments in formal knowledge representation (e.g., Description Logics [7], Common Logic [8]) aim to provide ways of concretizing conceptualizations into artifacts called *ontologies*. Because of their formal underpinnings, ontologies capture semantic information in a tractable and, most importantly, computable manner. This opens up the possibility of much greater automation support when dealing with language composition.

3   Our Approach

The potential for increased automation offered by formal ontologies as well as the need for a closer match between a DSML and its conceptualization were principal influencing factors in our approach to dealing with the problem of combining UML profiles. Rather than relying purely on implementation-polluted profile metamodels, we require the definition of an intermediate implementation-independent *domain model*, which serves as a kind of ontology. The semantics of a profile are then defined by *semantic mappings* of its symbols to corresponding elements in the domain model. At present, these domain models still use informal (natural language) specifications of semantics, since the choice of suitable ontologies, methods, and tools is still an open research issue. Ultimately, however, we hope to eventually evolve metamodels into true formal ontologies.

The central feature of our approach to combining UML profiles is to define a new language that eclectically *reuses* the concepts of all of its original "source" languages. This is illustrated by the abstract example in Fig. 2: given languages L_1 and L_2 whose respective conceptualizations C_1 and C_2 overlap, we want to define a new language L (and its corresponding concrete syntax E), whose conceptualization C:

— reuses some subset of the concepts from C_1 and C_2 (C_{Adopt})
— introduces new concepts not present in either C_1 or C_2 (C_{New})
— leaves out some subset of concepts from C_1 and C_2 (($C_1 \cup C_2$) \ C_{Adopt})

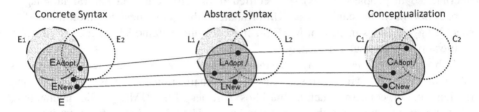

Fig. 2. Outline of the approach

Compared to designing a completely new language from scratch, this approach has the important advantage that it can potentially reuse much of the knowledge, experience, and tooling associated with its source languages. Of course, this means that we must deal with all three types of language composition issues described earlier (expression, syntax, and semantics).

Although it is likely that this approach can be generalized, we examine this problem only in the specific context of DSMLs defined as UML profiles. A common criticism of the profile mechanism is that the UML metamodel may limit the language designer, due to constraints stemming from both its semantics and its syntax. For this reason, many designers prefer defining "pure" DSMLs, which give them full freedom to tailor the language primitives. However, as noted earlier, unless specifically designed to be used in combination, such *ad hoc* approaches are likely to introduce incompatibilities when it becomes necessary to use them jointly for the same system. On the other hand, since all UML profiles share a common semantics foundation [2], the likelihood of both syntactic and semantic conflicts is greatly reduced and their resolution is generally simpler. Furthermore, given that the conceptualization and metamodel of UML contain relatively universal modeling concepts (e.g., class, association, behavior, etc.) the limitations that it imposes may not be too severe in many cases.

The approach we advocate, then, is to define a new profile that combines the required elements of its source profiles. Afterwards, if necessary, models based on this new profile can be translated back into models corresponding to the source profiles.

3.1 An Example Case Study

As a motivating example, we consider the joint use of the MARTE [9] and the SysML [10] profiles, a combination that is highly likely in the design of complex technical systems. Both profiles have been standardized as official technology recommendations by the OMG, which increases their visibility and use.

MARTE is intended for model-driven development of real-time and embedded systems. It is designed to be used throughout the development cycle for a variety of activities including specification, design, analysis, and verification and validation. For its part, SysML is a UML profile dedicated to systems engineering, that is, the design and development of complex heterogeneous systems or systems of systems. Both profiles have been designed as generic, anticipating the need for adaptation to specific problems and domains. For instance, MARTE may be refined to support specific types of model analyses, and SysML may be specialized to fit specific domains such aerospace or automotive.

For this particular case study, we used as inputs the following descriptions:

— The domain models of MARTE and SysML. These domain models were specified using the OMG's MetaObject facility (MOF). To allow us to convert these domain models into true ontologies that could then be manipulated by appropriate tools, we developed a UML to OWL-DL [11] transformation that is aligned with ODM [12]. The choice of OWL-DL is motivated by its widespread adoption and readily available tooling. Also, it is highly expressive while retaining computational completeness and decidability.

— The UML profiles definitions of MARTE and SysML provided in the corresponding OMG specification documents.

— The semantics mappings between concepts in the domain model and the corresponding language symbols (stereotypes) that represent them as well as the relations between the stereotypes and the concrete syntax (the expressions). Note that these had to be created, as they are not defined formally in the specs (although the MARTE specification includes a partial mapping, SysML does not even provide a domain model).

Using the semantic relations between the concepts introduced in the domain models, our objective is to generate a new "MARTE-SysML" profile that deals with the domains covered individually by MARTE and SysML.

The possibility of combining the MARTE and SysML profiles to model embedded systems and the resulting concerns raised by heterogeneity have been discussed in[13]. These two profiles are highly complementary, but, nevertheless, there is still some overlap between them.

Consider, for example, the FlowPort stereotype, which appears in both profiles (Fig. 3) and their definitions in domain models of SysML and MARTE (Fig. 4):

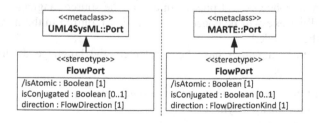

Fig. 3. The FlowPort stereotype definition in SysML and MARTE

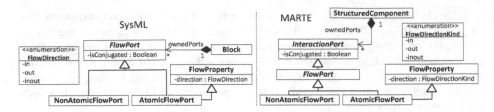

Fig. 4. FlowPort concept definition in domain models of SysML and MARTE

At first glance, these two appear to be almost identical. However, a simplistic merge of the two into a single concept would be inappropriate because there are important semantic differences between them that are not discernible from the metamodel or the domain model. Namely, the semantics of SysML state that a "FlowPort is an interaction point through which input and/or output of items such as data, material, or energy may flow", whereas in the semantics of MARTE "FlowPorts have been introduced to enable dataflow-oriented communications between components, where messages that flow across ports represent data items".

Because MARTE flow ports only allow data flows, we see that the MARTE concept is actually a *specialization* of the corresponding SysML concept.

This example clearly demonstrates that resolving language conflicts is not always trivial and that it often requires human intervention and especially so in the absence of formally specified semantics.

In future work, we also plan to assess our approach with a case study that aims at redefining EAST-ADL2 [14] as an extension of MARTE.

3.2 Details of the Approach

The process for deriving a new profile from two or more source profiles is a multi-step procedure.

In the initial step, a first-pass domain model is defined. This identifies the full set of concepts needed in the new "combined" domain.

Based on that, suitable source languages (profiles) are selected such that, between them, they cover a significant percentage of the domain concepts. As indicated by the FlowPort example, some of the "matching" concepts in the source languages will have to be refined or extended to fully satisfy the needs of the domain. Also, additional domain concepts, not present in any of the source languages, may have to be added. Finally, there will be concepts that are not required in the new domain and which need to be excluded.

Once the source languages have been selected, the language definition process involves:

1. Alignment of the ontologies (i.e., the conceptualizations),
2. Alignment of the abstract syntaxes,
3. Alignment of the concrete syntaxes.

As might be expected, this may require multiple iterations.

3.2.1 Aligning the Ontologies

This step involves identifying suitable concepts from the ontologies of all the source languages (C_{Adopt}) as well as, possibly, adding new concepts not found in any of them (C_{New}). It also involves defining the semantic relationships that exist between the original source concepts and the corresponding target language concepts. For example, in the case of the flow port concept, the target language would likely incorporate the SysML concept directly, and would then add a generalization relation for the special case required by MARTE.

Although some relations between source and target language concepts are relatively straightforward (e.g., equivalence, subsumption (is-a relationship), and meronymy (part-whole relationship)), we consider that, in the general case, these relations can be quite complex. Therefore, instead of relying solely on pre-defined relationship primitives provided in some transformation language (e.g., ATLAS Transformation Language [15] or QVT [16]), we introduce the notion of a *resolution*. This is a concept in the combined language that results from the sequence of elementary transformation operations (referred to collectively as the *resolution record*) by which it is derived from its source concepts.

For example, the following transformation fragment might be applied to define a FlowPort concept in the combined language, which directly matches the SysML concept and which has a specialization called DataFlowPort corresponding to the MARTE concept[1] (the resolution itself is shown in Fig. 5):

```
FlowPort=Merge(SysML::FlowPort,MARTE::InteractionPort){
    isConjugated=Merge(SysML::FlowPort::isConjugated,MARTE
    ::FlowPort::isConjugated);
    Set(MARTE::ownedPorts.memberEnd(MARTE::InteractionPort
    ),SysML::FlowPort);
    Set(MARTE::FlowPort.general(MARTE::FlowPort),SysML::Fl
    owPort);
}
Block=Merge(SysML::Block, MARTE::StructuredComponent){
    Set(MARTE::ownedPorts.memberEnd(MARTE::StructuredCompo
    nent),SysML::Block);
    Remove(MARTE::StructuredComponent);
}
ownedPorts=Merge(MARTE::ownedPorts,SysML::ownedPorts);
Set(MARTE::NonAtomicFlowPort.general(MARTE::FlowPort),S
ysML::NonAtomicFlowPort);
Set(MARTE::NonAtomicFlowPort.name,NonAtomicDataFlowPort
);
Set(SysML::NonAtomicFlowPort.name,NonAtomicFlowPort);
Set(MARTE::AtomicFlowPort.general(MARTE::FlowPort),SysM
L::AtomicFlowPort);
Set(MARTE::AtomicFlowPort.name,AtomicDataFlowPort);
Set(SysML::AtomicFlowPort.name,AtomicFlowPort);
Remove(MARTE::FlowPort);
```

---

[1] The language used here to denote the record of the composition could be any model transformation language.

```
FlowDirection=Merge(SysML::FlowDirection,MARTE::FlowDir
ectionKind){
   in=Merge(SysML::FlowDirection::in,MARTE::FlowDirection
   Kind::in);
   out=Merge(SysML::FlowDirection::out,MARTE::FlowDirecti
   onKind::out);
   inout=Merge(SysML::FlowDirection::inout,MARTE::FlowDir
   ectionKind::inout);
}
Set(MARTE::FlowProperty::direction.type,FlowDirection);
FlowProperty=Merge(SysML::FlowProperty,MARTE::FlowPrope
rty){
   direction=Merge(SysML::FlowProperty::direction,MARTE::
   FlowProperty::direction);
}
```

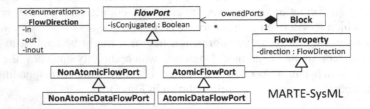

Fig. 5. A possible resolution that defines FlowPort, DataFlowPort and Block concepts

Note that such a resolution record can be easily inverted, so that it is possible to translate in either direction (although some inversions will be non-trivial).

In designing resolutions, one can choose to emphasize the characteristics of one of the source concepts while deprecating the others. In that case the chosen source concept is said to be *dominant*. This is usually manifested in that a larger proportion of its characteristics (i.e., features) are retained relative to all the other source concepts.

3.2.2 Aligning the Abstract Syntaxes

Once the new ontology has been defined, we must then define new symbols that represent the resolutions (which are part of C_{Adopt}) as well as the new concepts (belonging to C_{New}). Since we are focusing on UML profiles, this involves identifying which metaclasses will be extended by the new derived language concepts.

For new concepts, this is straightforward, since we are unconstrained by any source language considerations. However, the issue is more complex for concepts within C_{Adopt}, because the source concepts already have their corresponding metaclasses defined. Clearly, these specifications must be preserved to ensure that the original semantics are still present. In what follows, we assume that the semantic mappings between the original concepts in the domain model (ontologies) and the original symbols that represented them in the profiles (i.e., the original stereotypes) are already defined.

For a given resolution, if the original stereotypes of its source language concepts all extend the same set of metaclasses, the case is straightforward: the new stereotype simply needs to extend the same set of metaclasses. However, if these sets are different, then decision is non-trivial. In the situation where one metaclass is a specialization of another (e.g., Class and Classifier), there are two possible strategies. One is to define heuristics such as "always extend the most concrete metaclasses" or "only extend common metaclasses". Alternatively, the decision can be left to the language designer, who will make the choice on a case-by-case basis. The most suitable approach seems to be a combination of the two; that is, to provide a set of choices based on heuristics and then allow the language designer to either choose the most appropriate one or to define a new one.

Consider, for example, the hypothetical case in, where two source concepts, represented by symbols A and B, *which respectively extend two very different metaclasses*, are merged into a common resolution represented by the symbol R. In this case, depicted in Fig. 6, the decision was made to use both source metaclasses.

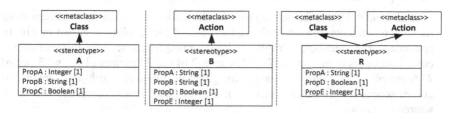

Fig. 6. Original representation of two source concepts A and B and a possible representation of the resolution R

3.2.3 Aligning the Concrete Syntaxes
This final step involves in selecting a concrete syntax representation of the symbols of the new language. For resolutions, it is possible to select one of the original representations used for the source symbols (e.g., the dominant one, if it exists), or to define a new one.

3.3 Ensuring Consistency and Interoperability

The approach described above leaves considerable leeway to combine concepts, define symbols, and select concrete representations. However, such unbridled freedom can increase the likelihood of inconsistencies in the language, which is certainly undesirable. This can be prevented by the imposition of rigid formal constraints and rules to control the language derivation process. But, such an overly paternalistic approach might not only limit expressive power but can also lead to inappropriate or even nonsensical resolutions. Instead, we prefer an approach that does not constrain design freedom, but provides assistance through various metrics and guidelines that can help improve consistency. In our opinion it is the language designers who are in the best position to decide which resolution makes sense in a given case.

For instance, the type of reasoning that led to the decision on the proper way to combine the two seemingly identical flow port concepts in SysML and MARTE is not something that can be easily automated. That would require that the subtle differences between these two source concepts be captured in a formal way within their respective ontologies so that they can be recognized and properly accounted for by a computer program. With current metamodel-based modeling languages whose semantics are specified informally, this possibility is still a long way off.

Consequently, the approach we have taken is to provide an arsenal of useful guidelines, heuristics and metrics that a language designer can utilize to increase the consistency of design choices made. It is important to note that all of these can be easily integrated into a tool and consulted when needed to provide an automated *decision support* facility (as opposed to a highly-automated but inflexible *decision-making* facility).

3.3.1 Heuristics for Ontology Alignment

The following two metrics can be used for ensuring semantic consistency:

— *Completeness*: This is the percentage of information that a resolution keeps from its source concepts. For example, in the case of the resolution shown in Fig. 6, removing the attribute PropB reduces completeness. (In this example, completeness is computed as 71% because 2 of the 3 features of A and 3 out of 4 features of B were retained.) In general, maintaining higher levels of completeness is preferred, since it indicates more complete preservation of source semantics.
— *Dominance*: This is the percentage of each concept kept by a resolution. In the above example, concept B is dominant because 75% of its features are kept while nothing is kept from A (except, of course, its metaclass). Dominance tells us to what extent we are favoring one of the source languages. As a general guideline, it is probably good practice to consistently favor one of the source languages, as opposed to having a mixture of dominances.

3.3.2 Heuristics for Abstract Syntax Alignment

For aligning symbols, the following heuristics can be helpful:

— *Metaclasses adequacy*: If the stereotypes that represent the source concepts extend different metaclasses and those metaclasses are not related by direct or indirect type-subtype relationships, then the resolution may be inappropriate. That is, if no such relationship exists, then this may indicate a fundamental semantic mismatch of the source concepts.
— *Properties adequacy*: If two source features are merged, then, in the ideal case, their types, multiplicities, visibilities, and default values should all be equal; otherwise, a non-trivial translation is needed.

In addition, the following is a non-exhaustive list of guidelines and metrics proposed in [6], which we find useful:

— *Completeness*: every concept should have a corresponding symbol (stereotype).
— *Soundness*: every symbol should represent a concept.
— *Conciseness*: every concept is represented at most once (in the metamodel).
— *Lucidity*: every symbol represents at most one concept.

— *Dominance*: if a source concept is significantly dominant over other source concepts, then this dominance should be matched in the symbol corresponding to the resolution.

3.3.3 Heuristics for Concrete Syntax Alignment

Finally, the following are some guidelines for consistency of concrete representations:

— *Completeness*: every symbol can be expressed with a representation.
— *Soundness*: every representation expresses a symbol.
— *Conciseness*: every symbol is expressed by at most one representation.
— *Lucidity*: every representation expresses at most one symbol.
— *Expression adequacy*: the representation should intuitively express the corresponding meaning; for instance, graphical containment intuitively expresses semantic containment.
— *Expression interoperability*: syntactically related symbols should have correspondingly related representations.
— *Dominance*: if a concept is significantly dominant over another, then the original representation of the dominant source symbol should be favored.

4 Discussion

As noted earlier, a key concern is the degree of automation that can be provided to support this approach. Although some automation support can be provided for the metrics and heuristics described above, the language definition process is still mostly manual. As noted earlier, current metamodels only describe the abstract syntax while domain models given in the specifications do not contain enough information in a form that can be processed by a computer. In addition, we evaluated several ontology matching frameworks (such as Alignment API [17]) with SysML and MARTE domain models as inputs. Our results and conclusions are aligned with those reported in [18]: the proposed alignments are mostly inaccurate or even absurd confirming thus the inadequacy of a fully-automated approach.

Consequently, we look forward to more formal definitions of semantics. Various initiatives based on shared formal ontologies [19] are likely to be useful. The approach used in the definition of the fUML subset of UML [1], where semantics are defined using CLIF [8], a first-order logic formalism, and are based on PSL [20], seems to be in this spirit. In addition to enabling and facilitating increased automation support, shared formal ontologies can be used to improve consistency. This is the direction we are considering for our future work.

The fact that language designers struggle when designing resolutions can be a problem: this will be reflected in the resolution record. However, it is not really an issue if we let the designers edit the record directly.

Also, when adopting standards, language designers may want to benefit from new revisions of these languages. The approach we propose offers version management facilities. Though that is not its primary goal, we can even apply the approach to only one language (create resolutions from only one language) and thereby track revisions. In that case, we can simply apply the transformations corresponding to the resolution record to simplify conversion of existing models.

One of the assumptions behind our approach is that we have at our disposal artifacts from the semantic domain: the semantic mappings and the mappings between representation and expression. However, this is not always the case, because these are often omitted or are defined using natural language. Therefore, an additional effort may be required to reach the necessary level of formality. Nevertheless, the dominant trend in the MBE community is to use MBE techniques to design languages. Consequently, the use of formalisms is increasing and is likely to provide us eventually with the right type of artifacts required by our approach.

Although we illustrated our approach using just two languages, it is possible that language designers will want to combine more than two DSMLs. There is nothing inherent in this approach that limits the number of languages that can be combined. Of course, for practical realization of this, suitable tool support will be crucial.

5 Related Work

There is much active research around the problem of combining modeling languages. In this section, we present those that inspired our approach and some that may support our future work.

The artificial intelligence, information systems, and semantic web communities have worked on ontology alignment to support information and semantic integration. Here, we can distinguish two not necessarily exclusive classes of approaches:

- *Shared ontology*: The key idea in these approaches is to determine semantic relations between two ontologies by using an *upper* (higher-level) ontology. DOLCE [21], SUMO [22] and PSL are notable upper ontology initiatives. In [19], the authors use PSL as shared ontology to translate process models between two DSMLs. We hope to adapt these results to provide automation support for the composition of domain ontologies of multiple DSMLs.
- *Heuristic and machine learning*: In contrast shared ontologies, these approaches do not require a reference ontology. Instead, to detect similarities, they apply heuristics based solely on syntactic, lexical, or structural information available in the ontologies. One example of this is PROMPT [23], which guides the user and suggests possible matches. Mappings designed both by the system and the user when merging ontologies are recorded to create a declarative mapping. Our approach is rather close to this, but adapted for profile composition.

In the MBE domain, we can mention the following related initiatives:

- AMW [24] proposes to store semantics relations between elements of different models or metamodels in a weaving model. Although the core weaving metamodel can be extended with new semantic relations, as noted earlier, we believe that it is infeasible to define *a priori* all possible resolutions for the different types of semantic relations.
- Various approaches have been proposed for model version management, such as EMF Compare or AML [25]. In general, those approaches have rather good results for versioning purpose. However, our experiments show that it does not give practical and accurate results when the ontologies are significantly distant.

In general, the approaches cited above are usually focused mostly on semantic equivalence relations. However, as our work showed, these are not always sufficient and it should be possible for language designers to define their own problem-specific semantic relations.

6 Summary and Conclusions

In the design of complex technical systems, different specialties will use different ontologies and different languages to deal with their concerns. Thus, whether we consider it wise or not, the use of multiple languages in such cases is a given. The issue then is how to deal with the problems that arise from such practices and, in particular, the problem of conflicts that arise from language incompatibilities. This paper focuses on a special but relatively common variant of that problem: the combined use of multiple domain-specific UML profiles.

The solution proposed is one distinguished by emphasis on reuse in order to take maximal advantage of existing tools and expertise. To achieve this, it suggests defining a "composite" profile that eclectically reuses concepts from each of its component profiles. Our experiments with language composition techniques indicate clearly that a fully automated approach is unlikely to be realized without *computable* semantic information that is both accurate and precise. In other words, the process of combining languages almost always requires human intervention and guidance (at least until more formal methods for defining language semantics are sufficiently evolved). Consequently, our solution does not rely on pre-defined and inflexible formal transformation rules, which, like those early natural-language translators, are likely to produce flawed and even absurd results. Instead, the choice of defining and selecting the most suitable transformations is left to the language designer, who is in the best position to make meaningful decisions. Yet, it is an approach that is still suited to automation, because it provides a set of guidelines, heuristics, and metrics that can be easily incorporated into an automated decision-support system.

It is fairly clear that much work remains to be done, including a more extensive assessment of the effectiveness and practicality of the proposed approach. An important next step is to investigate more thoroughly the applicability of formal ontologies to support increased levels of automation.

References

1. Object Management Group: Semantics of a Foundational Subset for Executable UML Models - Beta2 - ptc/2009-10-05 (2009),
   http://www.omg.org/spec/FUML/1.0/Beta2/
2. Selic, B.V.: On the semantic foundations of standard UML 2.0. In: Formal Methods for the Design of Real-Time Systems, pp. 181–199 (2004)
3. Ullmann, S.: Semantics: an introduction to the science of meaning. Barnes & Noble (1962)
4. Object Management Group: Object Constraint Language (OCL) - Version 2.0 - formal/2006-05-01 (2006), http://www.omg.org/spec/OCL/2.0/
5. Guarino, N.: Formal Ontology and Information Systems (1998)

6. Guizzardi, G.: On Ontology, ontologies, Conceptualizations, Modeling Languages, and (Meta)Models. In: Databases and information systems IV: selected papers from the Seventh International Baltic Conference, DB&IS 2006. p. 18. Ios Pr. Inc. (2007)

7. Baader, F., Calvanese, D., McGuinness, D.L., Patel-Schneider, P., Nardi, D.: The description logic handbook: theory, implementation, and applications. Cambridge University Press, Cambridge (2003)

8. ISO/IEC: ISO/IEC 24707 - Information technology - Common Logic (CL): a framework for a family of logicbased languages (2007)

9. Object Management Group: UML Profile for MARTE: Modeling and Analysis of Real-Time Embedded Systems - Version 1.0 - formal/2009-11-02 (2009), http://www.omg.org/spec/MARTE/1.0/

10. Object Management Group: OMG Systems Modeling Language (OMG SysML) - Version 1.1 - formal/2008-11-01 (2008), http://www.omg.org/spec/SysML/1.1/

11. Web Ontology Language (OWL), http://www.w3.org/2004/OWL/

12. Object Management Group: Ontology Definition Metamodel (ODM) - Version 1.0 - formal/2009-05-01 (2009), http://www.omg.org/spec/ODM/1.0/

13. Espinoza, H., Cancila, D., Selic, B., Gérard, S.: Challenges in Combining SysML and MARTE for Model-Based Design of Embedded Systems. In: Model Driven Architecture-Foundations and Applications, pp. 98–113. Springer, Heidelberg (2009)

14. ATESST: EAST-ADL 2.0 Specification (2008)

15. ATLAS Transformation Language (ATL), http://www.eclipse.org/m2m/atl/

16. Object Management Group: MOF 2.0 Query/View/Transformation Specification (QVT) - Version 1.0 - formal/08-04-03 (2008), http://www.omg.org/spec/QVT/1.0/

17. Euzenat, J.: An API for ontology alignment. In: McIlraith, S.A., Plexousakis, D., van Harmelen, F. (eds.) ISWC 2004. LNCS, vol. 3298, pp. 698–712. Springer, Heidelberg (2004)

18. Kappel, G., Kargl, H., Kramler, G., Schauerhuber, A., Seidl, M., Strommer, M., Wimmer, M.: Matching metamodels with semantic systems-an experience report. In: BTW 2007 Workshop Model Management und Metadaten-Verwaltung, Aachen (2007)

19. Ciocoiu, M., Nau, D.S.: Ontology-based semantics. In: Principles of Knowledge Representation and Reasoning - International Conference, pp. 539–546 (2000)

20. NIST: ISO 18629-11 - Process Specification Language, PSL (2005)

21. Gangemi, A., Guarino, N., Masolo, C., Oltramari, A., Schneider, L.: Sweetening ontologies with DOLCE (2002)

22. Niles, I., Pease, A.: Towards a standard upper ontology. In: FOIS 2001. ACM, New York (2001)

23. Noy, N.F., Musen, M.A.: The PROMPT suite: interactive tools for ontology merging and mapping. International Journal of Human-Computer Studies, 983–1024 (2003)

24. Del Fabro, M.D., Bézivin, J., Valduriez, P.: Weaving Models with the Eclipse AMW plugin. In: Eclipse Modeling Symposium, Eclipse Summit Europe (2006)

25. Garcés, K., Jouault, F., Cointe, P., Bézivin, J.: A domain specific language for expressing model matching. In: IDM 2009 (2009)

A Systematic Review on the Definition of UML Profiles*

Jesús Pardillo

University of Alicante – DLSI/Lucentia, Spain
jesuspv@dlsi.ua.es

Abstract. This article reports a systematic review on the definition of UML profiles in the research literature. Several exploratory statistical analyses have been performed in order to characterise both the idiosyncrasy of UML profiles and how they are reported in the literature. This study uncovers the differences between presentation styles for behavioural and structural domains, and shows how UML profiles based on **Class**, **Association**, and **Property** structural metaclasses clearly outnumber any other kind. Also, this review reveals how half of the examined UML profiles merely extend the abstract syntax, without adding neither icons nor constraints. The main contribution of this study is therefore a clear picture of the state-of-the-art in UML profiling, together with a set of open questions regarding its future.

Keywords: UML, modelling, profiles, review.

1 Introduction

In the last years, we have witnessed a number of articles whose main contribution was a UML profile [1] aimed at solving modelling problems in different domains. Most of them have been presented in conferences specialised in conceptual modelling and software engineering. However, they show a great disparity regarding both the profile definition process and the quality of the UML-profile presentation. This heterogeneity makes the presented UML profiles very difficult to compare, discuss and use, which most of the time are merely sketched.

In order to cast some light on this subject, this article presents a systematic review [2] of UML-profiling practices that tackles both the (abstract) profile definition process (metaclasses that they extend, practices regarding the definition of constraints and tagged values, etc.) and their presentation quality. Neither of these aspects have been tackled so far in the literature.

Next section describes the systematic-review protocol and variables studied (§2). Then, the findings of this study are presented (§3), and, later, discussed (§4). Finally, some concluding remarks are provided (§5).

* Supported by the FPU grant AP2006-00332 from the Spanish Ministry of Education and Science. Special thanks to Cristina Cachero who contributed to the systematic review and the MODELS' anonymous reviewers for their helpful comments.

D.C. Petriu, N. Rouquette, Ø. Haugen (Eds.): MODELS 2010, Part I, LNCS 6394, pp. 407–422, 2010.

2   Method and Materials

This review has followed the systematic review protocol proposed in [2]. The sources were selected by means of a first exploratory study on the ERA ranking[1], which indicated that the two major conferences in the field of general-purpose modelling were: the *International Conference on Model Driven Engineering Languages and Systems* (MODELS, ranked as B), formerly known as the *International Conference on the Unified Modelling Language* (UML, until 2004), and the *International Conference on Conceptual Modelling* (ER, ranked as B). For both UML/MODELS and ER conferences, the review also included the workshops.

These sources were reviewed for a 11-year period (1999-2009), *i.e.*, since the first contribution on UML profiles appeared in UML'99. The initial set of primary studies were selected by searching[2] in the title, abstract, and keywords of the articles, the following case-insensitive search string (square brackets stand for optionality, '|' for disjunction, and round brackets for grouping): (extend[ing|s] [the] UML)|(UML extension[s])|(UML profile[s]). The returned articles were manually filtered for novel UML profiles. Only articles that focused on the presentation of a profile were included in the study. For instance, [3] was discarded since authors presented not a novel UML profile but a technique for automatic UML profiling. Auxiliary resources supporting those articles (*e.g.*, technical reports) were also discarded.

Table 1 summarises this process output. A total of 63 publications were returned by the initial search. After a manual review of these publications, 39 of them were classified as reporting a UML profile.

Table 1. Statistics on the articles filtered

Venue	Total	Discarded	Selected
ER	6	2	4
ER Workshops	10	4	6
MODELS	11	6	5
MODELS Workshops	5	2	3
UML	31	10	21
Total	63	24	39

In order to analyse the state-of-the-art of UML profiles, two types of variables were manually gathered (see Table 6 in the appendix for the comprehensive list): those for characterising the abstract definition of UML profiles, such as the number of profiles by year, or stereotype count by metaclass, and those for evaluating the presentation quality of the profile description.

Concerning the abstract definition, the presence of several base UML-profiling characteristics were measured to study trends regarding the abstract definition

---

[1] http://core.edu.au

[2] The search engine used is located in 'http://dblp.l3s.de'

of UML profiles. Herein, C_G stands for the number of occurrences of the characteristic C by occurrence of the characteristic G. For instance, S_M stands for the stereotype count by metaclass[3]. Each characteristic is denoted for brevity with the first letter of its name, whenever it is unambiguous. In addition, some ratios over the former variables were studied. For instance, P_M/S_M stands for the ratio between the profile count and the stereotype count, both by metaclass.

Concerning the presentation of UML profiles, and after a preliminary study of the format of the contributions found in the literature, the quality indicators defined ($\mathcal{Q}$ variables) refer to the presence in the article of: (1) all the constraints that are introduced by the UML profile (whether they be coded in OCL or not; denoted as C), (2) a UML-profile diagram for representing the metaclass extension made by the stereotypes (D), (3) a definition of the profile formal semantics (whether they be axiomatic, denotational, etc.; F), (4) a metamodel diagram (whether it be a domain-specific or one specialising UML; M), (5) constraints formalised in OCL (O), and (6) any kind of template for systematically specifying the UML profile (*e.g.*, itemised list or a table; T).

3 Findings

Table 2 shows part of the exploratory statistics gathered by UML profile (quality-presentation indicators in §3.3 are omitted in this table due to the space constraints). There was a total of 406 stereotypes (variable S) and 46 distinct metaclasses (M) identified. In addition, the average number of tags identified by stereotype (T_S) was 0.7 and the median value was 0. Next sections further dive into the analysis of these data.

3.1   UML-Profiles Publication Trends

Our first analysis regards the profile count by year & venue ($P_{Y,V}$). Fig. 1 decomposes this variable distribution by venue and year. As the reader may already know, UML/MODELS is the venue where UML profiles began to appear. Interestingly, along the years, whereas this conference has decreased the number of accepted articles presenting UML profiles, MODELS & ER workshops have increased their number, with a peak in 2007. On the other hand, the ER main conference is the venue where less UML profiles were presented, with no profile published since 2005. It is interesting to also note that 2002, the most prolific year in UML/MODELS main conference, was also the year when the last (and current) main revision (2.0) of UML was presented. In this revision, UML profiles were further formalised in a specific metamodel that introduced the explicit definition of stereotypes for tagging model elements, as well as the transparent and dynamic extension of UML (without hard-coding UML profiles in the UML metamodel). Also, 2002 and 2007 were the most prolific years by aggregating all the studied venues.

---

[3] It is assumed that the reader is familiarised with the definition of UML profiles.

Table 2. UML profiles gathered and their number of stereotypes (*S*) and distinct base metaclasses (*M*), and the presence of icons (*I*), tags (*T*), and constraints (*C*)

Ref.	Domain	S	M	I	T	C
ER:						
[4]	XML	4	2	×	✓	×
[5]	security	20	8	✓	✓	✓
[6]	data warehouses	3	1	✓	×	✓
[7]	data mappings	7	4	×	✓	✓
ER Workshops:						
[8]	business processes	11	5	×	✓	✓
[9]	schema mappings	10	6	×	✓	×
[10]	constraints	4	1	×	✓	✓
[11]	business processes	19	4	✓	×	✓
[12]	requirements	30	5	✓	✓	✓
[13]	database usage	6	4	✓	✓	×
MODELS:						
[14]	signal processing	4	4	×	✓	×
[15]	time	12	11	×	✓	×
[16]	dependencies	2	2	×	✓	×
[17]	state machines	1	1	×	✓	×
[18]	airworthiness	30	4	×	✓	×
MODELS Workshops:						
[19]	railway	9	1	✓	✓	✓
[20]	homecare services	15	5	✓	✓	×
[21]	softw. architectures	5	2	×	✓	✓

Ref.	Domain	S	M	I	T	C
UML:						
[22]	quality of service	14	4	×	✓	✓
[23]	real-time syst.	1	1	✓	×	✓
[24]	ontologies	9	4	×	✓	×
[25]	hypermedia	20	4	✓	×	×
[26]	device capabilities	6	3	✓	✓	✓
[27]	time	4	3	×	✓	✓
[28]	softw. architectures	6	5	✓	×	×
[29]	complex topologies	2	2	×	×	×
[30]	manufacturing	7	4	✓	✓	✓
[31]	mobile syst.	13	9	×	✓	✓
[32]	hypermedia	13	4	✓	×	×
[33]	security	10	5	×	✓	✓
[34]	safety-critical syst.	11	6	×	✓	✓
[35]	data warehouses	8	3	✓	✓	✓
[36]	databases	31	7	✓	✓	×
[37]	interactive syst.	13	4	✓	×	✓
[38]	executability	9	7	×	✓	×
[39]	parallel applications	10	3	✓	✓	✓
[40]	reliability analysis	7	6	×	✓	✓
[41]	interactions	12	3	✓	×	×
[42]	reflection	8	4	×	×	×

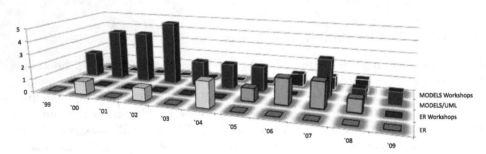

Fig. 1. Publication trends of the UML profiles by venue

3.2   Characterisation of the UML Profiles

This section presents the analysis of the variables related to the abstract definition of UML profiles.

Metaclass Extensibility. In order to assess the extension frequencies for each UML metaclass, the variables studied were the ratio between the profile count and the stereotype count by metaclass (P_M/S_M), their relative ranking ($S_M - P_M$), and the profile count by metaclass (P_M). First, P_M/S_M was analysed to identify differences in the metaclass extension by stereotype and profile in order to assess a reliable granularity for the grouping of the remaining features.

Fig. 2 shows the distribution of P_M/S_M, where whole bars represent the stereotype count (S_M) for which the black bar represent the profile count (P_M). It is perceived that there are indeed large differences between P_M and S_M depending on the metaclass. Some metaclasses have been extended in very few profiles, although with many associated stereotypes. For example, Collaboration ($\frac{1}{16}$, ◐) has been extended in only one of the 39 identified profiles, but sixteen stereotypes were defined for it. Another example is ActivityPartition ($\frac{1}{9}$, ◐), for which nine stereotypes were defined in the context of a single profile. Others appear in very few profiles, and also with a low number of stereotypes associated (see *e.g.*, Abstraction ($\frac{2}{2}$, ●), or AcceptEventAction ($\frac{1}{1}$, ●). As the reader may have noticed, in Fig. 2, three metaclasses are left out of this figure since their relative P_M, S_M detach from the median values (1.5, 4.5, respectively), thus breaking the scale of the figure: Class ($\frac{26}{141}$, ◐), Property ($\frac{15}{49}$, ◐), and Association ($\frac{16}{38}$, ◐).

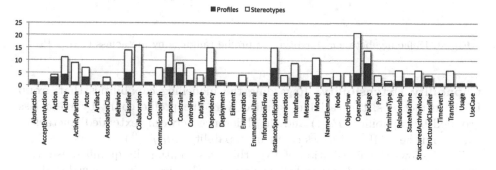

Fig. 2. Ratio between profile count and stereotype count by metaclass (P_M/S_M)

Fig. 3 ranks metaclasses by both S_M and P_M for comparison purposes. The main body of metaclasses is separated by vertical bars from the outliers (left-hand side of the figure) and from metaclasses with $S_M, P_M = 1$ in each case (right-hand, in italics and grey). This figure enriches the former view with both the absolute metaclass ranking by S_M or P_M (that shall be reviewed in the next paragraph) and the variations between both rankings. If we focus on large differences, we can detect biases due to particular profiles. For example, if we observe the Collaboration metaclass, we can see that it is ranked as fifth in S_M and 29th in P_M, that is, very few profiles extend from Collaboration, but they define a lot of different stereotypes for it. Conversely, the Action metaclass, which ranks 24th in S_M and 13th in P_M, is an example of a metaclass that has been extended in several profiles, but with few stereotypes associated in each one of them. In this figure, we can also observe how, no matter how we rank metaclasses, Class, Property and Association are the preferred subjects of extension. This fact can be further analysed in Fig. 4. In this figure, in which metaclasses have been ordered alphabetically, the reader can further analyse the frequency distribution of extension metaclasses. This figure depicts the fact that a large number of metaclasses are marginally extended (the median is 1.5 profiles per metaclass, and 4.5 stereotypes per metaclass).

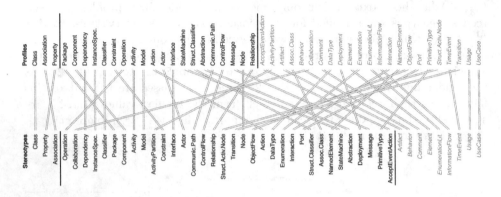

Fig. 3. Difference between stereotype & profile rankings by metaclass ($S_M - P_M$)

Capability Extensibility. Regarding the modelling capabilities that group UML metaclasses, the variables studied were the profile count by metaclass grouped by capability (P_{M_C}) and the difference between (extended) metaclass count and the UML metaclass count by capability (M_C/M_C^0).

Fig. 5 shows the distribution of P_{M_C} that was additionally qualified as structural (dark grey) or behavioural (light grey) capabilities. It is perceived that the P_{M_C} distribution is uniform but the Classes capability, which 69% of the UML profiles extend. For behavioural capabilities, Activities is the most extended.

Fig. 6 shows the distribution of M_C/M_C^0 ordered by descending M_C^0, where whole bars represent the UML metaclass count by capability (M_C^0) for which the black bar represent M_C. It is perceived that, for none of the capabilities, the metaclasses effectively extended are lower than a half of the total. The highest ratio is for Classes ($\frac{21}{55}$, ◖), being Activities far next ($\frac{6}{52}$, ◗). For the remaining capabilities, M_C is similar (median value is 2) independently of M_C^0.

Extension Expressiveness. In order to study the complexity of the extension, the variables studied were the presence of icons, tags, and constraints by stereotype and by profile ($\{I, T, C\}_{\{S,P\}}$ and the ratio between the number of icons and the number of stereotypes by metaclass (I_M/S_M). Due to the space limitations, it is a common profile presentation practice that a comprehensive list of constraints is left out of the articles. For this reason, C_S has been dismissed in this study, which has focused instead on the profile granularity (C_P).

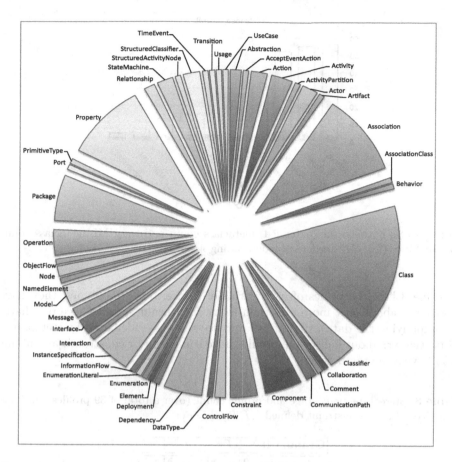

Fig. 4. Profile count by metaclass (P_M) over the sample of 39 profiles. The three most extended metaclasses are `Class` (26, 16%), `Association` (16, 10%), and `Property` (15, 9%). `Package` is next with 9 profiles (6%).

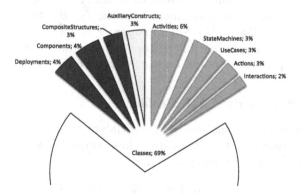

Fig. 5. Profile count by metaclass grouped by capability (P_{M_C}, structural-modelling capabilities are depicted in dark grey, and behavioural ones in light grey)

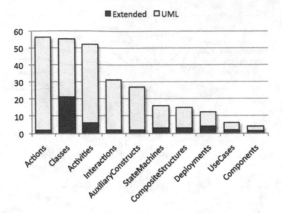

Fig. 6. Ratio between the (extended) metaclass count and the UML metaclass count by capability (M_C/M_C^0, ordered by descending M_C^0)

Table 3 lists the values of each variable. Concerning stereotypes, they have associated about 50% more tags than icons. Concerning profiles (see pie charts accompanying the data), the ratios are twice the ones calculated by stereotype. In particular, about half of the profiles have some icon or constraint, and about 75% have some tag defined.

Table 3. Stereotype percentage and profile count (over a total of 39 profiles) that has some icon, tag, or constraint defined ($\{I, T, C\}_{\{S,P\}}$)

Granularity	I	T	C
Stereotype	24% ◗	37% ◖	N/A
Profile	18 ◗	29 ◗	20 ◗

These values are significantly different when the study is focused on the three main base metaclasses. The `Class` metaclass, the I_M/S_M for the outlier metaclasses is: $\frac{60}{141}$ (◗) for `Class`, $\frac{19}{67}$ (◖) for `Property`, and $\frac{7}{42}$ (◗) for `Association`. In this way, none has significant differences (the remaining metaclasses were not extended by enough stereotypes to be worth mentioning them).

3.3 Presentation of the UML Profiles

This section presents the analysis of the variables related to the presentation issues of UML profiles in the literature. These variables were presented in §2 and are listed in Table 6 in the appendix.

Presentation Quality Trend. Fig. 7 shows the UML-profile presentation-quality trend in groups of two consecutive years since 2000 (Q_Y variables). It is perceived that there has been a cumulative increase of the presentation-quality

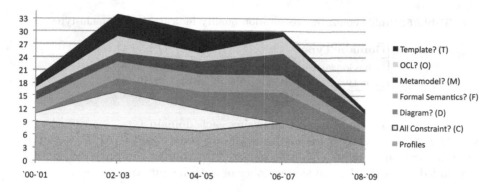

Fig. 7. Presentation-quality trend of the UML profiles

indicators along the first four years of publication. Then, the levels got stabilised until 2007, and have decreased in the last two years. Despite of the large cumulative values, when studied in isolation, the quality indicators have small values. Concerning specific trends, there are not significant differences between quality indicators, except for the presence of all the constraints, be them expressed formally or informally, in the studied profiles (C_Y). Since 2002-2003, such indicator has decreased its value until being completely missing in 2006-2007 (the low presence of OCL constraints, O_Y, does not help to ameliorate this trend).

Authorship Templating. Given the fact that there is no standard (neither official nor *de facto*) for the presentation of profiles, one aim of this study was to check whether authors had internally worked on a systematic way to present profiles. In order to check this possibility, UML profiles of the same first author were reviewed for commonalities (Q_A variables). Table 4 lists alphabetically the authors with P_A articles ($P_A > 1$) included in the study. For these authors, Q_A variables are classified according to the total number of presentation-quality indicators between profiles defined by the same first author that has either the same value ('=' column) or different value ('$\neq$' column).

Table 4. Commonalties count by first author having several UML profiles published

First Author	References	P_A	=	$\neq$
Cuccuru	[17,29]	2	2	4
Jürjens	[33,34]	2	4	2
Lujan-Mora	[35,6,7]	3	2	4

Domain-type Presentation Quality. Concerning the UML profile domain type (Q_D variables), a total of 25 UML profiles out of 39 modelled a structural domain (64%), whereas 14 (36%) modelled a behavioural one. Table 5 lists the percentages of profiles for each domain type, together with the set of

Table 5. Profile count by presentation-quality indicator and domain-type

Domain Type	C	D	F	M	O	T
Behavioural	5	9	8	5	4	4
Structural	10	8	8	11	7	10

presentation-quality indicators. Comparing each domain type, we can observe how $D, F > C, M, O, T$ holds for behavioural profiles, and $C, M, T > D, F, O$ for structural ones, where O can be obviated for comparison purposes, since it is included in the right-hand side member of both inequalities.

4 Discussion

This section discusses the main implications of the previous findings.

4.1 Publication Trends

MODELS/UML is the conference that agglutinates the bulk of published UML profiles, including the first profile ever published. This is not surprising, since this conference is the natural target of researchers aiming at publishing UML-related research. However, along the years, the interest of this venue on profiles has decreased. A similar trend can be observed in ER. Meanwhile, UML profiles have been gaining scope in their respective workshops. One possible explanation to this fact is that workshops, being forums of discussion, are less demanding. For this reason, one of the conclusions of this study is that the research focused on UML profiles is losing interest. Apart from the potential maturity of UML profiling, one of the causes of the decrease could be the advent of modelling tools that support 'heavier' metamodelling techniques, such as GMF (2006)[4], which seems to be narrowing the utility of UML profiles.

4.2 UML Profiling

The distribution of P_M/S_M points out that stereotypes in UML profiles are highly cohesive with regard to the extended metaclasses, *i.e.*, if a metaclass is worth extending, it will be extended multiple times. Importantly, the P_M distribution highlights the top extended metaclasses, namely, `Class`, `Association`, and `Property`. These metaclasses are indeed the backbone of class diagrams, which are in addition the most popular UML diagram in practice [43]. One possible explanation for this fact could be that these metaclasses are extended because of the same reasons. However, other explanations are also feasible; theoretically speaking, such results seem to go against the conception of a general purpose language, such as UML, since such usage and extension preferences are

---

[4] http://www.eclipse.org/gmf

very focused on a few set of metaclasses. Moreover, the widely-common extension of the same metaclasses in so different profiles and domains may also imply a neglect of the semantics associated to these metaclasses.

The distribution of $\{I, T, C\}_{\{S,P\}}$ shows that the presence of tags in UML profiles is more usual than icons or constraints. This means that tags are regarded as useful elements for profiles (*e.g.*, in order to add metadata to the extended metaclasses). This contrasts with the relatively low number of icons defined in the studied profiles. Further, the presence or not of icons does not depend on the base metaclass, as I_M/S_M points out. If we compare this fact with the number of metamodels with proprietary notation that have been proposed in the last years, it seems weird that so few profiles try to benefit from icons (being so simple to manage) to enrich the profile visualisation capabilities. We believe that the reason is that icons provide such a limited visualisation flexibility that only authors with low demands regarding notation opt by defining a profile instead of a brand new metamodel.

Interestingly, only about half of the profiles have some constraint defined. This could mean that profiles were defined informally, or just that simple labelling of the metaclasses is required (not changing their syntax nor semantics).

4.3   Presentation Issues

Concerning the quality-presentation trends, it is interesting to study the correlation between a the decrement of the publications and a decrement in their quality during the last years. The reason could be that UML profiling is becoming well known, and so researchers are giving more and more aspects for granted during their description. This would explain why fewer profiles have been published and, despite its increasing maturity, less formality is used to report them.

Regarding these presentation-quality indicators, it is especially worth mentioning how the definition of the profile formal semantics (F) is very rare. This is a clear indicator of the lack of rigour of UML profiling in practice, *i.e.*, the semantic mapping between domain-specific notions and UML metaclasses. In addition, the common lack of metamodels (M) stands for non-formal syntaxes, that in the case of specific domains (instead of UML pure extensions), could compromise the correctness of the constraints imposed by profiles over UML.

Summarising, profiles show in general a low level of presentation quality (even lower in the last years), with many elements missing from their definition. This may point out that the community pays low attention to formal presentation methods, whether it be by ignorance or necessity (*e.g.*, saving article space). This could have limited the (practical) applicability of UML profiles, since authors could have been centred on particular issues on UML profiling, but not on comprehensive and proven solutions. Concerning the lack of authorship-templating evidence, this may imply either that a rigorous presentation of profiles has not been an issue of concern or that authors do not indeed know how to present UML profiles properly, and they have learned by practice which presentation techniques are better.

With regard to the domain type, the presence of diagrams (D) and formal semantics (F) is higher for behavioural profiles. Conversely, the presence of all the constraints (C), metamodel (M), and templates (T) are higher for structural profiles. This result points out a presentation pattern for structural profiles based on the presence of C, M, and T. In contrast, behavioural profiles are preferred to be presented by showing the visual mapping to UML (D) instead of the domain-specific metamodels (M), and the domain-specific formal semantics (F) instead of providing all the constraint or some OCL code (O). This pattern also seems natural since UML itself has no formal semantics for their metaclasses (which are described in natural language), whereas behavioural modelling needs to be supported by their formal semantics to be useful. Conversely, structural domains (which usually represent vague notions) are defined more informally.

4.4   Limitations of the Review

The main limitation to the validity of this review is the manual gathering of the data, which may have caused some articles to be inaccurately discarded, or may have hampered the measurement precision. This hindrance has been controlled by a pair-review process, where every conflict of opinion between the reviewers has been discussed before making any final decision on the exclusion of any article and assigning marks to the quality indicators.

Also, in order to avoid the possibility of a selection bias, several combinations of the main keywords in UML profiling were identified and tested for completeness. Concerning the data extraction and analysis, every part of the process was piloted and tested multiple times.

5   Conclusion

This study has characterised the state-of-the-art of UML profiles in the top modelling conferences. Some important trends have been detected about how UML profiles have been defined and presented. Then, some theories on the findings obtained have been discussed. In particular, the distribution of extended metaclasses, largely unbalanced towards a small number of metaclasses, suggest the need for further research on the use of general-purpose *versus* domain-specific modelling languages. Indeed, both UML profiles and other 'model-driven' techniques still need comprehensive and empirically-assessed theories for understanding their success factors in software development. A good starting point would be the research accomplished on visual languages [44] or the conformity with the technology acceptance model (TAM) [45].

From this study, new research lines have been opened. First of all, concerning the large number of profiles extending `Classes`, both structural and behavioural, it remains an open issue whether such situation may be caused by UML being profiled for notational purposes; some preliminary exploratory research on this assumption has lead the author to formulate the hypothesis (yet to be quantitatively confirmed) that, instead of selecting extension metaclasses by their semantic closeness, many profiles extend metaclasses due to a notational closeness to the target language. In this sense, `Classes` `Associations`, and `Properties` provide very intuitive mappings. Also, the class diagram is the best known UML diagram. Has UML become too complex for designers to be able to find the most suitable extension metaclasses? If this is the case, is it possible that such complexity is one of the reasons behind the increasing popularity of MOF meta-models in detriment of UML profiles?

Last but not least, the low presentation quality point out the need of more formal methods and templates to present UML profiles. In this sense, additional studies on the theory of software modelling could help to improve both the quality of the UML profiling itself and its presentation. For instance, the application of techniques to study and manage ontologies could help to formally asses the mapping between domain-specific languages and UML notions.

As a final remark, we would like to encourage readers to question themselves about the very nature of UML profiling, and what makes a UML profile worth as research contribution nowadays.

References

1. Object Management Group: Unified Modeling Language (UML), version 2.2. (February 2009), http://www.omg.org/technology/documents/formal/uml.htm
2. Kitchenham, B.: Procedures for performing systematic reviews, pp. 1–28. Keele University and National ICT Australia Ltd. (2004)
3. Giachetti, G., Valverde, F., Pastor, O.: Improving Automatic UML2 Profile Generation for MDA Industrial Development. In: ER Workshops, pp. 113–122 (2008)
4. Conrad, R., Scheffner, D., Freytag, J.C.: XML Conceptual Modeling Using UML. In: Laender, A.H.F., Liddle, S.W., Storey, V.C. (eds.) ER 2000. LNCS, vol. 1920, pp. 558–571. Springer, Heidelberg (2000)
5. Fernández-Medina, E., Trujillo, J., Villarroel, R., Piattini, M.: Extending UML for Designing Secure Data Warehouses. In: Atzeni, P., Chu, W., Lu, H., Zhou, S., Ling, T.-W. (eds.) ER 2004. LNCS, vol. 3288, pp. 217–230. Springer, Heidelberg (2004)
6. Luján-Mora, S., Trujillo, J., Song, I.Y.: Multidimensional Modeling with UML Package Diagrams. In: Spaccapietra, S., March, S.T., Kambayashi, Y. (eds.) ER 2002. LNCS, vol. 2503, pp. 199–213. Springer, Heidelberg (2002)
7. Luján-Mora, S., Vassiliadis, P., Trujillo, J.: Data Mapping Diagrams for Data Warehouse Design with UML. In: Atzeni, P., Chu, W., Lu, H., Zhou, S., Ling, T.-W. (eds.) ER 2004. LNCS, vol. 3288, pp. 191–204. Springer, Heidelberg (2004)
8. Korherr, B., List, B.: Extending the UML 2 Activity Diagram with Business Process Goals and Performance Measures and the Mapping to BPEL. In: ER Workshops, pp. 7–18 (2006)
9. Kurz, S., Guppenberger, M., Freitag, B.: A UML Profile for Modeling Schema Mappings. In: ER Workshops, pp. 53–62 (2006)
10. Lagarde, F., Terrier, F., André, C., Gérard, S.: Extending OCL to Ensure Model Transformations. In: ER Workshops, pp. 126–136 (2007)
11. List, B., Korherr, B.: A UML 2 Profile for Business Process Modelling. In: ER Workshops, pp. 85–96 (2005)
12. Pardillo, J., Molina, F., Cachero, C., Toval, A.: A UML Profile for Modelling Measurable Requirements. In: ER Workshops, pp. 123–132 (2008)

13. Stefanov, V., List, B.: A UML Profile for Modeling Data Warehouse Usage. In: ER Workshops, pp. 137–147 (2007)
14. Daw, Z., Vetter, M.: Deterministic UML Models for Interconnected Activities and State Machines. In: Schürr, A., Selic, B. (eds.) MODELS 2009. LNCS, vol. 5795, pp. 556–570. Springer, Heidelberg (2009)
15. André, C., Mallet, F., de Simone, R.: Modeling time(s). In: Engels, G., Opdyke, B., Schmidt, D.C., Weil, F. (eds.) MODELS 2007. LNCS, vol. 4735, pp. 559–573. Springer, Heidelberg (2007)
16. Bernardi, S., Merseguer, J., Petriu, D.C.: Adding dependability analysis capabilities to the marte profile. In: Czarnecki, K., Ober, I., Bruel, J.-M., Uhl, A., Völter, M. (eds.) MODELS 2008. LNCS, vol. 5301, pp. 736–750. Springer, Heidelberg (2008)
17. Cuccuru, A., Mraidha, C., Terrier, F., Gérard, S.: Enhancing UML Extensions with Operational Semantics. In: Engels, G., Opdyke, B., Schmidt, D.C., Weil, F. (eds.) MODELS 2007. LNCS, vol. 4735, pp. 271–285. Springer, Heidelberg (2007)
18. Zoughbi, G., Briand, L.C., Labiche, Y.: A UML Profile for Developing Airworthiness-Compliant (RTCA DO-178B), Safety-Critical Software. In: Engels, G., Opdyke, B., Schmidt, D.C., Weil, F. (eds.) MODELS 2007. LNCS, vol. 4735, pp. 574–588. Springer, Heidelberg (2007)
19. Berkenkötter, K.: OCL-Based Validation of a Railway Domain Profile. In: Kühne, T. (ed.) MoDELS 2006. LNCS, vol. 4364, pp. 159–168. Springer, Heidelberg (2007)
20. Walderhaug, S., Stav, E., Mikalsen, M.: Experiences from Model-Driven Development of Homecare Services: UML Profiles and Domain Models. In: MoDELS Workshops, pp. 199–212 (2008)
21. Weisemöller, I., Schürr, A.: A comparison of standard compliant ways to define domain specific languages. In: MoDELS Workshops, pp. 47–58 (2007)
22. Aagedal, J.Ø., Ecklund Jr., E.F.: Modelling QoS: Towards a UML Profile. In: Jézéquel, J.-M., Hussmann, H., Cook, S. (eds.) UML 2002. LNCS, vol. 2460, pp. 275–289. Springer, Heidelberg (2002)
23. Apvrille, L., de Saqui-Sannes, P., Lohr, C., Sénac, P., Courtiat, J.P.: A New UML Profile for Real-Time System Formal Design and Validation. In: Gogolla, M., Kobryn, C. (eds.) UML 2001. LNCS, vol. 2185, pp. 287–301. Springer, Heidelberg (2001)
24. Baclawski, K., Kokar, M.M., Kogut, P.A., Hart, L., Smith, J.E., Holmes III, W.S., Letkowski, J., Aronson, M.L.: Extending UML to support ontology engineering for the semantic web. In: Gogolla, M., Kobryn, C. (eds.) UML 2001. LNCS, vol. 2185, pp. 342–360. Springer, Heidelberg (2001)
25. Baumeister, H., Koch, N., Mandel, L.: Towards a UML Extension for Hypermedia Design. In: France, R.B., Rumpe, B. (eds.) UML 1999. LNCS, vol. 1723, pp. 614–629. Springer, Heidelberg (1999)
26. Brenner, E., Derado, I.: UML Extensions for ASAM-GDI Device Capability Description. In: Evans, A., Kent, S., Selic, B. (eds.) UML 2000. LNCS, vol. 1939, pp. 148–161. Springer, Heidelberg (2000)
27. Cabot, J., Olivé, A., Teniente, E.: Representing Temporal Information in UML. In: Stevens, P., Whittle, J., Booch, G. (eds.) UML 2003. LNCS, vol. 2863, pp. 44–59. Springer, Heidelberg (2003)
28. Crettaz, V., Kandé, M.M., Sendall, S., Strohmeier, A.: Integrating the Concern-BASE Approach with SADL. In: Gogolla, M., Kobryn, C. (eds.) UML 2001. LNCS, vol. 2185, pp. 166–181. Springer, Heidelberg (2001)

29. Cuccuru, A., Dekeyser, J.L., Marquet, P., Boulet, P.: Towards UML 2 Extensions for Compact Modeling of Regular Complex Topologies. In: Briand, L.C., Williams, C. (eds.) MoDELS 2005. LNCS, vol. 3713, pp. 445–459. Springer, Heidelberg (2005)
30. Flake, S., Müller, W.: A UML Profile for Real-Time Constraints with the OCL. In: Jézéquel, J.-M., Hussmann, H., Cook, S. (eds.) UML 2002. LNCS, vol. 2460, pp. 179–195. Springer, Heidelberg (2002)
31. Grassi, V., Mirandola, R., Sabetta, A.: A UML Profile to Model Mobile Systems. In: Baar, T., Strohmeier, A., Moreira, A., Mellor, S.J. (eds.) UML 2004. LNCS, vol. 3273, pp. 128–142. Springer, Heidelberg (2004)
32. Hennicker, R., Koch, N.: A UML-based Methodology for Hypermedia Design. In: Evans, A., Kent, S., Selic, B. (eds.) UML 2000. LNCS, vol. 1939, pp. 410–424. Springer, Heidelberg (2000)
33. Jürjens, J.: UMLsec: Extending UML for Secure Systems Development. In: Jézéquel, J.-M., Hussmann, H., Cook, S. (eds.) UML 2002. LNCS, vol. 2460, pp. 412–425. Springer, Heidelberg (2002)
34. Jürjens, J.: Developing Safety-Critical Systems with UML. In: Stevens, P., Whittle, J., Booch, G. (eds.) UML 2003. LNCS, vol. 2863, pp. 360–372. Springer, Heidelberg (2003)
35. Luján-Mora, S., Trujillo, J., Song, I.Y.: Extending the UML for Multidimensional Modeling. In: Jézéquel, J.-M., Hussmann, H., Cook, S. (eds.) UML 2002. LNCS, vol. 2460, pp. 290–304. Springer, Heidelberg (2002)
36. Marcos, E., Vela, B., Cavero, J.M.: Extending UML for Object-Relational Database Design. In: Gogolla, M., Kobryn, C. (eds.) UML 2001. LNCS, vol. 2185, pp. 225–239. Springer, Heidelberg (2001)
37. Nunes, N.J., e Cunha, J.F.: Towards a UML profile for interaction design: the Wisdom approach. In: Evans, A., Kent, S., Selic, B. (eds.) UML 2000. LNCS, vol. 1939, pp. 101–116. Springer, Heidelberg (2000)
38. Pitkänen, R., Selonen, P.: A UML Profile for Executable and Incremental Specification-Level Modeling. In: Baar, T., Strohmeier, A., Moreira, A., Mellor, S.J. (eds.) UML 2004. LNCS, vol. 3273, pp. 158–172. Springer, Heidelberg (2004)
39. Pllana, S., Fahringer, T.: On Customizing the UML for Modeling Performance-Oriented Applications. In: Jézéquel, J.-M., Hussmann, H., Cook, S. (eds.) UML 2002. LNCS, vol. 2460, pp. 259–274. Springer, Heidelberg (2002)
40. Rodrigues, G.N., Rosenblum, D.S., Uchitel, S.: Reliability Prediction in Model-Driven Development. In: Briand, L.C., Williams, C. (eds.) MoDELS 2005. LNCS, vol. 3713, pp. 339–354. Springer, Heidelberg (2005)
41. da Silva, P.P., Paton, N.W.: UMLi: The Unified Modeling Language for Interactive Applications. In: Evans, A., Kent, S., Selic, B. (eds.) UML 2000. LNCS, vol. 1939, pp. 117–132. Springer, Heidelberg (2000)
42. Suzuki, J., Yamamoto, Y.: Extending UML for Modelling Reflective Software Componentsa. In: France, R.B., Rumpe, B. (eds.) UML 1999. LNCS, vol. 1723, pp. 220–235. Springer, Heidelberg (1999)
43. Dobing, B., Parsons, J.: How UML is used. Commun. ACM 49(5), 109–113 (2006)
44. Moody, D.: Theory development in visual language research: Beyond the cognitive dimensions of notations. In: VL/HCC, pp. 151–154 (2009)
45. Venkatesh, V., Morris, M.G., Davis, G.B., Davis, F.D.: User Acceptance of Information Technology: Toward a Unified View. MIS Quarterly 27(3) (2003)

A   List of Variables

Table 6. List of the studied properties and the notation for the associated variables

Property	Variable
General:	
How many stereotypes are in all the UML profiles?	S
How many distinct metaclasses are in all the UML profiles?	M
How many UML profiles have been published by conference and year?	$P_{Y,V}$
How many quality-presentation indicators are shared among all the author's profiles?	Q_A
How many profiles present a specific quality indicator by domain type?	Q_D
How many profiles present a specific quality indicator by year?	Q_Y
Stereotype:	
Is any icon defined?	I_S
Is any tag definition present?	T_S
Metaclass:	
How many stereotypes extend it?	S_M
How many stereotypes extend it in the context of the owning profile?	P_M/S_M
What is the difference between the rankings of S_M and P_M?	$S_M - P_M$
How many profiles contain some stereotype that extend it?	P_M
How many icons are defined for it in the context of S_M?	I_M/S_M
Modelling capability:	
How many profiles contain any stereotype extending an owned metaclass?	P_{M_C}
How many metaclasses are extended with respect to the ones provided by UML?	M_C/M_C^0
Profile:	
How many stereotypes are defined?	S_P
How many distinct metaclasses are defined?	M_P
Is any stereotype icon defined?	I_P
Is any tag definition present?	T_P
Is any constraint defined?	C_P
Presentation-quality indicators (Q):	
How many profiles present all the involved constraints?	C
How many profiles present a UML-profile diagram?	D
How many profiles present formal semantics?	F
How many profiles present a metamodel diagram?	M
How many profiles present any constraint formalised in OCL?	O
How many profiles present a textual template?	T

Author Index